Contemporary Britain

Contemporary Britain

An Annual Review 1992

Edited by

PETER CATTERALL

Assistant Editor

VIRGINIA PRESTON

Published for the
Institute of Contemporary British History
by Blackwell Publishers

British Library Cataloguing in Publication Data

Contemporary Britain: an annual review. 1991–
1. Great Britain, Social conditions.
I. Institute of Contemporary British History
941.0859
ISBN 0–631–18494–5
ISSN 0957–5960

Typeset in 10 on 12pt Times
by the Institute of Contemporary British History
Printed in Great Britain by
Athenaeum Press Ltd, Newcastle upon Tyne

Contents

Preface

Contemporary history provides the context in which to understand current issues. The third volume in this series of yearbooks describes and critically assesses current concerns and the prevailing trends and themes in British society and politics during 1991. It provides both a detailed record of the year, and an in-depth scrutiny of events and issues, their context and the policy responses adopted for the use of policy makers, businessmen, civil servants, journalists, academics and all those interested in the changing character of contemporary Britain. In the process it analyses the development of policy and its outcomes, and the social, political and economic setting in which it operates, with the object of ensuring that future policy making is based upon solid knowledge of the historical context, rather than ideological prescription or mythology. Each essay surveys an important aspect of British life and examines the major themes that have characterized 1991. Indeed, an additional article has been included this year on the Gulf war and its handling in the media. These essays are supported by detailed chronologies recording the development of the issues, the significant events and other notable occurrences of the past year.

This series forms part of the work of the Institute of Contemporary British History. The principal aims of the Institute, founded in 1986, are to promote the study of all aspects of post-war history at every level and to provide a guide to current issues for everyone from students to contemporary policy makers by demonstrating the way in which the recent past has shaped the present. A central objective of this series is therefore to provide the material with which an informed assessment of the contemporary state of, and future agenda for, Britain can be made.

I am very grateful to the Twenty Seven Foundation, in association with the Institute of Historical Research, for their generous assistance with the production costs of this series and their support for the project. Many individuals have also contributed to the creation of this book. The efforts and helpful suggestions of the contributors to this volume, who have done their best to mitigate the editorial burdens I have faced, must be gratefully recorded. My five month old daughter, Rebecca, has meanwhile done her best to distract me from these burdens. The project itself would be impossible without Alyn Shipton and Caroline Bundy of Blackwell Publishers. Caroline must also be thanked for the picture research she has conducted. Above all, I must thank my colleague Virginia Preston, who has speedily and efficiently borne the brunt of the task of typesetting, subediting and coordinating this volume. We hope that this book provides a detailed and authoritative portrait of the issues facing Britain in 1991, and a context and an analysis within and from which to approach the contemporary and future agenda.

List of Contributors

* ARTHUR, Paul. Lecturer in Politics at the University of Ulster at Jordanstown and the author of several books on Northern Ireland, including *The Government and Politics of Northern Ireland* and *Northern Ireland since 1968*, Blackwell, 1988.
* BALSOM, Dr Denis. Lecturer in Political Science, Department of International Politics, University College of Wales, Aberystwyth. A well known commentator on Welsh affairs for the BBC, ITV and press and also author of numerous academic articles concerning Wales.
* BAYLIS, John. Reader in International Politics and Dean of the Faculty of Economics and Social Studies at the University of Wales, Aberystwyth.
* BECKER, Saul. Director of Studies for the interdisciplinary masters degree in Policy, Organization and Change in Professional Care, University of Loughborough. Author and editor of numerous books, research reports and articles on the boundaries between social work and social security, and a former adviser to the Association of Directors of Social Services.
* BILSBOROUGH, Peter. Senior Assistant Director, Centre for Physical Education and Sports Development, University of Stirling. He is the author of a book and numerous articles on various aspects of physical education and sport in Scotland.
* BLOWERS, Andrew. Professor of Social Sciences, The Open University. He is a county councillor in Bedfordshire specializing in environmental issues. Recent books include *Nuclear Power in Crisis*, co-authored with David Pepper, and *International Politics of Nuclear Waste*, co-authored with David Lowry and Barry Soloman.
* BUTLER, Dr David. Is a Fellow of Nuffield College, Oxford. He has been associated with the Nuffield Election Studies since 1945. Recent publications include *British General Elections since 1945*, Blackwell, 1989.
* CATTERALL, Dr Peter. Director of the Institute of Contemporary British History. He is the author of *British History 1945–1987: an annotated bibliography*, Blackwell, 1990.
* CHERRY, Gordon E. Emeritus Professor of Urban and Regional Planning, University of Birmingham. He is a past President of the Royal Town Planning Institute, specializes in planning history and is Chairman of the Planning History Group, an international body of scholars working in that field. His latest book *Cities and Plans* was published in 1988. In 1991 he was elected to a fellowship of the Royal Society of Arts.
* DAVIE, Dr Grace. A sociologist of religion, holding an honorary research fellowship in the Department of Sociology, University of Exeter. She has

carried out a number of studies for the Church of England and has published *Inner City God*, Hodder and Stoughton, 1987.

* DAVIES, Alan. Chief Economist, Barclays Bank plc. Most of his career has been with Barclays, primarily in the Economics Department, where he has specialized in UK economic, banking and financial matters.

* DAVIES, Gary. Currently Post Office Counters Professor of Retailing at Manchester Business School, previously Fellow in Retail Marketing at Templeton College, Oxford. Author of a number of texts and monographs on distribution, most recently *Positioning Strategy in Retailing, The Independent Retailer*, and *Advertising in Retailing*.

* EVANS, B.J. Dean of the School of Music and Humanities at Huddersfield Polytechnic.

* GAUTHIER, Anne H. Currently a Prize research fellow of Nuffield College, Oxford. She has a doctorate in sociology from Oxford University and a master in demography from Université de Montréal. Recent publications include: 'Consequences of fertility decline: cultural, economic and social implications – The European experience' in J. Cleland (ed) *Impact of Fertility Decline on Population Policies*; 'Family policies in comparative perspective', discussion paper no.5, Centre for European Studies, Oxford.

* GEORGE, Stephen. Senior Lecturer in Politics, University of Sheffield. His research specialisms are the politics of policy making in the European Community and British policy towards the EC. His recent publications include *An Awkward Partner: Britain in the European Community*, OUP, 1990, *Britain and European Integration since 1945*, Blackwell 1991 and *Politics and Policy in the European Community*, OUP, 1991.

* GOODWIN, Dr P. B. Director of the Transport Studies Unit and Reader in Transport Studies at Oxford University. Member of SACTRA, the statutory body advising the Secretary of State for Transport on trunk road assessment methods, also a member of the Dover Harbour Board. Has published articles and books on transport topics for twenty years, and frequently advises national and local government and transport companies.

* HARDMAN, David. Senior Lecturer in Resources/Tourism and Head of the BSc (Hons) Environmental Management Degree in the Department of Environmental and Geographical Studies, Manchester Polytechnic. Extensive experience in tourism lecturing. Particular interests include National Parks as tourist attractions, mining and quarrying as a basis for tourism and urban tourism initiatives.

* HARLOW, Carol. Professor of Law at the London School of Economics. Author of *Compensation and Government Torts, Politics and Public Law* and (with Richard Rawlings) *Law and Administration*. She is currently working on a book on pressure through law and is also vice-chair of the Legal Action Group.

* HARRISON, Anthony. He has edited *Health Care UK* since 1984. He is now a senior health policy analyst at the King's Fund Institute, working on hospital policy.

* HENNESSY, Dr Peter. Visiting Professor of Government at Strathclyde; presenter, BBC Radio 4's *Analysis*; columnist, *Director* magazine; author of *Cabinet*, 1986, *Whitehall*, 1989, and *Never Again: Britain 1945–51*, to be published by Cape, autumn 1992.

* HEWISON, Robert. Author of four books on Ruskin, and of the trilogy *The Arts in Britain 1939–75*. His most recent books are *The Heritage Industry*, 1987 and *Future Tense*, 1990. He has written on the theatre for the *Sunday Times* since 1981 and is a regular presenter of the 'Issues' edition of Radio Three's *Third Ear*.

* HILL, Christopher. Montague Burton Professor of International Relations at the London School of Economics, where he specializes in British foreign policy, the external relations of the European Community, and theories of foreign policy making. He is the author of *Cabinet Decisions in Foreign Policy*, 1991 and editor/joint author of *National Foreign Policies and European Political Cooperation*, 1983.

* HIORNS, Dr B. M. He is deputy managing director and head of the research department for Kleinwort Benson Securities. He has been senior UK investment strategist and responsible for UK research since early 1987 and global research since 1991. Before this he was a partner (1983) with Grieveson Grant & Co. (the forerunner of Kleinwort Benson Securities) in the UK institutional equity department, having originally joined the research department in 1974.

* HOLDERNESS, Dr B. A. Reader in Economic and Social History, Department of Economics and Social Studies, University of East Anglia. A farmer's son, he has written numerous works on agricultural history since the eighteenth-century, including *British Agriculture since 1945*, MUP, 1985. He is currently working on a book on British agriculture in the twentieth- century.

* HYMAN, Professor Richard. Convenor of graduate studies at the Industrial Relations Research Unit, University of Warwick. He has written extensively on industrial relations; the fourth edition of *Strikes*, and a new study of *The Political Economy of Industrial Relations*, were both published by Macmillan in 1989.

* KELLAS, James G. Professor in Politics, University of Glasgow. Author of *the Scottish Political System*, 4th edition, 1989 and *The Politics of Nationalism and Ethnicity*, 1991.

* KENWARD, Michael, OBE. He is a freelance science writer who edited the weekly *New Scientist* between 1979 and 1990.

* LAYTON-HENRY, Dr Zig. He is a Senior Lecturer in the Department of Politics, University of Warwick. He has recently edited *The Political Rights*

of Migrant Workers in Western Europe. His next book will be *Immigration and Race in Britain since 1945*, Blackwell, 1992.

* MORGAN, David. After researching twentieth-century poetry at Birkbeck College, London, he is now teaching English at Bancroft's School.

* MORRIS, Terence. Professor of Social Institutions at the London School of Economics and a specialist in the areas of criminology and criminal justice policy. He is the author of, among other works, *The Criminal Areas*, 1957, *Pentonville: The Sociology of an English Prison*, 1963, *Deviance and Control: The Secular Heresy*, 1976, and *Crime and Criminal Justice since 1945*, 1989.

* MORRISON, David M. Research Director of the Institute of Communications Studies, University of Leeds. His most recent publication is *Television and the Gulf War*, 1992.

* MURIE, Alan. He is Professor of Planning and Housing at Heriot-Watt University, Edinburgh. He is editor of *Housing Studies* and joint author with P. Malpass of *Housing Policy and Practice*, Macmillan. He is also joint author with R. Forrest of *Selling the Welfare State*, Routledge, and with R. Forrest and P. Williams, *Home Ownership: Differentiation and Fragmentation*, Unwin Hyman.

* NEW, Bill. He is a research officer at the King's Fund Institute. He is currently completing an MSc in Public Policy and Public Administration.

* NORTON, Professor Philip. Professor of Government at the University of Hull. An officer of both the Study of Parliament Group in the UK and the Research Committee of Legislative Specialists of the International Political Science Association. His publications include *Dissension in the House of Commons*, 1975, 1980; *The Commons in Perspective*, 1981; *The British Polity*, 1984, 1991; *Parliament in the 1980s* (ed), 1985, *Parliament in Perspective*, 1987; *Legislatures*, 1990 and *New Directions in British Politics?* (ed) 1991.

* PINTO-DUSCHINSKY, Dr Michael. Senior Lecturer in Government at Brunel University. His books include *British Political Finance, 1830–1980*. He researched the foreign funding of parties for the Policy Planning Staff of the Foreign Office, 1988–90 and is vice chairman of the research committee on political finance and corruption of the International Political Science Association.

* REID, Margaret. A freelance financial journalist and author. Once a Treasury official she has worked for the *Financial Times* and the *Investors Chronicle* (of which she was Finance Editor), and has been Journalist Research Fellow at Nuffield College, Oxford. Her latest book is *Conversion to PLC*, 1991, about Abbey National's switch from building society to commercial bank status. It followed her *All-Change in the City*, 1988, and *The Secondary Banking Crisis 1972–75*, 1982.

* REINER, Robert. Professor of Criminology, Department of Law, London School of Economics. His books include *Politics of the Police, Chief*

Constables: Bobbies, Bosses or Bureaucrats and *Beyond Law and Order: Criminal Justice, Policy and Politics into the 1990s* (ed).

* SEYMOUR-URE, Colin. Professor of Government, Rutherford College, University of Kent. He has written widely on political communication and the mass media and is preparing a study of prime ministers' and presidents' relations with the news media in the UK, other parliamentary systems and the UK. His *The British Press and Broadcasting since 1945* was published by Blackwell in 1991.

* SINCLAIR, Dr Peter. He is a Fellow and Tutor in Economics at Brasenose College, Oxford, and Research Associate at the Oxford Institute of Economics and Statistics. He is a managing editor of *Oxford Economic Papers*. His most recent books include *Modern International Economics* (with S. A. Heffernan), 1990, and *Unemployment: Economic Theory and Evidence*, 1987.

* SMITHERS, Professor Alan. Director of the Centre for Education and Employment Research, University of Manchester. He is currently working on projects on teacher supply, education 16–19, graduate employment, vocational qualifications and technology in schools. Recent publications include: *Gender, Primary Schools and the National Curriculum, Staffing Secondary Schools in the Nineties* and *Beyond Compulsory Schooling*.

* STONE, Graham. Principal Lecturer in Tourism in the Department of Hotel, Catering and Tourism Management, Manchester Polytechnic. Extensive experience in lecturing to undergraduate and postgraduate tourism students and consultancy to the industry.

* SUTTON, Kathy. She is a researcher at the Labour Party and was previously Wages Rights Officer at the Low Pay Unit. She writes here in a personal capacity.

* TAYLOR, Dr Philip M. Deputy Director of the Institute of Communications Studies, University of Leeds. His most recent publication is *War in the Media: Propaganda and Persuasion in the Gulf War*, 1992.

* WALDEN, Neil. Lectured at Manchester Polytechnic and the University of Strathclyde, before moving to Jordan Hill College of Education, Glasgow. He has a particular interest in environmental decision-making and has been concerned with developments in energy policy for many years.

* WALSH, Kieron. Senior Lecturer, Institute of Local Government, University of Birmingham. Currently doing research on the impact of competitive tendering on local authority management. Author of a number of books and articles on public sector management, including *Marketing and Local Government*, Longmans, 1989.

* WILLIAMSON, Valerie. Senior Lecturer in Social Policy at Brighton Polytechnic and executive board member of East Sussex Family Health Service Authority. She has recently published 'Patient Satisfaction with General Practioner Services', *Journal of the Royal College of General Practitioners*, 1989.

List of Abbreviations

3i	Investors in Industry
ABTA	Association of British Travel Agents
ACOST	Advisory Council on Science and Technology
ACPO	Association of Chief Police Officers
AEU	Amalgamated Engineering Union
AIDS	Acquired Immune Deficiency Syndrome
ARCIC	Anglican Roman Catholic International Commission
BBC	British Broadcasting Corporation
BCCI	Bank of Credit and Commerce International
BR	British Railways
BSC	Building Societies Commission
BSkyB	British Sky Broadcasting
BT	British Telecom
BTA	British Tourist Authority
CAA	Civil Aviation Authority
CAP	Common Agricultural Policy
CBI	Confederation of British Industry
CCGT	combined cycle gas turbine
CCPR	Central Council of Physical Recreation
CDP	Committee of Directors of Polytechnics
CERN	Conseil Européen pour la Recherche Nucléaire
CID	Criminal Investigation Department
CLP	Constituency Labour Party
CNAA	Council for National Academic Awards
CND	Campaign for Nuclear Disarmament
CNN	Cable News Network
CO_2	carbon dioxide
CPAG	Child Poverty Action Group
CPGB	Communist Party of Great Britain
CPRE	Council for the Protection of Rural England
CPS	Crown Prosecution Service
CRE	Commission for Racial Equality
CSCE	Conference on Security and Co-operation in Europe
CTC	City Technology College
CVCP	Committee of Vice Chancellors and Principals
DE	Department of Employment

DES	Department of Education and Science
DHA	District Health Authority
DM	deutschmark
DMU	directly managed unit
DNA	deoxyribonucleic acid
DOE	Department of the Environment
DPP	Director of Public Prosecutions
DSS	Department of Social Security
DT fusion	deuterium tritium fusion
DTI	Department of Trade and Industry
DTp	Department of Transport
DUP	Democratic Unionist Party
EA	Employment Action
EC	European Community
ECGD	Export Credit Guarantee Department
ECU	European Currency Unit
EETPU	Electrical, Electronic, Telecommunications & Plumbing Union
EFTA	European Free Trade Area
EMS	European Monetary System
EMU	European Monetary Union
ENO	English National Opera
EOC	Equal Opportunities Commission
EPC	European Political Co-operation
EPOS	electronic point of sale
ERM	Exchange Rate Mechanism
ES	Employment Service
ESDA	electrostatic document analysis
ESRC	Economic and Social Research Council
EST	Eastern Standard Time
ET	Employment Training
ETB	English Tourist Board
EVSSG	European Value Systems Study Group
FA	Football Association
FAIT	Families Against Intimidation and Terror
FE	further education
FL	Football League
FoE	Friends of the Earth
G7	Group of Seven
GATT	General Agreement on Tariffs and Trade
GCSE	General Certificate of Secondary Education
GDP	Gross Domestic Product
GLC	Greater London Council
GMB	General, Municipal and Boilermakers Union

GMT	Greenwich Mean Time
GP	general practitioner
GPMU	Graphical, Paper and Media Union
HA	Health Authority
HAT	Housing Action Trust
HGV	heavy goods vehicle
HIV	Human Immuno Deficiency Virus
HMI	Her Majesty's Inspectorate
IGC	intergovernmental conference
IMF	International Monetary Fund
IPPR	Institute for Public Policy Research
IRA	Irish Republican Army
ITC	Independent Television Commission
ITN	Independent Television News
ITV	Independent Television
JET	Joint European Torus
LBGC	London Borough Grants Committee
LCA	life cycle analysis
LEA	Local Education Authority
LEC	Local Enterprise Council
LIFFE	London International Financial Futures
LMS	local management of schools
LTOM	London Traded Options Market
MAFF	Ministry of Agriculture, Fisheries and Food
Met	Metropolitan Police
MGM	Mirror Group Newspapers
MMC	Monopolies and Mergers Commission
MoD	Ministry of Defence
MP	Member of Parliament
MSC	Manpower Services Commission
MSF	Manufacturing, Science and Finance Union
NACAB	National Assocation of Citizens' Advice Bureaux
NACRO	National Association for the Care and Rehabilitation of Offenders
NAHAT	National Association of Health Authorities and Trusts
NAHT	National Association of Head Teachers
NAS/UWT	National Association of Schoolmasters/ Union of Women Teachers
NATO	North Atlantic Treaty Organization
NBA	Net Book Agreement
NCVQ	National Council for Vocational Qualifications
NEC	National Executive Committee (of the Labour Party)
NEDO	National Economic Development Office

NETRHA   North East Thames Regional Health Authority
NGA   National Graphical Association
NHL   National Home Loans
NHS   National Health Service
NIO   Northern Ireland Office
NRA   National Rivers Authority
NSPCC   National Society for the Prevention of Cruelty to Children
NTTF   National Training Task Force
NUM   National Union of Mineworkers
NUR   National Union of Railwaymen
NUT   National Union of Teachers
NVQ   National Vocational Qualification
NWWA   North West Water Authority
OECD   Organization of Economic Co-operation and Development
OFFER   Office of Electricity Regulation
OFTEL   Office of Telecommunications
OPCS   Office of Population, Censuses and Surveys
PACE   Police and Criminal Evidence Act
PC   Police Constable
PCFC   Polytechnics and Colleges Funding Council
PE   Physical Education
POA   Prison Officers' Association
POST   Parliamentary Office of Science and Technology
PR   proportional representation
PRC   People's Republic of China
PSBR   Public Sector Borrowing Requirement
PSI   Policy Studies Institute
QALY   quality adjusted life year
QC   Queen's Counsel
R&D   research and development
RAF   Royal Air Force
RAWP   Resource Allocation Working Party
RN   Royal Navy
RPI   Retail Price Index
RRC   Rapid Reaction Corps
RRF   Rapid Reaction Forces
RSC   Royal Shakespeare Company
RUC   Royal Ulster Constabulary
RUSI   Royal United Services Institute
SACTRA   Standing Advisory Committee on Trunk Road Appraisal
SDLP   Social Democratic and Labour Party
SDP   Social Democratic Party
SEAC   Schools Examinations and Assessment Council

SEAQ	Stock Exchange automatic quotation
SERPLAN	The London and South East Regional Planning Conference
SNP	Scottish National Party
SOGAT	Society of Graphical and Allied Trades
SPSG	Science Policy Support Group
SSA	Standard Spending Assessment
SSSI	Site of Special Scientific Interest
TAURUS	transfer and automated registration of uncertified stock
TDPA	tourism development action programme
TEC	Training and Enterprise Council
TEED	Trades and Enterprise Education Directorate
TGWU	Transport and General Workers Union
TIMs	transparent insulation materials
TUC	Trades Union Congress
UCATT	Union of Construction Allied Trades and Technicians
UCW	Union of Communication Workers
UDA	Ulster Defence Association
UDR	Ulster Defence Regiment
UFC	Universities Funding Council
UFF	Ulster Freedom Fighters
UK	United Kingdom
UKIAS	United Kingdom Immigrant Advisory Service
UN	United Nations
UNCED	United Nations Conference on Environment and Development
USA	United States of America
USAF	United States Air Force
USSR	Union of Soviet Socialist Republics
UUP	Ulster Unionist Party
UVF	Ulster Volunteer Force
VAT	Value Added Tax
VET	vocational and employment training
WEU	Western European Union
WNO	Welsh National Opera
YT	Youth Training

Introduction: The Year In Perspective

PETER CATTERALL

Great empires have been overturned. The whole map of Europe has been changed. The position of countries has been violently altered. The mode and thought of men, the whole outlook on affairs, the grouping of parties, all have encountered violent and tremendous changes in the deluge of the world, but as the deluge subsides and the waters fall we see the dreary steeples of Fermanagh and Tyrone emerging once again. The integrity of their quarrel is one of the few institutions that have been unaltered in the cataclysm which has swept the world . . . (Sir Winston Churchill)[1]

There have been dramatic changes in the geopolitics of Europe since 1989. By 1991 these were affecting not just the East-West divide in place virtually since the end of the Second World War (during the course of the year the Warsaw Pact was formally dissolved). National boundaries in eastern Europe, some of which had been in place since the peacemakers' deliberations after the great crisis of which Churchill wrote, the First World War, were also being redrawn in what, by the end of the year, were ceasing to be the Soviet Union and Yugoslavia. Civil war in the latter between Croats and Serbs became as much of a headache for the would-be peacemakers of the European Community as an enduring quarrel on the other side of Europe remains for the British government. Peter Brooke, the Northern Ireland Secretary, is to be congratulated on the persistence with which he pursued his talks initiative there. This effort, launched in January 1990, did at least bear fruit in his success in persuading all the Ulster parties in June, for the first time since 1974, to sit down together. The talks (Mr Brooke's rejected nominee as chairman, Lord Carrington, found himself leading the negotiations for peace in the new quarrel in Yugoslavia instead) proved however to be stillborn. In a situation where, as opinion polls showed, there continued to be little common ground between the Protestant and Catholic communities on their preferred constitutional solutions and where a mere 19 per cent favoured the British goal of devolution and power-sharing, there was little incentive for the politicians to pursue them.[2]

The Gulf War and After

Northern Ireland continued to be a problem, as the mortar attack on the cabinet in February and the disruption the IRA periodically brought to shopping centres and rail services (also disrupted in February by what BR described as the wrong type of snow and in the autumn by the annual leaf fall) demonstrated. It was hoped at the beginning of the year that the dominant concerns of the time, the Gulf crisis[3] and recession, would prove less enduring. The war in the Gulf, which broke out within twenty-four hours of the UN deadline for Iraqi withdrawal from Kuwait, was certainly mercifully brief. Few can have expected victory to have been accomplished so swiftly, and with so few losses. It was perhaps the first war won effectively in the air. Allied control of the skies was never fully contested, even before the flight of many Iraqi planes to Iran. Air supremacy greatly facilitated the speed with which the Allied ground offensive liberated Kuwait and drove into southern Iraq, whilst greatly hampering efforts to resist.

The liberation of Kuwait was however not the end of the issue. The UN objective had been speedily achieved. But the consequences of the war lingered on. The oil spillages into the Gulf and the firing of oil wells by the departing Iraqis ensured that the war had a major impact on the region's environment. It took most of the rest of the year to cap the burning wells. And the aftermath of the war posed the problem, not only of coping with this environmental disaster, but with human tragedy as well.

For the British and Americans, President Saddam Hussein of Iraq was the progenitor of the crisis, and little secret was made of their desire to see him replaced. He was seen as a major threat to the stability of the region, a view which was felt to have been borne out as the year wore on and more revelations emerged about the extent of the Iraqi nuclear weapons programme. The coalition which fought the war was not however the vehicle to remove him. Saudi Arabia, which had played host to the coalition forces, and the other arab armies, wanted to liberate Kuwait, but would not support a full-scale invasion of Iraq. The Allies, mindful of public opinion, were keen to bring their troops back as quickly as possible. Another, though lesser consideration was whether the fragile post-cold war unity of purpose in the UN Security Council, which had greatly facilitated the response to the invasion of Kuwait, would survive an attack on Iraq. Nor had the Security Council sanctioned such an unprecedented intervention. There was also fears that such an action would turn Saddam Hussein into a resistance hero. The Foreign Secretary's view was that 'some plot to get rid of Saddam Hussein . . . has to come from the inside'.[3]

Efforts on the inside to overthrow the Iraqi dictator in response to western calls however ended in disaster. What the West hoped for was a military coup. What they got was rather different. The Shi'ite rising in the south seemed, to western eyes, dangerously likely to work in favour of their fellow Shi'ites in Iran and the CIA had already advised against the toppling of Saddam Hussein for fear of producing a power vacuum in the region which would be filled by revolutionary Islamic Iran. This same concern blunted sympathy for the Kurdish rising in northern Iraq. The US indeed allowed Iraq to use its air force to crush the rebellions. It was the massive flight of refugees that resulted which prompted western response. Britain could do little about the situation without American co-operation. However,

John Major does seem to have played an important role in the initiative that led to the setting up of safe havens for the Kurds in April.[4] This succeeded in reversing the Kurdish flight and in July the troops that had been sent to accomplish this were once again withdrawn and replaced by a small multinational force just across the Turkish border with a watching brief. By the end of the year concern was however still being expressed about a Kurdish lack of supplies, and Saddam Hussein was still in control in Iraq.

Some of the other questions thrown up by the war, such as the slaughter of an Iraqi column withdrawing from Kuwait along the road to Basra in the final stages of the conflict, were more easily forgotten by the media and public. Others remained to be explored further, not least the role of British companies in supplying Iraq with material used in their chemical and nuclear weapons programmes.

Aid not Arms

The war also raised a number of other issues. At the same time that the end of the cold war helped to make it easier to police the proliferation of nuclear weapons, the Iraqi example made such policing seem more necessary. It is therefore ironic that the International Atomic Energy Agency, the body charged with policing the Non-Proliferation Treaty, warned in 1990 and again in September 1991, of serious financial difficulties.

The end of the cold war also meant the running down of the arming of Third World proxies. This helped to undermine repressive regimes at a time when the example of the way the demand for democracy had swept eastern Europe since 1989, the impoverishment resulting from the decline in world commodity prices and pressure for economic reform from the IMF and the World Bank were already weakening authoritarian governments across Africa. In the process this provided the opportunity for the West to support this trend towards democracy in the Third World. Western aid policy has reinforced this trend by being linked more and more explicitly, as the year wore on, with good government, advancement towards democracy and human rights. Britain has been one of the front-runners in this development, which was enshrined in an EC aid charter in November. The effectiveness of this linkage is enhanced by the fact that, with the territories of the former Soviet Union themselves in need of aid (another consideration for Third World countries competing for aid and investment), there is nowhere to turn for support but the West. The object is not only to prevent further dictators in the Saddam Hussein mould and promote stable government and economic improvement. Aid and the export of democracy is also an element in EC policy to contain the explosion in asylum applications of recent years, by reducing the flow at source.

Even Britain, which has the lowest rate in the EC in terms of land area, population or wealth, has experienced sharp rises in the number of asylum applications. Seeing many of these as economic migrants the government introduced, to widespread concern from the churches and lawyers dealing with immigration, an Asylum Bill, which places the burden of proof upon the applicant for refuge, as a means of stemming the tide. The problem is seen as one of sorting out genuine refugees from those seeking merely to improve their economic circumstances.

But it would be wrong, despite the received impression, to see Europe as the main area of the world having to cope with this problem. Famine, cold war proxy wars (not least in southern Africa), and repressive regimes have led to an explosion in the number of people seeking asylum across the globe, of which the Kurds were merely the highest profile example in 1991. Refugees pose an international crisis, not merely a European one. Indeed a totally unequal proportion of the burden is currently borne by the poorest countries. In Malawi, with an income per head one seventy-fifth of that of the UK, every tenth person is a refugee. In the circumstances it is no suprise that aid and immigration policy are becoming increasingly intertwined.

The Changes in the East

If anything the need for policies to ensure stability in and contain emigration from eastern Europe has been even greater. The Soviet coup in August, the failure of which turned out to have doomed the political structure, the Soviet Union, which it was designed to save, offered some sort of warning of the chaos, and risk of reversion to authoritarianism, that might ensue should the successor states that emerged by the end the year, fail. This is perhaps a major reason why the West was reluctant to accept that the Soviet Union was in the process of becoming history,[5] or, at least until his heroic stand against the coup leaders, to see President Yeltsin of the Russian Federation as a viable alternative to Mikhail Gorbachev. The fate of the Soviet Union's nuclear weapons, now controlled by Russia, Ukraine and Kazakhstan, was also a consideration.

The stability of these successor states is threatened by the social tensions bred of a ramshackle and declining economy. Money is needed if these tensions are not to be further exacerbated by high inflation. In early December President Yeltsin wrote to John Major, with whom he seems to have developed a considerable rapport at the time of the August coup and whose role as chairman of the Group of Seven gave him a high profile in East-West relations during the year, asking for help to establish a stabilization fund to support the rouble. At that stage Britain's aid remained confined to the Know-How Fund for providing technical and economic advice, and humanitarian aid, but Norman Lamont made strong representations for such a stabilization fund at the G7 finance ministers meeting in January 1992.

Resistance to the more generous support the Germans pressed for at the G7 summit in London in July was understandable given the number of economic controls and distortions that then remained in place, though it was subsequently argued in some quarters that greater generosity may have prevented the August coup. With the removal of most price controls and the rouble becoming convertible on 2 January 1992 these distortions were largely swept away and the currency came to need some sort of ballast, which only the West could provide, as Poland had had when it introduced convertibility in 1990.

Policing possible sources of instability and conflict, as these issues show, now presents new challenges and requires a different mix of aid, support for human rights and security policy, than during the cold war era. Notwithstanding the example of the Gulf war, the accent is now on the first two levers. This is because of the expense of the last. The Gulf war may have demonstrated the technological superiority of the West. However it also demonstrated the difficulty it had in funding even so short and limited a war. Both the US and Britain sought and received substantial support from other nations to cover their war costs. This not only reinforced awareness of the inability of middleweight powers such as Britain any longer to mount substantial out of area operations without the military (and probably financial as well) support of its allies but also showed that even the resources of the US are not unlimited. It is therefore not suprising that in the aftermath of the Gulf war, the accent shifted to less costly methods of policing involving the deployment of economic, rather than military might, such as aid policy.

Another facet of this shift, and also made possible by the end of the cold war, was the realization that there was no longer the need for standing armed forces of the scale (and cost) that had formerly been deemed necessary. Policy-makers on both sides of the Atlantic accordingly introduced substantial cuts, particularly in the forces based in Germany. These bases were a natural target, associated as they were with a vanished confrontation. What caused concern was that the plans in the British *Options for Change* review seemed to several commentators to reflect more the desire to make these cuts than a considered assessment of future needs and commitments.[6] The Gulf war certainly did not seem to deflect a review which was already well under way by the beginning of the year, or lead to a major reassessment of out of area capabilities.

In Britain the cost cutting was in fact modest, about 5.5 per cent in real terms by 1993–94, compared to 25 per cent over five years in the US. This will leave Britain still near the top of NATO in terms of defence expenditure as a percentage of GDP. Resources for redeployment will be relatively small and the hopes in 1990 of a considerable shift in the large proportion of government related R&D which goes on defence and of defence related engineering capacity towards civil activities now look exaggerated.

Recession

Of more immediate concern to most people in Britain than the dramatic changes on the international stage was the persistence of the recession. A revival of demand and consumer confidence was persistently scouted, but refused, just as persistently to appear. Modest signs of an upswing seemed to be starting to appear in the early autumn, but by the end of the year the rise in optimism this prompted amongst economic commentators was replaced by renewed gloom. The economy was bumping along the bottom and there was a general feeling that no sustained revival could be expected before the election due by July 1992 at the latest.

The recession was far from uniform in its effects. Some regions, such as the north east, benefiting from considerable Japanese investment led by Nissan, experienced at worst a moderate downturn. London and the south east, in contrast to the previous recession of 1980–91, was much worse affected, with some sectors already entering recession as early as 1989. Service industries, which had escaped largely unscathed in the early 1980s, were now hit at least as hard as manufacturing. In total some 47,000 businesses folded in the course of the year, the worst on record. Many of these, of course, were small businesses brought into being by the encouragement of the Thatcher government, which found themselves either over-borrowed or with inadequate cash flows when confronted with their first recession. Those small businesses which survived meanwhile complained of the premium built into the interest rates charged by banks as an insurance policy, and the unhelpful attitudes of both banks and large clients.

There were also larger disasters. Chicanery was associated with both of the most notable instances. BCCI, closed by central banks in July, was linked with fraud, money-laundering and drug smuggling. Its collapse left many depositors, including local government authorities, dreadfully exposed. And in December Robert Maxwell's business empire unravelled; within a month or so of his death one of his quoted companies was in administration and many of his labyrinth of private companies were in liquidation. This collapse was but the most spectacular example of the problems flowing from the high levels of corporate indebtedness built up in the 1980s.

It also raised questions about responsible corporate governance. As with Asil Nadir, the former head of Polly Peck who was declared bankrupt during the year and banned from playing any management role in companies, debt led to dubious practices to support companies in the Maxwell empire. Money was used from private companies to support the share price of the publicly quoted Maxwell Communications Corporation and from pension funds to service debts. This raised the question of the need to ringfence pension funds to prevent a recurrence of such practices. The revelations also disclosed the same sort of accounting malpractices for which Maxwell had been condemned as 'not in our opinion a person who can be relied on to exercise proper stewardship of a publicly quoted company' in a DTI report in 1973.

The recollection of this warning was no consolation to the banks who had fallen for the allure of the tycoon and lent so freely to Robert Maxwell. The 'Max Factor' added further to the bad debt that splashed red across the banks' balance sheets in 1991. Nor was it just the banks that were plagued by debt. At the end of 1990 the gap between corporate income and spending had widened to a record £26.9 billion.[7] The cost of servicing the resultant high levels of debt at still high interest rates restricted the prospects of company spending carrying Britain out of the recession. Membership of the ERM meanwhile restricted the government's ability to reduce interest rates swiftly enough to overcome this problem. With sterling at or near the floor of the ERM for much of the year and a steady rise of German interest rates (to, by the end of the year, just 1 per cent below the British rate) reducing the attraction of holding sterling funds, the government's room for manoeuvre was severely limited. This was not least because, with the current account stubbornly refusing to return to surplus even in the depths of recession, a most worrying sign, the currency was increasingly underpinned by foreign holdings of sterling. The steady decline in inflation during the year helped to keep this money in London, though even so sterling did come under pressure several times in 1991. Nevertheless the Chancellor, Norman Lamont, was not in the end faced with the unpalatable choice between the political disasters of either devaluation within the ERM or a rise in interest rates that a full-blown sterling crisis would have entailed.

These restrictions on room for manoeuvre also affected attempts to kickstart consumer spending. In the personal sector, as in the corporate sector, a major problem was an overhang of debt from the boom years of the 1980s. This was fuelled by the encouragement of home ownership in those years, together with the loosening of credit after the 1987 stock exchange crashes. With the tightening of credit from 1989 onwards to try and rein in the build-up of debt, many homeowners found themselves in difficulties. The resulting squeeze dried up the housing market, not least because the fall in prices that this encouraged left many owners with mortgage debts larger than the current value of their house. This was particularly true at the lower end of the market, where properties were more likely to have been bought recently by first time buyers at the height of the boom, and in the south east, where the housing boom had been strongest, contributing to the peculiar severity of the recession there. People at the bottom of the housing market were therefore less able to sell and trade up because of the burden of debt they would have to carry with them. Many also found increasing difficulties in meeting enlarged mortgage interest payments. During 1991 this led to concern about the economic (and social) consequences of the resulting growth of mortgage arrears and house repossessions. There was little prospect of a consumer led recovery in these circumstances, and little incentive for new household formations to buy as an investment rather than rent.

This situation also discouraged moves against mortgage tax relief, which came in for increasing criticism during the course of the year, although minor adjustments were made in the Budget. This tax relief was blamed by many commentators for the housing boom. It was also seen as a contributory factor to the damaging British propensity to invest in bricks and mortar, tying up a large proportion of the national wealth, relative to other European countries, in mortgage debt.

The problems in the housing market also continued to affect the rate of housing completions. House builders, with some regional variations, were already in difficulties in 1990. Meanwhile, with 3 million new household formations expected by 2010, a process furthered by the declining average size of households as a result of family break-up and increasing numbers of single young people setting up home on their own, a number of reports in 1991 pointed to a need to encourage building accommodation for rent.[8] Policy constraints however continued to prevent the public sector from filling the resulting vacuum.

The Election that Never Was

What the government did do, in December, was introduce measures to stimulate the housing market and thus the economy, whilst bringing pressure to bear on mortgage lenders to stem the tide of repossessions. This action was also driven by political considerations. In 1991 it was the government's misfortune that the conjunction of the electoral and economic cycles was not in its favour. Mr Major's predecessor might have been tempted to risk an election in the aftermath of the Gulf war. But the opinion polls, whilst demonstrating the new Prime Minister's personal popularity, with his approval rating peaking at a level higher than any Prime Minister since the Second World War at the height of the Gulf conflict, seem never to have been deemed sufficiently auspicious for his party. The run of Conservative by-election disasters also continued. So the decision that the parliament would run its full course was taken, and there was no election in 1991. The government was perhaps waiting for the upturn that Norman Lamont repeatedly promised. By December however, with the hope of recovery before the election fading, the government instead settled for second best, by trying to alleviate the plight, and thus to rescue the votes of homeowners.

Not Quite Goodbye To All That

By then the new Prime Minister had completed his first year in office. Policy-related problems, notably over the poll tax and Europe, had proved his predecessor's undoing in November 1990. John Major was widely seen as having set out on a new tack. Thus *The Independent* commented on his Citizen's Charter: 'It offers an agenda for action which neatly points up the difference between Thatcherism and the policies that the Prime Minister intends to make his own'.[9] This statement is based on the view that Mrs Thatcher 'battered and humiliated' public services, whilst Mr Major is seen as being much more favourable towards them. Mrs Thatcher may have given this impression. But is there such a difference between, for instance, the unpopular NHS reforms with which the government has persisted and the Citizen's Charter as this view implies? The NHS reforms are after all much more an exercise in management accountancy than the sinister subversion of the welfare state[10] that the Labour Party, capitalizing on the public's lack of understanding and instinctive distrust of Conservative health policy, so successfully conjured up in the Monmouth by-election in May. They nevertheless were a substantial part of the government's electoral problem throughout the year, prompting increasing spending on the NHS above the rate of inflation in order to try and contain the damage.

Whilst affecting less emotive policy areas, is the Citizen's Charter so different from the NHS reforms? Far from being, in the words of Liberal Democrat spokesman Robert Maclennan, 'an attempt to start correcting the mistakes and failure of the Thatcher years' it seems to be entirely consistent with Mrs Thatcher's aims. In so far as that over-worked word 'Thatcherism' has any meaning it indicates a commitment to managerial change. In both the private and public sectors Mrs Thatcher sought improved management, efficiency and service-delivery through competition and the disciplines of the market, through privatization, contracting out and increased responsiveness to consumer demand. To a large extent provisions of the Citizen's Charter such as the privatization of British Rail, the enhancement of competition in the mail services, extension of compulsory competitive tendering in the NHS and other devices to increase regulation and accountability in public services are not only of a piece with this but are seeking the same virtuous ends through the use of the same tools.

There are however two main differences. The objects are essentially the same but instead of using changes in budgeting, the management accountancy route pursued in the NHS reforms, the government is relying more on regulation. The main exception to this is the use of financial penalties to encourage motorway contractors to complete work on time. Otherwise the balance has shifted away from a reliance on the introduction of the market to deliver the goods. Instead there are instruments such as charters to lay down standards of service from the rail, gas, water, electricity and telecommunications services and league tables of schools, health and local authorities' performance. The second difference is therefore that instead of encouraging managers to decide on the best allocation of resources it seeks to lay down standards of service. Its intentions are thus not just managerial. The recipients as well as the providers of services are to have a role in assessing and improving service delivery.

In making the market more meaningful through compensating for the monopolistic position enjoyed by utilities not just by the introduction of market disciplines but by deliberately shifting power towards the consumers of public services, the Citizen's Charter is a progression from the policies of Mrs Thatcher. This does not mean that there has been a clear break, even in the policy areas which were most at issue in November 1990.

One reason for this is that the leadership battle did not mark a clear break with the past. Europe and the poll tax remained divisive issues in the Conservative Party. Each entailed a painstaking search for a way forward. This was not just because of tensions in the party, but also because the government wished to signal a new and more pragmatic and consensual approach to policy making in place of the conviction politics of the 1980s. The need to avoid policy disasters such as the poll tax, has perhaps played a considerable role in this shift. The Major government has therefore been at pains to consult more widely and to agonize visibly over policies. One facet of this is the resurrection of the Royal Commission, a device unused during the Thatcher years. The freeing of the Birmingham Six and a series of other events throughout the year drew attention to the need for such an inquiry into the criminal justice system. Problems with police handling of evidence to which these cases also pointed, did not however lead to a parallel Royal Commission on the police for which there were also calls. not least from the Police Federation.

Anxiety for swift results meanwhile meant Michael Heseltine was denied the opportunity of a Royal Commission on local government finance and had to make do with a rushed insider investigation conducted by civil servants. A desire not to return to domestic rates and widespread support in the party for, if not the poll tax then at least for the principle that everyone should pay something, were also very real limitations on his range of choices.

It should not be suprising that his council tax accordingly bore some resemblance to its predecessor. However, whilst the stress on the number of adults in a household retains an element of the poll tax, the council tax should, because of the household element, be easier to collect (houses are simpler to register and trace than people), whilst its banding provisions go some, if not all the way, to avoiding the perceived unfairness of the poll tax. In the meantime it has meant that local government finance has ceased to be such a contentious and unpopular issue. This was also the intention of the £4.5 billion to reduce poll tax bills announced in the Budget. The move to wider and lengthier consultation processes has also helped to dull controversy and reduce the electoral damage which resulted from the poll tax in 1990.

Major and Maastricht

Europe's potential to cause controversy, at least in the Conservative Party, however remained. Problems over Europe with Mrs Thatcher and the Bruges Group during the summer were defused when she announced her decision to retire from the Commons at the next election. Party divisions however re-emerged, and not just amongst the Conservatives, in the run-up to the December EC summit in Maastricht. These divisions were mainly over EMU and the social chapter, though the summit was also criticized by Euro-sceptics for failing to address the problems of Russia and eastern Europe and the issue of European competitiveness (except, in their view, detrimentally through the social chapter), not to mention long standing British grievances against the CAP.

The government's approach to Maastricht was strongly coloured by this political background. In the event, as far as domestic politics are concerned, its policy proved successful. Progress towards political union was limited. The treaty went further on defence than the government desired, but the need to ensure the maintenance of the American connection meant that NATO remained the lynchpin of European security. Britain meanwhile secured the excision from the treaty of the social chapter provisions (which the other 11 EC members acceded to in a separate protocol) for the harmonization of minimum wages, maximum hours, worker participation in industry and other aspects of labour law which Conservatives feared were likely detrimentally to affect the competitiveness of British industry.

An opt-out from the final stages of European monetary union was also obtained. This defused the threat of an electorally damaging split in the Conservative Party over the calls for a referendum on this issue from Euro-sceptics, led by Mrs Thatcher. These successes, only obtainable in part because Mr Major enjoyed a markedly better relationship with Helmut Kohl, the Chancellor of Germany, than had his predecessor, were less appreciated on the continent. It was, commented the Spanish daily, *El Pais*, progress by 'the lowest common denominator'.[11]

The question remained as to whether the resulting domestic peace had been dearly bought. Despite the opt-out John Major indicated that he intended to take a full part in the negotiations towards EMU, and there certainly remained the possibility of the British, as so often before, belatedly boarding the European train and joining EMU, on the basis that it is better have some influence over something that will necessarily have a major impact on Britain's economic policy rather than, as with the Germans (who have a similar impact at the moment), none at all. And the British are anyway committed to stages one and two of the process, to try to achieve convergence between economies on which progress to full monetary union can be agreed. The government's view is that this will pose enough problems for existing members by 1996–97 when the decision is to be taken, quite apart from for the new members it would like to see encouraged to join, and that it is therefore sensible to postpone a decision. On the other hand this continuing tendency to point to the drawbacks of Euro-ideals ignores the determination of its EC partners to press ahead.

Meanwhile the opt-out means that the British position will necessarily carry less weight in the design of a European central bank and economic policy. A further cause of concern is the impact of the opt-out on the future competitive position of the City. This, as the first ever visit by the Lord Mayor to Brussels and the inquiry set up under Stanislas Yassukovich showed, was finally becoming a cause for concern in the square mile. It will not be assisted by the uncertainty over the future of the currency. Neither will investment prospects. And any European central bank emerging from EMU will now almost certainly not be based in London.

There is also a potential debit side to the opt-out from the social chapter. With this, as with EMU, there were British doubts about its feasibility, though the harmonization it requires should be eased by the cohesion fund for the poorer EC members agreed at Maastricht. On the other hand harmonization is seen by Britian's partners as an element in the forging of the single market, of which the government is amongst the keenest supporters. This may mean pressure on Britain to join in the long term. Meanwhile Britain has abdicated any role in the decisions over the process of harmonization. This will go on, guided in large measure, ironically, by the labour laws Britain gave to Germany during the occupation following the Second World War. But Germany has a high wage, high skill economy, whilst too many of Britain's workforce are little or unskilled. In this context the social chapter, whilst it may not entail the return to the trade union problems of the 1970s that the government feared, perhaps did threaten to lock the

British workforce in this uncompetitive position, unless education and training can be improved.

Other Events

Progress in this area was however somewhat mixed during the year.[12] Whilst some new initiatives in training policy, such as training credits were mooted, the highest profile issue in education in 1991 was in the primary sector. It is in this sector that basic numeracy and literacy, the bases of further training, must be delivered if the other sections of the education system are to function efficiently. There was however growing concern, particularly about levels of literacy, increased if anything by the first results of the new standard assessment tests. This concern came to focus on whether what were seen as modish teaching methods were to blame, and an inquiry was ordered in December.

Literacy and training were not however the only issues. Another related area of concern was science and engineering. Whilst the Labour Party made much of this, calling for a more integrated governmental approach to science and design policy, more pressing issues were the funding problems that the research councils faced during 1991 and the need to redesign career structures to prevent the loss of researchers either to overseas, or to science altogether.

There was nothing new about concern in this area. An equally long-standing problem was the condition of the prison system. Lord Justice Woolf's report on the Strangeways riot of April 1990 was published in February. Although target dates for implementing some recommendations, such as an end to slopping out, were set, the Home Secretary suggested that other problems, such as overcrowding, were likely to prove more enduring. The new prisons being built should go some way towards meeting this problem. Some of these, as announcements during the year made clear, are to be run by private contractors, another example of continuity from and development of policies initiated during the Thatcher years.

With continuing criticism of the prison service a Home Secretary's life was unlikely to be easy. Kenneth Baker however endured a particularly awkward year. His worst moment was the escape of two IRA prisoners from Brixton in June. This brought pressure to accept ministerial responsibility and resign, pressures also felt at the same time by Peter Lilley over matters connected with trade with Iraq. Having resisted this Mr Baker went on to make history as the first minister found guilty of contempt of court. Fault was also found with his response to joyriding, a pastime of the unemployed youth of Northern Ireland for several years but which, with the associated problems of ram-raiding and, in the late summer, riots, only made the headlines on the mainland in a big way for the first time in 1991. A bill to deal with the problem was introduced. Nevertheless, car crime remains a potent source of moral panic. The government's solution is new sanctions. If however the Archbishop of Canterbury's suggestion, much criticized by the government, is correct that the problem is the social conditions that breed, though they do not excuse the problem, this is likely to prove at best a short term palliative.

A social malaise of a different kind was also prominent during 1991. Child abuse continued to be a major cause for concern. What was unusual was the extent to which attention focused on abuse of children in homes. The most prominent cases to come to light were the pindown regime in Staffordshire and the sexual abuses committed by Frank Beck in a series of Leicestershire homes. Both raised questions of therapeutic techniques, the training, staffing and supervision of homes, as well as concern as to how widespread such abuses were. The spate of reports and inquiries ordered as a result suggest that further unpleasant revelations might be expected to continue in 1992.

There is however a happier note on which to end. The year might have seen some new nightmares, such as pindown, uncovered or just beginning. It also saw, as with Northern Ireland, other nightmares continuing on their dreadful way. But for some men at least, 1991 brought the end of the nightmare. A more active policy on the part of the Foreign Office under Douglas Hurd, the turning of Syria and Iran towards the West and their declining value as bargaining counters with it; all this lay in the background to the release at last of the western hostages (with the exception of two Germans) in the Lebanon. Salman Rushdie remains in hiding. Nevertheless, with the release of John McCarthy, Jackie Mann and Terry Waite at least one painful saga was ended.

Notes

1 Winston Churchill, *The World Crisis Volume 6: The Aftermath*, Thornton Butterworth, 1923, pp 319–20.
2 I am grateful to Dr W Harvey Cox for much of this information.
3 Cited in *The Independent*, 27 December 1991.
4 See Sarah Helm, 'US and UK argue over who saved the Kurds', *The Independent*, 19 April 1991.
5 Douglas Hurd, speech to the UN General Assembly, 25 September 1991.
6 See pp
7 *The Daily Telegraph*, 22 March 1991.
8 See pp
9 *The Independent*, 23 July 1991.
10 For a detailed discussion see Ken Judge and Bill New, 'Health' in Peter Catterall (ed), *Contemporary Britain: An Annual Review 1991*, Blackwell, 1991, pp 280–93.
11 *El Pais*, 12 December 1991.

Central Administration

PETER HENNESSY

This was the year in which the central apparatus of state adjusted to an absence – Mrs Thatcher's. Within minutes of 'kissing hands' at Buckingham Palace, John Major talked outside No. 10 Downing Street of wanting a country 'at ease' with itself.[1] Within days he had created a more easeful society within his own direct labour organization, the civil service. 'Discussion is back. Argument, even, is allowed', declared a senior public servant in one of the central departments with conspicuous pleasure.[2] The new style was reflected, too, inside the Cabinet, which reverted to being a discussion-laden zone and remained one even though the Gulf emergency required the temporary creation of a small 'War Cabinet'.

There was more to Mr Major's first year than the absence theme. It had a flavour of its own – Chartism. The Citizen's Charter was very much the Prime Minister's own (though the two main rival parties each claimed prior paternity) and reflected strongly the important, but little noticed, speech he had made as Chief Secretary to the Treasury in 1989 on the theme of high quality public services as good in their own right not 'some kind of temporary phenomenon to be tolerated only until privatized'.[3]

Linked to the Charter was further progress in the Next Steps programme of rehousing large blocks of civil service work into freestanding executive agencies with substantial devolved managerial and financial freedoms. Mr Major shifted the direction and pace of the Next Steps process instructing the Treasury and the Cabinet Office that the onus would henceforth be upon them to justify withholding further freedoms from agency chief executives rather than the other way round.

The Labour Shadow Cabinet continued its preparations for a restoration to office in the 1990s. Proposals were brought forward to change the machinery of government in the area of science policy making and there was a special emphasis on women's rights and a new Ministry for Women was pledged. The Shadow Chancellor, John Smith, accepted the Next Steps notion and undertook to maintain the programme. The leader of the Opposition, Neil Kinnock, developed his thoughts on the kind of Cabinet 'think tank' he would create if elected and the party refined its plans for substantial constitutional change (assembly in Edinburgh, regional government of some kind for England and Wales, an elected second chamber to replace the House of Lords and freedom of information) while privately keeping an open mind about the possibility of proportional representation in some form.

In 1991 there were almost as many alternative constitutions on offer as there were charters. They ranged across the political spectrum from Tony Benn's Commonwealth of Britain Bill to the free market Institute of Economic Affairs. Intellectual research and development clearly anticipated a highly fluid political decade, and, for most of the year, the opinion polls suggested an electoral arithmetic that made it a distinct possibility for the first time since the mid-1970s. The prospect of substantial constitutional change by the turn of the century, perhaps induced by the European dimension (the notion of 'subsidiarity' was, after all, incorporated in the draft treaties which emerged from the Maastricht summit as the year ended) no longer seemed remote or especially alarming.

Cabinet Government

Mr Major kept Mrs Thatcher's Cabinet and Cabinet committee structure largely intact. The change was largely of tone, but one sufficiently substantial to have changed the ecology of Cabinet life. As the first anniversary of the change of premiership approached, Mr Major's colleagues were reported to be telling their Labour rivals that 'this is how Cabinet government ought to work'.[4]

The Prime Minister himself made a public virtue of this saying in a newspaper interview:

The Cabinet is a very young Cabinet; it is the youngest Cabinet of this century; we have been working very closely together, most of us, throughout the last ten years. So there is a very good series of personal relationships and I think that does help the nature of Cabinet discussions we have.
When we have had discussions people express views. There has been no single occasion in the 11 months I have been Prime Minister when we have had any difficulty in coming to a decision. Those who have won the argument have been satisfied. Those who have perhaps lost the argument have been content.[5]

The more even tenor of Cabinet relationships was reflected in a lower level of leaking than in recent years. The 'War Cabinet ' apart, perhaps the most important and politically taxing Cabinet committees of 1991 were the ministerial group on the poll tax abolition which met in the run-up to the budget and the standing sub-group of the Oversea and Defence Committee on Europe which met with frequency and intensity as the Maastricht summit approached. The Cabinet Committee on Science and Technology met more often under Mrs Thatcher. It was widely credited with the extraction of extra money from the Treasury for scientific research.[6]

Relationships between No. 10 and the Westminster political correspondents improved under the Major régime. His press secretary, a career civil servant brought with him from the Treasury, economist Gus O'Donnell, was willing for a more precise attribution of information to be made 'Downing Street' sources. The political correspondents of *The Guardian* and *The Independent* were instructed by their editors to rejoin the lobby system as a result.[7]

A substantial step towards a more routinely open system of government was taken with the publication of the first set of new style annual departmental expenditure reports replete with mission statements, plans and targets.[8] Though for the time being Mr Major declined to go beyond the precedent set by Mrs Thatcher in acknowledging in Parliament the existence of the four main standing committees of the Cabinet (Economic Affairs, Oversea and Defence, Legislation and Home and Social Affairs) he declared a willingness to contemplate further disclosure.[9] It was announced through his principal private secretary that he did not have 'a closed mind' about the possibility of emulating Australian practice by releasing a fuller Cabinet committee list and declassifying the Cabinet rulebook, *Questions of Procedure for Ministers*.[10]

The Cabinet
Prime Minister and First Lord of the Treasury
    Rt Hon John Major MP
Lord Chancellor
    Rt Hon The Lord Mackay of Clashfern
Secretary of State for Foreign and Commonwealth Affairs
    Rt Hon Douglas Hurd CBE MP
Lord Privy Seal and Leader of the House of Lords
    Rt Hon Lord Waddington QC
Chancellor of the Exchequer
    Rt Hon Norman Lamont MP
Secretary of State for the Home Department
    Rt Hon Kenneth Baker MP
Secretary of State for Wales
    Rt Hon David Hunt MP
Secretary of State for Defence
    Rt Hon Tom King MP
Secretary of State for Employment
    Rt Hon Michael Howard QC MP
Secretary of State for Trade and Industry
    Rt Hon Peter Lilley MP
Chancellor of the Duchy of Lancaster and Chairman of the Conservative Party
    Rt Hon Christopher Patten MP
Secretary of State for Health
    Rt Hon William Waldegrave MP
Secretary of State for Education and Science
    Rt Hon Kenneth Clarke QC MP
Secretary of State for Scotland
    Rt Hon Ian Lang MP

Secretary of State for Transport
   Rt Hon Malcolm Rifkind QC MP

Secretary of State for Energy
   Rt Hon John Wakeham MP

Secretary of State for Social Security
   Rt Hon Anthony Newton OBE MP

Secretary of State for the Environment
   Rt Hon Michael Heseltine MP

Secretary of State for Northern Ireland
   Rt Hon Peter Brooke MP

Minister of Agriculture, Fisheries and Food
   Rt Hon John Selwyn Gummer MP

Chief Secretary of the Treasury
   Rt Hon David Mellor QC MP

Charters

Transparency in government was a strong theme of the Prime Minister's *The Citizen's Charter*, published in July.[11] The Prime Minister was reported to have toyed briefly with the idea of adding freedom of information to the armoury of citizens' powers, but Whitehall orthodoxy prevailed.[12] The document's publication, however, was a significant constitutional event in its own right. For the first time we were described officially in a government document as *citizens* with *rights* rather than *subjects* with *duties*.[13] As the Labour and Liberal Democrat parties flaunted their charters,[14] there was much debate about how sharp would be the bite of the government's proposals. Would the citizen have any real financial redress if public utilities let him or her down or if the National Health Service failed to undertake the promised operation within two years of a patient being placed on the waiting list? By the autumn it had become plain that the Citizen's Charter had been drafted with care to minimize the possibility of judicial review in the courts. The senior official in charge of the Citizen's Charter unit inside the Cabinet Office said that: 'This is a concept that does not say that standards equal rights'.[15] Sir Kenneth Stowe, former Permanent Secretary at the Department of Health and Social Security, was not alone in arguing that: 'The effectiveness of a Citizen's Charter depends upon enforceability in the courts'.[16]

It was, however, historically significant that, thanks to Labour's policy reviews of the late 1980s and a tangible depolarization of British politics in the early 1990s, the nature of political competition changed. Instead of the argument concentrating almost exclusively on public versus private ownership or provision, the debate shifted to which party could deliver the best public services with greatest efficiency at lower cost. The duelling charters were the prime symbol of this changed political world.

Next Steps

The Next Steps programme crossed two significant benchmarks in 1991. First it fulfilled the intention of its civil service framers in achieving formally the status of political bipartisanship, ensuring thereby its durability. Following where the all-party House of Commons Select Committee on the Treasury and the Civil Service had led in 1990,[17] John Smith, Shadow Chancellor of the Exchequer, accepted it in a lecture to the Royal Institute of Public Administration in May.[18]

Second, Mr Major accepted the need for 'increased personal responsibility and authority for running their organizations' on the part of agency chief executives. Following up a report, *Making the Most of Next Steps*, prepared by his efficiency adviser, Sir Angus Fraser, the Prime Minister told the House of Commons that the 'agencies, delegations and flexibilities can be enlarged as their track record of performance is established, provided that essential controls on public expenditure are not jeopardized'.[20] He also accepted Sir Angus's advice that departments should set a 25 per cent target for cuts in headquarters staff now that so much work had been delegated to agencies.[21] Prodded by the Commons Treasury and Civil Service Committee, the government undertook in the autumn to review the staffing and functions of the management sides of the Cabinet Office and the Treasury.[22] The government also accepted that Next Steps agencies would be the chief instruments for delivering the civil service's contribution to the Citizen's Charter[23] and in November, in its *Competing for Quality* white paper, it extended the Charter's application to Whitehall by re-emphasizing the bias towards contracting out as much civil service work as possible with the regular subjecting to market testing of those functions that remained in-house.[24]

Permanent Secretaries of the Departments of State
Secretary of the Cabinet and Head of the Home Civil Service
     Sir Robin Butler KCB CVO
Lord Chancellor's Department
     Thomas Legg CB QC
Foreign and Commonwealth Office
     Sir Patrick Wright GCMG
     Sir David Gillmore KCMG
Home Office
     Sir Clive Whitmore GCB CVO
Treasury
     Sir Peter Middleton GCB
     Sir Terence Burns
Environment
     Sir Terence Heiser KCB
Defence
     Sir Michael Quinlan KCB CB
Education and Science
     Sir John Caines KCB

Transport
    Sir Alan Bailey KCB
    A P Brown
Energy
    G H Chipperfield CB
    J R S Guinness CB
Social Security
    Sir Michael Partridge KCB
Northern Ireland
    John Chilcot CB
Agriculture, Fisheries and Food
    Sir Derek Andrews CB CBE
Wales
    Sir Richard Lloyd Jones KCB
Trade and Industry
    Sir Peter Gregson KCB
Health
    Sir Christopher France KCB
Scotland
    Sir Russell Hillhouse KCB
Employment
    Sir Geoffrey Holland KCB
Chairman of the Board, HM Customs and Excise
    Sir Brian Unwin KCB
Chairman of the Board of Inland Revenue
    Sir A M W Battishill KCB

By the time the 1991 annual review of Next Steps was published in November 1991, 56 agencies had been established embracing over 200,000 staff (see Table 1). Among the agencies which had been up and running for a full year, of the 53 'quality of service' targets set, 37 had been met or surpassed, the same applying to 20 of the 26 'financial performance' targets and 28 of the 38 'efficiency' equivalents.[25]

In a lecture to the First Division Association on 15 October 1991, Sir Robin Butler, head of the Home Civil Service, reformulated the conventions of ministerial responsibility to take account of Next Steps. 'Ministers and the public', he said, 'are more likely to accept the delegation of responsibility which seems to me an essential element in running public services today if the delegation is buttressed by a knowledge on the part of those to whom such responsibility is delegated that their personal success or failure is in a direct sense dependant on the way in which they exercise those responsibilities.'[26]

Table 1. Next Steps agencies

Agency	Staff	Operating Costs £ million
Accounts Services Agency	90	2
Building Research Establishment	690	31
Cadw (Welsh Historic Monuments)	220	11
Central Office of Information	680	168
Central Veterinary Laboratory	600	20
Chemical and Biological Defence Establishment	600	30
Civil Service College	230	14
Companies House	1,100	27
Defence Research Agency	12,300	800
Directorate General of Defence Accounts	2,150	40
Driver and Vehicle Licensing Agency	5,250	157
Driving Standards Agency	2,100	50
Employment Service	34,500	708
Forensic Science Service	600	24
Historic Royal Palaces	340	27
Historic Scotland	610	31
HMSO	3,250	388
Hydrographic Office	870	25
Insolvency Service	1,500	36
Intervention Board	940	22
Laboratory of the Government Chemist	340	14
Land Registry	10,050	188
Medicines Control Agency	310	18
Meteorological Office	2,300	107
Military Survey	1,230	50
National Engineering Laboratory	380	22
National Physical Laboratory	830	48
National Weights and Measures Laboratory	50	2
Natural Resources Institute	420	25
NHS Estates	120	8
Occupational Health Service	100	4
Ordnance Survey	2,450	70
Patent Office	1,200	44
Queen Elizabeth II Conference Centre	70	6
Radiocommunications Agency	500	30
RAF Maintenance	13,000	633
Rate Collection Agency (N. Ireland)	270	5
Recruitment & Assessment Services Agency	260	13

Agency	Staff	Operating Costs £ million
Registers of Scotland	1,200	30
Royal Mint	1,050	109
Scottish Fisheries Protection Agency	200	10
Service Children's Schools (North West Europe)	2,330	70
Social Security Agency (N. Ireland)	5,500	99
Social Security Benefits Agency	65,600	1,700
Social Security Contributions Agency	7,200	110
Social Security Information Technology Services Agency	3,600	413
Social Security Resettlement Agency	470	26
The Buying Agency	80	8
Training & Employment Agency (N. Ireland)	1,700	25
UK Passport Agency	1,200	51
Valuation Office	5,250	139
Vehicle Certification Agency	80	3
Vehicle Inspectorate	1,850	52
Veterinary Medicines Directorate	80	4
Warren Spring Laboratory	310	13
Wilton Park Conference Centre	30	1

Source: Cabinet Office

Labour's Preparations

As the 1992 general elections approached, Labour was committed to enhancing the power of the Department of Trade and Industry *vis à vis* the Treasury, to renaming and retasking another two ministries (the Department of Health and Community Care; the Department of Food and Farming) and to creating six new ones (Ministry for Women, Ministry for Arts and Media, Department of Legal Administration, Department of Consumer Affairs, Department of Development and Cooperation and the Office for Science, Technology, Research and Statistics to be housed within the Cabinet Office).[27] In a radio interview, Mr Kinnock developed his plans for a 'strategic' think tank to assist a Labour Cabinet in policy formation. He stressed its ability to 'cross-fertilize' with outside research institutes thanks to the freedom of information legislation that would be introduced.[28]

Mr Kinnock also decided to avoid the appearance of politicizing the civil service by placing special advisers in ministerial planning units.[29] With the departure of Mrs Thatcher, the 'politicization' argument lost much of its validity. Very significant in this context was Labour's acceptance of Sir Terence Burns as the new Permanent Secretary to the Treasury after Sir Robin Butler had, with the Prime Minister's permission, consulted the Leader of the Opposition and the Shadow Chancellor before the decision was announced in April.[30] Unlike the run-ups to the 1983 and 1987 elections, the contacts between shadow spokesmen and permanent secretaries allowed for under the so-called Douglas-Home rules[31] seemed set not only to take place but in an atmosphere free of suspicious animosity.

A Fluid Decade?

With Buckingham Palace, No. 10 and the Cabinet Office discreetly preparing for a possible hung parliament and the shift to a multi-party system that might create[32] and no shortage of draft written constitutions on offer,[33] there was a distinct sense in Whitehall that old patterns of government and administration might not survive the century. Even if domestic politics remained in a 'steady state' there was a foreseeable prospect of harmonization of governing styles developing gradually alongside the growing political and economic integration of Europe. As David Williamson, a former Whitehall deputy secretary and now Secretary General for the EC Commission put it in a lecture in London in the autumn:

The European and national administrations are indeed living together before marriage . . . In the area of the implementation of major European Community policies we must look for development of the partnership between the European public service and the national civil services . . . We are going to need you even more than you need us.[34]

Table 2. Autumn Statement

Department	amount increase (£ billion)	spending 1990/91 (£ billion)
Social Security	5.60	70.60
Health	2.44	28.15
Arts and Libraries	0.05	0.61
Education and Science	0.63	7.95
Legal Departments	0.10	1.76
Home Office	0.26	6.00
DOE-Local government	2.75	31.02
DOE-Environment	0.08	1.29
DOE-Housing	0.15	7.78
DOE-PSA	−0.13	0.12
Transport	1.32	6.96
Employment	0.23	3.87
ECGD	−0.02	0.07
Scotland	0.82	12.54
Wales	0.55	5.81
Northern Ireland	0.55	7.03
Chancellor's Departments	0.23	5.03
Cabinet Office	0.05	0.45
European Communities	1.55	2.46
Defence	1.33	24.18
Foreign Office	0.07	1.12
Overseas Development	0.14	2.15
MAFF	−0.01	2.19
DTI	−0.02	0.94
Energy	−0.33	0.61

Notes

1 'Text of the Prime Minister's speech in Downing Street', *The Independent*, 29 November 1900.

2 Private information.

3 John Major, 'Public Service Management: the Revolution in Progress', lecture to the Audit Commission, 21 June 1989.

4 'Mr Nice Guy and his chums', *The Guardian*, 28 November 1991.

5 'Strength behind the Quiet Man', *Mail on Sunday*, 6 October 1991.

6 'A light in the gloom?' and 'Major tells universities to spend more on research', *New Scientist*, 14 December 1991.

7 'The Future of the Civil Service', *FDA News*, March 1992.

8 Andrew Likierman and Alison Taylor, *The Government's First Departmental Reports*, Chartered Association of Certified Accountants, July 1991.

9 Written Answer 212, House of Commons, 5 November 1991.

10 'Whitehall Watch: Major considers revealing hidden Cabinet workings', *The Independent*, 25 November 1991.

11 *The Citizen's Charter: Raising the Standard*, Cmnd 1599, HMSO, 1991, p.5.

12 'Freedom of information ruled out', *The Independent*, 5 July 1991.

13 'Whitehall Watch: Citizen's Charter will provide welcome challenge', *The Independent.*, 29 July 1991.

14 *Citizen's Charter: Labour's better deal for consumers and citizens*, Labour Party, 1991; and *Citizen's Britain*, Liberal Democrat Party, 1991.

15 'Whitehall Watch: Traditional language backed by "Exocets"', *The Independent*, 7 October 1991.

16 Sir Kenneth Stowe, 'Good Piano Won't Play Bad Music: Administrative Reform and Good Governance', Royal Institute of Public Administration Annual Lecture, 28 November 1991.

17 See Peter Hennessy, 'Central Administration' in Peter Catterall (ed), *Contemporary Britain: An Annual Review 1991*, Blackwell, 1991, p.21. During 1991 the select committee continued its tradition of reviewing annually the progress of the Next Steps initiative: Treasury and Civil Service Committee, Seventh Report, session 1990–91, *The Next Steps Initiative*, HC 496, HMSO, 1991.

18 John Smith, 'The Public Service Ethos', Lecture to the Royal Institute of Public Administration, 8 May 1991.

19 Efficiency Unit Report to the Prime Minister, *Making the Most of Next Steps: The Management of Ministers' Departments and their Executive Agencies*, HMSO, 1991.

20 He was replying to a House of Commons question put down by Terence Higgins MP on 16 May 1991.

21 Ibid.

22 *The Next Steps Initiative*, the government's reply to the Seventh Report from the Treasury and Civil Service Committee, Session 1990–91, Cmnd 1761, November 1991, p.3.

23 *The Citizen's Charter*, pp.36–7.

24 *Competing for Quality: Buying Better Public Services*, Cmnd 1730, HMSO, November 1991.

25 *Improving Management in Government: the Next Steps Agencies, Review 1991*, Cmnd 1760, HMSO, November 1991, p.6.

24

24 *Contemporary Britain*

Contemporary Britain

Contemporary Britain

24 *Contemporary Britain*

4 Apr: UN Commission on Human Rights criticizes Britain on immigration law, freedom of expression and privacy law.

8 Apr: *Executive Agencies: Facts and Trends*, Price Waterhouse, published.

10 Apr: Benefits Agency becomes an executive agency.

11 Apr: Stephen Haseler, *Britain's Ancien Regime*, Radical Society, proposes a written constitution, the end of the hereditary peerage with voting rights, open government and the removal of the constitutional functions of the monarch.

18 Apr: Sir Terence Burns is to replace Sir Peter Middleton as permanent secretary at the Treasury.

24 Apr: MORI poll for the Joseph Rowntree Trust finds widespread support for constitutional change.

16 May: Prime Minister's Efficiency Unit, *Making the Most of Next Steps*, HMSO, argues that the Next Steps programme still has a long way to run and that thousands of headquarters staff should go as a result of the programme.

20 May: Tony Benn presents his Commonwealth of Britain Bill to replace the monarchy with a presidency, disestablish the Church of England, introduce an elected second chamber, reduce the voting age to 16, introduce separate national parliaments in England, Scotland and Wales, withdraw from Northern Ireland, scrap the honours system, and radically alter the judiciary, the official secrets laws, the armed and security forces and police accountability.

6 June: *Citizen's Charter*, Adam Smith Institute, argues consumers must be offered guaranteed performance and rights of redress against services and utilities.

7 June: *United Kingdom Human Rights Concerns*, Amnesty International, criticizes Britain's human rights record over the criminal justice system, Northern Ireland, the treatment of political asylum seekers and the detention of Iraqis and Palestinians during the Gulf war.

24 June: Granada television's *World in Action* draws attention to the non-payment of taxes by the Royal Family.

2 July: Simon Hughes introduces a ten minute bill to highlight the Queen's exemption from taxes.

3 July: *Citizen's Charter*, Labour Party, outlines plans for a local government Quality Commission and an Education Standards Commission.

5 July: *Devolution and Democracy*, Labour Party, suggests regional authorities could have the power to raise taxes.

9 July: Justice's annual report calls on the government to appoint an independent commission to oversee privatized companies and public bodies.

11 July: *Citizen's Britain*, Liberal Democrats, promises a written constitution, a Bill of Rights, electoral reform and guaranteed consumer rights in respect of services and utilities.

22 July: Andrew Likierman and Alison Taylor, *The Government's First Department Reports*, Chartered Association of Certified Accountants, assesses the results of the move to departments producing annual reports, the first of which appeared earlier in the year, and criticizes the poor publicity in some cases and the general high prices of the reports.

Citizens' Charter, HMSO, the long awaited white paper is published. Its main points are the privatization of BR, and the introduction of a passenger's charter, guaranteed minimum waiting times from health authorities, the ending of the Post Office monopoly on the carriage of letters and the appointment of an independent regulator, more powers for the regulators of the gas, water, electricity and telecommunications industries, penalties on contractors for slow work on motorways to be extended to all major roads, utilities to be required to co-ordinate street repairs, better information on schools' performance, a parents' charter and league tables for schools, health and local authorities, an improved tenant's charter for those in council accommodation and the inclusion of compulsory competitive tendering for housing management, the introduction of clear complaints procedures in the public services, a right for individuals to take legal action against trade unions in the event of strikes, an extension of compulsory competitive tendering in the NHS to the distribution, warehousing and transport services, the dismantling of the barriers to contracting out in local and central government and the introduction of the better identification of public servants.

24 July: Civil service pay to be more closely related to performance.

26 July: Alan Budd appointed to replace Sir Terence Burns as Chief Economic Adviser to the Treasury.

5 Aug: Anne Davies and John Willman, *What Next? Agencies, Departments and the Civil Service*, IPPR, argues that Next Steps is not compatible with the traditions of a unified civil service.

Making Government Work, Liberal Democrats, proposes an independent central European bank, PR with fixed term parliaments and the state-funding of parties, freedom of information, regional government with tax-raising powers and local income taxes.

16 Sept: *The Constitution of the United Kingdom*, IPPR, in a 129-clause document suggests a bill of individual rights and freedoms, four-year fixed term parliaments, a second chamber elected by STV to replace the Lords, the election of the Commons by the additional member system, the election of the Prime Minister by the Commons, power-sharing with regional assemblies in Scotland, Wales, Northern Ireland and 12 English regions, personal taxes to go to regional governments, a Supreme Court, a lay-dominated commission to appoint judges, a broader base for judicial candidates, and a minister of justice.

23 Sept: Government to seek to impose a 4.5 per cent ceiling on civil servants and a one year delay in the report of the Top Salaries Review Body.

25 Sept: *Improving Government Statistics: Gaps and Discontinuities in Official Statistics*, Social Science Forum, argues that statistics on politically sensitive subjects such as unemployment, poverty, health, education and the economy are seriously flawed. It particularly identifies data discontinuities, changes in definitions, gaps in statistical runs and problems in accessibility.

21 Oct: *Competing with the World's Best*, CBI, criticizes the fragmentary nature of industry's policy on the environment and the lack of understanding amongst policy makers of manufacturing's problems, and calls for a new role for the DTI to promote manufacturing.

30 Oct: Liberty proposes a Bill of Rights to strengthen civil liberties, curb government powers and give parliament powers to review judicial decisions.

31 Oct: Queen's Speech outlines plans for a Barrage on Cardiff Bay, tighter regulation of offshore safety, the replacement of the poll tax with the council tax, the creation of the new offence of prison mutiny, the removal of colleges of further education from local authority control, the end of the division between universities and polytechnics, more

rigorous and independent inspection of schools, the publication of league tables of schools' performance, the protection of charitable donations, better service and more efficient redress from utilities, and more competitive tendering in local authorities.

3 Nov: *A Freedom of Information Act for Britain,* Campaign for Freedom of Information, suggests public rights of access to government records (with an independent review body which could force disclosure) and defines which records could be withheld by the government in the interests of security.

6 Nov: Autumn statement forecasts a rise in public spending in the next year of £11 billion and a PSBR of £10.5 billion.

18 Nov: The white paper, *Competing for Quality,* HMSO, identifies government services where competitive tendering is being considered.

19 Nov: Kenneth Baker found guilty of contempt of court in connection with the deportation of a Zairean refugee, the first minister to be so convicted.

21 Nov: Elections for the House of Keys in the Isle of Man return a clear majority opposed to legalization of homosexuality, making a constitutional clash with Whitehall increasingly likely.

1 Dec: Government sells bulk of ECGD to Dutch group NCM holdings.

17 Dec: A leaked document reveals that an insistence that EC regional aid be channelled through the Treasury rather than the regions is holding up the £109 million grant.

19 Dec: Graham Hart is to replace Sir Christopher France as Permanent Secretary of the Department of Health next February. France is moving in turn to replace Sir Michael Quinlan at the Ministry of Defence.

Parliament

PHILIP NORTON

During the year, Parliament experienced some notable debates. The most prominent were held in January on the situation in the Gulf. On 15 January, the House debated the issue on an adjournment motion. Nationalist and some Labour MPs opposed to the possible use of force divided the House. Government and Opposition MPs combined to carry the vote by 534 votes to 57.[1] Six days later, with troops in combat, the House again debated the issue. A government motion supporting the action was carried, with Opposition support, by 563 votes to 34.[2] The bipartisanship established between the two front benches was maintained throughout the conflict.

The rest of the year was notable more often for the absence of bipartisanship. Bernard Crick once characterized the House of Commons as the arena for a 'continuous electoral contest'. This contest became more pronounced as the prospect of a general election neared. Tension increased as the summer recess approached, some Conservative MPs favouring – and the Leader of the Opposition expecting – an election in the autumn. In July, the Prime Minister and the leader of the Opposition clashed in the Commons over what the Prime Minister knew about the Bank of Commerce and Credit International (BCCI) when he was Chancellor of the Exchequer.

The autumn witnessed a new situation. The Prime Minister let it be known that there would be no election until 1992. At the beginning of the new session, the Queen's Speech revealed a relatively heavy programme for what was to be a short session. The speech was delivered from the throne on 1 November. Even if the session lasted as long as was legally permissible, it would be no more than an eight month session. The general expectation was that it would last no more than six months. The relatively heavy legislative programme constituted a notable change from previous sessions and a significant feature of the year. The year was notable also for a feature that existed largely independent of the party battle: the pressure for a change in the procedures and sittings of the House. Also worthy of note, again independent of the party battle, was the continuing importance of private members' legislation.

The New Session

The Queen's Speech included a range of measures that were substantial and, in many cases, contentious. Among the most contentious were the Local Government Finance Bill, introducing the new council tax – guillotined in order to get it through by Christmas – and the Asylum Bill, introducing new procedures for refugees seeking asylum in the United Kingdom. Given that time was of the essence, the government lost no time in introducing the bills. The Local Government Finance Bill was taken for second reading on the first two available days, followed on the third day by the Asylum Bill, and by the Coal Industry Bill – paving the way for privatization – on the fourth. The same week, two bills – including the Offshore Safety Bill – were given second readings in the House of Lords.

Government business managers knew that it would be a short session. It was a situation that set them apart from their predecessors in previous Parliaments. Only three other post-war Parliaments had lasted a full five sessions and, as those had first assembled in August or October, it was possible for the final session to last until the summer.[3] What also set the session apart was the fact that the previous, full-length sessions had been relatively light ones. Sessions in the 1983–87 Parliament had been full ones. Most had seen the passage of at least 40 government bills (the number excludes consolidation bills, of which 30 were passed in the Parliament); in the full sessions of the 1987 Parliament, the number on occasion dipped below 30 (again excluding consolidation bills, of which again there were fewer). Some of the bills were substantial measures, such as the Education Reform Bill – which required 200 hours of parliamentary time – and the Water Bill, but the previous Parliament had also seen some substantial measures. In the final session, the government was almost reverting to its practice of the previous Parliament.

For the government, the legislative programme was potentially a double-edged weapon. On the one hand, most of the measures embodied in it enjoyed popular support.[4] On the other, seeing the measures through meant that many senior ministers – including the Home Secretary, Environment Secretary and Education Secretary – were having to devote considerable time to Westminster rather than stumping the country. Given that time was of the essence, there was also the risk of dissident backbenchers upsetting the tight schedule. If not a high-risk strategy, it was at least a risky one.

Pressure for Parliamentary Reform

There was growing pressure for changes in the practices, procedures and sittings of the House. During the Conservative leadership contest in November 1990, Douglas Hurd had made reform of working conditions in the Commons one of his principal goals. The following month, the new Prime Minister – John Major – was quoted as favouring more sensible hours and conditions. A number of MPs from all three parties then tabled an Early Day Motion calling for such changes to be made. A survey of MPs carried out for the House of Commons Commission discovered widespread dissatisfaction with working conditions.[5] Demands for reform grew in number and prominence during 1991. Several female Members, led by Harriet Harman (Labour, Peckham), argued the case for different – and less anti-social – hours of sitting. In July, Labour MPs expressed support for a four-day week in the Commons. The left-wing think tank, the Institute for Public Policy Research (IPPR), argued the case for a major increase in MP's support facilities. The Leader of the House, John MacGregor, made it clear he was not opposed to a change in the working practices of the House.

Various committees of the House proposed some changes to existing practices. In May, in its third report of the session, the Procedure Committee recommended various changes to the rules governing parliamentary questions, including abolishing the system of 'blocks' under which the Table Office has to decide whether a question falls within the categories on which departments will not answer questions.[6] In March, the Select Committee on Members' Interests proposed changes to avoid conflicts of interest on the part of Select Committee chairmen[7] and in October recommended the creation – by a resolution of the House – of a Register of Professional Lobbyists.[8] In its first report of the new 1991–92 session, it was expected to recommend changes to the Register of Members' Interests.

More importantly, the House established a new committee. Responding to the feelings of Members, Mr MacGregor proposed the creation of a select committee to consider whether changes to the sittings and business arrangements of the House were desirable. The Select Committee on Sittings of the House was appointed on 9 July with broad terms of reference. It was empowered to consider whether the public and private business of the House might be conducted more effectively by making changes to the order and timing of business, the hours of sitting, and the arrangement of the parliamentary year. As such, it was not covering matters that could not have been covered by the Procedure Committee, but given the workload of the Procedure Committee – and, in practice, the fact that it had lost its cutting edge in the present Parliament – it was felt that a new committee would be more appropriate to the task. When the new committee met, it decided to survey all MPs and a questionnaire was sent to every Member. Of the 650 Members, 444 responded. More than half favoured a reduction in the number of sitting hours; over 80 per cent wanted fewer late night sittings. Most also favoured a fixed parliamentary year.

Appearing before the committee in its first public evidence-taking session, the Leader of the House also nailed his reforming colours to the mast. 'Mr MacGregor made clear to the committee that he was committed to a new regime for the Commons.'[9] He recommended no Friday sittings, some morning sittings for private members' legislation, abolition of ten-minute rule bills, and further time limits on speeches. Further proposals for change were put before the committee in the form of both written and oral evidence. By the end of the year, there appeared to be every prospect of significant changes being recommended.

Nor was the prospect of change confined to the Lower House. The House of Lords also began to consider whether changes were necessary to its committee structure. In 1990, the Commons' Procedure Committee published a review of the workings of the departmental select committees after ten years of existence.[10] In 1991, the Lords decided, in effect, to undertake a similar enquiry, appointing a Select Committee on the Committee Work of the House. Under the chairmanship of Earl Jellicoe, it was given terms of reference 'to consider the committee work of the House and to make recommendations'. When it met, the committee adopted a far more active approach than had its Commons' equivalent the year before. It immediately started to invite evidence from selected academic observers and made clear that it wanted to look not just at existing modes of committee enquiry but also at whether the committee balance was right (given the existing emphasis on European Community legislation and on science and technology) and whether or not there might be a case for taking some government bills off the floor of the House. The committee began work in earnest in the autumn.

When the Leader of the House, Lord Whitelaw, had appointed a small working group at the end of 1986 to consider whether improvements could be made in the way the House conducted business, the group's report – in 1987 – had largely given the procedures a clean bill of health. 'We conclude that the current procedures are, in the main, satisfactory, and make only minor suggestions for change.'[11] Four years later, it looked as if the House might be prepared to consider slightly more than 'minor' changes to its committee structure.

Table 1. Chairmen of principal select committees: (C) = Conservative (L) = Labour

Agriculture	Members Interests
Jerry Wiggins (C)	Sir Geoffrey Johnson Smith (C)
Defence	Parliamentary Commissioner for Administration
Michael Mates (C)	Sir Anthony Buck (C)
Education, Science and Arts	Procedure
Malcolm Thornton (C)	Sir Peter Emery (C)
Employment	Public Accounts
Ron Leighton (L)	Robert Sheldon (L)
Energy	Social Security
Dr Michael Clark (C)	Frank Field (L)
Environment	Trade and Industry
Sir Hugh Rossi (C)	Kenneth Warren (C)
European Legislation	Transport
Nigel Spearing (L)	David Marshall (L)
Foreign Affairs	Treasury and Civil Service
David Howell (C)	Terence L Higgins (C)
Home Affairs	Welsh Affairs
Sir John Wheeler (C)	Gareth Wardell (L)
Health	
Nicholas Winterton (C)	

Private Members' Legislation

Private members' legislation occupies usually less than 5 per cent of the time of the House in any session. Yet within that time, usually between five and 15 bills will achieve passage. The number is normally closer to 15 than to five. The 1990–91 session was notable for the enactment of 18 private members' bills introduced in the House of Commons (see Table 1). Of the 18, 11 were introduced under the ballot procedure and the remaining seven were non-balloted bills introduced under standing order 58. As can be seen from Table 1, the measures enacted were diverse in subject matter.

Such legislation is variously criticized for being minor in character. It cannot make a charge on the public revenue. In practice, if it is contentious, it will require some measure of government support – in terms of votes and time – to get through. The largest single number of private members' bills that are enacted have their genesis in government departments, Members successful in the ballot having an opportunity to select bills prepared by departments but for which time has not been found in the government's programme for the session. The bills are modest but basically guaranteed to succeed.

What is noteworthy, though, are those measures which emanate from Members themselves or from outside interests, such as consumer groups, animal welfare organisations or groups formed to promote a particular moral issue. Even if a measure is not passed, the fact that it is debated on the floor of the House is valuable for raising the issue in an authoritative forum and helping put it more directly on the agenda of public debate. As such, Friday debates of private members' bills fulfil a valuable 'safety valve' function. This is especially so in the case of issues which are not usually accommodated in the partisan battle that dominates for most days of the parliamentary week.

Among the bills debated in the 1990–91 session which help illustrate the point were several affecting the welfare of animals. As Table 1 reveals, a number achieved passage. Some did not. Among the latter was the Pig Husbandry Bill, introduced by Sir Richard Body (Conservative, Holland-with-Boston) and supported by animal welfare organisations such as Compassion in World Farming. The bill helped put pressure on the government to bring forward the date by which dry sow stalls had to be phased out. The bill attracted significant lobbying in its support. A number of MPs subsequently revealed that they had received far more letters on the subject of the bill than they had on the Gulf war.

The new session beginning in November was less auspicious for those Members keen to achieve passage of a bill. The short session meant that the chances of success were smaller than would normally be the case. Nonetheless, some of the bills introduced by those who topped the ballot on 7 November ensured that the time was used to debate topical and contentious issues, ranging – not for the first time – from animal welfare to freedom of information.

Table 2. Private Members' Bills passed Session 1990–91

Procedure	Bill	Sponsor
Under the Ballot Procedure	Badgers	Roy Hughes
	Children and Young Persons (Protection from Tobacco)	Andrew Faulds
	Criminal Procedure (Insanity and Unfitness to Plead)	John Greenway
	Crofters Forestry (Scotland)	Calum Macdonald
	Local Government Finance (Publicity for Auditors' Reports)	Michael Mates
	Motor Vehicles (Safety Equipment for Children)	Michael Jopling
	Property Misdescriptions	John Butcher
	Radioactive Material (Road Transport)	Dudley Fishburn
	Registered Homes (Amendment)	John Butterfill
	Road Traffic (Temporary Restrictions)	William Cash
	Wildlife and Countryside (Amendment)	Donald Coleman
Under Standing Order 58	Age of Legal Capacity (Scotland)	Sir Nicholas Fairbairn
	Badgers (Further Protection)	Alan Meale
	Breeding of Dogs	Alan Williams
	Football (Offences)	Sir John Wheeler
	Forestry	Sir Hector Monro
	Smoke Detectors	Conal Gregory
	Welfare of Animals at Slaughter	Sir Richard Body

Overview

The year in Parliament was an interesting, and distinctive, one. Some features apparent in previous years continued throughout this one. Among them was the willingness of the House of Lords to amend measures against the wishes of government (see chronology). What was without precedent was the use of the provisions of the Parliament Act of 1949. The House of Commons again passed the War Crimes Bill. It was given a second reading on 18 March. On 30 April, the House of Lords again denied the bill a second reading. The bill was given the royal assent on 9 May under the provisions of the 1949 Act.

The Gulf war predominated at the beginning of the year but normal – partisan – activity soon resumed thereafter. A light legislative session – at least in terms of government bills – was replaced with a relatively heavy one for the short remaining session of Parliament. For private members' legislation, the position was the reverse.

By the end of the year, the issue of European economic and monetary union was again to the fore, the debate within the ranks of Conservative MPs spilling over into the election – again not for the first time – of officers of the backbench European affairs committee. Whereas two years previously, the pro-European chairman, Ian Taylor (Esher), had been defeated by Euro-sceptic William Cash (Stafford), the tables were now turned, with former Cabinet minister Sir Norman Fowler (Sutton Coldfield) being nominated to take on Mr Cash. In an election that attracted more than 200 MPs – more than ten times the number that would normally attend a committee meeting – Sir Norman was duly elected. Other Euro-sceptics also lost their battle to retain the other officerships of the committee. The election gave backbench committees a degree of public attention that normally they do not receive.

Attention then returned to the chamber and a two-day debate on 20 and 21 November on the forthcoming Maastricht summit, producing contributions not only from the present prime minister but also two former prime ministers, Margaret Thatcher and Edward Heath. The issue divided both parties: six Conservatives voted against the government – and a further nine abstained – in opposition to the government's negotiating stance and over 20 Labour MPs abstained on an Opposition amendment that they considered too supportive of European union.

As the year progressed, it was not just reform in Europe that attracted Members' attention. There was also reform of their own institution. By the end of the year, the prospects for change in the arrangements for Commons' business and sittings appeared bright, at least much brighter than it had for almost a decade.

Notes

1 HC Deb. Vol. 183, cols. 821-5.

2 HC Deb. Vol. 184, cols. 109-113.

3 See P Norton, 'Sessional Variations', *The House Magazine*, No. 534, Vol. 17, 4 November 1991, p. 14.

4 This was the finding of a MORI poll conducted on 1 November 1991. See D Hughes, 'Voters warmly approve Tories' new policies', *The Sunday Times*, 3 November 1991.

5 See P Norton, 'Reforming the Commons', *Talking Politics*, 4 (1), Autumn 1991, pp. 17-18.

6 *Parliamentary Questions: Third Report from the Procedure Committee*, Session 1990-91, HC 178, London: HMSO, 1991, paras. 110-14.

7 *Interests of Chairmen and Members of Select Committees: Report of the Select Committee on Members' Interests*, Session 1990-91, HC 108, London: HMSO, 1991.

8 *Parliamentary Lobbying: Third Report from the Select Committee on Members' Interests*, Session 1990-91, HC 586, London: HMSO, 1991.

9 *The Times*, 6 November 1991.

10 *The Working of the Select Committee System: Second Report from the Procedure Committee*, Session 1989-90, HC 19, London: HMSO, 1990.

11 House of Lords, *Report by the Group on the Working of the House*, Session 1987-88, HL 9, London: HMSO, 1987, para. 113.

Chronology

14 Jan: Death of Donald Coleman, Labour MP for Neath.

15 and 21 Jan: Debates on the Gulf war.

21 Jan: Commons Health Select Committee and Social Security Select Committee nominated to replace the Social Services Select Committee.

22 Jan: Government twice defeated in the Lords over the powers and duties of Scottish National Heritage.

28 Jan: Peers defeat the government on Statutory Sick Pay.

5 Feb: Six Tory backbenchers rebel over the Statutory Sick Pay Bill, protesting that small businesses were being burdened with extra costs when they could least afford it.

19 Feb: Government defeated at Commons committee stage of Export Credit Guarantee Bill.

7 Mar: Government defeated by 125 to 103 in the Lords over plans to change the benefits system for the disabled as 12 Tory peers rebel.

Bernard Weatherill, the Speaker of the Commons, announces that he will retire at the next election.

13 Mar: Select Committee on Members' Interests report urges new curbs on MPs' business links to allay concern over possible conflicts of interest involving chairmen of select committees.

19 Mar: Government plans to penalize single mothers who refuse to identify the fathers of their children to maintenance assessors are defeated in the Lords 110 to 106.

26 Mar: Select Committee on Broadcasting *The Arrangements for the Permanent Televising of the Proceedings of the House*, HMSO, endorses United Artists proposals for a dedicated cable television channel and reaffirms current regulations.

26-8 Mar: Legislation to introduce the £140 poll tax cut guillotined through parliament.

27 Mar: Government survives an opposition motion of no confidence by 358 to 236.

29 Mar: Sir John Stradling-Thomas, the Conservative MP for Monmouth dies.

8 Apr: Report by senior Labour MPs urges the party to discuss possible changes in voting rules, including the introduction of proxy voting, should there be a hung parliament.

1 May: Lords votes to reject the War Crimes Bill by 131 to 109. The government therefore invoked the Parliament Act to pass the legislation.

9 May: Royal Assent is given to the War Crimes Bill under the provisions of the 1949 Parliament Act.

27 May: Death of Eric Heffer, Labour MP for Liverpool Walton.

20 June: Cross-party demands that replies to MPs' questions to chief executives of Next Steps agencies should be published.

27 June: John MacGregor announces a review of the hours, procedure and workings of the Commons.

10 July: Select Committee on Procedure *Parliamentary Questions*, HMSO, calls on ministers to publish replies to parliamentary questions to executive agencies in Hansard. It also calls for the abolition of the 'Mayor of Sligo' rule under which, if a minister says he will write to an MP other MPs cannot ask for his reply, an end to planted questions allowing ministers to list their departments' achievements and an end to blocks on ministers answering on certain subjects.

17 July: The parliamentary Labour party calls for a four day week in the Commons.

22 July: IPPR report suggests the need for a major increase in MPs' secretarial allowances and the funds available for the opposition.

14 Sept: Death of George Buckley, Labour MP for Hemsworth.

17 Sept: Hansard Society recommends fixed term parliaments, publication of audited accounts by political parties, cuts in the number of parliamentary seats in Scotland, Wales and London and the creation of a standing electoral commission to take over the oversight of elections from the Home Office and incorporate the Boundary Commission.

30 Sept: Select Committee on Members' Interests, *Parliamentary Lobbying*, HMSO, recommends that committee chairmen should not be allowed to have commercial interests in areas which could conflict with their committee duties.

15 Oct: Government wins the vote in the defence review debate by 324 to 66. Seven Tories voted against the government and eight others abstained.

1 November: Queen's Speech.

5 Nov: John Macgregor suggests having morning sessions on backbench business in the House of Commons.

12 Nov: At least eight Tory MPs deliberately abstain on the first reading of the Local Government Finance Bill.

21 Nov: Six Conservatives vote against the government at the end of the pre-Maastricht summit debate and nine abstain.

2 Dec: Government defeated by 62 to 55 in the Lords on plans to extend compulsory competitive tendering in local government.

13 Dec: MoD refuses to release details on regiments to be merged or cut under 'Options for Change' to the Defence Select Committee.

19 Dec: Seven Tories vote against the government and about 20 others abstain in the Commons vote on the Maastricht treaties.

Political Parties

MICHAEL PINTO-DUSCHINSKY

Following the shock of Mrs Thatcher's dismissal in November 1990, the party scene was less dramatic in 1991. The two main parties manoeuvred and prepared for the forthcoming general election. Throughout the year the date of the poll and its outcome both remained uncertain. Neil Kinnock was the longest-serving of the leaders of the main parties. Apart from attacking the Tories, his main tasks were to continue his campaign against the far left, to consolidate the modernization of the Labour Party and to present himself and his team as a moderate and reliable alternative government.

For Paddy Ashdown, the objective was to guide the Liberal Democrat recovery after the disastrous split in 1987 between the Liberal and Social Democrat leaders of the ill-fated Alliance, David Steel and David Owen. The Liberal Democrats could hope to hold the balance of power in a new Parliament and to press ahead with their demands for electoral and constitutional reform.

The Conservative government had the advantage of a new leader and of control over the date of the election. But it also had to surmount the political problems posed by a deepening world economic recession, by public divisions among its MPs over European union, by problems of party organization and by the possible appeal of a change of government after 12 years of Tory rule.

The Conservative Party

The replacement of Margaret Thatcher as party leader and premier by John Major brought an immediate and sharp improvement in the Conservative rating in the opinion polls. Labour's large lead during 1990, which had been the outstanding cause of Mrs Thatcher's being ousted, evaporated. Though the change of Conservative leadership afforded some hope that Mr Major could win the general election (which he was obliged to hold by July 1992) he failed to establish a clear lead over Labour. This fact combined with the economic recession produced an atmosphere of political uncertainty and, in the end, led him to abandon the option of dissolving Parliament during 1991. Over the summer of 1991, the possibility of a November poll appears to have been seriously considered.

The limited time available to the new Prime Minister made it necessary for him to move rapidly to create a distinctive personal image and a new style of government. As if to respond to criticisms of Mrs Thatcher's forceful – to some strident – delivery, Mr Major spoke in a calm and friendly manner. There was to be no continuation of the former leader's verbal fisticuffs with her European colleagues. Mr Major went out of his way to establish cordial relations with the German Chancellor, Helmut Kohl, and to speak in warmer terms about Britain's commitment to the European Community in a speech delivered near Bonn to the Konrad Adenauer Foundation. He soon announced plans to replace the unpopular community charge, a tax to which Mrs Thatcher had been committed.

During 1991 the new Prime Minister emerged as a solid personality whose common touch could be seen in his passion for cricket and, more seriously, in his advocacy of a Citizen's Charter, designed to ensure that ordinary people received courtesy and punctual, efficient service from the utilities and public authorities. He was active and visible on the international stage, especially during the Gulf war, the brief Soviet coup in August 1991, as host to the G7 nations at a summit meeting in London, and during the highly publicized and contentious preparations for the European Community summit held in Maastricht, in Holland, in December 1991.

Mr Major was not only at pains to minimize disunity among Conservative MPs over policy towards the European Community but was also reported by insiders to have established a more collegial style with members of the Cabinet. The end of formal business would sometimes be followed by informal discussions about political strategy. There were frequent tactical meetings of a group of ministers who came to be known as the 'Musketeers': Richard Ryder (the Chief Whip); Chris Patten (the new party chairman); John MacGregor (Leader of the House); Lord Waddington (Leader of the House of Lords) and John Wakeham (the former Chief Whip and Secretary of State for Energy).

Mr Major appointed a new team of personal advisers at No.10 Downing Street. Sarah Hogg, a journalist and wife of the Foreign Office minister Douglas Hogg, became head of the Policy Unit and in this capacity was to play a key role in the formulation of the election manifesto. Judith Chaplin and Nick True took over the premier's political office and Gus O'Donnell replaced the controversial Bernard Ingham as press secretary.

During the 1987 general election, the frosty relationships between Mrs Thatcher's Downing Street staff and the party chairman, Norman Tebbit, had proved an unfortunate (and subsequently much publicized) feature of the Conservative campaign. This time No.10 and Conservative Central Office were to work together more happily, a result of the openness and informality which reportedly characterized Mr Major's contacts with the party chairman, Chris Patten.

Mr Patten was a popular choice as head of the Conservative Central Office. Before entering the House of Commons in 1979, he had devoted his career to the Conservative organization, rising to become the director of the Conservative

Research Department. He had proved indispensable to Mrs Thatcher despite his position on the 'wet' wing of the party and had been tipped as a possible future party leader. Nevertheless, he faced a hard job at 32 Smith Square. On the one hand, he needed to prepare for the possibility of a poll as early as spring 1991; on the other hand, he faced some serious organizational difficulties.

Mr Patten was confronted by what was probably the deepest financial crisis at any time in the history of the Conservative Party. The accounts published in autumn 1990, revealed a loss of £4.4 million in the previous financial year (April 1989 to March 1990). The position in 1990–91 was to be even worse. In June 1991, Mr Patten took the exceptional step of publishing four months earlier than normal accounts for the year to March 1991. They revealed that Central Office spending for the two previous financial years (1989–90 and 1990–91) had exceeded income by a staggering £9.4 million.

The problem had not arisen from a decline in income but from high spending. In 1989–90, Central Office spent £13.5 million (and received £9.1 million). In 1990–91, income rose to £13.0 million – a very high sum for a non-election year – but spending soared to £18.1 million. This compared with Central Office spending of £7.6 million in 1986–87 (the equivalent non-election year in the previous parliamentary cycle). Even in the election year of 1987–88, Central Office's combined spending on its routine activities and on the campaign had only reached £15.6 million. The high spending between 1989 and 1991 was only partly accounted for by the extension and modernization of the party headquarters (£3.8 million) and by the installation of a mainframe computer. There was considerable grumbling at the 1991 Conservative Party conference about extravagance and lack of financial control in this period.

During the previous financial crisis, after the 1979 general election, the Conservative treasurers had funded the party's deficit partly by arranging the sale and leaseback of the 32 Smith Square building. Loans from local party associations had helped to fund further deficits. But, by 1989–90, the new losses meant that Central Office was obliged to pay interest payments of £234,000. In 1990–91, the cost of interest charges reached £823,000. This was proof that the party was in the red to the tune of millions of pounds.

What made the financial position worse was that Central Office was about to enter the crucial campaign period of the electoral cycle when spending normally rises. Moreover, a late election, when the pre-election phase is prolonged, creates pressure for high spending. Sir John Cope, MP, an accountant by training and a former personal assistant to the party chairman in the 1970 election, was appointed as deputy chairman and treasurer. Control of expenditure was part of his brief.

A source of financial difficulty was that two of the main sources of Central Office income – corporate donations and payments from constituency associations – failed to keep pace with the escalating expenditures. In 1990–91, the total income published in the Central Office accounts amounted to £13.0 million. The sum collected was slightly greater since this figure is net of direct fundraising costs.

Constituency contributions to the centre amounted to only £1.3 million and a survey by the Labour Research Department of the director's reports of over 5,000 of the largest companies revealed donations of £3.4 million. Of the additional income not accounted for by these two sources (over £8 million), £1.2 million was raised by fundraising efforts such as the sale of exhibition stands at the annual party conference and by direct mail appeals. Some additional money also came from medium-sized and small companies not included in the Labour Research Department's survey. It is clear, however, that several million more came from individual donations, some of them in large amounts. A series of articles in the *Sunday Times* reported donations from Hong Kong businessmen, including £100,000 from Li Ka Shing and no less than £2 million from the Greek shipping tycoon John Latsis. In addition the Conservatives – like Labour – ran fundraising dinners, including an event at Blenheim Palace.

Central Office's increasing reliance on large donations from individuals was a source of concern and criticism both inside and outside the party. It reflected the failure over previous years at Central Office to put enough effort into the task of building up a sufficiently impressive list of small and medium-sized donors by means of direct mail.

Finance was not the only difficulty which greeted Mr Patten. The communication of Conservative policy and, in particular, the position of the party's advertising agency, Saatchi and Saatchi, Garland Compton, had been bones of contention in the 1987 election. Following adverse publicity, Saatchi and Saatchi announced that it did not wish to retain the Conservative Party advertising account. In the 1989 elections for the European Parliament, the agency employed for the unsuccessful Conservative campaign was Allen, Brady and Marsh.

Mr Patten appointed Shaun Woodward, a producer of the BBC's *That's Life* programme, as director of communications in succession to Brendan Bruce; Russ Pipe succeeded Harvey Thomas as director of presentation and Saatchi and Saatchi once again became the party's leading advertising agency. The services of the US pollster Richard Wirthlin were much reduced. Harris Research Centre continued to act as the main firm for private polls and additional work was commissioned from Gallup.

The campaigning department assisted in 1991 in a run of by-elections which, as usual for a governing party in mid-term, were disappointing. By early 1992, there were 276 full-time Conservative constituency agents, of whom 240 had completed the party's training. The party claimed to have placed an agent and a computer in every marginal constituency and to have encouraged the production of local party newspapers.

Though Conservatives prepared to enter the 1992 election as the only party with a substantial corps of professional agents, their doorstep advantage over Labour was possibly less pronounced than in most postwar elections. Conservative membership appears to have declined during the Thatcher era to about 0.75 million.

The Labour Party

In 1991 Neil Kinnock, like his predecessor Harold Wilson before the general election of 1964, continued to make it his central aim to present the party as a modern, competent alternative to the Conservatives. While proclaiming Labour's concern for 'the essential public services like health and education', and equal treatment for women, Mr Kinnock and his shadow economic team launched repeated attacks on the government's economic record. Labour promised to promote growth by encouraging industrial investment, by backing scientific and technological research and by improving the public transport system. Industry, training and the economy were major themes of the Labour Party political broadcasts.

Following the publication in 1990 of the policy document *Looking to the Future*, the party's campaign unit organized launches in 1991 of a *Charter of Rights, Building a World Class Economy* and statements of policy on science and technology, education, health, and on improvements in London.

Labour stressed its commitment to the European Community, which it contrasted with the 'Conservative's disarray over this issue'. At an organizational level, reforms were introduced as a result of which the European Labour Party was recognized in the constitutional framework of the British party. The 45 British members of the European Parliamentary Labour Party – also members of the Socialist Group in the European Parliament – restructured their secretariat and based four members of its staff in London. Labour's victory in the 1989 European Parliamentary elections promoted a powerful pro-European lobby of Labour MEPs and encouraged contacts between Labour leaders in England and their European counterparts. The European influence was to be seen in the interim report, issued in July 1991, of a working party established by the National Executive Committee in response to decisions taken in the 1990 party conference. Chaired by Professor Raymond Plant of Southampton University, the working party explored options for proportional representation in elections for the European and Westminster Parliaments, local government elections and the proposed regional assemblies. Final decisions about party policy on this contentious issue were postponed until after the general election.

The instinct for electoral success and political survival following three general election defeats made Neil Kinnock's position within the party as powerful as that of any modern Labour leader. Support in the National Executive Committee, the party conference and the major trade unions enabled him to press ahead with the attack on the Militant Tendency and with the modernization of the party organization. He also received backing for his emphasis on the task of electoral communication and on the use of advanced campaign techniques.

The 1991 party conference overwhelmingly endorsed the suspension of two Militant-supporting Labour MPs, Terry Fields (Liverpool Broadgreen) and Dave Nellist (Coventry South East) and of 25 members of the Brighton Labour Party. The conference also asked for a further investigation of the party in Birmingham Small Heath.

Development of the party organization involved a significant increase in the influence of the centre over the constituency Labour parties. This was seen not only in the NEC's control over the selection of candidates for parliamentary by-elections (agreed by the 1988 party conference) but in a number of other ways. In 1990 Head Office introduced the new membership system – a central, computerized register. According to the NEC's report to the 1991 party conference, this ran into a large number of teething problems. Nevertheless, the number of members increased from 293,723 in 1989 to 311,152 in 1990. The central organization claimed the lion's share of membership fees. It was agreed at a 1991 conference on party finances to increase individual membership subscriptions for 1992 to £15 and reduced rate subscriptions to £5. The introductory rate for individual members of trade unions would increase to £10. Sixty per cent of all these subscriptions would go to the Head Office and the rest to the relevant constituency parties. The affiliation fees paid by trade unions on behalf of blocks of members was to increase to £1.60 per member in 1992 (including 55 pence per member for the general election fund).

The Head Office played an important part in providing agents and full-time organizers for constituency parties. As the 1992 election approached, few local associations financed full-time agents. The Head Office met £263,000 out of the £430,000 spent on the long-established National Agency Scheme. In addition, the headquarters provided temporary organizers for up to two years in the constituencies designated as key marginals, of which 75 per cent had the services either of a full or part-time agent or of a temporary organizer. Head Office gave special attention to improving organization in constituencies in London.

The Head Office attempted to diversify and extend its sources of money. In addition to membership subscriptions and payments from affiliated trade unions, Labour expanded its distinctly untraditional Business Plan Fund. This had been set up in 1988 with the help of a loan of £500,000 from the Unity Trust Bank, underwritten by five affiliated unions (the GMB, NGA, NUR, TGWU and UCW). This Business Plan Fund included a 'high-value donors initiative' which involved a 'Gala Fundraising Dinner' in June 1991 and a further £500-a-plate gathering in February 1992. Other initiatives were an 'affinity' credit card and a list of sponsors. The party benefited from supporters who obtained a Labour Co-op Visa card. By 1991 this had raised £250,000 for the party. Labour received an initial fee for each card issued as well as 0.25 per cent of all payments made using the cards. Even more important than the 'affinity card' was the long-term strategy of building up 'sponsorship' of the party by standing orders. By 1991 the Head Office reported that it had some 20,000 individual sponsors. They were recruited by direct mail and telephone fundraising as well as through *Labour Party News*. Large sponsors received rewards such as biographies and novels of leading party figures and copies of *Opportunity Britain* signed by the full NEC. In 1990 these various fundraising efforts collected £1.6 million. Though most of this amount (£1.1 million) was absorbed by fundraising costs, it was hoped that such initial costs would decline as the sponsors list was built up and income increased.

Though these funding schemes represented an important change in style and policy, the Labour Head Office remained heavily dependent in the short run on its main traditional source: trade union political levy funds. Membership of affiliated unions continued to decline. In 1979 unions paid fees for 6.5 million members (though these fees did not mean that they had precisely this number of political levy-paying members). By 1987 the number was slightly under 5.6 million. The total fell further from 5.3 million in 1989 to 4.9 million in 1990. The drop in the size of these block affiliations was compensated for by the increasing amount paid on behalf of each member. In 1990 union affiliations provided £4.2 million for the party's income and expenditure account. On top of this, unions were responsible for most of the £1.8 million contributed to the general election fund as well as for other special donations.

Trade union levy funds provided about £6 million for Labour's Head Office in 1990. This was almost double the contributions made by the 5,400 largest companies to Conservative funds. Ron Todd of the TGWU, who chaired Trade Unionists for Labour, pointed out in July 1991 that unions' political funds remained strong. The total raised in these levies rose by one fifth in 1989, the most recent year for which statistics were available.

Labour's central income in 1990 amounted to £7.9 million. This total excludes (a) fundraising costs of £0.2 million, (b) the party's share of the 'Short money' (public funding for opposition parties in the House of Commons) and (c) the Business Plan Fund. If the Short money (£0.8 million) and income from the Business Plan Fund (£0.9 million) are included, total Labour income rises to £9.6 million. However, the money raised by the Business Plan Fund was all absorbed by fundraising costs. Expenditure from the income and expenditure account and the general election fund in 1990 amounted to £6.8 million. If the Short money and the Business Plan Fund are included, expenditure totalled £8.6 million.

From April 1991 onwards, Labour headquarters launched pre-election campaigns costing approximately £0.25 million a quarter. Its agreements with Trade Unionists for Labour led it to plan on the basis of a general election fund of £6 million by the start of the final campaign period. This concentration in the election was likely to produce a deficit on the general fund that would require staff cuts after the election. However, the party was committed to introduce legislation providing for extensive public funding of parties if it won a parliamentary majority.

While the forthcoming election was the main concern in 1991, planning for the gradual constitutional changes agreed at earlier party conferences went ahead. The 1991 party conference endorsed plans to increase the representation of women at all levels of the party and, in particular, to ensure that the proportion of women among Labour members of parliament would rise to one half over a period of ten years. Further plans involved the introduction of one member, one vote selection and reselection procedures for parliamentary candidates and a national policy forum. Both these reforms would gradually decrease the power of the major unions within party affairs.

The Labour Party
Leader
    Rt Hon Neil Kinnock MP
Deputy Leader, Home Affairs
    Rt Hon Roy Hattersley MP
Chief Whip
    Derek Foster MP
Chairman of the Parliamentary Labour Party
    Rt Hon Stan Orme MP
Trade and Industry
    Gordon Brown MP
Treasury and Economic Affairs
    Rt Hon John Smith MP
Energy
    Frank Dobson MP
Employment
    Tony Blair MP
Foreign and Commonwealth Affairs
    Rt Hon Gerald Kaufman MP
Defence, Disarmament and Arms Control
    Martin O'Neill MP
Transport
    John Prescott MP
Health
    Robin Cook MP
Social Security
    Michael Meacher MP
Scotland
    Donald Dewar MP
Leader of the House and Campaign Co-ordinator
    Dr John Cunningham MP
Chief Secretary to the Treasury
    Margaret Beckett MP
Environment
    Bryan Gould MP
    Ann Taylor MP
Women
    Jo Richardson MP
Food, Agriculture and Rural Affairs
    Dr David Clark MP
Education
    Jack Straw MP
Wales
    Barry Jones MP
Northern Ireland
    Kevin McNamara MP

Arts
    Mark Fisher MP
Development and Co-operation
    Ann Clwyd MP
Science and Technology
    Dr Jeremy Bray MP
Secretary to the Committee
    Bryan Davies
Leader of the Labour Peers
    Rt Hon Lord Cledwyn of Penrhos
Chief Whip, Lords
    Lord Graham of Edmonton
Peers' Representative
    Lord Dean of Beswick

Labour NEC elected at 1991 party conference
TU section (12 places)
    Vernon Hince (RMT) 4,681,000
    Gordon Colling (NGA) 4,675,000
    Tom Sawyer (NUPE) 4,665,000
    Bill Connor (USDAW) 4,654,000
    Eddie Haigh (TGWU) 4,639,000
    Tony Clarke (UCW) 4,490,000
    Tom Burlison (GMB) 4,455,000
    Nigel Harris (AEU) 3,727,000
    Richard Rosser (TSSA) 3,723,000
    Colm O'Kane (COHSE) 3,464,000
    David Ward (NCU) 2,910,000
    Keith Brookman (ISTC) 2,797,000
Socialist Societies (1 place)
    John Evans
Constituency section (7 places)
    David Blunkett 480,000
    Robin Cook 469,000
    Dennis Skinner 452,000
    John Prescott 425,000
    Bryan Gould 398,000
    Tony Benn 343,000
    Gerald Kaufman 316,000
Women's section (5 places)
    Margaret Beckett 5,405,000
    Joan Lestor 5,068,000
    Diana Jeuda 4,724,000
    Clare Short 3,594,000
    Brenda Etchells 3,464,000
Treasurer
    Sam McCluskie

The Liberal Democrats

Following the divisions and failures of recent years, 1991 proved a year of growing confidence for the Liberal Democrats. The party's morale was boosted by its sweeping victory in the by-elections held in October 1990 in Eastbourne and in March 1991 for the Ribble Valley seat vacated by David Waddington following his appointment as Conservative leader in the House of Lords. The party enjoyed a further success in the local government elections of May 1991, in which it scored a net gain of 487 seats. The final demise of the Social Democrats and David Owen's announcement that he would not stand for reelection at the succeeding general election closed the unhappy chapter of quarrels among the leaders of the former Liberal-SDP Alliance.

By 1991 the Liberal Democrats had largely recovered from the financial crisis of 1989. This resulted from growing membership and from economy measures taken by the general secretary, Graham Elson, and the finance controller, Matthew Bedford.

The pay roll at the Cowley Street headquarters was about 30 and there were also volunteers. The party maintained several additional offices. The party leader's and whip's offices in the House of Commons received £0.2 million in Short money as well as an additional contribution for research from the Asian Liberal Democrats. These had a staff of about 20. Liberal Democrat MPs used some of their parliamentary allowances to employ research staff to assist their work as party spokesmen. The Association of Social and Liberal Democrat Councillors employed several more at its office at Hebden Bridge in Yorkshire and the company responsible for party publications was based in Dorchester. Some 15 staff were employed by the Scottish and Welsh parties and by a limited number of regional organizations.

Membership rose from about 70,000 in 1989 to 92,000 by the beginning of 1992. Apart from membership subscriptions (which averaged nearly £10 per person) the party raised funds by direct mail. It had a data base, inherited from the SDP, including some 300,000 names (dating back over a decade) and a donor base of 30,000. The Liberal Democrats also ran an 'affinity' Co-op Visa credit card system similar to Labour's.

The income of the Social and Liberal Democrats totalled £1.4 million in 1989 (including £0.2 million in Short money) and £1.6 million in 1990 (including the same amount of Short money). Expenditure amounted to £1.6 million in 1989 and to £1.3 million in 1990. The party planned for a general election budget of £1.5 million. These statistics exclude the finances of the party's Scottish and Welsh offices as well as those of the Association of Social and Liberal Democratic Councillors and of some regional parties. On the other hand, a considerable proportion of central expenditure was devoted to the costs involved in maintaining the membership lists and in direct mail fundraising. These costs amounted to £0.2 million both in 1989 and in 1990.

The experienced campaigner, Des Wilson, continued to act as general election director, a position to which he had been appointed in 1990. He was supported by a general election planning group. Lord Holme directed preparations for the election manifesto. During the long pre-election period, the party organized a series of 'policy campaigns'. In May 1991, for example, it launched a campaign on environmental issues. The taxation of pollution was an important feature of Liberal Democrat policy. Plans for constitutional reform were a recurring and prominent theme. Other important issues were the economy (on which the Liberal Democrats stressed its policies for competition), European union and education.

Chronology

4 Jan: Cyril Townsend's Conservative constituency association in Bexleyheath votes to set up a selection committee in the light of discontent brought to a head by Townsend's support for Mr Heseltine in the 1990 Conservative leadership contest.

22 Jan: Tony Banks loses his front bench job after joining 33 other Labour rebels in voting against the party line of support for the Gulf war.

22 Jan: Tim Eiloart, the Green party secretary, is suspended from office.

1 Feb: Brian Griffiths succeeds Lord Thomas of Swynnerton as chairman of the Conservative think tank, the Centre for Policy Studies.

14 Feb: Clare Short is forced to resign her Labour front bench post after she publicly expressed disquiet about war aims in the Gulf.

15 Feb: Cyril Townsend wins a vote of confidence from his constituency association.

27 Feb: Liberal Democrat policy document, *Shaping Tomorrow, Starting Today* is published. It proposes higher personal taxes if necessary to improve education, a wide-ranging pollution tax, an independent Bank of England with sterling in the narrow bands of the ERM, restrictions on short-termist takeovers and tax reform to encourage growth in investment.

12 Mar: Conservative Way Forward launched as a new Thatcherite pressure group in the party with Mrs Thatcher as President.

13 Mar: Labour and Liberal Democrats publish their alternative budgets.

24 Mar: Labour expels four from Birkenhead CLP for belonging to Militant.

27 Mar: Communist Party to change its name to Democratic Left and adopt a new constitution.
Labour's NEC suspends 13 councillors in Lambeth, including Joan Twelves, the council leader, as well as the deputy leader and the chief whip.

28 Mar: Harvey Thomas resigns as Conservative party publicity officer.

11 Apr: Those attempting to introduce some structure to the Green party lose further ground at its spring conference.

16 Apr: *The Labour Way for the 1990s*, Labour Party, envisages requiring companies to spend 0.5 per cent of their payrolls on training, an immediate increase in child benefit and pensions, the retention of nuclear weapons whilst other countries retain them, the exploitation of the opportunities presented by Europe, and help for families to prosper in a fairer, safer society. It also waters down the party's commitment to tax cuts for the low paid.

19 Apr: MORI poll shows most Labour supporters favour PR.

25 Apr: Ealing Southall CLP deselects its sitting MP, Sidney Bidwell, in favour of Piara Khabra.

2 May: In the local elections in England and Wales, the Conservatives gain 245 and lose 1135 seats; the Labour Party gains 708 seats and loses 218 and the Liberal Democrats gain 750 and lose 230 seats.

5 June: John Underwood resigns as Labour's director of communications.

7 June: Militant decides to run Lesley Mahmood as a Real Labour candidate against the official party candidate in the Liverpool Walton by-election. Labour announces that any members openly supporting Ms Mahmood will be expelled from the party.

11 June: Bruges Group memorandum leaked to the *Evening Standard* criticizes the drift of the government's policy on Europe, provoking a storm of protest from all sides of the Conservative Party.

14 June: John Major seeks to reassert his authority in a speech to the Welsh Conservative Party conference after a week of sniping from right-wing critics, including Mrs Thatcher, over European policy.

17 June: Mrs Thatcher attacks moves towards federalism in Europe in a speech in Chicago, further fuelling the debate in the Conservative Party.

18 June: Ted Heath responds bitterly to Mrs Thatcher's recent comments.

21 June: Labour urges tighter controls on political advertising.

28 June: Mrs Thatcher announces that she is to retire as an MP at the next election.

3 July: *Just the Job*, Liberal Democrats, outlines plans for reducing unemployment through energy conservation, and the freeing of receipts from council house and land sales. It also outlines plans to allow small businesses to charge interest on debts not paid within 30 days.

5 July: Big purge of Militant promised by Labour in the wake of its rout of the rebel candidate in the Liverpool Walton by- election on 4 July.

8 July: David Hill appointed as Labour's new director of campaigns and communications.

11 July: Terry Fields, the left-wing Labour MP for Liverpool Broadgreen, is gaoled for 60 days for the non-payment of the poll tax.
Labour's conversion to multilateralism is signalled in an article by Gerald Kaufman in *The Guardian*.

12 July: Internal Labour Party report chaired by Professor Raymond Plant favours some form of electoral reform.

15 July: Labour orders an inquiry into Terry Fields' links with Militant. It also suspends 62 people with links with Militant.
Frank Field wins his battle against deselection in Birkenhead.

16 July: British Airways announces it is ending its donations to the Conservative party.

18 Aug: Liverpool Independent Labour party set up by the Broad Left in Liverpool to oppose the Labour Party.

26 Aug: Condemnation of a declaration on the rights of people with AIDS and HIV by the Conservative Family Campaign provokes resignations from and criticism of the group.

3 Sept: *Economics for the Future*, Liberal Democrats, aims to restrict mortgage tax relief to the needy, develop a stronger competition policy, regional pay bargaining, break up the high street banks, create a central European bank, and to set national savings targets, to be met by using tax and other incentives.

8 Sept: *Shaping Tomorrow's Local Democracy*, Liberal Democrats, suggests a huge devolution of power and taxation from central to regional government, with key

functions, including health, education, housing, planning and environmental powers, being transferred.

Liberal Democrats conference decides that the party would bring opted-out schools back under local authority control and condemns the proposed soccer super league.

10 Sept: Liberal Democrats conference endorses policy for wider share ownership, the ending of all unnecessary cruelty to animals, the protection of fur-bearing animals, and the prevention of water companies cutting off supplies to families with small children, elderly or disabled relatives without a court order.

11 Sept: Liberal Democrats conference agrees on energy taxes and calls for the government to make clear that any bid for ICI from Hanson will be referred to the MMC, argues that Slovenia and Croatia should be recognized by the EC and urges the strengthening of race relations legislation.

19 Sept: Labour attacks the Conservative Party over a £2 million donation from a Greek billionaire.

24 Sept: Labour pledges it will not increase the basic rate of income tax.

25 Sept: The Labour MPs Dave Nellist and Terry Fields are suspended from the party. So are 25 members of Brighton CLP.

29 Sept: Labour conference supports the suspension of Dave Nellist and Terry Fields.

Labour's NEC votes 21 to 4 to retain Trident.

Labour changes the procedure for selecting candidates, but continues to allow trade unions one third of the votes, as opposed to one member one vote.

30 Sept: John Major rules out a November general election.

Labour conference endorses a package of employees' rights including a safety tax on company payrolls to finance workplace inspections and the right to stop work when there is a risk of danger to life and limb, supports a proposal for a statutory minimum wage starting at half median male earnings, currently £3.40 per hour, reaffirms a commitment to regain a controlling stake in BT if the government stake remains at 49 per cent, rejects renationalization of water, gas and electricity in the first year of a Labour government, narrowly rejects phasing out of nuclear power in 15 years, rejects repeal of all trade union legislation of the Conservatives, endorses the reverse of the schools opt-out policy, the provision of nursery places for all three and four year olds, the reduction of class sizes and the payment of pensions at 60 for men as well as women.

1 Oct: Labour conference decides that by 1995 women must have at least 40 per cent representation at all decision-making levels in the party, to set up a policy forum of 194 seats (60 reserved for trade unions) to take much of the policy-making role from conference and involve MPs and MEPs in the process for the first time, votes against contesting seats in Northern Ireland and condemns the government's blocking of the EC directive protecting the rights of pregnant women at work.

2 Oct: Labour conference opposes the privatization of BR and the deregulation of London's buses, calls for increased police and legal sanctions against people involved in the distribution of racist material and threats and attacks against racial minorities, calls for a statutory right of reply to inaccuracies in the press and for the establishment of the crime of marital rape, approves the replacement of the Lords with an elected second chamber, changes to MPs working hours and childcare facilities so more women can become MPs, backs a Bill of Rights and measures to promote free speech, privacy and the right to join a trade union and engage in peaceful picketing, calls for an independent inquiry into the case of the Tottenham Three (imprisoned for the murder of PC

Blakelock in 1985) and for an end to convictions on uncorroborated confessional evidence, demands the return of privatized penal centres to the prison service, calls for an extension of legal aid, an end to capping legislation in local government and the restoration of the financial autonomy of local councils.

3 Oct: Labour conference calls for the dismantling of the internal market in NHS, the abolition of charges for dental check-ups, the introduction of a no fault compensation scheme in the NHS, an environmental protection agency and the reduction of defence spending to the level of other west European countries.

8 Oct: Selsdon Group manifesto calls for all pensions to be privatized, charging for social services, an insurance based health service and an NHS health tax which people with private cover could opt out of, and virtual withdrawal from the EC. This provokes several ministerial resignations from the group.

17 Oct: Derek Enright is imposed as Labour's by-election candidate for the Hemsworth contest instead of the locally selected Ken Capstick.

23 Oct: New Shadow Cabinet elected; Gordon Brown 150 votes (last year 138), Robin Cook 149 (125), John Smith 141 (141), Ann Clwyd 137 (102), Bryan Gould 136 (94), Margaret Beckett 134 (133), Frank Dobson 134 (96), Tony Blair 132 (115), Ann Taylor 126 (100), David Clark 122 (118), Donald Dewar 122 (115), Jack Cunningham 121 (99), Gerald Kaufman 121 (121), Jack Straw 119 (119), Michael Meacher 118 (111), John Prescott 118 (85), Barry Jones 113 (99) and Jo Richardson 107 (97).

8 Nov: Nicholas Ridley says on BBC Radio's *The Week in Westminster* that people should vote for candidates opposed to European union, even if they represent Labour.

13 Nov: Sir Norman Fowler elected to replace the Euro-sceptic Bill Cash as chairman of the Conservatives' backbench European Affairs Committee.

15 Nov: CPGB admits secret donations of up to £100,000 per year were made by the Soviet Union to support industrial disputes and protest movements during the period 1958–79 in an article by Reuben Falber in *Changes*.

21 Nov: Eighteen Labour MPs abstain on a Labour amendment urging qualified majority voting in the EC on social and environmental issues.

24 Nov: CPGB votes to change its name to Democratic Left.

5 Dec: Terry Fields, MP for Liverpool Broadgreen, is expelled from Labour for having links with Militant.

7 Dec: Dave Nellist, MP for Coventry SE, is expelled from Labour for having links with Militant.

18 Dec: Coventry SE CLP is suspended for continuing to support Dave Nellist.

23 Dec: Scottish Conservative and Unionist Association disbands the local party in Argyll and Bute.

Elections in Britain

DAVID BUTLER

The election omens were confused in 1991. From the beginning to the end of the year expectations about the date and the outcome of the general election fluctuated sharply. In actual voting tests – local elections and by-elections – the Conservatives fared ill. But opinion polls offered more comfort to the government and almost induced Mr Major to call an autumn general election. The year ended with the two big parties level pegging and with a sense that all was yet to play for in 1992 in a spring or summer election.

The government extended its losing streak in by-elections to seven. It lost two seats to the Liberal Democrats and two to Labour. In March Ribble Valley, its thirteenth safest seat in 1987, switched to Liberal Democrat and in May Monmouth went to Labour for only the second time in its history. The Conservatives' only consolation was that, when on November 7 they lost both Kincardine and Langbaurgh, the slump in their vote was less than in any Conservative-held seat since Kensington in July 1988. But the lesson that in a by-election nowadays no government seat can be safe was not lost on anyone.

One other by-election had significant repercussions. In the July battle for Eric Heffer's old seat, Liverpool Walton, the National Executive of the Labour Party had nominated Mr Peter Kilfoyle, a scourge of the local Militants, as candidate. The Militant Group then nominated Lesley Mahmoud, one of the expelled Labour councillors as a 'Real Labour' candidate. She only won 7 per cent of the vote but she and those who publicly supported her rendered themselves liable to expulsion from the party.

In the opinion polls John Major's honeymoon was short-lived. The lead which his election had won for the Conservatives in November lasted until April. But then anxieties over the poll tax and the health service pushed Labour into a lead, variously recorded between 4 per cent and 10 per cent, which lasted throughout the summer. In the last months of the year the advantage switched to and fro between the parties but seldom exceeded 1 or 2 per cent. The Liberal Democrats' vote shot up after their Ribble Valley triumph in March and, despite sharp variations in individual surveys, averaged a steady 15 per cent over the second half of the year.

Table 1. Parliamentary by-elections

Turnout %			Con	Lab	Lib D	Green	Nat	Other
72.2	Ribble	Lib Dem	38.5	9.4	48.5	1.0	–	2.6
–6.9	Valley Mar 7	gain	–22.4	–8.3	+27.1	+1.0	–	+2.6
64.0	Neath	Lab hold	8.6	51.8	5.8	–	23.4	10.5
–14.8	Apr 4		–7.5	–11.6	–8.3	–	+17.0	+10.5
76.0	Monmouth	Lab gain	34.0	39.3	24.8	–	0.6	1.0
–4.6	May 16		–13.6	+11.5	+0.7	–	–0.2	+1.0
33.4	Liverpool	Lab hold	2.9	53.1	36.0	–	–	8.1
–17.1	Walton July 4		–11.5	–11.3	+14.8	–	–	+8.1
65.4	Langbaurgh	Lab gain	39.1	42.9	16.1	0.9	–	–
–13.4	May 7		–2.6	+4.5	–3.8	+0.9	–	–
42.85	Hemsworth	Lab hold	10.5	66.3	20.1	–	–	3.1
–32.9	Nov 7		–6.7	–0.7	+4.3	–	–	+3.1
65.7	Kincardine	Lib Dem	30.6	7.7	49.0	1.6	11.1	–
–9.5	Nov 7	hold	–10.0	–8.2	+12.7	+1.0	+4.7	–

At the very end of the year there were uncertain signs of a new move towards Labour. But the Conservatives could take comfort in Mr Major's continuing substantial lead over Mr Kinnock in terms of personal popularity.

Table 2. Opinion polls 1991 (weighted average of published polls taken in each month)

	Conservative	Labour	Liberal Democrat	Other
Jan	44	41	10	5
Feb	44	40	10	6
Mar	41	38	16	5
Apr	41	39	15	5
May	37	41	17	5
Jun	37	41	17	5
Jul	38	41	17	4
Aug	39	40	16	5
Sep	41	39	16	4
Oct	40	42	13	5
Nov	39	42	14	5
Dec	39	40	16	5

Source: *The Financial Times*

The local elections in May involved all districts in England and Wales but left London boroughs and all of Scotland untouched. The Conservatives showed a slight recovery from the abyss of 1990 but they lost a net 890 of the seats they were defending (last fought in 1987). Labour gained 490 seats, and, to the general surprise, the Liberal Democrats gained 520 and were ahead of the Conservatives in a number of their target parliamentary constituencies such as Bath and Cheltenham. Labour's prize gains were Luton and Plymouth from the Conservatives and Blackpool, Cardiff and Darlington from no clear control. The Liberal Democrats took control in Cheltenham, Gosport, Torbay and Taunton. The Conservatives also lost control in Bournemouth, Derby and Northampton. They ended with fewer councillors than at any time since the new districts were established in 1973. Not surprisingly Mr Major described the results as 'disappointing but bearable'; Mr Cunningham saw them as 'a devastating defeat for the Tories' and Mr Ashdown as 'a stunning achievement for the Liberal Democrats'.

Local government by-elections provide a continuous monitor of how the parties are faring in actual polling booth situations. As always the Liberal Democrats fared a lot better than the opinion polls were suggesting.

Table 3. Local government elections May 1991: voting percentages

| | % of vote | | |
	Conservative	Labour	LD
Metropolitan boroughs	31.8	45.1	18.6
Change since 1987	+0.1	+2.5	–5.2
English and Welsh districts	35.4	35.8	23.3
Change since 1987	–4.8	+6.3	–4.3

These figures relate only to those districts where a third of the councillors retire every year.

Table 4. Local government elections May 1991: wards won

	Conservative	Labour	LD
Metropolitan boroughs	182	519	107
	–45	+27	+6
English districts	2519	1505	1220
	–580	+330	+235

Tables 3 and 4 are drawn from C Rallings and M Thrasher, *Local Elections Handbook 1991*, Local Government Chronicle elections centre, 1991.

Table 5. Local government by-elections 1991

| | Conservative | | Labour | | Liberal Democrats | |
	held or gained	net change	held or gained	net change	held or gained	net change
Jan-Mar	17	+7	11	–6	5	–
Apr-Jun	25	+6	34	–5	18	+1
Jul-Sep	20	+3	22	–3	17	+6
Oct-Dec	19	–3	33	+1	14	+5

Opinion polls and elections are watched not for themselves but for what they may indicate about the public mood and the way it will react when a general election, the ultimate choice of government, occurs. In 1991 with a new prime minister and an impending general election exceptional attention was paid to them. But, although the result in the Ribble Valley by-election or the May local elections pointed to total Conservative disaster, it is worth recording that the Conservatives remained ahead in the betting odds until the very end of the year.

Local Government

KIERON WALSH

The resignation of Mrs Thatcher and the return of Mr Heseltine as Secretary of State for the Environment has not led to any lessening of the pace of change in local government. A new agenda, focusing upon the further reform of local taxation, possible reorganization of local government, and the Citizen's Charter, has emerged over the last year. Other changes, in social services, education and environmental matters in particular, continue to work their way through the local government system. Two major bills were introduced into Parliament in November 1991 dealing with local government finance and with the organization and management of local authorities. The nature of change will depend upon the outcome of the general election in 1992, but, whatever happens, there will be major developments over the next decade. Local authorities have their own agenda for change, in addition to that of central government, emphasizing strategic management, the development of quality services, and the devolution of financial and management control. In this chapter I review the major changes that are proposed by the present government for the future of local government, and comment on more general developments in the operation of local authorities.

Local Government Finance

The community charge/poll tax, has, as many people predicted, turned out to be an administrative and political nightmare. Levels of collection are low in many authorities, and the experience of Scottish authorities has shown that the tax does not become any easier to collect over time. Authorities face financial difficulties as a result of the shortfall in local tax revenue. The Chancellor of the Exchequer announced in the 1991 budget that increased central government grant was to be provided to reduce community charge/poll tax bills in 1991/92 by £140. This move was funded by an increase in Value Added Tax by 2.5 per cent. The result is that very little local government spending, about 14 per cent, is now funded by local taxation, which results in high 'gearing'; that is, large increases in local taxation are needed to fund any spending above central government defined norms. Central control over local authorities consequently increases and, in effect, all local authorities now face capping on their spending. Nigel Lawson has proposed that the proportion of local authority spending funded by local government is now so low that local taxation should be abolished and funding taken over wholly by the centre. An alternative approach would be to increase local authorities' ability to raise their own revenue, for example by returning the business rate to local control.

The government proposes to replace the community charge/poll tax with the 'council tax', which will involve a mixture of property-based and personal taxation. The proposal is that property will be banded according to market value, and households in the same band in each council area will pay the same tax. The original proposal was for there to be seven bands, but an extra band has now been added to take account of high value properties. Those with properties in the highest band would pay a tax three times that of those with properties in the lowest band. The personal element in the tax would be based on the assumption that the norm was a two-person household and that half the tax related to property and half to the person. A single person household would then only pay half the normal personal element, involving a 25 per cent reduction in the total tax bill. There are to be rebates for people on low incomes, and no minimum payment as there was with the community charge/poll tax.

Few want to see the retention of the community charge/poll tax, but many fear that the council tax will bring its own problems. The first relates to the reduction in payment for single-person households. The government argues that this will not require registers, which have proved difficult to administer under the community charge/poll tax. But many in local government believe that a register will be necessary because of the frequent changes that are likely in entitlement. More generally, the retention of the personal element in the tax leads to many of the difficulties of the community charge/poll tax being retained. It is also likely that there will be bunching of properties in a few bands in many authorities. In London, for example, a high proportion of properties will be in the top bands, while in many northern authorities they will be concentrated in the lower bands. Conservative Members of Parliament have complained that people in the south-east of England will be unfairly treated because properties fall in the higher bands. The Labour Party has argued that the proposed tax is still regressive because the variation in payment between higher and lower bands is small.

The new tax is to be introduced by 1993, assuming no change of government, requiring a timetable which is tight, given the need to continue to collect the community charge/poll tax as well as introduce a new system. There will also be significant costs involved in introducing the new tax. The world of local taxation looks set to continue to be difficult in the future.

The government proposes to maintain the present arrangement for the non-domestic rate, under which it is controlled by central government and distributed to local authorities. Income from the business rate has fallen because of the recession. There are no proposals to change the approach by which central government grant aids local authorities. Under the present system variations in need are taken account of in the standard spending assessments (SSAs), which represent government's estimates of local authorities' need to spend. The consultative paper on the council tax argues that 'The SSA system is based on extensive research and provides about as fair a way of assessing needs as can be devised.'[1] Many in local government, particularly in shire district councils, would disagree, and there are strong feelings that the grant system is in need of revision, and local authorities dispute whether SSAs are an accurate estimate of local spending needs.

There is, perhaps, no system of local taxation and finance that would elicit universal approval. Few other countries experience the level of difficulty in local government finance that Britain has had in recent years. The result of the constant changes of the last decade has been a weakening of local government and confusion and obscurity in the operation of local finance. The community charge/poll tax did not bring the enhanced accountability that was argued to be one of its virtues. It is unlikely that the introduction of the council tax will solve the problems, or remove local finance from the agenda of central government's relations with local government.

Reorganizing Local Government

The second aspect of the review of local government that was instituted by Mr Heseltine involves proposals for the reorganization of local government. No set structure is proposed, though there are rather firmer proposals for Scotland and Wales than for England (no changes are proposed for Northern Ireland). The consultation paper on the structure of local government argues that issues of size are not as significant as they once were, and the presumption is that unitary authorities 'could often provide a better structure for an area'. The role of parishes might also be enhanced. The government proposes to establish a Commission which would review the structure of local government outside London and the metropolitan authorities. The Local Government Boundary Commission will be abolished and its functions taken over by the new commission.

The review of local government structure would take place on a region by region basis, without any national overview. Though there would be a presumption in favour of unitary authorities, two tiers might be acceptable in some areas. The basic argument is that single-tier local government would be better understood and would reflect the nature and interests of local communities more effectively. Staff commissions would be created to cope with the personnel issues that would be raised by reorganization. Residuary bodies might also be necessary to deal with the winding down of assets of authorities that ceased to exist. Certain areas of the country, for example Avon, Cleveland and Humberside, all counties newly established in 1974, are likely to receive earlier attention than others, but the whole process of review promises to take many years to complete.

It is easy to agree with the notion of a single tier of local government in theory, especially if the emphasis is on 'enabling', that is working through other organizations, through contracting out, and through partnership and other mechanisms. It may be much more difficult to attain in practice. Few, if any, advanced industrial countries have managed to develop a unitary system. Many have more than two tiers of local government. It is fairly clear that large cities, such as Nottingham and Portsmouth could well take on the full range of local authority functions. It is much less clear that unitary authorities would be feasible in many other areas, for example where population is sparsely distributed.

The concept of community itself is much debated and disputed. In some parts of the country people would identify with large areas such as 'Yorkshire' or 'Devon', as well as smaller, more local units. In others there might be no easily identifiable basis to community. The notion of 'community', given the different meanings which people attach to it, provides no unequivocal guidance to the appropriate structure of local government.

It may well be that a move to unitary authorities would, in practice, lead to increased centralization. The problems that might face smaller authorities in providing certain functions might lead to those functions being taken on by central government or by newly established regional government. Alternatively there might be a proliferation of joint bodies and committees to administer services on behalf of more than one authority. These joint arrangements can themselves constitute, in effect, a further layer of government and increase confusion in the minds of local residents. These questions would arise with regard to many of the most significant services now provided by local government such as fire, police, social services, education and planning. In some cases, notably that of education, the problems may be reduced by other proposals for change, notably local management of schools. But significant issues are still likely to arise in many parts of the country.

The experience of the abolition of the metropolitan counties and the Greater London Council illustrates some of the issues. In the case of London there is now much debate about the perceived need for there to be a voice for the city as a whole. There has also been significant centralization of functions. Problems of co-ordination across boroughs are only partly resolved by joint bodies and committees. In the metropolitan areas, too, there is, in effect, a second tier of government to deal with services such as police, fire and waste disposal, in the form of joint bodies.

It is unlikely that the 'big bang' model of reform, which was used in 1974, will be adopted in future. But the alternative is likely to be very slow change, as has been the experience of other countries. Different solutions are likely to be evolved for different parts of the country, through a process of extensive debate and negotiation.

Two other factors are likely to mean that any changes will tend to be slow and limited. First there is the issue of cost. There is debate over the costs or savings that have resulted from the abolition of the metropolitan counties and the Greater London Council, but any wholesale reorganization of local government is likely to be expensive. Second, the change is being proposed at the same time as many other changes are also being brought in for the administration of individual services. It may be that the service changes may ease reorganization in some cases, such as education, by reducing the power of local authorities. In other cases, such as social services, they may make reorganization more difficult. Service reorganization priorities may override more general changes in the structure of local government as a whole.

Management Change

The third field in which the local government review proposes change is that of the internal management of local authorities, both at the political and the officer level. This involves extending the competitive processes developed in the Local Government Act 1988, and a range of more general proposals. The consultative paper, *The Internal Management of Local Authorities*,[2] discusses the possibility of introducing directly elected mayors, a directly elected executive committee to run councils, or a cabinet system on the Westminster model. The existing committee system is seen as time-consuming and often wasteful, and approaches involving greater delegation are considered. Local authorities are encouraged to experiment with the use of different approaches.

The management of local authorities has been changing greatly in recent years, partly for reasons internal to local government, and partly because of the pressures of finance and legislative change. The work of the Widdicombe Commission, which examined the operation of local government in the mid-1980s, led to some changes, but there is certainly now room for a much wider consideration of the nature of local government management. Existing approaches are often out of step with the need for the ability to act quickly, and for a more strategic pattern of operation. The emphasis on variation and experimentation in the consultation paper contrasts markedly with the prescriptiveness that characterized the government's response to the Widdicombe Committee in the Local Government and Housing Act 1989. It may be possible to learn from the experience of other countries, for example Scandinavia, where there have been experiments with 'free' local authorities, intended to encourage innovation and change.

Any change in the operation of local authorities will need to recognize the problems of recruiting councillors. The difficulties that face local government are making it hard for all political parties to attract councillors in many authorities. There is also a need to recognize the need for democracy, for example in ensuring openness and accountability, and the tensions between representative democracy and participative democracy. Change will also need to recognize the distinctiveness of the British approach to local government.

The government's consultative paper on internal management concentrates strongly on the nature of the central management of the local authority, particularly the problem of establishing a powerful executive. But councillors also play a strong role in representing their constituents, expressing particular interests, and dealing with individuals' problems. These roles also have to be considered in restructuring local authority management. It is ironic that the emphasis of the consultation paper is on central mechanisms, when many of the pressures for change involve pressures to decentralize.

The Citizen's Charter

The Citizen's Charter has major implications for local government as the primary provider of public services. The Local Government Bill 1991 includes proposals intended to implement elements of the charter, namely:

- powers for the Audit Commission to gather, check and publish information on the performance of local authorities
- a requirement that more local authority services be subject to competitive tendering.

The bill proposes an enhancement of the role of the Audit Commission in overseeing the quality of local authority services. This will involve greater attention being given to standards of service and how they can be measured. There is likely to be an increase in the central definition of standards. It would seem that the government's intention is that there should be 'league tables' that will allow the service standards being attained by authorities to be measured clearly, and enable comparison to be made between one authority and another. The Audit Commission is to come forward with proposals for how this is to be done.

The search for the holy grail of effective measurement of the performance of public service has gone on throughout the 1980s and before. There have been significant advances in performance measurement and management, but universally accepted approaches have not been developed. The main problems are the measurement of relatively intangible aspects of service, notably quality, and the need to recognize the different starting points of different organizations. The quality of public service is inevitably a matter of debate, with different values and political viewpoints leading to varying judgements. It can also be argued that, for example, authorities with high levels of social deprivation will not be able to reach the same standard as those in more advantaged circumstances. In the case of education, for example, it can be argued that what should be measured is 'value added', rather than absolute levels of achievement. Whatever the rights and wrongs of this issue, there will, inevitably, be wide-ranging debate about the way that standards should be specified and performance measured. The trend is towards central government setting of standards for local services.

Local authorities, themselves, have, in many cases, been developing new approaches to quality management. Indeed, many of the approaches and ideas now being propounded by central government have been developed independently by local authorities. A number of authorities, for example York and Lewisham, have produced service contracts, detailing the service to be delivered, and means of redress for service users. There is also wide-scale development of complaints procedures in addition to the statutory procedure that has now been introduced in social services. The Citizen's Charter developments, therefore, are part of a developing debate on the way that the quality of public services can be monitored and improved.

Competitive Tendering

Compulsory competitive tendering has become an established, if contested, aspect of local government management. It is now proposed that competition should be extended beyond the services specified under the Local Government Act 1988 (it is also proposed that competitive tendering should be extended to Northern Ireland). The Local Government Bill 1991 contains proposals that competition be extended to a number of manual services, namely the cleaning of police buildings, the maintenance of police vehicles, the maintenance of fire service vehicles, and the provision of home-to-school transport. These extensions of competition largely involve the inclusion of services previously explicitly excluded from the provisions of the Local Government Act 1988 for security or other reasons. It is also proposed to extend competition to a number of direct services to the public, namely the management of arts facilities, aspects of library services, and the provision and management of parking services.

The government is also anxious to extend competition to the professional services of the local authority. The first services that will be affected are those involved in the construction work already subject to competition under the Local Government Planning and Land Act 1980. This development would involve competition for architectural services, engineering services and property management services. The government sees it as relatively straightforward to extend competition for construction related services since, the consultation paper on competition argues, the skills involved are well-defined and understood, client responsibilities are clear, and there is private sector capacity. There are, as yet, no proposals for competition for housing management services, though it is intended that they should be subjected to competition in due course.

The most controversial proposals are those to extend competition to central support and corporate services, that is the central management of the authority. The services involved are corporate committee and administrative services, legal services, financial services, personnel services and computing services. It is recognized that it would be difficult to subject these services to competition on a wholesale basis, given their centrality to the operation of the local authority, but it is argued that specific aspects of service, such as printing, conveyancing or the audit service, could well be put out to competitive tender. The government, therefore, proposes that a proportion of central support and corporate services should be subject to competition.

It is also proposed that central support and corporate services should be required to operate internal trading accounts. The development of trading accounts is seen as providing elected members and officers with a closer knowledge of costs, and more effective financial discipline. Many local authorities have been developing trading accounts as a result of competition, in the form of service level agreements.

This development has shown that there are significant issues in developing such agreements. First, there needs to be careful and accurate time-keeping so that central staff time can be correctly allocated. Second, there needs to be agreement between central and service departments on what are to be the services provided. Third, effective management accounting systems need to be developed.

The development of competition for professional services is seen as involving significant issues of quality. It is in the nature of professional services that their quality is difficult to assess or measure. Much depends upon reputation and relatively intangible aspects of service. It is seen as important that the introduction of competition for professional services should take account of quality. This will be done through requiring bidders to meet a quality threshold before the financial bid is considered. It is not clear how quality is to be assessed.

The extension of competitive tendering for local authority services raises three main issues. First, it is more difficult to specify professional services, such as law or accountancy, than such tangible services as refuse collection. There is very limited experience of tendering for such services, though a number of authorities have recently put legal and financial services out to tender, for example South Oxfordshire District Council, which has contracted out budget preparation.The second issue is the effect that the introduction of a multiplicity of trading accounts and contracts has on the overall management of a local authority. There is a potential for fragmentation and complexity. Third, it is not clear how the development of competition and internal trading will fit with attempts to develop more decentralized approaches to management. Contracts may prove to be constraints on change rather than enhancing it.

The Local Government Bill also provides for the tightening of the regulations that govern competition under the Local Government Act 1988. The client/contractor split is to be made obligatory. The approach to evaluating tenders is being more tightly specified. These changes result from pressure from private sector companies involved in competition, which have complained about what they see as unfair treatment.

Competitive tendering and contracting out are seen by the government as key aspects of the move to the enabling authority and the implementation of the Citizen's Charter. The experience of competition under the Local Government Act 1988 has been that there have been savings of about 6 per cent. Competition from the private sector has been increasing. Local authorities have, so far, won about 20 per cent of contracts, though there is likely to be advance by the private sector over time. The market for local authority services is relatively small in most cases, but, given the right conditions and incentives, can be expected to grow. The long term impact of compulsory competition may be very different from the experience so far.

Service Developments

As well as general changes affecting local authorities, individual services are also having to deal with significant developments. The trend of these changes is to introduce more decentralized financial control, competition, and clearer standards. In education the delegation of budgets to schools – the local management of schools – is in its first year. Headteachers and governors have generally welcomed the increased control over their financial affairs. There is some evidence that schools are underspending in the first year, in the knowledge that they can carry over spending from one year to another, and that smaller schools have benefited less than larger ones. It is proposed that the proportion of the budget for education that is delegated to schools should be increased over time. The role of the local education authority is being reduced. Local authorities are also to lose their responsibility for further education.

The emphasis on the quality of public services and users' rights has been reflected in education in the publication of the Parents' Charter. There are proposals to privatize the inspection of schools, and to involve parents in the inspection process. Local authority schools are to be encouraged to opt out and become grant-maintained.

Social services departments are involved in implementing the changes required by the Children Act, which have required extensive reorganization and revision of procedures. They are also preparing for the introduction of the provisions of the National Health Service and Community Care Act, which will increase their responsibilities. The intention behind the legislation is that there should be an assessment of individuals' needs and the development of a 'mixed economy of care'. Social services, like other aspects of local government, are to be required to move to a more market-oriented approach to service management, incorporating private and voluntary sector provision as well as direct local authority service.

Environmental services have been subject to change as a result of the Environmental Protection Act and the Food Act, which impose significant increases in responsibility on local authorities. It may be difficult to meet these new responsibilities, given financial constraints and shortages of skilled staff.

Legislation, Control and Centralization

Local government operates under the principle of *ultra vires*, which means that it may not do anything without statutory powers. In the past this rule has been relatively widely interpreted, but over the last decade the legislative and judicial limitation on local authority activity has become even tighter. When combined with the increase in the quantity of legislation in recent years, and the tendency for statutes to allow extensive powers to Secretaries of State to bring forward subsidiary legislation, local authority freedom has been significantly curtailed. The result is increasing central control of local government.

Two examples of the impact of legislation in the last year may be cited. First, the Law Lords have now ruled that all interest rate swaps are unlawful. It is, as yet, unclear what the implications of this ruling will be. There is likely to be a long drawn out process in settling the issue between the City and the local authorities involved. A second example is the ruling that authorities have no freedom to go beyond the statutory maximum level of payments when making redundancies, except in the case of London authorities, which are covered by specific legislation granting them the necessary powers. This ruling, if upheld, will make it difficult for authorities to make staffing adjustments by using redundancy packages as most other organizations would do.

The increasingly legalistic approach to the operation of local authorities, and to the relations between central and local government, has benefits and disadvantages. On the benefit side it creates a clear framework within which the local authority must work. But it also acts to constrict freedom, experiment and adaptation. A degree of ambiguity, particularly at times of changes, enables innovation to take place. In many European countries local authorities have a power of general competence, being able to do anything which they are not expressly forbidden to do. The British tradition is different, but the present highly restrictive limitations on local government might be reviewed with advantage.

The move to centralization is greatly compounded by the increase in central government control of local finance. The point has now been reached where there is virtually universal capping of local authority expenditure. Central control of local authorities has also been increased by the greater use of specific grants. In the last year the principle of competitive bidding by local authorities for grants, for example for urban regeneration, has been introduced.

Staffing

The Local Government Management Board, resulting from the amalgamation of the Local Authorities Conditions of Service Advisory Board and the Local Government Training Board, came into being from 1 April 1990. The new Board is responsible for encouraging a strategic approach to management in local government. It also continues to be responsible for industrial relations and negotiating at the national level. There has been some movement towards more localized bargaining in recent years, encouraged particularly by staffing difficulties in the south-east of England and the introduction of competitive tendering. There is little likelihood of the end of central bargaining for local government employees in the near future, but the trend towards more localized bargaining is likely to increase. There is also a continuing move towards performance-related pay which the government is encouraging, for example for teachers. Staffing issues are likely to become increasingly important as the process of change impacts on local authorities.

Conclusion

The government's approach to local government over the last 12 years has gone through three stages. In the first stage, from 1979 to 1987, the focus was upon the control of local government expenditure. In the second stage, from 1987 to 1990, the government brought forward legislation to change the way that local authorities, as a whole, worked, in the Local Government and Housing Act, and to reform individual services, such as education and social services. The third stage, on which they are now embarked, involves reform and reorganization of the system of local government itself.

The pattern of local government that emerges over the next decade and more depends, in part, upon the results of the 1991 general election. A Labour government would, for example, reintroduce the rates, and might create a regional level of government. The basic choice for change is, effectively, between two forms of the 'enabling' authority. The first involves a minimalist view of local government, seeing its role as the management of services using market mechanisms where possible. In this approach there would be extensive contracting out of services, with finance being devolved, wherever possible, to the point of service delivery. The local authority's role would be to develop and monitor standards of performance through contracts.

The second form of enabling is that which sees the local authority as a means of community self-government, attempting to create a strategic approach to the development of the local community. This form of enabling would involve contracting out, where appropriate, but also extensive working with and through other organizations. The emphasis would be upon partnership with central government and the private sector, the positive use of regulatory powers, and the encouragement of voluntary and other agencies.

Behind these two approaches to the development of the enabling authority lie differing concepts of the citizenship. In the first the emphasis is upon the citizen as consumer, and the authority as an agent for ensuring services are delivered effectively. In the second citizenship is seen as membership of the local community, with an appropriate set of rights and duties. The review of local government that has been launched in the last year involves the consideration of basic questions about the nature of the political system.

Notes
1 Department of the Environment, *A New Tax for Local government*, HMSO, 1991, p23.
2 Department of the Environment, *The Internal Management of Local Authorities*, HMSO, 1991.

Chronology
11 Jan: *The Administration of the Community Charge: Some Longer Term Considerations*
Audit Commission, warns that failure to monitor population movements is placing strains on registration and may necessitate a national identity scheme.

17 Jan: Government to use another £11 million to keep poll tax levels down.

24 Jan: Law Lords rule that all interest rate swaps by local authorities are unlawful, to considerable consternation in the City.

19 Feb: Announcement that service personnel and civilians in the Gulf will be exempt from the poll tax.

20 Feb: Dame Shirley Porter announces that she is resign as leader of Westminster City Council in April.

2 Mar: Move to take competitive tendering into white collar services is signalled by John Major at a Conservative local government conference.

7 Mar: Conservative defeat in the Ribble Valley by-election (won by the Liberal Democrats) after a campaign in which dissatisfaction with the poll tax featured prominently.

17 Mar: MORI survey shows councils in England and Wales recruited 11,600 extra staff to cope with the administration problems presented by the poll tax at an estimated cost of £232 million.

19 Mar: Budget announcement that poll tax bills are to be reduced across the country by £140. Domestic rates in Northern Ireland are also to be cut. To compensate local councils will receive increased government grants financed by increases in VAT.

21 Mar: Michael Heseltine announces the replacement of the poll tax with a local tax based on the number of adults in a household and the property's value, which he said would be fairer and easier to collect. The uniform business rate would be maintained.
Local government commission set up to investigate possible restructuring of some two tier authorities, review local authority organization and the extension of contracting out to housing, legal and computer services.

25 Mar: Announcement that all adults, instead of just two per household, are to benefit from the poll tax reductions signalled on 19 Mar.

3 Apr: Fourteen local authorities (11 Labour-controlled and three Conservative-controlled) are charge-capped.

10 Apr: *Opportunity, Quality, Accountability: The Better Way for Local Government*, Labour Party, outlines local government policy, including the fair rates proposal.

16 Apr: Liberal Democrats launch details of their local income tax scheme.

23 Apr: Government unveils plans to replace the poll tax with a council tax based on property which assesses properties in seven price bands with bills based on two adult households but with a 25 per cent discount for single adults.
Department of the Environment consultation paper suggests single-tier local authorities.

30 Apr: Government cancels a study into using nine rather than seven bands on the new council tax.
National Audit Office says that the government is using 41-year old guidance to assess local authority grants.

7 May: Government announces it will not retrospectively validate interest rate swap deals between banks and local authorities.

16 May: Lambeth, Warwickshire, Bristol and Wirral councils to be allowed to spend over their capped limits.

21 May: Announcement of emergency legislation enabling the Secretary of State for the Environment to cap more local authorities.

17 June: Local government associations complain to the Prime Minister that the government decision to cut the poll tax and fund 85 per cent of local government expenditure

centrally had made local discretion and accountability largely meaningless.

Proposals for all-purpose single-tier authorities in Scotland.

Consultations on the reshaping of local government in Wales announced.

23 July: Announcement that councils are only to have a 4.8 per cent increase in grant in the coming fiscal year and that there is to be an eighth band added to the council tax.

25 July: Audit Commission alleges that many food premises are escaping prosecution each year because environmental health departments are under-staffed, lack direction and have too few officers in the field.

30 July: Green paper, *The Internal Management of Local Authorities in England*, HMSO, suggests directly elected mayors, a directly elected executive committee to run councils, elected separately from the councillors who would concentrate on constituency cases, a cabinet system of executive appointments, more delegation of decision making to committee chairmen and the appointment of council managers to run authorities on a day-to-day basis.

7 Aug: Police seize council documents in the beginning of an inquiry into land deals and property development in Preston.

21 Aug: Labour-run Havering is the first council to put white collar services out to tender.

11 Sept: The chief executive and director of finance of Western Isles council, which lost £23 million on the BCCI affair, are suspended.

10 Oct: Announcement that councillors not paying poll tax will lose voting rights on budgetary decisions.

1 Nov: Bill to replace poll tax with council tax introduced.

5 Nov: Publication of Local Government Bill, to review its structure and introduce mainly single tier authorities, extend compulsory competitive tendering into professional services and introduce league tables of council performances.

26 Nov: New tougher poll tax capping rules announced, as well as ceilings on the spending of every council in England if they wish to avoid being capped.

20 Dec: High Court deprives seven Liberal Democrat councillors in Tower Hamlets, east London, of their seats and bars them from office for five years for distributing false election leaflets.

Britain and the European Community

STEPHEN GEORGE

In November 1990 Margaret Thatcher was replaced as prime minister by John Major. Although other factors were certainly involved in her downfall, the incident that precipitated the challenge to Mrs Thatcher was her attack in the House of Commons on the idea of European monetary union.[1] The new government faced the prospect of year-long negotiations on monetary union and political union in the European Community under the critical gaze of the former Prime Minister and her supporters, culminating in a European summit meeting in Maastricht in December at which changes to the founding treaties of the EC were agreed. In these negotiations the government adopted a distinctly more co-operative tone than had prevailed under Mrs Thatcher, although this did not necessarily indicate quite such far-reaching changes in the substance of policy.

Change of Tone

The change of tone was signalled by several ministers. In January the Secretary of State for Employment, Michael Howard, met in London with Vasso Papandreou, the Commissioner for social affairs, to outline the extent to which Britain could accept her proposed social directives. Howard stressed to the press that Britain was prepared to accept almost half of the proposed directives, and that it was the only member state to have implemented all 18 of the social directives already agreed. This positive tone was in marked contrast to the accusation that Howard had launched only four months earlier, that Papandreou was bringing the EC into disrepute with her proposals for directives on maximum working hours, rights for part-time workers, and harmonized maternity benefits.[2]

At a meeting of the intergovernmental conference (IGC) on monetary union in January, the Chancellor, Norman Lamont, stressed that the British plan for a 'hard Ecu' as a possible route towards monetary union was open to modification.[3] As the year wore on the British government increasingly emphasized that monetary union would have to be preceded by economic convergence, which seemed to imply that the British government could accept an eventual monetary union. This was a long step away from the position of Mrs Thatcher, who reiterated her opposition to monetary union in speeches in the United States later in the year.[4]

In those same speeches, Mrs Thatcher continued to criticize the idea that the EC should develop a security and defence dimension, perhaps by developing the Western European Union (WEU) into a bridge between the EC and NATO. Again the line of the new government began to diverge from that of the former Prime Minister. In February, giving the Winston Churchill memorial lecture in Luxembourg, Douglas Hurd made a distinction between security policy, which 'goes with foreign policy', and defence, which was 'a different matter'.[5] But he also accepted that 'Europe has to take on more responsibility for its own defence' and spoke of WEU being developed into 'a bridge between the Twelve . . . and NATO'.[6]

Shortly after Mr Hurd's lecture, the new positive tone was underlined by the Prime Minster in a foreword to a government white paper which described developments in the EC in the second half of 1990.[7] He stated his aims for Britain in Europe as being 'to help build and shape the future Europe – and to do so with enthusiasm. We need to be right at the heart of the Community, working closely with our partners, if we are to do that'. In March, Mr Major made a visit to Bonn, in an effort to mend Anglo-German relations which had reached a post-war low in the latter months of Mrs Thatcher's premiership.[8] While there he made a speech to the Christian Democratic Union, the party of Chancellor Helmut Kohl, in which he repeated that he wished to see Britain 'where we belong', at the very heart of Europe working with its partners with enthusiasm in building the future.[9] How far these changes of tone represented real changes of position is now examined in the light of developments in the debate on social affairs, and in the intergovernmental conferences on political union and on monetary union.

Social Affairs

The newly discovered harmony between Mr Howard and Mrs Papandreou did not last long. The emphasis which Mr Howard put on Britain's commitment to the social dimension of the EC was simply emphasizing the positive aspects of what had already been true under Mrs Thatcher. Although her Bruges speech in 1988 had convinced most people that Britain entirely rejected all social legislation, this was a misperception. The government had always accepted that the programme to free the internal market of the EC must be accompanied by the setting of minimum EC-wide standards on health and safety at work, otherwise employers might try to achieve a competitive advantage by reducing safety standards. All of the directives that had already been agreed were of this nature. What the British government did not accept was that there should be EC legislation on other matters such as working hours and employees' rights. On these issues there was no change of policy. When Mrs Papandreou produced proposals for directives on maximum working hours and maternity rights, the British continued to oppose them, and objected vigorously to the Commission's classification of them as measures involving health and safety at work, and therefore subject to qualified majority voting under the 1987 Single European Act.[10] In the IGC on political union, the suggestion was made in draft agreements prepared by both the Luxembourg presidency in the first half of the year and the Dutch presidency in the second half of the year that social affairs as a whole should come under majority voting. This position was rejected by the British.[11]

Here then there seems to have been little change of substance; and the reason for this can perhaps be seen in the speeches made to the annual conference of the Confederation of British Industry in Bournemouth in November, when speaker after speaker attacked the Commission's proposals as imposing unacceptable and unnecessary costs on industry that would make it less competitive in world markets.[12]

Political Union

Discussion in the IGC on political union appeared generally to go the way of the British government. The draft treaty produced by the Luxembourg presidency in April proposed a European union with three pillars, of which the EC would be one. The others, which would cover first internal security, and secondly foreign policy, external security, and defence, would be essentially intergovernmental in their procedures. When the Dutch presidency produced a more federalist draft in September, it was rejected by an overwhelming majority of the states, and had to be withdrawn, to be replaced with something much nearer to the Luxembourg draft.

This did not mean that there were no disagreements. On the question of whether immigration should be centrally controlled, for example, the Germans were determined that it should be, the British that it should not. There was also considerable wrangling over whether the preamble to the new treaty should describe the European union as having 'a federal goal'. The phrase had negative connotations in Britain, and although the Prime Minister at one stage suggested that it might be acceptable were the term 'federal' clearly defined, eventually it was replaced by the phrase 'creating an ever closer Union amongst the people of Europe' so as not to offend British political sensibilities.

On the question of a security and defence dimension for the EC, the experience of the Gulf war and of the civil war in Yugoslavia helped to produce a consensus that such a dimension was necessary. Although the French and Germans jointly produced a plan to put the process under EC rules, they so mishandled their case as to upset the other states.[13] A strong intervention from the President of the United States at the NATO summit in Rome in early November[14] also helped to sway the final proposals in the direction of the British view that defence and security should not be incorporated in such a way that there would be any rupture with NATO, despite French wishes for a more independent policy. Although these issues caused some discontent in domestic politics, especially the security and defence question, it was particularly the negotiations on monetary union that produced domestic political effects.

Monetary Union

At a meeting of finance ministers in May, Mrs Thatcher's old sparring partner Jacques Delors, the President of the Commission, suggested a formula that would allow Britain an 'opt-out' clause on movement to a single currency. This suggestion was taken up in the subsequent draft treaty presented by the Dutch presidency in early September. It proposed writing into the treaty a right for any member to consult its national parliament before actually adopting a single currency, thus putting off the final decision until such time as the process had reached full maturity.

This procedural device proved acceptable to some of the Conservative critics of monetary union. Teddy Taylor MP indicated that it would satisfy the doubts of the Tory Reform Group, a backbench group of some 70 Conservative MPs. But Nicholas Ridley, the former cabinet minister, attacked the proposal in a speech to the Bruges Group, and shortly afterwards a Bruges Group memorandum was leaked to the press which appeared to threaten a split in the Conservative Party if the Prime Minister did not veto a treaty on monetary union. Although this memorandum was repudiated by Bill Cash MP on behalf of the parliamentary 'Friends of Bruges', the issue did not go away. Norman Tebbit joined Mr Ridley in publicly attacking the whole concept of a monetary union, and Mrs Thatcher continued to make speeches in a similar vein.

In November the question was brought out into the open in a two-day debate in the House of Commons.[15] Margaret Thatcher used the occasion to call for a referendum on monetary union before Britain agreed to participate.[16] This intervention was unhelpful for the government, which had already indicated that it did not intend to put the Maastricht agreement to a referendum. The Prime Minister chose to interpret his predecessor's comments as a call for a referendum only at the point when the decision actually to enter the monetary union came to be made, and therefore a matter for a future parliament.

Maastricht

Britain did get an 'opt out' clause on monetary union written into the Maastricht agreement, but it referred specifically to Britain. This was something that the government had hoped to avoid, because it gave the impression that Britain was again the awkward partner in the Community, and it also led to the risk that industrialists would think twice before investing in Britain so long as a question mark remained over whether the country would eventually participate in the monetary union that would complete the single market. However, other member states were not prepared to accept a general opt-out provision because they feared that the German parliament might try to use it to take the deutschmark out of any future monetary union if it did not like the constitution of the proposed European central bank, thus causing the collapse of the whole project.

In the event the question of majority voting on social matters became the most difficult issue at Maastricht, and an agreement there only proved possible because the social chapter was dropped from the draft treaty, and replaced with a protocol in which the other eleven member states committed themselves to making progress on social issues, but Britain committed itself to nothing beyond those obligations already contained in the Treaty of Rome and the Single European Act. Because of these two derogations for Britain, Neil Kinnock accused the government of a 'double opt-out' which left Britain as a semi-detached member of the Community.[17] But Conservative backbench sceptics on Europe seemed prepared to accept the agreement that the Prime Minister had brought back, and criticism from within the party was muted. Even Mrs Thatcher kept quiet. It was generally agreed by observers that John Major had achieved quite a diplomatic and political success, which was likely to enhance his standing in his party and in the country.

What were less noticed were the concessions that Britain had made in other directions, particularly in agreeing to an extension of the range of issues on which there would be majority voting in the Council of Ministers, and increasing the powers of the European Parliament. There was also some doubt about whether the wording on security and defence was really more favourable to the British view than to the French view. Indeed, the agreement failed finally to settle many of the issues around which the negotiations had circled. An indication of this was the provision of a review clause to allow the whole structure of the new European union to be looked at again in 1996.

In some ways the Maastricht agreement was a less fundamental step in the evolution of the European Community than the Single European Act which Mrs Thatcher had signed in 1986. It was nevertheless a big step toward closer European unity, and perhaps a bigger step than many members of the Conservative Party realized.

Notes

1 Hansard, 30 October 1990, cols 872-3.
2 *The Independent*, 14 January 1991.
3 *The Independent* 29 January 1991.
4 Mrs Thatcher was touring the United States, and other parts of the developed world, to raise money for her 'Thatcher Foundation'. Her speeches in Chicago on 17 June and in Washington on 23 September were widely reported in the British press.
5 Transcript of The Churchill Memorial Lecture, Foreign and Commonwealth Office press release, 19 February 1991, p.13.
6 The Churchill Memorial Lecture, p.14.
7 HMSO, *Developments in the European Community, July to December 1990*, (Cm 1457), p.III.
8 On the incidents that caused a cooling of relations see Stephen George, 'Britain and the European Community', in Peter Catterall (ed) *Contemporary Britain: An Annual Review 1991*, Blackwell, 1991 p.77.
9 John Major, 'The Evolution of Europe', *Conservative Party News*, 11 March 1991, p.13.

10 *The Independent*, 31 October and 1 November 1991. Eventually a modified version of the directive on pay for pregnant women was passed without a vote, Britain abstaining along with Italy. The effect of the directive was not to increase maternity pay in Britain, *The Independent*, 7 November 1991.

11 *The Independent*, 24 September 1991.

12 *The Independent*, 5 November 1991.

13 *The Independent*, 7, 9 and 17 October 1991.

14 *The Independent*, 8 November 1991.

15 Hansard, 20 November 1991, cols 269-389 and 21 November 1991, cols 436-527.

16 Hansard, 20 November 1991, cols 297-8.

17 Hansard, 11 December 1991, cols 862-3.

Chronology

1 Jan: Luxembourg becomes President of the EC.

2 Jan: IEA report *Constitutional Change and Political Union in the EC* urges that EC powers should be shifted from Brussels to the national governments. It proposes that national parliaments should come together to influence the Community agenda, the restructuring of the European Commission (splitting some functions and removing its exclusive right to initiate policy) and the setting out of conditions of membership so that countries with appropriate democratic systems, human rights and market economies can join.

6 Jan: Mrs Thatcher agrees to become President of the Bruges Group.

14 Jan: Michael Howard meets Vasso Papandreou in London.

22 Jan: In a speech in Den Haag, Karl Otto Pöhl of the German Bundesbank attacks Britain's hard ECU proposals.
John Major calls for European financial aid towards the cost of the Gulf war and says that the EC response shows that it is not yet ready for a common defence and foreign policy, sentiments echoed by Neil Kinnock in a speech to RUSI the following day.

25 Jan: Alan Clark, the Defence Procurement Minister, launches a vitriolic attack on the response of EC states to the Gulf Crisis.

11 Feb: Gallup Poll shows 73 per cent of Britons want to make EC economically stronger and more competitive. The survey (conducted May-June 1990) also traced cross-national social behaviour and ownership of consumer goods.

19 Feb: Douglas Hurd, giving the Winston Churchill memorial lecture in Luxembourg, outlines steps towards common European defence and foreign policies.

27 Feb: Britain proposes common external policies based on consensus at the European intergovernmental conference.

28 Feb: EC Commission proposes a common defence policy agreed by majority voting.
Government white paper, *Developments in the European Community*, HMSO, outlines a more positive approach to Europe.

7 Mar: Jacques Delors outlines his vision of a common European defence strategy in a speech to the Institute of Strategic Studies, London.

11 Mar: At the Anglo-German summit in Bonn John Major signals greater warmth towards Germany and the EC than under Mrs Thatcher and a movement towards social market attitudes.

8 Apr: Special European summit in Luxembourg. John Major outlines plans to create 'safe havens' for Kurds inside Iraq.

10 Apr: Germany and Italy propose a radical increase in the powers of the European Parliament.

17 Apr: First draft treaty for European political union is submitted. Britain dissents from it. Jacques Delors meanwhile describes it as a betrayal of the Treaty of Rome.

23 Apr: Luxembourg launches compromise proposals on a central European bank.

11 May: Jacques Delors suggests a compromise whereby Britain could sign the EMU treaty at the end of the year but reserve the right to put the final decision to parliament before the EMU is established in the next five years.

3 June: Neil Kinnock rejects proposals for a single European socialist party.

12 June: Douglas Hurd gives evidence to the House of Commons Foreign Affairs Committee on the progress of the European intergovernmental conferences.

17 June: Luxembourg tables a draft treaty including explicit references to the federal goal of European integration.

Mrs Thatcher makes a speech in Chicago attacking European monetary union and the idea of WEU as a bridge between the EC and NATO.

19 June: *Citizens' Europe*, Liberal Democrats, argues for a common European citizenship, co-decision for the European parliament, the opening up of the Council of Ministers to public scrutiny, common European foreign and defence policies, enlargement of the EC to include all European liberal democracies, devolution in the UK, an independent European central bank and a single European currency.

24 June: Government refuses to allow a minimum VAT rate of 15 per cent to be fixed by EC law.

25 June: John Major signals possible willingness to accept some form of federalism provided the term is clearly and satisfactorily defined.

27-28 June: EC summit in Luxembourg.

1 July: The Netherlands becomes the president of the EC.

25 July: European Court rules that Britain cannot prevent Spanish vessels reregistering as British to gain access to British fishing quotas, thus overturning the 1988 Merchant Shipping Act.

20 Aug: Employment Select Committee report says the individual interests of member countries will ensure that most of the Social Charter will never be introduced.

23 Sept: Government makes clear its opposition to any extension of EC competence in the field of social policy.

24 Sept: New draft EC treaty calls for dramatic new powers for the European Parliament, a common foreign and security policy and explicitly refers to a federal goal.

26 Sept: Tory MEPs urge Major to concede more powers to the European Parliament.

30 Sept: EC foreign ministers meeting in Brussels force a withdrawal of the Dutch draft treaty after it is rejected by ten member countries.

4 Oct: Anglo-Italian defence plans suggest European defence is centred on WEU, to remain autonomous of the EC.

17 Oct: EC Commission begins legal proceedings against UK government for not carrying out environmental impact assessments on three civil engineering projects.

22 Oct: EC and EFTA agree on creation of a European Economic Area.

30 Oct: Labour statement on EMU stresses need for political control over a central European bank and real convergence on unemployment and growth rates before entry.

30 Oct–1 Nov: Douglas Hurd in Bonn for talks preparatory for December's Maastricht summit, joined by John Major on the last day.

31 Oct: Germans refuse to accept opt-out clause as part of EMU treaty.

18 Nov: Anti-federalist Conservative MPs call for a referendum on economic and political union (later to be supported by Mrs Thatcher).

20–21 Nov: Two-day debate in the House of Commons on Maastricht. Mrs Thatcher calls for a referendum on monetary union.

22 Nov: Ruud Lubbers, the Dutch Prime Minister, in London for pre-Maastricht talks.

27–28 Nov: John Major in Bonn and Rome for pre-Maastricht talks.

1 Dec: EC finance ministers meeting in Scheveningen in the Netherlands vote against any general opt-out for EC countries from EMU and instead specify a special opt-out clause applying only to Britain and Denmark.

2 Dec: President Mitterrand of France in London for pre-Maastricht talks.

4 Dec: Richard Shepherd introduces a private member's bill to allow a referendum on the Maastricht treaty.

9–10 Dec: Maastricht summit. Mr Major claims a triumph for Britain's negotiating position. He wins an option to opt-out at the later stages of EMU, timed to be completed by 1999 at the latest. The word federal is also purged from the treaty. The social chapter is also left out at Britain's behest, but the other eleven members sign a separate protocol incorporating it. The agreement goes further in the direction of the integration of WEU into the EC than the government would have liked, but retains a commitment to NATO. It also marks the beginnings of a common immigration policy. A cohesion fund was set up for the benefit of poorer members.

10 Dec: Exchanges between Neil Kinnock and John McGregor, Leader of the House, during Prime Minister's question time, concerning the social chapter.

11 Dec: Prime Minister's statement to the House of Commons on Maastricht.

12 Dec: Exchanges at Prime Minister's question time on Maastricht.

18–19 Dec: Two-day debate on Maastricht in the House of Commons.

The Media

COLIN SEYMOUR-URE

Mass media toiled in the recession of 1991. Innovations made possible in the press by the technical and management changes of the late 1980s had run their course. Cable and satellite TV made slow progress. ITV began the reorganization forced by the 1990 Broadcasting Act, and four of the sixteen companies lost their franchises. The BBC prepared for changes in its own role in a broadcasting system that would less and less embody the 'public service' philosophy of the old BBC and ITV duopoly. Against this background the Gulf war revived historic arguments about censorship but gave TV reporters fine opportunities to dazzle with new technology. Politicians provided their annual *leitmotiv* of complaints about broadcasting bias. Litigants continued to win large sums of money from libel juries. At the end of the year came the startling demise of the publisher Robert Maxwell, shortly followed by the collapse of his labyrinthine international empire.

The recession had accentuated Maxwell's indebtedness. In March he sold Pergamon Press, the scientific publishing group which was one of his earliest ventures, to the Dutch publisher Elsevier. In the spring too he floated 45 per cent of Mirror Group Newspapers, which he had owned since 1984. He promised they would continue to support the Labour Party – a very important pledge, since these papers (notably the *Daily Mirror*, the *Sunday Mirror*, and *The People*) were the only mass market papers which did so. While capital thus raised reduced his debt, Maxwell continued to extend himself, in particular by purchasing the troubled New York tabloid, *The Daily News*. Rupert Murdoch, the other high-profile media baron, was equally troubled by debt, especially due to the heavy losses of the BSkyB satellite TV service. Costs at Murdoch's newspapers were rigorously pruned. For a time, until he reached agreement with bankers, the viability of his entire international empire too seemed in doubt.

The recession gave extra edge to the already relentless campaign among the tabloid papers. the *Daily Mirror*, the *Sunday Mirror* and the *Sunday Express* all had new editors – two of them women. So did *Today*, as the by product of a relaunch in the spring. This was designed to move the paper away from the *Daily Express/Daily Mail* market towards a younger readership, further downmarket but, it was hoped, more 'serious' than that of *The Sun* and the *Daily Mirror*. The broadsheet papers were generally thinner, as display and recruitment advertising fell dramatically in the early months of the year. *The Independent* amalgamated its daily and Sunday operations and called on new capital to help cushion losses. *The Indy*, aimed at young readers, was closed. The regional press too was hard hit by the advertising recession – especially the free sheets. One of the new Scottish Sunday papers, the *Sunday Scot*, closed in July.

Magazines have traditionally been subject to greater fluctuations in popularity than newspapers, with births and deaths dependent on changes in specialist markets such as DIY, computers and video games. In 1991 net closures began to exceed net launches for the first time in decades. The closure of *The Listener* in January by the BBC, after some 60 years, was the end of an era. On the other hand, TV listings magazines blossomed. From 1 March the law permitted the publication of all channels' weekly schedules in a single magazine – ending the 35-year old nonsense (from the consumer perspective) of viewers having to buy both *Radio Times* and *TV Times* in order to get the full schedule. *TV Plus* entered the market but sank after three issues. The German publisher, Bauer, established *TV Quick* with sales of about 700,000 by the autumn. The *Radio Times* dropped by one third to sales of 1.5 million. *TV Times* more than halved; but its owner, Reed International, kept its market share by launching *What's on TV* in addition.

The recession hit ITV when the companies were already paring costs for the new franchise round. The result was that ITV jobs were expected to fall to 11,000 by the end of 1991 from 17,000 in 1987. Channel 4 cut its programme budget by 7 per cent. It also had the misfortune to lose £5 million in the crash of the Bank of Credit and Commerce International. It spent £1 million on 'golden handcuffs' – half of it for the chief executive Michael Grade – to prevent senior staff being lured to other companies in the franchise competition. All this had dire effects on the previously fast-growing sector of small independent production companies, many of whom found their turnover halved.

Book publishing faced different problems. Sales generally hold up quite well in a recession. This time, the downturn came when firms were still paying for the spate of takeovers in the late 1980s and when profit margins were being squeezed by the growing strength of the retail chains, such as Pentos and Waterstones. Firms therefore shed staff. Terry Maher of Pentos continued his campaign against the Net Book Agreement that enables publishers to enforce retail prices. Thwarted by legal injunctions in 1990, he succeeded this year in discounting selected titles and caused Waterstones to follow suit.

The recession may have had less to do with the apparent end of the video boom. For the first time, rentals of prerecorded cassettes fell in 1990, to 374 million from 396 million in 1989. The growth in the number of households owning video machines was slowing down and rental frequency is highest in the first six months of ownership. Ownership topped 15 million in 1991, compared with 6.9 million in 1984. Purchase of cassettes, distinct from rentals, continued to grow – to 40 million in 1991. The value of cinema ticket sales, with attendance estimated at around 100 million, was now less than one third of the value of the video rental market.

Video rentals were also hit partly by the growth of the Sky satellite movie channel. Research showed that subscribers typically gave up renting cassettes after taking out their subscriptions. But Sky's rate of penetration remained slow enough in 1991 for it continued losing money at an heroic rate. Its merger (effectively a takeover) with BSB in November 1990, stemmed the flow. By March, the combined company, cumbersomely named BSkyB, had shed 1,000 jobs under antipodean Murdoch management and operating losses were down to an estimated £1.6 million a week. BSkyB offered six channels. By the autumn they were available in nearly 8 per cent of households via satellite dishes and in 4 per cent via cable. People could also get access to a variety of other satellite channels, such as Lifestyle, Screensport and the Children's Channel.

Among Sky subscribers, audience research suggested that at the end of 1991 ITV (including TV-am) was still the most popular channel (nearly one third of total viewing time), followed by Sky (25 per cent) and BBC1 (22 per cent). Altogether, satellite subscribers seemed to be watching only about half an hour more TV per week than non-subscribers – nearly 29 hours.

The progress of BSkyB was part of the backdrop to a great guessing game – the ITV franchise competition, last held in 1981. The 1990 Broadcasting Act had introduced a radical new principle: each of the 16 franchises was to go to the highest cash bidder. Frantic lobbying persuaded the government to strengthen the 'quality threshold' which applicants must pass before the cash test was applied. By the 15 May closing date, 37 applications had been submitted for the 15 regional franchises and three for the national breakfast time licence. Each was accompanied by a sealed bid, stating how much the applicant would pay the Treasury per year for the franchise. Some companies, such as Carlton, bid in more than one region – and could in principle have been successful in each, provided they were not contiguous or large franchises. In three regions the existing franchise holder was sole bidder. One of these, Central TV, knowing the position, bid a derisory £2,000. Carlton, in contrast, had to bid £43 million to get the comparably valuable London weekday franchise.

The members of the Independent Television Committee spent the summer scrutinizing the applicants' programme proposals, business plans, ownership and engineering arrangements. The quality threshold involved judgements both about initial quality and about whether the level was likely to be maintained. Where more than one applicant passed the threshold, the Act also required consideration of whether 'exceptional circumstances' justified awarding the franchise to an under-bidder. The ritual bow to public opinion required a six week 'consultation period': 21,250 requests for application summaries were received and 2,278 individuals and organizations offered comments.

Decisions were sent to the applicants by fax on the morning of 15 October. Of the 13 contested franchises, nine went to the existing holders. The four losers were Thames (London weekday), TVS (south and south east), TSW (south west) and TV-am (breakfast). Thames was outbid by Carlton, an electronic and film conglomerate which had earlier sought to take Thames over. Its bid was one third higher (though slightly smaller than a third contestant who failed the quality test). There was little surprise at the failure of TVS, which had fared badly after investing foolishly in American TV. TVS bid highest (at nearly £60 million, the highest bid in the entire auction) and it passed the quality threshold; but the Commission did not believe it would be able to afford to maintain its proposed plans. TSW failed on the same basis, bidding twice as high as the winner.

TV-am seemed most stunned by its failure. It was hugely outbid by two competitors (£33/34 million to £14 million). Its flamboyant Australian chairman, Bruce Gyngell, declared that the winner would surely go bankrupt. There was irony in his defeat: his determination to eliminate overmanning and his success in strike breaking had made a fan out of Mrs Thatcher and had helped to entrench the auction principle as a cost-cutting incentive in the 1990 Act. Gyngell pulled a personal letter from Mrs Thatcher out of his pocket and spontaneously read it out in an after dinner speech. 'When I see how some of the licences have been awarded', she had written, 'I am *mystified* that you did not receive yours, and heartbroken. You of all people have done so much for the whole of television and there seems to be no attention to that. I am only too painfully aware that *I* was responsible for the legislation.'

Four of the bidders who successfully defended their franchises won by submitting the highest bid. The other five survivors were luckier, in the sense that they were outbid – but by companies which failed the quality test. In this way Granada was saved from the well publicized challenge of Phil Redmond, the creator of *Brookside*. (Granada is thus the sole survivor of the original ITV companies of the mid 1950s.) The new franchises run from January 1993. The possibility of litigation by unsuccessful applicants remained open at the end of 1991, when Lord Donaldson, Master of the Rolls, gave TSW the right to seek a judicial review. A week earlier, he forced the ITC to disclose documents explaining its reasons.

Insofar as the object of the new system was to make ITV pay more money back to the taxpayer via the Treasury, it may not have succeeded. The ITC chairman, George Russell, said that the effect of strengthening the 'quality' provisions was implicitly to 'put back' so much money into programme-making that the Treasury would be better off by only about £40 million a year – two or three per cent of the industry's turnover.

Much press comment on the allocation repeated the prevalent opinion when the Act was passed – that it would drive down programme quality. But the ITC was widely regarded as having done a fair job. The defeated companies were unlikely immediately to disappear. Several owned assets such as programme libraries and popular series, which they might still expect to market. Moreover, some of the new companies planned to operate as 'publisher/contractors' buying in programmes rather than making them all in-house. In this way as in others, TV will become a more plural industry as the 1990s develop.

Table 1. ITV franchises (bids in 1992 prices; viewing figures represent total possible audiences)

Region	Winner	Owners	Losers
National Breakfast 54.8m viewers	Sunrise TV Bid £34.6m	LWT (20%)/ Scottish TV(20%)/ Guardian and Manchester Evening News (15%)/ Walt Disney (15%)/ 30% to be placed.	TV-am (incumbent, £14.12m) Daybreak TV (£33.3m)
London weekday 10.57m viewers	Carlton Television Bid £43.2m	Carlton Communications (90%)/*Daily Telegraph* (5%)/Rizzoli Corriere della Sera (5%)	Thames (incumbent, £32.5m)/ CPV-TV (£45.3m, failed quality)
London weekend 10.57m viewers	LWT (incumbent) Bid £7.58m	Institutional investors, directors	London Independent Broadcasting (£35.4m, failed quality)
South and Southeast 5.044m viewers	Meridian Broadcasting Bid £36.5m	MAI (65%)/Central TV (20%)/Selec TV (15%)	TVS (incumbent, £59.8m, overbid)/ Carlton (£18.1m) /CPV-TV (£22.1m, failed quality)
Midlands 9.2m viewers	Central Independent Broadcasting (incumbent) Bid £2,000	Carlton (19.4%)/ D C Thomson & Co (19.2%)	Unchallenged
North West 6.33m viewers	Granada Television (incumbent) Bid £9m	Granada Group (100%)	North West TV (35.5m, failed quality)
Yorkshire 5.43m viewers	Yorkshire Television (incumbent) Bid £37.7m	Institutional investors	WhiteRose(£17.4m)/ Viking (£30.1m, failed quality)
East of England 3.858m viewers	Anglia Television (incumbent) Bid £17.8m	Institutional investors	Three East (£14.1m)/ CPV-TV (£10.1m, failed quality)
Wales and the West 4.298m viewers	HTV (incumbent) Bid £20.5m	Phillips & Drew (9.5%)/FMR Corp (6%)/Barclays Bank (7.6%)	C3W (£17.8m)/Merlin (£19.4m, failed quality) /C3WW (£18.3m, failed quality)
South West England 1.52m viewers	Westcountry Television Bid £7.8m	Assoc. Newspapers (20%) /Brittany Ferries (15%) /South West Water(20%) /Trilion (10%)	TSW (incumbent, £16.1m, overbid)/ TeleWest (£7.3m, failed quality)
Northern Ireland 1.4m viewers	Ulster Television (incumbent) Bid £1.02m	Institutional investors	TVni (£3.1m, failed business plan)/Lagan (£2.7m, failed quality)
North East 2.852m viewers	Tyne Tees Television (incumbent) Bid £15.1m	Institutional investors	North East Television (£5m)
North Scotland 1.095m viewers	Grampian Bid £720,000	Local businessmen	C3 Caledonia (£1.13m, failed quality)/North of Scotland TV (£2.71m, failed quality)
Borders 629,000 viewers	Border Television Bid £52,000	Local businessmen	Unchallenged
Central Scotland 3.557m viewers	Scottish Television Bid £2,000	Chase Nominees (8%) /Scottish Amicable (7%) /PhildrewNominees(6.7%)/ Bank of Scotland (6.6%)	Unchallenged
Channel Islands 135,000 viewers	Channel Television (incumbent) Bid £1,000	Channel Islands Communications (100%)	CI3 (£102,000, failed quality)

The BBC was subject to no such upheavals in 1991, but it was already preparing for an uncertain future. The compulsory licence fee is obviously at issue in a system with many channels. The government raised the fee in April to £77, 3 per cent less than the rise in the retail price index. In the financial year 1990–91 the BBC ran a budgeted deficit of £80 million (against an income of £1.4 billion). Production studios and staff were planned to shrink, as the government requirement to buy 25 per cent of programmes from independent companies came into force. The main architect of retrenchment was John Birt, the Director-General designate and deputy to Michael Checkland, whose five year term as Director-General was extended for a year until 1993. The chairman of the governors, 'Duke' Hussey, was appointed to a second five year term in April.

A more immediate problem than long term restructuring was the collapse of the BBC's audience share in the autumn. The peak time ratio of 40:44 per cent BBC1:ITV in autumn 1990 had changed to 34.7:44.4 per cent a year later, with BBC2 and Channel 4 splitting the remainder evenly. This was an inauspicious level from which to conduct the argument about the corporation's future, but it may be taken to epitomize the question how far old 'public service' values can or should be sustained, if necessary at the cost of audience share. There were pockets of BBC cheer in other directions, however. These ranged from the tribute by Mr Gorbachev to the World Service – his standby during Moscow's August coup – to the successful launch of World Service television in October. This latter, originating in Hong Kong, is within reach of a potential 2.6 billion people in 38 countries, and it could form part of a full World Service challenging America's Cable News Network.

The biggest news story of 1991 was the Gulf war. As usual, 'the story of the story' got mixed up with the story, and in the weeks of inactivity on the ground, journalists fretted about the limitations on their capacity to cover the war unsupervised and uncensored. The stars were those few, including a BBC correspondent, who were caught in Baghdad when the shooting started and were able, by the magic of satellite transmission, to send back vivid film. Unlike the Falklands campaign of 1982, which was exclusively 'Britain's war', the Gulf conflict did not lead to politicians impugning broadcasters' patriotism, if ever something more than a simple rehearsal of the official line was reported. Indeed John Major explicitly turned aside a backbencher's invitation to him in the Commons to criticize the BBC. Journalists agonized about the ethics of reporting the war from the enemy's camp. Many felt, at the end, that they had been skillfully orchestrated by the military to show the war the generals wanted shown; but few seemed to think they had compromised their integrity. The war was a triumph for CNN's round the clock news service. When nothing much was happening, radio proved a more suitable medium than TV for continuous coverage, and BBC Radio 4 attracted 1.5 million new listeners with such a service. For its part, the government organized daily press briefings by a member of the War Cabinet and avoided some of the infelicities and frustrations of Falklands press relations.

Table 2. Editors of leading daily newpapers and circulation figures

Editor	Owner	Circulation (Jul-Dec 1991 except where shown)
The Times Simon Jenkins	News International	387,386
The Independent Andreas Whittam Smith	Newspaper Publishing	372,240
Financial Times Richard Lambton	Pearson	287,120
The Guardian Peter Preston	Guardian & Manchester Evening News	409,660
Daily Telegraph Max Hastings	Hollinger Inc.	1,058,082
Daily Express Sir Nicholas Lloyd	Express Newspapers	1,518,764
Daily Mail Sir David English	Associated Newspapers	1,683,768
Daily Mirror Richard Stott	Mirror Group Newspapers	2,881,266
Today Martin Dunn	News International	459,621
The Sun Kelvin Mackenzie	News International	3,665,006
The Star Brian Hitchen	Express Newspapers	837,700
News of the World Patsy Chapman	News International	4,815,894
The People Bill Haggerty	Mirror Group Newspapers	2,215,465
The Mail on Sunday Stewart Stevens	Associated Newspapers	1,958,660
Sunday Express Eve Pollard	Express Newspapers	1,652,659
Sunday Mirror Bridget Rowe	Mirror Group Newspapers	2,816,935
Sunday Times Andrew Neil	News International	1,147,667
Sunday Telegraph Trevor Grove	Hollinger Inc	56,7497
The Observer Donald Trelford	Lonrho	548,305
Independent on Sunday Ian Jack	Newspaper Publishing	374,084
London Evening Standard Paul Dacre	Associated Newspapers	485,964
Glasgow Herald Arnold Kemp	G Outram & Co. (Lonrho)	123,656 (Jan–Jun 1991)
The Scotsman Magnus Linklater	Thomson Regional Newspapers	85,520
Western Mail & South Wales News John Humphries	Thomson Regional Newspapers	74,272
Belfast Telegraph R.Lilley	Thomson Regional Newspapers	132,816

John Major's first year saw generally less abrasive relations with media than those of the Thatcher administration, both at ministerial level and at that of press secretary Bernard Ingham. Ingham's successor, Gus O'Donnell, was an economist who had worked for John Major in the Treasury. His approach to the job seemed less ambitious. Even so, there were reports, as the year went on, of the Prime Minister complaining to broadcasting executives about unfair programmes. Conservative Central Office complained of bias, as did the Liberal Democrats over by-election reporting. Such complaints – especially in the months before a general election – are an inevitable result of the gradual expansion of political broadcasting. Equally, though, the broadcasters can be expected to resist them – as did John Birt, for example, both in public and in private. But broadcasters could do nothing, it may be noted, about the government ban on the broadcast voices of certain Irish extremists, now in its third year.

The propensity for the public to complain – to the Press Complaints Commission, the Advertising Standards Authority, the Broadcasting Standards Council and the like – continued to grow. The Broadcasting Standards Council also commissioned research into aspects of public taste and sensitivities. There was no particular *cause célèbre* involving the tabloids, and the threats of 'right of reply' or 'privacy' legislation heard in 1990 remained muted.

The unpredictabilities of the libel law threw up a variety of cases. In May the first case of a libelled child came before the courts, when a five year old boy branded by *The Sun* as the 'worst brat in Britain' was awarded undisclosed damages (probably up to £50,000). In November *The Sun*, again, paid £50,000 damages to the actor Bill Roache, who was described as smug and self-satisfied, like his long running screen character, Ken Barlow, in *Coronation Street*. Shortly before Christmas *The People* had to pay £250,000 to the broadcaster Esther Rantzen, for alleging that she kept quiet about the child abuse record of a school teacher. Ms Rantzen said the bulk of the money would go to the charity ChildLine.

In an echo of the secrecy trials of the 1980s, the European Court of Human Rights ruled in November that the government was wrong to prevent publication of the book *Spycatcher* by the former MI5 officer Peter Wright in 1987, once it had become available in the USA. The injunctions against publication up to that point, on the other hand, were ruled acceptable. The court's decision is not binding in Britain but it was regarded by lawyers as a 'small victory for press freedom'.

Media news in the last two months of 1991 was dominated by the consequences of Robert Maxwell's death. The whole chain of events conformed to the historical pattern of media magnates as idiosyncratic giants doing nothing by halves. The death itself came in truth-is-stranger-than-fiction style. Why did Maxwell fall off his luxury yacht in the Azores during the small hours of 5 November? Had he possibly had a heart attack first – or did he not so much fall as jump? This last sad possibility gained credence as the scale of his financial troubles and frauds became clearer. Tributes to his energy, acumen, ingenuity and philanthropy gave way to

vituperative stories of the 'now it can be told' type: he was ('let's face it . . . ?') a
bully, a liar and a cheat.

Any clarity in his affairs was purely relative. The structure of his businesses was
extremely complex. 'A global web of connections following four decades of
growth' was the headline to a *Financial Times* chart trying to make sense of them.
There were hundreds of companies stretching across Britain, north America,
western Europe, eastern Europe (Maxwell's birthplace), Israel, Japan, the Soviet
Union. The two pillars of the business were Maxwell Communications
Corporation, a diverse publishing group, and Mirror Group Newspapers, whose
chief assets were the *Daily Mirror* and its companion papers. Each company had
assets estimated at about £1 billion. The Maxwell family owned 68 per cent of
MCC and 51 per cent of MGN. A third pillar was AGB International, one of the
largest European market research businesses. These three companies were flanked,
as the *Financial Times* put it, by 'cascades of holding companies in the UK, US
and Channel Islands'. The businesses included publications of all kinds; printing
and newsprint, cable TV, aviation, property, engineering, football clubs.
Interlocking with the public companies, and parent of most of them, was the private
Maxwell Foundation. This was registered in Liechtenstein and not obliged to reveal
its ultimate beneficiaries.

Maxwell's two sons, Kevin and Ian, now in charge, saw the MCC and MGN
share prices plunge. Throughout November they sold off businesses, to shore up
bankers' confidence. After a month, MCC shares, standing at 121 pence on
Maxwell's death, were down to 35 pence. The brothers lost control and resigned
from both MCC and MGN on 3 December. The Serious Fraud Office launched a
wide-ranging investigation and administrators were appointed.

In December, all such complexities could be swept aside for the ordinary *Daily
Mirror* – or *The European* – reader by the brute simplicity of the disclosure that
Maxwell had misappropriated millions of pounds of Mirror Group pension funds.
Here was simple tabloid morality: you just do not rob the old folks. Maxwell's own
papers chased with appetite the tale of his fraudulence, while liquidators unravelled
the skeins of deception. It was a terrific story to see out the year.

Chronology

1 Jan: Press Complaints Commission under the chairmanship of Lord McGregor of Durris
replaces the Press Council.

6 Jan: On BBC's *See for Yourself* Sir John Harvey-Jones says the Corporation needs to cut
its wages bill by a third and halve its top management.

13 Jan: Jocelyn Stevens is appointed chairman of the Independent Television Commission.
ESRC report criticizes the government's telecommunications policy for concentrating
on choice rather than effectiveness.

14 Jan: BBC licence fee to rise by 7.9 per cent to £77 in April.
Report by Price Waterhouse for the government calls for a slimming down of the BBC
management and argues that savings and improved management could save £203
million.

16 Jan: National Consumer Council criticizes BT's arbitration scheme for customer complaints.

17 Jan: Press Council criticizes exaggerated press reporting of the riots in Strangeways Prison in 1990.

23 Jan: Complaints to the Advertising Standards Authority in 1990 rose by 17 per cent to a new record level of 9,972.

25 Jan: IEA report calls for price controls on BT to be relaxed.

28 Jan: John Major rejects calls for attributable Westminster lobby briefings.

1 Feb: Postal services should be deregulated and the Post Office split up into its existing centres of counters, parcels and letters and privatized according to a study by the Adam Smith Institute.

5 Feb: The Press Council received a record 1,588 complaints in 1990.

7 Feb: Lords reject legal challenges to the ban on direct-speech interviews with terrorist groups.

8 Feb: Thorn EMI makes a bid (which eventually fails) for Thames Television, in which it already held a 27.8 per cent stake.

18 Feb: National Consumer Council calls for a radical overhaul of British Telecom's pricing structure, which it argues discriminates against private customers and the less well-off.

19 Feb: Robin Morgan leaves the *Sunday Express* and is replaced as caretaker editor by Henry McCrory.

1 Mar: *The Indy*, the newspaper aimed at the teenage market, is closed by Newspaper Publishing.

3 Mar: Charles Wilson become acting editor of the *Daily Mirror*, replacing Roy Greenslade.

5 Mar: White paper on telecommunications policy proposes higher limits on price increases, a 10 per cent price cut in international calls from June, schemes to help low users, the elderly and infirm, greater choice in local telephone services, and the operation of local services through mobile systems.

10 Mar: A new Scottish tabloid, the *Sunday Scot* is launched.

12 Mar: Watchdogs strongly criticize use of cross-media promotion of other forms of media by firms with cross-media holdings.

28 Mar: Robert Maxwell to sell Pergamon Press to the Dutch group Elsevier for £440 million. David Montgomery is replaced as editor of *Today* by Martin Dunn.

2 Apr: Richard Stott becomes the new editor of the *Daily Mirror*.

11 Apr: The Lords rule that all media organizations can be silenced by an injunction against just one newspaper in a judgement against the *Sunday Times* over the *Spycatcher* affair.

14 May: Eve Pollard becomes editor of the *Sunday Express*. She is replaced as editor of the *Sunday Mirror* by Bridget Rowe.

15 May: *The Independent* and the *Independent on Sunday* are to integrate their operations. The 40 bids for the 16 ITV franchises are unveiled.

23 May: David Boulton, *The Third Age of Broadcasting*, IPPR, suggests the abolition of the BBC licence fee and its replacement by a sales tax on televisions and radio sets, to be channelled through a direct government grant.

25 May: Stephen Glover resigns as editor of the *Independent on Sunday* following the decision to move *The Independent* and its Sunday sister to seven day operations.

30 May: Routledge (part of International Thomson) buys HarperCollins Academic from News International.

3 June: Walter Allen and Peter Curwen, *Competition and Choice in the Publishing Industry*, IEA, calls for the abolition of the Net Book Agreement, which they argue has led to an inefficient publishing industry and a poor deal for readers.

27 June: BBC reveals it overspent by £80 million in 1990–91.

2 July: Government confirms that John Birt will replace Michael Checkland as director-general of the BBC in 1993.

4 July: Disclosure that John Birt has drawn up radical plans to close studios and production facilities at the BBC.

EC to probe price arrangements between European telecommunications companies.

8 July: Complaints about postal services fell 23 per cent in 1990 according to the Post Office Users' National Council.

Ann Shearer, *Survivors and the Media*, John Libbey for the Broadcasting Standards Council, says reports on tragedies and accidental deaths should be conducted with greater sensitivity and aim to cause as little distress as possible to relatives and survivors.

11 July: The *Sunday Scot* closes with losses of £3 million.

8 Aug: PSI report criticizes attempts to expand independent radio at the moment and suggests that the objectives of commercial radio growth laid out in the 1990 Broadcasting Act are unlikely to be achieved.

19 Aug: John Birt pledges to introduce an internal market into the BBC in an effort to increase flexibility and cut costs.

22 Aug: Centre for Policy Studies paper advocates the sale of the Royal Mail as 64 separate postal districts.

2 Sept: Revamped schedule for BBC Radio 4 announced.

11 Sept: Labour pledges to introduce a Freedom of Information Act, increased editorial independence in broadcasting, and the abolition of the Broadcasting Standards Council.

15 Oct: Results of ITV franchise bids announced. Four companies lose their franchises; TV-AM (to Sunrise), Thames (to Carlton), TVS (to Meridian) and TSW (to West Country Television).

20 Oct: Controversy over the possible connections of Robert Maxwell and of Nick Davies, the foreign editor of the *Daily Mirror*, to Israeli intelligence begins with the publication of Seymour Hersh's *The Sampson Option – Israel, America and the Bomb*, Faber.

24 Oct: The television transmission network and engineering arm of the IBA is privatized in a sale to Mercury Asset Management for £70 million.

28 Oct: Nick Davies is sacked by the *Daily Mirror*.

5 Nov: Robert Maxwell drowns off the Canary Islands.

14 Nov: Birmingham Post and Mail regional newspaper group bought by management from the American Ingersoll Group for £125 million.

26 Nov: European Court of Human Rights rules that the government should not have tried to prevent publication of allegations contained in Peter Wright's *Spycatcher* after it had been published in the US.

2 Dec: *The European* closes.

19 Dec: EC agrees standards for high definition television.

30 Dec: *The European* is reprieved, at least temporarily, by its administrators.

The Legal System

CAROL HARLOW

This year the media has fastened on to two sensational cases. The first involved rape. Modern caselaw has shown the courts gradually resiling from the hardline position of the common law that rape of a wife by her husband is impossible. As expressed in a statement from Sir Matthew Hale in 1736, the marriage contract was deemed to contain an irrevocable consent to intercourse. Modern cases ate into this rule by holding rape possible where, for example, the parties were separated. This year, the question reached the House of Lords for the first time in a case where a husband broke into the house in which his wife was staying and forced intercourse by 'squeezing her neck with both hands'.[1] The House ruled that the doctrine of irrevocable consent was 'no longer in existence'.

In the second case,[2] the plaintiff was the mother of a young girl who had been murdered some twelve years ago. An abortive trial had resulted in the acquittal of the daughter's young boyfriend who had admitted in court to helping the real criminal, his stepfather, to conceal the offence. The Director of Public Prosecutions declined to prosecute, probably on the ground that the statement was unreliable and lacked independent corroboration. Twelve years after the trial, the mother brought a civil action claiming damages against the alleged murderer for assault and battery. The first hurdle of the civil period of limitation, generally three years in actions for personal injuries, was overcome when the Court of Appeal ruled that time started to run only from the date when the mother learned of the possibility of a civil action; permission to proceed was therefore given. The trial judge went on to find the case proved against the defendant, thus effectively finding him guilty of the gravest criminal offence in a civil court before which he did not appear.

The favourable media reception for these cases, though understandable, allowed important arguments of constitutional principle to go unheard. Most important is the question whether the criminal law ought to be changed in this way by judicial fiat. This point has been addressed before by the House of Lords when asked to revive common law offences thought either to have been replaced by modern statute or to have fallen into desuetude. Too often the House has fallen into the temptation of acting as law reformer, overriding compelling reasons to the contrary.[3] But in a parliamentary democracy such as we profess to operate, it is surely for the legislature to define the parameters of a serious criminal offence. This time the argument against intervention was strengthened by the existence of a Law

Commission report cogently arguing the case for new legislation.[4] Again, it is a cardinal principle of the rule of law that no person should be convicted retrospectively of a criminal offence. In the instant case, the defendant had less cause to complain in that his retrospectively earned custodial sentence was amply justified by his excessive use of force. But the fact remains that the prohibition against retrospective criminality is one of the most important protections against arbitrary action by the state and ought not to be lightly set aside. If they are to indulge, courts must at the very least adopt the practice of 'prospective overruling' whereby penalties do not attach to acts retrospectively criminalized.

Only four days after a specially convened Court of Appeal had abruptly terminated marital immunity, the War Crimes Bill was passed by the Commons to extend the territorial jurisdiction of British courts to crimes of genocide committed outside the United Kingdom during the Second World War. Arguably this bill too suffers from the defect of retrospectivity, a point made by leading lawyers in both Houses during second reading debates. The issue was less than straightforward; it was procedural rather than substantive law which was changed (genocide is a crime by international law and homicide is always criminal). A more powerful argument concerned the danger of acting on stale evidence (the parties might have changed beyond recognition and memory faded over such a long period of time). Acting this time in its legislative capacity, the House of Lords had rejected the bill in defiance of the Commons which now reasserted the authority of the government Chief Whip.

Stale evidence was also a danger in *Halford v. Brookes* but it was not the only issue. Increasingly, the power of prosecution is seen as a state monopoly but English law permits both private criminal prosecutions and also civil actions in parallel to or instead of criminal prosecution. This position could be abused. Trial by jury in serious criminal cases is a constitutional right and the existence of an impartial prosecution service with a duty to filter out dubious cases is a further guarantee against wrongful conviction, and one which has only recently been instituted.[5] The rules of evidence and the standard of proof are also tighter in criminal cases. In civil cases, on the other hand, the limitation periods protect defendants against stale evidence, a protection which does not exist in criminal cases as 'no time runs against the Crown'. Even here, stale cases can be ruled out by the court as an abuse of process (as occurred recently in cases involving the Wapping riots of 1987) or may be rejected by the jury (as happened this year in the prosecution of Randle and Pottle for 'springing' George Blake from prison in 1967). So there are good reasons for the limitation rules and the Court of Appeal might have been wise to dispose of the case on this ground alone.

Miscarriages of Justice: the Saga Continues

The points taken so far might seem dry and legalistic if the number of convictions set aside this year as unsafe and unsatisfactory had not been so high. In March the release of the Birmingham Six was ordered by the Court of Appeal after confessions and forensic tests had both been shown to be unreliable. Instantly, the appointment of a Royal Commission chaired by Lord Runciman, a distinguished academic sociologist, to scrutinize the criminal justice system with a view to minimizing as far as possible 'the likelihood of such events happening again' was announced. The move came too late to prevent 100 backbenchers from setting down a Commons early day motion calling for the dismissal of the Lord Chief Justice but it did help to disperse the steam. After consultation with interested parties, the Commission announced its agenda. This is wide enough to embrace the whole of pre-trial procedure as well as the conduct of the trial, forensic and other scientific evidence, appeals and provisions to rectify and possibly compensate for any miscarriage. Arguably, the breaches of police procedure exposed are so great as to require a separate Commission on police powers and accountability.

For historians, there was a pleasing symmetry in that the last Royal Commission to report before Margaret Thatcher took office and the first to be appointed after her demise should both concern the operation of the criminal justice system. Civil libertarians resolved, however, that the symmetry should stop there. The 1979 Philips Commission, set up to consider the relationship of police powers with the rules of criminal evidence after an earlier miscarriage of justice, had generally been considered as incorporating substantial concessions to a too-powerful police lobby. This time, the opposing lobbies moved into position even before the members were nominated. There were rumours that the Home Office was pressing for reconsideration of the 'right to silence' and media advocacy of a continental-style inquisitorial system. The release in November of Silcott, Braithwaite and Raghip, convicted in 1975 of the murder of PC Blakelock during riots in Tottenham, added fuel to the fire. All three had been convicted solely on confession evidence obtained in breach of standard police procedures. In the Silcott case, as in that of the Birmingham Six, new forensic tests conclusively proved parts of the alleged confession to be forged. A statement on behalf of the three blamed police and press for the wrongful convictions and asked that 'convictions based on uncorroborated confessional evidence be outlawed'. Official police evidence to the Commission, inappositely published on the same day, demanded an end to 'the devices used by defence solicitors to gain an advantage over the prosecution', modification of the right of silence and 'closer cooperation between prosecution and defence in search of the truth', at least at the pre-trial stage. It is hoped that the criminal justice system will receive a thorough review and one not unduly tilted towards the kneejerk reaction of dismantling our traditional, adversarial model of criminal justice. This has not always served us well. There is, however, little evidence to hand that inquisitorial systems function any better.[7]

Justice Denied and Delayed

Events in the civil courts have moved less quickly this year (in more senses than one) as reforms pushed through in the last few years are beginning to come into effect (some would say, come home to roost). The Lord Chancellor's Department, preoccupied with the spiralling cost of legal aid, naturally tends to see the problem as one of holding costs down. The constantly changing eligibility test has now fallen to an all time low: a mere 45 per cent of the population is said to be eligible for legal aid.[8] In the meantime, the profession emphasizes falling standards, low recruitment and longer delays. Applications for judicial review, for example, have to be made to the prestigious Administrative Division of the High Court by means of a special procedure known as 'Order 53 Procedure' (the reference being to the Rules of the Supreme Court). Knowledge that such applications now take on average two years from the time when they are set down is in itself enough to justify the Lord Chief Justice's plea for more judges to clear backlogs. As predicted in 1989, the problem in county courts is now chronic, extending beyond the judges to a grave shortage of ill-paid court clerks and administrative staff. The simplest matters may now incur six month delays and London solicitors describe the system as almost in collapse. One answer is to move 'cases' out of the court system altogether; the Lord Chancellor's Department, for example, is currently considering a scheme of 'no fault' liability for small traffic accident claims. More consumer-oriented and more fashionable is the idea for a 'Courts Charter' floated by the Bar Council, which would set standards and provide compensation for losses caused by delay and inefficiency. The London Solicitors Litigation Association would go rather further, demanding a unified courts system in the charge of a government agency responsible to the Lord Chancellor for the administration of justice system save only for judicial appointments.

The question for the dissatisfied consumer is where to complain. The Parliamentary Commissioner has partial jurisdiction over the Lord Chancellor's Department, extending to those aspects of the courts system which are in no way attributable to the judiciary (listing, for example, is a judicial function, collection of fines administrative). There is no official system for handling complaints about the judiciary: in principle, the Lord Chancellor's Department deals with them on an informal basis. The Courts and Legal Services Act established for the first time a Legal Services Ombudsman. Michael Barnes, the first ombudsman, took office in January and, in the first nine months, received nearly 1,000 complaints about practitioners of which 50 per cent warranted investigation.[9] (With only 12 investigators and a backlog of 600 cases from the earlier complaints system, the ombudsman seems in danger of death by drowning). There is an obvious danger that complaints about different parts of a continuous process which must be referred to different places will be lost. A true 'Courts Charter' demands a Scandinavian-type 'justice ombudsman', to oversee the totality of the system. Complaints of serious miscarriage of justice could even be included!

The Biter Bit

Concern to control the legal aid budget is said to lie behind the Lord Chancellor's acquiescence in a controversial government decision to remove legal aid from asylum seekers, who may in future have to rely solely on the UK Immigration

Advisory Service.[10] This attack on a vulnerable section of the community, described by the chairman of the Bar Council as 'an action of which the government should be ashamed'[11] provoked a furore from world human rights groups as well as the profession. But, as the Asylum Bill, which further restricts refugees' access to the courts,[12] was before Parliament, the Home Secretary found himself answering for his department to the Court of Appeal. The Home Office had refused refugee status to a national of Zaire. His solicitor applied for judicial review. An undertaking to keep the man in the country pending the court's decision was given by counsel, despite which the man was flown out. The judge, alerted, asked for his return but the Home Secretary, acting on legal advice, declined. To his surprise, he was held personally liable for contempt of court. From a constitutional standpoint, the case was of capital importance and takes its place in history with the great 'General Warrant' cases[13] of the eighteenth century. The political threat was serious enough to prompt demands for resignation and to warrant a statement to the House of Commons.[14] All in all, a mixed year for the rule of law.

Notes

1 *Reg. v. R.* [1991] 3 Weekly Law Reports 767 (HL(E)).

2 *Halford v. Brookes, The Guardian,* 30 September 1991.

3 See particularly the celebrated dissent of Lord Reid in the controversial case of *Shaw v. DPP* [1962] AC 220, where the House revived the common law offence of conspiracy to corrupt public morals which the House of Commons intended to replace by the Obscene Publications Act 1959.

4 Law Commission Working Paper No 116, *Rape within Marriage,* 1991.

5 The office of Director of Public Prosecutions dates to the Prosecution of Offences Act 1879 while the Crown Prosecution Service, which separates prosecutorial from police functions, was set up by the Police and Criminal Evidence Act 1984.

6 The Royal Commission on Police and Criminal Evidence, Cmnd. 8092 (the Philips Commission) reported in 1981.

7 Particularly relevant is Anne Grosskurth, 'Scotland's Pitfalls', *Legal Action,* November 1991, p.7.

8 There is some dispute over the figures, though a baseline of 79 per cent in 1979 is generally agreed. The LCD works on a figure of 69 per cent, the Law Society of 45 per cent. See *Legal Action* October 1989, May 1991, November 1991.

9 Interview, *Legal Action,* November 1991, p.7.

10 UKIAS is a government funded body of lay advisers which presently offers specialist representation services in tribunals.

11 Anthony Scrivener QC, 18 August 1991. Legislation is nonetheless currently before Parliament.

12 The Bill is two-faced. It creates a right of appeal to a tribunal or 'adjudicator' where none previously existed but restricts access to the High Court by substituting appeal to the Court of Appeal on a point of law and with leave.

13 *Wilkes v Wood,* (1763), *Entick v Carrington,* (1765), *Leach v Money* (1765).

14 *M v the Home Office and Kenneth Baker, The Guardian,* 4 December 1991.

Chronology

8 Jan: Michael Barnes takes up office as Legal Services Ombudsman.

25 Feb: DPP says he no longer considers the prosecution of the Birmingham Six 'safe and satisfactory'.

27 Feb: Law Society presses the Lord Chancellor to change to appointments procedure for judges, claiming that it is discriminatory.

1 Mar: John Greenway's Criminal Procedure (Insanity and Unfitness to Plead) Bill is given an unopposed second reading. It aims to allow courts to hear cases and make judgements even if a person is found unfit to plead.

14 Mar: The Birmingham Six are released. The government announces the setting up of a Royal Commission under Lord Runciman on the criminal justice system, to 'minimise as far as possible the likelihood of such events happening again'.
Husbands' immunity from the charge of rape is swept away in a Court of Appeal ruling that the law has become anachronistic and offensive.

15 Mar: The law reform group Justice calls for the introduction of continental style examining magistrates to the British criminal justice system.

18 Mar: Commons early day motion signed by 100 MPs calling for the dismissal of Lord Lane as Lord Chief Justice in the wake of the release of the Birmingham Six.
Commons passes the War Crimes Bill, rejected by the Lords in 1990, on the second reading, by 254 to 88.

19 Mar: Mr Justice Peter Gibson, the head of the Law Commission, criticizes the government's failure to introduce recommended reforms.

26 Mar: First man in England and Wales to be convicted of raping his wife is gaoled for five years.

27 Mar: Survey by Michael Murphy of LSE shows that the number of people eligible for civil legal aid is at an all-time low.

1 Apr: Solicitors Complaints Bureau introduces major changes to improve its reaction time and make it more user-friendly.

2 Apr: Law Society applies to Lord Chancellor's Advisory Committee for greater involvement of solicitors at all levels of the court system in England and Wales.

15 Apr: Reforms to make pre-marital contracts legally binding in the event of divorce and to guarantee former partners a share of their spouse's pension is urged by the Law Society.

25 Apr: The use of facial mapping in the identification of suspected criminals is put in jeopardy by the CPS decision to withdraw the case against the first man convicted by the process.

10 May: Lord Donaldson suggests judicial tribunals should replace trial by jury in fraud cases because of the length of time the cases often involve.

15 May: Law Society advocates pre-marriage contracts as a way of expediting divorce settlements.
Lord Chancellor proposes 'no fault' compensation scheme for road accident victims to allow small injuries claims to be settled out of court.

18 May: Bar Council approves a radical equal opportunities policy to ensure that at least 5 per cent of members and pupils of chambers should come from ethnic minorities and that at least 5 per cent of work sent to chambers should be given to ethnic minority lawyers.

22 May: David Lockwood, chairman of the Police Federation, urges changes in the rules of evidence to allow an accused person's previous convictions to be made known to a jury.

28 May: Bar Council to set up a working party to consider the feasibility of courts sitting in the evenings and generally being more user-friendly.

2 June: Working committee of Justice says maximum penalties for making and supplying cannabis should be reduced, but opposes its legalization.

4 June: Lord Mackay suggests that would-be claimants of legal aid should have to pay a lump sum towards their legal costs and then have to undergo a means test before becoming eligible for legal aid.

24 June: Some solicitors are charging excessive legal aid fees and curbs are necessary to control spiralling costs according to the Legal Aid Board.

26 June: Pat Pottle and Michael Randle, on trial for helping the double agent George Blake to escape from gaol in 1967, are acquitted by the jury.
Court of Appeal rules that the convictions of the Maguire seven were unsafe.

9 July: Lord Lane, the Lord Chief Justice, criticizes the government's failure to provide sufficient judges to cope with increasing workloads.

16 July: Lord Mackay suggests a reorganization of the courts by the formation of an extra panel of judges in order to cut waiting times in the criminal division of the Court of Appeal.

26 July: In a judgement on Home Office handling of the case of a Zairean refugee the High Court rules that ministers are exempt from contempt of court. The Appeal Court later reverses this decision and the government decides to appeal to the House of Lords.

13 Aug: New guidelines on the appointment of magistrates published.

17 Sept: The case of Judith Ward, gaoled for an IRA bombing in 1974, is referred by the Home Secretary to the Court of Appeal.

26 Sept: The cases of those imprisoned for the murder of PC Blakelock at the Broadwater Farm riots of 1985 are referred to the Court of Appeal.

3 Oct: Sir Allan Green, the Director of Public Prosecutions, resigns after allegations of kerb-crawling.

23 Oct: Law Lords uphold the Appeal Court ruling that marital exemption from prosecution for rape was an 'anachronistic and offensive fiction'.

25 Oct: Dr Malcolm Smith receives record £150,000 damages for slander.

5 Nov: Charities Bill to regulate the activities of professional fund-raisers, enhance the powers of the Charity Commissioners and clarify the duties of charities' trustees is published.

25–28 Nov: Cases of the three men, Winston Silcott, Engin Raghip and Mark Braithwaite, convicted of the murder of PC Blakelock collapse when prosecution lawyers concede that the apparent dishonesty of the senior investigating officer destroyed their case. Winston Silcott is formally acquitted.

29 Nov: The BBC's *Public Eye: A Betrayal of Trust*, highlights the failings of the legal system when dealing with the sexual abuse of mentally handicapped people.

3 Dec: Solicitor-General rejects appeal for review of the law of contempt of court from Greville Janner, who had been named in the Frank Beck child abuse case but unable to refute accusations made against him whilst the case was being heard.

5 Dec: Appeal Court formally quashes the sentences of Engin Raghip and Mark Braithwaite for the Blakelock murder and apologizes for the shortcomings of the criminal law process.

13 Dec: Mr Justice Ognall at Manchester Crown Court conditionally releases two teenage rapists saying it had been a prank and there had been no lasting psychological damage to their victim..

Police and Public Order

ROBERT REINER

Policing used to be a consensus issue, one on which political parties – and the public – were in fundamental agreement. The police, like the monarchy, motherhood and apple pie, were sacred totems above the humdrum partisan fray. The advent of 1979, Thatcherism and all that, shattered this accord, together with so many aspects of the post-war political mould. By the mid-1980s the police were the pigs in the middle of a sharply polarized political debate. Generally they were the darlings of the Tories, and in conflict with Labour-controlled police authorities to which the national Labour Party threatened to make them more accountable.

In 1991, the first year of the post-Thatcherite era, there was good news and bad news for the police. The good news was the return of consensus about policing. The bad news was that the new consensus view was that the police were failing badly on almost every front, and in need of drastic reform. Once the preserve of the supposedly anti-police 'Loony Left', this was now the received wisdom even of the true blue press and politicians, staunch supporters of law and order. A *Guardian* cartoon on the 29th November, just after the Court of Appeal declared the convictions of the Tottenham Three to have been miscarriages of justice, summed it up well. Apologizing for being late for a date a man offers the excuse: 'I asked a policeman the time, and he lied.' As in 1989 and 1990, news about the police was dominated by scandals involving major miscarriages of justice. At the same time there was a steady background stream of revelations of police abuse, and failure to deliver adequate services. The news also contained many items which put the police in a much better light. However, these do not balance the impact of the 'bad news' on public perceptions, and indeed are not given equal weight in reporting. The same is true of the many ongoing efforts by the police service to improve its practices and image, which in a variety of ways have been steadily pursued since the shock-waves of 1981, the urban riots and the Scarman Report. It is increasingly apparent that the police feel trapped in a time warp. They are intent on reforms. However, the impact of these on public perceptions of the police is continuously being undercut by shocking revelations of skeletons in the cupboard, as well as unrealistic expectations of performance and probity built up in the bygone era when the lid was shut tight on scandals.

Miscarriages of Justice

The year began and ended with official acknowledgement of two major miscarriages of justice. In March, the Court of Appeal finally upheld the appeal of the Birmingham Six, who had been convicted in 1975 for the savage pub-bombings in Birmingham the previous year. Coming on top of the similar vindications in 1989 of the Guildford Four and in 1990 of the Maguire Seven, the case profoundly shook public confidence in the police and criminal justice system. So did the November decision upholding the appeal of the 'Tottenham Three' who had been convicted ot the murder of PC Keith Blakelock during the 1985 Broadwater Farm riots. By coincidence, the very same week as the Court of Appeal announced the Tottenham verdicts, one Met sergeant was murdered and two PCs seriously stabbed by a pair of suspected burglars. Whilst highlighting the dangers which the police routinely face, these tragic incidents did not avert severe damage to the police image and to morale.

The Home Secretary attempted to begin the process of recuperation by establishing a Royal Commission on Criminal Justice, chaired by Lord Runciman. This ended a twelve year hiatus for Royal Commissions, which under Thatcher had been dismissed as the acme of the despised consensus politics style. The last Royal Commission before the present one had been the Royal Commission on Criminal Procedure chaired by Sir Cyril Philips, (progenitor of the 1984 Police and Criminal Evidence Act (PACE)) which had been appointed in 1978 and reported in 1981. The setting-up of the new Royal Commission indicated the extent to which government acknowledged the depths of public concern about criminal justice, including the police. Many police representatives (notably the Police Federation) and commentators continued to press for a separate Royal Commission specifically on the problems of policing, but so far this idea has been rejected.

During the year several other prominent allegations of miscarriages of justice continued to surface. In September, the Home Secretary referred the case of Judith Ward, who had been convicted for a 1974 IRA bombing of a coach, to the Court of Appeal. Anxieties continued to be expressed about the men convicted of the murder of the newsboy Carl Bridgewater in 1978, and in December a new inquiry was set up.

The impact of the major revelations of recent years also continued to reverberate. One was the case of the West Midlands serious crimes squad, which had been broken up in June 1989 by the then chief constable Geoffrey Dear, following serious allegations of widespread malpractice in the handling of evidence. In January 1991 the Court of Appeal freed John Edwards, who had been serving 14 years for an armed robbery and who claimed he had been framed by the West Midlands serious crimes squad. In June three former members of the squad were acquitted on charges of concocting evidence in a robbery case in 1987, although the Court of Appeal had ruled in July 1989 that the conviction of the alleged robber (Keith Parchment) was unsafe. In July a fifth man was freed after his conviction on squad evidence was quashed, and the Civil Liberties Trust published a report detailing abuses attributed to the squad. In February the report of an inquiry by the Sussex police into the response to the squad scandal placed responsibility on Geoffrey Dear for failing to secure the squad's offices after disbanding it, which hampered the investigation he had initiated. In November some former members of the squad were placed by Ron Hadfield (the new chief constable) in a new unit to combat drugs, fraud and firearms offences, seemingly contrary to Police Complaints Authority recommendations.

Other continuing controversial cases included the Guildford Four. In February three detectives were charged with conspiracy to pervert the course of justice. The cases were blocked by the Bow Street stipendiary magistrate on 11 June, but in October the DPP challenged this ruling in the High Court. Also in October, four of the West Midlands detectives who investigated the Birmingham Six were charged with conspiracy to pervert the course of justice, and with perjury. There were police abuses established also in a number of less high profile cases. In July, for example, the Metropolitan Police paid £40,000 damages to a man who said they had beaten, racially abused and framed him.

Miscarriages of justice or abuses were also found in cases arising from some notorious public order incidents of recent years. In June the South Yorkshire police agreed to pay more than £500,000 compensation to miners who had picketed the Orgreave coke plant during the 1984 strike. In July a student who was filmed throwing bricks at the police during the Trafalgar Square poll tax demonstration on 31 March 1990 was acquitted after claiming this was self-defence. During another poll tax demonstrator's trial that month a Met PC was accused of perjury by the judge. In November last, the two Met Officers facing charges arising from the 1987 Wapping print dispute had their cases dismissed at the Old Bailey, after the judge ruled that the long delay prevented a fair trial.

Malpractice

In addition to the above cases of abuse of police powers leading to miscarriages of justice, numerous other forms of malpractice caused concern during the year. As in the last few years generally, there were a number of major scandals involving personal corruption for gain. The main example was reported in November, when the chairman, secretary and treasurer of the West Midlands Police Federation Joint Branch Board were all charged with stealing funds from their members' insurance scheme. As in other recent years, a number of cases of sexual malpractice were reported involving police officers. One Police Federation official was charged with using an official credit card for extra-marital liaisons. In August a West Midlands chief superintendent retired on medical grounds whilst facing disciplinary charges after having been filmed leaving a massage parlour.

More institutionalized forms of malpractice occurred in cases of race and sex discrimination. The saga continued of the action claiming sex discrimination brought by Merseyside Assistant Chief Constable Alison Halford, who had applied unsuccessfully for a series of deputy chief constable posts, together with her subsequent suspension following allegations of misconduct. In January 1991 Alison Halford lodged a formal complaint of neglect of duty against the chief constable of Merseyside. She was granted leave by the High Court to seek a judicial review of her suspension in July. This was adjourned in September, following an agreement by Merseyside Police Authority to reconsider her suspension.

In January PC Surinder Singh won £20,000 damages from Nottinghamshire Constabulary following an industrial relations tribunal decision that he had been refused a transfer to the CID on racial grounds, and other Asian officers also received compensation. PC Singh was subsequently transferred to CID. In July ten Nottinghamshire officers were disciplined as a result of the racial discrimination established in the Singh case. An orthodox Jewish PC won an undisclosed settlement from the Met in November, after an industrial tribunal supported his claim that it was racially discriminatory to have ended the practice of allowing him to exchange shifts with colleagues so that he did not have to work on Saturdays, the Jewish Sabbath. A black PC received £20,000 compensation from the Met in November following an industrial tribunal action about racist remarks by fellow officers.

Discrimination against gay people, inside and outside the force, was also a theme of 1991. In January four homosexuals won £30,000 agreed damages from Staffordshire police after claiming they had been maliciously prosecuted. In the same month, it was announced that a lesbian and gay police association had been established to fight prejudice within the force. The Met in August proclaimed a policy of monitoring attacks on homosexuals in London.

Police Effectiveness

During 1991 the police faced double-sided criticism. As already indicated, it was a year in which major and minor malpractices came to light. At the same time, their performance in dealing with crime and disorder was widely perceived and attacked as inadequate. Concern about police effectiveness and how it could be bolstered was a continuing preoccupation of policy-makers and politicians, in relation to the core police tasks of controlling crime and disorder.

Tackling Crime

During 1991 the previous year's record-breaking increases in the official crime statistics were matched or surpassed. In March it was announced that recorded crime had for the first time gone over four million offences. The Home Office Statistical Bulletin reported on 13 September that 4.9 million notifiable offences were recorded in the twelve months ending on 1 July 1991, a rise of 18 per cent over the previous 12 months. The previous increase between June 1989–1990 had itself been a record 13 per cent. Apart from a slight drop between 1987–9, recorded crime has increased in every year during the 1980s, but each of the last two years' rises has been far greater than any earlier years.

There were some major success stories. For example, in November the Lord Advocate announced that warrants had been issued for the arrest of two Libyans for the murder of the 259 people who died in the Lockerbie bombing in 1988. He singled out for praise the investigation by Dumfries and Galloway Constabulary, Britain's smallest force. However, the reporting of bad news as usual crowded out the good. The combination of unprecedented increases in crime with revelations of major malpractices in crime investigation has been of enormous embarrassment to the police. This has been exacerbated by similar criticisms of police performance in dealing with disorder.

Maintaining Public Order

The March 1990 anti-poll tax riots in Trafalgar Square had been the most serious outbreak of disorder since Broadwater Farm in 1985. A Scotland Yard report in March 1991 concluded that there had been many shortcomings in the Met's response which had led to their loss of control over the demonstration. It was noted earlier that several court cases established also that there had been malpractices in the handling of arrested anti-poll tax demonstrators.

The failure adequately to handle crowd control at the Hillsborough soccer stadium in April 1989 had been attributed by the Taylor inquiry primarily to inadequacies in the police operation. In July 1991 it was announced that Chief Superintendent Duckenfield and Superintendent Murray were to face disciplinary charges arising out of the disaster.

The most serious disorder of 1991 occurred at the very end of August and in early September, in a series of unrelated events in Cardiff, Handsworth, the Blackbird Leys Estate in Oxford, and the Meadow Well Estate, Tyneside. The first two incidents arose from racial tensions. The latter two were the result of police attempts to control joyriding and the crowds of people who assembled to watch the teenagers drive their stolen cars.

The joyriding episodes aroused enormous concern, and indeed set in train a 'moral panic' culminating in new legislation to increase the penalties for joyriding. What particularly caused anxiety and much soul-searching amongst media pundits was the absence of any manifest protest element such as had been clearly apparent in say the industrial or anti-poll tax disorders of the 1980s and even the 1981 and 1985 urban disorders (although this interpretation of the latter was contested by some Conservatives). Nonetheless a connection could be drawn between the Oxford and Tyneside disorders, which occurred on estates with relatively high levels of youth unemployment and social deprivation. When the Archbishop of Canterbury did draw this obvious connection in a widely publicized speech he attracted a furious response from the government and many Conservative commentators.

The police were also widely criticized in the political and media debate about the September disorders for alleged failures to control either the joyriding or the crowds which gathered around it. They were the unfortunate recipients of charges from different quarters that they under-reacted to law-breaking, and that they harassed the youths involved. As with crime control, so too with order maintenance, the police were attacked in 1991 both for failures to police effectively and at the same time for abuse of powers in their methods.

Organizational Reform

During 1991 the police continued to pursue strategies of reform which had been initiated in recent years to try and reverse their falling public support and perceived inadequacies. Politicians and commentators also promulgated a variety of reform proposals. Some were concerned to enhance police capacity and power to deal with crime and disorder. However, the main theme of both internal and external reform initiatives was consumerism: the search for demonstrably efficient and effective service.

In January the Home Secretary announced an increase in police establishments totalling 700 officers to try and meet their increasing problems. The Home Affairs Committee recommended in January that a DNA database and machine readable identity cards be created, to aid police investigations. In July it was announced that some Met patrol cars would routinely carry firearms. In November the police evidence to the Royal Commission on Criminal Justice called for an inquisitorial element to be introduced into pre-trial procedure, to facilitate the search for the 'truth', and claimed the present system allowed too many guilty people to escape justice.

However, most reform initiatives were concerned to achieve more adequate performance from given police resources rather than by enhancing them. The Audit Commission published reports in March and April suggesting value for money would be enhanced by giving senior officers more control over their own budgets, and by greater civilianization. The Adam Smith Institute argued in May for greater privatization of certain specific police tasks, and in October it was announced that the Port of London Police (one of the oldest forces in the country) would be privatized in effect by the replacement of the Ports of London Authority by a private company. The £4 million recruitment drive for special constables announced in January was condemned by the Police Federation as back-door privatization and 'policing on the cheap'.

The Home Secretary gave the annual Police Foundation Lecture in June, and called for better performance indicators to measure the quality of police service. He denied any plans existed to form a national police force, but did not rule out amalgamations in the pursuit of efficiency. In October, the HM Chief Inspector of Constabulary, Sir John Woodcock, wrote to all chief constables informing them of the introduction of new performance indicators, placing more emphasis on 'quality of service' rather than crime detection. A special issue of *Policing* was published in September attempting to chart the 'Way Ahead' for the next decade. All the contributions by the police élite indicated commitment to the new ethic of consumerism enshrined in the 1990 Common Statement of Purposes and Values of the three police staff associations. The tougher stance of HM Inspectorate of Constabulary was indicated by Geoffrey Dear's second consecutive unfavourable Inspector's report on the Derbyshire Constabulary, and his refusal in October to sign their certificate of efficiency.

More effective external means of accountability continued to be called for. In October the Labour Party announced plans to establish an elected police authority for the Met. In July the Institute of Race Relations called for a standing commission to deal with deaths in police custody. Many commentators continued to demand radical changes in the complaints procedure, and recruitment of senior officers from outside the service.

An Unhappy Lot

For the third consecutive year the police service has been assailed by falling public confidence due to a combination of scandals about police abuse and perceived ineffectiveness. Many comments from police sources reveal confusion and demoralization. A common response has been a call for a Royal Commission to examine the predicament of the service. Certainly there seems to be a need for an authoritative clarification of the police mandate and how it should be achieved, something which only a body like a Royal Commission could do.

Chronology

3 Jan: Alison Halford, the suspended Merseyside assistant chief constable, lodges a formal complaint of neglect of duty against her chief constable.

14 Jan: The family of a man killed in a road accident involving a police car in 1987 is awarded £50,000 damages.

Four homosexuals win £30,000 agreed damages and costs against Staffordshire police after claiming they were maliciously prosecuted.

15 Jan: Home Affairs Committee, *Annual Report of the Data Protection Registrar*, HMSO, suggests the creation of a DNA database of the male population to help police investigation, and the introduction of a machine-readable identity card.

16 Jan: Court of Appeal frees John Edwards, serving 14 years for armed robbery, who claimed he was framed by the disbanded West Midlands serious crimes squad.

17 Jan: A lesbian and gay police association is set up to combat prejudice in the force.

21 Jan: A £4 million recruitment drive for the special constabulary is launched. It was attacked by the Police Federation as 'policing on the cheap'.

28 Jan: PC Surinder Singh wins £20,000 damages after an industrial relations tribunal finds he was refused a transfer to the CID on racial grounds. Other Asian officers also receive damages awards against Nottinghamshire Constabulary. PC Singh was subsequently transferred to the CID.

5 Feb: Three detectives connected with the Guildford Four case are charged with conspiracy to pervert the course of justice.

24 Feb: Overmanning of police administration is criticized in an Audit Commission report.

4 Mar: Scotland Yard report concludes that failures in command systems, poor communications and role confusion between senior officers led to the Metropolitan Police losing control of anti-poll tax riots in Trafalgar Square in March 1990.

13 Mar: A judge is to receive £105,000 damages for malicious prosecution and abuse of public office from the Met.

14 Mar: Sir James Anderton (knighted in the New Year's honours list), Chief Constable of Greater Manchester, announces his retirement.
Court of Appeal upholds an appeal by the Birmingham Six. The Home Secretary establishes a Royal Commission on criminal justice as a result.

18 Mar: Audit Commission, *Pounds and Coppers: Financial Delegation in Provincial Police Forces*, HMSO, says that the police would be more effective if senior officers had more control over their budgets.

25 Mar: Fourth conviction based on evidence of West Midlands serious crimes squad is quashed by Appeal Court.
Murderer of Met PC Brown is sentenced to life imprisonment. He subsequently committed suicide.

26 Mar: Centre for Criminological Research, Oxford *A Study of the Police Complaints System*, Home Office, calls for a radical re-think of the system.

27 Mar: Court of Appeal blames the conviction of the Birmingham Six on corrupt police practices.
Home Office announces that recorded crime increased by a record amount in 1990.

16 Apr: National Audit Office, *Promoting Value for Money in Provincial Police Forces*, HMSO, suggests that civilian staff should take over more administrative police work.

9 May: War Crimes Bill receives royal assent, leading to the setting up of a police war crimes unit.

19 May: Calls for urgent action to deal with American pit bull terriers after a six year old girl is savaged by one in Bradford.

21 May: Ban on import of American pit bull terriers, Japanese tosas imposed and plans to ban the ownership of such dogs announced.
Ian Westwood of Greater Manchester tells the Police Federation conference that forces are losing control of the streets to vandals, lager louts and drug dealers, 'because of a shortage of uniformed officers on traditional patrols'.

24 May: In the face of objections to the mass destruction of dangerous breeds from vets and the RSPCA the government begins to retreat on such a condition.
Tony Mullett, Chief Constable of West Mercia, is appointed head of the new National Criminal Intelligence Service.

31 May: *An Arresting Idea*, Adam Smith Institute, argues that police should devolve their court duties, abnormal load escorts, training and registration of aliens to private security firms.

5 June: Dangerous Dogs Bill introduced to ensure that pit bull terriers and Japanese tosas are neutered, insured and registered by 30 November or destroyed. It will also empower the courts to impose muzzling or leashing orders on any dogs considered to be dangers to the public. Owners who do not comply or who allow their dogs to go dangerously out of control in public places face up to six months in gaol and/or a £5,000 fine, with heavier penalties if injuries result.

10 June: Home Affairs Select Committee, *Police Sickness*, HMSO, calls for measures to curb abuse of the police sick leave system.

11 June: Charges of conspiracy to pervert the course of justice against three Surrey police officers in connection with the Guildford four case are dropped by magistrates.

20 June: Three former members of the disbanded West Midlands serious crimes squad are cleared of fabricating evidence against a man convicted of robbery.

South Yorkshire police agree to pay more than £500,000 in compensation and costs as a result of clashes with pickets at the Orgreave coking plant during the miners' strike in 1984.

25 June: Home Secretary calls for better performance indicators to measure the quality of police service. In the Police Federation annual lecture he also denied plans to form a national police force, but did not rule out some amalgamations.

1 July: First permanently armed police patrol cars appear on London streets.

David Wilmot succeeds Sir James Anderton as Chief Constable of Greater Manchester.

Metropolitan Police pay £40,000 damages to a man who claimed he was beaten and racially abused by officers who then concocted a case against him.

10 July: Government confirms it is to ban the import and ownership of two more types of fighting dog, the dogo Argentino and the fila Braziliera, neither of which is yet in Britain.

12 July: Police pay £35,000 compensation to a man over wrongful arrest.

Chief Superintendent Duckenfield and Superintendent Murray face disciplinary charges arising from the Hillsborough stadium disaster in 1989.

16 July: Tim Kaye, *Unsafe and Unsatisfactory*, Civil Liberties Trust, examines the record of the West Midlands serious crimes squad which was disbanded in August 1989.

The deputy chief constable of north Wales retires following substantiation of two allegations against him which earlier cleared the chief constable.

18 July: Institute of Race Relations calls for a standing commission on deaths in police custody.

Ten Nottinghamshire officers disciplined over racial discrimination established in the case of PC Surinder Singh.

25 July: Metropolitan Police ordered to conduct an inquiry into claims that its officers faked evidence that led to Winston Silcott being convicted of the murder of PC Blakelock after the Broadwater Farm riots in 1985.

30 July: Geoffrey Cheetham becomes the fifth man convicted on the evidence of the West Midlands serious crimes squad to be freed by the Court of Appeal.

1 Aug: Metropolitan Police to begin monitoring attacks on homosexuals in London.

9 Aug: Scotland Yard establishes a special squad to tackle London based gangs involved in drugs related crime.

12 Aug: West Mercia police officers shoot dead a man who threatened them with an unloaded air pistol. This was followed by disturbances in Shropshire on the nights of 12-13 August.

30 Aug: Three nights of mob rioting and racial tension begin in Cardiff on the Ely housing estate.

Three nights of rioting in Oxford on the Blackbird Leys housing estate begin.

Rioting and looting in Handsworth, Birmingham.

3 Sept: Alan Eastwood, the chairman of the Police Federation, calls for the restoration of the 1714 Riot Act, which had been repealed in 1967.

9 Sept: Three nights of rioting on north Tyneside on the Meadow Well estate begins.

10 Sept: John Major calls for a full ministerial report on the riots on Tyneside.

13 Sept: Report by the Chief Inspector of Constabulary, Geoffrey Dear, condemns the inefficiency of Derbyshire police.

17 Sept: The case of Judith Ward, gaoled for an IRA bombing in 1974, is referred by the Home Secretary to the Court of Appeal.

19 Sept: In a speech which sparks some controversy the Archbishop of Canterbury associates the Newcastle riots with social deprivation.

16 Oct: Police Federations of England and Wales, Scotland and Northern Ireland call, in *The Policing Agenda*, for a Royal Commission into the crisis in the criminal justice system.

21 Oct: Three more convictions involving the disbanded West Midlands serious crimes squad are quashed by the Court of Appeal.

1 Nov: Report by Donald Shaw into the disbanded West Midlands serious crimes squad is published. It criticizes the lack of financial and other forms of accountability and recommends the retention of custody records for at least six years, a new form to indicate suspects' physical condition on arrival at police stations, standardized procedures for the use of documentary evidence in prosecution, the better supervision of the use of pocket books and an overhaul of overtime to prevent abuses.

20 Nov: Staffordshire police announce inquiries into the role of its Special Branch regarding the failure to prevent the escape of two IRA prisoners from Brixton in July, and into the 1978 Carl Bridgewater murder case.

25-8 Nov: Court of Appeal upholds the appeals of Winston Silcott and two other men convicted of the murder of PC Blakelock at Broadwater Farm in 1985.

29 Nov: A Met sergeant is fatally stabbed by suspected burglars and two other officers are seriously wounded in an associated incident.

5 Dec: Elizabeth Marks awarded £55,500 damages against Greater Manchester police for false imprisonment and malicious prosecution in 1985.

17 Dec: Police national computer inaugurated.

Crime and Penal Policy

TERENCE MORRIS

At the end of March the crime figures for England and Wales released by the Home Office showed that the volume of recorded crime, compared with the preceding 12 months, had risen by no less than 17 per cent to a gross figure of some 4.5 million offences; more crimes having been committed than in any other year on record. The bulk of these offences were against property, with auto crime – the theft of or from vehicles – amounting to almost a third of the total. This represented an increase of some 25 per cent on the previous year, while in burglary, another category of crime to which private citizens are highly sensitive, the increase was almost as great at 21 per cent. Not far behind was the level of criminal damage, up some 15 per cent on the previous year. Offences against the person in the form of sexual and other physical violence which have never been more than a small fraction of the total of all crime, in 1990–91 some 6 per cent, increased at a far lower rate. In the case of violence this was only 4 per cent – much less than in earlier years – and sexual offences showed a drop of 2 per cent. The average clear-up rate was 31 per cent but there were substantial variations around the country. The Metropolitan Police District was as low as 17 per cent while Cheshire had a 50 per cent rate and West Mercia 46 per cent. These data must be considered against the background of the sobering fact that the figure of recorded crime may represent no more than about 40 per cent of all the crimes actually committed.

The level of crime became, somewhat predictably, a subject for contention between government and Opposition, the latter's spokesman on Home Affairs, Roy Hattersley maintaining that the increase was 'shameful' and that government efforts to combat crime were 'gimmicks' while the Home Office minister John Patten argued that rising crime was a matter for society as a whole. In 1990 a Home Office research study had concluded that economic factors do indeed have a major influence on trends in both property and personal crime. In times of affluence property crime either increased at a lower rate or fell while interpersonal crime rose, often because people went out more and drank more alcohol. Privately, a number of Chief Constables were concerned about the extent to which stricter budgetary controls and manpower shortages had reduced police effectiveness. While the Home Office minister was at pains to emphasize that Britain was not becoming a more violent country and was less violent than some of our European neighbours, he argued that we were becoming more careless of our property and that this, especially vehicle crime, was not simply a problem for the police but one for the whole community. Vehicle crime is certainly a more serious problem in Britain than elsewhere in Europe. Some analysts have argued that the high proportion of company cars produces a lower level of consciousness about vehicle security but the heart of the problem would appear to lie in the relatively low level of security built into vehicles at the manufacturing stage. Manufacturers, for their part, were quick to point out that higher levels of security must inevitably be reflected in higher initial costs. How far such improvements might, if demanded by legislation, become marginal would require a comparable analysis with progressive requirements over the years for the provision of improved lighting, screenwashers, indicators and seatbelts.

There was more political embarrassment for the Conservatives' reputation as the party of law and order when further figures were published in the middle of December. These showed that in the year ending in September the annual increase had risen to some 19 per cent to a record total of 5.1 million recorded crimes. Thefts had risen by 19 per cent, burglaries by 24 per cent and criminal damage by 14 per cent. The rise in autocrimes was 23 per cent. The government response was proactive, John Patten denouncing the 'death riders, thieves and vandals' whose 271,000 additional offences accounted for a third of the increase in recorded crime. He took the opportunity to refer to the government's Aggravated Vehicle Taking Bill currently in the legislative programme which arose out of a series of well-reported incidents earlier in the year involving the theft of cars and some urban disorder.

The Yobs Go 'Hotting'

At the end of August there was, during the warm weather, an outbreak of disorders in a variety of urban locations, mainly on public housing estates, some, but not all, of which were characterized by the more severe forms of social deprivation, in Oxford, Birmingham, Cardiff and Newcastle.

The relatively prosperous Oxford housing estate of Blackbird Leys achieved an unexpected prominence as a result of four consecutive nights of disorder. The trouble had begun when the police had moved in to quell an outbreak of 'hotting' – the driving of stolen cars at high speeds combined with the dangerous use of the handbrake to cause the vehicle to turn violently in a cacophony of noise augmented by the stench of overheated tyres before an encouraging audience. In its combination of skills and crowd psychology 'hotting' bears a close affinity to 'banger' racing in which the crowd derives satisfaction not only from the destructive display but the risks to the drivers.

No sooner had the trouble in Oxford subsided than there was an outbreak of disorder and looting in the Handsworth district of Birmingham. A timber warehouse was deliberately set alight, resulting in a three hour power cut when an adjacent electricity substation was disconnected. More than 100 youths rampaged through the streets smashing the shutters that had been installed by shopkeepers after the riots of 1985 and looting thousands of pounds worth of stock. A number of local shopkeepers angrily protested at the two-hour delay while the police assembled a 200 strong riot squad. The West Midlands police reacted by saying that they had acted as quickly as possible, given the circumstances of the blackout and that rather than a riot there had been a series of sporadic disturbances in which opportunism played a major part. Nineteen arrests were made for a range of offences including theft, burglary, robbery, assault and public order matters.

In the meantime there was trouble on the Ely estate in Cardiff. Here the trouble had its origins in a dispute between two shopkeepers, an Asian grocer and his neighbour, a newsagent against whom he obtained an injunction requiring him to refrain from selling groceries, contrary to the terms of a restrictive covenant on the property. For two nights Abdul Waheed and his assistant were besieged in the flat above the shop while below the police fought to restrain a mob hurling bricks at his steel shutters. They finally abandoned the premises on police advice. Twenty-two people were charged with public order offences and trials were in progress in January 1992.

A week later there was rioting on the Meadow Well estate in Newcastle on Tyne. This was on a much more serious scale than the trouble in Birmingham, although an electricity substation was also damaged, causing power cuts. A school, a community centre, a warehouse and a house were set on fire and shops were looted and also burned. A road into the estate was blocked by trees and telephone poles that had been cut down with chainsaws. A contributory factor here was the death of two local youths aged 17 and 21 at the end of a 125mph chase in a stolen car. The police had recently moved on to the estate to investigate a series of so-called 'ram raids' in which stolen cars are driven at speed into the fronts of shops which are then looted, and the police believed that the two dead youths had been involved in such a raid. A relative of the elder youth was quoted as saying that the police were 'continually harassing' him and 'just could not handle the fact that [he] was the best ram raid driver in North Shields and they couldn't catch him'. The Meadow Well estate, unlike Blackbird Leys, is an area characterized by the direst poverty and unemployment and is adjacent to a multi-million pound luxury hotel and housing development currently under construction. The police records for the previous year show that of 179 cars stolen in the subdivisional area, no fewer than 135 were driven to Meadow Well and abandoned.

By now there had been also been trouble in Telford and on 11 September the Prime Minister, John Major, told reporters while on a visit to Scotland that events at Meadow Well had been unjustified lawlessness. 'There has been a small run of these incidents and that does occasionally happen. They all seem to have a different genesis. One often gets this copycat effect. It is not acceptable to behave in that way and they must recognize it.' Disturbances on Tyneside continued for three nights; after the Meadow Well eruption there were disturbances in the West End area of Newcastle and in nearby Elswick. A post office, cars, and derelict buildings were set alight and an attempt was made to firebomb the magistrates' court at

Blaydon. On the third night firemen had to deal with about 80 separate fires while being pelted with bricks and stones. The Prime Minister condemned the violence in terms reminiscent of Margaret Thatcher at the time of the Brixton riots in 1981, as ' . . . premeditated violence. There can be no excuse for that. There can be no reason that can be remotely acceptable to anyone.'

Meanwhile Opposition spokesmen and some senior churchmen, while condemning the violence, sought to emphasize the contribution of unemployment and social deprivation to the situation in which many of the inhabitants of these deeply depressing estates were locked into a cycle of poverty and despair and boredom which manifested itself in outward aggression towards the police.

There is little doubt but that the growing problem of autocrime is associated in some way with the attempts of bored, unemployed youths to find some relief in joyriding, especially in high performance cars that are by no means difficult to break into, but while this appears to be a national problem the worst incidence of 'ram raiding' has occurred in the north east. Because taking a car without the owner's consent is not, in law, the same as theft (which involves the intention permanently to deprive the owner of possession) the government considered that changes in the law were necessary in order to provide sterner punishments, hence the bill currently before Parliament.

The 'Irish Question' – Vindication and Humiliation

The collapse of the Crown case against the Maguire Seven in June 1990, coming after the Director of Public Prosecutions had argued less than a year before that the convictions of the Guildford Four could no longer be sustained, came as a great blow, not only to the criminal justice system as a whole and to the police in particular, but to the legal establishment, and the inquiry set up under Sir John May revealed a state of affairs that critics of the system regarded as being now demonstrably insupportable. Attention inevitably turned to the case of the Birmingham Six about which anxiety had continued to grow. Not only was the forensic evidence against them seriously challenged but there was little doubt that they had, at some time between arrest and their appearance in court, suffered injuries that suggested *prima facie* evidence of assault whilst in custody. Although by December 1990 their case was again before the courts it became clear that the kind of capitulation on the part of the Crown that had heralded the release of the Guildford Four and the Maguires was not about to be repeated. The Appeal judges announced shortly before Christmas an effective hearing date for late February 1991, but by 26 February the Director of Public Prosecutions was admitting that the convictions could no longer be considered satisfactory

What was to cause a sense of outrage was the reaction which declined to allow the appeal then and there but insisted on hearing a full appeal the following week. 'It is not enough', said Lord Justice Lloyd, 'for us to give our secret blessing to a view expressed by the Crown Prosecution Service'. Convicted 16 years before on the basis of what the trial judge, Mr Justice Bridge, had described as 'the clearest evidence I have ever heard' the case against the six had become increasingly suspect with the passage of time yet it seemed as if the criminal justice establishment became increasingly unsympathetic as the arguments for their innocence grew ever stronger. The spotlight now shifted from the forensic evidence and that of the men's confessions to the judges themselves. For Bridge the evidence was such as would in former days have sent them all to the gallows. Widgery, as Lord Chief Justice in 1976 had refused them leave to appeal, remarking that 'There is no evidence to suggest that the six had received any knocking about in custody *beyond the ordinary*' (my italics). In 1980 Lord Denning, then Master of the Rolls, in blocking the men's civil action against the police and the Home Office promoted an astonishingly instrumental view in saying

Just consider the course of events if this action is allowed to proceed to trial. If the six men fail it will mean that much time and money will have been expended by many people for no good purpose.

If the six men win, it will mean that the police were guilty of perjury, that they were guilty of violence and threats, that the confessions were involuntary and were improperly admitted in evidence and that the confessions were erroneous.

That would mean the Home Secretary would either have to recommend that they were pardoned or he would have to resubmit the case to the Court of Appeal. That would be such an appalling vista that every sensible person in the land would say: It cannot be right these actions should go any further.

Denning had been criticized in 1990 after the *Spectator* quoted him as saying that if the Birmingham Six had been hanged they would have been forgotten and the whole community would be satisfied.

But if Denning's remarks must be seen in their context as the probably ill-guarded words of a now frail nonagenarian, those of the Lord Chief Justice, Lord Lane in 1988, when he dismissed the men's appeal, which had finally reached the courts, were clear and unambiguous: 'The longer this hearing has gone on the more convinced this court has become that the verdict of the jury was correct'. After the capitulation of the Crown in February 1991, Denning's regrets were for the failure of the police: 'As I look back, I am very sorry because I always thought our police were splendid and first class and I am sorry that in this case it appears to be the contrary'. Lord Justice Lloyd whose attributed remark at the preliminary hearing of the appeal in December 1990 on hearing that there was a 'mindboggling' amount of material to read was 'I don't think we are going to let this spoil our Christmas' released the six on March 14 with the words 'In the light of fresh evidence which has become available since the last hearing in this court, your appeal will be allowed and you will be free to go as soon as the usual formalities have been discharged'.

The case against the Birmingham Six essentially collapsed not only because the forensic evidence against them was seen to be totally unreliable but because the evidence of the police emerged as fatally flawed by perjury. The new ESDA test (electrostatic document analysis) showed that certain police notes were not what they purported to be. Moreover, the men's lawyers maintained that no fewer than 16 of a central core of 25 officers were either liars or unreliable witnesses. Most of them had been members of the West Midlands Serious Crime Squad, which had been disbanded by the Chief Constable, Geoffrey Dear in August 1989 and about which a number of matters are still under scrutiny. But whereas (unlike Lord Denning) many criminal justice professionals recognized that corrupt practices in criminal investigations have been sufficiently widespread to justify fully the restrictions and safeguards embodied in the recent Police and Criminal Evidence Act, the focus of public criticism was upon the judges and the criminal justice system itself. For even as the six were about to walk free from the court the Crown sought to distinguish between convictions that were 'unsatisfactory' and those which were 'unsafe'; only in the latter case would it be able grudgingly to admit to their innocence. And while the court declined to accept this distinction, it equally declined an invitation from the men's lawyers to offer them an apology for what had been done to them.

The reaction of Kenneth Baker, the Home Secretary, was swift; for the first time since 1979 a minister announced the establishment of a Royal Commission, in this case to examine the whole criminal justice process under the chairmanship of the Cambridge sociologist and businessman Lord Runciman. This break with the practice during the regime of Margaret Thatcher, who never disguised her view of Royal Commissions, was itself a sign of the times and a recognition that the shortcomings of the system were now such as to produce a crisis in public confidence. Meanwhile criticism mounted against Lord Lane and over 100 MP's called for his resignation. This was the third major miscarriage of justice that the appeal system had been unable to detect or resolve without years of protracted litigation and campaigning and, insofar as the legal establishment seemed incapable of recognizing that the fault was internal, not external to it, the complaint that it was concerned with damage limitation rather than the pursuit of justice was widely echoed.

Three months later, on 27 June, Lords Justice Stuart-Smith, Mann and McCowan quashed the convictions of the Maguires in the Court of Appeal on the narrowest ground, namely that they had been 'innocently contaminated' with nitroglycerine, leaving the slur that someone else in the household had handled explosives. The representatives of the Crown seemed to be determined to pursue a course of damage limitation, no matter what the public obloquy incurred, and at the May Inquiry – which was of course still examining the circumstances surrounding the investigations upon which the case against them had been constructed – the solicitor for the Maguires walked out of the inquiry after Michael Hill, QC (a junior counsel at their trial) seemed to imply in his evidence that there were still suspicions hanging over the family and defended the decision to prosecute.

As if the Fates had not wrought enough devastation in the Irish cases, in November the Court of Appeal cleared Winston Silcott of the murder of PC Keith Blakelock who was hacked to death during riots on the Broadwater Farm estate in

Tottenham in 1985. In July 1991, Kenneth Baker specifically asked the Metropolitan Police to carry out ESDA tests on the interview notes in the case of Silcott who had been convicted of the killing, along with Engin Raghip, whose case had already been referred back to the Court of Appeal after expert witnesses had changed their testimony and agreed that he was mentally subnormal when he confessed, and Mark Braithwaite, whose confession was also disputed. By 26 November, the case against the Broadwater Three was in shreds. They had been convicted on uncorroborated confession evidence. The ESDA tests had revealed that the notes in Silcott's cases were not what they purported to be and the Crown conceded that it could no longer rely upon police evidence. Lord Justice Farquarson, sitting with Mr Justice Alliott and Mr Justice Cresswell, took less than two hours to clear Silcott and Raghip and Braithwaite were similarly cleared several days later. In 1988 Lord Lane, in dismissing an earlier appeal, had said that there were 'no lurking doubts' but while the Guildford Four, the Maguires and the Birmingham Six were denied any apology, one was to be forthcoming in this instance, although Silcott remains in prison convicted of a killing wholly unconnected with the death of PC Blakelock.

There remain a number of other cases concerning which disquiet grows rather than diminishes with the passage of time, notably those of the Bridgewater Four (the fifth having died in prison) convicted of the murder of a paper-boy, Carl Bridgewater, in 1978 which has twice failed before the Court of Appeal and of Judith Ward, convicted in 1974 of planting a bomb in an army bus which killed nine soldiers, a woman and two children. Judith Ward's case was referred by Kenneth Baker to the Court of Appeal in September. In its evidence to the Runciman Commission the National Association of Probation Officers claimed that as many as 700 men and women currently in prison could have been wrongly convicted.

The State of Prisons

Nothing in 1991 gave any cause for congratulation about the state of prisons, for in spite of the opening of a new London prison at Belmarsh near Woolwich which eased the pressure in the metropolis, conditions outside London remained largely unchanged. The publication of the Woolf Report in February, the inquiry having been set up after the riots at Strangeways and elsewhere in 1990, was accepted positively by government and largely incorporated into proposals in the white paper *Custody, Care and Justice* published in September, though it became clear that there were substantial discrepancies in the timetables envisaged by the Woolf team and by Kenneth Baker with regard to a strategy for ending overcrowding.

Meanwhile the government pressed ahead with its plans for the commercial management of prisons with the announcement in November that the new Wolds Prison on Humberside will be run by the Group 4 company, which already runs the immigration detention centre near Heathrow aerodrome. A second, as yet unfinished establishment in the west Midlands is also scheduled to be put out to contract management. Perhaps the most significant consequence of this policy will be to weaken the position of the Prison Officers' Association which has come to be regarded by ministers and some civil servants in a light not altogether unlike that in which the National Union of Mineworkers was regarded in the early 1980s, for industrial relations within the prison service showed little sign of permanent improvement until the very end of the year, when the new Director General of the Prison Service, Joe Pilling, indicated that he was ready to make a new deal with the POA after an almost unprecedented lull in industrial action by staff.

Two other matters presented problems of a political nature. The first was the escape from Brixton of two IRA suspects, Pearse McAuley and Nessan Quinlivan on 7 July with the aid of a gun which had been smuggled into the prison in the sole of a training shoe. As the story unfolded, it was seen to contain elements somewhat stranger than fiction. The Chief Inspector of Prisons was requested to make a report and Sir Raymond Lygo was commissioned to carry out a study and make a report on prison management. The political pressure on Kenneth Baker to resign was considerable and in evidence to the Home Affairs Select Committee in December he stated that he had not been informed until the day after the break out that Special Branch officers had known of the escape plans in advance and had passed the information both to the governor of the prison (who had taken early retirement) and a Home Office official as early as February. To date the men are still at large. The Lygo report was to recommend a form of agency status for the prison service, closely in line with ministerial wishes and not altogether distant from those of some penal commentators, who had indicated at the Woolf Inquiry that since the demise of the old Prison Commission in the early 1960s, the history of the prison service under Home Office control had been a largely dispiriting one.

The second was the continuing problem of prison suicides. Nineteen ninety-one showed a welcome improvement in that only 41 prisoners took their own lives, mostly by hanging – a reduction of some 18 per cent from 1990. But the basic problem for prison staff remained, being fundamentally related to the inability of the prison system as a whole and its slender psychiatric resources in particular, to deal with the growing numbers of mentally disordered and unstable people in the community who find themselves in what is often serious conflict with the law.

The year was also marked by concerns relating to the fate of young people, by no means necessarily offenders, in residential care. A regime known as 'pindown', carried out in a Staffordshire childrens' home and involving solitary confinement, was revealed to have held more than 130 youngsters in solitary confinement for varying periods during the preceding six years. Although the practice ceased in October 1989 it was the subject of an official report by Allan Levy QC and the child care expert Barbara Kahan. The government commissioned its own report by Sir William Utting the retiring Chief Inspector of Social Services, which appeared in August, revealing a decade of neglect by ministers and local authorities. Virginia Bottomley, the Minister of State for Health, accepted all its 22 recommendations. Claims for compensation by children who were the subjects of the 'pindown' regime, which involved the detention in solitary confinement of children as young as ten – some of whom were allegedly driven to self- mutilation – for periods as long as 84 days without respite, were reported as being substantial and possibly in excess of £2 million in total.

On 29 November, in an entirely separate matter, Frank Beck, the former head of three children's homes in Leicestershire, was sentenced to life imprisonment five times over in respect of 17 convictions including rape, buggery, indecent assault and assault causing actual bodily harm. In this, the greatest child sexual abuse scandal in children's homes ever to be prosecuted, no fewer than 200 former residents of the homes who were interviewed by police complained that they had been abused by Beck over a 13-year period up to 1986. One of his former deputies was sentenced to three years for various assaults. William Waldegrave the Secretary of State for Health immediately ordered two inquiries, a national one to look at the selection of staff for children's homes and the support and guidance available to them in their work and a second by Leicestershire County Council to examine how it was that such abuse had been possible for so long.

Chronology

9 Jan: Customs and Excise pull off Britain's largest drug seizure, cocaine with a street value of £50 million, in Ullapool, south west Scotland.

13 Jan: Pilot scheme to allow children to spend two Sundays a month with their mothers in Holloway Prison is launched.

14 Jan: Insurance bonds against dishonesty are to be subsidized by the government to encourage employers to take on ex-offenders.

18 Jan: Inquest jury returns a verdict that Anthony Hook, found hanged in a remand centre, killed himself 'in circumstances brought about by lack of proper care'.
Prisoners are to be exempted from standard poll tax on their empty homes.

20 Jan: NACRO warns that government plans to punish parents of young offenders could break up families and increase juvenile crime.

31 Jan: Dr Michael Levi at the Association of London Authorities conference draws attention to the growing problem of white-collar crime, including fraud, health and safety infringements and income tax offences.

4 Feb: Clause inserted into the Criminal Justice Bill to ensure that the state can step in to deal with riots in privately run gaols.
Plans to put juvenile offenders to secure units run by local authorities when on remand, rather than in adult gaols, are announced.

11 Feb: Prison Reform Trust accuses the prison service of failing to care properly for Aids sufferers.

18 Feb: Arson Prevention Bureau is launched by the Home Office and the Association of British Insurers to promote policies to deal with and research into a fast-growing crime.

21 Feb: A wide range of prison reforms, including improvements in contacts between prisoners and their families, allowing more activities and other changes in the prison regime, are promised in advance of the Woolf Report.

25 Feb: Lord Justice Woolf's report on the Strangeways riot of April 1990 is published. Key recommendations are that inmates should be enabled and encouraged to maintain links

with their families, an end to overcrowding and slopping out, the setting of national standards of what services prisons will provide and what behaviour is expected from inmates in return, greater powers for the Director General of Prison Services and greater autonomy for prison governors, and the co-ordination of the criminal justice system through new national and local Criminal Justice Consultative Councils.

4 Mar: Don Grubin and John Gunn, *The Imprisoned Rapist and Rape*, Home Office, finds that 59 per cent of rapists claim they were wrongly convicted. It endorses calls for special units inside prisons and provides an in-depth study of rapists' attitudes and their social background.

27 Mar: The level of recorded crime rose by 17 per cent in 1990 over 1989 according to *Criminal Statistics 1991*, HMSO.

A Digest of Information on the Criminal Justice System, HMSO, shows that according to the British Crime Survey crime is underreported by up to a factor of four and that the chances of being a victim of crime have risen sevenfold since the 1950s.

Court of Appeal rules that court orders are, in effect, impossible against youths under 17 because they cannot be enforced by the threat of gaol or fines.

7 Apr: Experimental Sunday visiting scheme for mothers imprisoned in Holloway which allows their children to spend all day with them is made permanent.

11 Apr: *Women and Prison*, Women's National Commission, says children's needs should be taken into account when women are sentenced and suggests the need for more mother and baby units and bail hostels.

Organizing Supervision and Punishment in the Community, HMSO, envisages a new liaison between the probation service, magistrates and judges, and will put the Inspectorate of Probation on a statutory basis.

17 Apr: In a letter to the Home Secretary prison governors warn of a crisis because of chronic staff shortages.

ACPO conference is warned of rising crime and violence relating to drug trafficking, with fights over territory taking place in some cities.

29 Apr: Campaign to abolish the prison medical service launched.

22 May: Police Federation conference overwhelmingly backs a mandatory 25-year sentence for criminals carrying guns and the introduction of a certificate of competence for legitimate firearms licence applicants.

29 May: Recorded crime in Scotland rose by 9 per cent in 1990.

7 June: Sex offenders gaoled for four or more years are to be offered therapy in prison.

14 June: Internal Home Office report urges the creation of a self-financing independent National Criminal Records Agency to replace the current fragmented criminal records system, and a massive extension of vetting.

17 June: Report by NACRO argues that too many non-violent prisoners are still being unnecessarily imprisoned.

21 June: Inquiry set up into alleged maltreatment of inmates at Ashworth special hospital.

24 June: The director and two staff at St Charles Youth Treatment Centre, Brentwood, Essex, are suspended for malpractice.

25 June: Government reinstates mandatory life sentences for murder into the Criminal Justice Bill.

26 June: Steady rise in computer hacking and fraud is revealed by an Audit Commission report.

7 July: Inquiry immediately ordered after two IRA suspects escape from Brixton prison.

18 July: Home Secretary predicts that it will take 25 years to implement the Woolf Report. Belmarsh prison for high-security inmates opens in London.

19 July: Survey in Bristol suggests that 30 per cent of offences are committed whilst on bail.

22 July: Joint letter to the Home Secretary from prison reform and health care bodies urges him to divert mentally disturbed offenders from prisons, where they form an estimated one-fifth of the inmates.

24 July: Highly critical report on Preston prison released by Stephen Tumin, the Chief Inspector of Prisons.

Sir Michael McNair-Wilson MP demands an inquiry into prison security after the Home Office discloses 297 prisoners who have escaped from custody in the past three years are still at large.

The House of Lords rules that prisoners have no legal right to know why they have been refused parole or to see reports on them.

4 Aug: Apex Trust reports on inadequate training and employment opportunities for ex-offenders.

5 Aug: Report on the escape of two IRA suspects from Brixton criticizes the failure of the Home Office to pass on police warnings of the likely method of escape.

8 Aug: Rudimentary psychiatric care facilities in prisons attacked in paper in *British Medical Journal,* which also argues that more than 14,000 prisoners have psychiatric disorders and about 10,000 need immediate hospital care.

14 Aug: Large secure units for teenagers to be built in Wales after the suicide of a 15-year old remanded in Swansea gaol.

18 Aug: Success of the Intermediate Treatment Initiative of community-based penalties for juvenile offenders is praised in a report for the Department of Health.

20 Aug: Riots at Lindholme prison in South Yorkshire. An inquiry under Peter Kitteridge is subsequently appointed.

21 Aug: Review of prison service management under Admiral Sir Raymond Lygo announced.

22 Aug: Police establish the Mutual Aid Co-ordinating Centre to co-ordinate the holding of prisoners in police cells.

30 Aug: Urgent inquiry into offending whilst on bail launched by the Home Office.

4 Sept: Survey by Northumbria police in North Tyneside in 1989 finds 40.1 per cent of detected crime was committed by offenders on bail.

13 Sept: Home Office figures show recorded crime rose by 18 per cent in the year to June to 4.9 million incidents.

16 Sept: The white paper, *Custody, Care and Justice – The Way Ahead for the Prison Service in England and Wales,* HMSO, incorporates all but six of the Woolf proposals but includes no mention of extra cash or timetables for implementation. It involves plans for a Criminal Justice Consultative Council to increase co-ordination between the penal and legal systems, a code of standards for prison conditions, a new offence of prison mutiny, the development of community prisons, greater control of their budgets and recruitment by governors and an end to slopping-out by 1994.

23 Sept: Superintendents' Association calls for a system of totting up offences to trigger automatic imprisonment or tougher punishment for juvenile offenders.

29 Oct: Home Office report suggests 1,100 prisoners need psychiatric treatment in special hospitals. There is a particular shortfall in medium security hospitals according to the report.

1 Nov: Political criticism of lack of mention of action against joyriding in the Queen's Speech.

Group 4 are given the contract to run Britain's first privatized prison, the Wolds on Humberside.

11 Nov: New guidelines emphasizing counselling and support for prisoners with HIV or AIDS, rather than segregation, are issued by the Home Office.

28 Nov: Employment Select Committee, *Employment in Prisons and for Ex-Offenders*, HMSO, urges higher pay and direct work for private employers in prisons. There should also be a strong element of training according to the report, leading if possible to NVQs.

3 Dec: Gywneth Boswell, *Waiting for Change: Section 53 Offenders*, Prince's Trust, argues that a large majority of serious juvenile offenders were abused as children and criticizes a lack of counselling and strategies for rehabilitation.

5 Dec: Announcement that the Blakenham prison currently under construction near Redditch will be privately managed.

9 Dec: Aggravated Vehicle Taking Bill to deal with the growing offence of joyriding is rushed through all stages of the Commons.

12 Dec: Home Office publishes a Council of Europe report on the three worst English prisons, Armley in Leeds, and Wandsworth and Brixton in London. It condemns overcrowding and the inadequacy of sanitary provision.

Chief Inspector of Prisons' annual report calls for in-prison training and fair wages in prison workshops.

15 Dec: OPCS survey into the prison population shows that 31 per cent were unemployed and 12 per cent homeless, 38 per cent had experienced family breakdown and nearly a quarter had been in local authority care as children. In 35 per cent of cases someone in their family had been in prison. Forty-three per cent had no educational qualifications and 15.6 per cent had a reading age of ten or younger. About a third suffered from some form of psychiatric illness. Only 3.6 per cent of prisoners are women. Nearly 20 per cent of male inmates are under 21 and two thirds are under 30. Ethnic minorities are over-represented, with 16 per cent of the prison population. Afro-Carribean sentences tend to 44 per cent longer than whites for adult males and 50 per cent longer for females. The survey also showed that magistrates are far more likely to remand defendants into custody if they do not have a job or a home.

16 Dec: Report by Sir Raymond Lygo suggests that the Prison Service should become an executive agency.

Britain and the Media in the Gulf War

PHILIP M. TAYLOR and DAVID E. MORRISON

Although Britain's military contribution to the multinational effort to expel Iraq from Kuwait in January and February 1991 constituted only about 5 per cent of the total forces available to the American-led coalition operating under United Nations auspices, Britain's war in the Gulf was characterized by several unique features. RAF Tornados, for example, flew dangerous low-flying missions against Iraqi targets at the start of the war, and suffered comparatively heavy losses in the process. Equally, British regiments and special forces made significant contributions to what General Schwarzkopf somewhat enigmatically described as his 'Hail Mary Play'[1] as allied troops swung rapidly to the west of Kuwait and moved swiftly into southern Iraq during the 100-hour ground war at the end of February. Codenamed Operation Granby, the British contribution also included four warships, three minesweepers and six supply vessels playing their part in the deception campaign to lead Saddam Hussein into believing that the coalition was planning a direct sea-borne assault as part of the campaign to liberate Kuwait. The known cost to British lives for both the six-month long Desert Shield and the two-month long war was 44 dead (25 in action) and 43 wounded. In total, less than 400 coalition soldiers lost their lives against what has been estimated to have been between 20,000 to 100,000 Iraqi deaths.

For those outside the military theatre of operations, the war began on television. Like President Bush, John Major, Prime Minister since replacing Margaret Thatcher the previous November, was even reported to be channel-hopping on Downing Street's TV set as coalition aircraft launched Operation Desert Storm on the night of 16 January.[2] It was certainly to be the start of the most high profile media war in history, with western correspondents – uniquely – transmitting from the enemy capital under fire, with over 1,000 journalists being husbanded in Riyadh by the Joint Information Bureau, with the launch of BBC Radio 4's Gulf War FM experiment and with television stations around the world going over to 24-hour news coverage, creating in the process a new breed of viewer suffering from what some psychologists described as 'Scudavision'.[3]

One of the most striking features of British involvement, however, was the degree to which public opinion was overwhelmingly behind the war effort, as revealed repeatedly by opinion polls and surveys which indicated a level of popular support greater than during the Korean and Suez conflicts and one that was at least as strong as at any time during the Falklands conflict less than 10 years earlier.[4] The degree to which such support was affected by near-saturation media coverage and exposure must remain a matter for some conjecture until research into this area is completed.[5] Thanks, however, to the role which television was to play in the conflict, the British public were able to feel that they themselves were actually involved in a war that was being enacted in their name on behalf of the New World Order. But how much of the war were they actually seeing? How much information was being withheld from them? How reliable were the media as a source of objective information about what was in fact going on? Given that in reality all news and information about the progress of the war was being tightly controlled by both the Iraqis in Baghdad and by central command in Riyadh, how far did the media coverage create an illusion of an open information policy which was in fact more akin to official propaganda? And how much did the public want to know anyway?

Such questions highlight an important point, namely that there were essentially two wars taking place: the 'real war' fought by the combined forces of 30 nations against the regime of Saddam Hussein and what may be termed the 'media war' that was being enacted for the benefit of a global television audience. The latter did not automatically reflect the reality of the former. Until the official records are opened, we have only the media record to evaluate, although certain post-war revelations are helping to fine tune our knowledge of some aspects of the conflict, such as the real extent of Iraq's nuclear programme. This at the time, however, remained a matter for some speculation. We do know that both sides placed great emphasis upon the televisual aspects of war coverage, with the Americans in particular being inspired by what they perceived to be the 'lessons' of the 'uncensored war' in Vietnam.

The arrangements made for the release of information about the progress of the war to the world's media gave the British a central position, thereby providing a media profile that was essentially disproportionate to their actual military contribution. Only British, American and French correspondents were allowed to join the official news pools attached to the troops at the front and only those countries, plus the Saudis, were permitted to conduct daily televised press briefings. These not only helped to bring a distant war into the living rooms of the British public, it also served to remind American television viewers that the British government and people were still their staunchest allies, consolidating still further the 'special relationship' that had flourished under President Reagan and Prime Minister Thatcher, especially during the difficult days of the Falklands conflict.[6]

Nonetheless, it is important to reiterate the point that until the official archives are opened for public scrutiny, much will remain unknown about the reality of the Gulf war – which might seem surprising in view of its unprecedented media profile. Much of the coverage, however, was given over to speculation by an army of pundits who were wheeled before the cameras to fill the time-guzzling nature of television.[7] It did not take long for John Naughton of *The Observer* to notice that the coverage resembled 'the journalistic equivalent of candy floss; delicious to consume but devoid of substance.'[8] The war was undoubtedly proving to be a major television event, in Britain as indeed elsewhere, with an estimated 20 million viewers per night tuning into the main evening news bulletins, as compared with about 16 million daily newspaper sales. For its part, the British press, with the marginal exception of *The Guardian* and the obvious exception of *The Morning Star*, was overwhelmingly pro-war, although the quality papers such as *The Independent* often carried articles by such journalists as Robert Fisk and Richard Dowden who refused to participate in the newspool arrangements drawn up by an American military inspired by the 'Vietnam syndrome' in conjunction with the censorship-minded Saudi Arabian authorities. Such journalists became known as the 'unilaterals' and their copy often provided stories which were not always in harmony with views expressed by central command in Riyadh. For the most part, however, thanks to its media guidelines, the coalition was able to structure the media agenda in its efforts to shape the way in which the war was being portrayed to the outside world, *inter alia* by releasing spectacular 'video game' type images of smart weaponry hitting their targets with pin-point accuracy.

The Baghdad Loophole

An alternative source of information for British audiences hungry for news about the war was the presence of journalists from coalition countries in the enemy capital under fire. Apart from again providing an illusion of a war being enacted for the benefit of television audiences, it is important to recognize that the Iraqis permitted western journalists to remain behind in Baghdad after war's outbreak in the hope that they would be able to utilize western television for propaganda purposes. Cable News Network's (CNN) ability to keep transmitting live audio reports throughout the first night of coalition raids mesmerized audiences and rocketed the Atlanta-based all news station once lampooned by rivals as 'Chicken Noodle News' to world prominence. It was an inspired propaganda ploy on the part of the Iraqis. However, because the coalition had deployed only precision-guided 'smart' weaponry in the form of cruise missiles and radar-evading F117A 'Stealth' bombers, journalists were able to report only of pin-point accurate hits on strategic targets rather than of massive civilian destruction. Western journalists were for the most part, therefore, told to leave on 19 January, leaving behind only CNN's crew and a few print journalists from countries such as Spain and Japan.

Throughout the first week of the war, the media event continued like a roller coaster,[9] with the Iraqis firing their Scud missiles at Israel and Saudi Arabia, the American Patriot anti-missile missile crews performing heroics in intercepting them, the release by the coalition of that highly telegenic video footage demonstrating the accuracy of their hi-tech weaponry, the parading of captured coalition pilots on Iraqi TV (with CNN duly retransmitting the pictures around the world, causing outrage) and the release of a massive oil spill into the Gulf waters. Moreover, as the coalition extended its air offensive against Iraq's NBC (nuclear, biological and chemical) installations, more and more stories of mounting civilian damage began to emerge from Iraq, including the infamous 'baby milk plant' at Abu Gurhaid which the coalition maintained was connected with the manufacture of biological weapons. By the end of January, the Iraqis permitted the re-entry of western journalists into Iraq, operating under the careful supervision of Iraqi Ministry of Information 'minders'. In the first ten days of February, crews from BBC, ITN and from other national broadcasting companies were escorted to alleged bombed civilian sites at Nassiriyah, Najaf, Fallujah, Kirkuk and other Iraqi cities. Although the damage incurred was nowhere near as severe as Iraqi propaganda maintained, it was clear that some 'collateral damage' was indeed taking place, especially to Iraqi water and electricity supplies, damage that was to take an even greater human toll once the war was over.

The Amiriya Bunker/Shelter Incident

Increased coalition concern about the question of civilian damage came to a head on 13 February when two laser-guided bombs smashed through the roof of an installation in the Al-Amiriya suburb of Baghdad, killing nearly 400 people. The coalition insisted that it had hit what it had been aiming at, namely a command and control bunker that had been transmitting signals to Iraqi troops in Kuwait. The television pictures, however, showed horrific scenes of carnage and the charred corpses of mainly women and children (even though they had been self-censored by western news organizations on grounds of 'taste' and 'decency'). Despite outrage in both the USA and in Britain – with CNN's reporter Peter Arnett being labelled the 'Lord Haw Haw' of the Gulf conflict and the BBC being described in the House of Commons as the 'Baghdad Broadcasting Corporation' – the pictures failed to shake public support for the war in those countries.

Audience Research

Drawing on the results of the survey of public attitudes to the Gulf war conducted by the Institute of Communications Studies at the University of Leeds – a representative sample of 1,000 adults lasting one hour per interview (the largest survey conducted on the Gulf war anywhere) 65 per cent of the population were shown to be in strong agreement about the use of force to eject Iraq from Kuwait, with a further 20 per cent showing some support for the use of force. Only 8 per cent of the population were firmly against the use of force – the remaining 7 per cent either did not know what their position was or hardly supported the use of force – 2 per cent and 5 per cent respectively. When asked to give an overall view, few people felt that the use of force against Iraq had actually been wrong. However, one in four still felt that sanctions and diplomacy should have been given longer to work. Finally, people were asked whether or not they thought that it was right for Britain to have joined the coalition in the war against Iraq. Almost nine in ten

(87 per cent) said it was right, with 67 per cent saying it was definitely right. Overall, then, relatively few people were against the war, or Britain's involvement in it.

Given that the war in the Gulf was the first war to be covered live by satellite telephones and by satellite television the response of the public to seeing images of the war is especially important in the light of the criticism that was made in America against television for supposedly undermining civilian support for the war in Vietnam by showing pictures of destruction. Four events of the war were asked about in the Leeds survey. Those chosen were all given wide media coverage, particularly on television: the bombing of the bunker/shelter at Amiriya; the coalition pilots captured by Iraq and displayed on Iraqi television broadcasts; the filming of Iraqi troops in abject condition surrendering; and the aftermath of coalition air attacks on Iraqi forces as they were withdrawing from Kuwait in the final days of the conflict. Each of these events attracted widespread coverage and considerable debate as to their morality and acceptability.

Majorities of viewers said they had seen television coverage of these events; 73 per cent saw coverage of the bombing of the Amiriya bunker/air raid shelter in Baghdad, 85 per cent saw the captured coalition pilots, 75 per cent saw pictures of Iraqi troops surrendering, and 57 per cent recalled seeing coverage of the results of the air attacks on Iraqi troops on the road to Basra. If nothing else, this does show the penetration of war information to the public via television. In each case, however, all those who said they had seen television coverage were further asked whether it had been right or wrong to have shown this on British television.

For three of the four scenes, most people who saw coverage thought it had been right to show these on television. However, in the case of the transmission of Iraqi film showing captured coalition pilots – including two Britons – the majority view was that this should not have been shown. The reasons given by viewers for saying that it was right to show coverage of these events centred mainly around showing the truth about war – what war is like, reminding people that war causes casualties, and the need to show both sides. In the case of the captured pilots, the main reasons why it was felt that such pictures should not be shown was that they would upset the relatives of the pilots. One of the important findings, therefore, about the war in the Gulf, is that the British public believes it has a democratic right to see what is happening in times of military conflict, and that seeing such images will not affect substantially public support for a war which is felt by the majority to be both justified and just.

This does, however, raise the question of how much of the war viewers were actually seeing. Critics of the coverage – small in number though they were – argued that the coalition's media and censorship arrangements ensured that a 'sanitized' view of the conflict was being taken, that the real horror of war was not being seen at all but rather a clinical, clean and bloodless 'video-game war' was being portrayed. In a sense, such criticism was misdirected. It was not for the media-conscious coalition authorities to permit scenes of carnage inflicted by the enemy – small in number though these were also. It was for the Iraqis to exploit such scenes for their own propaganda purposes and that they failed to do so, at least in the military theatre of operations, may be seen to have been a serious miscalculation on their part. On the other hand, given the findings of the Leeds survey especially in relation to the Amiriya installation, it is doubtful whether such scenes would have influenced western popular support. It has to be pointed out, however, that very little of the ground war was seen on British television, with pictures of the aftermath of the battle of Mutlah Gap, for example, emerging almost three days after the event. At the end, allied ground forces were quite simply moving so rapidly that it was virtually impossible for television crews in the military news pools to set up their satellite communications. In other words, the final stage of the war, the crucial land war in which perhaps half of the Iraqi ground forces were destroyed, evaded live television coverage. In this respect, the comparatively short length of the war may have been crucial but so undoubtedly was the ability of the coalition to keep the 'real war' off the screen.

The Ground War

Two days after the Amiriya bombing, the world was momentarily relieved as Iraqi radio announced that it was prepared to withdraw from Kuwait. However, it quickly emerged that it was only willing to do so on certain conditions – including the withdrawal of Israel from the occupied territories. President Bush described the 'peace offer' as a 'cruel hoax' while Prime Minister Major followed suit by terming it a 'bogus sham'. The initiative was dismissed as yet another propaganda ploy on the part of the Iraqis who were actually laying down conditions for their withdrawal from Kuwait, such as the Israeli withdrawal from the occupied territories. The media's enthusiasm to break the story before it had fully unfolded, before the full text of the 'offer' had become clear, revealed the dangers of instant media telecommunications when directed more at gaining a 'scoop' than at issues of judgement and understanding. On the same day, the countdown for the ground war began.

Coalition ground forces had already clashed with the Iraqis at the end of January at the Saudi border town of Ras Al-Khafji. Although the battle had eventually resulted in a coalition victory with General Schwarzkopf dismissing its military significance as a 'mosquito on an elephant', it was heralded by Baghdad Radio as a great victory. From a propaganda point of view, it almost certainly was, with even the BBC radio announcing that 'the day belonged to Iraq'.[10] Given that the very same day the coalition had proclaimed air superiority over Iraq and Kuwait – greatly aided by the flight of almost 200 Iraqi air force planes to Iran the previous week – how was it, journalists asked, that the supposedly battered, poorly-fed and badly led Iraqi conscript forces were able to launch an *offensive* into Saudi territory? The coalition accordingly stepped up its air offensive against Iraqi troop positions in the Kuwaiti theatre of operations and against its supply lines and bridges in an effort to reduce coalition ground casualties once the land war began.

Despite a number of diplomatic initiatives to call a halt to the fighting, by the Iranians and the Soviets amongst others, the ground war was launched at 4am local time on 24 February. Coalition forces moved swiftly into Kuwait and southern Iraq, the latter move including American, British and French mechanized divisions which would swing right in an enveloping manoeuvre to trap the Iraqi forces who had been ordered to evacuate Kuwait early the next morning. Despite a coalition news black-out, the allied advance went much better than expected and the news was simply too good to suppress. Even though advancing coalition forces were encountering minimal resistance, they were beginning to witness the consequences of a scorched earth policy adopted by the Iraqis with the firing of Kuwait's 600 or so oil wells.

Kuwait City was 'liberated' on 26 February. To the north, General Schwarzkopf announced that all the gates to southern Iraq had been closed. Three days later, television pictures were able to reveal what he had meant by this as the first footage of a massive convoy attempting to escape through the Mutlah Gap was transmitted around the world. Caught in a trap, allied air forces laid down an aerial barrage that one US pilot described as 'like shooting fish in a barrel'. By that time, however, the story had moved on. On 27 February, possibly in an effort to salvage what he could from what was proving to be a 'Mother of All Defeats', Saddam Hussein agreed to adhere to all United Nations resolutions concerning Kuwait, and President Bush declared 'a unilateral cessation of hostilities' – not a ceasefire, as the Iraqis maintained in order to proclaim victory – and a halt was called to the fighting at 8am local time on 27 February. General Schwarzkopf met with Iraqi commanders at Safwan airbase to lay down the coalition's terms on Sunday 3 March. The enemy commanders had no choice but to accede. However, the decision by the Americans to call a ceasefire before all of Saddam's forces were destroyed – which, according to some sources, ran contrary to British advice – meant that a substantial part of his army, especially the elite Republican Guard, managed to make it safely back to Iraq. If it is correct that Britain was hesitant about calling an early halt to the fighting then events following the war – the harassment of the Kurdish minority within Iraq – demonstrated that, at least internally, Saddam Hussein still possessed a powerful military base and one that was sufficient for him to sustain his political position inside Iraq. Moreover, given the findings of the post-war UN team of inspectors concerning the extent of Iraq's nuclear and biological programmes, all those pre-war and wartime anxieties about Saddam Hussein's true intentions in the region gained considerable confirmation.

Conclusions

So what issues emerged from the war that we can as yet evaluate with some degree of authority? First, because the war was mainly fought with air power, and because air power is a notoriously difficult weapon for the media to cover satisfactorily, what happened after the pilots had dropped their bombs, or more spectacularly, what happened after the video screens had gone blank, was not something which managed to penetrate the television coverage – despite the efforts of the Iraqis to exploit the issue of 'collateral damage'. On the one occasion when this did occur, at Amiriya, the full horror was not shown owing to broadcasting standards in Britain which militated against the showing of graphic scenes of carnage on grounds of taste and decency. The Leeds survey would also suggest that the public did not want to see such carnage and, if it had, that it would not anyway have altered public perceptions about the rights and wrongs of this particular war. As long as audiences believed that they were being told broadly what was going on, they were prepared to suspend their 'right to know' in favour of the publicly supported military's considerations of the 'need to know'.

The ground war, likewise, together with the seven week pounding of the Iraqi army by coalition air forces, was for the most part also kept off television screens, even though this was where the majority of the enemy casualties were sustained. Very little of the killing fields of Kuwait were seen, not least because the Iraqis prevented western film crews from visiting the front and because the coalition's news pool arrangements were organized in such a way as to keep the 'real war' well and truly away from what Sir Robin Day once described as the 'visible brutality' of television war. When Sir Robin addressed the question of the relationship between war and television in a famous *Encounter* article back in 1970, he had wondered whether 'if in future a democracy which has uninhibited television coverage in every home will be ever able to fight a war, however just'.[11] The Gulf war of 1991 demonstrated that an answer had been found.

Notes

1 We refer to General Schwarzkopf's description of the tactics employed in the 100 Hour Land War as enigmatic because, in American Football, the 'Hail Mary Play' is usually associated with a desperation measure whereby the quarterback lofts the ball high in the hope that one of his forwards will catch the ball and score a last ditch touchdown. Given the speed with which coalition forces moved forwards into Kuwait and Southern Iraq, and given the comparative lack of resistance put up by the Iraqis, the use of this analogy to describe the allied thrust is therefore unusual, to say the least.

2 *The Sunday Telegraph*, 20 January 1991.

3 For further details see Philip M. Taylor, *War and the Media: Propaganda and Persuasion in the Gulf War*, Manchester University Press, 1992.

4 *The Daily Telegraph*, 8 February 1991.

5 The findings in this article are merely preliminary; more detailed results will follow as part of the ESRC funded research project conducted by the Institute of Communications Studies into audience reactions to the media coverage of the Gulf war.

6 For an examination of the press coverage of the Falklands war see David E. Morrison & Howard Tumber, *Journalists at War: the dynamics of news reporting during the Falklands conflict*, Sage, 1988.

7 See Philip Towle, *Pundits and Patriots: lessons from the Gulf war*, Institute for European Defence and Strategic Studies, Occasional Paper 50, 1991.

8 *The Observer*, 20 January 1991.

9 The initial media euphoria at the prospect of a quick, one- sided victory prompted British and American spokesmen quickly to dampen down media statements. See US Secretary of Defence, Richard Cheney's briefing at the Pentagon, as reported in *The Financial Times*, 19–20 January 1991.

10 *The Sunday Telegraph*, 3 February 1991.

11 Cited in Philip M. Taylor, *Munitions of the Mind: War propaganda from the ancient world to the nuclear age*, Patrick Stephens, 1990, p.228.

Chronology

1990

17 July: Saddam Hussein accuses America of conspiring with Gulf states to cut oil prices.

27 July: OPEC raises oil target price.

2 Aug: Iraqi invasion of Kuwait at 2am local time; the Emir, Sheikh Jaber Ahmed Al-Sabah flees to Saudi Arabia; emergency session of UN Security Council passes Resolution 660 which condemns invasion and demands immediate Iraqi withdrawal; Iraqi and Kuwaiti assets in UK and USA frozen; Margaret Thatcher and George Bush make parallel tough statements from their joint meeting.

3 Aug: Iraq moves troops in Kuwait to Saudi border; puppet government established in Kuwait and Iraq claims it is helping a Kuwaiti uprising against Al-Sabah family; US Navy ordered to Gulf; US/USSR joint declaration in Moscow calling for arms embargo on Iraq.

5 Aug: President Bush announces 'this will not stand'.

6 Aug: UN Resolution 661 imposes trade embargo against Iraq (medical and humanitarian food supplies exempted).

7 Aug: 4,000 American troops from 82nd Airborne Division sent to Saudi Arabia; Turkey turns off Iraqi pipeline.

8 Aug: Iraq declares formal annexation of Kuwait; President Bush announces American foreign policy objectives in televised address.

9 Aug: UN Resolution 662 declares Iraqi annexation of Kuwait null and void.

10 Aug: Arab League in Cairo votes to send pan-Arab force to Saudi Arabia.

11 Aug: Douglas Croskery, a British citizen, shot by Iraqis while trying to escape Kuwait.

12 Aug: Saddam links any withdrawal from Kuwait with Israeli withdrawal from occupied territories, together with US withdrawal from Saudi Arabia and Syrian withdrawal from Lebanon.

15 Aug: Formal end to Iran-Iraq war announced.

18 Aug: Iraqi announcement of 'hostage' policy; UN Resolution 663 demands that all foreigners be allowed to leave Iraq and Kuwait.

23 Aug: Saddam meets hostages, shown on Iraqi TV's *Guest News*.

25 Aug: UN Resolution 665 authorizes naval blockade to enforce sanctions; BBC and CNN crews enter Iraq.

27 Aug: Austrian President Kurt Waldheim arrives in Baghdad for mercy mission and takes 80 Austrian hostages home to Vienna.

28 Aug: Iraq declares Kuwait to be its 19th Province.

1 Sept: 200 British women and children permitted to leave Iraq on mercy flights to London.

9 Sept: Helsinki summit; Presidents Bush and Gorbachev call upon Iraq to leave Kuwait.

13 Sept: UN Resolution 666 authorizes humanitarian food shipments if distributed through international aid agencies.

14 Sept: Britain announces it is sending its 7th Armoured Brigade to Gulf.

15 Sept: 4,000 French troops ordered to Gulf.

16 Sept: UN Resolution 667 condemns Iraqi raids on diplomatic premises in Kuwait.
Iraqi TV transmits, unedited, President Bush's speech to Iraqi people warning of dangers of war.

24 Sept: UN Resolution 669 asks Security Council to assist other nations affected by the embargo.

25 Sept: UN Resolution 670 bans all cargo flights to Iraq.

27 Sept: Britain and Iran renew diplomatic relations.

8 Oct: 21 Palestinians killed and more than 100 wounded on Temple Mount in Jerusalem, renewing linkage issue.

23 Oct: Iraq releases 330 French hostages; Edward Heath brings home 33 British hostages.

25 Oct: Dick Cheney announces that a further 100,000 American troops are being sent to join the 210,000 Americans already in Saudi Arabia; US active duty service for combat reservists doubled from 180 to 360 days.

29 Oct: UN Resolution 674 demands that Iraq stop taking hostages and calls for reparations and redress for war crimes in Kuwait.

3 Nov: James Baker begins seven nation tour to begin forming grand coalition.

8 Nov: President Bush announces that he will double the size of the US forces in the Gulf by despatching a further 200,000 US troops.

9 Nov: Willi Brandt leaves Baghdad with 180 west European hostages.

10 Nov: General Schwarzkopf (secretly) draws up preliminary plan to envelop Iraqi forces in Kuwait by a flanking movement.

28 Nov: John Major replaces Margaret Thatcher as British prime minister.

29 Nov: UN Resolution 678 sets deadline of 15 January for withdrawal and approves use of 'all necessary means' to expel Iraq thereafter.

30 Nov: President Bush tells US 'this will not be another Vietnam'.

1 Dec: Saddam visits his frontline troops and puts Palestine linkage on the agenda.

6 Dec: Iraq announces impending release of all hostages.

22 Dec: President Bush meets John Major in Washington.

1991

4 Jan: European Community invites Iraqi foreign minister to Luxembourg for talks.

6 Jan: John Major rules out the use of nuclear weapons in the Gulf.

9 Jan: Last ditch talks between the US Secretary of State, James Baker, and the Iraqi foreign minister, Tariq Aziz, in Geneva fail to make progress on a solution to the Gulf Crisis.

10 Jan: British ambassador leaves Baghdad.

12 Jan: Peace demonstrations are held.
Javier Peres de Cuellar, the UN Secretary-General, visits Baghdad in last ditch attempt to persuade Saddam Hussein to adopt UN Resolutions.
Both US Senate and House of Representatives back Bush.

13 Jan: Iraqi parliament endorses Saddam's rejection of UN deadline.

14 Jan: Guidelines issued to the media.

15 Jan: European Community concede failure of last ditch peace plan and a final French initiative also collapses; President Bush signs National Security Directive that formally

authorizes military action.

All but four Iraqi diplomats are expelled from London

MPs vote 534 to 57 to support war in the Gulf. The number of Labour rebels rises from 42 in the last debate on 11 December 1990 to 55.

16 Jan: At 5am London time the UN deadline to Iraq expires. Richard Cheney orders General Schwarzkopf to execute the Directive.

17 Jan: Air and cruise missile strikes on Iraq commence as the air war for the liberation of Kuwait begins. The first British Tornado is lost.

Fifty MEPs issue a statement deploring the use of force to end the Gulf crisis. Left-wing and anti-war groups condemn the outbreak of war. NOP poll shows 71 per cent support for sending troops to the Gulf but 53 per cent felt that sanctions should have been given longer.

CNN broadcasts for 17 hours live from enemy capital before having its plug pulled; Iraqi Voice of Masses Radio combined with Radio of Iraq Republic.

18 Jan: Iraq announces it has captured several allied air crew.

Iraq launches eight Scud missiles at Israel, injuring 12 civilians and prompting intensive allied diplomatic activity to try and keep Israel out of the war; 1 Scud fired at Saudi Arabia intercepted successfully by first ever combat launch of Patriot missile; six mobile launchers destroyed by 'Scudbusting' coalition aircraft; Turkey allows coalition use of its bases; first Iraqi PoWs taken on raids against Kuwaiti oil platforms.

President Bush warns against unwarranted optimism by media.

19 Jan: About 7-10,000 in a peace demonstration in London.

Most western journalists expelled from Iraq (but not CNN).

Three Scuds fired at Israel.

Sea Island Terminal starts leaking oil.

20 Jan: Bombing missions from Turkey begin.

Disastrous briefing at MoD prompts series of media attacks.

Alleged 'baby milk plant' bombed.

Captured allied airmen, including two RAF officers, are displayed on Iraqi television.

21 Jan: Allied governments protest at Iraq parading captured airmen on television, requiring them to make humiliating anti-war statements and threatening to use them as human shields by siting them at key military installations in defiance of the Geneva convention.

CBS crew go missing on the Kuwait-Saudi border; MoD imposes blackout on Met Office's release of Middle East weather forecasts.

First Kuwaiti oilfields, at al-Wafra, reported to have been fired by Iraqis.

Announcement that a Gulf Trust to aid those injured, and the families of those killed in the war, is to be set up.

Politics Today: The Gulf Crisis, Conservative Political Centre, argues that the use of force in the Gulf is justified by Christian teaching.

Foreign Office holds talks with representatives of Iraqi opposition groups.

22 Jan: Three killed by an Iraqi Scud missile attack on Tel Aviv. The Allies appeal to the Israelis not to intervene in the war.

23 Jan: Iraqi government stops sale of petrol to civilians without warning.

Cheney and Powell deliver most forthcoming briefing to date in which General Powell announces that coalition will 'cut off and kill' Iraqi army.

Island of Qarah liberated.

Iraqi papers start publishing photographs of civilian damage.

24 Jan: French air forces starts bombing missions against Iraqi targets, reversing a previous decision only to attack targets in occupied Kuwait.

Saudi pilots shoot down two Iraqi planes; reports that Saddam has had his air force commanders executed.

Iraq begins releasing millions of gallons of crude oil into the Gulf from storage tanks and tankers off the Kuwait coast, creating a massive oil slick.

Iraq opens border with Jordan temporarily releasing flood of refugees.

Peter Arnett of CNN escorted to civilian damage sites.

25 Jan: Iraqis cease parading captured PoWs.

26 Jan: Mina Al-Ahmadi oil refinery complex bombed by coalition precision bombs to stem oil flow.

27 Jan: US bombing raids destroy the manifolds (oil terminal pressure controls) to cut off the flow of oil into the Gulf.

Start of exodus of Iraqi planes to Iran.

28 Jan: UK begins emergency airlift of anti-pollution equipment.

Baghdad radio warns it will extend war through terrorist attacks throughout the world.

President Bush tells National Religious Broadcasters' Convention that it is a 'just war'.

Iraq announces that captured pilot injured in coalition bombing raid; first reports of border clashes.

29 Jan: French defence minister Jean-Pierre Chevenement resigns, stating 'the logic of war risks driving us further every day from the objectives fixed by the United Nations'.

Saudi town of Khafji occupied by Iraqis.

30 Jan: Coalition declares 'total air superiority'.

CNN starts transmitting pictures live from Baghdad.

Germany offers Britain DM800 million towards the cost of military operations in the Gulf.

Britain repeats US offer of ceasefire if Iraq withdraws from Kuwait and does not seem poised to re-invade.

31 Jan: UK to be used as a base for B-52 bombing raids on Iraq.

Khafji retaken by coalition.

1 Feb: Coalition-media relations turn sour over Khafji.

2 Feb: Western journalists in Iraq escorted to Diwaniya.

Ramsay Clark mission enters Iraq.

Faylaka Island retaken by coalition.

3 Feb: New coalition media arrangements announced.

First Iranian peace offer coolly received at White House.

4 Feb: Iraqis continue to escort journalists to sites of alleged civilian damage.

5 Feb: Voice of the Gulf begins transmitting black propaganda.

6 Feb: Four Iraqi soldiers surrender to unilateral journalists.

Iraq accuses coalition of trying to 'expel Iraq from the 20th century' and severs diplomatic relations with the USA, Britain, France, Italy, Egypt and Saudi Arabia.

French claim 30 per cent of Republican Guard destroyed.

7 Feb: Physicians for Human Rights report on Iraqi atrocities in Kuwait published.

8 Feb: Iraq invites UN fact-finding mission to investigate 'baby milk factory' episode.

Coalition bombing of Nassariyah.

Ramsay Clark leaves Iraq.

9 Feb: Dick Cheney and Colin Powell begin visit to central command in Riyadh.
Primakov arrives in Baghdad as Gorbachev expresses worries that coalition is going beyond UN mandate.

11 Feb: Iran denounces Iraq for failing to take up its peace initiative.
Iraq announces that thousands, not hundreds, have been killed by coalition bombing and that it will never accept a ceasefire.

12 Feb: Non Anglo-American journalists write open letter complaining to King Fahd.
Saddam Hussein informs Primakov that he is prepared to consider pulling out of Kuwait under certain conditions.

13 Feb: Allies kill hundreds of Iraqi civilians in an air attack on what they claimed was a command and control bunker at Amiriya.
Primakov leaves Baghdad.

14 Feb: Iraqis launch Scud attack at Hafer Al-Batin; RAF mistakenly bombs market in Fallujah.
Renewal of campaign concerning Iraqi atrocities in Kuwait.

15 Feb: Coalition rejects Iraqi offer to withdraw from Kuwait to which a string of unacceptable conditions are attached.
Ground war countdown begins.

17 Feb: RAF admits that a bomb veered off course and struck the town of Fallujah during an attack on a bridge; Baghdad endures one of heaviest air raids of war.

18 Feb: Soviet peace plan for the Gulf launched with Tariq Aziz meeting President Gorbachev in Moscow.

19 Feb: Allied tanks begin making forays into Iraq.
French TV crews temporarily boycott covering the war.

20 Feb: Allied minimum terms for a ceasefire returned to Moscow. Labour's response is much more positive than the government's.
US announces that Iraq must withdraw by 23 February, 8pm local time; 450 Iraqis desert.

21 Feb: Soviet Union announces that Iraq has accepted its peace terms; President Gorbachev telephones President Bush with details; Saddam Hussein makes defiant speech on Baghdad radio.
Twenty three Labour MPs and two Plaid Cymru MPs register a protest vote against the Gulf war in the Commons.

22 Feb: President Bush says Soviet peace plan does not go far enough and warns Iraq to comply with all UN resolutions by 12pm EST on 23 February.
Belgium agrees to provide financial aid towards British and French war costs.
Iraqis set fire to Kuwait oilfields.

24 Feb: Ground war begins at 4am local time as coalition launches a three pronged ground offensive into Iraq and Kuwait.
News blackout imposed.
About 400 British Muslims march in London in protest at the beginning of the ground offensive.

25 Feb: Scud missile kills 27 US servicemen and injures 98 in Dhahran; Iraqis start to evacuate Kuwait.

26 Feb: Iraq announces it is withdrawing from Kuwait; Kuwait city liberated; start of battle of Mutlah Gap.
UN Security Council goes into closed session at the request of the Soviets.

27 Feb: Iraq says it accepts all UN conditions and demands; President Bush announces victory and end to offensive allied operations and declares a cessation of hostilities to begin at 5am GMT, 8am local time.

28 Feb: Ceasefire arranged in Gulf war. Iraq agrees to exchange of prisoners.

580 Kuwaiti oilfields reported on fire.

1 Mar: First television pictures of devastation on road north to Basra come through.

3 Mar: General Schwarzkopf and staff meet Iraqi commanders to agree permanent ceasefire for which Iraq agrees to all Allied terms.

Shi'ite Muslims rising begins in Southern Iraq.

4 Mar: Kurdish rebellion begins in Northern Iraq.

Sheikh Saad Al-Sabah, Crown Prince of Kuwait, returns home.

9 Mar: British troops begin to pull out of the Gulf.

14 Mar: Emir Sheikh Jaber al Ahmed al Sabah returns to Kuwait.

22 Mar: UN embargo on food and essential goods for Iraq lifted.

23 Mar: Iraqis begin to regain ground against the rebels in the south.

25 Mar: Survey of the impact of the media coverage of the Gulf war and of people's attitudes towards it is published by Centre for Security Studies, Hull.

27 Mar: US peace plan offers Iraq a chance of using its air force to crush rebellion in return for signing humiliating peace terms involving the destruction of all chemical and biological weapons.

31 Mar: Kurdish rebels driven back by Iraqis and Kurdish refugees begin to flee into Turkey and Iran.

1 Apr: US Treasury publishes a blacklist of 89 suspected Iraqi front-organizations, more than half of which are based in Britain.

2 Apr: Turkey closes its borders to fleeing Kurds.

3 Apr: UK urges Turks to open borders to Kurds and calls for international humanitarian aid.

3 Apr: UN Security Council resolution 687 imposes ceasefire terms on Iraq, that will force it to pay reparations and strip it of chemical and biological weapons, but does not mention Kurds. A French amendment aimed at safeguarding the Kurds is rejected by the US, USSR and China.

Iran opens its borders to all Iraqi refugees.

5 Apr: US and UK announce beginning of airlift of aid to northern Iraq.

Iraqi embassy in London occupied by Kurds for four hours.

7 Apr: President Bush indicates greater willingness to urge the UN to protect the Kurds.

8 Apr: US/UK airdrop of aid to northern Iraq begins.

John Major urges the creation of a UN enclave in northern Iraq to protect the Kurds.

9 Apr: US shifts to favouring military protection for the Kurds and warns Iraq not to use ground or air forces anywhere in the Kurdish areas of the country.

10 Apr: Kuwait proposes a UN enforced safe haven for the Shia refugees in southern Iraq.

15 Apr: EC pledges to seek ways to put Saddam Hussein on trial for crimes against humanity.

16 Apr: Britain, France and US are to send troops to northern Iraq and establish secure encampments on the plains of Kurdistan to aid the Kurdish refugees.

17 Apr: Allies begin to establish refugee camps in Kurdistan.

24 Apr: Kurdish leaders announce they have signed a deal with Saddam Hussein on Kurdish autonomy.

26 Apr: UK puts plans for UN police force in northern Iraq to Security Council with EC backing.

7 May: The American General Charles Horner blames a British air controller for the death of nine British infantrymen from US 'friendly fire' during the Gulf war in an interview in the American magazine, Air Force Times.

US troops pull out of southern Iraq.

17 May: A British engineer, Douglas Brand, is gaoled for life by the Iraqis for espionage. Britain immediately launches a diplomatic offensive via the UN warning Iraq that it is in breach of two UN resolutions and imperilling its chances of sanctions being lifted.

17 June: Douglas Brand is released after the intervention of Ted Heath.

21 June: European pressure leads to suspension of Allied withdrawal from northern Iraq.

1 July: Foreign Affairs Select Committee warns against the consequences of complete military withdrawal from Iraq.

8 July: Iraq admits that it had a secret nuclear weapons programme.

11 July: Allies discuss military strikes to destroy Iraq's nuclear installations.

15 July: Allied pull-out from Kurdistan completed.

25 July: Ministry of Defence report lays the blame for the deaths of nine British infantrymen killed by friendly fire in the Gulf war with the US aircraft responsible.

26 July: Revelation that the government continued to permit exports of nuclear materials and chemicals to Iraq until three days after the invasion of Kuwait in an annexe to evidence submitted by the DTI to the Trade and Industry Select Committee.

30 Aug: Eight RAF Jaguars are to be deployed to Incirlik in eastern Turkey to join the Allied air force stationed there.

24 Sept: Announcement that the UN investigation team has discovered details of Iraq's nuclear programmes. Iraqi troops detain them in a bus parked in central Baghdad, demanding the return of documents and videotaped evidence.

27 Sept: The siege of the UN investigators ends.

16 Oct: Charles Allen, *Thunder and Lightening - The RAF in the Gulf: Personal Experiences of War*, HMSO, says that the Americans kept the British largely in the dark about war plans after the theft of secrets from the car of Wing Commander David Farquhar in December 1990. Farquhar was later court martialled.

Foreign Policy

CHRISTOPHER HILL

Fifty years ago the United States and the Soviet Union entered the Second World War and in doing so they not only guaranteed Britain victory over Hitler but also began the superpower era in which Britain could hope for no more than a supporting role. Yet 1991 demonstrated that Britain has not only managed to retain a surprisingly prominent position in international relations, but that it continues to take on foreign policy responsibilities. This was evident in two of the year's three major foreign policy developments – the Gulf and the collapse of Soviet power – while the third, the European Community (EC), demonstrated the corollary of a preference for a continuing leading role, namely a suspicion of change. Elsewhere, particularly in relation to east Asia, Britain continued to be preoccupied with the fallout from its past imperial status, no doubt another factor inhibiting the making of common cause with the other eleven members of the EC.

Reverberations from the Gulf

The Gulf war dominated international relations during the first half of 1991. As such, it had considerable impact on Britain and British foreign policy. Not only had British citizens been prominent among those held hostage by Saddam Hussein during the phoney war period and British troops second only to the Americans in delivering the blows which led to Iraq's expulsion from Kuwait, but British relations with both Iran and the Arab world (at best delicately poised) stood to be profoundly affected by this renewed intervention in the region. In particular, the fate of the hostages in the Lebanon seemed more than ever at the mercy of great and intractable events.

The first half of January saw Britain stand aside from the last spasms of the peace diplomacy with which France and the Soviet Union sought to avert a war in the Gulf. In retrospect it seems clear that London (like Washington) had resigned itself to a military showdown from a much earlier stage in the crisis. Certainly when the air attacks on Iraq began on 17 January, the Royal Air Force took a prominent part, and there was no attempt made by the Major government to hide behind the skirts of the Bush administration, despite the risks to Britain's wider international position. Given the constitutional difficulties over German 'out-of-area' deployments, and France's ambivalence over being at war with one of its principal friends in the region, Britain also took the leading role in the coordination of European naval movements in the Gulf through the Western European Union (WEU). In fact the collective European response to the invasion of Kuwait was not perceived as either moral or effective in Washington, and this had the effect of breathing new (if only temporary) life back into conceptions of the Anglo-American special relationship.

The devastating victory of the allied forces in the short-lived February land war brought more kudos for Britain's armed forces as well as a political success for the government. But these were soon overshadowed by the new round of problems which the end of a war inevitably brings. In the case of the Kuwait campaign, the immediate concerns were threefold: firstly, victory came at the cost of perhaps 100,000 Iraqi lives, sacrificed mainly through Saddam's savage indifference towards the shedding of blood, but also because the allies were determined to take no risks and to employ overwhelming force. Although John Major lacked the relish for triumphalism of his predecessor, the tragedy of the 'turkey-shoot' on the road to Basra ensured that relief at the ending of the war was diluted by unease at some of the means which had been employed to achieve it.

This was also true, but in an inverted sense, of the second issue that arose from the restoration of Kuwait. It was soon evident that Saddam's defeat was not automatically going to be accompanied by his overthrow from within, as the Americans and British seemed to suppose. In fact the passing of the weeks served only to confirm that however decisive the military success, it had not in itself been able to remove one of the prime causes of the conflict, namely the current Iraqi regime. Britain may have regretted the decision to call off the campaign without advancing on Baghdad itself, but at the time it almost certainly accepted the logic of the argument that states such as China and the USSR, which had only allowed a UN operation to go ahead so as to expel the invader from Kuwait, would not sanction interference in the internal affairs of Iraq, and that it was important not to endanger international consensus on this and many other issues by seeking to determine the future of Iraq.

The third development which complicated western (and therefore British) foreign policy in the aftermath of the war was the condition of the Kurds in northern Iraq. Long determined on national self-determination, the Kurds interpreted American remarks about the likelihood (and desirability) of Saddam being removed by his own people, as a green light for their own insurgency, only to be dismayed to find both that enough of the Iraqi armed forces was intact to renew their suppression, and that the West was prepared to stand by and watch as thousands of Kurds were forced to flee in nightmarish conditions towards the Iranian and Turkish borders. An unwillingness to be dragged into another potential quagmire, plus a concern not to alienate Turkey, led the Major government into a deafening silence on the matter, despite rising media attention and an evident moral responsibility for what was happening in Kurdistan. It was left to former Prime Minister Thatcher, (incidentally precipitating criticisms from the Bruges Group of governmental weakness and indecision) to call for humanitarian assistance to the Kurds. This may finally have tipped the balance in favour of British and other allied troops being sent to monitor Iraqi treatment of the Kurds and ensure their eventual return home. In so doing, 'safe havens' were created which breached long-standing international norms of non-interference in the domestic affairs of other states, however seemingly just the cause. These are norms which Britain has traditionally made much of, and it remains to be seen whether the safe havens represent a precedent for interventions on the grounds of outstanding humanitarian need. It seems certain at least that Britain could not envisage such an intervention alone, wherever the possibility might arise.

Not only did the Gulf war not damage Britain's relations with the other states of the region (as many had feared); it actually seemed to free them up. This was part of the general trend by which the United States came to reassess its policy on the Arab-Israeli conflict, and many of the enemies of Israel decided to get onside with the United States, now demonstrably the world's only superpower. Relations with Syria (an ally in the war) and Iran (glad to see Saddam humiliated) were both restored, thus ending the situation where Britain had been at loggerheads with all four radical states in the Middle East. Now – apart from Iraq – only Libya remained a pariah (and the pressure on Colonel Ghadaffi was actually increased during 1991, as demands were made for the extradition of two of his agents to face trial for the Lockerbie air disaster of 1988). There were even slight signs of a lessening of Anglo-Iraqi tension towards the end of the year, as Baghdad released Ian Richter, a businessman who had been imprisoned on bribery charges, and Britain unfroze Iraqi assets in London.

Similar releases facilitated the development of British relations with both Tehran and Damascus. In April Iran released Roger Cooper, an alleged spy, after six years in prison without trial, and it became clear that the Rafsanjani government was also willing to exert pressure on those holding British hostages in the Lebanon, to bring that long saga to an end. Syria was also keen to use its good offices, after the restoration of diplomatic relations in February. In consequence, all three of the remaining British hostages (and indeed all the Americans) found themselves literally on the road to Damascus (and the inevitable press conference) before the end of the year. For John McCarthy, Jackie Mann and Terry Waite this was the end of more than five years in which they had paid the price of decades of deteriorating relations between the West and the world of Islam and Palestinian nationalism. If their release comes to symbolize the beginnings of more realistic attitudes on both sides of the divide, they may yet feel that their ordeal was not wholly in vain. The fact that a Middle East peace conference actually did begin in Madrid in November, and at the time of writing the peace process has not yet broken down, is a small sign of progress. Since 1980 Britain has consistently worked with its European partners for a settlement on the basis of guarantees for Israeli security in return for some kind of Palestinian homeland, and the Madrid conference is in no small part the consequence of persistent European pressure over the last decade – on the

Americans and Israelis as well as the Arab states. Of course this did not prevent undignified European squabbles over which of the twelve member states should be represented at Madrid. In the end Britain followed the French lead, and sent an official to monitor the actions of the presidency on behalf of the Community as a whole.

European Foreign Policy

In any other year, the European Community's Intergovernmental Conferences (IGCs) would have been the central issue in British foreign policy. As it is, if they were not the main priority behind the scenes history may well judge that they should have been. For what was at stake in both was the extent to which Britain would continue to preserve a separate identity and capability in international affairs. In the conference on political union in particular, a central point of dispute was the extent to which a single European foreign policy should be forged, through the mechanism of majority voting and through the development of a Community defence identity. Given Britain's still prominent international position, and historical experience, this debate touched on the most sensitive aspects of the key values of sovereignty and security, and it was hardly surprising that the Major government saw little merit in changing the existing arrangements whereby independent governments harmonize their diplomacies voluntarily and retain the right to step outside collective procedures when consultation shows that fundamentally different interests are at stake.

The victory claimed by John Major at Maastricht was in fact only partial in the area of foreign policy. The principle of majority voting was admitted into what had previously been an impregnable citadel of intergovernmentalism for the first time. It is true that this is only in relation to technical matters of implementation, and that the British government clearly does not expect it to become a working, everyday, principle for many years, if ever. But the Rubicon has been crossed, and the theoretical concession may turn out to have embarrassing practical consequences, given that other member states may well be willing to force majority votes if states like Britain are perceived to be persistently obstructive. Votes may not even be necessary, as the German ability in December to stampede the Community towards recognition of Slovenia and Croatia demonstrated. It is hard to believe that this move was not against Britain's better judgement, and it demonstrated the strong pressures for conformity which now characterise the foreign policy system of the Community.

The other major innovation on the foreign policy side of the Maastricht agreement was the recognition that the Community was moving inexorably towards a defence identity – something that had been virtually a taboo subject until the collapse of the cold war alliance structure. The change took the form of not only moving the semantic debate on from 'security' (which had been considered to be part of foreign policy consultations since at least 1981) to 'defence', with its military connotations, but also formalizing the convergence (which had become evident since the Gulf war) of EPC and the WEU. The WEU is a grouping of nine of the twelve member states which was revived in 1984 so that the Europeans could formulate strategies on the very two questions which NATO denied them – namely towards the United States itself, and on 'out of area' threats beyond the north Atlantic region.

For Britain this trend posed delicate dilemmas.Given that the United States was at best suspicious about the damaging effects which a developing WEU might have on western unity, London showed no enthusiasm for proposals to merge EPC and the WEU. It was made clear that talk of a European defence policy, let alone European armed forces, was premature and that national defence raised the sovereignty problem even more powerfully than did monetary policy, on which Britain was simultaneously insisting on an escape clause in the other intergovernmental conference.

Thus Britain ensured that the WEU's new role in relation to the Community went no further than that of bridge between the Twelve and NATO, although it should not be supposed that this outcome displeased the majority of member states. In the run-in to Maastricht there was a good deal of rhetorical posturing on all sides, and most governments were aware of the need for a certain amount of caution in the new fluidity of international relations. The main plank of British policy in this context was to ensure that the rundown of NATO forces in Europe took place smoothly and that the United States did not become decoupled from European affairs. As much as with the sovereignty question, Britain was concerned with a European defence entity falling under the sway of German pacifism just at a time when new threats might be emerging. Nor does Britain wished to see raised the questions of her nuclear weapons and permanent seat on the UN Security Council.

In 1991 therefore, the old balancing act between Washington and continental Europe continued to characterize British foreign policy. The arrival of a new, Anglophile American Ambassador to the Court of St James (and a professional diplomat to boot), Mr Raymond Seitz, showed that the Bush administration had no intention – as many had supposed – of letting its closest friend in the Community drift further offshore. The Gulf war was the most dramatic demonstration of continued common views of international politics, but in the Middle East, southern Africa, and Indo-China there were also signs of the two states working discreetly in harness. On the other hand, of course, Britain was embroiled ever more closely in the diplomacy of managing Europe. In the course of the year's dramas over the Gulf, eastern Europe, and the IGCs, Britain lost some of its traditional closeness to states like Portugal and Denmark, where Euro-enthusiasm was on the upsurge, and Spain continued to press over the Gibraltar question. Paradoxically however (given Rome's commitment to integration) Britain became temporarily aligned with Italy during the debate over the WEU. The endless raft of Franco-German initiatives tended to irritate those excluded from the inner circle. This also applied to the Dutch, who as President of the Community during the second half of the year often showed themselves surprisingly sensitive to British concerns. In the end it can be argued that the IGCs came down to a power struggle between Germany and Britain and their competing views of the Community. The result was a hard fought draw, but Britain was undoubtedly on the defensive, and the next round of the contest will not be long delayed.

The Disintegration of Soviet Europe

British pragmatism was tested to the limit by the continued avalanche of change occurring in eastern Europe during 1991. In truth the British tradition in foreign policy has only partly been to do with recognizing unpalatable realities or dealing with those who hold power rather than those one would prefer to hold it.It has also centred on dealing with states rather than nationalities, and on the importance of stability in the interstate system. The last twelve months, therefore, have all but provoked a crisis of conscience in British foreign policy.

The secession of the Baltic republics from the Soviet Union was difficult enough, but at least there the illegal annexations of 1940 (never recognised by Britain) provided clear grounds for the re-establishment of diplomatic relations once it became clear that not only was power draining away from Moscow but that Mr Gorbachev was also prepared to accept the fact. As it was, Britain took far longer to acknowledge the three new states than their supporters would have wished, (it did so together with its Community partners on 27 August) and to some extent came under criticism for effectively rewarding a hardline response from the Soviet government. German enthusiasm for the revived principle of national self-determination was hardly shared in London, where the main concern was to avoid the destabilization of eastern Europe and the Soviet Union.

It was increasingly on the USSR that world attention focused as the year wore on. As the nature and depth of the contest between Mikhail Gorbachev and Boris Yeltsin became clear, Britain like the other principal powers had to engage in a subtle balancing act whereby Yeltsin was courted without Gorbachev being abandoned. This came to a head during the August coup in Moscow when John Major and the Foreign Office first got it right by standing out against the plotters (unlike President Mitterand) but then had to acknowledge that the real victor of the counter coup had been Yeltsin, and that Gorbachev, in so many respects a personal ally of Britain since his first visit to Downing Street in 1984, was now a burnt-out case.

And so it proved, although the support of Britain and other western states was no doubt vital to Gorbachev in enabling him to leave power with dignity and to manage the transition (at least) between the Soviet Union and the new Commonwealth of Independent States with remarkable smoothness. Britain reluctantly came to accept that the disappearance of the second superpower was inevitable and to make arrangements for a new era of relations with the successor states. In this context it became evident that here too there was scope for the further 'Europeanization' of British foreign policy, as Britain and Germany agreed to cooperate over consular representation in Kiev (this before the Ukraine became independent) and pressure then built up for wider EC-based cooperation over the setting up of missions in the newly independent republics.

Parallel to the decline of the Soviet Union was the even more agonizing break-up of Yugoslavia, where no amount of diplomatic even-handedness could prevent civil war. British policy here was rather like Northern Ireland policy turned inside out, namely that of keeping the violence down to an irreducible minimum and allowing the secessionists no prospect of recognition. To Whitehall, it was a case of clinging to Yugoslavia for fear of something worse, despite the increasing pressure from domestic as well as German opinion to recognize those seeking to break with Belgrade. Slovenia, westernized, small and relatively self-contained soon became less of a problem than Croatia, whose war with Serbia has complex historical and demographic roots. As suggested earlier, Britain was hustled into a collective EC announcement at the end of the year that the breakaway republics would be recognised in January 1992 (if they fulfilled various conditions), preferring to risk inflaming Serbia than to endanger European unity on a vital security interest which the United States had conspicuously left to the Europeans to settle.

The Further Horizon

When such momentous events as those of 1991 hold the gaze, it is not uncommon for other questions, of hardly less significance in the long run, to become neglected, despite the fact that before they have reached the point of crisis, they may be more susceptible to influence. Britain was aware of this in the rest of eastern Europe, struggling to channel 'know-how' funds and expertise to countries which might easily sink back before long into stupor and chaos. But the same dilemma existed as with the Soviet Union, and indeed with the homeless who now throng London streets: does financial aid trap people in their existing orbit, or does it provide the crucial booster thrust to allow an escape velocity to be achieved? For Britain this theoretical dilemma is largely resolved by a lack of sufficient resources to do more than influence post-communist development at the margins, but with Bonn preoccupied with absorbing the former DDR, London's voice certainly became more important in the debate about what the west could do.

Outside Europe and the Middle East, it was difficult in 1991 to establish a case for any issue to become a burning priority in British foreign policy. The Commonwealth conference for once passed off (in Harare) without Britain either attracting or provoking acrimonious criticism, and John Major succeeded in placing on the agenda the idea that member states should live up, even in their internal affairs, to agreed standards of behaviour. (Later, Britain also began to exert pressure on the Moi government in Kenya over the suppression of civil liberties.) As something of a sweetener, Britain had announced that it intended unilaterally to implement the Trinidad Terms Initiative (of September 1990) providing for the writing off of two thirds of the bilateral debts of the poorest of the world's poor countries so long as they met IMF performance indicators. This too represented an important change from Mrs Thatcher's style in north-south relations. From a domestic British viewpoint, however, the conference was more remarkable for keeping the Prime Minister in Zimbabwe for as long as a week at a time when affairs in Europe were at their most pressing.

In Asia the question of Hong Kong and China continued to be vital for Britain but (perhaps fortunately) somewhat less in the public eye. China's increased leverage after its diplomatic cooperation during the Gulf war meant that Britain had little choice but slowly to rebuild relations with Beijing, and the Prime Minister even swallowed the bitter pill of being the first western head of government to be seen shaking hands with those responsible for the Tiananmen massacre of 1989 in an official visit to the PRC in September. All this, of course, is in the interests of consolidating the Sino-British agreement on the guaranteeing of Hong Kong's capitalist way of life after its handover in 1997. That some slow progress is being made to this end is indicated by the joint suggestion from London and Beijing that the sessions of the International Monetary Fund and World Bank in 1997 should take place in Hong Kong, to build up business confidence in the colony's future.

Slow change has also taken place in British relations with Vietnam, where an agreement has been reached to send back more boat-people against a background of a more sympathetic British approach to aid and trade with Hanoi, and over Cambodia, where the UN-sponsored peace agreement has brought to an end a sordid episode in British, indeed western, foreign policy. Now, insofar as Britain notices Cambodia, (and an envoy has been sent back to Phnom Penh for the first time in 15 years) it should be able to concentrate on helping to rebuild that shattered country, rather than pressurizing its isolated government. It also means that when Britain criticizes the human rights abuses of neighbouring Burma, as it is currently doing over the detention of Aung San Suu Kyi, it will have to worry less about the beam in its own eye. This more positive approach is largely the product of the world's changed diplomatic landscape since 1989, but it may also owe something to the arrival as Foreign Secretary of Douglas Hurd. After an uneasy period at the Home Office, Mr Hurd has settled into the less clear cut moral universe of international relations as if to the manner born. Less arrogant by temperament and necessity than some of his predecessors, the Foreign Secretary is hardly any less active. For better or worse Britain is still deeply immersed in what must now be called the management of the international system.

Acknowledgement

The research on which this article is based has benefited from the expert help provided by the staff of the Library of the Royal Institute of International Affairs, which I acknowledge with gratitude.

Ambassadors to selected countries
Argentina – The Hon Humphrey Maud CMG
Austria – B. L. Crowe CMG

Belgium – R. J. O' Neill CMG
Brazil – M. J. Newington CMG
China – Sir Alan Donald KCMG
    Sir Robin McLaren KCMG
Cuba – A. L. S Coltman
Czechoslovakia – P. L. O'Keefe, CMG CVO
    A. D. Brighty CMG CVO
Denmark – N. C. R. Williams CMG
Egypt – Sir James Adams KCMG
Finland – G. N. Smith CMG
France – Sir Ewen Fergusson KCMG
Germany – Sir Christopher Mallaby KCMG
Greece – Sir David Miers KBE CMG
Holy See – J. K. E. Broadley CMG
    A E Pelmer CMG CVO
Hungary – J. A. Birch CMG
  Iran (Chargé d'Affaires) – D. N. Reddoway MBE
Ireland – Sir Nicholas Fenn KCMG
    D. E. S. Blatherwick CMG OBE
Israel – M. Elliott CMG
Italy – Sir Stephen Egerton KCMG
Japan – Sir John Whitehead KCMG, CVO
Kuwait – Sir Michael Weston KCMG CVO
Luxembourg – Mrs J. J. d'A Campbell CMG
    The Hon Michael Pekesham
Netherlands – Sir Michael Jenkins KCMG
Norway – D. J. E. Ratford CMG, CVO
Poland – S. J. Barrett CMG
    M. J. Llewellyn Smith CMG
Portugal – H. J. Arbuthnott CMG
Saudi Arabia – Sir Alan Munro KCMG
South Africa – Sir Robin Renwick KCMG
    A Reeve CMG
Soviet Union – Sir Rodric Braithwaite KCMG
Spain – Sir Robin Fearn KCMG
Sweden – Sir John Ure KCMG LVO
    R. L. B. Cormack CMG
Switzerland – C. W. Long CMG
Turkey – Sir Timothy Daunt KCMG
United States – Sir Anthony Acland GCMG KCVO
    Sir Robin Renwick KCMG
Yugoslavia – P. E. Hall CMG

Governors of selected Dependent Territories
Bermuda – Sir Desmond Langley KCVO MBE
Falkland Islands – W. H. Fullerton
Gibraltar – Admiral Sir Derek Reffell KCB

Hong Kong – Sir David C. Wilson GCMG
St Helena – R. F. Stimson
   A. N. Hoole OBE

High Commissioners to selected Commonwealth Countries
Australia – B. L. Barder
Canada – B. J. P. Fall CMG
India – Sir David Goodall KCMG
   Sir Nicholas Fenn KCMG
Kenya – Sir Roger Tomkys KCMG
Malaysia – Sir Nicholas Spreckley CMG
New Zealand – D. J. Moss CMG
Nigeria – A. C. D. S. McRae CMG
Pakistan – Sir Nicholas Barrington CMG CVO

Chronology
5 Jan: John Major begins a four day visit to Saudi Arabia, Oman and Egypt.
11 Jan: Douglas Hurd begins a four day visit to the Gulf.
13 Jan: John Major in Paris for bilateral talks.
21 Jan: Britain begins to withdraw from selected missions in Asia which are expected to be the targets of Iraqi-backed terrorist attacks.
22 Feb: Bomb explodes outside British embassy in Guatemala.
25 Feb: Syria and Britain exchange ambassadors, formally restoring diplomatic relations.
4 Mar: John Major makes an official visit to Moscow.
   Foreign Affairs Select Committee report calls for an early end to all economic sanctions against South Africa and British pressure for the restoration of international sporting links.
5 Mar: John Major makes an official visit to Kuwait.
11 Mar: Successful Anglo-German summit in Bonn marks post-Thatcher rapprochement.
13 Mar: Dropping of charges against an Iranian student in London is seen as helping to pave the way for the release of British hostages in the Middle East.
16 Mar: Anglo-American talks between President Bush and John Major in Bermuda.
17 Mar: Dalai Lama begins a five day visit to Britain.
19 Mar: Douglas Hurd begins a four day visit to the USSR.
2 Apr: Douglas Hurd visits Hong Kong.
   Roger Cooper, the British businessman held for five years in Iran for alleged spying, is released.
3 Apr: Douglas Hurd begins a six day visit to China.
4 Apr: Britain is urged by UN Commission on Human Rights to ensure that irreversible human rights are in place in Hong Kong before the colony is transferred to China.
10 Apr: Bruges Group statement accuses John Major of a foreign policy of wobble and gesture, saying Mrs Thatcher would have stood against premature withdrawal from the Gulf. This was repudiated by Mrs Thatcher.
22 Apr: Antarctic conference on the question of mining in the continent begins.
   John Major urges Israel to release the Muslim cleric kidnapped from the Lebanon two years ago.

22-3 Apr: President F. W. de Klerk of South Africa meets John Major and Neil Kinnock at the start of a European tour.

23 Apr: Lech Walesa, President of Poland, begins a three day state visit to Britain.

24-5 Apr: Nelson Mandela meets John Major and Neil Kinnock in London.

29 Apr: Antarctic treaty countries produce a blueprint for international agreement to guarantee a ban on mining in the continent for 50 years and provide a basis for a comprehensive environmental protection regime.

1 May: Douglas Hurd begins a four day visit to Kuwait, Egypt, Jordan and Saudi Arabia.

7 May: Felipe Gonzalez, Prime Minister of Spain, begins a two day visit to London to discuss EC matters, the Middle East and Gibraltar.

8 May: Spain proposes an Anglo-Spanish condominium in Gibraltar.

13 May: Fatos Nano, the Albanian Prime Minster, arrives in London for talks about the restoration of diplomatic relations.

22 May: Britain agrees to restore diplomatic relations with Albania.

27 May: Peace talks open in London between the Ethiopian government and rebel factions.

30 May: David Gladstone, the British High Commissioner, is expelled from Sri Lanka, for criticizing Sri Lanka's human rights record.

3 June: Mikhail Gorbachev is invited to attend the forthcoming G7 summit in London.

6 June: Britain rejects Libyan overtures for a restoration of diplomatic relations.

7 June: Michael Manley, the Jamaican Prime Minister, begins a visit to Britain.

1 June: Government accepts linkage between Lebanese hostages in Israel and the release of British hostages in Lebanon for the first time.

21 June: Charles Haughey, Taioseach of the Irish Republic, meets John Major in London.

23 June: Antarctic treaty declaring the continent an area 'for peace and science' and banning mining there indefinitely is signed in Madrid.

24 June: Anglo-French summit in Dunkirk.

26 June: Government admits it gave military training to the Cambodian resistance for six years up to 1989.

3 July: UK freezes £13 million of aid and restricts arms sales to Sri Lanka in the light of its human rights record and the recent expulsion of the British High Commissioner.

4 July: Britain and China agreed on arrangements for a new airport in Hong Kong.

5 July: Central Television's *Cambodia: The Betrayal*, accuses the government of trying to suppress details of covert training for the allies of the Khmer Rouge in Cambodia.

8 July: Douglas Hurd begins a three day visit to South Africa.

12 July: Kurdish demonstrators storm the Turkish embassy in London.

15-17 July: G7 summit in London.

15 July: G7 agree on measures to strengthen the UN and increase its powers to interfere in the internal affairs of sovereign states.

16–17 July: Mikhail Gorbachev in London for a meeting with G7.

17 July: G7 offers a limited aid package to President Gorbachev.

22 July: Douglas Hurd begins a two day visit to Turkey.

23 July: President Mubarak of Egypt begins a four day state visit to Britain.

31 July: Norman Lamont begins a four day visit to advise the Soviet Union on the transformation of its economy.

5 Aug: Government orders the deportation of Krishna Kumar, a member of the central committee of the Tamil Tigers.

8 Aug: John McCarthy released after being held hostage in Lebanon for more than five years.

14 Aug: Rapid response plans for disaster relief are announced.

19 Aug: Government suspends aid to the USSR in the light of the hardliners' coup against President Gorbachev.

22 Aug: Review of G7 aid to the USSR instigated by John Major in his role as current G7 chairman.

EC aid to USSR unfrozen as coup there fails.

27 Aug: John Major begins a three day visit to the USA.

EC formally recognizes the independence of the Baltic states.

31 Aug: John Major visits Moscow to see Boris Yeltsin, the President of the Russian Republic, and President Gorbachev on a fact-finding mission for G7.

29 Aug: UK/US pledge to send economic experts to USSR to try and stem its economic chaos.

31 Aug: Douglas Hogg, Minister of State at the Foreign Office, visits Lithuania.

2 Sept: John Major begins a two day visit to Peking.

3 Sep: Lord Carrington is to chair an EC arranged peace conference on Yugoslavia.

John Major criticizes the human rights record in China in a speech in Peking.

4 Sep: John Major visits Hong Kong.

11 Sep: Douglas Hurd visits Kenya. During his visit he indicates British sympathy with the movement for multi-party democracy there.

13 Sep: Douglas Hurd visits Zimbabwe.

15 Sep: United Democrats of Hong Kong win a landslide victory in the first elections for the 18 of the 60 seats on the colony's legislative council which are directly elected.

24 Sept: The French Premier, Edith Cresson, visits London for talks.

Jackie Mann released after more than two and a half years as a hostage in Lebanon.

Eduardo dos Santos, President of Angola, visits London.

27 Sept: Anglo-Argentine joint commission to study oil exploration round the Falklands is set up.

16-19 Oct: Commonwealth Heads of Government meeting in Harare, Zimbabwe.

16 Oct: The Prime Minister offers to train ANC supporters in Britain for roles in a future non-racial civil service in South Africa.

17 Oct: Britain to write off £500 million of debts from third world countries.

21 Oct: Britain and Vietnam sign an agreement on the forcible repatriation of Vietnamese refugees from Hong Kong.

28 Oct: EC threatens trade sanctions against any Yugoslav republic not accepting the EC peace plan by 5 November.

14 Nov: Two Libyan agents named as responsible for the Lockerbie bombing of December 1988.

18 Nov: Terry Waite is released after nearly five years as a hostage in the Lebanon.

Britain, France and Italy offer to send warships into Yugoslav waters to protect 'humanitarian corridors' leading to cities under seige in the civil war between Serbia and Croatia.

Britain asks Libya to extradite two men charged with responsibility for the 1988 bombing of a PanAm jet over the Scottish town of Lockerbie.

23 Nov: Iraq frees Ian Richter (who returned to Britain two days later) in exchange for the unfreezing of £70 million of Iraqi assets.

28 Nov: EC signs charter saying future development aid should depend on respect for democracy and human rights and try to encourage a shift from defence to social spending.

2 Dec: Dalai Lama meets John Major in London.

Douglas Hogg, Minister of State at the Foreign Office, begins a visit to Tunisia and Egypt.

16 Dec: German pressure for the recognition of Croatia results in the EC setting a timetable and conditions by which the former Yugoslav republic can be recognized as independent.

Defence Policy

JOHN BAYLIS

During the past year those responsible for the formulation of British defence policy have wrestled with the implications and consequences of three major events: the war in the Gulf; the end of the cold war; and the movement towards greater political and economic integration in Europe. All three have created uncertainties and contributed to an era of transition which has produced considerable problems of adjustment for defence planners. As a result British defence policy in 1991 was controversial and not always wholly coherent.

The Gulf War

In January and February the main focus of British defence policy centred on the military campaign to liberate Kuwait from Saddam Hussein's occupying forces. For the first time since the Korean war Britain found herself part of a major multinational force operating under the auspices of the United Nations and commanded by an American general. On this occasion, however, the victory was achieved much more quickly and at a significantly lower cost than in the early 1950s. Following an air campaign which lasted from 17 January until 24 February a brief ground war was fought from 24 to 28 February resulting in the large scale destruction of Iraqi forces and Saddam Hussein's acceptance of all of the UN resolutions.

For Britain the war reflected some of the consistent themes which have characterized British defence policy over the past forty years. Like many other conflicts fought during the post Second World War era the Gulf war of 1991 reflected the British government's determination to play its role in what it regarded as a grave threat to international stability. A notable feature of government statements in Britain and the United States during the war was the comparison with the 1930s. The British Prime Minister, Mr Major, and the US President, Mr Bush, emphasized their belief that the lessons of appeasement indicated that aggressors had to be confronted if the fabric of international order was to be preserved. Saddam Hussein, like Stalin and Nasser before him, was compared to Hitler. In 1948 with the Berlin blockade and in 1950 with the Korean war it was Stalin who was regarded as the new dictator challenging the whole basis of international stability. In 1956 Nasser was regarded as the 'Hitler of the Nile'. In 1991, with the cold war over,

Saddam Hussein's invasion of Kuwait was regarded as the first major test of the new international order which was beginning to emerge. For contemporary policy-makers, like their post-war predecessors, the failures of the past had to be avoided. In this respect the Gulf war demonstrated the continuing hold of the 'Munich analogy' on the minds of both John Major and George Bush (and their advisers).

The Gulf war demonstrated continuity in British defence policy in another respect. For policy-makers since the Second World War the 'special relationship' between Britain and the United States, especially in the military field, has been of crucial importance. After the lull in the relationship during the Wilson and Heath governments, Margaret Thatcher had put great store on re-establishing close ties with the United States under Ronald Reagan. With the disappearance of both Reagan and Thatcher from the scene it appeared that the 'special relationship' might once again begin to wither. For President Bush the events of 1989 indicated that Germany would be the key player in the new European order. For Britain, despite the continuing importance of the United States, John Major seemed more inclined to adopt a different, more positive role towards Europe than his predecessor. During the Gulf war, however, the limited German role and the inability of the European Community to coordinate its response, helped to resuscitate close military ties between Britain and the United States. For the British, the Gulf war provided a welcome opportunity (like the Korean war) to demonstrate to the American government and people that Britain was a reliable and supportive ally during times of international crisis.

There was also one further way in which the Gulf conflict reflected a consistent theme in British defence policy. Operation Granby, Britain's contribution to Operation Desert Storm, involved the deployment to the Middle East of 45,000 men and women from the three services. During the conflict Britain played an important role in each of the key facets of the campaign – in the air, at sea and on the ground. As a result in the white paper published after the war the government was able to claim: 'Our decision to maintain balanced forces, able to meet the unexpected with a skilful and effective response has been completely justified'. The concept of balanced forces has been at the heart of British defence policy since 1945 and in the debate which was to follow the Gulf war the government continued to argue that one of the most important lessons of the conflict was that such balanced forces would be necessary in the uncertain period ahead.

Options for Change

Introducing his white paper on the defence estimates before the House of Commons on 9 July, the Secretary of State for Defence, Tom King, argued that the past year had 'been the most momentous for defence since the Second World War'.[1] The end of the cold war, the collapse of the Warsaw Pact and the Conventional Forces in Europe (CFE) agreement, meant that the major preoccupation of defence policy since the Second World War (the Soviet threat) was now of increasingly less significance. The major concern of the white paper therefore was with the impact of the major structural changes taking place in international politics. The fact that Britain had recently fought a highly successful campaign as part of a multinational alliance to recover Kuwait from Iraqi occupation appeared to have little significance for the future of defence policy. The general direction of the government's *Options for Change* proposals announced in 1990 were set to continue. The Army was to be reduced by 4,000 more troops to 116,000, the Navy by 5,000 more to 55,000 and the RAF was to be reduced to 75,000.[2] In line with previous announcements the Navy was to have a planned force of 40 destroyers and frigates and 16 nuclear and conventionally-powered submarines. The key determinant, however, remained the fundamental changes in the nature of East-West relations and the fact, according to the Defence Secretary, that the warning time for an attack on the West was now two years rather than two days.[3]

According to the white paper defence spending would be reduced by 6 per cent in real terms by 1993–94 following the trend set from 1986 onwards. Although Britain was continuing to spend more as a percentage of gross domestic product on defence than any of its western allies, with the exception of the United States, Greece and Turkey, the reduction to 4 per cent of GNP represented the lowest level of the post-war era and brought Britain closer to her major European partners.

The emphasis in the white paper was on the restructuring of British forces, particularly the Army, to meet the wider range of possible threats. The most notable changes were to occur in European defence. Despite the reduction of forces from 55,000 to 25,000 on the Continent, it was announced that Britain would play a key role in the new Rapid Reaction Forces (RRF) which were being set up. The multinational Rapid Reaction Corps (RRC) – NATO's most immediate response to the dangers of instability in Eastern Europe and the Balkans – is to be under British command and two of its four (or five) divisions will be British. The other two divisions will be drawn from western and southern European members of the alliance with the possibility of a fifth division provided by the United States. According to the Defence Secretary, the RRC would be 'able to move anywhere in Europe'.[4]

The Rapid Reaction Corps is designed to be part of wider Rapid Reaction Forces which will consist of six multinational corps, two led by Germany, one by Belgium, one by the Netherlands and one by the United States, together with a German/Danish corps to defend the Baltic approaches. A seventh purely German corps will be stationed in the former territory of East Germany. The RRC makes up the eighth corps to be deployed in the central region of Europe.

Criticisms of *Options for Change*

The central role of the British forces in the new NATO formations was welcomed by the Army but widespread concern was increasingly expressed from July onwards both inside the services and outside about the scale of the cuts that had been announced. Unlike the Nott Review of 1981 which had singled out the Navy for the biggest reductions, this time the Army was likely to be hardest hit, with proposed cuts of 40,000, raising deep-seated anxieties and protests about regiments disappearing, and amalgamating, together with redundancies, particularly amongst the officer corps. It was not long before the government was faced with extensive lobbying from the senior backbenchers, regimental associations and apparently even members of the royal family, designed to reverse and limit the reductions which had been announced. Prince Charles who is Colonel in Chief of three regiments scheduled to disappear, was reported in the press to be 'astonished, angry and amazed' by the 'drastic reductions' being planned.[5] It was also reported that the Queen had made clear her dismay and had privately told senior Tories that she was very unhappy 'with the way the defence review had been conducted'.[6] This unprecedented intervention was compounded by criticisms of government policy by the previous Prime Minister, Mrs Thatcher, the Conservative- dominated Commons Select Committee on Defence, and the Chief of the Army's General Staff, General Sir John Chapple.

In the early stages of the coup in the Soviet Union in August, which briefly toppled Mikhail Gorbachev, anxieties about the continuation of the recent improvements in East-West relations were voiced by Margaret Thatcher. This suggested that Britain would have to look again at its defence needs. The former Prime Minister agreed that: 'Those cuts which were going to be implemented, should not be implemented now. This is not the time for weakness . . .'.[7]

At much the same time as Mrs Thatcher's broadside, the government was faced with a very critical report from the Commons Select Committee on Defence which found that the government was in danger of creating a serious imbalance between commitments and capabilities. The report argued that: 'Either sufficient resources must be found or the government must acknowledge its inability to meet all the commitments, and take the political decision to reduce or abandon some of them'.[8] In a stinging indictment of Tom King's management of defence policy the report went on to claim that: 'There remains a yawning gap between shared perceptions of what has changed, and the role of the British armed forces in the new order'.[9] The problem, the report suggested, was that the government had singularly failed to carry out any strategic overview of Britain's defence needs.

The government's embarrassment was made worse by the publication of a letter in October from the Chief of the General Staff, General Sir John Chapple, to Tom King, exposing deep concern within the Army itself about the cuts. In his letter Sir John told the Defence Secretary that 'the most strongly felt and most vehemently expressed view across the whole spectrum of ranks and regiments, is that the Army will not have enough men or units to carry out its peacetime tasks and duties without greater overstretch or unacceptable penalty'.[10] Officers and men, he argued, had lost confidence in the Army Board and ministers. 'The Army thinks we have got it wrong, gone too far and that ministers don't understand.'[11] Sir John went on to argue that the thing that aggravated the Army most was the often expressed comment from the government that *Options for Change* was 'not Treasury-driven'.

'This really strains the confidence and credulity', he argued.[12] Opinion was also sceptical about government promises that the Army would be 'smaller but better'. They saw this, he said, as something of a 'con-trick'.

These views by the Army's top general echoed similar sentiments expressed by two former Chiefs of the Defence Staff during the summer. Lord Bramall, Chief of the Defence Staff from 1982 to 1985, told the House of Lords in June that the Treasury were 'calling the shots' over defence cuts and there was a danger that the armed forces would not be capable of protecting Britain's interests for the remainder of the 1990s.[13] Lord Fieldhouse, who succeeded Lord Bramall as CDS expressed similar views. He argued, in the same debate, that the changes would make it exceedingly difficult to maintain 'a broad platform of forces, realistically structured, well equipped and properly supported' which wars since 1945 had shown to be so necessary.[14]

These divisions in the ranks of the Conservative Party and the defence establishment not surprisingly were exploited by opposition parties. Despite the renewed bipartisanship on defence in the run-up to the next election, the Labour Party did allow itself a rare condemnation of Tory defence policy in August. John Reid, a Labour defence spokesman, argued that the government and the Defence Secretary had been humiliated by the findings of the select committee and he argued that the failure to carry out a major strategic review was at the root of the difficulties Mr Major and his colleagues were facing. In his view 'the setting of arbitary spending targets ruled out any prospect of producing a coherent and logical defence policy for the 1990s. What we are left with is a shambolic tangle of short-term cost-cutting measures and face-saving compromises'.[15] This was a view which was shared by the Liberal Democrat spokesman on defence, Menzies Campbell. He accused the defence ministry of being 'led by the nose by the Treasury'. *Options for Change*, he argued, was 'rapidly turning into a political disaster with no proper military logic behind it'.[16]

A more objective, but no less damaging, critique came from Lawrence Freedman, the Professor of War Studies at King's College, London. In an article in *The Independent* in July he argued that the central problem with government defence policy was that there was no clear conception of the threat to British security or how British forces were likely to be deployed in future. In his view *Options for Change* was

... geared only to the transition from the cold war to whatever may succeed it. The flaw is that it sets in motion a dramatic restructuring of Britain's armed forces without attempting to describe the circumstances in which they will be most likely to operate. The review will be properly complete only when this restructuring has been related to the emerging international system.[17]

This criticism that British defence planners have put the cart before the horse by initiating the restructuring of the armed forces before completing an overall

reassessment of their tasks in the changed international circumstances is one which
was repeated by a number of commentators during the year.

The Government's Reply to its Critics

Faced with these wide-ranging and embarrassing criticisms the government's
response was in general at least to stand firm. Faced with Mrs Thatcher's plea for
a pause in the implementation of the reductions in August neither the Defence
Secretary nor the Prime Minister was prepared to give ground. Tom King rejected
the idea that the defence cuts depended on Mr Gorbachev's survival: 'we did it',
he argued, 'on the basis of the massive strategic changes that are taking place in
the Soviet Union and the disappearance of the Warsaw Pact'.[18] The Prime Minister
echoed the point that, even if the coup succeeded, the changes which had taken
place already were so momentous that the cuts should go ahead. There was no
reason, he argued to take a fresh look at *Options for Change*. Defending the
government's defence policy, John Major pointed out that:

The prospects of events in the Soviet Union were amongst those matters that were
considered. Changes in our defence posture were made as a result of changing circumstances,
changing needs, changing capacity and changing nature of weaponry, so there were a whole
series of other reasons for making the changes that were in hand.[19]

The subsequent failure of the coup in the Soviet Union and the return of Mikhail
Gorbachev to power was seen by the government as a further reinforcement of its
decision not to suspend the changes announced in July.

Faced with the persistence of criticisms amongst Conservatives, however, the
Defence Secretary was prepared to compromise on one of the most controversial
of his cuts. Initially he intended to cut the number of infantry battalions from 55 to
36. Many of his critics argued that at least 41 would be needed to allow the Army
to rotate its forces in Northern Ireland and perform its wide range of commitments
in Europe and elsewhere. In July, Tom King announced that he had decided to
retain 38 battalions, including two Gurkha battalions, and to make more use of the
three Marine Commandos (equivalent in strength to infantry battalions) in Northern
Ireland.[20]

Despite this modification of policy the Defence Secretary continued to defend
his reforms robustly against continuing opposition within his party. In the highly
charged atmosphere of the defence debate in the House of Commons in October
Tom King and Alan Clark, the defence procurement minister, managed to head-off
a Tory back-bench revolt by arguing that even after the reforms were implemented
Britain would still retain the capability to fight a Falklands or Gulf-style operation
in the future if the need should arise. Concern about the proposed reductions,
however, were to rumble on within the Conservative Party for the rest of the year.

NATO, the WEU and the Future of European Defence

While the government was defending its policies against domestic critics another argument emerged about the focus of European defence in the new post-cold war era. As the year wore on these debates became increasingly embroiled in the wider discussions about political union in Europe which culminated in the Maastricht summit in December.

Ever since the cold war ended European governments had debated the future structure of European security and the responsibilities of the existing institutions. During 1991 this debate intensified as a result of the failure of the European Community to pull together effectively during the Gulf conflict and its failure (together with the CSCE) to resolve the civil war in Yugoslavia. The repercussions of those events reinforced two contradictory tendencies already evident in the debate about the future of European security.

On the one hand there were those who pointed to the inadequacies of the EC in dealing with these matters as evidence that the European Community was not a suitable organization to act as the central focus of the new structure of European defence which was beginning to evolve. Much the same was true of the CSCE, it was argued. Instead the key institution, at least for the time being, had to be NATO. The North Atlantic Treaty was tried and tested and had the virtue of tying the United States firmly into European security. This view tended to be associated with the British position.

The other school of thought, more closely associated with France and Germany, was that the failure of the EC in the Gulf war and the Yugoslav crisis demonstrated, not the inherent weakness of the organization as such, but the pressing need to improve the ability of the Community to deal with defence and security matters. This could best be done as part of the process of economic and political union which was gathering pace.

The different perspectives were highlighted in October when two plans were unveiled both designed, in their different ways, to chart the way forward on European defence. In early October an Anglo-Italian plan was launched which stressed the primacy of NATO and suggested that the WEU should act as a bridge between the alliance and the European Community. The plan, however, moved a little way towards the views of Paris and Bonn by accepting the long-term perspective of a defence role for the European Community.

This attempt by the British and Italian governments to gain the high ground in the debate was short-lived. Within two weeks a rather different Franco-German plan was produced which sought to absorb the WEU into the EC, to establish 'joint action' in key foreign policy fields, and expand the existing Franco-German joint Army Brigade into a larger Army Corps as a nucleus for a European defence force.[21]

The British reaction to this initiative was to describe the proposal as 'useless and dangerous'.[22] In particular there was concern that such a European defence pillar would duplicate and supplant, rather than complement the responsibilities of the Atlantic Alliance. Despite French and German denials that NATO would be undermined if the Franco-German plan was accepted British officials pointed to a statement by President Mitterrand which they argued highlighted the real French intention of establishing an alternative to the Atlantic alliance. At the end of October the French President declared that 'the new proposals will gradually take on greater significance because we cannot imagine that the United States will always be in the front-line ready to take over from Europeans in their own defence'.[23] Similar anxieties to those of the British about the Franco-German proposals were expressed in NATO headquarters and in the United States, even though some other European States, including Spain, favoured the move towards greater integration in the defence field.

The NATO Summit

The question of the new European defence identity figured prominently at the NATO summit meeting held in Rome from 7–8 November. The British position, stressing the continuing primacy of NATO was strongly supported by President Bush. In a blunt warning to his allies the President challenged them on the future of an American military presence in Europe. 'If you have something else in mind' he argued, 'if you want to go your own way, if you don't need us any longer, say so now.'[24] The warning was aimed particularly at President Mitterrand and his ideas of establishing a European defence identity with only tenuous links with NATO. As such it led to a ringing endorsement from the allies of the continuing importance of the alliance and the American role within it. For the French President, however, although NATO remained 'a good alliance' it should not be regarded as a sacred or 'holy alliance'.[25] The issue of the form a new European identity should take remained unresolved. It was left to the Maastricht EC summit in December to try to resolve the difficulties. The outcome of Maastricht represented something of a compromise between the French and British position which left the issue in a somewhat ambiguous state. According to the agreement the European Union would be able to 'request the WEU, which is an integral part of the European Union to elaborate and implement decisions and actions of the Union which have defence implications'. The French interpreted this as a victory for their view that the WEU would be subordinate to the 12 EC states which would allow them to pursue a common defence policy. The British, however, claimed that their view had prevailed because the WEU was to remain relatively autonomous and the treaty emphasized that European defence cooperation would be compatible with the NATO alliance. How exactly these new arrangements were to work in practice, however, remained unclear.

Progress was achieved, however, with the adoption of a new strategic concept to replace MC 14/3, the 'flexible response' Strategy, which had been in force since 1967. The new concept, designed to act as a blueprint for the alliance in the post-cold war world, acknowledged the fundamental changes which had taken place in Europe since 1989 and indicated the need for a wider, more political, definition of security. The risks to allied security were now seen as arising less from calculated aggression against allied territory, than from 'the serious economic, social and political difficulties, including ethnic rivalries and territorial disputes, which are faced by many countries in central and eastern Europe'.[26] In political terms this meant an enhanced role for NATO in managing a wide range of unspecified military and political crises which might occur. In military terms it meant that there was to be significantly reduced reliance on nuclear weapons (which would still nevertheless have a role) and, confirming earlier announcements, a need to prepare military forces for 'diverse and multi-directional risks', 'with fewer numbers of mobile multinational troops'.[27]

It was significant that, despite the continuing difficulties over European defence, the new strategic concept was accepted by all 16 NATO states, including France. This new consensus appeared to be the result of the vagueness and flexibility of the new concept. General Sir Brian Kenny, one of NATO's two Deputy Supreme Commanders, described it as 'a strategy for all seasons'.[28] As such there was no significant difference between the new NATO strategy and the Gaullist doctrine of *tous azimiths* in which defence was directed 'towards all points of the compass'.

For Britain the new strategy was welcome because it finally provided the doctrinal context for the multinational rapid reaction forces in which Britain is to play a leading role. Up until the Rome summit Britain had been engaged in a restructuring of her armed forces without any clear public reference to national or allied tactical and strategic planning. Although the details of the new strategic concept remained classified it was a little clearer after the summit how Britain's armed forces would fit in to alliance strategy as a whole.

Conclusion

The November summit, however, left a large number of issues still unresolved. In particular it was not clear where the alliance thought the major threats to European security might come from in the future. Was it to come from the still powerful Soviet armed forces? Was it to come from the spill-over effects of the disintegration of the Soviet Union, including the prospects of nuclear-armed independent republics? Was it to come from instability in eastern and southern Europe? Or was it to come from the Mediterranean and north Africa? How these threats impinged on European security and how NATO might respond remained unclear.

Nor was it clear exactly how NATO might develop in a political direction to deal with the broader spectrum of threats to security which existed in the more ambiguous post-cold war environment. How NATO might relate to the countries of what used to be Eastern Europe had only been partly resolved by the decision to set up a forum to discuss security issues with Poland, Czechoslovakia and Hungary. The medium and longer-term relationship with these ex-Warsaw Pact states was still uncertain. How the Soviet Union, or what remained of it, might fit into the 'variable geometry' of the emerging European security architective also remained a difficult problem for the future.

For Britain, however, by the end of the year, the issue which confused the future of defence policy most was the continuing disagreement over the relationship between NATO and the proposals for a European defence pillar. The resolution of this dispute was crucial for the future of British foreign and defence policy. *Options for Change* had emphasized the traditional balance of Britain's armed forces, albeit at lower levels. The new NATO strategic concept allowed Britain to avoid a fundamental review of defence by providing a framework for broadly based forces capable of high-intensity warfare on land, sea and air in defence of alliance interests. Significantly, it also provided a justification for retaining the kind of armed forces which allow independent military operations in defence of Britain's national interests.

The pressure for a more autonomous European security plan, however, challenged the whole basis of this approach on which British defence planning had been based since 1945. Service chiefs feared that the Franco-German proposals would push Britain into what one official described as an 'ill-thought out, niche-player role'.[29] If these plans were accepted it was believed that Britain would be forced to accept a division of labour in which European states concentrated on those areas of traditional expertise: in Britain's case naval warfare. Such an unbalancing of military capabilities would in turn lead to the loss of independence in the broader field of foreign policy. Britain would no longer be able to undertake operations like the Falkland campaign or indeed the Gulf conflict independently of her European allies. In this sense the future of British defence policy remained inextricably interwoven with the broader debate about European political and economic union.

Notes

1 *Statement on the Defence Estimates: Britain's Defence for the 1990s*, Vol 1, Cmnd. 1559-1, (London HMSO), p.5.
2 'Cuts leave UK with smallest Army since 1830', *The Independent*, 24 July 1991.
3 *The Independent*, 25 July 1991.
4 See *Statement on the Defence Estimates, op. cit.*, pp. 40–50.
5 'Royal Family and generals unite to fight army cuts', *The Sunday Times*, 13 October 1991.
6 *Ibid.*
7 *The Independent*, 20 August 1991.
8 *Defence Committee 11th Report, Statement on the defence estimates, 1991*, HoC paper 394, HMSO, 1991.
9 *Ibid.*
10 *The Sunday Times*, 13 October 1991.
11 *Ibid.*
12 *Ibid.*
13 *The Independent*, 13 June 1991.
14 *Ibid.*
15 *The Independent*, 17 August 1991.
16 *Ibid.*
17 'Whom are we defending, and against what', *The Independent*, 10 July 1991.

18 'Thatcher call on defence rejected', *The Independent*, 20 August 1991.

19 *Ibid.*

20 Former members of the Army, however, continued to argue that a force of 116,000 would not be enough. See the letter from General Sir Martin Farndale, former C in C BAOR to *The Times*, 18 October 1991.

21 *The Times*, 17 October 1991

22 *The Independent*, 17 October 1991

23 *The Guardian*, 24 October 1991

24 *The Daily Telegraph*, 8 November 1991

25 *Ibid.*

26 *Ibid.*

27 *Ibid.*

28 *The Guardian*, 4 November 1991.

29 *The Sunday Telegraph*, 3 November 1991.

Chronology

2 Jan: Royal Navy asks 2,500 reservists to volunteer for duty during the Gulf crisis.

14 Jan: Nineteen women on *HMS Brilliant* become the first women in the Royal Navy to sail to war.

16 Jan: National Audit Office, *Ministry of Defence: Fraud and Irregularities at Defence Establishments*, HMSO, finds many MoD establishments have failed to take adequate anti-fraud measures.

24 Jan: Announcement that women are to be allowed to be pilots in Fleet Air Arm.

7 Feb: National Audit Office, *Ministry of Defence: Initiatives in Defence Procurement*, HMSO, backs further savings measures in the Ministry of Defence including modifications to the profit formula which gives non-competitive contractors a guaranteed profit level.

20 Feb: Intention to close the Rosyth naval base at Fife in Scotland is leaked.

26 Feb: Warsaw Pact formally dissolved.

1 Mar: National Audit Office estimates that Britain lost the equivalent of £400 million in the division of the rewards of the British/German/Italian Tornado jet fighter programme.
Defence Select Committee publishes a critical report on the procurement of the army's new multiple rocket launcher.

21 Mar: Defence Select Committee calls for a review of the *Options for Change* proposals to reduce the surface fleet to about 40 ships by 1995 in the light of the Gulf War.

8 May: Public Accounts Committee, *1989 Statement on Major Defence Projects*, HMSO, criticizes delays and cost overruns on defence projects. It urges greater use of fixed-price contracts and the withholding of payments until targets are achieved.

10 May: Three RAF tornado squadrons to be disbanded.

17 May: USAF to leave RAF Bentwaters and RAF Woodbridge in Suffolk.

28 May: British troops to lead the new NATO rapid reaction corps.

6 June: Extension of the submarine notification scheme off the west coast of Scotland announced following the Antares inquiry.

10 June: Julian Brazier MP, *Sharpening the Sword*, Bow Group, suggests improvements in the quality of the Territorial Army are necessary as the regular army shrinks, which

could be achieved by the creation of TA divisions, a role in disaster relief and reserve units on the US model.

12 June: Defence Select Committee criticizes the proposed cuts in the RAF, arguing they are motivated by concern about resources more than by considerations of future security needs.

17 June: Death penalty restored to military legislation for servicemen assisting the enemy or mutinying in wartime by an amendment to the Armed Forces Bill, wiping out a government defeat on the same issue in April.

21 June: Announcement that the Vickers Challenger II will be the army's new main battle tank.

25 June: Plans to develop a new series of submarines scrapped in favour of updating existing designs.

27 June: Tenders for three Type 23 frigates and a new anti-air warfare frigate are invited but plans for seven minehunters and the new SSN-20 nuclear powered attack submarine are shelved.
Defence Select Committee *Royal Navy Submarines* HMSO, argues for the production of the SSN-20 and the retention of six diesel-electric submarines and criticizes government policy towards submarines as 'bizarre'.

1 July: Warsaw Pact dissolved.

2 July: RAF regiment to be cut by one-seventh.

4 July: Ministry of Defence announces plans to cut 35,000 civilian jobs.

9 July: The defence white paper, *British Defence in the 90s*, HMSO, outlines plans to axe 19 battalions, reducing the army to 36.

10 July: Defence Select Committee, *The Progress of the Trident Programme*, HMSO, reports good progress but expresses concern at the risk of accidents.
Revised civil defence guidelines and cuts in spending announced.

11 July: Announcement that the army is to procure a new anti-tank helicopter overseas by the end of the decade.

16 July: Rosyth naval base reprieved.

23 July: Announcement in the white paper *The British Army in the 90s*, HMSO, that the army is to be cut to 36 UK and two Gurkha battalions, cutting manpower from 156,000 to 116,000. The Territorial Army is cut from 75,000 to 60–65,000. A new army structure will begin in 1995 and a further Gurkha battalion will go with withdrawal from Hong Kong in 1997. The service corps and Royal Artillery are also to be reduced. The Royal Army Ordnance Corps, Royal Corps of Transport, Pioneer Corps and Army Catering Corps are to merge, as are many infantry and cavalry regiments. Cuts in the Royal Navy and the RAF are also announced.

24 July: Tom King says that the warning time for an attack on the west has increased from two days to two years.

31 July: Public Accounts Committee, *Ministry of Defence: Nuclear Research and Support Services*, HMSO, accuses the Atomic Weapons Establishment of cost-inefficiency and weak management.

2 Aug: Defence Select Committee, *Procurement of Upholder Class Submarines*, HMSO, reports on major faults in this, the first new class of submarines to be developed for 30 years.

8 Aug: Defence Select Committee, *Preliminary Lessons of Operation Granby*, HMSO, draws attention to how stretched British capabilities were during the Gulf war and

argues that this shows that the UK can no longer manage out of area operations without allied support.

National Audit Office report criticizes poor planning of computer projects at the Ministry of Defence and urges it to improve planning and to organize and manage projects better.

16 Aug: Defence Select Committee, *Statement on the Defence Estimates*, HMSO, criticizes the failure to conduct overall review of defence policy and to produce any coherent strategic overview of defence needs and concludes that either more must be spent or defence commitments must be abandoned.

2 Sept: IBM appointed prime contractor on the £1.5 billion RN contract for 44 EH-101 Merlin anti-submarine helicopters.

9 Sept: CND launches appeal in face of considerable financial difficulties.

11 Sept: Gunner Vic Williams, who refused to fight in the Gulf war, is convicted of desertion and gaoled for 14 months and dismissed from the army with disgrace by a court martial.

1 Oct: UK withdraws from joint venture with France and Germany to develop anti-tank weapons.

15 Oct: Safety review of Britain's nuclear stockpile announced.

16 Oct: Franco-German plans for European defence published and rejected by the UK as involving duplication of NATO.

Public Accounts Committee, *Fraud and Irregularities at Defence Establishments*, HMSO, complains that significantly less than half the people found guilty of fraud or theft from the MoD have been dismissed or even disciplined.

22 Oct: Inquiry into the Antares criticizes HMS Trenchant for ignoring RN drill and procedure and inadequate command procedures. The government also increases the distance submerged vessels must keep from fishing from 2,000 to 3,000 yards.

2 Dec: Anglo-French project to develop a new naval air-defence frigate for the next century announced.

16 Dec: Stella Rimington is to become head of MI5 in February in place of Sir Patrick Walker.

Economic Policy and Macro-Economic Developments

ALAN DAVIES

Nineteen ninety-one was a year of deep recession, the 2 per cent decline in output being the second sharpest one-year fall since the war. The extent of the recession can be explained by the painful adjustment undertaken by the personal and corporate sectors following the substantial accumulation of debt in the late 1980s. As inflation declined rapidly during the year, the government sought to reduce interest rates in order to revive the flagging economy. Despite the possible constraints imposed by sterling's position within the Exchange Rate Mechanism (ERM), interest rates fell from 14 per cent to 10.5 per cent during the year; but it remained unclear whether this would prove sufficient to restore consumer confidence in particular. Moreover, the year ended with further interest rate reductions looking unlikely following a rise in German interest rates which suggested that moving out of recession would be a slow and painful process.

Recession

The UK entered 1991 firmly in the grip of recession. However, at the time, its severity and likely duration were still in doubt. The Treasury's forecasts published the previous November acknowledged that the economy had experienced a technical recession, in that output appeared to have actually declined in the second half of 1990; but growth was expected to resume early in 1991, with GDP forecast to increase by 2 per cent during the course of the year, or 0.5 per cent in year-average terms. Nor was the Treasury view of a relatively mild, short-lived recession atypical. The regular survey of independent forecasters at the turn of the year indicated a similar profile for economic activity. In the event, the recession was to prove far more severe than the mainstream view. The unexpected severity of the recession is emphasized by the scale of the rise in unemployment. At the start of the year, unemployment was around 1.8 million and consensus forecasts envisaged a rise during 1991 to around 2 million. The outcome was a rise to almost 2.6 million by the end of 1991, with no early expectation of the peak being reached.

Why did economic forecasters fail to predict the extent of the downturn? There is always one major problem which confronts forecasters; which is that statistics on the performance of the economy are always produced considerably in arrears and are subject to frequent, and often substantial, revision. Thus, not until late in February were preliminary figures released for the change in output in the fourth quarter of 1990. This was the first clear confirmation that the economy had entered recession in the second half of 1990. Nonetheless, the scale of the forecasting errors in 1991 cannot be explained by the delays in publishing information on the state of the economy. A second source of major uncertainty surrounding economic developments at the start of 1991, was, of course, the situation in the Gulf. A specific economic worry concerned oil prices which had soared to over $30 per barrel in the latter months of 1990 and had contributed to the rise in UK inflation to almost 11 per cent. More generally the likely ramifications of all-out war cast a dark shadow over the international economy, with business and consumer confidence plummeting. However, the relatively short-lived and successful outcome to the Gulf war and the rapid fall in oil prices suggests that the overall effect on economic activity in 1991 was relatively modest.

What was undoubtedly at the heart of the severe recession was the aftermath of the rapid build up of debt during the late 1980s. In the case of the personal sector, borrowing had increased by over 20 per cent in 1988 alone. The borrowing boom had been fuelled by relatively low interest rates and sharply rising real incomes (which together facilitated the ability of individuals to service much larger debt levels). At the same time, substantial increases in house prices were both a result of the borrowing upsurge and also enhanced it by raising individual wealth. This in turn reduced the perceived need to save, and the personal sector's rate of saving plummeted to 5 per cent, a 20 year low. All of this might, at an early stage, have been expected to end in tears. But interpretation of these apparent financial excesses was complicated by the fact that the 1980s were a period of financial deregulation and of major changes in the housing market. Thus, the free availability of credit and mortgages would have been expected to result in a substantial increase in debt following years of rationing, and this financial adjustment was not necessarily a source of concern. At the same time, the rapid rise in home ownership meant that apparently disturbing record high levels of debt in relation to income had to take into account the fact that much of the debt build up represented mortgages by new home owners which were replacing rental commitments. This meant that there was understandable difficulty in predicting the scale of financial adjustment that the personal sector would undertake once interest rates were raised to 15 per cent.

We now know that the adjustment was dramatic. Borrowing slowed sharply and the saving ratio recovered rapidly to around 11 per cent. The result was recession in the housing market, with house prices falling by 20 per cent or so in parts of the country. At the same time consumer spending was sharply reduced, registering an outright decline of some 1 per cent for 1991 as a whole. For many individuals, financial adjustment involved the painful experience of having their homes repossessed; for 1991 as a whole repossessions are likely to total a record 80,000.

If consumer retrenchment precipitated the recession, it was the financial vulnerability of the company sector to a downturn in demand which reinforced it.

The corporate sector, too, substantially raised its borrowing in the late 1980s and was suddenly caught in the pincer of low turnover and rising costs (including interest rates). Companies reduced stocks, slashed investment and shed labour in order to limit their borrowing and reduce debt servicing costs. However, for many companies financial adjustment was not possible to ensure survival and, even if the 1991 recession was not as severe in terms of output loss compared with the early 1980s, the number of company failures rose to unprecedented levels. The scale of the problem was due to the record number of new businesses that had been set up in the heady days of the late 1980s. New businesses are always vulnerable in their first few years of operation and this was especially the case given the scale of borrowing which had been undertaken when interest rates were comparatively low.

The Policy Response

Although retail price inflation was still running above 10 per cent in the autumn of 1990, the authorities cut interest rates by 1 per cent when sterling joined the ERM of the European Monetary System (EMS) in October 1990. This suggested that the economic downturn was already sufficiently entrenched to be consistent with lower inflation and an easing of monetary policy. As the recession gathered force, lower interest rates were deemed to be the necessary response. However, lower rates were now subject to the overriding need to keep sterling within its ERM limits. For a while, it appeared that domestic and external needs would be seriously at odds, for shortly after ERM membership sterling fell to the bottom of the system. In part, this seemed to be because the markets were already discounting a substantial fall in UK interest rates; but it also reflected the need for sterling to establish its ERM credentials and specifically for devaluation to be ruled out as a policy option. The latter was assisted not just by official statements but also by a lack of widespread criticism that sterling had joined the ERM at too high a rate, a view which was reinforced by a relatively robust export performance in Europe, notably to the booming German economy.

By February, the authorities felt sufficiently confident to begin edging interest rates down and seven successive 0.5 per cent interest rate reductions were achieved by September without any serious problem for the exchange rate. This was even more remarkable given that the pressure of German interest rates had been upwards. As a result by the time that sterling celebrated its first full year of ERM membership, UK interest rates of 10.5 per cent were just 1 per cent above German rates, an unusually low differential. At this stage, at least, it was possible to say that our ERM experience had been a success, facilitating a lower level of interest rates than might otherwise have been possible without experiencing a sharp decline in the exchange rate. (A minority view still favoured a much more aggressive approach of substantial cuts in interest rates accompanied by a sterling devaluation).

By the time of the budget in March, the Treasury's forecasts were acknowledging the severity of the economic downturn. However, as in previous years, the Chancellor reiterated the government's commitment to a medium-term framework for the conduct of fiscal policy. Broadly speaking, this envisages a balanced budget over the medium term and eschews the use of fiscal policy for short-term demand management. However, the medium-term approach does imply that government borrowing will rise in recessions and fall in upswings. The severity of the recession meant that, after several years of budget surplus, the government was prepared to tolerate a return to borrowing of some £8 billion in 1991–92 and around £12 billion in 1992–93. Despite this large saving in government finances, it could be argued that they did not allow sufficiently for the extra costs and loss of revenues associated with the recession. In any event, the overall fiscal changes were broadly neutral in their impact. Instead the most dramatic feature of the budget measures was the decision to cut poll tax bills by £140 in 1991–92, a measure to be financed by a rise in VAT from 15 per cent to 17.5 per cent.

Inflation

The introduction of the poll tax in 1990 had wrought havoc with the measurement of retail price inflation rate, and the switch from poll tax to VAT in 1991 caused further complications in assessing accurately the rate of inflation. Nevertheless, by the spring, it was clear that inflation was on a sharply declining trend. The 'headline' RPI inflation rate was down to 6.4 per cent in April compared with its peak of almost 11 per cent the previous autumn. The downturn continued through the rest of the year to around 4.5 per cent in the fourth quarter. This was a downturn which actually exceeded the forecasts made at the beginning of the year. The extent of the decline in the headline RPI was in part due to reductions in mortgage interest rates which are included in the RPI. This means that the 'underlying' inflation rate is somewhat distorted by changes in interest rates, exaggerating the rate of inflation when interest rates are rising; and the converse. However, even excluding mortgage payments, the inflation downturn was impressive – from 8.5 per cent at the start of the year to around 5.5 per cent by the end of 1991. Moreover, there was mounting evidence that the reduction in inflation was soundly based and could be held at the lower levels delivered by the recession. Initially, lower inflation was primarily associated with the weakness of economic activity which prevented manufacturers from fully passing on cost increases in final prices. However, during the course of the year, cost pressures abated sharply. In particular, wage settlements in manufacturing fell to around 5 per cent by the end of 1991 compared with almost 9 per cent a year earlier. It is also worth noting that, despite the sharp decline in output, the extent of the shakeout in the labour market meant that productivity was rising during 1991, which suggested that the underlying improvement in productivity growth experienced during the 1980s was still evident.

Overall, we may say that 1991 saw Britain's inflation rate converge rapidly towards those of its ERM partners, which was a vital requirement if Britain was not to lose competitiveness. Not that ERM membership can be held to have played much, if any, of a part in the disinflationary process. Rather, it was the depth of the recession in general and the rise in unemployment in particular which had brought inflation down. A critical issue will be whether low inflation can be sustained during the upturn at anything other than high levels of unemployment; or whether ERM membership will influence restraint in pay bargaining. The issue is particularly relevant given that low inflation is one of the key convergence criteria agreed at the Maastricht summit on economic and monetary union (EMU). At the time, Britain actually met the inflation criteria and was close to German levels. However, Germany's 4 per cent inflation rate reflected a peak following an unprecedented economic boom. Britain's low inflation rate followed a deep recession. German inflation will surely decelerate, and just how the UK will fare, and at what cost, will be a critical issue during the economic upswing.

Recovery

The performance of UK inflation during the economic upturn begs the question of when recovery will actually get under way. This question of when the recession would end and the nature of the upturn dominated economic debate during 1991.

At the time of the Budget, the Chancellor acknowledged the extent of the fall in output; and the Treasury forecasts pointed to a 2 per cent decline in GDP in 1991 compared with the 0.5 per cent rise envisaged the previous autumn. However, the year-on-year figures concealed a relatively encouraging profile. The Chancellor held that the fall in output was coming to an end and that there were 'good reasons to expect that the recovery will begin around the middle of this year, although initially it may be slow'.

The precipitate decline in output did, indeed, come to an end during the summer months. However, during the second half of the year the frequent cliché used to describe the economy was 'bumping along the bottom'. Hopes were pinned on a consumer led recovery. This was because investment always lags the economic cycle and the international background was distinctly unfavourable for export led growth. The US economy was not emerging from recession with any rigour and towards the end of the year seemed more likely to turn down again. At the same time, the strength of the German and Japanese economies was rapidly running out of steam. The prospect of a resumption of consumer spending rested on the substantial decline in interest rates and the lower inflation rate which meant that pay increases were outpacing price increases. However, there were widespread fears that the consumer would continue to retrench. The painful experience of rapid debt accumulation in the 1980s and the bursting of the house price bubble might suggest that it would take some time before confidence returned, while rising unemployment would also sap consumer confidence. Nonetheless, surveys generally recorded rising consumer confidence during the course of the year; and by the time of the autumn statement the Chancellor still felt able basically to reaffirm the economic forecasts made at the time of the Budget. However, the risks of an even weaker upturn were acknowledged and few were prepared to say that the forecasting errors of previous years were not to be repeated. In short, 1991 was a year of painful adjustment after the excesses of the late 1980s. Whether the adjustment had further to run was the dominant question as the year ended.

Chronology

2 Jan: Sterling strengthens slightly after a statement by Norman Lamont. The overriding influence on interest rates would be the pound's position in the ERM. He ruled out devaluation or an early move to a narrow band.

A *Financial Times* survey of economic forecasters reveals forecasts of negligible GDP growth in 1991, and 2 per cent growth in 1992. Retail price inflation predictions average 5.4 per cent for 1991 and 4.5 per cent for 1992. Unemployment is forecast to rise sharply.

6 Jan: John Major suggests that the government is 'coming to grips' with economic difficulties and inflation is coming under control. Dismisses suggestions that the recession will be as bad as those of 1930s or early 1980s.

7 Jan: New car registrations showed their sharpest ever fall of 28 per cent in the year to December.

8 Jan: Sterling is replaced by French franc as weakest member of the ERM, closing the day at DM2.92.

14 Jan: Share prices slide across the world and oil prices rise by $3 a barrel as fears of war heighten. The Governor of the Bank of England warns the government not to relax monetary policy before a decisive downturn in inflation is achieved.

15 Jan: The UN Secretary General makes a final plea for Iraq to withdraw from Kuwait just hours before the UN Security Council deadline of 5am GMT on the 16 January.

16 Jan: Allied forces begin massive air attack on strategic military targets in Iraq and Kuwait.

17 Jan: The apparent success of allied air attacks leads to speculation in the markets that Saddam Hussein will be defeated rapidly. Oil prices drop by over $8 a barrel to $21 per barrel, world stock markets record steep rises of 2.5 per cent to 5 per cent and the dollar weakens to close at $1.92 from $1.90 against sterling.

18 Jan: The Bank of England announces the first issue of gilt-edged stock in 28 months to help fund the government's spending programme.

21 Jan: Evidence of a deepening recession emerges, with manufacturing production falling by 2.7 per cent between the three months to November and the previous three months – the worst fall since 1991.

31 Jan: The Bundesbank raises interest rates by 0.5 per cent, further postponing cuts in UK interest rates. The pound loses 2 pfennigs to close at DM2.905

1 Feb: The US Federal Reserve cuts its discount rate by 0.5 per cent to 6 per cent. The pound gains a cent to close at $1.98.

6 Feb: The pound rises to $2 for the first time in a decade as the dollar falls to a post-war low of DM1.45, despite concerted central bank intervention.

7 Feb: John Major says ERM membership is not acting as a straitjacket in preventing interest rate cuts, as sterling would need to be stable regardless of ERM membership.

11 Feb: A rise in manufacturing output price inflation from 5.9 per cent to 6.3 per cent in January, though viewed as an aberration, depresses hopes of rapidly falling inflation and consequently falls in interest rates.

13 Feb: Bank base rates are cut from 14 per cent to 13.5 per cent and sterling strengthens slightly to close at DM2.90.

14 Feb: The Council of Mortgage Lenders repossessed 44,000 homes in 1990, the highest level on record and over three times greater than the number repossessed in 1989.

20 Feb: UK recession is confirmed as fourth quarter output-based GDP figures record their second successive fall. Output fell 0.9 per cent on the quarter and by 1.1 per cent on the year, the first year-on-year fall for a decade.

25 Feb: CBI Survey reports that manufacturers' expectations of future output are at their lowest levels since December 1980. A balance of only 6 per cent of companies said they would increase prices in the next four months, the second lowest figure since the survey began in 1975.

26 Feb: CBI manufacturing pay survey finds that settlements for the year to date have slowed to 8.3 per cent from 9 per cent in the fourth quarter, a significant deceleration.

27 Feb: Mortgage rates are cut after the Bank of England cuts interest rates by half a point to 13 per cent.

6 Mar: Stock markets reach record levels following the ending of the Gulf war and investor optimism that interest rates would be lowered and economic recovery accelerated. The FTSE-100 rises to a record level of 2463.7 during the day. The electricity generators privatization offers close heavily oversubscribed.

14 Mar: The Cabinet decides to scrap the poll tax in favour of a combined property value and occupancy tax.

The Budget statement. The Chancellor, Norman Lamont, raises VAT by 2.5 per cent to 17.5 per cent in order to cut £140 off every community charge bill in April. Mortgage relief is limited to the basic rate of tax and taxes on company cars are extended. The main rate of corporation tax is cut by 1 per cent to 34 per cent for 1990–91 and to 33 per cent in 1991–92.

Economic forecasts include a 2 per cent fall in output during 1991 with recovery beginning in mid-1991 and inflation falling to 4 per cent in the final quarter of the year. The target for MO growth is set at 0–4 per cent for the coming financial year and a return to deficit forecast with a PSBR of £7.9 billion following a predicted £800 million surplus in 1990–91. There is little immediate response in financial or currency markets. Michael Heseltine formally announces the replacement of the poll tax in 1993–94 by a household tax.

22 Mar: Bank base rates are cut by half a point to 12.5 per cent, despite only a modest 0.1 per cent fall in inflation to 8.9 per cent in February.

26 Mar: The pound closes above its central rate of DM2.95 at DM2.96 for the first time since shortly after joining the ERM.

2 Apr: The March CBI survey shows an increase in confidence among manufacturers, with a balance of 24 per cent believing output would decline in the coming four months, compared with 36 per cent in February. Only 4 per cent intended to increase prices for domestic orders in the coming four months.

12 Apr: Base rates are cut by half a percentage point to 12 per cent shortly before the announcement of a fall in retail price inflation to 8.2 per cent in February. Mortgage lenders respond with cuts of 0.75–1 per cent bringing mortgage rates down to around 13 per cent.

15 Apr: The pound briefly breaches the DM3 level during the day, having been the second strongest currency within the ERM for over two weeks.

18 Apr: Seasonally adjusted unemployment reaches the 2 million level in March after the largest rise in unemployment, 112,900, ever recorded. Manufacturing output figures

for February reveal a fall of 1.6 per cent on the month, down 6 per cent since February 1990.

22 Apr: Retail sales rise sharply in March as consumers attempted to beat the April VAT increase. The 3.7 per cent jump is also accounted for by the timing of Easter, but the underlying trend appears flat.

23 Apr: The government sets out detailed proposals for the tax to replace the poll tax, the 'council tax'. It consists of seven bands based on capital values, with a 25 per cent discount for single-person households.

30 Apr: The CBI *Quarterly Survey* reports a sharp improvement in business optimism rising from a balance of –51 to –17. The current economic climate for manufacturers is reported to be worsening but recovery in the second half of the year is forecast.

14 May: The Governor of the Bank of England reiterates his call against cutting interest rates too rapidly and risking any achievement in bringing down inflation, after producer output price inflation rises to 6.4 per cent in April from 6.2 per cent in March. However this is largely put down to the rise in excise duties in the Budget.

17 May: Retail price inflation falls to 6.4 per cent in April, mortgage rate cuts and the poll tax reduction more than offsetting rises in excise duties and the VAT increase.

22 May: First quarter GDP figures indicate the third consecutive quarter of recession, output falling by 0.6 per cent on the previous quarter and down 2.5 per cent on the level a year ago.

24 May: Base rates are cut by half a point to 11.5 per cent.

28 May: Leading banks are attacked for widening lending margins while interest rates are cut, which they claim is to take account of greater business risks.

30 May: Norman Lamont rejects a fixed timetable for economic and monetary union, but says he does not want Britain to be in the slow track of a two-speed move towards EMU.

10 Jun: The CBI release figures showing that average pay settlements in manufacturing averaged 6.8 per cent in April compared with 8.1 per cent in the first quarter, the largest fall since the autumn of 1980.
Producer output prices for May provided optimistic news about underlying inflation. Manufacturers' output prices slowed from 6.2 per cent to 6 per cent, and excluding food, drink and tobacco, fell to 5.5 per cent.

17 Jun: Douglas Hurd rejects a draft treaty of the rewritten Treaty of Rome, because of a reference to a 'federal goal' for member states. Sterling falls further to DM2.925 largely due to domestic political difficulties.

20 Jun: John Major once again confirms that sterling will move to a 2.25 per cent band within the ERM.

23 Jun: The Chancellor Norman Lamont reaffirms that he expects output to recover in the second half of this year.

24 Jun: The June CBI *Monthly Trends Survey* suggests that the worst of the UK recession may now be over. Manufacturing expectations have improved with a balance of 11 per cent of firms expecting output to fall over the next four months compared with 18 per cent in May. Moreover, on balance firms were not expecting to increase their prices over the next four months, the most subdued response for 24 years.

8 Jul: There were 2,136 receiverships in the first half of this year compared with 2,634 in the whole of 1990.

9 Jul: Producer output prices excluding food, drink and tobacco fall by 0.3 per cent to 5.2 per cent in June, the lowest level since December 1988.

Although the full ramifications are not yet known the defence white paper shows that the Gulf war cost the UK £2.5 billion, £2.03 billion of which will be paid for by other countries.

12 Jul: Base rate cut 0.5 per cent to 11 per cent and the main building societies cut mortgage rates by the same amount to 11. 95 per cent despite inflation remaining at 5.8 per cent in June. Sterling gained 1 pfennig to take it above its DM2.95 central level and is now the fifth strongest currency in the ERM.

16 Jul: A lower than expected PSBR in June together with an upbeat statement on the prospects for world growth from the G7 meeting spurred the FTSE-100 past its previous April high, taking it to 2556.8. Sterling gained ground within the ERM to become the third strongest currency.

22 Jul: CBI/FT *Distributive Trades Survey* indicates that the fall in retail sales is bottoming out, supported by official retail sales data for June.

23 Jul: An extra £1.1 billion grant to local authorities contributes to an emerging concern that the government will overshoot its planned public expenditure and thereby PSBR in 1991–92 and 1992–3.

24 Jul: The government is to move ahead with its planned privatization of a second tranche of BT shares in November.

26 Jul: Bank of England moves to provide liquidity to head off any shortage for small banks following the closure of BCCI, which is estimated to have resulted in a loss of £70 million of local authority funds, and the need for National Home Loans recently to seek funds from its banks.

29 Jul: The FT all share index, benefiting from optimism from Norman Lamont's view of the progress of the economy, reaches its highest level since 16 July 1987.

5 Aug: CBI figures show the largest fall in manufacturing pay increases for ten years. In the second quarter wages rose by 6.5 per cent compared with 8.1 per cent in the previous quarter. Moreover, service sector settlements fell from 8.9 per cent in the second half of last year to a provisional 7.3 per cent in the first half of this year.

13 Aug: A rise in manufacturing output of 0.2 per cent in June supported indications that the UK recession may have touched bottom.

15 Aug: In its *Quarterly Bulletin* the Bank of England describes the economy as bumping along the bottom.

Bundesbank announces a 1 per cent rise in discount rate but only a 0.25 per cent rise in its Lombard rate.

Repossessions rise by 34 per cent in the six months to the end of June compared with the previous six months and are double the repossessions in the first six months of 1990.

19 Aug: Mikhail Gorbachev removed as Soviet president by coup. Dollar responds by rising, especially against the Deutschmark, sterling gains almost 3 pfennigs and financial markets worldwide decline: the Dow Jones by 2.4 per cent in Frankfurt by more than 10 per cent, in London by 3 per cent and in Tokyo by nearly 6 per cent.

Output data for the second quarter shows a slowing in the pace of decline in activity, and with retail sales in July increasing by 0.3 per cent points to optimism that an upturn, albeit meagre, may have begun.

21 Aug: Coup collapses. Mikhail Gorbachev returned as Soviet president, but the balance of power clearly shifts towards Boris Yeltsin, the democratically elected Russian president. World financial markets respond immediately.

27 Aug: Figures released by the Association of British Chambers of Commerce, on behalf of the DTI, suggest that insolvencies rose by 67 per cent in the second quarter compared with a year earlier. Indeed, in the year to the end of June 1991, 2 per cent of all active companies became insolvent.

1 Sep: MORI puts the Conservative Party 2 points ahead of Labour in an opinion poll, the Tories' first lead for four months.

2 Sep: FTSE-100 receives a further fillip, rising to 2679.6 in response to the Tory lead in the opinion polls. Sterling gains 0.5 pfennig against the deutschmark.

4 Sep: Base rate reduced by 0.5 per cent to 10.5 per cent. Halifax Building Society reduces its basic mortgage rate by 0.45 points to 11.5 per cent and other building societies are expected to follow.
Halifax Building Society figures show that house prices fell by 0.5 per cent on average in August, after declining by 0.9 per cent in July, evidence that the housing market remains subdued.

5 Sep: Gallup opinion poll puts Conservatives 4.5 points above Labour, fuelling speculation of a November general election. However, a larger poll conducted over the whole of August shows Labour still ahead by 0.3 points.

10 Sep: More encouraging news that inflation is being successfully tackled emerges, as manufacturing output prices fall to an annual 5.6 per cent in August. Moreover, excluding food, drink and tobacco, a widely accepted measure of underlying inflationary pressures, the annual increase falls to 4.8 per cent, its lowest rise since August 1988.

12 Sep: Average earnings growth falls to 7.5 per cent in July from 8 per cent in June, the sharpest drop since 1982.

16 Sep: Manufacturing output increases by 0.3 per cent in the three months to July, the first quarter-on-quarter increase for a year, adding weight to the view that the recession is bottoming out. However, a fall in retail sales of 1.4 per cent in August offers less encouragement of a significant consumer-led upturn.

17 Sep: PSBR moves into sharp deficit in August and the accumulated deficit for the first five months of the current financial year has now reached the government's projected figure of £7.9 billion for the year as a whole. The government argues that revenue should benefit from now on as a result of VAT increases in the March budget.

18 Sep: Robin Leigh-Pemberton, the Governor of the Bank of England delivers an upbeat assessment of the state of the UK economy.

22 Sep: Latest MORI opinion poll puts Labour Party back in front of Conservatives.

23 Sep: CBI *Trends Survey*, for September suggests that for the first time in 16 months there are more manufacturers expecting to increase output than to reduce it.

27 Sep: A Gallup poll for the European Commission shows consumer confidence in Britain's economic situation is at its highest since October 1987.

30 Sep: According to Dun and Bradstreet there were 33,532 business failures in the first nine months of the year, 71 per cent higher than the same period in 1990.

7 Oct: Manufacturers' pay settlements slow to an average annual growth of 5.5 per cent in the third quarter according to CBI figures, the lowest rate of increase for four years.

Moreover, John Banham, CBI Director-General, points out that pay settlements are now below those in Germany.

9 Oct: The Halifax Building Society reports a fall in house prices of 0.8 per cent in September. Average house prices are now 2.5 per cent lower than a year ago.

10 Oct: Sterling falls to the bottom of the ERM league, following disappointment that the UK does not move to the narrower 2.25 per cent band and worry over the government's prospects in the next election.

15 Oct: Manufacturing output falls by 1.1 per cent in August reflecting weak car and engineering production.

18 Oct: M4, a broad definition of the money supply, grows by an annual 6.4 per cent in September, the lowest figure for some 20 years. MO, essentially notes and coins, grows by an annual 2.2 per cent.

21 Oct: Both the CBI/FT *Distributive Trades Survey* and the London Chamber of Commerce survey indicate that any upturn in activity is at present very patchy and only modest. According to 3i, the UK's largest venture capital group, confidence among small businesses is at its highest for two and a half years.

29 Oct: The October CBI *Industrial Trends Survey* paints an upbeat picture for the economy, with more firms being optimistic than pessimistic for the first time in three years.

31 Oct: In the Queen's Speech for the last parliamentary session before the general election, the government pledges to follow firm financial policies, maintaining its chief aim of reducing inflation within the framework of the ERM. Public spending will be reduced over time and there are plans to privatize British Rail and British Coal.

In his Mansion House speech the Chancellor, Norman Lamont, maintains that the UK is now on the road to recovery, claiming that increased confidence is being derived from falling inflation, improved cost controls by British business, the prospect of increased profitability and rising UK share of world trade.

Norman Lamont announces a programme of government-backed three year Treasury notes denominated in ecus.

3 Nov: MORI opinion poll puts the Conservative Party one point ahead of the Labour Party, the Tories' first lead for six weeks.

6 Nov: In the autumn statement the Chancellor forecasts a 2.25 per cent increase in GDP in 1991, compared with a decline of 2 per cent for this year. Inflation is projected to be 4 per cent next year and the current account deficit is estimated to widen to £9.5 billion from this year's £6.5 billion. Expenditure on health, education, social security and transport is increased with the result that the PSBR is estimated to record £10.5 billion in 1991-92 compared with 1991 budget projection of £7.9 billion. There is an assumption that the PSBR will rise to around £19 billion in 1992-93, but the Chancellor maintains that his policy remains balancing the budget over the economic cycle.

8 Nov: Gallup opinion poll shows an 8 per cent lead for the Labour Party.

11 Nov: At the Lord Mayor's banquet at the Guildhall, John Major says that while it would be wrong to accept now the principle of a single currency, it would be equally mistaken 'to decide now that in no circumstances will we ever do so'.

12 Nov: Producer prices in October show a further easing in inflationary pressure. Excluding food, drink and tobacco output price inflation declines to an annual 4.2 per cent, the lowest figure for more than four years.

14 Nov: Unemployment increases by a seasonally adjusted 15,700 in October but the pace of increase continues to slow, resulting in the smallest monthly rise since September

1990. The Bank of England in its latest *Quarterly Bulletin* detects signs of a modest but sustainable upturn in the economy.

Sterling declines below to DM2.898 its lowest level against the deutschmark since mid-February. There are no reports on this occasion that the Bank of England resists the fall below DM2.90.

15 Nov: Retail price inflation falls to an annual 3.7 per cent in October, the lowest figure since March 1988. More importantly, underlying inflation continues to decline.

18 Nov: CBI October *Distributive Trades Survey* shows some signs of pick-up in trading conditions in retailing, but the picture is still very patchy and modest.

An increase in French interest rates, together with disappointing retail sales data for October, pushes sterling to the bottom of the ERM league.

Retail sales volumes fall in October by 0.5 per cent, indicating that the economy is not yet emerging buoyantly from the recession. This is an additional dampener on the stock market which reacts nervously to a fall on Wall Street, the FTSE-100 falling by 44 points to 2502, its lowest since 12 July.

19 Nov: Provisional output based GDP figures show a rise of 0.3 per cent in the third quarter. However, this increase is entirely due to oil production, with non-oil GDP declining by 0.3 per cent.

20 Nov: The Treasury confirms its forecast that GDP will grow by 0.75 per cent between the first and second halves of this year.

22 Nov: Sterling shows its biggest one-day fall against the deutschmark since October 1990, falling almost 3 pfennigs to close at DM2.84, its lowest for 18 months. This reflects a combination of a strong deutschmark, nervousness that there is little hard evidence the economy is recovering, and uncertainty in the run up to Maastricht and the general election.

Norman Lamont has agreed that the European central bank, envisaged for the final stage of monetary union, should have independent charge of interest rate policy.

25 Nov: It is speculated that the Bundesbank supports sterling, which steadies around DM2.85. There are also reports that the French and Italian banks intervened to help sterling.

26 Nov: Ford manual workers vote to accept their lowest pay increase for a decade. The deal is worth 5 per cent in the first year and 5 per cent or inflation + 0.5 per cent, whichever is the greater, in the second year.

4 Dec: According to the Halifax house price index, average house prices fell by 0.8 per cent in November, and are now 2.4 per cent lower than a year ago. The average price of new homes fell in November by 1.4 per cent.

5 Dec: According to the CBI's Smaller Firms Council, small businesses reported an improvement in orders in November, but most still do not expect a sustained recovery before the second half of 1992.

According to the Society of Motor Manufacturers and Traders, new car sales recorded their lowest November total since 1980 at 100,608, 14.4 per cent lower than in November 1990.

6 Dec: Gallup opinion poll for the *Daily Mail* puts the Conservative Party 2.5 points ahead of the Labour Party.

9 Dec: Summit on European economic and monetary union begins in Maastricht.

11 Dec: Agreement is reached in Maastricht on the convergence criteria for EMU. Under the agreement the entire social chapter is dropped at Britain's insistence. However, the

other 11 member states have reached a separate agreement to enact legislation affecting workers' rights. Other features of the agreement include a limited form of majority voting in foreign affairs, the powers of the European Parliament are to be extended, and the EC's right to legislate is to be widened.

12 Dec: The latest CBI/FT *Distributive Trades Survey* points to poor sales for this time of year in the retail, wholesale and motor trade sectors.

13 Dec: Retail price inflation rises to an annual 4.3 per cent in November. The increase reflects a rise in seasonal food prices, together with the falling out of the annual comparison of both last November's petrol price increase and reduction in mortgage rates.

Norman Lamont reaffirms the government's commitment to move sterling into a narrow 2.25 band in the ERM at its present central rate of DM2.95, thus ruling out any depreciation in the currency. Sterling rises by 1.5 pfennigs to DM2.87.

26 Dec: A bleak picture for the economy's prospects of recovery in the next few months is reported in the CBI's December *Monthly Trends Survey*. There is now a balance of 5 per cent of firms expecting output to fall in the next four months, whilst export prospects are also worse than last month reflecting problems in the key markets of the US and Germany.

Evidence of a still sluggish economy emerges as CSO figures show a 0.4 per cent reduction in manufacturing output in October, with a fall of 1 per cent in the latest three months. More encouraging news comes from retail sales, which show a provisional increase of 1.2 per cent in November following October's 0.6 per cent fall. However, the CSO warned that the November figure may have been inflated by up to 50 per cent due to factors connected with its method of collecting data.

The City

MARGARET REID

Just how intertwined are the fortunes of Britain's finance sector are with those of the wider economy was amply shown in 1991. As industry and commerce fought what bankers called the sharpest recession since the war, their troubles rippled through to the providers of financial services. The fact that sterling had been locked in October 1990 into the European Community's exchange rate mechanism denied the government the recourse so familiar in the past to business-boosting ploys which would have risked raising inflation and hitting the pound.

True, key interest rates were cut from their 15 per cent peak to 10.5 per cent, but in the prevailing atmosphere of squeeze and rising unemployment, confidence proved slow to rekindle. Businesses, faced with low demand in a toughly competitive environment, embarked on a radical retrenchment which, the Bank of England noted, involved 'all aspects of companies' operations and . . . included labour shedding and cost cutting, reduced capital expenditure, substantial destocking'. For many stronger groups, this response led to considerable economies in bank borrowing. At the same time, smaller firms, often too weak to resist recession pressures, and finding the banks taking a more critical line on lending, went to the wall on an unprecedented scale.

Individuals too faced harsher conditions, in which many, having lost jobs, were engulfed by mortgage and other loan problems. In hard statistical black and white, the switch from the heady consumer credit boom which had over-fired the economy in the late 1980s to a harder money climate is readily charted. Over the four years to November 1990, personal lending by the nine top British banks had almost doubled, soaring by 94 per cent to £78 billion. But whereas growth was as high as 26 per cent in 1986–87, it had by 1989–90 slowed to 11 per cent, much of that accounted for by inflation, and has since continued to be sluggish (see chart 1).

It is not hard to understand the effect on the financial industry of this troubled setting. For the banks, it has meant a dramatically heavy crop of bad debts, one leading analyst predicting late in 1991 that the big four clearers, Barclays, Lloyds, National Westminster and Midland, would have to set aside £4 billion in that year for losses on UK domestic lending, to the serious detriment of their earnings. Losses have been worsened by the scale of the bank loans, up to over £2 billion, at risk through the Robert Maxwell empire's collapse in December, a black date in the City's calendar. The banks face other, smaller, charges for the partial compensation of depositors in the Bank of Credit and Commerce International (BCCI), whose closure by the Bank of England in July was another shock event of the year. The spectacular collapses of the Maxwell and BCCI groups, both to the accompaniment of allegations of major fraud, spotlighted issues over the conduct and regulation of companies and banks, and left a trail of doubts and disquiet.

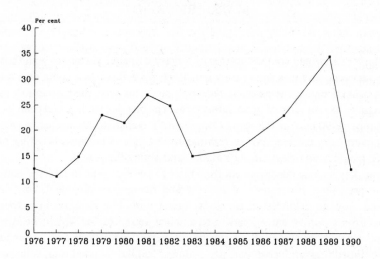

Source: 'The performance of major British banks, 1970–90', Bank of England Quarterly Bulletin, November 1991. Relates to all UK banks, not just 'Big Four'.

Chart 1. UK Banks: annual growth rates of domestic bank lending

Other financial bodies have equally felt the recessionary draught. With peak numbers of home buyers unable to pay on their mortgages, repossessions have soared to 85,000 in 1991 (five time the 1989 level) and will go higher. Forced sales of the houses, often at discounts, have depressed property prices and discouraged people from moving. All this has been a blow to the building societies and has caused severer problems to certain smaller independent mortgage lenders. The closely-regulated societies have however survived the storms successfully, with the aid of some defensive mergers.

Cutprice sales of repossessed homes have also had harsh repercussions in the insurance field. A number of leading insurers had built up a large business in covering societies and other lenders against the danger of loss through non-repayment by borrowers, a risk previously thought slight. But, in the event, many people who had bought houses, particularly at high late-1980s prices, have unexpectedly defaulted. Heavy loss liabilities, estimated at up to £3 billion over some two years, have thus arisen on the mortgage indemnity policies, throwing large losses on the insurers. Elsewhere in insurance, the centuries-old Lloyd's insurance market has faced unprecedented withdrawals of its underwriting 'names' after a spell of poor results.

Despite these various recession-linked problems, the City has been preparing optimistically for the more open EC single market, due in operation from the start of 1993. The pound's newly closer tie to other EC countries is welcomed in the City as helpful to its planning for a competitive future in financial services, an arena in which London still feels confident of outclassing resurgent EC rivals. Among its other activities, the stock market has continued to develop its market-making in European shares, so that 90 per cent of Europe's turnover in international stocks is now transacted through the City's market. Eastern Europe's affairs and the need for gradual integration of the former Soviet bloc into the wider European economy have not been overlooked. The new international organization to help these countries, the European Bank for Reconstruction and Development, has been launched, with a London base, under its chairman, the French economist and adviser to President Mitterrand, Jacques Attali. An increasing number of City institutions, including firms of accountants and lawyers, now have offices in Russia and eastern Europe, while the City's central authorities are providing advisory services to this newly capitalist area.

Banking and Finance: Counting the Cost

For Britain's big banks, 1991 confirmed that the unsustainable boom time party of the late 1980s was truly over and that the time for far-reaching changes in business had come. A larger than expected harvest of domestic loan losses had also to be absorbed, in what Sir Nicholas Goodison, chairman of the British Bankers Association and of TSB Group, described in mid-year as a prolonged period of severe recession. In this environment, the process of retrenchment on which the banks had already embarked assumed a more radical character. Over 1991–93, the large high street clearers are set to shed 30,000 jobs and to close hundreds of branches. Although the pace and scale of this strict housekeeping owes much to pressures on profits from shaky debts and flagging business, it also brings the organizations into the more compact shape made feasible by technology developments permitting much marketing and processing of transactions to by-pass branch networks. The current need for economy has been the greater because of the variety of pressures which have been at work to reduce bank profits. For instance, the fact that competition has raised the cost of deposits to fund lending has for some years been squeezing interest margins, the difference between cost of funds and interest on loans. In reply, the banks have often tried to recoup higher outgoings by raising, where possible, the level above base rate at which loan interest is set.

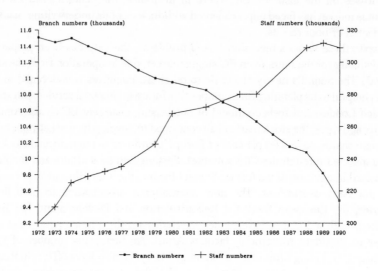

Source: British Bankers' Association.

Chart 2. 'Big Four' UK Banks: branches and staff numbers

There were signs of this trend in the first half of 1991, when it sparked off a storm of complaint that banks were not passing on to their small business customers (4.5 million with £40 billion of borrowings) the benefits of general interest rate cuts. After an intervention by the Chancellor of the Exchequer, Norman Lamont, an official probe took place, which at least exonerated the banks from colluding in the matter. It found that about 30 per cent of small business customers who used bank loans might have been subject to some increase in the margin charged over the base lending rate, but that in the vast majority of cases the extra was only 0.5 per cent. A later study by the Office of Fair Trading found the banks had acted 'insensitively' towards some customers. Codes of good practice vis-à-vis small business customers are now being issued by individual banks, while an agreed joint code regarding personal customers has been hammered out after consultation with consumer interests.

It is now clear that the banks, partly in response to the Thatcher government's wishes, expanded their financing of small businesses too rapidly in the 1980s and are now paying the price, after numerous such firms have collapsed. Barclays, the largest bank, has been providing for losses on small business loans at the rate of £1 million per day. In effect, the banks have been unintentionally providing equity capital to many concerns and often losing it. Barclays' chairman, Sir John Quinton, has warned that it is time for the banks to rein in such lending to 'more traditional levels' and other banks are following suit.

In further measures to remedy their predicament, the banks have been striving to boost their fee (as distinct from loan interest) income, which now accounts for about 40 per cent of revenues, against 20 per cent in 1980. For example, all the big four banks have imposed annual charges for credit cards, a change which, at Barclays, fostered a swing for the relevant retail services side from a £12 million loss in the first half of 1990 to a £23 million profit a year later.

The persistent recession has dashed hopes that bank profits would revive after the large bad debt provisions set aside in 1990. Still higher debt charges – including the estimated £4 billion for domestic losses at the big four banks – are in prospect for 1991. This implies a cut in the top quartet's £1.9 billion pretax profit total in 1990 to a little over £1 billion for the following year.

Small business collapses and lending to distressed property and building companies and to a range of larger troubled groups, all boosted the debt tally, which included many personal loan losses. But the heaviest single item in the bad debt provisions, totalling at least many hundreds of millions of pounds for the leading UK banks, came from the failure of the Maxwell empire, latterly nourished on bank credit and a very heavy borrower from both British and foreign banking groups. The shock of this big customer's collapse has been a chastening experience for bankers, who now appear as having been excessive lenders to dominant, over-ambitious tycoons, always ready with borrowing propositions when traditional groups have prudently battened down. Standard Chartered, one of the top nine UK banks, with a large overseas clientele, has acknowledged its earlier over-commitment to big-name entrepreneurs. On top of other bad debts, the banks have also had to provide up to £500 million for losses on the local authority swap deals in the money markets, made by councils later held in the courts to have exceeded their powers.

Slower growth of bank assets has been an inevitable trend, not only because of shrinkage of demand but as a result of the difficulties of building new capital. Rights issue calls on shareholders are virtually excluded after an earlier spate, while the thinness of profits has limited retained earnings. Compliance with the 8 per cent minimum ratio of capital to adjusted assets required under the Basle international concordat thus means a new caution over balance sheet expansion. While no 'credit crunch', in the sense of a loan famine for sound borrowers, exists, banks are vetting their portfolios more prudently. Brian Pearse, who was recruited from Barclays to run the loss-making Midland Bank as part of a major shakeup at the top there, said after his appointment: 'With the state of the country at the present time . . . I don't expect any bank balance sheets to grow very much'.

One means of boosting capital is through selling assets for cash. Having raised £1 billion through disposing of their Yorkshire Bank to National Australia Bank in 1990, the big UK banks plan in 1992 to float off their jointly-owned 3i industrial finance company for perhaps £1.5 billion. New acquisitions have been muted in the harsh climate, but further bank links with insurance have been formed in line with the Europe-wide trend to *allfinanz*. Abbey National, the former building society which is now Britain's fifth largest bank, has, for instance, acquired the Scottish Mutual life insurance company.

Merchant banks have had mixed experiences, with the ebbing of the merger boom hitting corporate finance work, but activities like the £5.35 billion privatization of remaining BT shares providing major work to houses including the government's lead adviser, S G Warburg. (The BT sale was done through a novel auction process to save the underwriting costs of earlier issues.) S G Warburg, which from its original merchant bank business has constructed one of the largest integrated investment banks as a result of the 1986 Big Bang stock market reforms, raised its 1991 first half profits by a third to £89 million, while Barclays' BZW, another large house, achieved a 43 per cent rise to £40 million.

For the building societies, which have 60 per cent of the mortgage market, compared with the banks' much enlarged 30 per cent, the worst housing recession for 60 years has meant slower growth. Assets, which had risen by 18 per cent in 1989–90, increased only 13 per cent in the year to September 1991. With house prices down around 2.5 per cent, and people made cautious by job insecurity, business has been sluggish, with deals in the house property market being 40 per cent lower in 1991 than the 1988 peak. Substantial increases in the societies' loan loss reserves of some £700 million at the end of 1990, were inevitable, despite the cushioning of mortgage indemnity cover. Generally, however, the building society sector is weathering the recession, thanks partly to the tight control on its activities maintained by its regulator, the Building Societies Commission (BSC) and partly to a string of mergers. Already the number of societies has been cut by amalgamations to 95 from 273 in 1980, and some experts foresee further reductions to no more than 30 in due course. In one case, the BSC stepped in during 1991 to promote a shotgun marriage in the shape of the effective takeover of Town & Country, the fifteenth biggest society, by the Woolwich, the fourth largest. Town & Country, lacking mortgage indemnity insurance, was facing losses due to bad debts which could have sapped savers' confidence.

Less traditional mortgage lenders have been more heavily caught in the recession crosswinds, notably some newer, so-called 'central' lenders, without branch networks, which had grown swiftly in the late-1980s boom. Mortgage Express was closed by its owner, TSB, and National Home Loans (NHL) was provided with a special £200 million loan facility, put together by the big banks under Bank of England sponsorship, amid talk of a possible recurrence of the mid-1970s secondary banking crisis. NHL, facing losses, has heavily scaled down its business. Another lender, First National Finance Corporation, a revivified casualty of the mid 1970s, has made a protective en bloc sale of debt.

Taking a long term view, the largest societies, hampered in their expansion ambitions by legal curbs, are lobbying for an amendment to the Building Societies Act 1986 to allow them to operate with wider scope as banks, but still with no-shareholder mutual status. In the prevailing climate, however, dialogue on this topic will at best be slow. Meanwhile, it is notable that no other building society has followed Abbey National, previously the second largest, in its 1989 conversion into a plc company with authorized bank status.

The Stock Market: Still Evolving

Five years on from its crucial Big Bang reforms in trading methods and structure, London's stock exchange is still considering adjustments to the key changes then made, successful as many have been. The scrapping of fixed commissions in 1986 has benefited large investors by halving commission payable by institutional investors to about 0.2 per cent and sometimes less. Indeed, some large customers pay no such charge at all, so valuable to dealers is the spread or 'turn' on business transacted for them. However, dealing costs to small investors have gone up (save on mass-market privatizations), loading the dice against the 'shareholder democracy' so dear to the Conservative government's heart. Worse still, the swift and smooth throughput of trades in major companies' shares is not so readily available for the less frequently dealt shares of small quoted concerns. For them, the spread of over 10 per cent between buying and selling prices is a marked deterrent to investors. To remedy this 'stickiness' in trading, a departure is being considered for smaller companies' shares from the five year old 'electronic notice board' system through which competing market-makers advertise on the Stock Exchange Automatic Quotation (SEAQ) screen-based service the prices at which they will deal by telephone. Instead, the idea is that specialist traders would be entrusted with matching buy and sell orders in lesser shares in the style familiar on foreign bourses.

More generally, the 1986 changes, which also allowed broker and dealer functions to be linked under the same roof, and led to the formation of broad-range investment groups, mainly owned by large commercial banks, have come a step nearer to fulfilling their creators' hopes. Higher share prices and brisker trading in 1991, when London's FT-SE index rose 25 per cent by September, before dropping back on recession worries, helped stock exchange firms make a fair start to the year, after long spells of loss or thin profitability. Whereas they had lost £353 million in aggregate in 1990, the first half of the succeeding year yielded £189 million of profits. As often in rising markets, dealing profits were a major contributor. In particular, the gilt-edged market in UK government bonds has livened up, with the renewed issue of paper following the budget swing into deficit after the exceptional surpluses of the Thatcher years.

Altogether, the number of market-makers, which dropped in the difficult years of 1987–89, had stabilized at 25 in domestic shares (against 32 at Big Bang) and 18 (27) in gilt-edged stock. After some, including American banks, had pulled out, the large groups which had invested heavily in London's securities markets have proved reluctant to throw in the towel and are holding on for better times. There is also new interest in entering the market, notably by Germany's big DeutscheBank (owner of the Morgan Grenfell merchant bank) and by brokerages from Japan, whose large Nomura and Daiwa houses are already market-makers.

Table 1. Financial statistics for Stock Exchange member firms

		Revenue £m	Expenditure £m	Profit before tax £m	Staff (000s)	Capital employed £m
1987	Q1	613	493	120	20.0	n/a
1987	Q2	785	572	213	20.6	n/a
1987	Q3	716	650	66	24.0	n/a
1987	Q4	269	644	–375	24.5	n/a
1988	Q1	542	473	69	24.3	n/a
1988	Q2	606	563	43	24.9	n/a
1988	Q3	400	538	–138	25.5	2,589
1988	Q4	420	589	–169	24.8	2,487
1989	Q1	747	599	148	24.6	2,736
1989	Q2	788	676	112	24.4	3,238
1989	Q3	885	724	161	24.1	3,250
1989	Q4	864	781	83	24.4	3,447
1990	Q1	507	664	–157	22.1	3,160
1990	Q2	670	658	12	22.2	3,244
1990	Q3	564	647	–83	21.8	3,130
1990	Q4	599	724	–125	21.4	3,175
1991	Q1	775	684	91	20.1	3,249
1991	Q2	824	726	98	20.8	3,404

Source: *Stock Exchange Quarterly with Quality of Markets Review*, Autumn 1991.

One of the unquestioned successes of Big Bang has been the SEAQ international screen service, which now handles the great bulk of Europe's international equity trade. At roughly £1.2 billion a day, its turnover is little short of the domestic market's £1.4 billion. There is now a possibility that the stock exchange will seek to bring the SEAQ domestic and international services closer together, with improvements in reporting procedures and perhaps participation by Continental dealers. A continuing shortcoming of the London system, and one which is proving slow to remedy, lies in its archaic paper-based settlement arrangements. Introduction of the more modern TAURUS (Transfer and Automated Settlement Registration of Uncertified Stock) electronic replacement has been repeatedly delayed but is now due to start by April 1993. A development scheduled for March 1992 was the launch of the combined financial futures market and the options market under the new title of London International Financial Futures and Options Exchange.

The City   179

Other Matters - and Regrets with Hindsight

Much sombre stocktaking took place in the City in 1991, following the previous deregulation spree in financial markets and the over-the-top spirit of competition it had sometimes fostered. The sharp economic recession, succeeding an excessive credit boom, and a premiership of less mettlesome tone than Mrs Thatcher's, highlighted the turnaround from the brash 1980s to the gentler 1990s. Not all the accompanying reassessment was a comfortable exercise for the City's leaders. The collapse of Robert Maxwell's group, after the dramatic death at sea of the secretive financier tycoon, taught the banks fresh lessons on the need for a more critical stance towards certain big borrowers. Following the apparent illicit siphoning off of £350 million from the group's pension funds, new regulations on the handling of such funds are also likely.

Further reappraisal of the spirit of the 1980s has been prompted by several lengthy trials consequent on events in that decade. Notable among them have been those concerning the conduct of the hard-fought 1988 takeover by Guinness of Distillers. Four leading personalities were convicted (and three of them jailed) in 1990 at the end of one trial, the first of three. Officials and former officials of County NatWest, a National Westminster subsidiary, have also been among those before the courts, charged with market-rigging offences in connection with the 1987 Blue Arrow rights issue. In these and other cases, questions about attitudes towards the need for careful compliance with the law have arisen.

Looming large in the past year has also been the decision by the Bank of England and its overseas counterparts to close BCCI, a large and publicity-shy group with tentacles in many nations, on 5 July 1991. The shutdown action was taken because of what a US prosecutor alleged to be the biggest fraud in banking history. It was the most dramatic move ever made by the world's increasingly co-ordinated official bank supervisors, though it took place to a barrage of criticism both that it was excessively harsh and, alternatively, that it was unduly delayed. BCCI, founded in 1972 by a Pakistani banker, Agha Hasan Abedi, had 800,000 depositors in 70 countries, including many individuals and small shopkeepers of Asian origin in Britain. The controlling shareholding was latterly in the hands of the ruler of Abu Dhabi, Sheikh Zayed bin Sultan al-Nahyan, from whom it was later claimed that vast sums had been robbed through the bank. At the end of the year plans were under negotiation by which Sheikh Zayed might put up money towards compensating depositors beyond the amounts available through the UK deposit protection scheme. Abu Dhabi had not been brought into the secret discussions by regulators elsewhere before the closure of the bank on 5 July. Mr Swaleh Naqvi, latterly BCCI's chief operating officer, is said to be under a form of custody in Abu Dhabi. In the US, criminal charges were launched within weeks of the shutdown against various people, including Mr Abedi and Mr Naqvi, associated with BCCI, often nicknamed the 'Bank of Crooks and Cocaine International'. In Britain, the Serious Fraud Office is pursuing its own enquiries about the group.

Meanwhile, the world's bank supervisory procedures have come under close public scrutiny following the BCCI debacle. In the UK, an independent enquiry headed by Lord Justice Bingham has been set up by the Chancellor of the Exchequer and the Bank of England to look into the supervision of BCCI and see whether the official actions taken were appropriate and timely. There has however been some disquiet that this non-statutory enquiry cannot compel witnesses to give evidence or to produce documents.

In a totally separate field, Britain's investing institutions – the pension funds, insurance groups and suchlike bodies which hold two thirds of UK shares – have further extended their watchfulness over managements of poorly performing companies. While operating in a low-key way, they have been instrumental in pressing successfully for shakeups at the top, as for example at the companies Asda, Burton and Tace. They have also been specially insistent on changes where, as at Granada and British Aerospace, they have been asked to support rights issues by cash-needy groups viewed as disappointingly managed. In December, the Institutional Shareholders' Committee, representing the main investor groups, issued a new statement of guidelines, 'The Responsibilities of Institutional Shareholders in the UK'. This called for more communication between institutional shareholders and company boards (though without the passing of price-sensitive information), together with a greater use of the institutions' voting rights and a more active role for them in the selection of non-executive directors.

With the former Soviet empire now developing on a non-communist basis, the City of London is both offering tuition on western methods through key institutions and extensively selling commercial advisory services. The Bank of England has made what its Governor, Robin Leigh-Pemberton, has described as a major commitment in setting up a new Centre for Central Banking Studies, concentrating particularly on 'the emerging market economies, including the [former] Soviet Union'. The stock exchange is also holding out a helping hand, with training courses, starting with one for Czech officials, in the financial services industry. Merchant banks too are playing a part in bringing western investment to formerly state-owned enterprises throughout eastern Europe.

Chronology

14 Jan: New rules governing share disclosures and classification come into force on the ISE.

21 Jan: Committee of Inquiry, *Report into Investment Performance Measurement* (chaired by Maurice Stonefrost), National Association of Pension Funds, makes recommendations relating to short-term investment, the assessment of investment performance and the responsibilities of trustees of pension funds.

25 Feb: ISE launches its FT-SE Eurotrack 200, incorporating the top 100 continental companies and the constituents of the FT-SE index, to be calculated in ecus.

5 Mar: Sir Kit McMahon is to be replaced as chief executive of Midland Bank by Brian Pearse, recruited from Barclays at the behest of the Bank of England. Sir Peter Walters replaces Sir Kit as chairman.

14 Mar: FT-SE index hits new closing high of 2,500.6.

19 Mar: Government outlines plans for high street share shops in the Budget.

20 Mar: Robin Leigh-Pemberton predicts that independence for the Bank of England will be forced on Britain by the pace of moves towards EMU.

3 Apr: FT-SE index reaches new closing high of 2,519.1.

4 Apr: FT-SE index reaches new closing high of 2,524.5.

5 Apr: FT-SE index reaches new closing high of 2,545.3.

15 Apr: European Bank for Reconstruction and Development inaugurated.

1 May: City Research Project to investigate the competitive position of the City of London, is launched.

2 May: Group of 30 report points to need for City to modernize its settlements systems.

7 May Government announces it will not retrospectively validate interest rate swap deals between banks and local authorities, leaving banks holding losses estimated at some £500 million.

15 May: DTI's draft regulations on Taurus published.

5 June: National Westminster Bank announces it is to cap interest rates for small businesses after its chairman, Lord Alexander, was summoned to the Treasury to discuss claims that banks were overcharging small companies through their policy of imposing extra margins on the supposedly greater risks involved.

17 June: Forum of Private Business, the small business pressure group, calls for the introduction of written contracts between banks and small businesses to ensure that no company could find its borrowing reduced or removed without due cause, which should then ensure that lending rises and falls with companies' performances.

1 July: Bank of England/Treasury report criticizes the banks' approach to charges for their services and their handling of customers in difficulties.

5 July: Bank of Credit and Commerce International (BCCI) is shut down by the Bank of England and other central banks and its assets are frozen.

8 July: Abu Dhabi, 77 per cent owners of BCCI, accuses the Bank of England of torpedoing a £6 billion plan to rescue the bank.

15 July: An attempt by Labour to insert a new clause into the Finance Bill requiring banks to supply the Treasury with reports on their interest rates is defeated by 316 to 213.

16 July: FT-SE index reaches new closing high of 2,556.8.

22 July: Lord Justice Bingham is to conduct an independent inquiry into the handling of the BCCI affair.

23 July: Fears of a secondary banking crisis in the wake of BCCI prompts National Home Loans to arrange large new borrowing facilities.

FT-SE index reaches a new closing high of 2,587.9.

26 July: FT-SE index reaches new closing high of 2,589.3.

29 July: FT-SE index reaches new closing high of 2,595.

BCCI and its founder, Mr Agha Hasan Abedi, and its former chief operating officer, Mr Swaleh Naqvi, are charged in the US with swindling up to $20 billion (£11.9 billion) from depositors around the world through fraud, falsifying bank records, money laundering and larceny.

30 July: Sheikh of Abu Dhabi places £50 million on deposit in London to save BCCI from immediate liquidation.

High Court refuses the Bank of England's request for an immediate winding up order against BCCI. It grants a four month delay to allow exploration of an Abu Dhabi project to help UK depositors and employees.

30 July: FT-SE index reaches new closing high of 2,595.6.

2 Aug: FT-SE index reaches new closing high of 2,601.7.

Secret report on BCCI prepared by Price Waterhouse for the Bank of England is released. It confirms the massive scale of the fraud by BCCI.

8 Aug: The large Woolwich Building Society agrees to 'stand behind' the small Southdown society, following rumours which have touched off a run of withdrawals from some Southdown branches.

14 Aug: FT-SE index reaches new closing high of 2,608.8.

15 Aug: FT-SE index reaches new closing high of 2,617.2.

16 Aug: FT-SE index reaches new closing high of 2,621.

22 Aug: FT-SE index reaches new closing high of 2,623.

23 Aug: FT-SE index reaches new closing high of 2,640.7.

30 Aug: FT-SE index reaches new closing high of 2,645.7.

2 Sept: FT-SE index reaches new closing high of 2,679.6.

16 Sept: Report by the London Chamber of Commerce and Industry surveys attitudes of foreign banks towards the City and finds them increasingly critical of London's infrastructural defects, lack of co-ordination and quality of life, and points to resulting problems in maintaining London's competitive position.

25 Sept: Abbey National to buy the Glasgow based life insurance office, Scottish Mutual, for £285 million.

30 Sept: Charges against two of the defendants in the Blue Arrow City trial were dismissed by the judge at the Old Bailey.

2 Oct: New rules on building society lending introduced.

3 Oct: Abu Dhabi owners of BCCI announce 1,100 redundancies at the bank in the UK, implying abandonment of attempts to resuscitate the group.

9 Oct: Control of Hoare Govett, a leading City stockbroker, is to be sold by the US bank Security Pacific, now merging with Bank America.

17 Oct: Announcement that the implementation of Taurus is to be delayed by a further 12 months.

24 Oct: OFT criticizes banks for 'insensitive and high-handed behaviour' towards small firms but clears them of collusion.

5 Nov: Robert Maxwell is found dead in the sea off the Canary Islands. The event triggers a major crisis for his shaky media empire, with billions of pounds of bank debts.

7 Nov: Bank of England calls for dividend cuts where trading conditions warrant.

19 Nov: Loss-making Town and Country Building Society is to be taken over by the Woolwich Building Society.

25 Nov: Banks led by National Westminster agree to a short term freeze of repayments on £850 million loans to the Maxwell family interests.

26 Nov: Southdown Building Society is to be merged into the Woolwich Building Society.

28 Nov: Complaints to the banking ombudsman increased in the year to September 1991 by 62 per cent to 6,327.

1 Dec: Britain's government-controlled short term export credit business is sold to NCM, the Dutch private sector credit insurer, and is renamed NCM Credit Insurance.

2 Dec: High Court grants the provisional liquidators of BCCI a further adjournment of winding up proceedings to give them more time to negotiate a deal with Abu Dhabi on behalf of creditors.

3 Dec: Kevin and Ian Maxwell resign as chairmen respectively of the family's quoted companies, Maxwell Communications Corporation (MCC) and Mirror Group Newspapers (MGN).

4 Dec: Serious Fraud Office launches investigation into potential losses of about £350 millions from MCC and MGN pension funds through lending to Maxwell family private interests.

12 Dec: Voluntary code of banking practice to set minimum standards of treatment for personal customers agreed.

16 Dec: MCC files for protection from its creditors under US bankruptcy law.

17 Dec: Five broking firms are fined in disciplinary moves following a market-rigging scandal at London Fox, the commodities futures and options exchange.

19 Dec: Regulations are laid before Parliament to provide the framework for TAURUS, the Stock Exchange's much- delayed paperless system of share ownership and trading, scheduled for introduction from APril 1993.

30 Dec: Federation of Small Businesses accuses the high street banks of accelerating the rate of business failures. Business failures are estimated to have increased by 65 per cent to 47,777 in 1991.

31 Dec: High Court approves an arrangement covering MCC's administration in the US, removing power from the MCC board. The decision allows an orderly administration of the company in the context of both UK and US insolvency law.

FT-SE index closes the year at 2,483.1, a rise over 1991 of 15.3 per cent. The year's highest point was 2,679.6 on 2 September; its lowest 2,054.8 on 16 January.

Industry's View of the Economic Background

B. M. HIORNS

There are years in the trade cycle which company chairmen and shareholders would prefer to forget, and 1991 was such a year. It was a year of dashed hopes, the optimistic feel that recession would be short and the landing soft was quickly extinguished as doubt and depression took control as the year progressed. All the signs of healthy financial markets, price volatility, takeover and merger activity and healthy dealing volumes slowed. Only rights activity was vigorous, especially in the first part of the year. It was a year of waiting for recovery, but where that recovery would come from became increasingly unclear. The dramatic events in Russia and in the Middle East filled the stage, and economic and financial events, since they told only of drift and decline, engaged international attention as an embarrassment to the political and military victories of the capitalist democracies. At the very moment when capitalism was savouring the defeat of the Marxist autocracies, and just when the struggling proto-democracies of eastern Europe were taking their first unsure steps into the new world of free markets, so too the first doubts about the resilience of Western capitalism were appearing to frighten the faint hearted.

The confident and surging growth in the world economy ended with the October 1987 crash. Too much credit had been extended, too much debt accumulated, savings ratios were too low and a period of retrenchment was plainly in the offing. Throughout 1989 and 1990 world credit was aggressively reduced. A regime of high interest rates and of much tighter money rapidly reduced available credit throughout the world. In the UK 1990 had evidenced the early stages of resulting economic slow down: unemployment started to rise and house prices in particular fell by up to 25 per cent in the boom area of south east England. They had not fallen elsewhere in the UK because the full impact of the recession had not then developed. If the recession was the result of the massive worldwide credit squeeze then a good indicator of underlying change for the better would be the end of the decline in credit. That happened in the last quarter of 1990. A clear signal was given that the world economy could swing into a period of expansion as long as the politicians generated an improved level of demand and world bankers provided credit. Confident that that would occur, the US stock market showed a sharp rise in February 1991, and this was rightly followed by the main western European markets; and even Japan, still in turmoil after the collapse of mid-1990, managed to rise from its unstable depths. But the subsequent history of the various national markets accurately described the course of disillusioned expectations during 1991. Optimism was, and remains, at its greatest in the United States, although this is a relative statement because having recovered to its old high level (around 3000 on the Dow Jones Industrial Index), the index then traded sideways until mid-November when, disappointed that real economic recovery was so long in coming, the market collapsed. The Federal Reserve Bank soon acted to cut the discount rate so that the year ended on a high note as the US market renewed its confidence that recovery would come.

The British index has, as has been usual since 1987, closely tracked the US index in terms of direction and inflexion point. The FT-SE 100 index has however shown some unusually volatile behaviour in terms of its value relative to the US index in 1991. Until June it tracked the US index very closely but then during the summer outperformed the US. This was perhaps a period of misplaced optimism as the opinion polls showed a swing to the Tories and as a measure of confidence that economic recovery was underway entered public perception. Both were, however, misplaced so that by the end of the summer the FT-SE 100 index declined from its near-2700 high in August to a low of 2350 just before Christmas. Although exhibiting the usual lagged behaviour relative to the US market, the FT-SE recovered further in the first days of 1992. Economists now order the recoveries from recession as follows: the United States, the United Kingdom, France, Japan and Germany. It is of analytical interest that the behaviour of the respective stock markets reflects this order of prospective recovery, confirming the utility of markets as forecasters of the behaviour of the real economy.

The key message from both the international and domestic stock market was that after a surge of confidence in January that world and national recovery was on its way, disillusion and growing fear that recession would turn to depression set in by the end of the year. In the United Kingdom the looming general election heightened market tension and exaggerated market movements. Numbers and indices alone do not entirely describe markets and in the UK since the underlying sentiment was at best neutral for much of the year, excitement, when it came, was generally transient and prurient interest in scandal and failure.

A Year of Reckoning

All great booms collapse to leave a trail of unhappiness and suffering. This collapse has been particularly characterized by the number of bankruptcies and failures which have resulted. The first wave of bankruptcy during 1990 took the weak, the firms that were inherently failing, and cruel though it may seem, this is a healthy economic process. Nineteen ninety-one took those firms which survived the initial stress but which did not possess either the reserves or the strategy to survive in tight conditions. It is now clear that 1991 was unusual in its savagery, a record rise of

45 per cent having occurred in the numbers of bankruptcies. Nineteen ninety-two will take those survivors which do not possess the balance sheet strength nor sufficiently strong cash flow to survive the stress of expansion under conditions of slowly growing credit. The thousands of small businesses which had developed during the years of the Thatcher boom continued to be culled viciously during the recession but they were not alone, 1991 saw several major failures, none of which was as rapid or as dramatic as that of Maxwell Communications.

Robert Maxwell joined the ranks of major financial criminals and the demise of his empire will come to symbolize the dark side of the eighties boom. The fact that a major business collapse of this type should occur is not of great significance historically; it is inevitable that the 'tight money' phase of a recession will generate some major collapses which will be dealt with through the normal process of liquidation, those parts of the broken firm which remain viable falling into the hands of new and more efficient owners. The uniqueness of the Maxwell collapse lay in its very ordinariness and raised the question as to why such an obvious disaster was not anticipated by the City. This is a serious question for the City because one of its purposes is to anticipate problems of the Maxwell kind and either to deal with them beforehand or to police and control the resulting debacle to minimize damage. Why then was Maxwell able to survive the various monitoring systems for so long?

Robert Maxwell was a financier of massive personal charisma and power and he positioned himself at the centre of a web of interlocked companies. His central position and his character ensured that the normal process of sceptical exchange among the directors of a well-run company was absent. It was well known that the investment analysis of any one of the Maxwell companies raised serious questions. It was certainly known that analysis of the group as a whole raised even more serious questions as to the financing of these operations. The precise ownership of the Liechtenstein parent was a mystery and the primary sources of Maxwell capital an enigma. Nevertheless, the analytical system failed to establish the true nature and extent of the decay of his companies. The nature of Robert Maxwell's business practices was also thoroughly well-known throughout City and business circles. The question that arises is why, when all this was known and when so many historical precedents were available, did so many banks lend Maxwell companies money and why had all of this disparate information and knowledge not gelled together to result in media or stock market retribution much earlier?

The most distasteful aspect of Maxwell's reign was his use of the personal intimidation of those who sought to expose him. It is a frightening fact that in a modern democracy individuals can be subjected to stress by the use of the law and by manipulation of the media. Robert Maxwell had established an atmosphere of real fear in which critics knew that they would suffer personal attack. If the first isolated criticisms of those individuals who bothered to establish the sordid facts of Maxwell's behaviour could be halted successfully then the whole process of formation of public opinion could be delayed. That perhaps explains why public concern never reached the level it should have and why better-informed people in the City never generated the level of concern which should normally have evolved. The stimulus to the whole process, informed individual comment, had been stifled.

It will not be known for many months, if indeed it will ever be known, when Robert Maxwell started the process of moving money, liabilities and assets from company to company, but it is clear that his actions become increasingly desperate during 1991. He had announced his interest in buying the *New York Daily News*, in March, but sold Pergamon to Elsevier in April for £440 million and announced the flotation of Mirror Group Newspapers at the same time. It had become quite clear in 1990 that the game of borrowing cheap and abundant money from Japanese and American banks to finance acquisitions, carried out with ample application of creative accounting, had ended. It is unclear why Maxwell should have continued to attempt to make overstretching acquisitions when the rest of his tycoon peers were either bankrupt or retrenching. Maxwell created an empire in which he was individually pivotal. He did not recognize that the moment for inactivity arrived in 1989 and he would presumably accept no internal advice that would limit his activities. The normal checks and balance of corporate life were absent. Maxwell pursued expansion in a world where bankers had loosened their usual criteria for lending. He lacked the flexibility to change his ways in time, and so his empire collapsed, as all empires do, ephemeral once the despot departs.

The City shrugged but rightly saw Maxwell as peripheral to the more serious matter of unrelenting recession, but beyond the financial aspects of collapse other issues were raised by the Maxwell affair and other scandals. The City and its institutions are in a difficult phase of transition from internal self-regulation to full legislative control. The operation of existing legislation has not yet matured nor is current legislation yet sufficiently developed to deal with affairs like Maxwell. Maxwell successfully manipulated his share price for a period and the policing and correctness of some of the operations associated with this probably require re-examination, while the plundering of Mirror Group's pension fund points to the necessity for strengthening of legislation in this vulnerable area. But the law can only go so far in protecting the innocent. The City has a duty both to itself and to society to ensure that the quiet policing of both its own affairs and those who use its institutions is effective. In the case of Maxwell it failed, as did government, the media and markets.

Among the various collapses, that of Maxwell naturally stands out because of its Napoleonic scale and character. BCCI brought with it more widespread suffering, affecting as it did a wide spread of depositors. At least on this occasion the Bank of England acted with judgement and caution, although it inevitably attracted criticism. Once again it had been well known for many years that the affairs of the bank were unsatisfactory but the collection of real proof takes time and involves the banking systems and politics of many countries.

A Change in Market Structure?

The equity market has traditionally enjoyed its role as a useful historical measure of financial health and as an instrument of prediction because it reflects the investment activities of the great savings institutions. This role was particularly apt in the United Kingdom where 75 per cent of equity is owned by the professionally managed savings funds – by insurance companies, corporate pension funds and banks. In America, although the proportion of institutionally held funds is rising the role of the individual investor is still paramount. In continental Europe the analytical significance of markets varies. In France it is as valid a measure of underlying economic reality as in the UK, but for various structural reasons the other national markets are perhaps less so.

The purport of this is that the economic historian has, since the mid-1950s and especially since the early 1980s, been able to use the performance of the stock market as a valid indicator of the performance and expectations of the savings side of the national economy. This in turn is of use to the historian since it is the measure of the most skilled and practised professional opinion as to which way the economy was expected to develop. This opinion represents an amalgam of both the short and long term. The basic requirement of investment, to ensure that the long-term liabilities of the fund are met, generates the long-term requirement to provide long-run real returns of at least 3 per cent. The investment behaviour of the professional investor always has been and always will be tailored to meet this end. The future time horizon which the professional investor takes within this definition lies between five and 25 years. Such a long view is of little use to the historian since many aspects other than the flow of events will control the fund manager's motives and investment actions.

It is the short-term behaviour of the professional investor which raises historical interest. In addition to the need to provide long run real returns the fund manager must also generate short-term performance. This arises because competitive peer pressure forces the fund manager to seek to outperform his rivals, and this is manifest in a percentage outperformance of the relevant market index. It is this Darwinian selective pressure which ensures that the fund manager buys or sells the market in reaction to political or economic news. It is this behaviour, especially the element of anticipation and hence forecasting, which is of interest to the historian. So the precise mechanism which the historical observer uses is the anticipatory behaviour of professional fund managers operating under competitive stress in buying or selling ordinary stocks or shares in the equity market. Changes in the structure of the London market are now eroding the integrity of that definition.

For some time two 'derivatives' markets have existed in London. A 'derivative' is a traded instrument such as an option, warrant, convertible or future. The definition of these types is technical and anyway irrelevant to our purpose. In one form or another they provide the fund manager with the facility to buy or sell his view of the future development of an individual stock, share or, importantly, market, without having to invest in the underlying equity which is traded in the stock market. This is attractive to the fund manager because volatility, the rapidity with which the instruments rise or fall is generally greater. If he is confident of his investment ability he can thus execute his policy quickly and often with substantial gearing or leverage.

Markets in the various types of derivative have existed for some time, although the opening of the London International Financial Futures Exchange (LIFFE) market in September 1982 stimulated a significant change in the attitudes of the savings institutions. The institutions had historically regarded derivatives operations as either a means of optimizing yield income or as a far from respectable casino. However, changes in tax laws and the development of sophisticated computer models to value derivatives with greater accuracy helped change these attitudes. In particular, the realization that index futures allowed the fund manager to exercise his view of likely markets and economic progression in a much less cumbersome way than through the purchase of traditional equities resulted in a marked shift of institutional activity from traditional equities to index figures. Equities still account for the major part of institutional cash flow but index futures are increasingly used to generate performance.

From the historical analytical point of view this implies that the observer must in future use the combination of both underlying equity market and the futures market as his source of data.

The use of stock options and derivatives has been developing for several years but 1991 was undoubtedly the watershed year in which futures established themselves as flexible tools for the fund manager. The rise in use of futures has coincided with the decline in use of stock options. The administration of the LIFFE has, since its inception, been efficient and enlightened. The same cannot be said of the LTOM market and 1991 was marked by the merger of the two markets. Like most mergers LIFFE effectively took over LTOM and the new options market remains to be tested in its new environment although it is unlikely that options will ever develop as well as futures. It is an interesting characteristic of the options and futures market that 'locals' continue to play a significant role. A local is either an individual or small company who uses his own capital to deal in the instruments of the market, he is the purest form of short-term speculator in that he has close access to the market and its information but because he is under-capitalized his market positions must generally be held for a short period of time. He does not generally deal with the retail or institutional client side of the market so that his views are short-term. The very volatility of the market, which gives it its short-term attraction, is thus enhanced by this group of individuals. However, questions exist as to the resilience and dependability of a market of this kind and there exist proponents of electronic dealing systems for these markets. The large integrated houses which provide the bulk of the capital to finance these markets would tend to prefer such systems for the faltering stock option market while the successful futures markets will probably continue as an 'open outcry' market.

While 1991 saw both the formal merger of the two principal derivatives markets and a real watershed change in use and significance of the futures market, the other change in nature of the London market was more insidious. In October 1986, the London Stock Exchange started a market known as SEAQ International, its purpose being to establish a market to trade in the stocks and shares of the principal continental European companies. This market has developed in a highly successful way, capturing about 40 per cent of the total volume of European exchange turnover. The market is used not only by British institutions investing overseas (the general weakness of the domestic economy and the more international attitude of British fund managers encouraging their use of SEAQ International) but by European fund managers as well. It is not coincidental that SEAQ International has developed in recent years, it having been planned that London should establish a strong position in international equity markets as the competition to become the principal European financial centre develops. This in turn reflects the growing integration of the European economy, the pace of which quickened during 1991. SEAQ International owes much of its success to its lesser 'transparency', which means that large stock movements can occur in conditions of less exposure to the whole market. Some market theorists are offended by such restrictions on information flow and their views hold partial sway in the normal SEAQ market in UK shares. There is no doubt that the liquidity and activity of the UK equity market has been restricted by the dogmatic attitude of the various overseeing bodies of government. The success of SEAQ International and the continuing integration of the European corporate sector are beginning to bring pressure upon the members of the UK market to think more internationally and to consider means of encouraging more active development of the UK market in its European context. If this does not occur then it is probable that London's equity markets will atrophy to provincial status.

While the economic cycle has imposed a quiet trading year upon the London market the two structural influences outlined above, the one clear and immediate in its influence, the other in its early stages, will ultimately radically change the nature of business methods in London. The influence upon the companies that comprise the market will be complex. The largest UK stocks will increasingly be compared with their European comparatives and the professional investor will probably expect to deal in the main European corporate stocks in the same large and efficient market. The lesser corporate stocks in each national market will continue to trade in the respective natural market but their ratings or market value may well become less related to the major companies within their industrial sector. This may affect their access to and cost of capital. Nineteen ninety-one was a year of apparent market boredom but of highly influential long-term underlying change in capital markets.

Why Are We Waiting?

The February market surge held its ground only in the US. Elsewhere, including the UK, the delayed appearance of recovery-generated market recession began in the autumn. In America the politicians were certain that enough had been done to regenerate growth. In the United Kingdom a rise in consumer spending was expected to generate sufficient demand within the economy to stimulate growth in 1991. It was true that the savings ratio had risen and that potential consumers possessed sufficient ability to gear up their debt to generate the beginnings of recovery but the process of cooling demand during 1989 and 1990 was too successful in blunting consumer confidence. In particular the continuing decline in house prices damaged the morale of the consumer and prevented any increase in activity in the housing markets. New house sales also failed to recover. If consumer spending was to fuel the recovery then confidence would have to be much greater. But the problems of the failed recovery are not limited to the UK. They reflect an international problem. The world credit crunch, necessary to control the inflationary problems of the late 1980s has left the world banking system bereft of both money and willingness to lend to finance a new expansion of credit. Internationally the banking system is still dealing with problems of asset devaluation and bankruptcy. In Japan, the possibility of another collapse in property prices continues to limit the availability of Japanese funds, while the restructuring of the American bankings system against a continuing background of bank failure also limits willingness to lend. The availability of banking funds in international markets is thus much lower than two or three years ago.

In the United Kingdom it is claimed that availability of credit would not limit recovery but the major clearing banks were suffering their own adjustment to the new reality. In March the four major clearers made a total provision of £3.4 billion to cover the bad debts generated by business and mortgage failure. In Midland's case the poor results caused the departure of the chairman and a halving of the dividend. Those insurance companies which specialized in insuring mortgages similarly suffered damage as policy holders claimed as unemployment rose, although commercial mortgages caused the major part of the damage. In circumstances like these a rapid turnaround in both consumer and banker confidence was never likely. The continuing high level of German interest rates limited the ability of the British government to reduce rates now that we were members of the ERM and consequently government's ability to stimulate the economy through rate decreases became limited. All of these factors emerged through the summer and autumn to erode confidence and to engender a developing sense of gloom.

The underlying economic reality seems to impose an inertia all of its own and the sceptical observer easily doubts the claims of politicians to control events. During the eighties the much maligned President Reagan and (domestically) Mrs Thatcher oversaw expansionist policies and were highly visible in so doing. No such high profile lead became apparent during 1991.

It is natural that 1991, probably the bottom of the economic and stock market cycle, should have engendered a mood of disappointed cynicism, but markets found it hard not to feel that Mr Micawber was in charge and that his policy was as always 'something will turn up'!

Industry's Year – The Slough of Despond

Nineteen ninety-one was always going to be an unpleasant year for corporate managers, they would be reporting the downturn of 1990, cutting back their operations, and, as the year progressed, forecasting unrelenting gloom in 1992. For some of them 1991 would mean early retirement.

For the building sectors there had been hope of recovery early in the year but by the second quarter the industry was forecasting that house construction would fall 11 per cent in 1991 and by a further 5 per cent in 1992. Advances by building societies fell to the lowest for some time. Commercial property construction, which had held up well, also collapsed. The absence of the hoped-for upturn then forced a series of rights issues from cash-starved companies. Not all rights issues stemmed from weakness, Redland raised £280 million in March presumably to indulge its usual strategy of acquisition at the bottom of the cycle. As an indicator, the building industry and its tribulations well exemplified the history of the economy as a whole through 1991.

The engineering industry's fortunes were equally predictable. British Steel's earnings fell 65 per cent in 1990 but it maintained its interim dividend and warned that its final dividend was not sacrosanct. In September new car sales were 17 per cent down on the same month a year before. Hawker Siddeley was taken over by BTR, ending a long period of investor disillusion with Hawker's poor management record. British Aerospace raised £432 million by way of a rights issue. It subsequently sharply reduced its profit forecast and then lost its chairman, Professor Smith, who was replaced by Sir Graham Day.

The conglomerates, for which 1991 would be a test of one of the principal rationales for diversification (that earnings volatility is thereby reduced), did not entirely justify themselves. BTR reported its first fall in earnings since its humble beginnings in the sixties, but it did at least complete two acquisitions, one small, Rockware, and the other of more majestic scale, Hawker Siddeley. Hanson acquired its now legendary holding in ICI in mid-May. To this day it is not clear what Hanson's intentions were. ICI's defence was vigorous and ruthless and by the year-end Hanson was confirming that it would not bid for ICI, although it still holds its original stake. P&O suffered a severe 31 per cent fall in profits, mainly through its property interests, in particular its holding in Bovis the house builder.

The utilities sector was joined by the electricity generators, floated early in the year, and by the Scottish electricity companies. In market terms the whole group of utilities began the process of becoming a united sector. The common theme that became increasingly obvious during the year was that of 'regular risk'. Ofwat, the water regulator, adopted a particularly aggressive stance in attempting to control profit, acquisition policy and dividend growth for the water companies. Ofgas was met by resolute resistance from British Gas, but came back fighting so that the British Gas share price now moves in response to this battle of powerful personalities. BAA successfully saw off the CAA. BT attracted public criticism for its profit increase even though it has consistently met Oftel's demands. The electricity industry is, as yet, too young for the battle lines to be drawn up, although the large industrial customers of the generators were plainly preparing a well-organized lobby to object to the price rises they were enduring as the year ended. The role of the regulators and the true extent of their regulatory power will be tested in the years ahead. The role of the utility in the professional investor's portfolio was established permanently as the utilities reported good profit and dividend growth in marked contrast to almost all other sectors apart from pharmaceuticals.

The normally defensive and profit resilient components of the consumer sector, food manufacturing and retailing, stores and breweries, all lost their recession-proof quality; a measure of the severity of recession in 1991. The food retailers Sainsbury, Tesco and Argyll raised £1.1 billion in rights issues by the middle of the year to finance the further expansion of floor space. Just as the stores sector had committed the classic blunder of bringing into commission excess capacity just at the top of the demand cycle some two years earlier, so the food retailers appeared to be intent on the same course. By mid-year the first signs of a competitive price war were appearing. The brewers did not escape the cycle this time either and Bass raised £558 million by way of rights. Allied Lyons had the embarrassment of losing £150 million in currency markets, but Guinness, after its problems, broke the trend with a phase of major recovery. For the stores sector the year was equally grim. Marks and Spencer reported a 4 per cent rise in profits, but Next showed a net loss of £223 million, which gives the range of experience for the sector.

If the trade cycle brought its problems for all they were at least predictable. For the TV contractors the 1991 licensing auction brought the random chance of the roulette wheel to the fight for survival. TVS and Thames lost their franchises while Yorkshire TV paid £38 million to retain its licence, £20 million more than the closest losing bid. Central and Scottish TV paid only £2,000 for their licence while Meridian paid £37 million for the south and south-east of England. The Treasury had at least raised £40 million a year.

In absolute terms the conditions businesses met in 1991 were the most vicious since the early 1970s. A year better forgotten.

Chronology

2 Jan: According to Dun and Bradstreet a record 24,442 businesses failed in 1990.

7 Jan: DTI inspectors appointed to investigate at Norton.

25 Jan: ICI protests to the DTI about the MMC inspired block on the sale of its loss-making fertilizer division to the state-owned Finnish company Kemira.

31 Jan: MMC gives go-ahead to merger between the missiles divisions of British Aerospace and the French company, Thomson-CSF.

Williams Holdings gains control of Yale and Valor in an agreed deal worth £330 million.

11 Feb: *Company Cars: An International Perspective*, NEDO, urges companies to use bicycles as perks instead of company cars.

EC clears the pubs for breweries swap deal of Grand Metropolitan and Courage (formerly Elders IXL).

19 Feb: Government to provide £48 million for two schemes to assist innovation in small firms.

20 Feb: Pentland Industries sells its stake in Reebok for $616 million.

21 Feb: Trade and Industry Select Committee, *Sale of Rover Group to British Aerospace*, HMSO, arraigns government of seriously misleading parliament over the use of financial sweeteners during the sale of Rover in 1988.

25 Feb: *Modern Manufacturing Strength*, Labour Party, outlines plans for tax breaks for investment in manufacturing and research, compulsory investment in training, cancellation of the Business Expansion Scheme, the creation of regional development agencies, technology trusts to help transform innovation into products, more support for market research, the renationalization of the British Technology Group (to be rechristened British Technology Enterprise) and to give tax allowances for investment in science parks.

4 Mar: *Bonjour Europe – Languages and the British Manager*, British Institute of Management, reveals an appalling lack of linguistic ability amongst British business managers.

Coats Viyella bids £193.7 million for Tootal.

19 Mar: Corporation tax reduced by 1 per cent to 34 per cent in 1990 financial year and by a further 1 per cent in 1991. Upper profit limit to qualify for smaller company rate of 25 per cent raised to £250,000. Carry-back period for companies to offset trading losses against later profits extended to three years. Period in which companies have to wait before reclaiming VAT on bad debt halved to one year.

8 Apr: EC launches a monopolies investigation into four large European steelmakers, including British Steel.

10 Apr: Accounting Standards Board suggests companies should have to calculate earnings per share before rather than after allowing for extraordinary items.

29 Apr: EC industry ministers meet in Luxembourg to discuss ways of reviving the European electronics industry.

30 Apr: Coats Viyella lifts its bid for Tootal to £248 million.

7 May: Sir Gordon Borrie calls for clarification of the 'Lilley doctrine' of blocking takeovers of British companies by state-owned foreign firms after the MMC cleared four out of five such takeovers.

14 May: Hanson raids 2.8 per cent of ICI's shares for more than £200 million, prompting bid rumours.

29 May: Japanese owned ICL to buy Nokia Data of Finland for £330 million.

30 May: Sir Adrian Cadbury is appointed chairman of a new Committee on Financial Aspects of Corporate Governance.

10 June: First UK R&D scoreboard published by the Innovation Advisory Board.

Chris Pratten, *Company Failure*, Institute of Chartered Accountants of England and Wales, argues the underlying problem is the competitive position of the UK economy.

25 June: Trafalgar House bids £114 million for stricken Davy Corporation.

27 June: Report by the David Hume Institute, chaired by Sir Alan Peacock, concludes that on average there is no evidence takeovers improve the performance either of the companies involved or of the national economy. To discourage takeovers it recommends changes to the company tax system including the abolition of corporation tax and a shift of shareholding away from institutions to private hands, requiring an end to tax privileges for insurance companies and pension funds.

28 June: Tate and Lyle wins its A$325 million battle for the Australian sugar miller, Bundaberg.

6 Aug: Whyte and Mackay bids £286 million for Invergordon distillers.

12 Aug: KPMG Peat Marwick pays Ferranti £40 million in settlement of damages relating to the ISC fraud.

12 Aug: MMC urges the end of the traditional arrangements in the soft drinks trade.

16 Aug: Electronic Data Systems claims victory in its £161 million battle to takeover SD-Scicon.

23 Aug: BTR makes a £197.2 million agreed takeover bid for Rockware.

16 Sept: Hanson makes a £351 million agreed bid for Beazer.

Racal Electronics demerges its Vodaphone subsidiary.

17 Sept: Williams Holdings launches a £700 million bid for Racal Electronics.

20 Sept: BTR bids £1.45 billion for Hawker Siddeley.

25 Sept: Sir Roland Smith is ousted as chairman of British Aerospace in the wake of an unsuccessful £432 million rights issue and profit warnings and replaced by Sir Graham Day.

10 Oct: Whyte and Mackay lifts its (ultimately unsuccessful) bid for Invergordon to £350 million.

15 Oct: Labour motion for government aid to help arms manufacturers to diversify is defeated by 345 to 238.

17 Oct: Lasmo bids £1.2 billion for Ultramar.

5 Nov: Robert Maxwell drowns at sea.

7 Nov: BTR increases its bid for Hawker Siddeley to £1.5 billion.

18 Nov: SFO confirms it is investigating Headington Investments, one of the largest private companies in the Maxwell empire.

19 Nov: Swiss Bank Corporation's calling in of a £60 million loan begins the unravelling of Maxwell's business empire.

20 Nov: Northern Foods buys Express Dairy and Eden Vale from Grand Metropolitan for £326 million.

22 Nov: BTR claims victory in its bid for Hawker Siddeley.

26 Nov: Ford of Britain transfer ownership of Jaguar to the US company to relieve it of the burden of servicing the cost of the purchase.

Asil Nadir of Polly Peck declared bankrupt, disqualified as a company director and forbidden to hold management positions.

2 Dec: Shares in Maxwell Communications Corporation and Mirror Group Newspapers suspended over worries concerning the finances of the private side of the collapsing Maxwell empire.

3 Dec: Maxwell sons Kevin and Ian quit the boards of his two quoted companies, Maxwell Communications and Mirror Group.

4 Dec: SFO launches an investigation into private companies controlled by Robert Maxwell following the discovery that £600 million had been transferred to them from the Mirror Group pension fund and public companies in Maxwell's control.

5 Dec: Two key Maxwell private companies, Headington Investments and Robert Maxwell Group, are placed in administration.

Government's privatization sale of a £5.5 billion stake in BT closes.

6 Dec: Racal rejects increased bid of £746 million from Williams.

7–8 Dec: Further 31 Maxwell companies are placed in administration.

9 Dec: New BT shares make their stock market debut.

10 Dec: Redland makes a £576 million bid for Steetley.

11 Dec: *Manifesto for Business*, Liberal Democrats, outlines plans to move to the narrow bands of the ERM, make the Bank of England operationally independent, regulate more strictly hostile takeovers, merge OFT and MMC and make them independent of the DTI and break up BT and British Gas.

17 Dec: Maxwell Communications Corporation to be placed in administration.

18 Dec: Lasmo clinches its bid for Ultramar.

19 Dec: Trade and Industry Select Committee recommends legislation to ringfence pension funds in takeovers, that unsuccessful bidders should pay half the defence costs of their targets and that the Takeover Panel becomes a statutory body.

21 Dec: Williams admits defeat in its bid for Racal.

27 Dec: Dun and Bradstreet say 47,774 companies and self-employed people went out of business in 1991, a 65 per cent increase on 1990 and the highest figure by far since comprehensive records began in 1980.

Energy Policy

NEIL WALDEN

In this review last year, I suggested 'the possibility that in 1991, energy policy may begin to move in a sensible direction'.[1] As the year began, there was evidence of a change of views likely to influence the government – the Confederation of British Industry called for 'sustainability' to be included in the goals of energy policy, and made recommendations such as a compulsory energy rating system for all existing buildings when sold or let. By late in the year there was evidence of some government action: full-page newspaper advertisements aimed at persuading domestic consumers to save energy.

Electricity Privatization

First things first, however. The priority remained selling off public assets into private hands. In this the government had a measure of success – the sale of 60 per cent of the shares in National Power and PowerGen to the public in March was nearly four times oversubscribed, and early sellers made a premium of up to 30 per cent. The Labour Party pointed out however that more money would have been raised if PowerGen had been sold to Hanson Trust, as mooted in 1990. The sale of shares in Scottish Power and Hydro-Electric in June was more than three times oversubscribed, and the government announced its intention to complete the privatization of electricity by selling off the Northern Ireland industry in 1992.

The privatized industry managed to keep the lights burning, using 'the pool' or spot market in which power generators bid at half-hourly intervals to supply electricity. Pool prices soared, with major industrial customers faced with rises of up to 40 per cent. This led them to call for a Monopolies and Mergers Commission inquiry into power generation. Meanwhile, Professor Stephen Littlechild, director general of the Office of Electricity Regulation (OFFER) launched an inquiry into pool prices.

Another initiative of Professor Littlechild forced the 14 recently privatized electricity companies in England, Wales and Scotland to compensate customers for poor service as from July. This was in line with John Major's ideas for a 'Citizen's Charter'. One example would be failing to restore electricity supplies within 24 hours, for which a domestic customer would receive £20 and a business customer £50.

In the summer, widespread publicity was given to pay rises for chief executives in the industry – for example the near tripling of salaries at PowerGen and Yorkshire Electricity. Many senior executives clearly did very well out of privatization; at the same time the industry substantially reduced the number of people it employed, closing some power stations and mothballing others. One reason for the closure of older stations was the construction of new stations using more efficient technology. In October, Lakeland Power became the first operator of a combined-cycle gas turbine (CCGT) power station to supply electricity to the national grid. Several other stations using this technology are currently under construction. In December, Friends of the Earth (FoE) criticized three-quarters of these plants for failing to use combined heat and power systems to capture waste energy and use it to provide heat.[2] FoE deplored the government's failure to adopt a rigorous energy policy which would safeguard against the squandering of natural resources and protect the environment.

Table 1. Status of combined cycle gas turbine projects in England and Wales (November 1991)

Project	Developer	Size (MW)	Efficiency %	Co-generation?	Status?	Commissioning date
Angle Bay, Dyfed	Texaco Ltd/ MissionEnergy	1,100	51	Yes	Proposed	Mid 1995
Avonmouth, Avon	British Gas	1,200	50+	No	Proposed	Mid 1995
Barking, London	Thames Power Ltd	1,000	48	No	Proposed	Early 1995
Brigg, South Humberside	Regional Power Generators	240	48	No	Firm	November 1993
Calder Hall, Sellafield	British Nuclear Fuels plc	170	68-75	Yes	Firm	October 1993
Chelsea, London	Scottish Power	370	c.45	UC	Prospective	1997
Connah's Quay, Clywd	PowerGen plc	1,350	50+	No	Proposed	1995–98
Corby, Northants	East Midlands Electricity	350	c.50	No	Firm	October 1993
Coryton, Essex	Eastern Electricity	450	c.60	Yes	Proposed	January 1995
Deeside Industrial Park, Clywd	Lakeland Power	450	c.50	No	Proposed	1994
Didcot, Oxfordshire	National Power plc	1,500	c.50	No	Proposed	Late 1994
Ellesmere Port, Cheshire	Associated Octel	120	N/A	Yes	Prospective	1994
Greenwich, London	Scottish Power	370	c.45	UC	Proposed	Late 1996

Project	Developer	Size (M/W)	Efficiency %	Co-generation?	Status?	Commissioning date
Isle of Grain, Kent	AES Electric	700	c.50	No	Proposed	1995
Keadby, Humberside	Energy Resources Co Ltd	670	54	No	Proposed	1994
Killingholme, Humberside	PowerGen plc	900	50+	No	Firm	1992
Killingholme, Humberside	National Power plc	650	c.50	No	Firm	Late 1993
King's Lynn, Norfolk	Eastern Electricity	380	c.50	No	Prospective	Late 1995
Lawford, Essex	Eastern Electricity	380	c.50	No	Proposed	Early 1995
Little Barford, Bedfordshire	National Power plc	650	c.50	No	Proposed	1994
Newcastle-on-Tyne	Merz & McLellan	150	c.80	Yes	Proposed	1995
Peterborough	Eastern Electricity	360	c.50	No	Firm	Mid 1993
Plymouth, Devon	PowerGen plc	450	50+	No	Prospective	1994
Port Clarence, Cleveland	Hydro-Electric	1,000	N/A	N/A	Prospective	Late 1996
Roosecote, Cumbria	Lakeland Power	224	c.50	No	In operation	October 1991
Rugby, Warwicks	E Midlands Electricity	380	c.50	No	Prospective	Late 1995
Rye House, Herts	PowerGen plc	680	50+	No	Firm	1994
Sheffield	Sheffield Heat and Power	120	80+	Yes	Proposed	October 1996
Spondon, Derbyshire	Mowlem	170	c.70	Yes	Proposed	1995
Stallingborough Humberside	IVO Energy	1,100	51	UC	Proposed	1996
Stayhope, Notts	National Power plc	1,500	c.50	No	Proposed	Late 1994
Wilton, Cleveland	Enron Power UK	1,875	c.50	Yes	Firm	April 1993

Source: Friends of the Earth[2]

British Coal

British Coal warned that the CCGT projects planned by 1994 could wipe out 40 per cent of its market. However, changing technology is only one of the reasons why British Coal faces an uncertain future. Contracts with National Power and PowerGen to supply between 65 and 70 million tonnes of coal a year expire in March 1993, and unless new long-term contracts are agreed, the very existence of a British coal industry of any significant size is questionable. During the year, both the generating companies took steps to enable them to import large quantities of coal, and were not prepared to sign new contracts. The resulting uncertainty in British Coal's future size and profitability threatens the government's plans to privatize it after the 1992 general election.[3] A government-commissioned report by the merchant bank N M Rothschild in which one option was the closure of all but 12 deep pits and the loss of 43,000 jobs was leaked to the press. In November, senior managers in the industry asked the Prime Minister to intervene in negotiations between British Coal and the electricity industry to guarantee the future of the industry by backing an orderly move to a deep mine capacity of 50-55 million tonnes, 75 per cent of the present figure. In this area as in so many others, Britain's relations with the European Commission may be crucial – the Commission proposes that member states be permitted to subsidize coal mined at below a reference price of 90 Ecus a tonne (about £50), and this would include British Coal's output. At the end of the year, the government's response to these issues was unclear, as indeed was the future of British Coal – although a buy-out by the Union of Democratic Mineworkers is one of the likely scenarios if the Conservatives are returned to power.

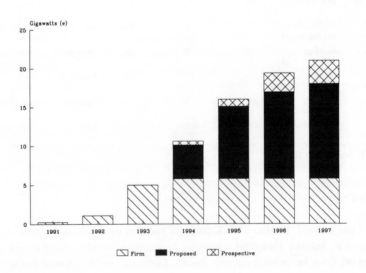

Source: Friends of the Earth[2]

Chart 1. Total Installed Capacity from CCGTs in England and Wales

British Gas

In March British Gas increased prices for its main industrial customers, the electric power generators, by 35 per cent, saying it wanted to choke off demand. Ofgas, the gas regulator, immediately condemned the price rise and asked British Gas to revise its schedule. In September, British Gas responded by cutting prices by 9 per cent, but warned that supplies could run out in 1995.

The Nuclear Power Industry

With a moratorium on nuclear power projects except Sizewell B until after the government review scheduled for 1994, the industry spent time and money trying to improve its image. Glossy advertisements in the colour supplements attempted to persuade the public of the benefits of nuclear power,[4] and senior executives in the industry pressed the government to try to secure its economic future.[5] They called for the establishment of a sinking fund for the decommissioning costs of new power stations, to be funded by electricity consumers.

Meanwhile, problems continued to plague the nuclear power industry. Both Nuclear Electric and Scottish Nuclear made overall losses, because of the large provisions necessary for liabilities (although they claimed power could be generated for 3 pence per kilowatt hour if they were relieved of these). The Nuclear Installation Inspectorate reported six years late on their long term safety review of the magnox reactors, stating concern about 'unexpected damage' in the condition of welds in the reactor pressure vessel. In Wales, a report kept secret since 1988 revealed that the lake next to Trawsfynnd power station – closed since February because of embrittlement problems – has radioactivity levels higher than anywhere else in Britain except Sellafield, and will remain a health hazard for many years into the future.[6] And the Scottish nuclear industry announced in December that the Hunterston A reactor – once Britain's best performing nuclear power station, but closed in 1989 as uneconomic – would not reopen, due to lack of a market for its output.[7]

Nuclear fusion made headlines in November, just days before the Joint European Torus (JET) programme budget was to be considered by the member nations. The stage had been reached where the project was actually generating energy – for a few minutes. The problems of getting from this stage to a commercially viable source of power are enormous, and it may well take 50 years to discover if it can be done. In the words of one commentator, 'Science couldn't devise a harder way to boil a kettle'.[8] It is highly questionable whether the $5 billion next stage is worth pursuing – almost certainly the resources would be better devoted to alternative energy technologies. It is quite possible, for example, that within ten years small solar panels could provide households' lighting needs. The price of photovoltaic modules has fallen by 80 per cent in the last ten years, and researchers believe that within two or three years these will be an economically viable replacement for glass cladding on the south-facing walls of office blocks in Britain.

War in the Gulf

Various commentators argued that the war in the Gulf – with all its horrors and destruction, and the many thousands of Iraqis killed – was really about ensuring the West's continued access to Middle East oil. At the start of the year, when it was not clear whether there would be war or not, oil was priced at $26 a barrel – down from a peak of $40 at the end of September 1990 as a result of fear of war occurring. When war broke out in January, the predicted very high oil price failed to materialize. After the crushing victory of western technology, a lead article in *The Guardian* called for 'a massive and long-term energy conservation programme' to remove the West's overdependence on this source of energy.[9] Suggestions included putting VAT on energy, penalizing gas-guzzling company cars, and a progressively rising 'carbon tax' on fossil fuels. Needless to say, no such measures were introduced.

Carbon Tax

In September, the European Commission called for member states to levy taxes, starting in 1993, that would raise the price of oil by $10 a barrel by the year 2000, in order to meet the target of stabilizing carbon dioxide emissions. While this particular proposal was unsuccessful, the idea of a carbon tax is now clearly on the agenda.

Alternative Energy Issues

The Gulf war and privatization of the electricity supply industry stimulated consideration of alternative fuels, the former because it highlighted the west's dependence on Middle East oil, and the latter because of the Non-Fossil Fuel Obligation. The Non-Fossil Fuel Obligation requires the regional electricity companies in England and Wales to secure generating capacity from renewable energy sources, and the government set six separate technology bands to reflect the variation in development of different sources, with premium prices ranging from 5.7 pence per kilowatt hour for landfill gas to 11 pence for wind energy.[10] These premium prices clearly encouraged interest in the possibility of using renewable sources, and the number of applications to do so exceeded government expectations.

In July, Energy Minister Colin Moynihan launched what is claimed to be the world's most advanced wave energy installation (an oscillating water column) on the island of Islay. In November, the government more than doubled its renewable energy targets and approved 122 new wind, wave and other projects to generate electricity from natural sources.[11] These included wind farms in Cornwall, Devon and Wales, the largest being a cluster of 100 wind turbines. The biggest single project is a proposed £200 million waste incineration power station on the south bank of the Thames. Incineration, unlike windpower, is not necessarily pollution free, and there was opposition to this proposed station from Bexley council and Greenpeace on the grounds of the threat to public health.

The current government target for renewables is 2 per cent of electricity production by the year 2000. Greenpeace has argued that the target should be 10 per cent, and it produced three scenarios showing different ways this could be met. The benefits would be 23 million tonnes less carbon dioxide released every year, 160,000 tonnes less sulphur dioxide and 100,000 tonnnes less nitrogen oxides. Such a proposal appears to have wide support – a British Market Research Bureau survey in August revealed that 67 per cent of the 1,000 people surveyed would be prepared to pay an extra £7 on their annual electricity bill to achieve this, and also wanted to see cuts in the current subsidy to nuclear power (currently £17 per annum per household).

In the short-term future we are likely to see increased emphasis on the generation of energy from waste – and increased debate over the health hazards of incineration.[12] In the longer term, wind and wave power seem likely at last to be properly developed, now that the government has finally accepted that these are particularly suited to British weather conditions. Unless the nuclear lobby can again exert a stranglehold over British energy policy-making, it is likely that renewable technologies will sound the death knell of the nuclear power industry.

Energy Efficiency

There were signs that the design of office buildings was at last responding sensibly to ecological concerns.[13] Major developers made good use of the Building Research Establishment environmental assessment method to evaluate the design of their buildings, which increasingly incorporated emphasis on good working conditions and energy-conscious design. In the domestic sector, two energy-rating schemes for homes were launched. It is likely that we will see increased emphasis on human scale, naturalness and simplicity in the spaces created by architects, but also the use of advanced technology materials to trap sunlight and provide insulation. Transparent insulation materials (TIMs) which both provide heat and prevent heat loss are rapidly being developed – one estimate suggests they could meet more than two-thirds of global heating needs.[14]

Osram continued successfully to promote its electronic light bulbs to the domestic market, pointing out that each one would save £45 worth of electricity in its 8,000 hour life, and describing them as 'a bright investment – for you, and for the planet we all live on'. Sales of such bulbs rose dramatically, much to the surprise of the manufacturers, and late in the year they were struggling to keep up with demand.[15]

In November, the government launched an energy-saving publicity campaign entitled 'Helping the Earth begins at Home'. This is a three-year £10 million campaign, and included full-page newspaper adverts asking 'What can any one person do about Global Warming?' and featuring 'relatively straightforward changes in the way we use energy at home' ranging from fixing dripping taps to installing a new (more efficient) central heating boiler. While clearly a step in the right direction, it was seen by critics as far from sufficient. Indeed, it was in many ways similar to the 'Save It' campaign by the government in 1976, and indicated how little energy policy in this country has progressed over the last 15 years.

The Environment Secretary's own advisory committee on business and the environment, composed of senior industrialists, called for much more radical action: minimum energy standards for electrical appliances, a single officially-backed rating system for measuring each house's energy performance, and a cut in VAT on energy-saving items such as insulation or heating controls. Earlier in the year, reports from the House of Lords, the Commons Energy Committee and the Bow Group Conservative think-tank had all made similar calls. The response was words rather than effective action – John Wakeham and Michael Heseltine conceded that energy conservation is 'the quickest, most promising and most cost-effective way of combating global warming', but did little to bring it about. Andrew Warren, the director of the Association for the Conservation of Energy estimated the 1991 Dutch government expenditure on energy conservation as £9.60 per head, the British figure as 75 pence.[16]

Conclusion

Change is in the air, and for once industrialists appear to be ahead of the government in seeing the need for change, and if necessary legislation. There is evidence of a widespread realization that business must become 'sustainable' and start to produce and use energy sensibly. So far, however, there is no reason to believe the government treats the issue as urgent, and this is in step with the short-term nature of British politics – energy policy clearly will not be an issue in the 1992 general election. Yet the very real problem of global warming will demand action from whichever party is elected to power, and painful decisions will have to be taken.

In 1991 there was increasing evidence that energy use was on the agenda of businesses – the question for 1992 is whether it will at last receive serious attention from government. Frank Dobson, the shadow Energy Secretary, made the Labour Party's views clear in November: 'We must make sure that (the electricity industry) promotes energy saving rather than sales; that its fuel policies reflect the need to husband our oil and gas reserves and promote the use of renewables; that, like Sweden, Germany and the United States, it invests in clean-coal technology; and that it reflects the need to help the balance of trade'.[17] It will be worth watching to see whether we are any nearer these goals by the end of 1992.

Notes

1 Neil Walden, 'Energy Policy' in Peter Catterall (ed) *Contemporary Britain: An Annual Review 1991*, Blackwell, 1991.
2 Friends of the Earth press release *'Dash for Gas' heads for second-rate design along third-rate policy track*, 3 December 1991.
3 Martin Waller, 'Sale of coal will inflate power prices', The Times, *10 June 1991*.

4 For example: *You* magazine, 10 November 1991.

5 Simon Beavis & Keith Harper, 'Coal managers plead with Major to save industry', *The Guardian*, 15 November 1991.

6 Paul Brown, 'Lake radiation peril will outlive N-plant', *The Guardian*, 8 July 1991.

7 Alan Dron, 'Hunterston restart plans are abandoned', *The Scotsman*, 3 December 1991.

8 John Vidal 'New monsters and masters of the universe', *The Guardian*, 15 November 1991.

9 'The Cost of Cheap Oil', *The Guardian*, 19 March 1991.

10 Colin Moynihan, 'The Wind of Change', *The Observer*, 1 December 1991.

11 Crispin Aubrey, 'Plugging into Nature Power', *The Guardian*, 22 November 1991.

12 *Burning Questions. Incineration in the UK* Greenpeace, November 1991.

13 David Nicholson-Lord, 'Healing the Sick', *Independent on Sunday*, 10 November 1991.

14 Peter Spinks, 'Seeing the Light on Heat Loss', *The Guardian*, 4 January 1991.

15 Crispin Aubrey, 'Glimmer of hope', *The Guardian, 8 November 1991*.

16 Andrew Warren 'Scrimp and Save', *The Guardian*, Friday 8 November 1991.

17 Frank Dobson 'How the Tories have ripped off the public', *The Observer*, 17 November 1991.

Chronology

9 Jan: Government to sell off only 60 per cent of the electricity generating companies. The advertising campaign for this privatization cost £6–8 million.

10 Jan: Widow of a former nuclear plant worker who died of leukaemia is awarded £150,000 compensation by British Nuclear Fuels, believed to be the largest payment by the nuclear industry for a radiation-induced death.

Controls lifted on the movement of sheep in the Lake District affected by the 1987 Chernobyl disaster.

28 Jan: Plans to develop the Lyell and Saltire oil fields in the North Sea at a cost of £600 million are given the go-ahead by the Department of Energy.

18 Feb: British Coal plans for a super pit at Hawkhurst Moor near Coventry are rejected as environmentally damaging by the Secretary of State for the Environment.

20 Mar: Northern Ireland power industry to be privatized and broken up.

7 May: Public Accounts Committee, *New Headquarters Building for the Department of Energy*, HMSO, denounces the delays and mistakes in moving to a new London headquarters costing millions of pounds.

8 May: Seven pits to close with the loss of 5,500 to 7,500 jobs.

29 May: Health and Safety Executive discloses plans for a dramatic increase in fines for breaches of safety rules and for the quadrupling of the number of inspectors on North Sea oil installations.

5 June: National Power announced the closure and mothballing of power plant at three stations and the loss of 300 jobs. This is in addition to the 1,700 jobs shed in 1990 and 2,000 white collar jobs which will go in 1992.

11 June: Energy Secretary John Wakeham, speaking at the annual conference of the Union of Democratic Mineworkers, puts pressure on the coal and electricity industry to settle swiftly terms for new coal contracts, conceding that the government's hopes of privatizing British Coal depended on investors being able to see a long-term future for the industry.

12 June: *Energy Conscious Planning*, Council for the Protection of Rural England, claims that a government commitment to change the law and issue new guidelines to planning authorities to discourage over-intensive developments which waste energy, had not been honoured.

17 June: The £2.9 billion Scottish electricity shares offer attracted 2.2 million investors, only a quarter of the applicants being Scottish.

1 July: Sir Graham Day, chairman of PowerGen, tries to defend the increase in pay of the chief executive, Ed Wallis, from £75,690 to £200,000. Labour's energy spokesman, Frank Dobson, described Mr Wallis's rise as an 'unjustified product of greed' and urged the government to use its stake to vote against it.

11 July: British Gas announced ambitious plans to move into electricity generation in South East Asia, revealing that it had set aside £125 million to put into projects over the next five years.

17 July: Energy Select Committee calls for subsidies and protection for the coal industry.

24 July: British Coal announces its first profits for 13 years and a further 7,000 job losses.

29 July: Lords Select Committee on Science and Technology calls for the re-equipping of existing buildings to make them energy efficient, the removal of VAT on energy saving equipment, the enhancement of the Energy Efficiency Office and its move from the Department of Energy to that of Environment so as to put greater emphasis on the environmental aspects of energy efficiency, but rejects a carbon tax as too blunt an instrument.

5 Aug: Government sets up an advisory group on renewable energy and orders a far-reaching review of its strategy in this area.

7 Aug: Energy Select Committee report urges a speed up of the implementation of the recommendations of the Cullen Report on safety in the North Sea oilfields.
Three injured in explosions on Shell's Fulmar Alpha platform in the North Sea.

14 Aug: *Costing the Earth*, Liberal Democrats, suggests an escalating 10 per cent a year tax on coal, oil and gas, along with higher petrol duties and the introduction of VAT on electricity consumption.

20 Aug: Department of Energy's Coal Task Force calls for £200 million investment in clean-coal burning technology.

11 Sept: National Power launches a joint venture to develop wind power farms.

13 Sept: Ofgas suggests an increase in gas prices to pay for better insulation for poorer households.

16 Sept: Frank Dobson claimed that more than two thirds of British Coal's 61 pits and 35,000 jobs will be lost under the government's privatization plans.

25 Sept: EC proposes an energy tax regime, to be phased in from 1993.

22 Oct: N M Rothschild report advises that the government must shoulder £5 billion liabilities if it is to privatize British Coal successfully.

8 Nov: Competition and Services (Utilities) Bill to improve services and the handling of complaints in the gas, water and telecommunications industries and abolish British Gas's monopoly of supply to domestic and small business customers is published.
Lessons from the Netherlands, Association for the Conservation of Energy, produces a report showing how much Britain has to learn about energy conservation.

9 Nov: The Joint European Torus fusion research reactor at Culham, Oxfordshire produces for a few minutes from 700 million watts of electricity, two million watts of fusion energy, mostly in the form of heat.

13 Nov: Members of the 7,000 strong British Association of Colliery Management call on the government to intervene into negotiations between British Coal and the electricity industry in fixing long-term contracts to replace a deal expiring in March 1995.

14 Nov: Coal Industry Bill which removes limits on the length of shifts miners can work underground and doubles to £3 billion the grant the government can make to British Coal towards redundancy, redeployment and retraining costs, is given a second reading.

2 Dec: It is announced that Britain's most efficient nuclear power station, Hunterston A in Ayrshire, is to remain shut because Scottish Nuclear cannot sell the electricity it would produce.

4 Dec: National Radiological Protection Board announced new lower limits for permitted radiation doses for workers and members of the public living near nuclear installations. These limits are to become law via a EC directive after a consultative period running until March 1992.

19 Dec: British Gas agrees to cut its share of the contract gas market from 90 to 40 per cent by 1995 and hive off its transmission network into a separate unit after pressure from Ofgas.

Transport

P. B. GOODWIN

Changes in Transport Policy

The author has been a participant, not only an observer, in the process of redefining directions of transport policy in recent years, and the 'participant-historian' needs to be particularly careful about the interpretation of developing events. It may be useful now to review expectations of how things were likely to develop, and compare the actual outcome.

Two years ago, this chapter in the 1990 edition of *Contemporary Britain* suggested that 1989 was 'a watershed in transport policy development'. The argument was that a sort of invisible revolution was taking place, marked by a downgrading of the central importance of road-construction as the cornerstone of solving the problems of traffic growth, and its substantial but not total replacement by a combination of improved public transport, traffic engineering, traffic calming to reduce the total amount of traffic and make it more environmentally friendly, and road pricing. Last year, the chapter suggested that consideration of environmental issues, both local and global, gave increased impetus to the same policy approach.

In March 1991, the line of argument was expressed in a report produced by the author and colleagues, entitled *Transport: the New Realism*. The underlying reason was summarized as follows:

In 1989 the Department of Transport issued revised traffic forecasts [which] suggested that economic growth and existing trends would result in traffic levels by the year 2025 that would be between 83 per cent and 142 per cent higher than in 1988 – that is broadly double the current levels . . .

The single most important conclusion of the resulting discussion was the proposition that there is no possibility of increasing road supply at a level which matches the growth rates in demand. It follows logically that (a) whatever road construction policy is followed, the amount of traffic per unit of road will increase, not reduce, that is congestion will get more severe or more widespread, and (b) demand management would therefore become the centre of transport policy; if supply cannot be matched to demand, demand has to be matched to supply.

This was the first step which allowed the possibility of a new consensus to be developed. That process is still continuing, and it is an important feature that the traditional alignment (road lobby versus public transport lobby) has given way to a new and more fluid search for common interests . . . In many towns and cities there are also signs of cross-party agreement on transport policy.[1]

In the event, it is clear that many of the developments of the year are consistent with such an interpretation, but there are mixed signals and conflicting tendencies.

Traffic Calming

Stonham – publisher of a new technical journal, *The Urban Street Environment*, whose launching in December signifies a new interest in quality of life at a local level – commented:

Just a couple of years ago, the normal vocabulary of those concerned with local highway planning and management in Britain hardly featured the words 'traffic calming'. Now it seems they are on everybody's lips – linked with everything from child accident reduction to combating crime, and the concept is apparently seen as a kind of multi-purpose answer to many of the environmental, social and economic problems of traffic in urban areas. The latest MORI poll for Lex indicates that even 90 per cent of motorists support some form of traffic controls in residential areas.[2]

Most of these schemes are initiated and implemented at local authority level, which involves collaboration (not always straightforward) between district and county councils. The Department of Transport has given some mild encouragement, but not produced the sort of detailed national guidelines that have had an important effect in the Netherlands and Germany, though the official Transport and Road Research Laboratory has produced a translated version of a Dutch manual. It is significant that Devon County Council has produced a beautifully illustrated book aimed at encouraging widespread implementation of traffic calming, and that the main legislative initiative during the year, aimed at removing the uncertainty of highway authorities about their powers to implement non-standard road humps, chicanes, pinch points and speed cushions, only arose because Conservative MP Keith Mans came second in the ballot for Private Members bills, and chose this 'non-controversial' topic.

In the same mode of non-governmental initiative, the main source of collated information about the schemes which have actually been implemented is from a survey carried out by a private consulting company specializing in the field, Environmental and Transport Planning (whose principal, Carmen Hass-Klau, introduced the phrase 'traffic calming' as the translation of the German *Verkehrsberuhigung*), supported by a charitable trust, the Rees Jeffreys Road Fund;

the same team are currently producing what is expected to be an influential manual and design guide for local authority engineers.[3]

The survey identified around 200 local schemes which had already been implemented, and a similar number being planned for the near future. Most of the schemes related to minor roads in residential areas; town centre pedestrianization, though in sympathy with the same intentions, is not called 'calming' by most engineers. Most were successful, liked by residents, and accepted (sometimes with resignation) by drivers. It is commonplace now that local authorities are faced with more requests from local residents to implement new schemes than they have the resources to carry out.

It has to be said that the ambitious, area-wide schemes common in Europe are still the exception rather than the rule in Britain. It is also the case that the importance of the *design* aspects is insufficiently appreciated; the good schemes make it immediately apparent how necessary are the right colours, shapes, materials, surfaces and details. The badly designed schemes typically use cheap concrete and tarmac and badly placed signs, quickly looking shoddy and unattractive. An even more important weakness is that the schemes rarely involve substantial associated measures to improve public transport or make more than token improvements aimed at changing the balance of car use, cycling and walking. This has led some of the green supporters of traffic restraint to see traffic calming as a 'sell-out', aimed at increasing effective parking capacity and making cosmetic rather than substantial changes. A related question arises when considering bypasses, which is discussed below.

The question – has traffic calming a role in Britain? – has now been settled, I think irreversibly. There now exist a wide range of well-established techniques, and an increasing range of experimental ones, which can slow traffic to acceptable speeds in residential areas, and enhance the quality of street life. It has taken hold of local politics. But while it is very frequently supported with references to wider changes in local transport policy, it is not yet implemented in that way.

Environmental Issues in Transport

After the important ideas signalled in the 1990 environment white paper, there has been a feeling of marking time. Major shifts in British and European policy are repeatedly signalled, but left unresolved. Some important research projects had been set up, including one on using land-use planning methods to reduce the overall amount of travel, and these could have important long-term consequences, but while the research is progressing there has been a tendency to wait for its results. At the time of writing there is still uncertainty about three important developments.

First, a statutory advisory body, the Standing Advisory Committee on Trunk Road Appraisal (SACTRA), presented a report in November to the Secretary of State for Transport, on how environmental effects were to be taken into account in assessing the case for new road schemes. There had been nearly two years of discussion and consultation about this report. The chairman of the committee,

Derek Wood QC, had addressed a seminar in September with some personal statements which were widely interpreted as indicating the main line of argument of the report; in particular, there would be a need for stronger treatment of the environmental impact of new roads, and (which would be a radical departure in policy analysis) there should be a formal assessment not only of the impact of specific schemes on a project-by-project basis, but also assessment of the cumulative impact of the roads programme as a whole. The press speculated that subsequent delays in publishing the report reflected a difference in view between departments of Transport and the Environment – the latter favouring such an approach, but the former fearing that it would cause difficulties for the road programme, though it can be said that no such indications were given to the committee itself. In any case, it is likely that a large-scale revision of the DTp *Manual of Environmental Appraisal* will be required, it is possible that some changes in the scale of the roads programme may follow, and almost certain that those roads schemes that continue to gain support will be those that are justified by arguments of environmental improvement (such as some bypasses) rather than relief of congestion *per se*.

Here there has already been a significant shift of emphasis; a further development has been the linking of proposed new urban bypass roads with extensive traffic restraint, pedestrianization and traffic calming *within* the bypassed area. Six small and medium-sized towns have been selected to spearhead this approach – Berkhamsted, Dalton-in-Furness, Market Harborough, Petersfield, Wadebridge, and Whitchurch. The idea is to take active steps to prevent traffic quickly returning to towns that have been promised relief; there is a window of opportunity when a bypass opens, that does not necessarily last for long. It seems likely that this is a policy which will command very wide support – that is, where there is a bypass, it should be accompanied by environmental improvement measures within the bypassed area. However, there is a converse argument (that bypasses are a necessary condition for such measures, and therefore environmentally friendly in themselves; or, equivalently, that it is not possible to implement urban traffic restraint schemes without a bypass) that remains one of the most disputed and controversial issues.

The second area of uncertainty concerns the European Communities. Brussels is an increasing source for detailed legislation affecting the transport sector, much of it on questions of detail that are not covered in the present survey. Not all of this is heading in the same direction: for example, the orientation of the Transport Directorate is largely on questions of competition within the transport industries, whereas the Environment Directorate has shown an increasing interest in transport at the policy level. The EC Directive 85/337, which came into force in 1988, requires an environmental assessment of certain types of major development to be carried out and discussed before development consent is granted. The Department of Transport took the view (and I think still does) that its existing procedures were consistent with that directive. However, a number of groups challenged that. The

Twyford Down Association objected to plans for the extension of the M3 near Winchester, and other protest groups were concerned with the east London river crossing, the Hackney-M11 link, and the Colne Valley link in Watford. The Council for the Protection of Rural England made a formal complaint in September about a planned link from Sheffield to Manchester, and three bypasses, for Hereford, Hindhead, and Melbury Abbas.

In September EC Environment Commissioner Carlo Ripa di Meana wrote to the Department of Transport saying that Britain was in breach of the Directive, and the schemes should be stopped. There is continuing argument about the status of this statement itself, about whether the environmental assessments carried out were adequate, and about the legal implications of assessments, even if inadequate, which were initiated before the Directive came into force. Further court action is expected. Meanwhile, there is an additional EC Directive in draft about strategic as distinct from project assessment of transport schemes, and its ramifications are still unknown.

The third uncertainty is about the scale of the environmental problem itself, with many people finding themselves uneasily switching between dismissing the most pessimistic forecasts as scaremongering, and being scared. On 13 December 1991 air pollution levels in London reached the highest levels since records began in 1976. The Department of the Environment issued a press notice appealing to people to use public transport wherever possible, and said 'Cars are the main cause of this problem. If people have to use their cars they should avoid revving, drive economically, and use the car as sparingly as possible.' While some other countries (notably Holland, Denmark and Greece) have on occasion restricted car use when dangerous air pollution levels are reached, this was the first time in Britain that such a statement had been made from a government department.

Public Transport

There were some encouraging signs for public transport during the year. A major new urban rail system in Manchester, and approval for another in Sheffield, represent the fruition of long campaigning by the local authorities in those areas for government support for schemes which contribute to the relief of congestion, though such support is quite restricted, both in scale and scope. There are a hundred or so proposals for such urban systems, and it is difficult at present to believe that more than a handful will ever see the light of day.

It may well be that some less dramatic signs of a shift in attitude towards buses may become more important. One of the reasons for the growth in local support for light rail schemes was that, after the 1985 Transport Act, the deregulation and privatization of the bus industry removed it from the perception of local authorities as an arm of transport policy. They thought that the buses were no longer 'ours', but simply one more category of essentially selfish road user, causing pollution and congestion. This was reinforced by the majority of bus companies becoming inevitably more concerned with commercial than social questions, and a minority behaving in a less than helpful way in the towns where they operated. Some of the traffic calming schemes (which in principle ought to be helpful to buses, and helped by them) were designed in a way which caused operating difficulties, or even damage to vehicles, and this was another point of tension between operators and authorities. Some movement during the year started to shift opinions on this matter.

The Bus and Coach Council, an industrial body representing the bus companies, undertook a public relations campaign designed to argue the advantages of buses in assisting congestion, pollution, economic efficiency, and mobility. The message that buses were more cost-effective in achieving these aims than new urban rail systems was also argued, albeit more gently. It is a very strong case indeed, as the biggest advantage of rail systems is that brought about by their reserved track – which is also the main cost. Achieving advantages of reserved track for buses can be done at a small fraction of the cost, by a variety of new systems and in the last resort by white paint and strict enforcement. The message is also one which fits the shortage of money in most local authorities, and for some, measures can be carried out using local powers without the need for national approval.

Roger Freeman, the minister responsible for public transport matters, approved a package of experimental schemes, and encouraged local authorities to apply for government funding for bus priority measures in the annual round of Transport Supplementary Grant submissions. Around 50 local authorities did so. It seems quite likely that – being cheap and quick to implement – the next two years could see a rapid growth of measures designed to make bus services more attractive in urban areas. What is still to be demonstrated is whether such improvements can actually be sufficient without major expenditure on vehicle design, high quality interchanges, bus stops and information systems, and more difficult political decisions on restrictions in on-street and off-street parking.

What is very much less clear is what is going to happen about British Rail. In a series of well-publicized speeches, government spokesmen made it clear that privatization was a strong priority, but there was no agreement on exactly how this would be done – as a single unit, as separate units based on transport function (such as freight, Intercity), as units based on geographical area (including a return to the pre-nationalization companies, thought to be favoured by the Prime Minister) or by a difference of function so that one agency would own the track and various competing companies would pay for the right to run trains on it. A common view of those professionally engaged in the transport sector and its policy is that privatization of British Rail should not really be understood as a transport policy at all since it does not derive from consideration of mobility and congestion, but from the government's general views on industrial organization and ownership.

London

Similar points may be made in relation to plans to deregulate buses and privatize the tubes in London, which have not excited a great degree of support as ways of improving the transport problems of the capital. However two other policy developments in London are more closely related to transport policy issues.

First, 'red routes'. Originally the red routes were little more than roads with parking bans that were strictly enforced. A pilot scheme was set up in north and east London between Archway and the Commercial Road, and research studies showed that, as intended, traffic speeds were significantly higher, not only for cars and lorries but for buses as well. There is a special unit within the Department of Transport to extend the scheme very much more widely, establishing a network of interconnected roads on which the delays caused by illegal parking would be virtually non-existent. However, there have been some problems. First, urban streets are not only routes for moving vehicles, but places for carrying out activities. Some local shops have been very hard hit by the loss of trade which, they say, depended on a rather relaxed view about very short-term parking. Secondly, there is some difference of judgement about the sustainability of the speed increases; if they derive from a once-for-all increase in effective capacity due to the removal of parked vehicles, then either traffic growth or traffic induced by the speed increase itself might swiftly fill up the space provided. In that case, measures to control the overall amount of traffic would be a necessary condition for longer term success of the red route experiment (though, if taken, making the red routes less necessary).

The other major development was the decision by the government to launch a large scale feasibility study into the case for, and possibilities of implementing, road pricing in London. Transport experts and professional institutes had in large numbers been coming round to the view that charging for the use of road space was efficient and could be made fair, but the government was, and remains, very cautious indeed. It is difficult to imagine that the new study will recommend against the implementation of road pricing, and the issue will be a big one in the first year of the new government's term of office.

Notes

1 P. B. Goodwin, S. Hallett, F. Kenny and G. Stokes, *Transport; the New Realism, Report to the Rees Jeffreys Road Fund*, Transport Studies Unit, University of Oxford, March 1991.

2 P. Stonham, 'Traffic Calming', *The Urban Street Environment*, No.1, December 1991.

3 Environmental and Transport Planning, *Traffic Calming; the First National Survey* and *Traffic Calming Manual*, both 1992.

Chronology

4 Jan: The Institute of British Geographers annual conference is told by Dr John Whitelegg that switching tax to fuel is the only way to deal with rising road congestion.

7 Jan: Red routes schemes to cut traffic congestion in London by restricting parking along certain routes start operation.

8 Jan: Railways Inspectorate launches an investigation into a train crash at Cannon Street station in London which killed one and injured 248 people.

16 Jan: M40 extension from Oxford to Birmingham opens.

Transport Select Committee report recommends compulsory smoke hoods, rear-facing exits and stricter restraints on cabin luggage for civil airliners.

18 Jan: Three BR workers killed by a train whilst repairing points in Liverpool.

22 Jan: EACO-Route study argues the need for an extension of the M11 from Cambridge to Newcastle-upon-Tyne to ensure the revival of the East coast economy.

CAA report calls for Heathrow airport to be deregulated and opened to competition from any airline.

6 Feb: Ferry safety standards are attacked in a Consumers' Association report in *Which?* calling for an independent transport safety commission, the presentation of passenger certificates only after ability to evacuate in under an hour is demonstrated, and standardized safety announcements and signs.

7 Feb: Proposals to fit lorries over 7.5 tonnes gross weight with speed limiters to restrict them to a 60 mph speed limit are announced.

12 Feb: Lords Select Committee on the European Communities, *A New Structure for Community Railways*, HMSO, argues private operators should be offered the chance to run railways whilst most railway infrastructure and management remain state-run.

BR promises to launch an investigation into the high rate of train failures (35 per cent) in the recent severe weather in the Network SouthEast area.

17 Feb: Sir Bob Reid, chairman of BR, calls on the government to allow increased spending of up to £2 billion a year on improving the rail network.

18 Feb: IRA bomb attacks at Paddington and Victoria stations in London, killing one person at Victoria, leading to questions as to why the latter was not evacuated earlier.

19 Feb: Bomb threats cause widespread disruption for London commuters.

20 Feb: Hoax bomb alerts again disrupt stations.

25 Feb: IRA bomb blast on the main line between London and St Albans.

26 Feb: All party attempts to incorporate random breath testing in the Road Safety Bill are rejected in the Commons by 265 to 157.

27 Feb: Proposals for a new trunk road from Cambridge to Newcastle-upon-Tyne announced.

6 Mar: Plans for a £1 billion international airport in Wales near Newport are announced.

16 Mar: Liberal Democrats special conference supports the liberalization of rail services and the use of privately operated lines.

19 Mar: Tax relief on construction costs of private roads announced in the Budget.

28 Mar: John Major pledges the privatization of BR.

8 Apr: Company car parking should be taxed and the revenues used to subsidize public transport for employees instead says a NEDO report.

13 Apr: Trial on the 1989 *Marchioness* disaster collapses after the jury is unable to reach a verdict and is dismissed.

28 Apr: Malcolm Rifkind promises the privatization of BR with open access to the permanent way on BBC's *On the Record*.

1 May: Jubilee line to be extended south of the Thames to Greenwich and then back north of the river through docklands and Canning Town to Stratford by Bow.

2 May: Public Accounts Committee criticizes the privatization and break-up of the National Bus Company.

Lords reject by 87 to 41 Lord Clinton-Davies's attempt to introduce random breath testing.

3 May: Health and Safety Executive is to hold an inquiry into the number of deaths caused by passengers falling from high speed trains.

10 May: HGVs to be fitted by law with speed control devices to prevent them exceeding 60mph.

17 May: Proposals outlined for the improvement of the handling of bad weather by the transport services, including a review of manpower and salt levels necessary to keep roads open, better procedures for assisting and removing motorists with broken down vehicles, better communications between the relevant authorities and a range of technical improvements to BR rolling stock.

20 May: Proposals for a £20 million rail link round London to relieve commuter congestion floated by Labour.

21 May: One in four roads will need to be closed or heavily disrupted for repairs in the next five years according to a National Audit Office report which censures the Department of Transport for its failure to monitor the extent of road closures and traffic restrictions.

28 May: Government outlines plans for the end of BR's monopoly of rail freight services, a tripling of government grants towards the building of rail freight sidings where these would provide worthwhile environmental benefits and a more positive attitude towards rail than hitherto.

6 June: Government promises BR more money for investment.

14 June: BR fined £250,000 with costs after admitting failures in safety measures were responsible for the Clapham rail crash in December 1988.

25 June: London Borough Associations/Association of London Authorities statement on transport in the capital calls for an end to tax relief on company cars, expresses doubt about bus privatization and argues for further investigation of road pricing.

28 June: Link-up between British and French halves of the Channel Tunnel.

1 July: Seat belts must be worn by adults in the rear of cars, providing belts are fitted.

8 July: Amendment introduced to the Road Traffic Bill to ensure applicants for taxi or private hire licences are checked on whether they have criminal records.

9 July: Calls for the development of the commercial use of the Thames are made at the London Rivers Association conference.
CAA imposes price curbs on BAA plc.

10 July: BR announces compulsory drug tests for would-be train drivers after revelations that the driver involved in the January Cannon Street crash had apparently been smoking cannabis.

11 July: Increased borrowing limits for BR rushed through the Commons after its first operating loss in four years.

18 July: Train driver killed in the collision of two trains near Exeter.
Trafalgar House sells its Cunard Ellerman container shipping interests to P&O for £62.5 million.

22 July: Royal Town Planning Institute report suggests car free areas agreed by local veto to curb traffic growth.

21 July: Rail crash at Newton near Glasgow kills four.

25 July: Road Traffic Act, which will extend red routes in London and lead to the appointment of a London traffic director, enforce compulsory retests for those convicted of the new offence of dangerous driving, increase penalties for speeding, introduce a voluntary rehabilitation course for drunken drivers, and the more effective use of cameras to detect traffic offences, is given the Royal Assent.

25 July: BR publishes its proposed Channel Tunnel rail link, now renamed New Kent Main Line in an attempt to beat a government ban on subsidies for tunnel-related projects.

29 July: Plans for a £40 million new runway at Manchester airport announced.

30 July: *Future Rail*, BR, unveils plans for £1 billion investment per year over the next ten years, new 155 mph Intercity trains, an east-west link in London between Paddington and Liverpool Street and between Paddington and Heathrow, improved commuter lines on Network South East, 60 miles of new or reopened line, further electrification, 100 new stations and a new rail link to Manchester airport, and £200 million investment on safety each year, including a system to prevent trains passing through red signals. It does not however specify how these are to be funded.

31 July: Second trial on the 1989 *Marchioness* disaster fails after the jury fails to return a verdict.

6 Aug: Central Transport Consultative Committee says BR needs more money to prevent the deterioration of current services and argues that government policy to cut public service obligation funding completely from Network South East and drastically reduce it to regional railways is a disaster.

12 Aug: Anglo-Italian consortium wins a contract to build the first new toll road, a 30 mile Midland Expressway round the north of Birmingham.

13 Aug: Plans to privatize Tees and Hartlepool port are announced.

15 Aug: Official report on the *Marchioness* disaster condemns the design of both boats involved in the accident and the Department of Transport as the responsible regulatory authority.

22 Aug: Bristol City Council privatizes its port, selling it to First Corporate Shipping for £36 million.

29 Aug: Health and Safety Executive says safety on the London underground has improved over the last two years, despite having only fully implemented eight of the 26 recommendations of the Fennell Report that followed the King's Cross disaster.

4 Sept: Announcement that the M25 is to be converted into a four lane motorway throughout its length in both directions.
King's Cross tube station is still a potential disaster area according to a report issued by staff four years after the fire that killed 31 people.

5 Sept: Doubling of grants to London's underground, recommended by the MMC, is rejected by the government.

16 Sept: *Switch on our Trains*, Railway Development Society, suggests that BR should aim to electrify half (as opposed to the current 27 per cent) of its 10,500 miles of track by 2000, cutting its fuel bill by 20 per cent and also reducing environmental damage.

27 Sept: Approval given to an extension of the runway at London City Airport and to the revised plans for the East London River Crossing.

9 Oct: Announcement that the government has rejected BR's favoured route for the Channel Tunnel link and instead preferred Ove Arup's link going through the east and terminating at Stratford in east London, because of plans by Michael Heseltine to develop a corridor city in East London and to minimize the environmental costs in Kent. It will however take longer to construct and cost £750 million more.

30 Oct: Dartford bridge carrying the M25 across the Thames is opened by the Queen.

31 Oct: NEDO suggests a doubling of parking fines, dedicated superbus routes, more traffic wardens and taxes on company car parking spaces as short-term measures to ease traffic

congestion in London. Longer term measures include greater investment in public transport and road pricing.

7 Nov: *Towards a Sustainable Transport Policy*, Association of County Councils, wants a strategy to limit road building, encouragement of greater use of public transport and better planning of the location of high demand public buildings, such as supermarkets, to take account of transport considerations.

13 Nov: Newcastle's Metro link to the city airport opens three months ahead of schedule.

18 Nov: BAA confirms that it is going ahead with £1 billion plans to build a fifth terminal at Heathrow and a rail link to the airport.

5 Dec: Labour's transport plans for London include evening and weekend lorry bans, an orbital rail route, improved public services, promotion of travelcards, a moratorium on new road schemes, traffic calming and green routes where buses have priority.

16 Dec: A Powell Duffryn subsidiary is to buy Tees and Hartlepool Port Authority, the first trust port to be privatized.

17 Dec: Britain is to defy an EC block on the East London River Crossing, the M11 link to the Blackwall tunnel and the M3 extension.

19 Dec: Independent inquiry into the DTI's handling of river safety is announced.

Home Affairs Select Committee, *Fire Safety and Policing of the Channel Tunnel*, HMSO, criticizes the proposed safety regime.

Retailing

GARY DAVIES

Discounting the Retail Sector?

Towards the end of 1991 retailers were looking forward to Christmas, not just because the final quarter of the year traditionally saw retail sales rise by some 50 per cent above the year average, but because the extra volume would compensate for what had been yet another disappointing year. This slightly more bullish view on the High Street by November was based on two precepts; that Christmas 1991 could surely not be as difficult as Christmas 1990, and that attempts by government to stimulate the economy in the run-up to a general election would, finally, take effect. A Gallup poll in October had shown an increase in consumer confidence over the year[1] following a gradual fall in interest rates and despite rising unemployment. But a return of some vestige of confidence amongst Britain's shopkeepers failed to disguise the effects of tighter margins caused by rising costs and the price cutting of almost every retailer in trying to stimulate demand.

Shops as well as merchandise went up for sale. In August the ailing Burton Group sold Harvey Nichols, a London Department Store, to a buyer based in Hong Kong.[2] Sears sold one of their menswear chains, Horne Brothers, to its management for a 'nominal price'.[3] In April the Corporate Intelligence Group reported that more than 100 of the UK's top 600 retailers had recorded losses during the previous year.[4] Next reported losses of £40.7 million. Harrods planned to shed up to 15 per cent of its staff. Department store group Lewis's went into receivership. Ratners put 35 of its 235 Salisbury's handbag and costume jewellery shops up for sale and planned a reduction of 1,000 in staff. Menswear chain Dunns closed many of its outlets and sold the rest.

Few retailers continued to record the profit levels of earlier years and, inevitably, heads rolled at board level. John Hardman left the top job at Asda in June. Asda's share price fell steadily during the year. A rights issue to raise £357 million, of shares issued at 35 pence, to cut Asda's debts of £931 million, attracted 90 per cent support in November – somewhat to the surprise of the business press. Two years earlier Asda's share price had held steadily at well over £2. In September Gateway's chief executive David Smith left along with finance director Liz Hignell. Gateway were still struggling with the reconstruction of a food retail business formed some years before from a number of individual chains.

Two other leading food retailers, Tesco and Sainsbury, had both gone to the financial markets during the year to raise funds for expansion, but discomfort about the prospects for even these businesses was being voiced by the end of 1991.[5] Part of the concern stemmed from doubts about the prospect for further expansion by the leading superstore businesses. Question marks were drawn alongside the logic of ever larger numbers of, seemingly identical, superstores being built by all the major food multiples, despite attempts to differentiate their owners through increased levels of media advertising.[6]

Less of a self imposed problem was the issue of selling prices in food stores. Price had been a major weapon for every multiple in its growth strategy against the independent and cooperative sectors in the 1970s and 1980s. But non-price factors such as design, good car parking, convenient location, and a wide selection of exotic and fresh products were seen as a better way of competing in the 1990s. However the cost of food in Britain was now being claimed to be high by European standards.[7] A report by the Consumers Association, published in their magazine *Which?*, queried the uniformity of selling prices between supermarkets and a price check towards the end of the year identified substantially lower selling prices in newcomer Aldi, a limited range, no-frills, discount store from Germany, with, albeit, a very small market share in Britain.

Isosceles, owners of the Gateway supermarket chain launched their own discount business, Food Giant. CRS experimented with a discount format, 'Co-op Pioneer'. Tesco and Sainsbury both announced price promotions. By the end of 1991 there was still a very real possibility of the price war in the food sector that had been mooted in the press a year earlier.

Margins in much of non-food retailing were much higher, reflecting the lower rate of stock-turn, leaving more room to manoeuvre on price, with heavy discounting remaining very much to the fore throughout the year.[8] Shoppers were encouraged by the media to 'haggle'. Fixed prices had been the norm in Britain since the turn of the century, now any reasonable offer was considered. The designer-created face of British retailing looked somewhat jaded as non-food retailers reverted to price promotion. B&Q, the leaders in DIY, chose television to advertise a 25 per cent discount off anything in their stores for one day. Some observers of retailing wondered whether such tactics merely served to move purchases of high ticket items further forward in the year. Others saw such actions as part of an established trend, pointing in turn to the return of the market traders to one end of Oxford Street in London, the one time heart of the retail sector, with their appeals to the passing shopper to sell them something 'not for five pounds, not even for four, but to you, how about 50 pence?!' The British marketplace was said to be ready for the discount formats that had been so successful in America for some years.

To trade in the longer term, that is to say strategically rather than tactically, by discounting, a retailer needs to have lower costs than its competitors. To achieve a cost advantage a retailer can negotiate lower prices from suppliers or, alternatively, reduce its overheads, the largest elements of which tend to be site costs and labour. The ratio of site costs to turnover had risen in the 1980s as developers increased rental values and retailers sold their freeholds and leased them back so as to release capital to fund expansion. One survey calculated a ratio for rent to turnover for fashion houses Next and Etam of around 10 per cent[9] compared to Marks and Spencer (who owned most of their freeholds), at just above 1 per cent. Turnover fell in the recession, but most rental agreements did not allow for any reduction. In May retailers in London's Mayfair organised a strike over rents[10] and by June a survey by chartered surveyors Hillier Parker recorded the first fall in shop rents for 'at least 25 years'.[11]

No review of 1991 should omit reference to Ratners, the UK's leading jewellers. In an address to the Institute of Directors, chairman Gerald Ratner referred to the quality of his merchandise using a four letter word implying less than top quality. Remarkably Ratner's share price rose the following day. By the end of the year, however, the price had slumped, reflecting not so much its chief executive's candour but a financial position laced with debt.

The Independent Sector

The problems in the multiple sector must have been greeted with a few wry smiles by the independent retailers who as a group had dominated retailing until the 1980s. The number of privately owned shops had been in decline since before the abolition of resale price maintenance in the 1960s, a move that allowed the larger retailers to discount in most sectors. One report predicted the continued decline of the grocer, the baker and the butcher but saw those with a wide, but carefully chosen, product mix as having a brighter future.[12] An alternative approach for the would-be retail entrepreneur was to join a voluntary chain such as Spar or a franchise. Many of the hundreds of franchised businesses were retailers and the entire franchise sector was said to be growing by 10 per cent each year. Results from individual retail franchises were mixed in 1991. Tie Rack repossessed 19 of its outlets (which had failed) but Pentos, the franchisor for Athena art shops and Ryman office supply stores, claimed an increase in profits for the year.[13] Ironically Pentos, through its Dillons chain one of the leading bookstore multiples, found themselves at the centre of a dispute that threatened one still protected preserve of the independent, book retailing. The Net Book Agreement was one of the few remaining examples of retail price maintenance left in Britain. It acted as a restraint on retailers' selling books at prices other than those determined by publishers. In September Dillons cut 25 percent off the price of 20 titles, including half the Booker Prize list.[14] Dillons claimed that their sales increased by 10 per cent as a result of their price promotion and advertising.[15] Rival booksellers Waterstones responded in October with discounts on 40 titles – as did the much smaller chain of Books Etc. Malcolm Gibson, president of the Bookseller's Association, forecast that smaller bookshops would soon be unable to compete on equal terms.[16]

Sunday Trading

One source of competitive advantage for the independent retailer had been their willingness to open all hours, and, if possible, on a Sunday. Attempts to liberalize Sunday trading in England and Wales had failed in previous years and retailers themselves were at odds on the idea. DIY retailers in particular were in favour, whilst Marks and Spencer opposed liberalization. In March a private member's bill was presented in the House of Commons[17] seeking to extend the range of goods that could be retailed on the Sabbath, but without success. In May the Court of Appeal lifted a ban on B&Q and Wickes from trading in West Yorkshire on a Sunday. The court's ruling was not one in favour of Sunday trading, more a result of the local authorities concerned being unwilling to give undertakings to compensate the retailers for losses incurred from not trading on a Sunday if the retailers won any appeal, because the law allowed only for a maximum £1,000 fine rather than a ban or closure.[18] The following week DIY stores around the country opened on the Sunday, as did retailers in Oxford Street, London. The week after, B & Q appealed to the Law Lords that the key legislation in the Shops Act of 1950 was incompatible with Article 30 of the Treaty of Rome. The House of Lords referred matters back to the European Court. In June the Home Office declined to propose any changes in legislation over Sunday trading before the decision from the European Court, something unlikely to be forthcoming until 1993. In the meantime many retailers decided to open on Sundays and many food retailers announced they would do so on the Sunday before Christmas. In October the opponents of Sunday trading appeared to gain support from a decision by an industrial tribunal in Bury St Edmonds that an agricultural worker had been unreasonably dismissed for refusing to work on Sundays[19] even though he had accepted his employer's conditions of work for 15 years.

By the end of the year the situation on Sunday trading resembled that of a Whitehall farce. The law did not allow Sunday trading in most categories of merchandise but local authorities, who were responsible for enforcement, could only seek a fine for each infringement. The government, despite its protestations over ceding powers to any centralized European authority as a general principle, found it convenient to await the decision of the European court before it would consider any change in legislation. Sunday trading continued in Scotland quite legally but identical businesses in England and Wales opened on the same day in clear violation of the law.

A Greener Consumer?

Despite the recession retailers seemed convinced the public's taste for environmentally sound products, even at higher prices, would grow. Tesco were reported as discussing a range of garments made from reclaimed or recycled yarns[20] and a number of market research organisations pointed to a section of affluent consumers who were insisting on a greener lifestyle.[21] The Coop introduced a pilot programme to seek to limit pesticide use and planned to lobby government on a range of safety matters connected to pesticides.[22] A Mintel report on the so-called 'ethical' consumer identified a number of issues that shoppers might feel strongly enough about to stop them from purchasing. The three leading factors were animal testing, damage to the ozone layer and irresponsible marketing by suppliers.[23]

Technology

Much of retailing had changed gradually to self service after the second world war, mirroring a general trend towards the industrialization of the service sector and the substitution of labour, but retailing remained relatively untouched by advanced technology until the 1980s. By 1991 laser scanning at checkouts had become standard practice. The Article Number Association, responsible for the bar-code system, could report that 7,000 stores now had EPOS (Electronic Point of Sale).[24] EPOS provides better data to retailers and does it more quickly than conventional methods of sales and stock analysis. In theory it also allows automatic re-ordering from suppliers, if the latter are given access to the aggregated EPOS data.[25] By 1991 KwikSave was employing 'auto replenishment' for some of its range and both Tesco and Sainsbury were known to be experimenting with the idea.[26]

How shoppers paid for goods was affected by changes to legislation during the year allowing higher prices to be charged when purchases were made using credit cards. Greater use of debit cards was expected to follow any such increases.[27] Sainsbury introduced the facility to withdraw cash when paying in their outlets with a debit card. Many retailers offered their own credit cards in competition with the leading names Access and Mastercard. However the credit squeeze in 1990/91 had discouraged shoppers from leaving monthly statements unpaid. As a consequence the profit potential of store credit cards reduced. Some retailers, notably the John Lewis Partnership, chose to operate their cards more as a service or convenience card than as a source of revenue in its own right.[27]

The Outlook

Towards the end of 1991, forecasters were presenting a mixed view of the future for retail business. Verdict saw costs rising faster than profit, further squeezing margins and favouring the low cost operator.[28] The one buoyant sector they saw as being electrical retailing. The Corporate Intelligence Group predicted increased cost pressures resulting from EC legislation including statutory minimum wages, increased protection for part-time workers, tighter controls on food safety and new consumer rights.[29] Times, it would appear, would get harder for the high cost retailer and the central question appeared to be whether the era of the discounter had returned?

Some retailers began, yet again, to look outside of Britain for their future success. What was new were the countries being considered. Littlewoods were opening in Russia and Mothercare in eastern Europe. Many of the founders of British retail companies had emigrated from eastern Europe in the past. Perhaps it was fitting to see some of the retail sector they had helped to shape looking in the opposite direction for profit in the future.

Notes

1 G Bowditch, 'Signs of a cheap and cheerful Christmas boost retailers', *The Times*, 31 October 1991.
2 J Thornhill, 'Burton sells Harvey Nichols', *The Financial Times*, 16 August 1991.
3 N Turpin, 'Sears sells Horne Brothers for a song', *The Independent*, 14 August 1991.
4 J Thornhill, 'Trading losses seen for more retailers', *The Financial Times*, 5 April 1991.
5 F Walsh, 'Shakeout at the check-out', *The Sunday Times*, 22 September 1991.
6 G Davies, *Advertising in Retailing*, Longman, Harlow, 1990.
7 M Skipworth and J Gerard, 'Supermarkets push British food prices to top of league', *The Sunday Times*, 11 August 1991; F Walsh, 'Fat years end for supermarkets', *The Sunday Times*, 12 May 1991.
8 A McCall, 'The great bargain jamboree', *The Daily Telegraph*, 18 July 1991.
9 J Randall and R Olins, 'Rent hikes "killing" high street shops', *The Sunday Times*, 9 June 1991.
10 R Hardman, 'Mayfair shops strike over rising rents', *The Daily Telegraph*, 14 May 1991.
11 V Houlder, 'Shop rents down for first time in 25 years', *The Financial Times*, 17 June 1991.
12 R Clancy and R Faux, 'Shopkeepers must adapt and diversify to survive', *The Times*, 19 August 1991.
13 D Baillieu, *The Times*, 13 May 1991.
14 R Snoddy, 'Discounting of books heralds end to retail price agreement', *The Financial Times*, 28 September 1991.
15 A Rawsthorn and R Snoddy, 'Final chapter for book price accord', *The Financial Times*, 30 September 1991.
16 R Snoddy, 'Book price war draws in third shop chain', *The Financial Times*, 9 October 1991.
17 N Timmins, 'Tories seek compromise on Sunday Trading Law', *The Independent*, 4 March 1991.
18 Rice, R, 'Sunday trading may grow after appeal court ruling', *Financial Times*, 1 May 1991.
19 J Rees, 'Worker wins fight to take Sundays off', *The Daily Telegraph*, 7 October 1991.
20 CWS Ltd, *Retail Review*, No.174, item 43.
21 J Fuller, 'Roddick's boredom pays off', *The Financial Times*, 8 June 1991.
22 CWS Ltd, *Retail Review*, No.172, item 10.
23 Mintel, *Retail Intelligence*, Vol.3 p.4, 1991.
24 CWS Ltd, *Retail Review*, No.173, item 6.
25 CWS Ltd, *Retail Review*, No.169, item 10.
26 CWS Ltd, *Retail Review*, No.170, items 5 and 6.
27 Mintel, *Retail Intelligence*, Vol.5, p.2, 1991.
28 *Verdict on Retailing 1995*, Verdict Research Ltd, London, 1991.
29 *Retailing in Europe in the 1990s*, Corporate Intelligence Research Publications, London, 1991.

Chronology

9 Jan: Sir Ian MacLaurin, chairman of Tesco, is named 1990 Retailer of the Year by County NatWest WoodMac.

18 Jan: Andrew Faulds' Children and Young Persons (Protection from Tobacco) Bill to raise the maximum fine for selling cigarettes to under-16s from £400 to £2,000, empower courts to remove cigarette vending machines used by children and require local authorities to enforce the existing law more rigourously, is given an unopposed first reading.

20 Jan: Midland Bank to shed 900 staff as part of a radical restructuring of the bank's retail operations.

4 Feb: Next announces the sale of its Grattan mail order subsidiary to the German company Otto-Versand for £140 million, a sale eventually confirmed after a subsequent lengthy struggle by Sears to buy Grattan.

8 Feb: Midland Bank to introduce a £10 annual fee for its credit card holders.

18 Feb: Report by Corporate Intelligence Group points to the success of convenience shopping on petrol station forecourts.
Volume of retail sales slumped in January by 1.3 per cent.
Barclays Bank announce staff cuts of 15-20 per cent.

25 Feb: DAKS Simpson to be sold to the Japanese Sankyo Seiko for £65 million.

19 Mar: Tobacco, petrol and derv duties raised by 15 per cent. Alcohol duties raised in line with inflation.

20 Mar: Lewis's, the regional department store group that went into receivership in January, is to be broken up,

22 Mar: Banks and building societies launch a campaign against cheque and credit card fraud.

25 Mar: Sears to expand into Europe through a joint venture with the French retailer, Group AndrQ.

19 Apr: Andrew Faulds' Children and Young Persons (Protection from Tobacco) Bill, which increases the maximum fine for selling tobacco to under-16s to £2,500 and requires local authorities to scrutinize enforcement of this at least once a year, wins an unopposed third reading.

22 Apr: Retail sales rose 3.7 per cent in March as a result of Budget changes.

23 Apr: Gerald Ratner, head of the Ratner's jewellery chain, condemns the quality of his own merchandise in a speech to the Institute of Directors.

30 Apr: Appeal Court ruling effectively bars local councils from enforcing the Sunday trading laws against retailers unless they undertake to compensate them for lost sales.

7 May: John Marshall's attempt to exempt video shops from the Sunday trading laws rejected in the Commons by 71 to 38.

14 May: Lords to seek further guidance from the European Court on the legality of the Sunday trading laws.

20 May: Retail sales fell 3.5 per cent in April.

24 June: Coronary Prevention Group complains of misleading 'health' claims on food labels.

27 June: Association of District Councils suggests a compromise over Sunday trading, allowing DIY shops and garden centres to open from noon until 6 pm and removing restrictions from newsagents, corner and video shops.

1 July: Soil Association criticizes the plethora of misleading 'green' labels on food.
> Institute of Trading Standards Administration finds short measures of beer are widespread and calls for new laws to ensure full measures are served.

4 July: New consumer rights bill requiring goods to be free of defect, safe and durable, is announced by the government.

8 July: Food Commission calls for stricter labelling of food products to cut unhealthy excessive salt consumption.

15 July: *Drinking in England and Wales in the late 1980s*, argues that levels of consumption have not been affected by all day opening hours.

22 July: Retail sales rose 1.3 per cent in June.

15 Aug: Burton sells Harvey Nichols to the Hong Kong based Dickson Concepts for £60 million.

19 Aug: Retail sales rose 0.3 per cent in July.

5 Sept: Environment Select Committee calls for the introduction of an official eco-labelling system.

9 Sept: Retail sales figures revised to show a 1.5 per cent rise in June and 0.7 per cent in July.

16 Sept: August's retail sales figures fell by 1.4 per cent.

27 Sept: Three publishers secure a high court injunction barring Pentos from breaking the Net Book Agreement on four of the 27 titles on which discounts have been announced.

30 Sept: Asda launches a £357 million emergency rights issue.

7 Oct: Norman Lamont appeals to the EC to extend duty-free shopping until 2008.

21 Oct: Retail sales, having fallen 1.2 per cent in August, remained unchanged in September.

24 Oct: *Children - The Influencing Factor 1991*, Mintel International, shows children have increasing influence on shopping habits and on the greening of the consumer.

18 Nov: Retail sales fell by 0.5 per cent in October (later adjusted to a 0.6 per cent fall).

22 Nov: US firm Blockbusters pays £75 million for the UK's largest video chain, Cityvision.

26 Nov: Tesco, Asda and Safeway are to defy the Sunday trading laws and open on the Sabbath in the weeks up to Christmas.

27 Nov: Sainsbury's announce that they are to join the Sunday trading revolt after the Attorney-General announced that he would take no action against stores that open illegally. In the following days a number of other retail groups also begin to defy the Sunday trading laws.

16 Dec: Retail sales volumes rose by 1.2 per cent in November.

20 Dec: Asda, Sainsbury's and Tesco say they will move indefinitely to Sunday trading, opening 400 of their largest stores seven days a week.
> Implementation of S43 of the Weights and Measures Act 1985, requiring public houses to have lines on glasses showing full measures exlcusive of beer froth, is announced.

Tourism

GRAHAM STONE and DAVID HARDMAN

The turbulence in the international economy predicted in the review of 1990 has been further exacerbated in 1991. The economies of western Europe and North America (responsible for the generation of 85 per cent of tourist flows) moved deeper into recession as a result of deflationary practices and high interest rates. The impact of the Gulf war in the first quarter of the year further affected tourism by adding fears of international terrorist acts to the existing squeeze on discretionary incomes. This caused a reduction of 25 per cent in international tourist flows. Although subsequent quarters have seen some restoration of visitor numbers, the outcome of the year suggests a level of activity below that of 1990.

Domestically, the reduction of the headline rate of inflation from 10 per cent in January to less than 4 per cent in December allowed a managed fall in interest rates and an easing of monetary policy in the UK. The economy has been officially declared to be in recession. Despite efforts to 'talk up' future confidence and claims that growth will begin over the winter of 1991/92, confidence and consumer expenditure levels have remained low, particularly when measured through retail sales. Unemployment is expected to continue to rise, perhaps at a decelerating rate next year due to a depressed home market. Opportunities to export are also constrained by membership of the Exchange Rate Mechanism.

Against this backcloth, tourist activity during the year has fluctuated greatly from heavy initial falls to some recovery during the second half of the year, making predictions extremely hazardous. Most forecasters anticipate that 1991 levels of tourist expenditure may be up to 5 per cent below 1990 figures, with at best expectations of a very weak recovery during 1992 (see Table 1).

Visits Abroad by UK Residents

In the decade prior to 1990, the level of UK visits abroad increased by nearly 60 per cent, whilst expenditure over the same period nearly doubled. This is indicative of a high propensity to travel (67 per cent) in the British market. Despite difficulties both at home and abroad, the first six months of 1991 saw an increase of 3 per cent in the outbound market. This figure obscures wild variations; for example, visitor flows to the eastern Mediterranean area, particularly Malta and Cyprus fell dramatically. Conversely, visits to western Europe increased, to France by more

than 50 per cent, whilst UK visitors to Spain fell by 10 per cent. These figures can
obscure a number of longer-term trends in the market – a fall in the inclusive tour
(package) holidays, a growth in second and third holidays, particularly short breaks,
more independent travel and a growing interest in 'newer' destinations.

Trends observable during the second half of the year suggest that the earlier growth
in visitor numbers will continue but with very limited growth in expenditure terms.
One of the factors which makes forecasting difficult is that of identifying
underlying trends in the package holiday market. Currently this sector accounts for
more than 60 per cent of outbound visitors from the UK. Numbers peaked 1988–9
with more than 12 million packages sold – largely air-inclusive trips. In 1990 the
numbers declined to less than 10 million. In 1991 summer sales (7.5 million) have
shown a fall of 5 per cent. However the level of bookings for the winter season
1991–2 is currently showing a growth of 17 per cent and should result in 2.5 million
sales. Within this context, the collapse of the International Leisure Group in March
1991 removed from the marketplace such major players as Intasun and Air Europe.
This has been of benefit to other major tour operators with respect to market share,
sales and profitability. In 1990, the top 30 tour operators made a profit on turnover
of 1.5 per cent (the best result for five years). Recently Airtours announced a profit
increase of more than 300 per cent. Thus the exit of ILG preempted the possibility
of a price war in 1991 due to excess capacity.

Table 1. Forecast for tourism to and within the UK to 1995.

	1990	1991	1995	% change 1995/90
International				
Visits (million)	18.0	18.0	22.3	4.4
Spending (£ billion at current prices)	7.8	7.9	11.6	8.3
Domestic				
Total visits (million)	95.5	–	105.0	1.9
Holiday visits (million)	58.5	–	63.0	1.5
Spending (£ million at current prices)				
Total visits	10,460.0	–	14,700.0	7.0
Holiday visits	7,350.0	–	10,100.0	6.6

Domestic spending estimates are rounded to the nearest £25 million.
Sources: British Tourist Authority; English Tourist Board

There are indications that the market for package holidays is changing to meet a demand which seeks greater sophistication and independence. Thus operators are offering more flexible packages to include greater choice, more exotic destinations, self-catering facilities, two-centre experience and flight-only seats. In terms of destinations, 90 per cent of packages are short haul with a sun, sea, sand orientation. Although the long haul market is showing signs of growth, it sill only represents 10 per cent of the total, with Florida accounting for 50 per cent of all long haul holidaymakers. The year should show sales in line with 1990, (see Table 2) but with a significant growth in winter holidays offsetting an anticipated fall in summer excursions.

Overseas Visitors to the UK

For incoming tourists to the UK 1991 has been a difficult year. Estimates suggest that the number of overseas visitors in 1991 will be 17.5 million (2 per cent less than 1990) with expenditure at £7.75 billion (a fall on 1990 levels).

The first half of the year saw visitor numbers and expenditure down by more than 5 per cent on the equivalent period in 1990. Within this figure, however, there were differential changes according to the countries of origin. Visitor traffic from north America fell by 14 per cent, with expenditure down by more than 17 per cent. As north American visitors constitute approximately 25 per cent of all tourist inflows into the UK and given their concentration in the south east and London area, there was a disproportionate effect on sales and consequently employment in these areas. Particularly during the first quarter of the year, London hotel occupancy rates fell dramatically, despite heavy price discounting to maintain market shares.

Long haul traffic in the first half of the year was down by 12 per cent, but this was compensated for to an extent through an increased per capita spend by visiting western Europeans (a third of the total visitor numbers). Thus the existing depressed business market (down 8 per cent on 1990) was reinforced by a decline in leisure visits. The second half of the year saw a slow recovery from the earlier period, but this recovery was weak and will continue to be so into 1992. Some estimates suggest that recovery will be delayed until 1993.

Table 2. Expenditure/visits by UK residents abroad

	£ million expenditure at current prices	Total visits (million)	North America	Western Europe	Rest of world
1990	9,916	16.89	1.22	13.8	1.81
1991	9,925	17.45	1.23	14.75	1.65

Source: International Passenger Summary

This market is heavily influenced by external political and economic variables such as the forthcoming elections in the UK and USA, relationships with and developments in Europe and the performances of the German and American economies – through exchange rates. All these and other factors will influence future flows in 1992 and 1993.

The Tourist Industry in Great Britain

The decline in tourist activity has required the industry to consider a range of defensive strategies in an attempt to protect their market share. Some were unsuccessful. One major casualty of the recession was the collapse of International Leisure Group in March 1991, with Air Europe and Intasun ceasing to trade, adding 7,000 to the unemployment totals. The depression in the market was highlighted by the fact that companies within the group were not acquired by other operators. This was an indication of the critical margins operated by ILG. The collapse benefited other operators who acquired increased market shares. Airtours became the third biggest tour operator and commenced their own airline operation whilst Dan Air increased its load factors at the expense of Air Europe. Currently the three major tour operators, Thomson, Owners Abroad and Airtours, share 60 per cent of the total market.

A similar form of concentration is happening in the travel agency sector where the five largest companies, A T Mays, Hogg Robinson, Lunn Poly, Pickfords and Thomas Cook, account for more than 50 per cent of inclusive tour sales with only one third of the outlets. Lunn Poly (Thomson) dominates this group with 25 per cent of sales. The market is being further consolidated – Carlson Travel acquired A T Mays and W H Smith travel, Airtours are likely to acquire Pickfords travel. However the joint operating agreement promised between Wagon-Lits and Thomas Cook has not transpired.

The picture is very similar in airline operators. The downturn in demand has led to reduced profits/losses, failures and consolidation. Eastern Airlines ceased trading in January, whilst the continuing problems of PanAm resulted in an end to operations in December 1991. Other airlines have sought forms of cooperation and cost cutting through joint operating agreements. SAS, Swissair and Austrian Airlines have continued to strengthen the European quality alliance. British Airways have been seeking closer operational links with KLM and Northwest. The drive to such development has been reinforced by the imminence of European deregulation in 1992–93. A major response has been the development and implementation of hub-spoke operations in Europe. This system, prevalent in the USA, enables airlines to develop collection points for passengers for onward transmission with greater flight frequency and from more convenient locations. Their operations require the establishment of major airports and there is currently much debate as to which airlines will consolidate their operations at which airports.

The result of these developments will have a major effect on European air transport in the next century.

Domestic Tourism

In 1991 the continued recession in the UK and the impact of the Gulf war combined to keep many potential foreign travellers at home, thus giving a much-needed boost to domestic tourism. The significance of this opportunity is clear when judged in the context of a £2.5 billion deficit between the money spent by the British abroad and that earned by tourism at home.

English coastal resorts remained popular destinations, accounting for some 40 per cent of stay holidays taken by the British in England. The quality of seawater is however still under debate following the publication of three separate reports. Those of the National River Authority (NRA) and the EC both indicate improvements since 1990 whereas that produced by *Holiday Which?* is less complimentary, claiming contamination of the sea by viruses on many popular beaches.

Blackpool is still preeminent yet even here bookings by July were 15 per cent down on 1990 and the resort was thus more dependent than usual on its conference market. An increasing dependence on day and short-stay visitors is possible in future which emphasizes the extension of the season via the illuminations. Positive steps are also being taken to retain its position as market leader. The tower is currently being refurbished by First Leisure Corporation while the pleasure beach opened its new Ocean Boulevard retail development. In November the pleasure beach also gained planning permission for the world's largest (1 mile) highest (235 feet) and fastest (85 mph) rollercoaster, its proximity to Blackpool airport requiring Civil Aviation Authority permission. Serious pollution on the Fylde Coast will also be much reduced by the construction of a new treatment plant by the North West Water Authority at Fleetwood Marsh.

The future of England's smaller seaside resorts was the subject of a special report based on a review of Weymouth, Bognor Regis, Skegness and Morecombe. It concluded that such resorts are suffering from a 'legacy of neglect' after 25 years of market decline and that a cooperative marketing effort is needed immediately. Elsewhere, tourism development action programmes (TDAPs) will provide the focus for tourism initiatives at Weston-super-Mare and Brighton. Coastal resorts in general are also to be targeted via a promotional campaign (£1 million pa for three years) and aimed at mid-market families with young children.

Coastal development has also proceeded rapidly with the emphasis on marina complexes usually with associated leisure and recreational facilities. These have stimulated an interest in boating activities throughout the UK. Eighty-four examples now exist along the south coast between Ramsgate and Poole and Associated British Ports are now developing such complexes at 12 out of 21 of their ports, their principal activities being centred at Southampton, Plymouth and Hull. On Merseyside, Liverpool Yacht Harbours has spent £10 million creating a 290-berth marina with over 100 waterside homes and computerized lock gates at the entrance to the Mersey.

Such developments can however bring environmental costs as well as socioeconomic benefits. A review of the UK's 155 estuaries revealed that 85 per cent of estuarine environments are being damaged by human activities which include the construction of marinas, tourism infrastructure and popular recreational activities (sailing, fishing, jet-skiing). Twenty-six of these are important international wildlife sites which the UK is obliged to protect under European legislation.

In rural areas changing land ownership is beginning to cause problems of public access. Currently this cannot be guaranteed where Forestry Commission land has been sold to private landowners and a similar problem may exist on land owned by the privatized water authorities. National Parks are under increasing visitor pressures but their attempts to treat the problems of impact and congestion are not always immediately successful. In Borrowdale an attempt by the Lake District special planning board to persuade visitors to use public rather than private transport failed because of local community objections to potential loss of income. In south west England the new Dartmoor area tourism initiative is seeking to develop an environmentally sensitive type of tourism in a region which has major conservation values and where at least 25 per cent of farms already provide some sort of tourist facility. The ETB are currently addressing many of these issues through their recent publication *Tourism in National Parks: a guide to good practice.*

Early in 1991 Scotland had one of its best winter sports seasons for three decades with perfect Alpine weather. Aviemore, Glenshee and Aonach Mor all reported good business and road access has been improved, the Glasgow-Fort William journey now taking just over two hours. Figures from the Highlands and Islands Enterprise suggest skiing is worth at least £15 million to Scotland in an average year.

Last year over 600 million day visits were made by the British generating £5.3 billion (20 per cent of the total British tourism income). However there is increasing evidence that coastal and rural destinations are now attracting less than one third as many day trippers as inland towns and cities and with only one tenth of such excursions being made by public transport. This focuses attention on the growing importance of urban-based tourism, the importance of the day trip market, the potential for city breaks and the need for related infrastructure such as car parks and budget hotels.

In Merseyside tourism has grown by 53 per cent in five years, now netting £350 million pa and supporting 14,000 full-time jobs. 30 million tourists visit Liverpool each year, 4 million of which stay overnight. Albert Docks (5.1 million visitors pa) is the major attraction with the Maritime Museum, Tate Gallery and Beatles Story as important components: the two cathedrals and the revamped Mersey ferries provide other foci.

Despite initial financial uncertainties the World Student Games at Sheffield provided an excellent example of how such an event can provide a stimulus for tourism. Hotel occupancy was up 25 per cent on 1990, the £147 million investment in new sporting facilities is now a springboard for further events, such as the European Swimming Championships in 1993 and the city now has a more positive image to market. It is also significant that the ETB are now backing Manchester's bid to stage the 2000 Olympics.

The 1986 Stoke Garden Festival provided a similar stimulus for tourism which has now diversified by location ('Peaks and Potteries') and industry ('Do China in a Day'). In Leeds a new TDPA centred on the waterfront is aiming to attract new tourism investment as a basis for economic regeneration and environmental improvement. A planned £0.5 million programme has attracted funding from the city council, British Waterways, Leeds Development Corporation and the private sector while a new museum at Clarence Dock, using material from the Royal Armouries Collection will provide a major focus. Carlisle's new Tullie House Museum of the Border represents a further excellent example of local authority investment (£6 million) in tourism.

Conference and exhibition tourism had a tough year with the recession eating into marketing budgets. Nevertheless the UK exhibition industry is still worth well over £1 billion pa and business tourism in England still accounts for 8 per cent of tourist overnight stays and 17 per cent of total tourist spending. The most significant development of 1990 was the opening of the International Convention Centre at Birmingham based on £120 million of local authority investment and a £30 million grant form the EC. Five thousand new jobs in five years are envisaged and at the same time the NEC is embarking on a £100 million project to increase its exhibition space.

The popularity of historical sites has continued to rise in 1991. However a rise in visitor numbers can lead to a decline in the visitor experience and a need for improved management. This problem is epitomized by Stonehenge which is a world heritage site and, with 700,000 visitors pa, English Heritage's main source of revenue. A plan has now been drawn up by English Heritage and the National Trust to create a 1400 acre archaeological park and involving the resiting and screening of an improved visitor centre as well as the diversion of part of the A344: the main aims are 'to improve the spectacle of the stones' and increase the length of stay (and thus visitor spend).

At Avebury the NT has also won an important battle to prevent the development of an Elizabethan Experience at Avebury Manor which would have caused damage to the 16th century house and threatened the adjacent neolithic monuments. Warwick Castle too is currently threatened by plans to build a new hotel, leisure centre and two golf centres.

The success and popularity of created heritage attractions is clearly demonstrated by awards made in 1991. The National Railway Museum (York) was named as National Heritage museum of the year, the York Archaeological Resource Centre as best museum of archaeological and historical interest and the National Waterway Museum at Gloucester as best museum of historic or social interest, all by the ETB. Dover's £14 million 'White Cliffs Experience' became England's visitor attraction of the year as well as receiving the British Award of the British Guild of Travel Writers. Proposals for 1992 include the development of a 'living museum' at the Lady Victoria Colliery, Newtongrange and the conversion of Alexandra Palace ('the birthplace of TV') into an electronic tourist attraction. The number of heritage attractions has doubled in the last five years, clearly indicating the demand for the product while at the same time raising issues of authenticity and selectivity. It can perhaps be said that after 2,000 years of making history, the British have now developed the skill of remaking it! However, it can also be argued that anything which acts as an entry point to history is good in principle.

Zoos have also found 1991 a difficult year, particularly those where large animals are kept in cramped conditions, a fact now unacceptable to many people. Reduced attendances and the need to improve outdated infrastructure have brought about economic problems. London Zoo in particular has been the focus of attention: it is still the eighth most visited tourist attraction in London but its 1.3 million visitors pa is well down on the 3 million pa of the 1950s. It is losing £2 million pa and it will be some time before one can tell if the new emphases on conservation and education will allow the zoo to operate profitably as well as retain its significance as a tourist attraction.

Theme parks are a relatively new tourist phenomenon in the UK. The key is investment to support the search for 'bigger and better' developments in an increasingly competitive situation. However declining visitor figures in 1991 have produced little profit for reinvestment in new rides which in turn stimulate return visits. There is also an increasing need to meet environmental standards: indeed Lightwater Valley claim their theme is 'everything is carefully integrated into the landscape'. Within the UK the Tussaud's Group dominates the market, owning Madame Tussaud's (London), Alton Towers (which combines 'white knuckle' rides with a stately home) and the Chessington World of Adventure, that is, three of the UK's top five attractions. The importance of such developments in economic terms is also shown by the portfolio of the Yorkshire and Humberside Tourist Boards which advertises 20 large sites suitable for the development of cultural and heritage attractions, leisure complexes or theme parks.

However perhaps the most significant theme park in terms of its likely impact on domestic tourism is being built outside the UK. EuroDisney, 20 miles east of Paris, is expected to attract 11 million visitors in its first year, including 1.5 million from the UK. Defined as 'a classic example of US cultural imperialism', it will set new standards that UK theme parks will have to follow. It will also become a major competitor for tourist attractions in south east England as the journey from London via the Channel Tunnel will only take just over three hours. The need for a comparable international attraction in the UK has already been recognized by the BTA and ETB but it is claimed that parochial attitudes and red tape make investment on such a scale unlikely in the UK. Indeed, Universal Studios' plans to build such a complex on Rainham Marshes (Essex) have been all but abandoned.

Domestic tourism has therefore experienced a difficult year on the whole. Despite the 'stay at home' influence of the Gulf war, the limited spending power of the home market and the frequent lack of ready capital for investment have both had negative effects on the industry. Government support to organizations and buildings serving the tourist industry has also declined and is likely to remain at levels well below those of other European countries. As a result admission charges have been introduced or increased at many museums and historic buildings in order to generate enough income for economic survival. Polluted beaches, litter, congested roads and archaic Sunday trading laws have also combined to produce an environment within which tourism cannot function at maximum efficiency.

There is also the likely effect of the Channel Tunnel to consider, emphasized by the opening of EuroDisney in April 1992. The ease of access to the continent could mean, at least initially, the loss of much of the south east market to Wales, Scotland and the north of England. It is also possible that flow through the tunnel may be biased in one direction with outgoing British tourists far exceeding the incoming continentals. Problems could also arise for Kent in general and Folkestone in particular as 'gateways' to and from the continent.

These and other problems have already been recognized by the BTA in *Guidelines for Tourism in Britain* and by the ETB in *Planning for the Future: a tourism strategy for England* which both look forward to the 1991–95 period. Four key themes emerge:

a) There will be a 12 per cent fall in the number of 15–24 year olds in the next five years. This will affect the labour force and the industry's ability to recruit and the gradual trend will be towards an older, more affluent market.

b) There is a need to develop a major international attraction capable of competing with EuroDisney. Six new countryside-based tourism villages are also suggested.

c) Public transport networks need investment, development and more effective integration.

d) A more symbiotic relationship is need between tourism and its environment. Tourism is the UK's most important industry generating £25 billion pa: it employs 6 per cent (1.5 million) of the labour force and is currently generating 20,000 new jobs pa. These figures would suggest that solutions to the above problems are crucial to the future economy of the UK.

Chronology

7 Jan: Consumers' Association condemns safety standards on holiday beaches in *Holiday Which?*.

13 Feb: Publication by NCC of review of the UK's 105 estuaries and associated developmental pressures.

18 Feb: Britain urges EC to strengthen draft laws on consumer protection to curb high-pressure timeshare marketing.

Thomas Cook asks 7,300 staff to take voluntary pay cuts of up to 10 per cent as part of a package of savings to cope with the impact of the Gulf war and recession.

3 Mar: Bankruptcy of International Leisure Group, operators of Air Europe and Intasun, announced.

8 Mar: Administrators appointed to International Leisure Group.

11 Mar: Opening of new 'Ecology' gallery at Natural History Museum.

13 Mar: Tour operating elements of International Leisure Group go into liquidation.

21 Mar: British Airways offers 50,000 free tickets for worldwide flights on 23 April in an attempt to reverse the damage done to the travel industry by the Gulf war.

Collapse of Sun Living Ltd, the ski holiday firm, leaves ABTA needing to call for funds from its members to cover its liabilities.

7 Apr: News leaks of the grave financial situation at London Zoo.

11 Apr: ABTA cancels its annual convention, to have been held in Orlando, Florida, for economic reasons and also announces measures to restore depleted funds.

Government refuses to subsidize London Zoo.

1 May: *Tourism and the Environment: Maintaining the Balance*, HMSO, says that the tourist industry must help to control the damaging impact of visitors on historic buildings and landscapes.

9 May: £10 million scheme to create an archaeology park around Stonehenge, Wiltshire, announced by English Heritage and the National Trust.

10 Jun: Hotel star ratings are criticized as an inadequate guide to room prices in a survey by Expotel.

19 Jun: Survey for Visa International finds 64 per cent of Britons take an annual holiday and spend £17 billion on travel. Thirty-five per cent of Britons take package holidays.

20 Jun: London Zoo unveils plans to become a wildlife conservation site and cut the number of animals on its London site.

22 Jun: BTA publishes *Guidelines for Tourism in Britain 1991–95*.

26 Jun: £50 million to tranform London Zoo into a conservation park announced.

30 Jun: British tourists are evacuated from fighting in Slovenia.

8 Jul: Survey of young women's attitudes to sex on holiday published in *Company*.

23 Jul: English Tourist Board announces plans for six countryside holiday villages and a campaign to boost tourism revenues by 50 per cent in five years in their new strategy document, *Planning for Success: a tourism strategy for England 1991–95*.

13 Aug: *Holiday Which?* claims that the government has misled bathers over hygiene standards on Britain's beaches.

28 Aug: Proposals from the tourism and leisure section of NEDO for a new public holiday in October are rejected by the government. The report also suggested a fixed date for Easter, staggering the start of the school holidays and eventually moving to a four term school and academic year to encourage people to take two holidays a year.

Thomson Holidays predict an autumn price war.

19 Sept: Keith Prowse, the theatre ticket agency and travel company, collapses.

27 Sept: Birmingham based TransEuropean Airways UK ceases trading.

29 Oct: Plans revealed to develop Alexandra Palace as an electronic tourist attraction within a £95 million development complex.

7 Nov: Planning permission given for construction of world's longest, highest and fastest roller-coaster at Blackpool pleasure beach.

9 Nov: Dover's White Cliffs Experience wins the British Award of the British Guild of Travel Writers.

3 Dec: Airtours announce 30 per cent increase in profits.

4 Dec: PanAm suspends operations.

Agriculture

B. A. HOLDERNESS

Are there signs of recovery in agriculture? It would be a sanguine person who predicted an end to the long period of decline in the 1980s. The problems of agriculture in the West and *a fortiori* in Britain, are not cyclical, even though recession has aggravated their effect; nor, in the conventional sense are they structural, which is to say that it is not matter of building a new edifice using fresh material but on the same foundations. In the 1870s, British agriculture was overcommitted to cereal production, and especially to wheat, and high cost arable farming could not compete with cheap imports of breadstuff. But options for change existed and were easily apprehensible. Low corn prices meant cheap animal feed; rising living standards increased demand for meat and dairy produce, for fruit and vegetables; and rail transport meant that fresh deliveries could be made to the towns daily. Moreover, the progress of technology enabled agriculture to benefit from cheaper fertilizers and implements and also added to its repertoire by facilitating canning and preserve-making. The adjustments that had to be made were often painful and sometimes reluctant but they followed an inescapable logic. In the past six years difficulties have accumulated that are not all of the same type. Even the principle of comparative advantage, so clearly evincible in the late nineteenth century, is ambiguous in the late twentieth. Neither a movement towards more arable food production nor towards greater livestock enterprises is foreseeable as a way out of the impasse. What the future holds is *economically* uncertain as it is *politically* threatening. British farmers suffer from the less firm resolution of their government towards the preservation of agriculture as a social institution: all other EC governments and most elsewhere in Europe favour their agricultural interests as they had formerly cherished their peasant subjects. In Britain the legacy of free trade and the uneasy acceptance of subsidization in the prosperous years from 1955 to 1972 together with the general weakness of agriculture *vis à vis* both industry and government, set all by the ears. The malaise in other words is partly attitudinal. Moreover the CAP is a political millstone round the neck of *British* agriculture.

The Decline of Agriculture

The rationale for protecting and supporting agriculture in Britain is weakly expressed in public discourse. Farmers may not be unpopular, but the dissociation of idealized rusticity from efficient agribusiness confuses the town-bred consumer of food and of the countryside. However, the real problem is that farming is now so marginal to the total economy. Few Britons have first hand experience of farming and the rural constituency of politicians is scarcely if at all agricultural. The trend of course is the same everywhere in the developed world, but in Britain the subordination of agriculture began so much earlier and had gone so far even by 1900 that only enthusiasts saw much hope of its restoration as a force in society. In times of national emergency the supply of food becomes critical; production at all costs may then be attempted. But the trend towards marginalization has been inexorable for a century or more. In 1914 the agricultural sector contributed about 6 per cent of GDP; in 1938 5 per cent; and despite the efforts of wartime planning still only 6 per cent in 1945. By 1975 the figure was 2.8 per cent and in 1990 1.4 per cent. Employment fell even more dramatically. The agricultural workforce in 1931 numbered 1.16 million including part-time workers; in 1981 0.65 million. In the past decade the actively engaged workforce fell by 20 per cent. In 1990, however, half a million farmers and their employees delivered about twice as much per capita in real terms as the agricultural manpower achieved in 1972. But superficially the British would hardly notice if husbandry ceased. Indeed, were the land to be utilized for leisure, afforestation or home-building, it is possible to argue that the contribution to the national product would be higher. There is of course no infinite appetite for recreation or accommodation and the law of diminishing returns would soon come into force. Land itself, however, may become a drug on the market and its agricultural purpose may not signify any more than other uses.

The dismemberment of the industry will not be difficult to achieve. Farmers with heavy debt charges, alert to the prospects of global overproduction of temperate foodstuffs, are clearly diversifying into other businesses or selling land for development. The recession has slowed the process and frustrated many desperate land owners from the finding of new uses for their property, but the current is running even among the rocks. Britain is well placed for 'disagriculturation'. The small size of the workforce and the large size of the farms, the fewness of farmsteads and their suitableness for conversion, set few obstacles in the way of golf courses, forest, or country craft complexes, while the craze for turning barns and cattle yards into dwellings, although probably past the meridian, shows how easily fixed capital can be recycled.

Farming may not be arduous in modern circumstances, but offsetting the savings on labour so far achieved, is the high cost of acquiring and maintaining capital equipment. The ratio of output to operating capital declined between 1974–76 and 1987–89 by about 12 per cent. That is to say that in spite of steadily increasing production (up in gross by 65 per cent) the charge upon capital rose in a greater proportion. There is a problem: I am unaware whether anyone knows how much value can be attached to property diverted from agricultural use. My figures are based on the recorded annual costs of acquiring and maintaining plant and equipment, stock in trade and relative agricultural land values. It is a crude measure that ought to be refined more than I have had the time to do, but it rather suggests that the cost squeeze in agriculture is deep seated. The industry is still too highly 'geared'. Entrepreneurial incomes have fallen steadily since the early 1980s in spite of falling numbers engaged in the business of farming.

Table 1. Output to capital ratio (index based in 1975)

	Agg. gross product *ad valorem*	'Capital', rent and long term liabilities (50:20:30)
1974–76	100	100
1981–83	145	246.5
1987–89	165	305

Another option, to attune one's business to the vicissitudes of CAP intervention, to stay loose and flexible, by skinning the land or by catching every slight breeze of opportunity, is equally impracticable, because most farmers cannot change direction quickly and cannot despoil their own property for fear of wasting their real assets. Farming is not one business in any event, and to re-equip an undertaking to gain a transitory or provisional advantage is both imprudent in purpose and unattainable in fact. Those in this mood who can, seem to prefer to stay liquid, not to become too venturesome. Most being burdened with debt can scarcely exercise such an aleatory choice.

The Detrimental Effects of CAP

Has British farming gained less from the provisions of the CAP in recent years than its competitors elsewhere in the EC? This is a difficult question in spite of common opinion. The CAP was designed to address diverse problems, but it was devised without reference to British conditions, except in a sense negatively, as when the participating governments refused to contemplate subsidies by way of deficiency payments – the British system of the period. Deficiency payments were predicated on the assumption of continuing free trade in agricultural products; on the continent the legacy of varied kinds of protectionism and state-driven reconstruction had to be harmonized so as to preserve the agriculture of every country while giving some precedence to France as the agrarian counterweight to German industrial preeminence. As with all schemes patched up to support divers little producers, the greatest beneficiaries were the larger commercial farms. Britain should have done well thereby, but agriculture in this island was pitched on too narrow a front to obtain all the advantages that accrued to continental producers.

This was visible but not conspicuous for a decade when general inflation and official anxiety about primary product supplies delivered agriculture from the necessity of sharing out insufficient rations. The 'good years' that coincided with the period of transition to the CAP disarmed former critics and all but silenced remaining sceptics. In an age of scarcity the bias in favour of production in the CAP was hardly unreasonable; except of course for the fact that scarcity, if it had been real, was short-lived. The downward pull of world agricultural prices soon resumed and in the mid 1980s the mismatch of production and price trends began to recreate tensions in the system that were essentially political. The change such as it was for the CAP, from supervising agricultural autarky within a regime of social reconstruction, to settling competitive claims upon less liberally found resources, without sacrificing the purpose either of subsidizing the small producer or of rationalizing his existence, was incomplete because governments would not believe that reform necessarily entailed economy. In the UK, however, when agriculture played little part in the macro-economic, or macro-social, determination of public policy, the CAP was both incubus and reproach. Fighting to keep one's share of the budget in the 1980s may have been valiant, but it was not conducted with much conviction. Farmers and even the public deduced that the UK stood at a disadvantage in the allocation of CAP funds. The conclusion was not correct, except in the sense that intervention and subsidies were more narrowly focused on British agriculture because so much of the funds were not appropriate to conditions in the UK. *Pro rata*, whether in the equivalence of price support for comparable levels and types of production or in proportion of the size and manpower of the agricultural sector, the UK share was at least as substantial as on the continent in the period. Only in the relative share of the fiscal contribution returning to this country was the UK disadvantaged, and even there the government struck an assortment of deals. This is not to defend the CAP which is in general indefensible; it is merely an effort to point out that the debate in Britain on the role of agricultural intervention has been conducted from false premises. There is, moreover, a narrower truth which farmers either do not see or find uncomfortable, that EC subvention has been a source of profit to most agriculturalists in the UK just as was the system of deficiency payments in the old days. In effect the income of British agriculture has for long borne an unfortunate likeness to the actual level of aggregate subsidization. Not only has it been paid to turn out produce for which government or Commission would guarantee good prices, but it has also been the case that maintaining the appearances of agricultural efficiency, as in France, owes more to public support than to the discipline of the market. The consequent distortion, towards conspicuous investment, over-gearing and a sclerotic response to price fluctuations has produced significant difficulties for agriculturalists, but their problems *arising out of the CAP*, have been less marked than those of consumers of food in Britain, since the greatest change wrought by the CAP in the 1980s, when plenty again abounded in the developed world, was to raise British food prices. The fact, if not the method, of subsidies for farmers remained constant after 1947. Consumers, however, had for 20 years the opportunity of buying food drawn from world markets at prices little higher than prices obtaining in the primary producing zones of the world. Farmers did not suffer because of the system of subsidy. After 1973, and more clearly after 1980, the continental practice of supporting agriculture without recourse to deficiency payments was foisted upon the British public.

The scandal of the CAP, however, is that intervention is unnecessary *sub specie aeternitatis*. It tends merely to magnify production whatever the means adopted to direct the flow of intervention.

Problems in Marketing

The problems are not so much institutional as entrepreneurial. The collapse of British farmers' incomes in real terms by about 50 per cent in the past ten years is not due to the decline of intervention, except insofar as the British government both applied more vigorously the rules agreed by EC heads of government to contain agricultural spending and sought fewer concessions and little virement in allocating the subsidies. The conviction that continental governments were not playing the same game is therefore justified. The view from France of course is different; there farmers are certain that British intransigence over successive CAP budgets in the late 1980s has undermined their livelihood. But French and German farm incomes have not fallen by so much as half the rate of decline in the UK, while Danish, Dutch and Belgian agricultural incomes have held up remarkably well.

Entrepreneurial shortcomings in British agriculture are of long standing. In the exploitation of changing demand schedules for foodstuffs British farmers have been outmanoeuvred by continental producers as they were before 1900. Even in sections of the industry once untouched by overseas competition, in liquid milk distribution or in the production of temperate vegetables for freezing, the past 20 years have seen a reversal of fortunes. Since British farmers have held their own in the British market in the sense that the country is now more self-sufficient in the supply of agricultural produce, the issue of market penetration is equivocal, but in most of the new areas of demand success has been elusive for British farmers as a body. Worse, their impact on continental markets has also been negligible. Farmers are unorganized in marketing. Their dependence upon distributors, whose organization betrays signs of rigid inflexibility, such as the Milk Marketing Board or certain commercial wholesale businesses, belies the efficiency of firms such as Sainsbury or Tesco in disposing of agricultural produce. Efficient marketing has tended to bypass British producers in favour of more ruthlessly organized producer groups on the one hand or of those who can deliver more attractive, fashionable or exotic commodities on the other. British agriculture in the 1990s is the victim of its own feeble bargaining position.

Chronology

10 Jan: Controls lifted on the movement of sheep in areas of the Lake District affected by fall-out from the 1987 Chernobyl disaster.

21 Jan: NFU says that British agriculture is in the worst recession for more than 50 years as the government publishes statistics revealing that the total farm income shrank by 14 per cent from £1,513 million in 1989 to £1,296 million in 1990.

22 Jan: Disclosure that three people had died in a salmonella outbreak in Southampton.

25 Jan: Forestry Commission announces that forest planting has slumped by a third as a result of the ending of tax privileges for private woodland owners in 1988 and higher than expected land prices.

29 Jan: Public Health Laboratory Service report says cases of salmonella in poultry, eggs and meat rose by 25 per cent in 1990.

4 Feb: Britain rejects plans for the radical reform of CAP as a blueprint for turning Europe into 'an agricultural museum'.

13 Feb: David Naish elected unopposed to succeed Sir Simon Gourlay as president of the NFU.
EC Commission exempts British fishermen from new regulations requiring them to tie up their boats in port for eight consecutive days a month providing they use nets with a mesh size designed to conserve fish stocks.

14 Feb: Warnings about hamburgers after 14 people were affected by escheria coli 0157 in Preston.

21 Mar: NFU suggests that a set aside land scheme to deal with food surpluses should be voluntary, not compulsory.

15 Apr: Figures show that the number of food poisoning cases almost trebled 1989–90.

26 Apr: Sir Richard Body withdraws his Pig Husbandry Bill after the government introduces draft regulations requiring pig farmers to phase out stalls and tethers within eight years and move to more humane methods.

15 May: Survey for Vegetarian Society by Bradford University argues 7 per cent of adults now claim to be vegetarian.

13 June: MAFF confirms an outbreak of blue-eared pig disease in Humberside.

19 June: Agriculture Select Committee expresses concern at proposals by EC Commission to weaken British rules protecting livestock transported to the continent for slaughter.

26 June: EC Agriculture Commissioner, Ray McSharry, outlines proposals for cuts of 14–18 per cent in beef prices, reductions in milk quotas for large farms, price cuts of up to 35 per cent in cereals, with balancing compensation. Initial reaction in Britain sees this as discriminating against large, efficient farms.

1 July: Trawlers required to use larger mesh nets to help conserve stocks of cod and haddock.

9 July: EC agriculture plans for 35 per cent cuts in minimum guaranteed prices to cereal producers, 10 per cent to milk producers and 15 per cent to beef producers are formally approved. Financial incentives to use environmentally friendly husbandry and encourage, or in the case of large farms, oblige the development of land for non-farm use are also agreed. So is a related compensation and retirement package.
Panel on Dietary Reference Values of the Committee on Medical Aspects of Food Policy, *Dietary Reference Values for Food Energy and Nutrition in the United Kingdom*, HMSO, outlines recommended levels and types of food intake.

29 July: Agriculture Select Committee calls for subsidies to animal waste rendering industry so that smaller charges are made for the removal of carcasses, making the burying or dumping of them uneconomic.

17 Sept: Report by World Wide Fund for Nature recommends a cut of 40 per cent in the North Sea fishing fleet, with accompanying retirement incentives and licensing of all boats.

24 Sept: The French Prime Minister promises protection of lamb exports and compensation for attacks.

6 Nov: Payments to farmers for conservation work in designated Environmentally Sensitive Areas are to more than quadruple in the next three years.

15 Nov: *Our Farming Future*, HMSO, outlines schemes to set up 12 Environmentally Sensitive Areas.

18 Dec: EC to restrict the North Sea cod and haddock catch to 100,000 tonnes in 1992 and require vessels to stay in port either eight days per month or 135 days in the year. It also requires a change in net sizes to allow young fish to escape.

Britain's Foreign Trade, Payments and Exchange Rates

PETER SINCLAIR

Sterling and European Monetary Arrangements

Nineteen ninety-one was the first full year of Britain's participation in the Exchange Rate Mechanism of the European Monetary System (EMS). Twenty years of free or managed floating for the pound came to an end in October 1990. Sterling was not completely fixed, since it could rise or fall within a wide band of up to 6 per cent either side of its central parities against the European Currency Unit (the ECU) and the other European Community currencies of which it was composed. The EC currency group was of course also still floating against the US dollar, the Japanese yen and other world currencies. As a whole, 1991 was a year of greater currency stability in the foreign exchange markets than most previous years. The dollar appreciated in the first few months, only to drop back later in the year when the US authorities lowered their interest rates sharply.

The year saw no currency realignments within the EMS. Realignments had in any case become increasingly rare and modest since the first few years after the system's inception in 1979. The pound fluctuated within narrow limits against its key currency, the Deutschmark, for most of the year, generally somewhat below the parity rate of DM 2.95. The British authorities felt able to lower the banks' base rate, to which all sterling short-term interest rates were linked, in a series of steps from 15 per cent at the start of the year to 10 per cent by the autumn. This success appeared to vindicate those who had been advocating sterling's entry into the ERM. But opponents argued that ERM participation was preventing the authorities from reducing sterling interest rates still further. In the United States, key short-term interest rates were brought down to 4 per cent to combat the recession and secure a dollar depreciation that gave welcome relief to America's exporting and import-competing industries.

In December, Germany raised its short-term interest rates to combat rising inflation there – German inflation had risen above the British rate in October, for the first time for over 35 years – and France, Italy and Spain followed suit. The Chancellor opted to hold UK interest rates unchanged, at only 0.5 per cent above German levels. This decision, influenced in part by electoral concerns, brought sterling down close to the bottom of its ERM exchange rate bands. Swift and firm denials of any plan to realign (devalue) sterling were issued to allay foreign exchange market participants' fears about the strength of Britain's commitment to hold the exchange rate. The Chancellor also announced that Britain intended, at an unspecified date, to follow other EC currencies in limiting sterling's ERM exchange rate bands to 2 per cent either side of the central parities as opposed to the 6 per cent band currently in force for the UK and Spain. These statements helped to limit speculation against the pound, but the Bank of England still had to intervene to prevent sterling from slipping too far.

For much of the year, EC governments were occupied by plans and negotiations that preceded the Maastricht summit in December. A majority of countries favoured the Delors proposals for eventual European Monetary Union (EMU). The idea was that this should be achieved in a series of steps. EC central banks would establish a central council to supervise the harmonization of monetary policies, exchange rates would be irrevocably fixed, a European system of central banks would be set up, and then finally the separate national currencies would be replaced by the ECU. EC governments differed in how quickly they thought these steps should occur, and what prior conditions should be set down for individual countries to adopt the EMU. There were also disagreements about ddefence, an issue rendered urgent by the collapse of the Warsaw Pact, agricultural policy, extending the powers of the European Parliament at Strasbourg, and a wide range of other matters, including social policy.

The British government's attitude to most of these issues was one of scepticism, tempered by a desire to avoid any open breach and the isolation from future discussions that could follow from it. On some matters it enjoyed support from other EC countries. Belgium, Denmark, Italy and the Netherlands shared Britain's desire to retain a strong defence role for NATO; Denmark, Germany and Portugal shared some of Britain's reservations about EMU; Britain and France were agreed in opposing some of Germany's proposals for increasing the powers of the Strasbourg Parliament. At home, the Prime Minister was caught in strident crossfire between his two predecessors as Conservative leader, Margaret Thatcher and Edward Heath: Heath supported the Delors plans wholeheartedly, while Thatcher roundly attacked them. The Liberal Democrats, and to a lesser extent the Labour Party, were pressing for most aspects of the Delors proposals while a vociferous minority of Conservative backbenchers, and a few Labour MPs, were resolutely opposed.

John Major secured what he took to be two central objectives: Britain could stand aside from the social chapter, with its provisions for minimum wages and employer-financed social security rights for workers, and would retain the right of UK Parliamentary veto over Britain's eventual entry into EMU. The timetable agreed for EMU, with its deadline for the final stage of 1999, was more protracted than the original Delors proposals had envisaged. Certain strict conditions were laid down for any EC country to qualify to participate in EMU. Its budget deficit could not exceed 3 per cent of national income; its inflation rate could not be more than 1 per cent, and long term interest rates not more than 2 per cent, above the average of the lowest 3 countries in the group; its ratio of national debt to national income could be no more than 60 per cent; qualifying countries must also have maintained the narrow 2 per cent exchange rate band, and avoided devaluation for at least the previous two years. These conditions were stringent: France and Luxembourg are the only countries that pass all of them at the time of writing.

The major arguments in favour of European Monetary Union were these. Intra-EC trade was inhibited by the retention of individual national currencies and the banks' commissions in foreign exchange transactions that these necessitated. The real resources employed in exchanging francs for marks, and pesetas for crowns, could be released for more productive use. Even the chance of intra-EC exchange rate changes, however remote, made trade risky or called upon traders to incur the costs, burdensome costs for small firms, of hedging against such risks. There would be gains from pooling foreign exchange reserves, where economies of scale are evident, and no one would need to hold reserves to meet payments imbalances, or transfer capital movements, within the EC area. For those EC countries with relatively unhappy monetary experience in the past – particularly Europe's inflation-prone south – EMU offers prospects of greater financial stability. Reducing inflation, and keeping it down, would be easier when a centralized monetary authority could build upon the reputation for sound money established by Germany. The Brussels officials responsible for organizing and operating the EC's Common Agricultural Policy see great merit in having a single currency in which to work. A single European currency would also offer its issuer the benefits of 'seigniorage' from ECU holdings in the rest of the world: foreign traders, governments and businesses would need to hold ECUs, often at low or zero interest rates, and on a much bigger scale than national EC currencies are held at present.

The case against has several strands to it. European countries differ markedly in their tax régimes, budgetary positions, living standards, traditions and values. Inflation is a tax on money. The sets of taxes that different countries apply, on everything from high and low incomes, alcohol, gasoline, housing, transport and food, could be seen as the outcome of a political marketplace – and this is just as true of inflation taxes on money as of any other tax. Presumably, in some sense, countries 'choose' to have these divergent, often sharply divergent tax rates. So why should uniformity be imposed upon them? Given sufficient similarity in supply and demand conditions, and social attitudes, harmonization would bring gains; but can we be sure that differences in tax rates reflect political mistakes rather than differences in underlying conditions? There is also the point that removing present financial barriers to intra-EC trade – modest as these barriers are – could lead to inefficient diversion of trade away from non-EC countries. Furthermore, for Germans, for example, an EMU that could represent a blend of sound marks and unsound, debt-plagued Latin currencies is a step back, not a step forward. Opponents of EMU may also argue that the grotesque, and apparently insoluble, inefficiencies of the Common Agricultural Policy – to which the EC Commission devotes almost two-thirds of the resources given it by the nation states – bode ill for EC institutions' ability to achieve intelligent compromises between conflicting interests in the much more important arena of monetary and fiscal policy. The nightmare for an inflation-prone country, such as Britain, is the possibility that British workers would press for something closer to German wage rates before raising their productivity enough to justify them. Within a common currency, the options of devaluation or interest rate cuts to offset the resulting unemployment would have gone, and severe restrictions would be placed on Westminster's freedom to fight unemployment with budgetary measures. In the absence of a Europe-wide regional policy to alleviate such problems, EMU seems an unattractive gamble.

To most observers in continental Europe, the case for EMU appears incontestable. It is in Britain that the scepticism runs deepest. These different attitudes are forged on the anvil of history. The six founder-members of the EC – France, Italy, West Germany and the Benelux countries – all suffered humiliating military defeat in the 1940s, and the collapse of their national institutions. Commercial, economic and even political union is seen as a heaven-sent opportunity to ensure that such disasters never recur. They are close neighbours and rely very heavily on trade with each other. Britain was an undefeated victor in the Second World War. Its record of political continuity and freedom from invasion stretches back many centuries. It has strong links with north America and other continents, and a long tradition of free trade and cheap imported food. In Britain, European entanglements and decrees from officials in Brussels are rarely accepted with enthusiasm. However, British supporters of EMU argue that post-war experiences with an independent currency have been markedly less successful than Germany's, that monetary sovereignty is in any case severely restricted by international capital movements, and that sterling devaluations have little if any enduring effect upon unemployment.

UK External Payments and Trade

The high interest rate policy that Britain maintained after 1988, and relaxed in 1991, had been partly a response to the unwelcome surge in inflation which peaked at over 10 per cent in 1990. It was also partly motivated by the very large deficits on the current account of the balance of payments which began in 1987. In each of the years 1988, 1989 and 1990, these deficits represented nearly 3 per cent of national income. They reflected the strong boom in British private sector consumption and investment spending of the mid and late 1980s, fuelled by tax cuts, rapid monetary and credit expansion, and the massive increase in household wealth in the form of house values with which these were associated. Private demand had outpaced the growth of domestic supply, and spilled over into imports. In 1991 the current account deficit fell sharply, to a little over 1 per cent of national income.

The main factor that brought down Britain's current account deficit was the UK recession. Imports are highly sensitive to national income in the UK, particularly close to the peak of a business cycle boom. British national income reached its peak, relative to trend, in late 1989, but for much of 1990 domestic demand remained high. In the autumn of 1990, British output began to slide. Private sector investment spending and housebuilding were especially depressed, and consumer retail spending weakened too, particularly in the durables sectors. Since as much as half of UK residents' spending out of income is devoted, at the margin, to imports, a sharp check to the rapid growth which UK imports had displayed since the mid 1980s was inevitable.

The British recession of 1990–1 could be attributed in part to a correction of some variables which had become badly out of line with long-term trends during the later 1980s. House prices fell back by an average of nearly 30 per cent in real terms in the two and half years from mid-1989, restoring their 1984 ratio to average household earnings. Private sector saving recovered from 4.5 per cent of disposable income to nearly 9 per cent in the same period (close to its average value in the first half of the 1980s). Private investment similarly registered a sharp drop, falling back to its 1984 share of national income. But the major trigger that provoked all these developments, and explains why they happened when they did, was the high interest rate policy adopted by the British authorities from late 1988.

UK exports were strengthened to some degree in 1990 and much of 1991 by the boom in Germany in 1988 and 1991. West Germany's growth rate more than doubled from its 1980–8 average of barely 2 per cent. The German expansion filtered through to many of its neighbours, strengthening UK exports to much of continental Europe in 1991. In north America, however, the pattern of recession resembled Britain's in both timing and magnitutde. UK total exports to non-European markets stagnated in 1991, and fell steeply in certain categories (such as car exports to the United States). The autumn of 1991 witnessed a sharp drop in exports, mainly reflecting the end of the German boom and an unexpected secondary weakening of demand in the United States. Exports of manufactures for the three months from September to November were 5 per cent down on their value from June to August.

The year 1991 registered a major improvement in Britain's balance of payments deficit on current account, it was just £10 billion, while the visible trade deficit (the excess of imports over exports of goods) was 60 per cent lower in 1991 than in 1989. For income, which was some 17 per cent higher in nominal terms in 1991 compared with 1989, the improvement was still greater. However, the current account deficit, at 1.2 per cent of national income, was still above the European Community average, and this in spite of the severity of the UK recession. The deficit would have been smaller had Britain entered the Exchange Rate Mechanism of the EMS at a lower exchange rate for sterling.

Contemporary Britain

Table 1. UK Current Account Statistics, 1989–91 (figures in £ billion).

	Visible trade balance	Invisibles balance	Total current account balance
1989	−24.6	+4.2	−20.4
1990	−18.7	+3.5	−15.2
1991	−10.1	+4.2	−5.9
1991			
quarter 1	−3.0	+0.3	-2.7
quarter 2	−2.1	+2.0	−0.1
quarter 3	−2.3	+1.0	−1.3
quarter 4	−2.7	+0.9	−1.8

Source: Central Statistical Office and author's estimates

The invisibles balance in 1991 is estimated to have been in surplus. That favourable balance, at £4.2 billion, compensated for nearly half of the visible trade deficit. Britain has traditionally enjoyed an invisibles surplus, reflecting overseas earnings on banking, insurance, net foreign investment income, and other services. In 1991, as in many past years, this allowed Britain to import more goods than it exported. The size of the invisibles surplus was greatly reduced, however, by the scale of Britain's current account deficits from 1987, which entailed net borrowing from overseas of some £70 billion. But for the interest charges on these borrowings, the 1991 invisibles surplus would presumably have been much higher. The official estimates, upon which the statistics in Table 1 are based, are built upon an assumption that excludes interest paid abroad on *unrecorded* foreign borrowing. For most years in the 1980s, the balance of payments statistics add a large positive balancing item to reconcile the accounts. Some observers argue that the official estimates therefore underestimate interest payments to foreign creditors, and that the true invisibles surplus may be much lower. There are also concerns about the scale of overseas liabilities of UK insurers, which could imply that net foreign earnings on insurance are lower than they appear in Table 1.

Trade statistics for the first half of 1991 reveal that 57.1 per cent of UK exports went to its EC trading partners. Germany was Britain's largest export destination, with 13.7 per cent of total UK exports, followed by France (11.3 per cent) and the USA (10.7 per cent). Other leading destinations were the Netherlands (8 per cent), Italy and Belgium (including Luxembourg) with 6 per cent each, Ireland with 5 per cent, and Spain (4 per cent). Sweden took a 2.4 per cent share of British exports, and Japan and Switzerland accounted for 2.2 per cent each. Britain was nearly as reliant on the rest of the European Community for its exports as the other members were on each other. The strength of UK exports to western Europe in 1991 partly reflected the buoyancy of the German economy (at least until the last few months); north America, suffering from deep recession, cut back its imports from Britain.

It was noteworthy that, of her EC partners, only Denmark and Germany accounted for a larger share of Britain's imports than exports. Britain enjoyed trade surpluses with France, Belgium (including Luxembourg), Ireland, Italy, Greece, Spain and Portugal, while trade with the Netherlands was close to balance. By contrast, Britain ran sizeable trade deficits with the United States and Japan. Japan's exports to the UK were nearly three times higher than her imports from Britain. Just over half of Britain's imports came from the EC, as against an EC average of 59 per cent. Germany (14.7 per cent), the USA (13.1 per cent) and France (9.2 per cent) accounted for the largest shares of UK imports, followed by the Netherlands (7.7 per cent) and Japan (5.4 per cent).

Turning from the geographical to the commodity composition of UK overseas trade in goods, the year was marked by a strong performance of British exports of machinery and transport equipment. These accounted for 41.1 per cent of exports in the first half of the year, as against only 35.7 per cent of imports. Indeed, trade in this category was approximately balanced. The recession depressed Britain's car sales and imports, while strong demand in Germany and other EC countries led to a redirection and stimulus to exports. An adverse trade balance on transport equipment and machinery had contributed much to Britain's large current account deficits in the later 1980s. Britain ran its traditional trade surplus in chemicals (where exports exceeded imports by a margin of 5 to 4) and beverage and tobacco (a 5 to 3 margin). Fuel exports fell with production cut backs in North Sea oil. Although fuel still accounted for a higher share of exports than imports (6.5 per cent as against 6.3 per cent), there was an adverse trade balance on oil for the first time in nearly a decade. (See Table 2).

All in all, 1991 was a year when unfavourable developments in the 'real' aspects of the domestic economy (severe recession, and rising unemployment) coincided with increasing stability in the monetary and external sphere. Inflation fell. The balance of payments deficit came down. Exchange rates for sterling were steadier than in the past, and in terms of north American and far eastern currencies as well as the European Community currencies to which sterling was now tied more closely through the Exchange Rate Mechanism. The increasing integration with Britain's partners in the European Community was reflected in their rising share of British exports. The process of integration was strengthened by the Maastricht summit in December, which laid down a timetable and conditions for monetary union. But Britain's future participation in that union remained doubtful: the British Parliament would have to sanction it, and Britain would have to qualify to be accepted for it.

Table 2. Commodity Composition of UK visible exports and imports for the first half of 1991

Category	UK exports (% share)	UK imports (% share)	Imports to exports ratio
Food	4.4	8.7	0.43
Beverage, tobacco	2.7	1.4	1.68
Raw materials	2.1	4.0	0.44
Fuel	6.5	6.3	0.88
Oils and fats	0.1	0.3	0.27
Chemicals	13.6	9.3	1.25
Manufacturers classified by material	15.4	17.5	0.75
Machinery and transport equipment	41.1	35.7	0.98
Miscellaneous manufacturers	12.4	14.6	0.72
Goods not specified elsewhere	1.7	2.3	0.63

Source: Eurostat (Statistical Office of the European Communities)

Chronology

22 Jan: The bill to privatize the Export Credit Guarantee Department receives its second reading.

25 Jan: The current account deficit in December 1990 fell to £844 million.

19 Feb: Announcement that the trade gap in automotive products, the largest single contributor to Britain's trade gap, shrank from £6.55 billion in 1989 to £4.58 billion in 1990.

20 Feb: Uruguay Round of GATT resumes in Geneva.

25 Feb: Current account deficit in January widened to £1.228 billion.

13 Mar: Revised invisibles figures slash the fourth quarter current account deficit in 1990 from £2,974 million to £843 million.

15 Mar: Report by British Invisibles shows arts and culture brought in £6 billion overseas earnings in 1990.

25 Mar: Current account deficit in February drops to £192 million. The deficit in January is revised to £783 million.

23 Apr: Current account deficit in March widened to £432 million.

23 May: Current account deficit in April fell to £339 million.

11 June: Current account deficit in the first quarter revised up to £2.6 billion because the invisible surplus was revised down from £1.5 billion to £231 million.

24 June: Current account deficit increased to £523 million in May.

1 July: Announcement that the government is to sell the ECGD to the Dutch insurer, NCM Holdings, a transaction completed later in the year.

10 July: Britain suggests that the EC lifts its embargo on arms sales to Syria.

18 July: Japanese/EC trade summit in the Hague.

22 July: June saw the first current account surplus for over four years, of £23 million. The surplus in manufactured goods was £117 million, the first since 1984.

26 July: EC agrees to limit Japanese car imports to 1.2 million per year, but protects British interests.

22 Aug: Current account returned to a deficit of £165 million in July.

11 Sept: Net overseas assets fell in 1990 to £29.6 billion.

23 Sept: Current account deficit widened in August to £543 million.

22 Oct: Current account deficit fell from a revised figure of £596 million in August to £529 million in September.

22 Nov: Current account deficit fell in October from a revised figure of £702 million for September to £601 million.

11 Dec: Surplus on invisibles revised up for the first three quarters, reducing the current account deficit for the period by 20 per cent to £4.2 billion.

23 Dec: Current account deficit of £587 million in November posted.

Trade Unions and Industrial Relations

RICHARD HYMAN

Industrial relations in 1991 continued to display the contradictory features which had distinguished Britain throughout the 1980s. Trade union membership was still declining, though the losses had become less serious than a decade earlier. Strikes, once widely castigated as the 'British disease', diminished to the point of virtual insignificance. Yet the notion that the removal of union influence in the labour market was the recipe for a supply-side economic miracle seemed increasingly hollow. While unemployment climbed throughout the year, the goal of enhanced productivity seemed as distant as ever. To many observers, the stridency of government insistence on excluding continental norms of industrial relations from a national system in evident disarray seemed bizarre.

The Labour Market

For the second year running, unemployment increased substantially. The November figures (released in late December) showed a total of 2.51 million registered as unemployed and claiming benefit, or 8.8 per cent of the UK labour force; the figures 12 months earlier were 1.73 million and 6.1 per cent. Whereas in some previous years a rise in unemployment was associated with an expansion in the labour force, this was no longer the case. The workforce stabilized at 28.4 million, slightly below the peak of the late 1980s; rising unemployment was wholly attributable to a fall in the numbers of workers in employment. The OECD 'standardized rate' put the UK percentage unemployed in September 1991 at 10.1, compared to 9.5 in France, 4.6 in Germany, 10.0 in Italy, 7.8 in Belgium, 6.5 in the Netherlands and 2.8 in Sweden.

Though the British unemployment rate is once more among the highest in Europe, the labour market still exerted little evident downwards pressure on pay. Compared to a median level of settlements of almost 10 per cent at the end of 1990, rises did indeed moderate during 1991, to a median of just under 6 per cent. However, the much faster deceleration in price increases – the rise in the retail price index falling from roughly 10 to 4 per cent during the year – meant that the real value of pay settlements actually increased during 1991. In addition, average earnings rose somewhat faster than settlements, ending the year at a rate of increase of some 7.5 per cent. As for most of the 1980s, those at the top did better than the rest: surveys indicated that remuneration of senior executives was rising on average at a rate of 14 per cent. Some cases of much larger increases, particularly in recently privatized companies, attracted publicity during the year: notably the 43 per cent increase to £536,000 in the salary of Iain Vallance of British Telecom. An analysis by Labour Research showed average pay rises of 65 per cent for top executives in the privatized utilities.

In previous years, there had been evident disparities in pay movements between the private manufacturing and public service sectors; some of the main disputes which occurred were reactions to perceived inequities in treatment. In 1991 such differences were less of an issue, largely because the impact of the recession was most immediate in the manufacturing sector. Some companies faced by particularly serious cash problems imposed a pay freeze, or delayed annual increases, as an economy measure.

The government's explicit objective of dismantling national pay determination in the public sector, and allowing the development of differentiated pay structures reflecting local labour market factors, achieved only modest results. One notable innovation was at HMSO, which has been assigned the status of an autonomous agency within the civil service; at the beginning of the year a separate pay structure was negotiated, to replace the centrally negotiated civil service arrangements. In much of the public sector, however, centralized negotiations remain of primary importance for pay negotiation – though with scope for local flexibility, and moves towards personalized contracts for some senior managers. For another substantial public sector group, schoolteachers, the government had previously announced its intention to restore in 1991 the collective bargaining rights withdrawn in 1987. However, another change of policy occurred: the Teachers' Pay Bill published in April provided for the introduction of a pay review body instead. Following the passage of the legislation the review panel was established in the autumn, chaired by Sir Graham Day.

The annual *New Earnings Survey for 1991* indicated that the gender gap in pay continued to narrow slightly: full-time women employees earned 70 per cent of male weekly earnings and 78 per cent of their hourly earnings (the difference between the two figures reflecting greater overtime working by men). The gender differential however remains larger than in many other European countries and is moreover accentuated by the particularly high proportion of women in Britain employed part time, often with distinctive pay arrangements. A detailed study by Industrial Relations Services and the Equal Opportunities Commission showed that men and women remain largely segregated in distinct types of jobs with different pay structures and unequal scope for earnings enhancement.

It is widely believed that employers – partly in response to principles of 'human resource management' – have increasingly attempted to link pay to performance and productivity. However, a survey by the Institute of Personnel Management at the beginning of the year showed that in only one pay settlement in four did employers claim that efficiency or productivity measures were built into the agreement – though roughly half insisted that they maintained some connection between pay and performance. Two thirds of employers believed that productivity was improving in their organizations – though less than half actually claimed to measure productivity! These findings are consistent with the conclusions reached by many critics of British industrial relations, that most managements pay little more than lip service to issues of employee performance and commitment. One indicator of this attitude is training: the 1991 publication of official training statistics showed that only 15 per cent of British employees received job-related training. The British figures compare miserably with the level of investment in training in most other European economies, and are reflected in shortages of key skilled workers despite the overall level of unemployment. For example, Jobcentre figures showed that in September 1991, vacancies for skilled machine operators in the UK took 5–6 weeks to fill on average, and twice as long in Greater London. The picture of the British labour market – after a decade of deregulation – is marked by a weak skill base and low productivity, with relatively low wage levels but high unit labour costs.

Industrial Disputes

Final statistics for 1990 showed a total of 620 officially recorded stoppages – the lowest level since 1935. Fewer workers were involved in strikes than in any year since 1950, and working days lost were the lowest since 1963. In the first nine months of 1991, recorded strikes were lower still: the rate was little more than half that of 1990. Almost certainly, the year's total will show 1991 to be one of the most strike-free years since statistics were first officially compiled a century ago.

Strikes are not the only form of industrial action: survey evidence from previous years suggests that such tactics as overtime bans and working to rule are more commonly used, and that such non-strike sanctions proved more resilient than strikes in the 1980s. One novel form of action was proposed by the Inland Revenue Staff Federation in December: a 'work-to-charter', involving the literal application of the government's exhortation in its Citizens' Charter for public employees to provide a customer-friendly service. Priority would be given to checking for cases of overpayment of tax, and arranging prompt refunds, rather than pursuing cases of underpayment – at considerable cost to the Treasury.

The year provided a notable demonstration of the fact that industrial disputes are not necessarily attributable to the actions of workers and trade unions. In May, Rolls Royce issued dismissal notices to 34,000 of its workers, and offered re-employment on new contracts. The aim was to avoid giving pay increases to which the firm was contractually committed. The unions concerned resisted the company's plan, but held back from strike action. It soon became clear that the stratagem was flawed on legal as well as industrial relations grounds, and Rolls Royce was obliged to back down.

Trade Union Organization

The latest available statistics of trade union membership compiled by the certification officer – for the end of 1989 – showed a continuing decline, with 10.158 million members in 309 unions. This represented a fall of 2.1 per cent during the year, and of 24 per cent from the peak of 13.3 million achieved in 1979. The results of the 1990 labour force survey, published in April 1991, showed that union density in Britain had fallen to 38 per cent. Membership of the 74 unions affiliated to the Trades Union Congress amounted to 8.193 million at the end of 1990, a fall of 2.7 per cent.

Over the past decade the number of British unions has fallen by a third, largely because of amalgamations, and this process continued in 1991. The most notable merger brought together the two main print unions, SOGAT and NGA, to form the Graphical, Paper and Media Union. The amalgamation of the two unions in broadcasting took effect at the beginning of the year, while the Tailors and Garment Workers merged with the GMB general union, and the unions of footwear and hosiery and knitwear workers amalgamated. Detailed planning continued for an amalgamation of the three main unions in local government and the NHS, which if successful will create a new organization with 1.5 million members – the largest union in the country. Discussions between leaders of the AEU and EETPU overcame a major hurdle at the end of the year, when merger plans were approved by the engineers' national committee, paving the way for a ballot in the new year – and opening the prospect of the electricians' return to the TUC. Arrangements for an amalgamation of the two main unions in postal and telecommunications services proceeded smoothly. On the other hand, merger proposals from the TGWU were rejected by the mineworkers, who agreed however to continue talks.

A number of significant leadership elections took place in 1991. In the largest union, the TGWU, Bill Morris won the ballot to succeed Ron Todd as general secretary: when he takes over in early 1992 he will be the first black leader of a British union. In the election for his own successor as deputy general secretary, the veteran communist Jack Adams defeated the Kinnockite Jack Dromey. The new leadership will inherit a serious financial crisis: the union's executive was told in November that expenditure would exceed subscription income by over £10 million in 1991. In the EETPU, Paul Gallagher was elected to succeed Eric Hammond, easily defeating a challenger who called for rapprochement with the TUC.

Women fared badly in two important elections. Brenda Dean, who as secretary of SOGAT was the leading woman trade unionist in Britain, was narrowly defeated by Tony Dubbins of the NGA for the post of general secretary of the new GPMU; she became deputy general secretary. In the white collar union MSF, Roger Lyons beat Barbara Switzer to succeed Ken Gill in 1992.

In the courts, the case against NUM leaders Arthur Scargill and Peter Heathfield – charged by the certification officer with failure to keep adequate accounts – collapsed when the magistrate refused to allow information in the *Lightman Report* to be used as evidence against them. The general secretary of the construction union

UCATT, Albert Williams, obtained an injunction in the High Court against the decision of the left-dominated executive to suspend him from office, after he had pursued allegations of ballot-rigging in the executive elections. The severity of the union's internal crisis was demonstrated when 14 full-time officials defected to the GMB. The latter union was dissuaded by the TUC from recruiting UCATT members, but the dissident officials then joined the EETPU, which opened a construction section. Another general secretary at odds with his executive was Steven Turner of the Journalists – elected in 1990 as an opponent of merger with the print unions – who was removed from office in July.

Unions, the TUC and the Labour Party

After a decade of defeat and decline, unions collectively have been forced to address questions of strategy which in more favourable times were traditionally neglected. Two major documents were issued by the TUC in the first part of 1991, and approved by Congress in September.

The work and priorities of the TUC itself were reviewed in a consultative document entitled *TUC Towards 2000*, drawn up with the assistance of advice from sympathetic academics. It argued that the structural changes which had created difficulties for unions in the 1980s – the shift from manufacturing to services, the trend to smaller workplaces, the growth in part-time and other 'atypical' forms of employment – would continue in the 1990s, as would management policies posing challenges to traditional union methods. In assisting unions to respond constructively, the TUC – itself facing serious financial problems – would need to focus on a limited number of realistically attainable objectives. These included encouraging unions to co-ordinate the setting of their subscription levels, assisting with recruitment in areas with potential for extending union organization, and extending the range of financial and other services available centrally to trade union members. Vocational training, health and safety, equal opportunities and trade union education were all identified as priority issues for TUC work in the 1990s.

In its document *A Collective Bargaining Strategy for the 1990s*, the TUC called for the twin pursuit of enhanced productivity and improved real wages. It advocated greater co-ordination of collective bargaining, reversing some of the trend to decentralization apparent during the 1980s. The document endorsed Labour Party plans for a national economic assessment – involving annual tripartite discussions to clarify the macroeconomic framework within which collective bargaining would take place. The goal of a statutory minimum wage was also reaffirmed. Partly in response to the pressure of unions representing higher-paid staff, such as the AEU and MSF, the TUC explicitly insisted that the synchronization and co-ordination of collective bargaining, while desirable, should not be imposed; and that the national assessment was not a formula for pay restraint, and in particular would not specify norms for pay settlements. A nationally co-ordinated programme *including* explicitly norms for pay increases had been advocated in a document *Pay Strategy for the 1990s* published in March by the Institute for Public Policy Research, the think tank linked to the Labour Party.

The TUC's somewhat ambivalent position was unanimously endorsed at the September congress, through a lengthy composite resolution. The familiar TUC desire to evade or suppress internal divisions was strongly apparent in the final annual congress before a general election. Most unions rallied behind the broad policy consensus hammered out in the previous two years between the TUC and Labour Party leaderships. On the emotive issue of trade union law, a motion from Arthur Scargill and the NUM which called for total repeal of the Conservative legislation was defeated by almost three to one. Scargill was however successful in winning support for a motion calling for nuclear power to be phased out. The central theme of many of the debates was the continental principle of social partnership. John Edmonds of the GMB insisted that the traditional system of British industrial relations was irredeemably flawed, and should be adapted in the light of European models. His call for the TUC to explore the possibility of a statutory system of works councils in Britain won strong support. Also notable was a resolution which criticized the industrial relations practices of some overseas firms, notably Japanese companies which have imposed restrictive conditions for trade union recognition. The issue was particularly topical since four TUC unions were competing with the EETPU for recognition by Toyota at its new Derbyshire plant: the AEU, viewed as favourite to achieve a single union deal, opposed the resolution.

Government Policy and the Law

Any thought that with the 1990 Employment Act – the seventh major piece of industrial relations legislation in a decade – the government might have exhausted the scope for further legal changes was dispelled with the publication of a new green paper in July. Four main groups of changes were proposed.

Firstly, yet more restrictions would be imposed on the legality of strike action. All strike ballot papers (at least where more than 50 workers are involved) would have to be distributed as well as returned by post, and counting overseen by an independent scrutineer who would produce a formal report. Employers concerned would have to be notified of the intention to hold a ballot, and provided with a sample voting paper, and should subsequently be informed of the result. After a successful ballot, a union would further have to give written notice at least seven days in advance of the dates when action would take place, and specify the workers involved. In the case of public services, actual or potential customers (and not only, as at present, the employer) would have the right to take legal action against a union where unlawful industrial action was alleged.

Secondly, the legal regulation of unions' internal affairs would be extended. Changes would include a more detailed scrutineer's report on ballots, increased access to union membership records, and enhanced powers for the certification office. Ballots on union mergers would have to be fully postal. Of more substantial import, the TUC 'Bridlington' principles which for half a century have regulated inter-union conflict over recruitment and representation would be undermined by a new legal provision guaranteeing an employee 'freedom of choice' of which union to join.

Third, restrictions would be placed on the operation of the 'check-off', the system of deduction of union subscriptions from employees' pay which increasingly applies where trade unions are recognized. The new proposals are that written consent to check-offs would need to be reaffirmed annually and would be invalidated by any change in subscription levels. While disruptive of union financial stability in general, this proposal may perhaps have been particularly motivated by a desire to hamper payments to unions' political funds – an emotive issue for many Conservatives, but not explicitly addressed in the green paper.

Finally, it was proposed that the current legal presumption that collective agreements are not legally enforceable should be reversed – as was attempted two decades earlier with the Industrial Relations Act.

The three months allowed for responses to these proposals brought few expressions of support. A poll commissioned by the TUC found two thirds of respondents opposed to further industrial relations legislation, with only 18 per cent supporting additional laws. One of the most notable responses to the green paper came from the Institute of Personnel Management: it argued that changes to the check-off were unnecessary, that undermining Bridlington could prove destabilizing, and that legal enforceability of agreements was not 'a constructive way to conduct industrial relations'.

By the end of the year, the government had not announced how it intended to proceed. No doubt the employment secretary, Michael Howard, was fully preoccupied with the fruitless search for EC allies in resisting the 'social chapter' eventually agreed (with one exception!) at the Maastricht summit. For much of 1991, Howard appeared to be conducting a one-man crusade against social and legal regulation of the labour market and of individual employment rights. Draft directives emanating from Brussels – whether on detailed issues like work with visual display units, or broad institutional reforms like the proposed European works councils in multinational companies – attracted furious denunciations. The same was true of domestic proposals for reforms analogous to continental social protections: most notably, the TUC-Labour Party advocacy of a statutory minimum wage. The government strove vigorously to fashion evidence that a legal minimum would create job losses, and made remarkable attempts in September to 'spike' the reports of an employer, commissioned by the Institute of Personnel Management, which found little basis for the government's warnings.

EC regulation had one major impact on British employment policy in 1991, with the gradual responses to the previous year's judgement of the European Court of Justice in the 'Barber' case that discriminatory pension arrangements were unlawful. Discussion of unifying the pensionable age of men and women thus received an important impetus. However, the government proposal (in a discussion document at the end of the year) to introduce a unified retirement age of 63 disappointed those who had hoped for a flexible system of retirement opportunities with pensions available from the age of 60.

Another issue central to EC employment regulation is health and safety – indeed it is notable as the one area of industrial relations explicitly covered by qualified majority voting. In this context it is significant that in December – coinciding with Maastricht – the director general of the Health and Safety executive revealed that investigations showed that two thirds of legally notifiable accidents were not reported. Some employers, he argued, were 'little better than villains or cowboys'. Under-reporting meant that the official statistics of accidents seriously understated the extent of the problem. This vignette perhaps exemplifies the state of British employment relations after a decade of decollectivization and deregulation and indicates why the EC social chapter was not without British enthusiasts.

Chronology

7 Jan: Industrial Society paper draws up proposals to end the distinction between workers and managers in British industry.

21 Jan: Report by Income Data Services shows pay deals remaining around the 10 per cent mark.

23 Jan: Labour Research Department survey argues it is a myth that British workers are pricing themselves out of a market, showing that in total labour costs terms the UK is only the eighth most expensive in Europe, whilst hourly labour costs in Germany are the highest in the EC.

3 Feb: IDS report argues that wage demands will remain high because of the need to keep up large mortgage payments as long as interest rates remain high.

14 Feb: House of Lords Select Committee on the European Communities, *Working Time*, HMSO, warns of the health and safety effects of working long hours in the NHS and other services.

4 Mar: Pay rises in the first quarter were running at around 9 per cent according to Income Data Services.

5 Mar: Announcement that a study into the efficiency of the industrial tribunal system has been ordered.

8 Mar: Survey by the Low Pay Unit and Birmingham City Council finds 43 per cent of children in Birmingham between 10 and 16 have jobs and 75 per cent are working for low pay and long hours.

11 Mar: TUC publishes its proposals on collective bargaining.

12 Mar: John Grieve Smith *Pay Strategy for the 1990s*, IPPR, calls for a Pay Advisory Commission and a return to a national pay policy.

19 Mar: Incentives for profit-related pay and employee share schemes announced in the Budget.

4 Apr: Assistant Masters and Mistresses' Association and Professional Association of Teachers begin merger negotiations.

22 Apr: *In the ERM: Achieving Full Employment in the 90s*, Campaign for Work, suggests the need for co-ordinated and synchronized pay settlements.

24 Apr: Despite some misgivings the trade unions largely endorse Labour's pay strategy.

15 May: Rolls Royce issues dismissal notices to all 34,000 employees before immediately re-employing them as a ploy to impose an across-the-board pay freeze.

30 May: Graphical, Paper and Media Union formed by the merger of the National Graphical Association and SOGAT 82 with Tony Dubbins of the NGA as its first general secretary.

7 June: Bill Morris elected as successor to Ron Todd as general secretary of TGWU.

13 June: Unions at British Nuclear Fuels negotiate the first nationally agreed 35-hour week in return for more effective bell-to-bell working, improved attendance, increased flexibility, the payment of wages into bank accounts and an end to 'Spanish practices'.

19 June: The case against Arthur Scargill and Peter Heathfield over the NUM's alleged failure to keep proper accounts collapses.

26 June: Government asks National Training Task Force to involve the trade unions in talks aimed at ensuring employees are rewarded for qualifications.

1 July: Paul Gallagher elected to replace Eric Hammond as general secretary of the EETPU.

3 July: In 1990 there were 630 disputes and 1.9 million working days were lost, the lowest levels since 1935 and 1963 respectively.

13 July: Steve Turner, the general secretary of the National Union of Journalists, is dismissed by his national executive.

16 July: NUPE launches a campaign for equal pay and conditions for part-timers.

26 July: *Industrial Relations in the 1990s*, HMSO, a new green paper, suggests a new right for the public to bring actions over unlawful disputes disrupting public services, the need to give seven days notice of any action, the right to join the union of one's choice, individual consent to union dues, greater influence for members over union affairs, including greater ability to combat fraud and vote-rigging, the right to independently vetted ballots before strikes, postal ballots on union mergers, collective agreements to be legally binding unless they include provisions making them unenforceable, new powers for the certification officer to investigate union finance and higher penalties for trade union leaders who fail to keep proper accounts.

21 Aug: Institute of Fiscal Studies reports that the government's initiative to spread profit-related pay has been a failure because of insufficient incentives for employers and because employees are unattracted by the downside of lower pay when profits fall. AEU and EETPU to recommence merger negotiations.

3 Sept: TUC conference endorses measures to improve the representation of black people in trade unions and the TUC.

4 Sept: TUC unanimously backs Labour's proposed national minimum wage of £3.40 per hour.

5 Sept: TUC reaffirms the Bridlington rules which are designed to prevent the poaching of members.

9 Sept: Research by Business International ranks Britain twelfth out of the 16 EC/EFTA countries in terms of labour costs, with costs below that of either the US or Japan.

10 Oct: High Court rules that statutory rights to protection against unfair dismissal and redundancy pay do not apply to part-timers working less than 16 hours per week.

18 Oct: Labour announces that it would set up a specialist police unit to investigate deaths and serious injuries in the workplace.

21 Oct: Survey of absenteeism in British industry, the highest in Europe, demonstrates that British companies show little initiative in tackling the problem.

31 Oct: AEU signs a single union deal with Toyota.

16 Dec: BT is ordered to pay £6,000 compensation to two former VDU operators in an important test case concerning repetitive strain injury.

18 Dec: AEU National Committee votes to recommend merger with EETPU.

Health

ANTHONY HARRISON and BILL NEW

There can be little doubt that the principal event in 1991 was the implementation, at least in part, of the National Health Service and Community Care Act[1] from 1 April onwards. Consequently, the bulk of our review concentrates on the first effects of this restructuring. However, in June 1991 the government followed its main reform with a consultative document, *The Health of the Nation*,[2] which, for the first time for England, suggested a range of health targets, the achievement of which would require action across most parts of government. If implemented, this is as potentially revolutionary as the reforms of provision, so we continue our review of the events of the year with an assessment of its significance. Next we turn to what was presented at the time as the government's 'big idea' for the next election. After 12 years of Conservative attempts to cut back the public sector, the new Prime Minister sought to identify himself with a positive approach to public services with the introduction of a Citizen's Charter,[3] followed later by a Patient's Charter[4] for the NHS. Finally we look at the debate surrounding Labour's charge that the Conservative reforms were intent on privatizing the NHS. The exchanges between government and Opposition generated more heat than light, but important issues involving the boundaries of appropriate NHS provision were nevertheless highlighted.

Creating Competition

The central concept underlying the reforms introduced on 1 April 1991 was the creation of a competitive market within the framework of public provision and finance. In a broad sense, district health authorities were in competition with each other before 1 April 1991, since GPs could refer patients to any consultant in the country willing to see them, but it is doubtful whether that was sufficient to create the competitive pressures which result from knowing that poor performance will lead to loss of income. To implement the new system, a series of interrelated measures was required, each one of which might have been regarded as a radical departure.

Purchasers and Providers

The first essential step towards creating a competitive market involving the NHS is the requirement that all district health authorities in England and Wales, and their counterparts in Scotland and Northern Ireland, should divide themselves into a purchasing arm on the one hand and a provider arm on the other, except where, as we go on to discuss below, providing units become independent trusts. Henceforth districts will be expected to concentrate on their purchasing or commissioning functions, which will involve assessing the health care needs of their population, identifying the services to meet those needs and setting priorities when resources are insufficient to meet all identified needs. GP fundholders represent the other main innovation on the purchasing side. Purchasing requirements are expressed through contracts which define what the providers are to do and the prices at which they will be paid for doing so. As Chart 1 shows it is these contracts which are the centre piece of the new system. The government envisages that different forms of contract may be needed in different situations. Three broad classes of contract have been identified. These are described below.

Block Contract. Under this form of contract, the GP or district health authority would pay the hospital an annual fee, in instalments, in return for access to a defined range of services. The contract would be viewed as funding a given level of capacity, particularly with respect to the treatment of urgent cases. The level of capacity would be agreed reflecting past and expected future referrals where immediate treatment was required. Such contracts should additionally reflect a variety of performance aims, for example an increase in the proportion of day cases, which is often a more cost-effective form of treatment. Waiting times, reduction in length of stay and turnover intervals may also be specified. The contract should set out what services would be provided, how the hospital proposes to meet standards for customer service, how the quality, efficiency and where possible the outcome of the services would be judged, including the role of medical audit, what changes might be introduced during the course of the year, and the respective roles of the health authority or hospital in monitoring performance.

Cost and Volume. Under this approach, hospitals would receive a sum in respect of a baseline level of activity, defined in terms of a given number of treatments or cases. Beyond that level, funding would be on a cost per case basis; the cost per case, which would be agreed in advance, could reflect either average or marginal costs – the latter being the cost of each additional patient. For the hospital a guaranteed baseline of activity would assist planning. From the point of view of the purchaser, contracts must specify a maximum volume of cases or treatments in order to maintain expenditure control.

Cost per Case This type of contract would be used to fund referrals which did not fall within either of the two previous forms of contract. An example would be where the GP or district health authority did not have a regular contract with a specific hospital or where additional treatments were purchased from a contracted hospital outside the terms of the contract. The payment would be on a case by case basis, without any prior commitment by either party to the volume of cases which might be so dealt with.

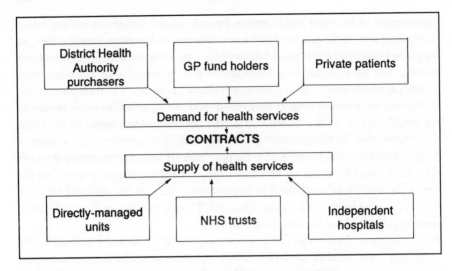

Chart 1: The New Health Care Market

Initial Impact

Despite their central role, the introduction of effective contracts has been slow. As the possible implications of moving to a managed market became clearer, the Chief Executive of the NHS, Duncan Nichol, announced before implementation was nominally due to start, that in the first year of the new system health authorities should aim for a steady state, that is, contracts should reproduce the existing pattern of activity and referrals: finance was allocated for 1991–92 to allow this. They remain for the most part validations of the status quo.

Nevertheless, the novelty of the new arrangements has meant inevitably that there have been some teething problems. A NAHAT survey of purchasers and providers[5] found that 82 out of 100 responding authorities reported problems of some kind. The data suggest that the sheer task of managing the financial consequences of contracts is proving difficult, despite the apparent degree of certainty that the 'steady state' was intended to provide. Table 1 shows that in almost 20 per cent of cases provider units had been able to negotiate extra contracts to make use of spare capacity. A larger number had been forced to restrict activity, while half had had to make larger than anticipated efficiency improvements.

The (almost) steady state has meant that authorities have had a further year of preparation, not just of contracts but also of their internal organization. There can be little doubt that they need it: as with the introduction of contracts for ancillary services nearly a decade ago, authorities in general were simply not geared up to writing the kind of contracts which the Secretary of State appears to want.

GP Fundholders

An important innovation on the purchasing side of the contracting system is the introduction of GP budgets. In contrast to the measures taken at district level, this element in the managed market was more experimental. Only practices with over 9,000 patients were allowed to become fundholders, and out of those only 306 were implemented. On average these contained 5.6 GPs per practice and 12,200 patients. Overall, they cover 3.6 million patients and £404m expenditure – 1 per cent of the Hospital and Community Health Services budget.

Unlike health authorities, which receive budgets to cover the full range of hospital and community health services, GP fundholders' budgets cover only hospital diagnosis and investigations, out-patient services and a range of elective surgical procedures. Nevertheless – see Table 2 – the allocations they received more than doubled the resources under their control. The budgets themselves appear to have been allocated on a fairly crude basis in order to get the scheme launched. The information necessary to identify precisely what use existing patients were making of hospital services was not always available, so allocations were made on a rough and ready, but on the whole generous, basis. (See Table 2).

While GP fundholding may have begun on a small scale basis, there are signs that it is already proving effective in improving care standards. These signs come from research supported by the King's Fund by Howard Glennerster and colleagues at the London School of Economics.[6] In a number of case studies they found that GPswere 'shopping' around for orthopaedic, ophthalmological and gynaecological services in order to get better services for their patients and were bringing hospital consultants into their surgeries for outpatient clinics, again to the benefit of their patients.

Table 1. In order to achieve a break-even position on income and expenditure this year, do you anticipate you will need to take any of the measures outlined below?

Measures Planned	Provider Units responding 'yes' to one or more categories			
	Directly Mgd Units	Trusts 1st wave	Trusts 2nd wave	Total
Renegotiate contracts (eg prices)	19	6	5	30
Restrict activity	36	9	7	52
Seek efficiency savings above contract agreements	61	12	18	91
Seek additional contract work	18	8	8	34
Numbers responding 'no'	42	5	18	65
Number in sample	122	21	40	183

Table 2. GP Fundholders' Budgets

Fundholder	£ million
Hospital services	208.3
Prescribing	162.5
Staff	30.6
Total	£404.4

Source: Department of Health

Unlike health authorities, which have had to conform to the 'steady state' requirement, general practitioners appear to have been ready to upset the steady state by striking deals which they consider more attractive for their patients. In some cases, GPs have attempted to negotiate contracts which allowed their patients to jump the waiting list queue. The NHS Executive responded to this by issuing a directive[7] designed to rule out such 'favouritism', but anecdotal evidence suggests that this has not been entirely effective.

While any appraisal of the effects of GP fundholding must be tentative at this stage, it has become clear that it has the potential to be the single most important reform of all. If GP fundholding became widespread, as the government appears to intend, with only a few single-handed practices omitted, the primary care sector would become the prime purchaser of hospital services, particularly of elective surgery. The role of the district, as set out above, would be diminished since nearly all the resources under its direct control would be absorbed by emergency and other activities over which it would have little discretion. With the number of fundholders due to double in 1992, this possibility is a real one.

Trusts

In December 1990, the government announced that 57 trusts were to be created in England. These provider units were to be administratively separate from the district in which they operate but remaining within the NHS. The bulk were large acute units. During the year, further announcements have been made of second and third wave trusts, with the result that the number will rise to 103 on 1 April 1992. The government has made it clear that, as far as larger units are concerned, it would like to see them all with trust status.

The central idea lying behind trusts is that greater independence from district and regional management would yield better performance. As the Department of Health puts it:

Trusts have the freedom to: acquire, own and dispose of assets to ensure the most effective use is made of them; make their own cases for capital developments direct to the NHS Management Executive; borrow money, within annually agreed limits, primarily for new building and equipment and for upgrading existing buildings; create their own management structures; employ their own staff, determine their own staffing structures, and set their own terms and conditions of employments; advertise their services, within the guidelines set down by professional codes of practice on such advertising.[8]

If the intention is to increase the chances of competition emerging between different providers, then the aim of spreading trust status is appropriate, since it reduces the risk that purchasers will 'favour' their directly managed unit. If they are to enjoy a genuine degree of independence, trusts must enjoy a wider range of discretion than their directly managed counterparts do at the moment.

A comparison of the arrangements governing them shows that in many respects the two forms of organization are quite similar; most importantly, both must gain contracts to survive. If major differences are to emerge, they must spring from two main sources: freedom to raise capital and freedom to set their own wage rate and manning levels. In practice, however, the government has already shown some reluctance to let the trusts be genuinely independent in these key areas. Although the trusts escape control by district and regional health authorities, their numbers have necessitated the creation of a separate 'local' arm of the Management Executive to administer them. It will be responsible for, among other things, the supervision of their capital programmes.

One test of the trust regime is superior performance. Ministers were quick to claim that trusts were proving successful by quoting figures for increased activity and shorter waiting lists. Some unofficial surveys have confirmed that trusts are being innovative, others that some of their finances were rocky, despite the 'steady as she goes' regime. Of this latter group of trusts, the case of Guy's attracted most attention as it had to make 400 compulsory redundancies – and lost its financial director as well.

But all this – both the official and the unofficial – carries very little weight. It is simply too soon to come to any reasoned or evidenced conclusions of the significance of the trust regime. In particular, it remains to be seen whether an otherwise bullish survey in Newchurch & Company's 1991 *Guide to NHS Trusts* is correct in its conclusion: 'The greatest single concern for trusts is, however, a creeping reintroduction of bureaucratic controls, particularly through regions. Virtually all chief executives remained unconvinced of the Department of Health's capacity to deal directly with the growing number of trusts and fear a reimposition of local, excessive, control by regions.'[9]

Resource Allocation

The final plank in the new arrangements is the way that finance is to be allocated. Under the old arrangements, originating from the Resource Allocation Working Party (RAWP), money did follow patients, but only imperfectly and with a considerable lag, so a district taking on more work did not find that reflected in its budget. The essential step is the creation, through contracts, of a tighter link between activity and income for health care providers. The formula by which resources are allocated to regions and then to districts has not been substantially altered under the new arrangements: finance is to be allocated to purchasing districts on the basis of their resident population. However, the introduction of contracts means that adjustments for cross-boundary flows are no longer necessary.

Limits of Competition

We end this section on a cautionary note. Most analysis of the reforms are couched in terms of competition and the economics of creating an 'internal market'. This is undoubtedly apposite and instructive, but it runs the risk of giving the impression that the NHS reforms are simply about grafting private sector incentives onto a public service. The reforms also mirror a more general development in public administration, in this and other countries, during the 1980s. Put at its simplest, this involves a separation of the two main activities of government: the making of policy, and its administration. The creation of the so-called 'Next Steps' agencies offers the clearest example of this process operating in other areas of government. Reforms in the education field, where schools now largely manage their own administrative affairs, also follow this pattern. Sweden has organised most of its government functions in this way: central policy-boards 'commission' administratively separate agencies, within the public sector, to carry out and implement central policy. Viewed in this light, the reforms described above separate the 'administrators' – the hospitals and other provider units – from the policy-makers – the purchasing authorities. Competition is not an essential element in this process. The clarification of roles, the creation of smaller management units and the setting of clear targets for health care activity – these could be argued to represent the key changes.

We would not like to suggest that competition is not important. However, if the new arrangements fail to demonstrate 'true' competitive conditions this should not lead us to prematurely decry all elements of what is a more general administrative reform.

Public Health Strategy

In June, the government published a green paper, *The Health of the Nation*, for consultation, which the Department of Health called at the time the first ever health strategy for England. The consultation period ended in October; the white paper is due sometime in 1992. At the same time, a health strategy steering group was announced for England to oversee the development of the green paper's proposals. A shift from a preoccupation with health care to concern for better health is of course one that the government's critics have long urged on it. If such a shift were to be made, it would represent as great a revolution as the organizational and financial reforms we have already described. Moreover, the two 'revolutions' can be seen as complementary. The creation of purchasing units free from day-to-day responsibilities for running health services opens the way to policies for achieving better health based on prevention rather than treatment. They have always been available, but in practice the amount of resources devoted by health authorities to prevention has been minimal.

The implications of this new approach are very wide. As the Secretary of State's announcement indicated, when launching the green paper, the new approach has two elements. First, selecting key areas for health improvements. These range from major causes of premature death, such as coronary heart disease, to causes of ill-health such as diabetes and mental illness. Other important areas, such as the health of pregnant women and food safety, are also covered. The second element is setting clear objectives and targets in each key area and monitoring progress. If the new approach is to work, a number of conditions must be satisfied. The single most important one is that those responsible for drawing up plans in particular areas and choosing between alternative policy mixes must know what works, that is what actions are likely to achieve in practice the desired outcomes. It is notorious that many health care interventions are of unproven validity; the same is true of many of the courses of action which do not involve health care services. But without such knowledge, the very notion of a health strategy breaks down. The necessary knowledge cannot of course be created overnight, but two steps have been taken to improve utilization of such knowledge of the effects of different policies which already exists. The first is the UK Clearing House for Information on the Assessment of Health Services Outcomes, the second the proposed series of effectiveness bulletins which are designed to spread knowledge of procedures of proven value – a small proportion of the total in use.

Independent of these initiatives, the Faculty of Community Medicine of the Royal College of Physicians published its own report[10] of UK levels of health, which attempted to identify the information available at national level which would adequately describe the 'level of health' of the population. Not surprisingly, this initial report found many gaps in the available information. The most glaring of these is the lack of any regular information on ill-health or handicap. Again, there are new initiatives such as the new Office of Population Censuses and Surveys' health needs surveys, which represent an intelligent start to some of the challenges thrown up by the new framework. But there are many others further down the line, as the green paper turns to white and implementation begins in earnest. Some lie outside the service, some inside.

The main merit of the green paper's approach is that, potentially, it recognises the contributions of all government departments to the promotion of health. But experience with cross-departmental initiatives shows that actually to marshal those contributions is a massive task. The Central Policy Review Staff argued in 1975 that: 'many of the most intractable problems affect more than one department, and involve central government, local authorities and other bodies', exactly the case in health.[11] But that initiative foundered, as have many other similar ones, on the interests of each minister and department.

The omens for this vigorous implementation of the green paper's proposals are not good. For one thing, the government, again perhaps with an eye on an election, has set out a leisurely time-table. For another, it has managed to defeat a European Community proposal to ban cigarette advertising on the grounds that voluntary restrictions were effective – which is dubious. Furthermore, the specific proposals made in the green paper have attracted a good deal of criticism. Whole client groups such as the elderly have been given short shrift. More fundamentally, the document fails to address the central issue of poverty and its association with poor health status. According to Malcolm Dean in *The Lancet*, the Secretary of State considers inequalities in health to be too long-lasting and complex for a reduction in them to be set as a target.[12] The government has throughout the 1980s pursued a policy of breaking the link between social security payments and real income, as a means of creating incentives in the economy. This is obviously at odds with a truly wide-ranging public health strategy. The government would of course claim that the performance of the British economy in the 1980s justified the sacrifice.

Serving the Consumer

During 1991, the government took a number of initiatives right across the public sector which were pulled together in the Citizen's Charter, designed to make public service providers more attentive to the needs of users. Although these initiatives were presented as the government's next 'big idea', the central concern, that public sector providers tended to serve their own interests rather than those of users, was not new. Soon after the government came to office it published a white paper, *Patients First*, which suggested that the largely administrative reforms it was then intent on producing were designed to overcome producer domination of the service. The title of the white paper in which the reforms introduced ten years later were originally set out, *Working for Patients*, maintained the rhetoric. However it proposed no new rights for patients: but the introduction of separate purchasers was intended to create 'proxy' consumers who would have sufficient muscle to countervail the power of entrenched producer interests and hence be freer to select a pattern of services which better fitted the needs of their residents.

However, before the new arrangements could begin to take effect, the government in effect jumped the gun. With the publication of the Citizen's Charter in July, the government declared its intention to require all public services to meet specific service standards. In the case of health, that involved a shortlist of specific standards, with a general promise of more to come in patients' charters for England, Scotland and Wales.

In October, England's Patient's Charter was announced. It begins by listing seven existing rights and adds three new ones:

- a maximum waiting time for elective surgery (maximum waiting times in out-patients are regarded as a standard and not a right);
- access to information on services; and
- full and prompt treatment.

Several service standards are set out which 'are not legal rights but major and specific standards which the government looks to the NHS to achieve as circumstances and resources allow.' The Charter also emphasizes that every citizen has the following established National Health Service rights:

- to receive health care on the basis of clinical need, regardless of ability to pay
- to be registered with a GP
- to receive emergency medical care at any time, through your GP or the emergency ambulance service and hospital accident and emergency departments
- to be referred to a consultant, acceptable to you, when your GP thinks it necessary, and to be referred for a second opinion if you and your GP agree this is desirable
- to be given a clear explanation of any treatment proposed, including any risks and any alternatives, before you decide whether you will agree to the treatment

- to have access to your health records and to know that those working for the NHS are under a legal duty to keep their contents confidential
- to choose whether or not you wish to take part in medical research or medical student training

To promote a National Health Service, to quote from the Charter, 'that always puts the patient first' is hard to fault as an objective. However, its language is flabby and imprecise in areas where it should be the opposite. The first and fundamental right, that to treatment free at the point of use regardless of the ability to pay, does not actually exist now in that form. Some services are charged for and have been since virtually the beginning of the NHS. If people are deterred by charges, as the evidence suggests, then health care is not being provided purely on the basis of need. Furthermore, this first right does not set out what is included within the ambit of 'health care'. In fact the line between social care (not free) and health care (free) is very hard to draw in practice.

We would not like to suggest that the Charter is therefore entirely without merit. Most users of out-patients would indeed appreciate the replacement of a system which valued their time at a slightly higher level than zero and that of medical staff at infinity. But other measures taken in 1991 are much more significant; the most significant are not covered in the Charter at all – the potential of the purchaser-provider split to counter producer interests. Thus if, as it would seem from the Audit Commission's report,[13] people prefer day surgery to in-patient care, the Charter will not help them. Purchasers may influence service patterns in ways which are much more fundamental than those covered in the Charter, in particular, they can get at what is most important, clinical performance, helped by the effectiveness bulletins already mentioned. But if purchasers are to act 'for consumers' it would be wrong to assume that all consumers will benefit: quality of care may be increased, so fewer are treated. One form of care may be chosen in favour of another: some consumers will gain and others lose. For purchasers must work within cash limits, and that reflects the fact that, however well consumer interests are taken into account in the delivery of services, the taxpayer interest can never ultimately be denied. The government's policy during the 1980s, reviewed by Anthony Harrison in last year's edition of *Health Care UK*,[14] has been to attempt to ride both horses simultaneously by getting sufficient efficiency gains out of the NHS to improve services while keeping tax burdens down. But such a policy can only work if patients are not always put first: waiting lists operate through the rationing procedures adopted by clinicians as part of their way of working within the resources limits.

This fundamental conflict has been with the NHS ever since its inception. But some of the elements of the new system have served to bring out that conflict between consumer choice and resource limitations in ways that perhaps the government had not anticipated. The Charter is explicit that patients can be referred to a preferred consultant subject to GP agreement but it does not specify how that preference will be embodied in financial arrangements that guarantee it. A case involving Kettering District Health Authority highlights the difficulties. The authority initially refused to fund a referral for which no existing contract existed. It argued that its funds for extra contractual referrals, that is referrals to authorities not specifically included in written contracts, had run out. This case was resolved by ad hoc intervention from the Department of Health, but the general issue remains.

In the final analysis, though, and whatever impression the Charter gives, individual patients are not going to be able to choose the range of services which constitute a 'comprehensive' service. At zero price at the point of consumption this would place an impossible strain on NHS resources. Some form of rationing will always be necessary, and it is to these issues we now turn.

Privatization?

As the prospect of an election came closer, so did the intensity of public debate on whether or not the government was intent on privatizing the NHS. That debate served to illuminate at least one point: that privatization has several quite distinct meanings. Any attempt to clarify these meanings must begin with the key distinction between the privatization of finance and the privatization of supply. The policy of competitive tendering for ancillary services, introduced as far back as 1983, clearly fell into the second category. Whatever the merits of that policy, it has not affected the basic nature of the NHS, in particular it had no impact on the accessibility of the services to its users. However, the new system clearly widens the scope for private supply, not just of ancillary or professional services, but also health care itself. The field is open for private hospitals to bid for contracts – just as it is for NHS provider units to offer private health care facilities, such as pay beds. Such contracts were rare before 1991 and continue to be so. Even if they became more common, that in itself would not change the fundamental conditions of access as far as patients were concerned.

Labour Party spokesmen alleged of course that the creation of trusts and the purchaser/provider split were the prelude to the sale of NHS assets to the private sector; again, that would represent privatization of supply, not finance. Even if that were to take place, it would not have a direct effect on the conditions of access enjoyed by patients. Nevertheless, despite the shadow-boxing round and about the question of what the government really intended, there were important developments in 1991 which did bear on the central question of the conditions governing access to services and which did involve privatization of supply, at least in the sense of 'rationing-out' certain health-care interventions from public provision.

The first indication that the use of explicit rationing procedures would constitute a significant theme in the health policy debate was provided by the leaked decision of North East Thames Regional Health Authority (NETRHA) to remove five procedures from its waiting lists: varicose vein operations, the removal of non-malignant lumps and bumps, the extraction of symptomless wisdom teeth, in-vitro fertilization, and the removal of tattoos.[15] This is except in cases where there is 'overriding' clinical need.

The context in which this decision was taken has two important elements. Firstly, there is the long term tendency for NHS resources to fall behind its ability to provide treatment, as evidenced by waiting lists which continue to rise. There are well-rehearsed reasons for this: an aging population presenting greater morbidity; new drugs and medical and surgical techniques which allow for the treatment of conditions previously 'untreatable'; widening conceptions of ill-health to include more 'social' illness such as cosmetic, reproductive and minor psychiatric problems; and economic factors such as the relative price effect which results from the inability of the public sector to match private sector productivity gains, making public services relatively more expensive through time.

The second element in NETRHA's decision was the implementation of the NHS reforms. The resulting administrative split between purchasers and providers has meant that districts and regions have largely been freed from managerial responsibilities, and have been encouraged to concentrate more on issues of policy, particularly the assessment and prioritizing of the health needs of their areas. NETRHA's recommendations are the first explicit reaction to these twin developments, and as such caused considerable debate. Implicit rationing has of course been a feature of the NHS since its creation. The treatment of non-emergency conditions has been limited by forcing patients to wait until resources became available; waiting times vary between conditions, but the expectation has always been that one's 'turn' would finally come, as long as clinical necessity was underwritten by a GP and hospital consultant. The system thus attempted to satisfy two contradictory demands: it was, on the one hand, impossible to treat all the medical demands made on the NHS simultaneously; on the other, the concept of 'free and comprehensive' care meant that no individual, or group of individuals, could be excluded altogether. Furthermore, the fact that waiting times vary between different conditions reveal that there has been an implicit acceptance by those who manage waiting lists, essentially the hospital consultants, that some forms of treatment could achieve greater health benefits than others, even if we are only considering non-urgent cases. Up until the present no attempt has been made to establish a consensus on this issue, and consultants have been left free to make their own assessments of the relative importance of various states of ill-health.

It might be argued that this circle could not be squared indefinitely. If it was accepted that some treatments produce greater health benefits than others, why treat some minor conditions at all, given that the resources thus released could be used to greater effect? Seen in this light, NETRHA's decision is unsurprising, if politically contentious: for the first time certain individuals will no longer be able to call on the NHS to treat a medical complaint.

It is not precisely clear how the five treatments excluded from NETRHA's lists were arrived at, however. NETRHA appear to have taken a rather intuitive assessment of what conditions could most easily be removed from waiting lists.

However, there is no reason to suggest that explicit rationing should restrict itself to these five conditions when there may be many more which satisfy the same criteria, whatever these may be. It is worth describing two other explicit attempts at rationing which have sought to clarify these criteria. The first is theoretical and involves the use of 'quality-adjusted life years' (QALYs); the second is practical, the so-called 'Oregon initiative' in the USA. Each generated considerable discussion in the media during 1991.

It was suggested above that there was an implicit acceptance that certain interventions are of greater benefit than others. QALYs are an attempt to quantify with more precision the expected health benefits to be gained from treating various forms of ill-health. They take into account both survival (in terms of gains in life expectancy) and 'quality' (in terms of increased health status) resulting from a treatment. Thus, if the expected length of life is unchanged after treatment – it remains at, say, 20 years – but the 'quality' of that life in terms of health status is increased from 50 per cent of full health to 100 per cent, then the individual concerned would be said to gain 10 QALYs (50 per cent of 20 years). Combine this with the cost and a 'cost per QALY' figure can be calculated. To maximize the total number of QALYs (the total amount of 'health gain') a health system can produce, health care should be provided such that the marginal cost per QALY is equal across all treatments.

Although in the context of a different finance and delivery system, the Oregon initiative attempts to put a QALY-type system into practice. The origin of the process was an attempt to widen the number of individuals who could benefit from the Medicaid budget, by limiting the number of procedures which were to be performed. The process involved a significant public input into the ranking of various 'condition-treatment' pairs on a cost-utility basis – the precise nature of this process remains unclear, however, since the rankings were not accompanied by scores and the final listing was produced in private. The rationale was precisely the same as that behind QALYs, though: greater health outcomes could be achieved with the same resources by concentrating on certain treatments and conditions.

It is clear that NETRHA's action has nothing like the ambition of either of these developments, but the contrast between the two reveals a potentially interesting divergence in the paths of the rationing debate: NETRHA appear to have concentrated on removing provision of health care for conditions which could be described as 'social' in their character, involving cosmetic and reproductive problems which would impair individuals' ability to form relationships, whereas QALY and Oregon methods concentrate on all (physical, psychiatric and social) health-related conditions, but remove or restrict provision for those which nonetheless do not produce a cost-effective increase in health-status. There are numerous philosophical and practical problems with these approaches. But both are in some sense explicit: they name treatments which will not, or are less likely to, be provided by public provision. The alternative, for rationing to remain implicit, providers would somehow have to continue to convince an increasingly informed and health-conscious public that everyone who falls ill has a chance of getting to the front of the queue, even as resources fall further behind the demands made on them.

Conclusion

Nineteen ninety-one contains elements of paradox. The largest reform ever in the NHS was due to come into effect but its main provisions have been deferred or put on hold. Radical changes in responsibility for community care have been postponed; the new health strategy remains only an outline. So if we look only at what has happened, what we find amounts to not a great deal. Yet there is little doubt that the existing mould has been shattered. If nothing else, a large number of mental barriers have been broken. Initiatives have been taken at local level which would never have occurred before and ideas have been aired for further changes which until recently would have been unthinkable.

The wider implications of GP fundholding, district purchasing, the shift to a public health emphasis and so on, are yet to be fully worked through. Policy has undoubtedly moved in a new direction – and will continue to do so even if there is a change in government. Quite where it is going is hard to see. But it is certainly moving somewhere. The familiar dilemma, how to reconcile limited funding with open-ended access, remains. However, the reforms may serve to encourage explicit rationing processes which were once implicit. That in the end may have the most significant impact of all.

Notes

1 *National Health Service and Community Care Act 1990*, HMSO, 1990.
2 Cmnd 1523, *The Health of the Nation. A consultative document for health in England*, HMSO, 1991.
3 Cmnd 1599, *The Citizen's Charter*, HMSO, 1991.
4 Secretary of State for Health, *The Patient's Charter*, Department of Health, 1991.
5 National Association of Health Authorities and Trusts, *Autumn Survey of Financial Position of DHAs and Provider Units: 1991. Part 2: Financial and Contractual Position of Purchasers and Providers*, NAHAT, 1991.
6 Howard Glennerster, Pat Owens and Manos Matsaganis, *A Foothold for Fundholding. A Preliminary Report on the Introduction of GP Fundholding*, King's Fund Institute Research Report No.12, 1992.
7 NHS Management Executive, *Joint Guidance (NHSME/JCC) to Hospital Consultants on GP Fundholding*, EL(91)84, 1991.
8 *NHS Trusts: a working guide*, Department of Health, 1990.
9 *The Newchurch Guide to NHS Trusts, 1991*, Newchurch and Company, 1991.
10 Faculty of Community Medicine of the Royal College of Physicians, *HFA 2000 News*, 12, May 1990.
11 Central Policy Review Staff, *Joint Approach to Social Policy*, 1975.
12 Malcolm Dean, 'Who is satisfied with WHO's targets?', *The Lancet*, 16 June 1991.
13 Audit Commission for Local Authorities and the NHS in England and Wales, *Measuring Quality: the Patient's View of Day Surgery*, NHS Occasional Papers 3, May 1991.

278 *Contemporary Britain*

14 Anthony Harrison, 'Cost Containment in the NHS, 1979–1990', in Anthony Harrison and Shirley Bruscini (eds), *Health Care UK 1990*, Policy Journals, King's Fund Institute, 1990.
15 Malcolm Dean, 'End of a Comprehensive NHS?', *The Lancet*, 337, 351–352, 9 February 1991.

Chronology

1 Jan: Professor Michael Peckham takes over as Director of Research and Development at the Department of Health.
2 Jan: Report by the Association of Community Health Councils calls for a national strategy to reduce inequalities in health care between social classes.
Report by the Medical Research Council suggests improved housing may significantly reduce deaths from stomach cancer.
A report on neonatal fatalities by Dr Tony Lee and published by the Association for Non-Smokers' Rights says that there are more than 8,000 unsuccessful pregnancies a year as a result of mothers smoking.
3 Jan: Consumers' Association report in *Which?* argues that hospitals are failing to follow recommended steps to keep radiation to a minimum.
National Kidney Research Fund press conference argues that over 1,000 die needlessly each year because there are not enough specialists or facilities to treat kidney patients.
7 Jan: Report by Dr Andrew Herxheimer in *Drugs and Therapeutics Bulletin* argues that doctors do not spend enough time explaining drug treatments or their side effects to patients.
9 Jan: Government is to more than double its funding of the hospice movement to £17 million.
A leading private health insurance company blacklists the AMI chain of private hospitals for over-charging private patients.
£71 million allocated for 1991–92 for Nursing 2000.
10 Jan: *Aids and HIV Infection*, Royal College of Surgeons, sanctions surgeons testing high risk patients for Aids without their consent if they consider that they or their staff may be at risk.
BMA survey declares a 'no fault' compensation scheme for victims of medical negligence.
16 Jan: £35 million allocated for reduction of waiting lists to be supplemented by matching regional fund.
21 Jan: Professor George Teeling Smith, *Patterns of Prescribing*, Office of Health Economics, argues that thousands of people with high blood pressure suffer strokes because their conditions go untreated.
22 Jan: Report of joint working party on women doctors and their careers, recommending several measures to increase numbers of women in surgery.
23 Jan: Campaign launched to encourage women qualified as doctors to develop careers in medicine.
25 Jan: *Health Service Journal* publishes a survey of family practices to be given their own budgets.
26 Jan: NETRHA proposes to remove certain minor operations from waiting lists.
1 Feb: Scheme to introduce independent arbitration in cases of alleged medical negligence is announced.

3 Feb: Jane Griffin, *Dying with Dignity*, Office of Health Economics, argues that many NHS staff lack training in looking after the terminally ill.

4 Feb: Furore begins over the refusal of managers at the Christie Hospital, Manchester to pay for a new drug (eventually supplied) which could save the life of a seriously ill cancer patient.

7 Feb: Government declares support for the general principle of nurse prescribing.

13 Feb: Closure of 25 mental handicap and 32 mental illness hospitals over next five years announced .

14 Feb: National Audit Office, *NHS Outpatient Services*, HMSO, criticizes waiting times for outpatient appointments.

2 Mar: Health authorities required to examine working hours of junior doctors.

13 Mar: Audit Commission reports that the NHS needs to spend £2 billion bringing its buildings up to standard.

26 Mar: Audit Commission report says NHS could save £30 million a year by improving energy efficiency.

27 Mar: £10 million allocated to capital costs of improving services for the mentally ill.

28 Mar: Calls to combat the shortage of organs for transplant by requiring people who do not wish to donate to opt out are rejected by the government.

1 Apr: Internal audit in NHS comes into effect.
Prescription charges rise by 35p to £3.40.

12 Apr: Association of Optometrists claims that one in five people are avoiding eye tests because of the cost.

18 Apr: Voluntary agreement with the tobacco industry to remove 50 per cent of shop front advertising over the next five years.

21 Apr: New working group to draw up guidelines on cancer treatment announced.

24 Apr: National Audit Office, *National Health Service Supplies*, HMSO, criticizes the NHS's fragmented supplies policy.
Cancer research to get top priority in a new strategy for medical research unveiled by the government.

25 Apr: Storm over 600 job losses at the new Guy's self-governing hospital trust in south London begins.

6 May: Businessmen now outnumber doctors by three to one on district health committees according to a survey by the BMA.

8 May: *The First Report of the Effects of the NHS Reforms on Medical Education and Research*, Universities Funding Council, warns that teaching hospitals, especially in London, may become financially unviable.

13 May: Talks on junior doctors hours break up over consultants' refusal to agree shorter hours for all juniors.

15 May: Audit Commission survey of patients' views show that most would prefer day surgery to hospital admittance.

16 May: Department of Health statistics show that AIDS is now spreading fastest amongst the male heterosexual population.

17 May: Tory attacks on Labour claims that hospitals would be forced to opt out of the NHS, a claim which played a part in the Conservatives' Monmouth by-election defeat on 16 May.

21 May: Health boards in Scotland are encouraged to go ahead with 'patient hotel' plans. Working party of the General Medical Council recommends a shift away from a factual to a more intellectual approach to medical education.

22 May: Review of NHS Low Income Scheme announced.

30 May: A national waiting list helpline is established.

31 May: College of Health's *Guide to Hospital Waiting Lists 1991*, shows 200,000 in England have waited more than a year for an operation.

4 Jun: Britain helps block an EC proposal to ban tobacco advertising.

Green paper on *The Health of the Nation*, HMSO, sets outs the government's aims in preventive health care.

5 Jun: *Financial Management and the Family Health Service*, Chartered Institute of Management Accountants, examines the implications of the NHS reforms on management accounting in the family health service authorities.

8 Jun: Study in *The Lancet* shows that health inequalities are due to salary, not occupation.

12 Jun: Announcement of plans to phase in reductions in junior doctors hours to 72 per week by 1997.

13 Jun: Monitoring and reporting arrangements for community care announced, plus advisory group of NHS managers and directors of social services to advise of steps needed for successful implementation.

19 Jun: Joint committee to review the working of the new NHS announced.

20 Jun: Interim Licensing Authority says fertility clinics should be required to publish their success rates.

27 Jun: Report in *The Lancet* warns of a rapid increase in HIV rates amongst sexually active women, with the rate in London doubling every 12 months.

28 Jun: New annual health audit of the nation based on interview samples is announced by the government.

30 Jun: Survey by Mintel International finds one in four people have put off eye tests since charges were introduced in 1989.

1 Jul: Charges for dental check-ups are increased by 30p to £3.75 as Labour publishes a document pledging to abolish dental charges, set targets and timetables for the fluoridization of the water supply, establish nutritional guidelines on school meals, set a code on labelling the sugar contents of foodstuffs and permit dentists to prescribe fluoride tablets.

2 July: Inquiry into causes of still births and infant deaths launched.

3 July: Government to stop publishing waiting lists for individual hospitals.

11 Jul: Tougher health warnings on smoking announced for implementation in 1992.

23 July: Lack of co-ordination between authorities in handling the outbreak of salmonella in north Wales in 1989 is criticized in a report by the Welsh Affairs Select Committee.

24 July: Report by the Department of Health says thousands of people are avoiding Aids tests because they believe they will penalized by insurance companies.

Richard West, *Organ Transplantation*, Office of Health Economics, analyses the cost-efficiency of transplants.

Survey of regional variations in child tooth decay is published by Leeds University's Department of Child Dental Health.

30 July: Review of NHS family planning services is ordered.

31 July: *Nursing Costs and Benefits,* Institute of Manpower Studies, University of Sussex, argues more and better qualified nurses would be cost-effective because patients would recover more quickly with less chance of relapses.

1 Aug: Public Accounts Committee, *NHS Outpatient Services,* HMSO, criticizes the waiting times for outpatients and expresses concern that the reforms in the NHS could exacerbate the situation.

Equal Opportunities Commission report on *Equality Management – Women's Employment in the NHS* is published, criticizing the NHS for wasting women employees by not giving them greater opportunity to combine work with parenthood.

5 Aug: Another 113 applications to become NHS trusts are announced.

6 Aug: Central supplies authorities are to be set up in the NHS to save on costs.

9 Aug: Survey of first year of GP contracts shows 90 per cent are hitting health targets.

21 Aug: Audit Commission report criticizes the lack of financial information on the running of the NHS.

3 Sept: Labour pledges to reverse hospital opt-outs.

11 Sept: The proportion of under-16s who are regular smokers is increasing according to OPCS, *Smoking amongst secondary school children in 1990,* HMSO.

13 Sept: Norwich Union Healthcare is appointed to buy comprehensive healthcare for Guernsey by the island's government.

26 Sept: Health strategy group established to examine how co-operation can be achieved between government, statutory and voluntary bodies, national and local organizations.

9 Oct: Reforms announced providing for reduction of junior doctors' working hours from 80 to 56 per week.

10 Oct: Announcement of an independent inquiry into health care in London under Sir Bernard Tomlinson.

School Meals Campaign set up to try and get nutritional guidelines reinstated.

18 Oct: 103 second wave NHS trusts approved.

30 Oct: *Patient's Charter,* HMSO, guarantees treatment within two years and a better system for dealing with complaints.

31 Oct: John Major pledges to increase health spending every year in real terms if the Tories win the next election.

1 Nov: Access to Health Records Act comes into force.

Bill to shift funding of nursing training to DHAs published.

5 Nov: *Enjoy Healthy Eating,* Health Education Authority, gives nutritional guidelines.

6 Nov: In his autumn statement the Chancellor announces an extra £2.2 billion for the NHS.

17 Nov: Ron Akehurst et al, *Health of the Nation: An Economic Perspective on Target Setting,* Centre for Health Economics, University of York, criticizes government health targeting as based on inadequate evidence and lacking the necessary mechanisms. They suggest higher cigarette taxes and cast doubt on the cost effectiveness of screening for breast and cervical cancer.

27 Nov: Code of practice issued to local authorities on how to inspect Crown premises for public health.

3 Dec: Audit Commission, *The Virtue of Patients: Making the best use of ward resources,* HMSO, says nurses' time is ineffectively used.

King's Fund report recommends statutory registration of osteopaths.

4 Dec: Three Scottish hospital trusts approved.

11 Dec: *Lord President's Report on Action against Alcohol Misuse*, HMSO, says 7 million adults regularly drink more than the limits set by medical advice, but the government is prevented from putting warnings on bottles by EC rules.

14 Dec: BMA announces support for making GP fundholding generally applicable.

Acknowledgment

This article is a reduced and revised version of 'Health Policy Review, 1991' which appears in *Health Care UK 1991*, edited by Anthony Harrison.

Social Security Policy

KATHY SUTTON

Breaking with the Past?

As 1990 drew to its close, few people seriously believed that Conservative policies had assisted in trickling wealth down from the rich to the poor. The rejection of state intervention to redistribute wealth from the rich to the poor and their proclaimed faith in the power of the market to provide wealth throughout society had created the conditions for growing inequalities in Britain. In many respects the gap between rich and poor appeared never to have been wider. This was exacerbated by the furore surrounding the introduction of the poll tax earlier in the year and its resounding and continuing unpopularity – directly attributable to the fact that the government had broken a fundamental rule of taxation, that it should be linked to the ability to pay.

Government ideology on social security in the 1980s sought to break the 'welfare dependence' of the British people; the purpose of social security was no longer social integration but social control. The Conservatives believed that the social security system deterred economic progress by creating a culture of dependence. According to the Tories, the state should break this dependence and promote the positive ethos of individualism, self-help and family values. This ideology was supported by policies which sought to control public expenditure; provide incentives for the privatization of benefits and undermine the state's contributory benefits system; replace universal and contributory benefits with means-tested benefits and use these as a hidden subsidy to employers.

The irony of the government's approach was that far from reducing people's dependence on state benefits, its policies led to increased poverty and unprecedented numbers of recipients reliant on means-tested benefits. As a means of controlling public expenditure, increasingly the government aimed to 'target' means-tested benefits away from the 'undeserving' – the young and the unemployed – to the 'deserving' – the family with children and the disabled, for example. At the same time as demand for benefits had increased, their real value had fallen dramatically since the Tories came to power.

The poll tax crystallized the discontent of British people. It showed a nation hardly at ease with itself. The fact that even the poorest must pay a 20 per cent contribution infuriated not only those affected but those whose sense of justice was betrayed. The question, then, on many people's lips as 1991 commenced and the new Prime Minister became accustomed to taking the helm was how far this year would be a break from the past.

The Reestablishment of One Nation Toryism?

The new Prime Minister spoke a new language and adopted a style distinct from the Thatcher years in which he – and his colleagues – had played an integral role. It was a return to the old one nation Tory philosophy shaped in the language of the 1990s.

Nineteen ninety-one should be remembered for the four 'c's that impacted, in some shape or other, on social security: the Prime Minister's vision of a classless society in which society was at ease with itself; the Prime Minister's Citizen's Charter; the Prime Minister himself who sought to persuade us that he was the common man but who sometimes appeared to have lost the common touch; continued chaos in the benefits system. It was a year of increasing poverty, as a result of the deep recession, on which was superimposed a new government sponsored-language that promoted 'buzzwords' (stolen from its critics) such as opportunity, fairness and rights. And it was the year in which the Conservatives continued to resist European pressure to extend Community powers to determine social security policy in member states.

Continuity in Policies

There was much in 1991 that reflected continuity in social security policy. In June the Disability Living Allowance and Disability Working Allowance Act received Royal Assent. Claimed by the government to be a major step forward, they were criticized by others as shoddy public relations exercises disguising cuts in both rights and benefits. The new Disability Working Allowance, based on the government's flagship benefit 'Family Credit', was a new means-tested benefit which would be payable to disabled people in low-paid employment. Critics believed that such benefits merely act to provide subsidies to low-paying employers and do nothing to harness economic efficiency. The new benefits would be introduced in April 1992.[1]

A month later the Child Support Act 1991 received Royal Assent setting the scene for the establishment of the new Child Support Agency and the collection and enforcement of maintenance payments. Despite widespread opposition, the punitive penalty clause for women who failed to reveal the name of the father of their child without good cause remained.[2] The Act also provided for an extension of Family Credit by reducing the threshold at which people could qualify from 24 hours to 16 hours. An attempt by the government later on in the year to force unemployment benefit claimants to take up part-time jobs of 16 hours or more or lose benefit failed after widespread political opposition and rejection of this by the Social Security Advisory Committee.

The Classless Society?

At the end of the year *The Guardian* wrote: 'the social security reforms . . . which were aimed at producing less dependency and less fraud, have combined with the indexing of social security to prices and not wages, to produce levels of mass poverty to rival those of the nineteenth century'.[3] Earlier in the year, a number of studies had indicated the rising trend of poverty and the myth behind the 'trickle down' effect. In April, the findings of a new 'Breadline Britain' survey for London Weekend Television showed that the number of poor had increased from 7.5 million people in 1983 to 11 million in 1990 – from 14 to 20 per cent of the population – and the numbers in severe poverty from 2.6 million to 3.5 million (from 4.8 per cent of the population to 6.3 per cent). This survey defined poverty in relation to the inability to afford basic essentials such as heating and hot meals. It also showed that 70 per cent considered that the government was doing too little to help the poor and that three quarters would be prepared to pay more tax to help it do more.

A month later, a Social Security Select Committee report showed that in 1988 11.8 million people or nearly 22 per cent of the population were living in poverty – defined as below half average income after meeting housing costs. The report showed that after housing costs, the poorest tenth of the population had received only slight increases in their income. Between the years 1979–88 their income had risen, in real terms, by 2 per cent as compared to 35.5 per cent for the rest of the population.[4]

Despite the different measurements of poverty the conclusions drawn by the two studies were strikingly similar – one in five of the population was now in poverty. The Institute for Fiscal Studies estimated that 3 million children (25 per cent of all children) were in households below half average income and a third of these were actually in households where one parent was in full-time work, indicating that low pay remained a major cause of poverty.

The reasons for the growing level of poverty were primarily linked to the Thatcher government's economic philosophies. Under Major, there appeared to be little prospect of shifting some of the more fundamental tenets adopted in the Thatcher years: unemployment remained a price worth paying for the lowering of inflation; low pay remained a price that the unemployed must accept if they wanted a job. Further deregulation of the labour market remained on the government's agenda. And as the recession hit deeper, 1991 witnessed relentless, persisting and increasing levels of unemployment hitting the Conservative heartland of the south east and affecting service industries as well as manufacturing.

A Budget for the Low Paid

Some had predicted that the first budget under the premiership of Mr Major would be one that would assist the low paid as the first step towards his vision of the classless society. But the reality was different. The one partial success story was child benefit. For three years running the Conservatives had frozen this popular and universal benefit. In October 1990, the government had made a minor concession in announcing an increase of £1 for the eldest child. In the budget the policy on child benefit was all but reversed – with a further increase of £1 for the eldest child and 25 pence for second and subsequent children to be paid from October 1991 and a commitment that child benefit would be index-linked from April 1992.

It was a resounding victory for those who had campaigned so hard to keep child benefit on the political agenda. But it was only a partial victory. As the Child Poverty Action Group pointed out, the 1991 increases did not compensate wholly for the three year freeze and there was a major anomaly in treating second and subsequent children as of considerably less worth. The new levels of benefit to be introduced in October would be £9.25 for the eldest child and £7.50 for second and subsequent children. The Low Pay Unit, in its budget analysis, calculated that in spite of the increases child benefit had still been cut by 6.6 per cent for the oldest child and over 24 per cent for second and subsequent children since 1979.[5]

A commitment to end the despair of the poll tax was followed up by a maximum £140 reduction in poll tax bills. But whilst the maximum reduction amounted to £2.69 per week, it was estimated that the poorest – those on full rebates of 80 per cent – would receive as little as 58 pence a week from this change, far lower than the announced increase on VAT.[6] Cuts in the poll tax were to be achieved by the transfer of some local government services to central government and an increase in VAT from 15 to 17.5 per cent. This increase in indirect taxation falls most heavily on those least able to pay. This was in line with the traditional government policy of the Thatcher year. Over the years, despite decreases in income tax, the overall tax burden had risen due to increases in indirect taxation and national insurance contributions. The Low Pay Unit calculated that the increase in VAT would add about £2 to the cost of living of the low paid. A further 15 per cent increase in excise duties on tobacco and petrol would cost the low paid a further £2.05 per week.[7]

Before the budget there had been much speculation that the Chancellor would increase personal allowances over and above inflation. His failure to do this meant that more low-paid workers would be drawn into tax in the year ahead, resulting in an increase in the number of families caught in the poverty trap of taxes and means-tested benefits and an increase in the tax burden on the low paid. His inaction on this point has to be judged against the over-indexation of the threshold at which the higher (40 per cent) rate of tax became payable – over 5 per cent over the level for indexation.

The April Upratings

One of the direct reasons for the growing inequality between the rich and poor in Britain was as a direct result of cuts in the value of social security benefits. Far from the social security system being a means of redistribution its purpose was to provide a basic minimum. The government has so sought to remove its responsibility for unemployment and used the benefits system increasingly as a means of controlling and directing the unemployed into low paid work through increasing restrictions on the rights to claim unemployment benefit and income support.

In April unemployment benefit rose to a basic £41.40 per week. Its value has fallen dramatically during the period of Conservative rule. A report published by the Labour Party, based on official statistics, showed that unemployment benefit rates were lower in Britain than in any other country in the European Community. It showed that Britain was the only country which did not pay unemployment benefit based on recent earnings. As a result, the impact of being thrown out of work in this country was far worse than in the rest of the Community.[8] Only a minority of the unemployed actually receive unemployment benefit and most have to rely on means-tested benefit because of the increased restrictions on claiming and because levels are inadequate to support a family.

Although the increase in child benefit had received much publicity, few noticed that one parent benefit payable to single parents had been frozen. This is payable to around 750,000 single parents. By the winter it was reported that seven out of ten single parents were living on income support. Family Credit, viewed originally by the Conservatives as the benefit to replace child benefit, was treated far more favourably – credits for children were raised above the rate of inflation. Family Credit had been the jewel in the crown of the government's reformed benefits system in 1988. A means-tested benefit, it is payable to families of the low paid who are in regular low-paid employment. It is a cash benefit which acts as a subsidy for low-paying employers.

In the same month, the government announced details of its new council tax which would replace the poll tax in 1993–94. The new council tax reproduced much of the unfairness of the poll tax, with discounts for single people irrespective of their ability to pay. Although the government admitted defeat by accepting the need for the reintroduction of 100 per cent rebates under the new system, despite widespread calls and recommendations – even from within its own political ranks in local government – it refused to accept the case for full rebates under the poll tax. This was despite the fact that the cost of collection often exceeded the actual poll tax owing and that non-payment of the poll tax grew to exceptional levels so that by the end of the year the whole exercise was being described as the biggest debt collection recovery exercise ever in the world!

Caring for the Claimant? – The Citizen's Charter

In July, after much inter-departmental deliberation and to much applause in the media, John Major launched his new initiative intended to distinguish his leadership from that of his predecessor. The Citizen's Charter promised better standards in public services and rights of redress. The Charter made reference to the rights of social security claimants. Doubts, however, were expressed that it could be effective in this area without significant costs.⁹ All the signs were in 1991 that the system was failing to provide an effective service.

Three months prior to the Charter, the government had introduced laws restricting the rights of benefit claimants to claim arrears due to them due to official mistakes. The government proposed to exclude any errors made before 1988 under the old benefits system. Later on in the year it was announced that £63 million in national insurance contributions had been written off as bad debt, showing a serious under-resourcing of the National Insurance Inspectorate.

In February, the National Association of Citizens' Advice Bureaux drew attention to how the benefits system operated against the interest of black claimants. The same month a National Audit Office report on the social fund criticized inconsistency in decisions and the effects of the fund in creating multiple debt for claimants. If anything was at odds with the principles behind the Citizen's Charter it was the social fund which had replaced the regulations-based single payments scheme. The major element of the fund is its discretionary cash limited scheme. Two thirds of it is paid out in interest free loans repayable directly from income support. It is costly to administer – representing around 0.5 per cent of social security benefit expenditure but taking up 4.2 per cent of DSS labour and 2.8 per cent of running costs. There is no statutory right of appeal against refusal and as the NAO pointed out, it forces people to live below subsistence rates. The 1991–92 budget for the social fund was set at £228 million – around £20 million below the rate of inflation. With the increases in VAT announced in the budget the real value of the fund fell – despite increasing levels of unemployment and extra demand on the fund. The conclusion of some experts was that it was all a question of pot luck whether or not an application to the fund was successful or not.¹⁰ In 1991 applications for the social fund shot up – applications for budgeting loans, for example, rose from 933,185 in 1988–89, the first year of the fund's operation, to 521,064 in the first five months of 1991 – running to an average of 1.25 million claims. An increasing number of these claims were rejected, from 38 per cent to 48 per cent in 1991 and an increasing number of people were unable to repay the loans.

In June, the new head of the Benefits Agency, established in April of this year, was publicly stating that increasing levels of unemployment and demands placed upon the service were affecting the level and quality of the service. Finally, in November, for the third year running the Comptroller-General refused to endorse the Social Security Account pointing to errors in Family Credit and income support.

Opting Out of the European Social Agenda

Despite a political agenda that emphasized the message of opportunity, under Major's premiership the government continued to resist the attempts of the European Community to develop harmonization and improvements in social security benefits. The government had refused to sign the Social Charter in 1989 which contained provisions concerned with 'social protection' and finally in

December opted out of any agreement on social provisions contained within the original social chapter of the draft Maastricht treaty. Whilst all the other 11 European partners planned to proceed with developing the programme in the Social Charter, Mr Major's government stood alone in rejecting it.

Although many were surprised at the formula reached at Maastricht, few could be surprised at the government's stance. Previous directives on 'untypical working', which, amongst other things, had proposed to give part-time workers employed over 8 hours per week equal pro-rata rights to social security benefits, had been vigorously attacked by the government on the grounds that they would create heightened unemployment, particularly for women, who would be most affected by these proposals.

At the end of the year, before Maastricht, the government appeared to have reached a compromise on maternity pay for women. In October 1990, the European Commission published proposals for a directive on the protection at work of pregnant women or women who have recently given birth. Its main proposals would have provided pregnant women with the legal right to 14 weeks of maternity leave on full pay as well as the right to return to their work following the birth of a child. Member states would be given the powers to restrict this right to women who are in work or registered unemployed at the beginning of their pregnancy. The UK is bottom of the maternity pay league, as Table 1 shows. Based on average earnings, statutory entitlement in the rest of the European Community is 14.5 weeks – 6.5 weeks longer than the best statutory provision that the UK offers. Many women are excluded from Statutory Maternity Pay because their earnings are below the national insurance lower earnings limit or they fail to benefit from the higher rate of Statutory Maternity Pay (paid at 90 per cent of earnings for six weeks and 12 weeks at the basic rate) because they have not worked for their employer for two years (five years if they work between 8 and 16 hours). Only 45 per cent of pregnant women qualify for the higher rate and only 22 per cent qualify for the basic rate of Statutory Maternity Pay (paid for 18 weeks).

Instead of the original proposal, the Council of Ministers reached a compromise that pay should be no less generous than national sick pay arrangements. Although the Conservatives failed to support this proposal, preferring to abstain, it had been reached largely as result of the Conservative government's rigid opposition to the original proposals. The Statutory Sick Pay scheme is itself discriminatory – it is paid at two rates, dependent upon the level of earnings. People with earnings below the National Insurance Earnings Limit (£52) are excluded. Most of these are part-time women workers. In recent years the government has introduced draconian cuts in statutory sick pay – the majority of those affected have been women. In 1989 and 1990 the government announced details about the restructuring of SSP. This amounted to a leap from £84 to £185 in the threshold for the lower rate of payments. In total 4.9 million workers lost out as a result of this 'restructuring' – 70 per cent of whom were women.[11] In the 1991 annual upratings, Tony Newton announced that the higher rate of SSP had yet again been frozen at its current level.

Table 1. Paid maternity leave in the European Community as a multiple of weekly earnings

Country	Statutory Pay	Total Maternity Pay Equivalent in full weeks[1]
Denmark	14 weeks – 90% salary further 10 weeks to either parent – 90% salary	22
Italy	5 months – 80% salary	17
Luxembourg	16 weeks – 100% salary	16
Greece	16 weeks – 100% salary	16
Netherlands	16 weeks – 100% salary	16
Germany	14 weeks – 100% salary	14
France	16 weeks – 84% salary	14
Portugal	90 days – 100% salary	13
Spain	16 weeks – 75% salary	12
Belgium	4 weeks at 82% salary then 10 at 75% salary	11
Ireland	14 weeks – 70%	10
UK	6 weeks – 90% salary then 12 weeks flat rate or 18 weeks flat rate	8 4

[1] Rounded to nearest full week

Source: European Commission information updated by IDS European Report – IDS Study, February 1991

In June, the government published its consultation document on equal treatment in state pensions appearing to come down in favour of an equal retirement age of 63. The need to consider equal treatment had been forced on the government because of the successful case of *Barber v GRE* in the European Court which had held that occupational pensions are part of pay and had to be equal in the future at least. Whilst the decision required employers to equalize the age at which pensions became payable for women and men, a number of outstanding issues remained to be considered by the European Court on the position of employees who had made contributions to works pensions before the date of the judgement in May 1990. Employers, in particular, were concerned that they would have to equalize benefits for all those who were in a scheme at the date of the judgement. At Maastricht, however, following pressure from both the British and the Dutch governments an agreement was reached to amend Article 119 of the Treaty of Rome (which provided for equal pay for women) to the effect that occupational pensions contributions paid before May 1990 would not constitute pay, arguably cheating British pensioners out of their rights to equality. We would have to wait until 1992 to see if the European Court of Justice would accept this apparent attempt to opt out of equality.

The Common Touch?

At the end of the year, Mr Major's government was facing a highly critcial media and political protest from dispossessed home owners, due in part to his own previous policies as a junior social security minister. The dream of home owning had turned into a nightmare in 1991 as interest rates soared and the housing market collapsed. Of the 80,000 who had lost their homes, it was calculated that four fifths were in Conservative seats. As social security minister, John Major had introduced reforms to the social security system so that those who were newly unemployed received only half the support with mortgage interest payments that they had hitherto. Indeed, it was he who had originally proposed that claimants should lose all state benefit help for the first six months of unemployment.[12]

Critics of Mrs Thatcher had claimed that she was out of touch with the common person. It is arguable that the high level of popularity that Mr Major enjoyed throughout 1991 was due to the fact that he claimed to the British people that he was the common person. But, at times, he proved to be dangerously out of touch with how common experiences had been changed – not least by his own policies. In June, for example, Mr Major cited how important unemployment benefit had been for him, following a period when he had given up work to care for his sick parents. His critics countered that he had been a social security minister when regulations were tightened up to prevent people who became voluntarily unemployed from claiming benefit.

Conclusion

Under Major's first full year of government, the direction of social security policy, as determined under the Thatcher years, remained largely intact. Public expenditure was closely controlled, the burden of taxation was shifted further on to those with low incomes, means-tested benefits acting as subsidies to low paying employers were extended and the role of Europe in the development of social security rejected.

Any concessions – and there were concessions – were mostly concerned with tinkering around the edges of the social security system rather than a drastic about-turn in government direction on social security policy. But these concessions – for example over cold weather payments for the elderly – combined with a new language of consensus, were important in helping to create in the public's mind an impression that policy was changing and could change. But whilst, in one sense, the language had changed, the message remained much the same. Despite the fact that the numbers living on low pay had reached unprecedented levels, poverty and unemployment were increasing relentlessly, public services declining and homelessness rising, the government sought to avoid underlying responsibility, blaming conditions on the world market. In 1992, the Conservatives would face the ultimate test when erstwhile supporters who had faced unemployment, increasing financial hardship, homelessness and debt would have to choose between the reality that they knew and the perceived rhetoric of the political parties.

Could Conservative rhetoric persuade people that the reality of recession was not so bad after all? And that the rhetoric of the other parties would lead to a life far worse than the hard realities under Conservative rule?

Notes

1 For a fuller discussion of this see Kathy Sutton, 'Social Security Policy' in P. Catterall (ed.), *Contemporary Britain, An Annual Review 1991*, Blackwell, 1991, pp297–9.

2 Ibid, pp301–2 for a fuller discussion.

3 *The Guardian*, 30 December 1991.

4 Social Security Committee, *Low Income Statistics: Households below average income tables 1988*, HMSO, 1991.

5 'A budget for a classless society', *The New Review*, April/May 1991, p.7.

6 Ibid.

7 Ibid. pp.7–8.

8 Michael Meacher, Press Release, Labour Party, July 11 1991.

9 See, for example, Fran Bennett, 'A Window of Opportunity', in *Windows of Opportunity: public policy and the poor'*, Child Poverty Action Group, 1991, p.93.

10 Hilary Arnott, 'Pot luck', *Legal Action*, July 1991, p.9.

11 *In Sickness and in Poverty*, LPU, November 1990.

12 *The Guardian*, 23 December 1991.

Chronology

13 Jan: *Happy Families? Four Points to a Conservative Family Policy*, Centre for Policy Studies, calls for an increase in child benefit for the under-fives, a new child tax allowance, nurseries to be zero-rated for VAT purposes and for changes to make it easier for private providers of child care to obtain planning permission.

25 Jan: National Audit Office, *Support for Low Income Families*, HMSO, argues that social security officials are paying out the wrong amounts to thousands of people including mistakes on more than one in five claims for Family Credit. It also says Family Credit is not achieving its aim of getting people back to work and that most people on income support cannot return to full-time work because of child care difficulties.

Social Security Advisory Committee condemns plans to cut benefits from single mothers who refuse to name the absent fathers of their children because of their fear of violence.

5 Feb: *Barriers to Benefit: Black Claimants and Social Security*, NACAB, argues that people from ethnic minorities are badly served by the social security system, which does not cater well for poor speakers of English.

6 Feb: Help the Aged appeals for elderly people to get heating allowances automatically in severe weather, rather than only when they apply.

7 Feb: Prime Minister announces that cold weather payments are to become immediately available without the seven day qualifying period during the current cold spell and that they will be raised from £5 to £6 a week.

12 Feb: National Audit Office, *The Social Fund*, HMSO, points to growing numbers of people in debt to the social fund, inconsistencies in its application, and millions of unspent pounds despite 780,000 people being refused help. The fund is also by far the most expensive social security benefit.

19 Feb: *Beyond the Limit*, NACAB, draws attention to the inability of many elderly people in residential homes to meet the bills from their state pensions.

21 Feb: In a test case the Court of Appeal rules that the government can amend disability payment regulations and disqualify claimants from severe disability premiums.

19 Mar: Announcement in the budget that child benefit will rise by £1 in October to £9.25 per week, on top of the £1 rise already due in April.

21 Mar: Sean Stitt, *Of Little Benefit: A Study of the Adequacy of Income Support Rates*, Campaign Against Poverty, argues that state benefits to pay for food provide only about half the recommended nutritional requirements for families.

27 Mar: Income of the poorest 20 per cent fell by just under 5 per cent between 1979 and 1989 according to Peter Townsend, *The Poor and Poorer*, Statistical Monitoring Unit, University of Bristol.

10 Apr: Benefits Agency becomes an executive agency.

17 Apr: High Court upholds a government decision to deny social fund clothing grants to psychiatric patients moved into the community.

23 Apr: *Family Prosperity*, Labour Party, pledges to restore child benefit to its 1987 value and immediately raise pensions.

1 May: Public Accounts Committee report finds that the subsidy for people to leave SERPS was equivalent to a 1.5 per cent cut in income tax and that whilst savings of £3.4 billion have been made the costs have been £9.3 billion.

6 May: Family Policy Studies Centre argues six out of ten children of lone parents will be no better off under the current Child Support Bill and criticizes proposals to dock the equivalent of the maintenance due from absent fathers from the benefits of mothers who refuse to reveal the father's identity.

7 May: EC introduces a non-legally binding measure requiring all member states to guarantee all citizens a minimum level of income.

16 May: Social Security Select Committee, *Low Income Statistics: Households below average income 1988*, HMSO, shows that the number of people with incomes below half the average rose from 5.4 million to 9.1 million between 1979–88, and finds that the poorest 20 per cent of households were slightly worse off in 1988 than in 1981.

10 June: Survey for the DSS finds that more than 60 per cent of children of lone parents never see their fathers and less than one third of one parent families receive regular maintenance. Thirteen per cent of them said that they would refuse to give details of former partners if pressed by the DSS and 94 per cent of them relied on the state for most of their income.

24 June: *Meaningful Statistics on Poverty 1991*, Statistics Monitoring Unit, University of Bristol, argues that government statistics misrepresented the fall in income of millions of people, the changes in living standards of the rich and the poor and the non-existence of a trickle-down effect from the rich to the poor in the 1980s.

26 June: Public Accounts Committee, *The Social Fund*, HMSO, argues that the social fund is indefensible in the way it treats people with the same needs for essential items differently, solely because of where they live, and that it has not delivered the greater flexibility of provision that its creators promised.

17 July: Statistics reveal that more than 27,000 people were refused social fund loans in 1990 because they were too poor to repay them.

22 July: National Children's Home survey reports on the poor diet of families on income support.

23 July: *A Survey of 16 and 17 year old applicants for severe hardship payments*, MORI, finds that the payments are failing to meet the needs of claimants.

22 Aug: Department of Employment fraud inspectors reveal that some companies are underpaying workers and then giving them time off work to claim benefit to make up the difference.

1 Nov: Reports by the Low Pay Unit (pointing out that one in six adult full-time workers in London earn less than the Council of Europe's decency threshold of £178 per week) and by CPAG (pointing out up to 1 million people in the capital depend on income support) are published.

National Audit Office, *Appropriation Accounts 1990–91 Vol 9: Classes XIII and XIV*, HMSO, estimates that more than 650,000 families and individuals have been wrongly assessed for benefit by social security staff.

14 Nov: Social Security Select Committee, *The Financing of Private Residential and Nursing Home Fees*, HMSO, argues that elderly people whose income support fails to cover bills for private residential care must be allowed to top up social security payments to avert the threat of eviction and relieve pressure on charities, and that there must be more investment in community-based care which allows them to remain in their own homes.

Employment Policy

B. J. EVANS

'Nineteen-ninety-one has been a year of upheaval and uncertainty in the world of unemployment and training: the rise of TECs, changes to the Employment Service, rapidly increasing unemployment and lengthening queues for training opportunities.' This was the view that the Unemployment Unit and Youthaid expressed in the course of promoting their *Unemployment and Training Rights Handbook*. It may be true, from the perspective of the unemployed job or benefit seeker, that the changes in both training and employment policy in 1991 were substantial and bewildering. From the perspective of the student of policy studies, however, the changes were rather more incremental in character, and the work of both the Training and Enterprise Councils (TECs) and the Employment Service (ES) followed on logically from the policy initiatives of the previous year. Training policy was particularly marked by the successful completion of the TEC network with all 82 in England and Wales in place by the middle of the year, the acceptance by government of training targets which it had previously dismissed as incompatible with a free-market approach, and the announcement that the youth credits pilot initiative was to be short-circuited by the extension of the credit principle to the whole country by 1996. Training policy remained a high profile political issue in 1991 and a matter of contention between the two main political parties. The dispute between the government, which was satisfied that its training policies were succeeding, and the opposition Labour Party which continues to believe in the need for compulsion through a training levy, continued to simmer.

Employment policy was dominated by the undoubted slowing down of the labour market, the continuing rise of the seasonally-adjusted unemployment figures, the development of the Employment Service as an independent agency rooted in the 1986 Next Steps report and the ministerial resistance to European employment directives. As always there is close interaction between employment and training policies, and this was most apparent in the Employment Department's view that training was of diminishing value in assisting the unemployed back into the labour market, and that the various activities of the Employment Service such as Jobclubs were better suited to the purpose.

Training Policy

It was argued at the end of 1990 that the omens for the future of training in Britain would be more favourable if government could overcome 'its caution both about setting training targets and investing more resources. The litmus test is the degree to which employers increase their investment.'[1] These three criteria are clearly measurable at the end of 1991.

The CBI Targets

The first criterion is easily tested because in June 1991 the government overcame its aversion to target setting when the Secretary of State, Michael Howard, accepted the CBI's World Class targets which had emerged with the full approval of the trades unions, the Institute of Personnel Management and the TECs. The previous year Howard renounced the targets which had been announced by Sir Norman Fowler, his predecessor. This was said to have been at the behest of the then Prime Minister, Margaret Thatcher, and it was justified on the grounds that the government was unwilling to proclaim targets which it was leaving to others to achieve and which were, in any event, unenforceable because they did not place specific responsibilities on particular groups to ensure that they were met. An unstated reason was also a sense of trepidation about public spending costs.[2] The pressure from leaders in the training field, including the CBI itself and the TEC movement, however, compelled a reevaluation, and facilitated by the change in the Conservative Party leadership, Howard endorsed the ambitious targets which the CBI proclaimed.

The targets were for young people, adults and employers alike. In foundation learning the target was that 80 per cent of all young people should achieve NVQ level II or its academic equivalent by 1997, and by the year 2000 half of the age group should attain NVQ level III. For adults the principle of lifelong learning required that by 1996 all employees should take part in training or development activities as the norm, half of the employed workforce should aim for NVQ qualifications within the context of individual action plans with employer support and by 1996 half of the medium and larger-sized organizations should qualify as 'Investors in People' as awarded by the TECs.[3] The CBI considered targets to be necessary in order to build a qualified society, because the UK, despite being on an upward trend, has the lowest proportion of 17 year olds in education and fewer qualified managers, engineers and other key workers than its major competitors.[4] The CBI defined the responsibilities which the fulfilment of the targets required, with the TECs playing their role in partnership with educationalists and local authorities, and employers embracing their full responsibilities. Although employers were already spending £20 billion, more than ever before, further investment and greater cost-effectiveness was necessary. The evidence that a firm was carrying out the required policy was its acquisition of the Investors in People award. The government too was urged not to reduce funding for Youth Training (YT) below present levels. 'Resources must be adequate for the objectives set.'[5]

There was a consensus behind the targets encompassing even the trades unions, and such providers as the Committee of Directors of Polytechnics (CDP) expressed their enthusiasm. In one sphere of training policy at least, consensus politics was returning.

Investment of Public Resources

There is no evidence to support the idea that the government increased its investment in training during 1991, and it is a cause for disappointment that there was so little for training in the Chancellor's autumn statement. A leaked letter from the Chief Secretary to the Treasury, David Mellor, had suggested that there were to be savage cuts in the funding of training, and the autumn statement at least demonstrated that the worst fears which the leaked letter had aroused were misplaced, and that Michael Howard had fought his corner well in the weeks between September and November.[6] Yet the majority of the money to be made available for 1991–92 was not earmarked for the government's two main programmes, Youth Training and Employment Training (ET). Rather, some £189 million of the £470 million was accounted for by Employment Action (EA) which was an emergency work-experience scheme introduced in October 1991 as a response to rising unemployment. The problem was that many TECs had refused to co-operate with EA because they regarded it as an irrelevance to training as it was based upon the idea of people working for benefit plus £10. Leeds and Sheffield TECs were two examples of TECs which took a negative attitude towards EA, which they regarded as a distraction from improving the skills of young people.[7] The House of Commons Employment Committee also criticized EA as it was a retrograde shift from the training of unemployed workers. Its report noted that trades unions were opposed to the scheme.[8] The North Derbyshire TEC also refused collaboration with a scheme that its chief executive described as a temporary work-experience programme which failed to match the TEC objective of promoting economic growth by stimulating investment in training and business development.[9] As north-west London joined the TECs refusing participation in EA, the Employment Department expressed its intention of inviting neighbouring TECs to receive EA funding and to undertake the work of the recalcitrant TECs.[10] Once more the government had the capacity to prevail because of its control of the purse strings.

Yet the Employment Department was effectively undermining the policy which Howard had expressed earlier in the year, of encouraging the unemployed to look to the activities of the ES such as Jobclubs, rather than to training programmes. The news of cutbacks in government training programmes was revealed in February 1991 when detailed figures for the 1991–92 expenditure programmes were announced. ET particularly was affected with a cut from £1062 million in 1990–91 to £757 million in 1991–92, amid statements from the Secretary of State that ET was not the best way to assist the unemployed. This marked a major shift from the views of his predecessor, Sir Norman Fowler.[11] The Shadow Employment spokesman, Tony Blair, described the cuts as 'savage'.[12] The political pressures which followed led to the restoration by the government of £120 million of the £365 million cut.[13] Yet Eric Dancer, the leader of the Group of Ten) chairmen of TECs, pointed out that this returned money was merely a fraction of the earlier 30 per cent cut and so ET remained underfunded.[14] Even *The Economist* was critical and pointed out that the ET cutbacks would have major effects.

The businessmen who dominate the TECs are usually more interested in solving the skills shortage than in running a chunk of the welfare state. And even the most tender-hearted among them have a huge incentive to cream off the most easily-trained jobless: a quarter of TECs income will be related to the getting of qualifications . . . Training cuts will not only ensure that most unemployed people will remain unemployable. They will also scupper the government's attempts to cut the size of the prison population. The Department of Employment once put it rather well: 'If you think training is expensive, try ignorance'.[15]

Worried by such arguments the Employment minister began to shift his position and to criticize the TECs for neglecting the needs of the long-term unemployed. As the possibility of a November general election then loomed the government was becoming concerned about the electoral fallout of rising unemployment, which explains why it soon unveiled the EA scheme.

The position of YT was also adversely affected during 1991 although the recession, and the effects that it had upon the capacity of employers to provide placements, combined to put the government's training guarantees in jeopardy. In July Sainsbury's ceased the provision of YT placements, as the recession led them instead to extend the employee status version of YT to its own workers.[16] A month later the Humberside TEC complained that the recession was leading to fewer employers offering YT placements.[17] By November evidence from 60 TECs showed that 32 of them were unable to carry out their contractual obligation with the government to provide a YT place to all 18 to 24-year olds out of work for more than six months, but less than a year. In Manchester, for example, between 1,200 and 2,000 young people were likely to be denied a place before Christmas. Nor was the recession the sole reason, as shortage of public funding was also responsible. The YT budget fell from £1.2 billion in 1988 to £833 million between 1990 and 1991. The situation was serious, therefore, even if David Mellor's leaked letter about £100 million of cuts was merely part of a haggle over spending rises. The combined effect of inadequate funding and the fall in the supply in the number of employers prepared to provide the work placements that are supposed to be an important element in YT activity led TECs so to concentrate their work upon meeting guarantees that they had to wind down their efforts to stimulate business and in-work training. A representative comment from the TEC world was that of Ron Evans, head of training and education for the North-West Wales TEC, who asserted that, 'we are seeing an erosion in both quality and quantity and a total lack of investment by providers'.[18]

The government clearly adhered firmly to its position of encouraging employers and employees to respond to market pressures and to invest in training, and concentrated its own efforts on enticements rather than further direct funding. The 1991 Budget introduced a tax advantage, so that those on training courses received a 25 per cent discount on their fees, simply by deducting and retaining the basic rate tax from the fee charged. Training providers can then claim the tax back from the Inland Revenue. Yet the verdict of industry and the training bodies was that the tax concession was not ambitious enough and should have been extended to books, equipment and travel.[19]

Employer Investment in Training

The extent to which employers can be encouraged to invest in the training and human resource development of their own workforce is the ultimate litmus test for the effectiveness of government policy, and so far the evidence appears inconclusive. The CBI's training officer is convinced by the encouraging data which his organisation has produced in its *Quarterly Survey of Industrial Trends*. The data repeatedly shows an excess of employers intending to increase their investment in training over those who predict a reduction of expenditure, as well as revealing that there has been a 50 per cent increase in the numbers of employees who report that they have undergone training in the recent past.[20] The CBI also points to Employment Department research undertaken between February and May 1991, in a survey of 4,000 employers, which demonstrates that 92 per cent of the respondents reported that training investment was then at the same or at a higher level than in the previous year, and 66 per cent were operating training plans as compared to 60 per cent in 1990.[21] The government's view is similar, with the permanent secretary at the Employment Department confidently asserting that this is the first economic recession when employer investment in training has been maintained.[22] The DE's own labour force survey reported in October that while the percentage of employers intending to spend more on training fell from 40 per cent in April to 26 per cent in October, that still constituted a higher figure than the 21 per cent who intend to spend less.

Yet a quite different interpretation is also possible. First, the evidence is sparse and is based upon survey samples which themselves deal with intentions rather than quantification of expenditure undertaken. Second, there is anecdotal evidence that small and medium-sized firms are not investing on the same scale as the bigger firms, and that the TEC boards, which are composed of chief executives of large firms, are unable to provide role models for the smaller employing organizations. Stronger evidence to counter CBI and government confidence can also be cited. First, Ken Mayhew of the National Economic Development Office (NEDO) urged that the TECs should be allowed to impose training levies on companies, so as to *require* a specified amount of training. He argued that undertraining resulted from 'line managers' making decisions and because training was not fully integrated into general company planning.[23] Also the report of the Industrial Society, *Training in the Workplace*, suggested that the growing interest of employees in training was unmatched by employers. Rhiannon Chapman said that many companies took the view, despite their recognition of the importance of the National Vocational

Qualifications (NVQ) initiative, that the old approach would suffice. In recessionary times companies were tending to cut out external training providers first, and then to ignore the needs of mature blue-collar workers in the interests of training new and younger workers.[24] It is apparent that more evidence, impartially interpreted according to the canons of policy analysis, is required, and that it will take several years before it is clear whether or not there has been a true training revolution. There are many close to the centres of policy-making, however, who are sceptical about the rhetoric of the training revolution and of a great leap forward, because of the difficulty of reconciling what needs to be done with the government's non-interventionist approach. It is not just the opposition political parties, therefore, who continue to advocate various forms of compulsion by means of a training tax or levy.

The Employment Department published a report which reveals a clear perception of how it wishes to secure further improvements in employer investment in training. The proposals range from the government's inspirational role as a very large employer, the use of forums such as the National Economic Development Council, measures to stimulate the provision of market intelligence, and the department's mediation of employers' views of what they need from the education system through its increased leverage over the FE system. But primarily the 'TEC initiative is our main instrument for further encouraging employers to train'.[25]

The TEC Initiative

The TEC network was completed in 1991, ahead of schedule, with all 82 fully operational. The theory underpinning the local organization of training orientated to the perceived needs of employers in specific labour markets, formally dated back to the December 1988 white paper, *Employment in the 1990s*. Yet the idea was implied as early as 1984 in the *Competence and Competition* report, and it was piloted by the co-operative work locally of Chambers of Commerce in the emergence of the Local Employer Networks (LENs) after 1985. Certainly, an employer-led local labour market-based system of organizing the delivery of training and capable of replacing the 'tripartite' quango of the MSC was bound to appeal to the Thatcher Conservative government. The new Prime Minister, John Major, continued to promote the cause of the TECs in 1991, and he hinted at an increased role as well as expressing sympathy for their impatience of government supervision.[26] The Labour Opposition also are converted to the TEC cause, despite the Scottish TUC's decision to refuse to co-operate with their more powerful counterparts in Scotland, the Local Enterprise Councils (LECs). Certainly the LECs have a wider remit which adds to training responsibilities a whole range of enterprise and economic development duties.[27] While indicating that trades union representation may be more substantial on TEC boards under a Labour government, the Shadow Employment spokesperson, Tony Blair, expressed his commitment to the retention of TECs.[28] The TECs did not enjoy an untroubled year, however, and their ambiguous relationship to the Employment Department and the Treasury remains unresolved. In 1990 the disquiet felt by many TEC leaders had led to the establishment of the Group of Ten (G10) to negotiate with the Secretary of State.

Theoretically, the TEC arrangement could work well with the Employment Department laying down strategic guidance on VET which the TECs could implement in various ways according to local need. The guidelines are essentially those outlined in *The Skills Decade*, which the department published in October 1990. Government is committed to providing national standards of excellence through NVQ, National Training Awards and the new Investors in People kitemark. Employers are to establish incentives and pay structures to reward training. Individuals should learn the merits of self-investment and TECs are to implement the strategy by encouraging company training provision. TECs are particularly charged with creating market-led solutions, so that education and training is relevant to the local economy. The entire document is redolent of a limited government, market-based approach to training policy. Yet TECs increasingly felt as the year developed that they were underfunded and subject to a great degree of supervision and constraint by government. The year began badly when Judith Donovan, chairwoman of the Bradford TEC and the only woman on G10, resigned from the group because she was tired of 'the cosy male atmosphere' which existed between G10 and government. 'She had been sickened by the fact that meetings of G10 convened before they saw ministers expressed strong views, only to be diluted when they saw the Secretary of State.'[29] Partly to counter this bad publicity the government launched an advertising campaign in spring 1991 costing £10 million to turn the TECs into a household acronym. The TECs enjoy a certain flexibility in tailoring national schemes and the new credit system to local needs and are encouraged to engage in flexible targeting on the basis of local labour-market intelligence. Yet their role and relationships are somewhat confining.

TECs operate under the corporate plan that they negotiate with government. The problem for the TECs is that they only receive government funding for a year at a time. This annual system of funding makes the TECs particularly vulnerable to the vagaries of the public expenditure round and creates difficulties for their agencies and for their own capacity to plan their affairs. The Labour Party is pledged to exempt the TECs from the normal rigours of annuality, in order to provide funds for three-year planning periods. This pledge emanated both from the party's training spokesman as well as from the party leader Neil Kinnock in a meeting with G10 chairs.[30] Yet this issue, which has still not been resolved to the satisfaction of the TECs, is merely a symptom of the problem, that TECs are (they protest) not allowed, owing to the problems of financial accountability and bureaucratic rules, to introduce appropriate private sector methods into their operations. On one occasion the permanent secretary of the Employment Department, Sir Geoffrey Holland, appeared to join them, when it was revealed in a leaked departmental document that unless the TECs were funded so that they could properly carry out government guarantees to the unemployed, then the whole credibility of the TEC movement would suffer.

By the spring, the resentment of the TECs reached the point where Michael Howard commissioned a study to investigate the relationships between TECs and the department. The study was intended to clarify the roles of the competing parties. Yet the obstacles to overcoming the tensions between government and TECs are, in the words of a further leaked memorandum, 'increasing rather than diminishing', since the 'present relationship is not sustainable'.[31]

The TECs are likely to survive and their responsibilities might increase. Their own main concern is with their discretionary power, however, and the government is unlikely to grant them any release from annual financial accountability.[32] There is also evidence that they have not overcome all of their bridge-building problems at a local level, with such interests as training organizations and Chambers of Commerce complaining that 'TECs consider themselves to be the only show in town'.[33] There are also complaints from such national organizations as the Print Federation and Sainsbury's about the difficulty of negotiating with 82 different TECs, which is scarcely mitigated by the limited central-brokerage system performed by the Central Providers Unit which attempts to facilitate a standard operating agreement.[34] The TECs have a further problem in that the National Audit Office criticized their poor spending controls, which resulted in the misappropriation of £47 million intended for ET and YT, because the inadequate auditing of accounts allowed money to be improperly paid to trainees and firms.[35]

Some mention should also be made of the further powers which government has given to the National Training Task Force (NTTF), partly as a result of criticisms that the TECs left out the national dimension in policy. The NTTF, chaired by Bryan Woolfson, and dominated by businessmen, has a strategic responsibility in advising the Secretary of State, assessing TEC performance against local and national objectives and overseeing the implementation of the Investors in People (IiP) initiative. Howard looks to the NTTF 'to ensure that standards are universally and rigorously applied so that IiP is recognized as a national symbol of excellence in employer training'.[36]

Training Credits

In November 1991 Michael Howard announced a new initiative for adult workers, particularly those with low skills, to give them assistance to improve their jobs under a £2 million a year scheme. The aim is to provide vouchers of £120 to be spent on professional careers counselling. While this is a pragmatic response to pressures from TECs to pump-prime projects to help adults to upgrade their skills, it also represents a 'U-turn', in the sense that government is willing to invest directly in the training of adults, rather than leaving it entirely to individual responsibility. Mr Howard argued that the scheme was compatible with the government policy of making individuals responsible for their own development. The Secretary of State claimed that a lower drop-out rate at work would ensue.[37] While the idea of credits was not an original one in 1991, since it had been gestating in new-right publications and 'think-tanks' for years and had specifically been proposed for young people by the CBI in its 1989 document *Towards a Skills Revolution*, it was in the government white paper of summer 1991, *Education and Training for the 21st Century*, that the intention to universalize what had previously been a narrow pilot scheme became apparent.

The white paper asserted that training credits would stimulate young people to train to higher levels, and defined a credit as a 'voucher showing a money value, typically at least £1,000, put in the hands of young people leaving full-time education . . . It entitles them to vocational education and training, and buys them the opportunity to qualify with a National Vocational Qualification at NVQ Level 2 (or its equivalent) or higher'.[38] It is significant that the white paper referred to credits as enhancing 'the market in training provision'. The extension of the youth credits scheme so soon after a pilot initiative had been introduced, and before it could be effectively evaluated by anything more than anecdotal evidence, was the result of its ideological consistency with market principles. A further round of applications was invited to extend the principle further and 31 TECs have been awarded the opportunity to do so. There were opponents on some TEC boards, but they were defeated by the attractions of the funding that would accrue and by an enthusiastic commitment by most Board members to the empowerment of young people through credits. The successful TECs have the opportunity to grant vouchers up to the value of £5,000 from April 1993.

Employment Policy

The two main trends in employment policy in 1991 were the substantial growth in recession-related unemployment and the development of the Employment Service (ES) as an independent Next Steps agency.

Unemployment

The slowdown of the labour market became marked in 1991 and the signs at the end of the year are that unemployment will continue to rise even after the 1990–91 recession technically ends. The recession of 1980–81 led to ever-increasing unemployment until 1986. Since the 1990–91 recession has affected the service sector of the economy at least as much as manufacturing, however, it is possible that the 'lagged' effect upon unemployment will be less, since it is easier to reopen a shop than a foundry. The predictions for unemployment at the end of 1991 varied from a peak of 3 million in 1993 to 3.25 million in 1994. The growth in unemployment presents a bleak picture, although Michael Howard claimed that the figures for October, in which the month's rise in seasonally adjusted unemployment was the smallest since September 1990, 'confirmed that the recession was ending'.[39] In the same bullish vein the Employment Department commented that most regions experienced small rises and that female unemployment fell for the first time since September 1990. Equally, the number of 'new vacancies notified to Jobcentres and the number of people placed into jobs by the Employment Service rose in October for the second month running'.[40] Certainly the number of available vacancies has historically been the best guide to unemployment trends.

The fact remains, however, with 2,472,900 unemployed at a rate of 8.7 per cent of the workforce, that the figure was continuing to increase at the year's end. The figure in January 1990 was 1,704,800, a rate of 6.7 per cent of the workforce, and the increase had continued for two years. The Unemployment Unit's figure shows the October 1991 total to be 3,549,700.[41] The unit exists to campaign for full employment and to secure better benefits and training for unemployed people. It engages in its own research programmes, however, and its 'alternative' index measures the broader levels of unemployment by estimating the figures on a pre-1982 basis and by taking account of the 30 changes in the compilation of figures which have occurred since 1979. It also estimates that the Exchequer cost of unemployment has risen to £8,900 for every out of work benefit claimant, and this excludes indirect social and personal costs.[42] Another perspective on this otherwise gloomy picture is that the British workforce in employment, at 25.6 million in September 1991, was 2.6 million higher than when the upward trend in employment began in 1983.[43]

Yet the composition of the workforce continued to change in 1991, if mainly by an acceleration of trends which began back in the 1970s. Service sector employment continued to displace manufacturing industry, and the decline in the number of young school leavers was compensated for by the increased participation in the labour force by women. The Employment Department projects that by the year 2001 women of working age are likely to comprise 44 per cent (12.4 million) of the total labour force.[44] The government is implicitly acknowledging its own misperceptions, as well as those of organizations such as the CBI, when in the late 1980s there was concern about a demographic time-bomb and resultant labour shortages in the 1990s. The perception has been undermined by the recession coupled with the rise in the size of all age groups over 25 and the increased propensity of women to return to the labour market. It is also evident that there is under-utilized talent in the ethnic minority population.

A surprising characteristic of the 1990–91 recession is that while affecting all regions, and continuing to undermine the manufacturing base of the economy, it has hit particularly hard in the service sector and the south-east of England, which were both relatively unscathed in earlier recessions. Yet the congestion and expense of developing manufacturing industry in London suggests that the best prospect for reducing unemployment in the London labour market remains with service industries. Yet even in the service sector, 'job opportunities for unskilled workers will continue to fall. In all areas the drive is to obtain greater value added from fewer workers. People with low levels of marketable skills will be increasingly disadvantaged as the decade progresses. They will be forced . . . into an alternating pattern of insecure, low paid work, spells on government schemes and unemployment'.[45]

The Employment Service (ES)

The ES experienced its second year of existence during 1991 as an integrated organization which unites the Jobcentre network and the unemployment benefit service. The chief executive, Mike Fogden, asserts that ES has raised standards of service, enhanced job satisfaction and obtained greater value for money. Despite the recession he draws satisfaction from the ES record of placing 1.4 million clients in employment, which represents only a slight fall from the previous year as well as achieving a £13 million, or 2 per cent efficiency gain. The ES also made progress in integrating Jobcentres and unemployment benefit offices under one roof to provide a 'one-stop' service to clients.[46] As an executive agency within the Employment Department the ES operates as a Next Steps agency, which is to say that its objectives are set by government, but it enjoys autonomy in the methods by which it uses its budgets and appoints its staff, and is monitored for its performance against objectives after a three-year period. While it has been suggested that the government was motivated by a desire to change conditions and remuneration for agency staff, most employees have noticed little alteration in their work to date.[47] Treasury officials are reported by Employment Department officials to be ambivalent on the issue since they are unsure about the financial consequences of independent pay negotiations for 37,000 employees.

The ES provides a wide range of services to the unemployed. These include advisory interviews to help the unemployed to get back to work quickly, the payment of unemployment benefit and income support on behalf of the Secretary of State for Social Security (DSS), job referral services, Jobsearch seminars and Job Review workshops. It can also provide additional help through Jobclubs, an ES programme to provide job hunting and interviewing advice, Restart courses, job interview guarantees and travel to interview schemes.[48]

The ES agreed an operational plan for 1991–92. Its targets included finding situations for 1.3 million clients, placing long-term claimants into at least 16 per cent (208,000) of total placements, unemployed people with disabilities into 2.4 per cent (31,200) and unemployed people in inner cities into 34 per cent (442,000). The plan also aimed at a referral to start ratio on ET of 25:1 and the achievement of the £19.2 million efficiency savings agreed by HM Treasury. The details of 91 per cent of new claims should be entered into the National Unemployment Benefit Service computer within six days of being made, and the total value of correct payments of unemployment benefit should be more than 95.5 per cent of the total value of payments.[49]

The ES's chief executive has a list of responsibilities to manage staff and budgets, but one of his responsibilities demonstrates the impossibility of cleanly separating policy-making and policy-implementation functions. He is required to 'contribute to the development of the Employment Department Group's top management cadre'.[50] In short, the chief executive has a direct input into the policy-formulation process *before* the Secretary of State receives policy advice. This is a rational recognition by the department that good policy implementation requires the participation of those charged with the execution of policy. The converse also applies, however, since because unemployment is such a high-profile issue ministers naturally retain a strong interest in the execution of policy.

The ES is committed to implementing the idea of the Citizen's Charter to ensure a quality service for its clients in line with the government white paper of July 1991 which introduced performance targets and complaints procedures.[51] This has been applied by the ES in a number of ways: for example, reducing waiting times for clients to see advisers, obtaining rapid responses to telephone enquiries, prompt and accurate payment of benefit and the wearing of badges by ES staff except where there is a threat to their safety. Like much of the Citizen's Charter there is great emphasis upon procedural improvements in service delivery, but no attention to such substantive issues as creating more jobs or rectifying incorrect decisions about benefit eligibility. The Unemployment Unit offers a searching critique of the changes. 'Unemployed people are not consumers, able to move elsewhere if they are unhappy with the quality of the service. They are legally obliged to sign on, attend regular compulsory interviews and show that they are available for and actively seeking work . . . Whilst compensation might be given to rail travellers whose journeys are disrupted, this principle will not be extended to benefit claimants whose weekly income can be denied them on the basis of "insufficient evidence".'[52] Compatibly with the fashionable emphasis upon quality assurance, the ES conducted a customer satisfaction survey in 1990/91. The evidence from the survey is ambiguous in detail although the ES can draw comfort from a high degree of satisfaction overall. Yet the Unemployment Unit justifiably points out that the survey does not raise such broader questions as what the unemployed might want from the public employment service.

It appears as if the Citizen's Charter approach to public service delivery is having a beneficial effect on the ES's work, and the face-to-face treatment of the unemployed is more sympathetic and the open plan offices in which it is occurring are pleasanter than before. Problems remain with the Next Steps agencies, however. First, the ES faces the same dilemma as the Secretary of State, in that both are praised or blamed according to the overall level of job opportunities or unemployment benefits, and yet neither determines policy on these matters owing to Treasury domination and other external factors which are beyond their control. Second, it is clear that Parliament is alarmed at aspects of agency operations. The Treasury and Civil Service committee which previously had given cross-party support to the initiative has become critical of the 'lack of strategic thinking and direction about the role of the civil service'. The concerns include the lack of accountability of the agencies to Parliament, problems in setting targets for the agencies and the lack of a national career civil service. The government accepts the need for consistent terminology in target-setting, but rejects a standardized vocabulary recommended by the committee, saying agency targets must reflect the specific nature of the tasks they perform. If Parliament is concerned about agency shortcomings, and particularly about the lack of Parliamentary accountability, then it is a major matter of concern because there are 55 agencies other than the ES, employing over 200,000 civil servants, and a further 32 are under consideration. By the end of 1993 the government intends to transfer all executive functions to agencies.[53]

Other Employment Issues

The government is persisting with the policy of maximum deregulation of the labour market, in order to free up the economy, so as to enhance profitability and create employment opportunities. This has been demonstrated by the draft framework of a new white paper on individuals in the labour market, and by attitudes towards the European Social Charter. The 'draft framework' of the white paper was approved by the Employment Secretary at the end of July, and it develops an under-noticed theme in the 1988 white paper *Employment in the 1990s*, that of the supercession of trades unions in the 1990s by individual negotiation between employers and workers. A leaked draft document on the white paper on individuals in the labour market, received by the Unemployment Unit, stresses the supremacy of the individual, wants pay to reflect individual skills and capacities, but also wants individuals to negotiate their own terms and conditions and to consult with employers directly rather than through the medium of unions, since individuals in the labour market cannot be treated as an undifferentiated mass with identical interests at work. The draft criticizes compulsory and regulatory approaches, particularly the minimum wage. After this criticism of the Labour Party's policy the draft also condemns the EC's approach as 'too inflexible and regulatory'.[54]

The Employment Department favours a single market within the European Community (EC) in which the social dimension should 'help almost 15.5 million unemployed people in the Community to find jobs'.[55] This does not require regulation of employment and social issues, as many of Europe's employers recognize. The solution lies in recognizing the principle of subsidiarity, so as to allow each country to pursue its own strategy towards employment legislation and employee rights. But the British government is adamant that the regulations and burdens placed upon employers by an over-interventionist social dimension will lead to increased unemployment.[56] This was one of John Major's 'bottom lines' at the Maastricht negotiations on closer union at the end of 1991.

Employment Policy-making

Most of the employment policies implemented during 1991 were the result of decisions taken in earlier years. Even the unexpectedly high unemployment rate was the result of economic and financial decisions taken by the government in the two years which surrounded the 1987 general election. But the persistence of unemployment thoroughly undermined the widespread platitudes about labour shortages in the 1990s which had been the conventional wisdom until the year began. In the training field it was only the decision to transform youth training credits from a small scale pilot project to universal national practice in the *Education and Training* white paper which challenged the normal incrementalist style of British policy-making. There were two reasons for the Secretary of State's cursory dismissal of the canons of rational policy analysis. First, while credits demonstrated to ideologically committed Conservative supporters that market principles still prevailed, they also appeared to be a dramatic attempt to address the training and youth unemployment crisis in a manner likely to appeal to the mass of the electorate. There is also evidence that the government was persuaded by a CBI analysis which revealed that credits would cost the Exchequer no more than the YT scheme which it would replace. Finally, there is evidence from the activities of the G10 group of TEC chairs, the NTTF and the CBI, which is back in from the relative 'cold' of the Thatcher years, of the emergence of a close-knit, consensual, single-interest (business) and interactive training-policy community. Training is a major issue which involves many interests in a loose issue network, but it is evident that those groups which share the Employment Department's agenda and priorities enjoy a privileged access. It is also apparent, however, that the relationship is asymmetrical. It is the Employment Department and the Treasury which possess the greater resources of power.

Notes

1 Brendan Evans, 'Employment Policy' in P. Catterall (ed.) *Contemporary Britain: An Annual Review*, Blackwell, 1991, p 315.
2 *The Financial Times*, 25 March 1991.
3 CBI World Class Targets, press release, June 1991, paragraph 2.
4 Ibid. paragraphs 10–14.
5 Ibid. paragraphs 44–51.
6 *The Financial Times*, 7 November 1991.
7 *The Financial Times*, 12 September 1991.
8 House of Commons Employment Committee, *Training and Enterprise Councils*, Fifth Report, vol.1, HMSO, 1991.
9 *The Financial Times*, 23 August 1991.
10 TEC officials in conversation.
11 *The Financial Times*, 6 February 1991.
12 *The Guardian*, 7 February 1991.
13 *The Guardian*, 16 March 1991.
14 *The Independent*, 1 March 1991.
15 *The Economist*, 6 April 1991.
16 *The Financial Times*, 3 July 1991.
17 *The Financial Times*, 2 August 1991.
18 *The Guardian*, 4 November 1991.
19 *The Observer*, 24 March 1991.
20 CBI Training Officer in conversation with the author.
21 *Labour Market Quarterly Report*, November 1991, pp.5- 6.
22 Sir Geoffrey Holland at Huddersfield Polytechnic, 23 October 1991.
23 *Financial Times*, 4 April 1991.
24 *Ibid.* 17 June 1991

25 'Employers Investment in Training'. Note by Training Strategy and Secretariat Branch, Director General's Board, OGB/91/43, 1991.
26 *Training Briefing*, Employment Department Library, Moorfoot, Sheffield.
27 *The Guardian*, 9 January 1991.
28 *The Financial Times*, 16 April 1991.
29 *The Independent*, 9 January 1991.
30 *The Financial Times*, 25 October 1991.
31 *The Financial Times*, 19 July 1991.
32 Views of TEC officials in conversation.
33 *The Financial Times*, 18 July 1991.
34 CBI Training Officer in conversation.
35 *The Guardian*, 7 November 1991.
36 Employment Department, Press Notice, 11 April 1991.
37 *The Financial Times*, 12 November 1991.
38 *Education and Training in the 21st Century*, London, HMSO, 1991, 6.4-6.6.
39 Employment Department, Press Release, 14 November 1991.
40 Ibid.
41 Unemployment Unit Course Notes, 1991, p.28.
42 Unemployment Unit, October 1991, p.1.
43 Employment Department Press Notice, 14 November 1991.
44 *Labour Market Quarterly Report*, Employment Department, November 1991, p.1.
45 Unemployment Unit, *Unemployment and Changing Labour Market*, 1991, p.28.
46 Employment Service, *Annual Report and Accounts, 1990/91*, Foreword.
47 Staff in conversation with the author.
48 *The Employment Service: An Introduction to its Services.*
49 *Employment Service Operational Plan, 1991/92*, pp.7-9.
50 *Employment Service: A Framework Document for the Agency*, 7.2.
51 *The Citizen's Charter*, HMSO, 1991, p.20.
52 Unemployment Unit, *Working Brief*, November 1991, p.3.
53 *The Financial Times*, 12 November 1991.
54 Unemployment Unit, *Working Brief*, November 1991, pp.1-2.
55 The United Kingdom in Europe, People, Jobs and Progress, Fact Pack on the European Commission's Proposals, Fact Sheet 1.
56 Ibid. Fact Sheets, 9-16.

Chronology

7 Jan: NEDO report points out the lack of pay differentials for skilled men compared with Germany and argues that they need to be widened. A report by Karin Wagner of the Technical University in Berlin points to the lower qualifications of British workers compared with Germany and France.

8 Jan: Judith Donovan resigns from the G10 committee of TEC chairmen and government in disgust at the 'cosy male atmosphere'.

17 Jan: Seasonally-adjusted unemployment in December rose by 80,400 to 1.844 million.

21 Jan: *Can TECs cope with Recession?*, Employment Institute, finds lack of commitment to training amongst the companies of TEC chairmen.

31 Jan: *Britain in 2010*, PSI, predicts a fall in unemployment in a tighter job market and some rise in the labour force in the manufacturing sector as a result of new high-technology industries by 2010.

5 Feb: Government confirms that there will be substantial expenditure cuts in both Youth Training and Employment Training.

14 Feb: Seasonally-adjusted unemployment rose in January to 1.89 million.

26 Feb: £120 million increase in funding for adult training announced.

4 Mar: TEC leaders are to set up their own secretariat, independent of the government.

11 Mar: Philip Virgo, *Training for Jobs: Not Jobs for Trainers*, Bow Group, suggests that training costs should be treated as a loan to trainees. Employees on recognized training schemes should be made exempt from national insurance and the problem of poaching should be dealt with by introducing training contracts involving financial penalties for those who leave their companies. Child and family care expenses should be made tax deductible and it should be possible to offset personal spending on training against tax. There should be generous tax relief for corporate donations for education and research and a more interventionist government approach to TECs and industry training organizations.

14 Mar: Seasonally-adjusted unemployment in February rose to 2.045 million.

1 Apr: Payments under the Enterprise Allowance Scheme to encourage unemployed people to set up their own businesses are increased from £40 to £90 per week.

5 Apr: Ken Mayhew of NEDO calls for compulsory training levy on employers.

10 Apr: National Training Task Force is divided into three groups, the most important of which will attempt to evolve a national strategy on training, whilst another will monitor the efforts of the TECs.

18 Apr: Seasonally adjusted unemployment rose in March by 112,900, the largest monthly increase since current records began in 1971, to 2,092,900.

25 Apr: Roy Hattersley commits Labour to full employment.

26 Apr: *A New Policy Framework for Unemployed Adults*, Full Employment UK, urges the introduction of a US style workfare system compelling those unemployed for more than a year to work on a community benefit programme in order to obtain benefit. It also outlines alternatives to Employment Training.

15 May: More than half the 66,000 training places for the unemployed provided by charities and voluntary organizations have been axed because of government cuts according to a study by the National Council for Voluntary Organizations.

16 May: Seasonally-adjusted unemployment rises to 2,175,000.

20 May: *Education and Training for the 21st Century*, HMSO, proposes that within the life of the next parliament every 16 and 17-year old should be offered a training credit of £1,000 for them to buy vocational or educational training from the provider they choose. Two new diplomas are aimed at ending the academic/vocational divide. Sixth forms will be able to admit part-time students and adults and to charge fees. Further education and sixth form colleges will become autonomous institutions.

24 May: Employment Institute report argues that the concentration of redundancy schemes at the upper ends of the age range is damaging the economy, with many skilled workers never returning to work.

28 May: NIESR report argues that training emphasis is being directed at the wrong levels and that the situation at the crucial craft level is actually worse than ten years ago.

Leaked document from TEED in which Sir Geoffrey Holland says that the reputation of TECs and the government depends on more being done to assist the unemployed.

29 May: John Ermisch in the NIESR review criticizes the social charter as unnecessary as transnational labour mobility in Europe is low anyway and it is much better and fairer to decide social benefits for labour at the national level.

4 June: *Training: Negotiating the New Agenda*, GMB, is the first sign of trade unions grasping that high wages for young people deters training.

6 June: Study announced by the Secretary of State into TEED and G10 relationships.

13 June: Seasonally-adjusted unemployment rose to 2.244 million in May.

17 June: According to a Institute of Manpower Studies report self-employment rose from 7.5 per cent to 12.2 per cent of the workforce in the 1980s.

19 June: Announcement of new 60,000 place Employment Action scheme providing work experience on local projects.

8 July: Report by Coopers and Lybrand Deloitte draws attention to an increasing gulf between government and the TECs.

Vacancies for graduates have fallen by 20 per cent since a year ago and starting salaries are rising only slowly according to a survey by the Association of Graduate Recruiters.

11 July: TUC threatens to boycott a training initiative to promote national vocational qualifications because it says the CBI has watered down the programme.

18 July: Seasonally-adjusted unemployment in June rose to 2.3 million.

25 July: Government, CBI and TUC set new training targets for 1997 of four out of every five young people having four GCSEs or NVQ equivalents, and of 50 per cent of young people achieving two A level passes or their NVQ equivalents by 2000. They also aim to restructure education and training to develop self-reliance and flexibility as well as skills, provide training and development for all employees by 1996, use the new NVQ system for half the training provided for the workforce by 1996 and create a new Investors in People award for companies achieving set minimum standards of training.

29 July: Institute of Personnel Management suggests statutory transfer fees and training contracts to discourage the poaching of trained staff.

31 July: Investors in People initiative to be administered centrally by NITF and the Employment Department rather than by the TECs.

5 Aug: Survey by BDO Binder Hamlyn argues companies assess training in terms of costs and courses rather than in terms of meeting business needs.

Institute of Public Policy is critical of the performance of all the Next Steps agencies, including the Employment Service.

15 Aug: Seasonally-adjusted unemployment rises to 2.368 million.

20 Aug: Employment Select Committee criticizes the lack of a mandatory training element in Employment Action, the government's temporary work scheme. It also calls for an urgent review of whether the guarantee of a place on Youth Training for all school leavers is being fulfilled.

23 Aug: North Derbyshire TEC joins those of Leeds and Sheffield in refusing to participate in Employment Action.

27 Aug: Training, Industry and Commerce Company, which took over four privatized skills centre in 1990, goes into liquidation.

12 Sept: Seasonally-adjusted unemployment rose in August to 2.43 million.

TECs are expected to be asked to undertake EA work for neighbouring TECs which refuse to participate.

22 Sept: *Paying for Skills*, Norfolk and Waveney TEC, finds that relatively small charges are discouraging people from taking up training. Nevertheless 60 per cent of adult training is financed by the individuals themselves.

24 Sept: Leaked memorandum from David Mellor, Chief Secretary to the Treasury, provokes concern about cuts in Employment Training.

25 Sept: *Performance and Potential: Education and Training for a Market Economy*, Institute of Directors, urges the introduction of a right for schoolleavers to day-release in the first couple of years in work, tax relief for adults wishing to retrain, the designation of master workers in companies responsible for in-house training on the German model, more vocational subjects in the National Curriculum and the acceleration of the opting-out of schools.

30 Sept: Prime Minister hints at increased role for TECs.

17 Oct: Seasonally-adjusted unemployment rose in September to 2.46 million.

The first 28 Investors in People awards are granted.

23 Oct: PSI report on policies to combat unemployment suggests increased statutory notice periods, programmes to encourage part-time jobs and self-employment, priority training for the least qualified, income support which does not prevent casual work and lifetime training credits for adults.

25 Oct: Neil Kinnock tells TEC chairs that under a Labour government they will receive triennial funding.

28 Oct: Labour Force Survey shows 15.4 per cent of employees received training in the previous week, as opposed to 9.1 per cent in 1984.

29 Oct: Opportunity 2000 to promote women in the owrkplace launched.

7 Nov: National Audit Office finds more than £100 million training money has been misspent by the Employment Department.

12 Nov: Michael Howard announces a government U-turn on training for adults by offering vouchers to unemployed adults for up to £2 million per year.

14 Nov: Seasonally-adjusted unemployment rose to 2.472 million in October.

19 Nov: Long-term unemployment (people out of work for more than a year) reached 654,000 in October, up 146,000 on a year earlier.

3 Dec: Concern is expressed at the possible precedent the suggestion that the Treasury is considering payments of £50,000 to civil servants made redundant by privatized Skill Centres might make.

19 Dec: Seasonally-adjusted unemployment rose in November to 2.513 million.

Personal Social Services

SAUL BECKER

The 1980s marked the discovery of poverty's impact on the work of personal social services.[1] By 1991, this realization had transformed itself into professional concern and anxiety. On a daily basis social workers witnessed the harsh realities and destructive consequences of widespread material and financial deprivation. But as far as popular consciousness was concerned, poverty remained invisible and hidden from public view; a private pain rather than a public issue. In September, however, poverty briefly materialized as a cause for wider concern, as rioting spilled out on to the streets of Newcastle, and the debate was opened once more, not least by the Archbishop of Canterbury, as to the links between social deprivation and wrongdoing.[2]

Social Work and Poverty

There is no doubt that poverty increased dramatically during the 1980s. Taking one proxy measure – the number of people living below half average income – by 1988 (the latest year for which figures are available), just under 12 million people or 22 per cent of the population could be said to be in poverty. This was a rise from just under 5 million in 1979. Other measures show a similar pattern: the numbers of people living on or below supplementary benefit (now income support) during the same period rose from 6 per cent of the population to 19 per cent; the number of people unable to afford at least three basic necessities (such as an indoor toilet or damp-free accommodation) also rose to one in five of the population.[3]

Personal social services have always been services for poor people. That is not to say that the better off don't use these services – they clearly do – but some personal social services are used far more by people on low incomes. Nine out of ten users of social work services are claimants of social security benefits and the majority of new referrals to social workers are concerned with financial and benefit-related problems.[4] More and more people are becoming social work clients simply because they are poor. Some of these people choose to make use of personal social services. Others are reluctant or even hostile clients. This is perhaps more clearly shown in social work interventions into cases of child abuse and neglect – a growth area of activity in 1991 – and one which continued to dominate the headlines of the popular press and professional journals alike.

The Abuse of Children

On both sides of the Atlantic there has been a growth of interest, professional and academic, about the associations between child abuse, receptions into care and financial poverty. About one quarter of all children born in the United Kingdom are now born into poverty.[5] Research in this country has shown that 'debts, marital discord and unemployment are most commonly cited by parents as triggers which preceded the abuse of children',[6] while American studies[7] have reported significant correlations between local rates of unemployment and the number of cases of physical child abuse seen by child protection teams. Similarly, Holman[8] and others[9] have shown how, for some families, financial poverty creates barriers for the achievement of accepted child care objectives, and precipitates children being taken away from parents and being brought into care. The message from these studies is stark: almost all the children brought into care, for whatever reason, are children of the poor.

Many of these children are not necessarily protected in care either. Throughout Great Britain there were a number of residential child care scandals in 1991. These included 'pindown' in Staffordshire, Brock Youth Centre in central Scotland, Ty Mawr in Gwent and the Frank Beck case in Leicestershire. What all these had in common was the alleged physical or sexual abuse of vulnerable children by their social work carers, often under the cover of treatment and care ('pindown' in Staffordshire, 'regression therapy' in Leicestershire). The Frank Beck affair was perhaps the most frightening. For more than a decade Beck sexually and physically abused many children in his care, and some of the social workers employed in his children's homes. Following a ten week trial and after being found guilty of 17 charges of abuse – including buggery, rape, indecent assault and actual bodily harm – Beck was sentenced in November to five life terms plus 24 years.

These and other horrors led to the establishment in 1991 of a number of official child care reviews. In May, a report by Allan Levy QC and Barbara Kahan dissected the pindown saga and the inadequacy of Staffordshire's management techniques.[10] A review of residential child care facilities, chaired by Sir William Utting, reported in August.[11] It recommended a £30 million package to remedy training deficiencies. It also proposed that all heads of children's homes must be appropriately qualified by 1995; that one third of staff should be qualified by 1997; that care plans for children's services should be published and that all secure accommodation should be subject to the Secretary of State's approval. Additionally, Sir William wanted new powers for inspection units, so that any future incidents would be uncovered more quickly and effectively. Another inquiry, chaired by Lady Howe, is yet to report. Following the Beck case, the Health Secretary, William Waldegrave, announced another two separate inquiries. One, to be set up by Leicestershire County Council (similar to the Cleveland inquiry), would investigate how Beck was able to operate as he did between 1973 and 1986, despite at least four police investigations of his activities. The other inquiry, to be chaired by Mick Warner, former director of Kent social services department, would examine national procedures for the selection and appointment of staff in children's homes, and look at the support and guidance available. Additionally, the Warner inquiry will look at how treatment regimes such as pindown and regression therapy were brought into children's homes without adequate safeguards and monitoring.

Ritualistic Abuse: The Crucible Revisited

The debate about the etiology of child abuse took new forms as Satan continued to seize the headlines in 1991.[12] Yet more alleged incidents of 'ritualistic' and 'satanic' abuse were added to the ever growing repertoire of evils committed against children. Nineteen ninety-one saw the continuation of a furious existential battle of wills between social workers, the NSPCC, the police, the media and others, as to the reality, and definition of this emerging social problem. What was consistent in the reporting, however, but rarely noticed, was that many of the estates where these ritualistic or satanic abuses were alleged to have taken place were amongst the most deprived in the country. The Nottingham case, which generated numerous articles in the press, a number of documentaries and a wave of accusations and recriminations between the police and social services department, centred on the Broxtowe estate. Described by the media as 'a deprived area . . . a rundown estate of redbrick council houses',[13] Broxtowe ranked amongst the top three deprived areas in the county, on the council's own deprivation indicators.[14] The Langley estate in Rochdale, with its '12,000 inhabitants, boarded up shops, featureless houses, abandoned flats and disconsolate patches of dead greenery'[15] was described as a place 'where the poorest have to fight authority and sometimes fight each other to survive'.[16]

None of this media or professional concern focused on *why* these suspected ritualistic abuses were all allegedly taking place amongst the poorest families in the land. Such a discussion would require a penetrating analysis of the etiology of child abuse in its widest sense; the consideration of areas of broader socio-political significance, some of which are not directly child-related, such as unemployment, low incomes and substandard housing, as well as a traditional focus on individual cases and the selective application of individualized treatment methods. Informed discussion and analysis went into retreat. Attention turned away from the heated issue of the objective reality and definition of ritualistic abuse, to a more generalized and familiar attack on the unjustified interference of the state in domestic and family life. Naïve social workers with 'fevered imaginations',[17] dragging screaming children from their beds and from their parents in military-style dawn raids, were defined as the *real* social problem which required government action. And coverage also worked to discredit child witnesses, who were sometimes characterized in the press as 'dyslexic and retarded', who also had 'fevered imaginations'.[18] The message generated by this constant barrage of words and images was that social workers, the NSPCC and poor children could not be trusted to tell the truth. Complex individual and structural issues were reduced to the lowest common denominator – denial of any ritualistic or satanic problem and, literally, blaming the victims and social work professionals. In October 1991, guidelines on dealing with victims of suspected ritualistic abuse were issued to social workers, the police and charities by the Department of Health. These stressed the need for closer co-operation between all organizations working with children. Staff were told to keep an 'open mind' and, where ritualistic abuse is thought to exist, the timing of investigations must be agreed by all agencies involved – an attempt to stop the grosser excesses of dawn raids. In the same month, the Children Act was implemented – a landmark in the social welfare legislation for children and their parents, and discussed in some depth in the previous volume of *Contemporary Britain*.[19]

Cash and Care

Policy formulation and implementation in personal social services has generally ignored the single characteristic which most users of social work services have in common – dependency on social security benefits. Social workers and their departments have been uneasy about their role and responsibilities *vis à vis* people in poverty, and have never come to terms with policy and procedural issues around money, income maintenance and welfare rights. This is perhaps more surprising as many of the skills and techniques that are now the essence of professional social work were originally evolved within nineteenth century agencies such as the Charity Organization Society, for which the relief of poverty was a fundamental concern. Today, many social workers, their managers and educators, are reluctant to acknowledge the inescapably close professional contact they have with some of the poorest in society. In terms of public policy and social administration, this disjunction can be traced back to 1948, when an important distinction and division of responsibility was clarified. Policies of income maintenance were to be the responsibility of the central government, which would finance and administer nationwide programmes of social security. Meanwhile, there would be many people whose needs were of a different kind, not so much for *cash* as for *care*. Personal social services, as caring organizations, were to be organized, administered and delivered locally, responsive to the expressed wishes and assessed needs of the individual, and delivered by face-to-face contact between service provider and client. Professional social work, as it has evolved for the past 40 years, is deeply rooted in this local, decentralized and individualized perspective. Many social workers have distanced themselves from the material and cash problems of their clients, which, if they are acknowledged at all, are seen as the proper responsibility of other agencies, particularly the social security bureaucracies, or other specialists such as welfare rights advisers. But in 1988, coinciding with the major reforms of social security, and amidst a climate of fear and suspicion between agencies concerned with cash and care, many local authority social services and social work departments began monitoring the impact of the benefit changes on the operation of departments and the practice of social work.

The findings of a number of these projects became available in the final months of 1990 and early 1991.[20]

These studies reveal that personal social services are being inundated with pleas for help from people in poverty. As the gap between personal needs and income widens, many vulnerable people have turned to social workers for assistance, advice, advocacy and support. The 1988 social security reforms, and the introduction of the discretionary social fund in particular, have generated serious financial consequences for many claimants, who have turned in large numbers to social workers and charities for help. About one quarter of all financial-based problems confronted by social workers now directly relate to the social fund. This scheme replaced single payment grants available to supplementary benefit claimants with a cash-limited, and (most often) loan-based system of payments relying on the use of administrative discretion. It is perhaps the most controversial and criticized of the 'Fowler' reforms.

Cash and Community Care

Paradoxically, the reforms in social security and the introduction of the social fund, and the impact on personal social services and their users, have provoked new professional interest in the appropriate boundaries between personal social services and income maintenance. This concern has coincided with, and to some extent been precipitated by, recent developments in community care policy and legislation.[21] With the phased implementation of the legislation has come a flurry of activity in 1991, where professional social work advisers and the local authority associations have attempted to come to grips with the complex technical, policy and procedural considerations involved in the transfer of financial and income-maintenance responsibilities to social services and social work departments from the Department of Social Security.[22] For many years, directors of social services had rejected any attempts to blur the boundaries between cash and care, but in the initial community care bravado of 1989 and the belief that directors were to get more power and resources, many lost sight of the fact that finally and unequivocally, personal social services were to become income maintenance as well as care agencies. Issues of cash and care have now become inseparable in the brave new world of community care – with its emphasis on performance indicators and quality for money. But, as it has become increasingly apparent that resources are unlikely to be sufficient to provide a truly effective network of community care, social services departments have looked to strategies for maximizing their incomes and minimizing their costs. Issues of means testing and charging policies reared their ugly head.[23] Welfare rights, considered a maverick part of the social work task for most of the 1980s, became vaguely respectable in 1991, as departments saw the potential, for their clients and themselves, of income maximization and the pursuit of welfare rights.

This stemmed partly from a realization that most of the current and future users of community and residential care services are claimants of one social security benefit or another. It is women, most often living on benefits, who provide much of the formal and informal community care to other vulnerable people on benefits. There was growing concern, especially amongst welfare rights advisers to social services departments, that the reality of community care for most people would be that the poor, mostly women, would look after other poor people, and personal social services, as enabling authorities, would arrange it.

With a transfer of funds from the Department of Social Security to local authorities, and the financial battle lines being drawn between definitions of social care and health care,[24] local authorities increasingly looked for ways to maximize the incomes of those living in residential and community care, especially as part of those incomes would be put towards the costs of social care. Case managers with welfare rights expertise or support might be needed. One respected principal welfare rights adviser wrote, 'our expertise is being used to generate the income specifically so that it can be clawed back in part or full by the authority . . . but people use those benefits to supplement inadequate basic benefits . . . attendance allowance does not represent spare cash for care that the local authority can lay claim to'.[25] As personal social services move ever nearer to taking on cash *and* care responsibilities in 1993, the need for the profession to come to terms with complex issues of poverty and social divisions will become more critical, particularly for the poor users of social work services, and especially for their vulnerable children.

Notes

1 R. Lister, 'Poverty trap', *Insight*, 25 March 1988, p.15.

2 'Carey says riots linked to poverty', *The Guardian*, 20 September 1991.

3 J. Millar, 'Bearing the cost', in S. Becker (ed.), *Windows of Opportunity: Public Policy and the Poor*, Child Poverty Action Group, 1991, pp.23–37.

4 S. Becker and S. MacPherson, *Poor Clients: The Extent and Nature of Poverty amongst Consumers of Social Work Services*, Nottingham University, Benefits Research Unit, 1986.

5 J. Millar, op cit, p.27.

6 *Families Affected by Unemployment*, National Children's Homes, 1986.

7 See, for example, R. D. Krugman *et al*, 'The relationship between unemployment and physical abuse of children', *International Journal of Child Abuse and Neglect*, 10:3, 1986, pp.415–418.

8 R. Holman, *Inequality in Child Care*, Child Poverty Action Group/Family Rights Group, 1980.

9 See, for example, P. Hardiker and M. Barker, 'A window on child care, poverty and social work', in S. Becker and S. MacPherson (eds), *Public Issues, Private Pain: Poverty, Social Work and Social Policy*, Insight Books, 1988, pp.105–117.

10 A. Levy and B. Kahan, *The Pindown Experience and the Protection of Children. The Report of the Staffordshire Child Care Inquiry 1990*, Staffordshire County Council, 1991.

11 Department of Health, *Children in the Public Care: A Review of Residential Care*, HMSO, 1991.

12 See also A. Webb, 'Personal social services', in P. Catterall (ed.), *Contemporary Britain: An Annual Review 1991*, Blackwell, 1991, p.321.

13 *The Mail on Sunday*, 21 October 1990.

14 *Disadvantage in Nottinghamshire: County Deprived Area Study 1983–84*, Planning and Transportation Department, Nottinghamshire County Council, 1984.

15 'Children speared on the horns of a demonic dilemma', *The Sunday Times*, 30 September 1990.

16 'Hard man's rage turns to despair', *The Observer*, 16 September 1990.

17 *The Sunday Times*, 30 September 1990, op.cit.

18 *The Mail on Sunday*, 9 September 1990.

19 See A. Webb, op.cit.

20 See, for example, S. Becker and R. Silburn, *The New Poor Clients*, Reed Business Publishing/Community Care, 1990; Social Security Research Consortium, *Cash Limited, Limited Cash*, Association of Metropolitan Authorities, 1991.

21 See A. Webb, 'Personal social services', in P Catterall (ed.), *Contemporary Britain: An Annual Review 1990*, Blackwell, 1990, pp.314–328.

22 See, for example, *Community Care: Consultations over Funding and Related Matters*, Association of County Councils, circular, 30 October 1991.

23 See, for example, S. Balloch, 'Local authority charging policies', *Benefits*, issue 2, 1991, pp.40–41.

24 *Care in the Community: Definitions of Health and Social Care – Developing an Approach*, National Association of Health Authorities and Trusts, 1991.

25 G. Vaux, 'Charges and the rights brigade', *Benefits*, issue 2, 1991, pp.34-35.

Chronology

3 Jan: Cheshire County Council is to transfer its homes for the elderly to a newly formed trust which will mean that, unlike previously, their residents will each qualify for DSS income support payments of up to £155 per week.

17 Jan: *Living Dangerously: Risk-Taking, Safety and Older People*, Centre for Policy on Ageing, argues that welfare workers should not overprotect pensioners because half of them enjoy risky hobbies for a 'stimulating and satisfying life'.

30 Jan: *Not Such Private Places*, Counsel and Care, argues that elderly people in some institutional homes are regularly humiliated by a lack of privacy.

31 Jan: National Care Homes Association says that homes for elderly people are going bankrupt and residents may be evicted because state support is insufficient.

27 Feb: A number of children on the Orkneys are taken into care over allegations of ritual child abuse.

5 Mar: Hearing begins on the Orkney ritual abuse case.

7 Mar: Mr Justice Douglas Brown dismisses the ritual child abuse cases in Rochdale and condemns social work practice in the area.

8 Mar: Gordon Littlemore, director of Rochdale's social services, resigns.

11 Mar: Government to issue new guidelines on diagnosing and handling child abuse.

18 Mar: NSPCC repeats its view that ritual child abuse is widespread and launches a new helpline for adults concerned about abuse.

19 Mar: New guidelines are to be issued on the running of children's homes after a series of scandals.

4 Apr: Ritual abuse cases in Orkney collapse.

8 Apr: Police and social services launch a joint inquiry into allegations of ritual child abuse in Nottinghamshire.

9 Apr: Daphne Statham, director of the National Institute for Social Work, says social workers need a professional council along the lines of those for doctors and nurses. Measures to reform Scotland's children's panels in the wake of the Orkney child abuse case are called for by David Miller, the secretary to the Association of Reporters to the Children's Panel.

10 Apr: *Physical Signs of Sexual Abuse in Children,* Royal College of Physicians, advises that all health districts should have a special group of doctors prepared to examine children for signs of sexual abuse and seeks to lay down a national standard for examination procedure. It warns however that in two thirds of cases there will be no evidence that can be used.

12 Apr: DES announces measures to prevent child sex abuse in private schools in the wake of the gaoling of the headmaster, Ralph Morris.

16 Apr: Revised guidelines on fostering produced.

19 Apr: Judical inquiry into the Orkney child abuse case is announced.

22 Apr: Department of Health report finds police, social workers, health visitors and doctors are still failing to work together to prevent child abuse deaths.

6 May: Study for the International Bar Association criticizes UK authorities dealing with families trying to adopt children from abroad as racist and obstructive.

16 May: Government to set up new central agency to oversee the adoption of children from overseas.

24 May: TUC, *Charter for Carers,* suggests that working people caring for elderly or disabled relatives should be entitled to special leave or career breaks and flexible working, with part-timers receiving the same benefits as full-time staff. It also suggests the extension of Invalid Care Allowance to people caring for an adult for more than 35 hours a week.

25 May: Satanic abuse case collapses in Grampian.

27 May: National inquiry into residential child care demanded after allegations of multiple suicide attempts and abuse at Ty Mawr children's home, Abergavenny, Gwent.

28 May: Government inquiry into children's homes ordered, to be conducted by Sir William Utting.

30 May: Report by Allan Levy QC and Barbara Kahan on the 'pindown' regime followed in Staffordshire residential children's homes in 1988–89 condemns the damage and humiliation imposed by this system and recommends a strict logbook-keeping and complaints system, statutory visits without notice, a named person to be given responsibility for children's education, annual supervision and evaluation and a five year staff training strategy.

31 May: Welsh Office announces an inquiry into the management and control of children's homes in the Principality.
Local inquiry ordered into Brock Youth Centre, a children's home in Central Scotland, after allegations that it had been following a sort of pindown regime.

3 June: All social service departments ordered to check for evidence of abuses such as those uncovered by the Levy Report.

4 June: Review of children's homes in Scotland, to be carried out by Angus Skinner, ordered.

11 June: Stephen Hempling writes of alleged child ritual abuse in East Sussex in Child Abuse Review.

12 June: Appeal against the dismissal of the Orkney child abuse hearings in April is upheld in the Court of Sessions in Edinburgh.

Rooftop protest at Ty Mawr residential children's home in Gwent.

17 June: Report by Calouste Gulbenkian Foundation argues the need for a special children's commissioner to oversee children's welfare.

24 June: Major improvements in the quality of training of residential childcare staff are urged by Sir William Utting, the Chief Inspector of Social Services.

25 June: Langton House, a private nursing home in Dorset, is to close after concern is expressed by the Mental Health Act Commission.

27 June: A legal loophole that allows local authorities to privatize old people's homes so that fees are paid by the DSS is to be closed.

8 July: *No Place like Home*, NALGO, details neglect and abuse in private old people's homes.

12 July: A private old people's home is closed in West Sussex after its licence is revoked because of low standards of care and safety.

17 July: Health Select Committee, *Public Expenditure on Personal Social Services: Child Protection Services*, HMSO, argues that children's social services are underfunded.

18 July: Naomi Pfeffer and Anna Coote, *Is Quality good for you?*, IPPR, argues for a range of policies in welfare services, involving a mixture of consumer choice, regulation and effective local democracy.

22 July: Association of Directors of Social Services says a shortage of social workers is jeopardizing children at risk of abuse.

24 July: *Equal Shares in Caring*, Socialist Health Association/Ruskin College, criticizes employers and unions for a lack of understanding of the needs of employees who also care for elderly or disabled relatives.

25 July: New rules for the conduct of local authority children's homes are published, but inspection is still not to be made mandatory.

1 Aug: Inquiry on pay and standards and conditions for residential care workers chaired by Lady Howe begins.

20 Aug: *Children in the Public Care: A Review of Residential Child Care*, HMSO (chaired by Sir William Utting), recommends £30 million programme to remedy training deficiencies, that all heads of children's homes must be appropriately qualified by 1995 and one third of the staff by 1997, the publication of care plans for children's services, that all secure accommodation should be subject to the Secretary of State's approval, and new powers for the new inspection units.

21 Aug: Report by Arthritis Care/RADAR argues that some councils are ignoring their legal obligation to provide home help for elderly and disabled people whilst others are wrongly charging for the service.

29 Aug: *Children First*, Association of Metropolitan Authorities, calls for greater co-ordination at local and central government levels between health, education and social services.

11 Sept: Peter Newell, *The UN Convention and Children's Rights in the UK*, National Children's Bureau, examines Britain's apparent shortcomings against the 1989 UN Convention on the Rights of the Child, which Britain has yet to ratify.

4 Oct: Department of Health report condemns unacceptable standards and incidents of abuse in Sheffield's children's homes.

8 Oct: Inquiry into children's homes in Bradford finds instances of prostitution, sex abuse, attempted suicide and generally poor accommodation.

12 Oct: Children's Act comes into effect.

15 Oct: *Blind and Partially Sighted Adults in Britain: The RNIB Survey Vol. One*, HMSO, shows that blind people are poorly served by social service departments and isolated and under-supported in the community. Many are in poverty and experience discrimination in the labour market.

25 Oct: First social services official in Staffordshire sacked in association with pindown.

9 Nov: Epping Forest satanic abuse case collapses at the High Court in London.

20 Nov: More than one third of child sex abusers are themselves children, a significant minority of them under 13, according to research disclosed on Channel 4's *Despatches*.

29 Nov: Frank Beck given five concurrent life sentences for sexually and physically abusing children in his care in Leicestershire homes he headed from 1973–86. Two inquiries are ordered, one to examine the selection of staff of children's homes and the other to look at why Beck was able to continue to abuse children for so long.

5 Dec: A house parent at a school for the deaf in Wandsworth, south London, is convicted of sexually abusing 11 boys over a seven-year period.

24 Dec: New guidelines on closing down substandard private nursing homes are being prepared after a report found that three elderly patients died within a month of the emergency closure of a home in Surrey.

Housing

ALAN MURIE

In early post war Britain housing was high on the political and electoral agenda. However, by the mid 1970s problems of housing shortage were generally regarded as a feature of the past. Cuts in housing public expenditure did not generate a substantial reaction and further cuts followed through the 1980s. Housing was increasingly seen as most appropriately left to the market, and privatization policies involved not just the sale of publicly owned dwellings but a more general promotion of home ownership and move towards market pricing and financing. The right to buy had been an important issue in the general elections of 1979 and 1983. The Labour Party's reservations on this policy were silenced by electoral defeat in 1983. Housing had settled back to being a low-ranking political issue not often referred to by politicians or in the media. Academic debates were about why housing had so easily been downgraded and why housing pressure groups had been so ineffective in opposing attacks on council housing and housing investment.[1] Although the consequences of the policies pursued since the 1970s were widely forecast and problems associated with the right to buy, an unreformed system of housing finance, the pattern of public expenditure and homelessness have each been thoroughly analysed for a number of years no major policy response emerged.

By the 1990s this picture had begun to change. Rising levels of homelessness and especially the visibility of people sleeping rough in major cities were a cause of concern and in 1990 government acknowledged this with a small programme directed at those sleeping rough in London. But housing had also attracted increasing attention as the house price boom between 1986 and 1989 collapsed and ushered in a period of unprecedented problems in the home ownership sector. By the end of 1991 problems associated with mortgage arrears and repossessions were dominating newspaper headlines and government and building societies were constructing emergency packages to deal with the crisis. The links between the performance of the housing sector and the economy more generally aroused continuing comment and were central to government's concern. Developments in housing were widely regarded as having been a key factor in the inflationary spiral leading to recession. Similarly the housing sector in 1991 was seen to be delaying economic revival and prolonging recession. The problems of the construction industry and building materials and related manufacturers as well as those of mortgage lenders and insurers were only likely to be resolved if the home ownership sector recovered from its recession.

Home Ownership in Recession

Some 68 per cent of dwellings in Great Britain in 1991 were owner occupied. This compares with 57 per cent in 1981. The very different structure of the housing market has implications for the impact of economic recession.[2] More of those affected by redundancy and unemployment are likely to be home owners than was the case in earlier recessions.

The career of the recession of the 1990s and of housing market changes are closely linked. House prices in the UK doubled between 1985 and 1989 but have fallen back since then. The high house prices, in a period of economic buoyancy, encouraged higher borrowing relative to income – especially in the south of England. Financing house purchase in these conditions increasingly involved more than one income and (until this was abolished in 1989) sometimes involved multiple tax relief. The rise of house prices and borrowing associated with housing contributed to rising general inflation and interest rates. Building society mortgage interest rates rose from below 10 per cent in mid-1988 to 15.4 per cent in early 1990. The succeeding period was marked by stagnant or falling house prices and a low level of transactions.[3] The affordability problems associated with high house prices were only slowly eroded – and economic recession reinforced problems. Difficulties of both buying and selling were increasingly apparent. They had a particular impact on house building and on the level of mortgage arrears. High rates of interest began to have their effect on inflation and employment. They particularly affected house purchasers with high outstanding debts, especially in the south and east of England. The reduction in mortgage interest rates from 15.4 per cent in February 1990 to 14.5 per cent in October 1990 and through five small reductions in 1991 to 11.5 per cent in September relieved the beleaguered borrower. However, problems associated with high rates of interest gave way to problems associated with unemployment generated by these high interest rates. Although interest rates fell mortgage arrears rose with unemployment and repossessions became more important. In the first half of 1991, 36,610 properties were taken into possession. This compared with 43,890 in the whole of 1990, 15,810 in the whole of 1989 and 26,390 in the previously highest year of 1987. The trend in mortgage arrears was similar and led most commentators to anticipate an increasing level of repossessions into 1992. The high level of repossessed properties for sale was also argued to be depressing the housing market and forestalling a general recovery. While this argument may be exaggerated it is likely to be one of a number of factors involved in a continued depressed market. House price indices underlined the weakness of the housing market. Average house prices were falling in 1991 and this pattern resulted particularly from falls in the East Midlands, East Anglia, the south east, south west and Wales. The number of property transactions presented a similarly depressed picture declining from 2.1 million in 1988 to below 1.4

million in 1990 and in 1991. Again there are regional variations with the south and east showing the most violent contractions. These regions continue to be marked by the highest house prices but the greater differences which emerged between 1986 and 1988 were being reduced. Nevertheless the increase in possession orders in 1991 was marked in all regions. Repossessions remained small in relation to the number of outstanding loans (0.5 per cent in 1990). However it was no longer possible for the building societies to regard them or the number of mortgages in substantial arrears as acceptable. Problems with mortgage repayments associated with rising interest rates or with crises occasioned by relationship breakdown or loss of income or employment are coped with in various ways. For those entitled to income support mortgage interest would normally be covered in full after three months. For others (where perhaps one income remained) rescheduling payments could often only buy time and, depending on the lender's practice, action for repossession followed. Criticisms related to how lenders managed this process and to the tendency for repossessed properties to remain unsold and subject to decay as empty properties for lengthy periods.

In this environment housebuilding continued to contract. Public sector completions had fallen from over 100,000 in 1980 to below 30,000 in 1989 as a direct result of public policy. A small recovery in 1990 was not sustained in 1991 and government's public expenditure plans did not promise a reversal. Private sector completions had risen from 115,000 in 1981 to 197,500 in 1988. By 1990 they had fallen to 154,200 and they continued to fall in 1991. This contributed to falling profits and failing businesses and calls from the housebuilders for the abolition of stamp duty and increase in mortgage tax relief to boost activity. In 1991 the construction industry was in serious difficulties and demands for a revival of public investment were influenced by this as well as a desire to revive the economy and relieve housing need.

The weakness of the housing market did not only affect the construction industry. Estate agency continued to be depressed and affected by business failure. The striking new element in 1991 was the impact of repossessions on insurance companies. Those companies which had provided mortgage indemnity insurance found their accounts badly affected. For example, Eagle Star and Sun Alliance reported losses from this activity. Sun Alliance referred to losses around £320 million from mortgage indemnity business and stood to benefit considerably from any mortgage rescue schemes.

These factors also affected building societies. Repossessions and defaults could mean losses in an environment of falling house prices. Where mortgage lenders were not using mortgage indemnity insurance they experienced difficulties. A number of building societies were in this position – the biggest being Town and Country, then the 12th largest society. Its possible mortgage losses were reported to be in excess of £40 million and the Woolwich Building Society was requested by the Building Societies Commission to take it over.. Other societies experienced difficulties and the new mortgage lenders which emerged in the 1980s did not prosper. National Home Loans announced a £48 million loss in 1991 and was looking for a buyer.

Repercussions

The repercussions of these changes took various forms. Some of the first indications of rethinking related to the extent to which the practices of major lenders had contributed to the volatility of the housing market. The governor of the Bank of England expressed his view that steps should be taken to ensure that the inflationary spiral set off by house prices was not repeated. No doubt lenders agreed and hoped that restraint in lending, or self-regulation, would be sufficient. However, the intention to intervene if it was not was evident.

Building societies responded to the changing environment in other ways but the most important issues arose in relation to repossessions. The rising tide of repossessions resulted in some innovative local authority and housing association mortgage rescue schemes. As the 1991 and 1992 forecasts for repossessions increased building societies were reported to be developing mortgage rescue packages in partnership with housing associations and mortgage indemnity insurers. Linked to this the Council of Mortgage Lenders was involved in discussions with ministers concerning arrangements involving DSS payment of income support in respect of mortgage interest direct to lenders. Ministers expressed concern at rising repossessions (in contrast to earlier statements) but wanted a solution with no cost to the exchequer. The pace of activity was stepped up with the Prime Minister's desire to announce a rescue package before the Christmas Parliamentary recess. Lenders were given 48 hours to produce a satisfactory package. The package which emerged involved £200 million from the Halifax and £60 million from the Abbey National to fund mortgage rescue schemes. Other private funds followed and the total had passed £750 million before Christmas. The funds would enable housing associations or others to purchase repossessed properties and relet them. The government's part of the package was initially only to allow direct payment of the £750 million of income support paid for mortgage interest. This was quickly followed by the suspension of stamp duty associated with house purchase. This last act was the first time in twelve years that a tax change had been announced outside of the annual March budget.

This whole episode represented the most dramatic intervention in the operation of the home ownership market since the late 1970s. What effect the suspension of stamp duty will have is uncertain. The scale of the mortgage rescue package was seen to be sufficient to prevent repossessions causing a further deepening of the problems in home ownership. The costs to government and lenders are very small and could be more than offset by their impact on house prices and transactions. Doubts were expressed over whether home owners faced with repossession would be helped. The rents emerging could be beyond the means of most households and the problems for households whose income has fallen dramatically but who do not qualify for income support will remain. In this context the mortgage rescue package could prove merely to represent a decision by financial agencies to maintain a stake in the equity of their property and organize resale rather than suffer the losses associated with previous practice. At the same time the whole episode has focused attention again on the treatment of mortgage interest for income support.

Parallel Debates

If housing in 1992 became dominated by problems in home ownership this was not the exclusive concern. Homelessness continued to be a major issue and those pressing its importance were assisted by the crisis around repossessions. Shelter's figures indicated that in 1990–91 some 2,700 persons were sleeping rough. Other estimates put these figures much higher. The numbers sleeping rough in February 1991 were estimated at around 7,000 and at least ten of these are believed to have died from the effects of the bad weather in that month. A large proportion of rough sleepers are young people and the general analysis of homelessness identified low income and problems of access to housing as of key importance. The numbers of households accepted as homeless in England rose from 60,000 in the first half of 1989 to 71,000 in the first half of 1990 and 74,000 in the first half of 1991. The numbers in temporary accommodation continued to increase – to over 55,000 in June 1991 with 13,000 in bed and breakfast hotels. Concern at these high figures was expressed by various organisations including the House of Commons Environment Committee and the Public Accounts Committee. In addition to concern about the inadequacy of housing provision, bed and breakfast provision was again criticized as bad value for money. The government in 1990 had introduced a three year, £96 million scheme for rough sleepers in London. Other grants were made to over 80 voluntary organisations in England and similar provision was made in Scotland, Wales and Northern Ireland. The problems of 16 and 17 year olds continued to be affected by their treatment under the income support scheme. While the government's package and other actions increasing housing provision were generally welcomed by organisations concerned with the homeless they continued to stress the need for more action on both housing and benefits if circumstances were not to deteriorate further.

A constant theme of commentators in recent years has been that the underlying problems in housing derive at least to a substantial extent from an inequitable and inefficient housing finance system. The important decision of government in the March budget to abolish tax relief on mortgage interest at any rate other than the standard rate of tax can be seen as a product of this argument. At the same time the argument for a more thorough-going reform was put forward in the second report of the *Inquiry Into British Housing* chaired by the Duke of Edinburgh.[4] The likelihood that such a reform will emerge does not, however, seem very great. The housing preoccupations of government remained with extending home ownership. While increased public expenditure for housing associations is emerging local authorities remain out of favour and there is no strategy for a significant revival of rented housing. In spite of problems in home ownership the sector will continue to grow. The right to buy continues to be a major route in to home ownership and a source of erosion of the rented housing stock and properties available for letting to the homeless. By 1991 some 32 per cent of the local authority stock in England had been sold with sales highest in the south east outside London, the east Midlands and the eastern region.

The highest selling authorities and district councils in England generally were expressing concern at the decline of rented housing. One response was to take advantage of arrangements for voluntary transfer of council stock. Sixteen authorities in England had done this and another three were in process by the end of 1991. Another 100 were said to be contemplating such a move. The framework of public expenditure controls and tenants' rights brought these issues to the fore, but how substantial a change emerges is likely to depend on electoral outcomes and government's stance. These voluntary transfers have emerged from the tenants' choice ideas introduced in the Housing Act 1988. Other elements of this package have also been adapted to find a successful formula. Housing Action Trusts as initially formulated have not emerged but a modified version was introduced in Hull. And the emphasis on consumer choice continues in a revised tenants' charter and the development of rent to mortgage schemes. In England a new approach to local authority capital allocations involved competitive bidding designed to improve management performance. An enhanced estate action programme was also designed to concentrate resources on the most run-down local authority estates.

Emerging Issues

By the end of 1991 it is reasonable to argue that housing policy was in disarray. The problems of homelessness and repossessions had tarnished the successful image of a policy package built around home ownership and the right to buy. How far this would have electoral consequences or have long term impacts on attitudes to home ownership is uncertain. Survey evidence in 1991 did suggest some loss of interest and confidence in home ownership. And the coincidence of rising unemployment in high house price areas already hit by high interest rates could have an electoral impact. The responses which have been adopted may help to revive the housing sector and relieve some pressures on the housing industry. The housing consumer may not benefit so clearly. The long standing existence of an affordability problem alongside stagnation is not a familiar situation and for most commentators represents the consequences of previous policies – consequences which were anticipated but ignored by government.

The revival of private landlordism continues to be elusive and only seems likely with substantial fiscal support. Again the survey evidence does not suggest that this option is favoured by consumers. The increased funding available to housing associations will not on its own be sufficient to meet the need for rented housing. Furthermore there are issues related to the increasing coincidence between poverty and rented housing. A housing element exists within the civil disturbances on council estates in 1991 in Wales, Oxford and Tyneside. These also captured headlines and focused attention on urban deprivation. While commentators differed in their explanation of these disturbances social polarization linked to housing was increasingly evident. Current policies will not reverse this trend.

Notes

1 P Malpass and A Murie, *Housing Policy and Practice*, 3rd edition, Macmillan, 1990.
2 R Forrest, A Murie and P Williams, *Home Ownership: Differentiation and Fragmentation*, Unwin Hyman, 1990.
3 Council of Mortgage Lenders, *Housing Finance*, quarterly.
4 *Inquiry into British Housing, Second Report*, June 1991, Joseph Rowntree Foundation.

Chronology

4 Jan: Nationwide Anglia Building Society says house prices fell by 10.7 per cent in 1990.

8 Jan: Announcement that people offering bed and breakfast to six people or less as a subsidiary use of their home are to be exempt from business rates from 1 April.

21 Jan: A £3 million scheme to provide housing advice and emergency shelter in provincial cities is announced.

5 Feb: Law Commission argues that sending in bailiffs to seize goods from tenants in rent arrears should be banned.

6 Feb: The two largest building societies claim that house prices began to recover in January.

14 Feb: Announcement that the number of homes repossessed because of mortgage arrears trebled in 1990 to 43,890.

5 Mar: Halifax Building Society says house prices are still falling.

18 Mar: Channel 4's *A Plague on your house* shows in a survey of 70 environmental health departments that complaints about insect infestation of homes has increased by 40 per cent between 1989 and 1990.

25 Mar: Robin Leigh-Pemberton, the Governor of the Bank of England, says the Bank will consider direct curbs on mortgages if another house price boom threatens the economy.

27 Mar: Sir George Young, Minister of State for the Environment, announces an extra £115 million for local authorities to help homeless families.

6 Apr: Mortgage tax relief restricted to basic income tax rate as a result of budget changes whilst the threshold remains £30,000.

12 Apr: Tenants in Hull vote to set up the first housing action trust.

29 Apr: Law Society complains about the lack of a requirement to disclose a commission when building societies and banks enter the conveyancing market in 1992.

17 May: Announcement that the number of homeless on London streets sleeping rough has halved to less than 500 since £96 million programme to improve and increase hostel places began in January.

23 May: Labour signals some rapprochement with the private rented sector. Instead of imposing rent controls it will encourage lower rents by tax breaks and improvement grants.

3 June: National Federation of Housing Associations predicts homelessness will worsen over the next decade unless the level of housebuilding for rent is more than doubled.

5 June: Government plans to bring some of the 600,000 empty private homes into use by encouraging owners to let through housing associations are launched.

10 June: Glen Bramley, *Bridging the Affordability Gap*, Association of District Councils/House Builders Federation, argues that less than half of new household

formations can afford their own home and that the number of new homes being built to meet demand for rented housing needs to triple.

13 June: Salvation Army's 'Strategy for Change' aims to create 250 self-contained units for London's homeless within five years.

19 June: Environment Select Committee denounces 'dumping' of families in bed and breakfast accommodation.

20 June: Public Accounts Committee warns official records of the rise in homelessness to about 300,000 may 'significantly understate' the problem. They urge greater use of 31,000 empty state-owned properties and criticize bed and breakfast accommodation as bad value for money.

25 June: According to Shelter a record 47,490 homes were repossessed in 1990.

27 June: Report by the National Federation of Housing Associations chaired by the Duke of Edinburgh says mortgage interest tax relief should be phased out over the next ten years, suggests the replacement of all personal housing subsidies with a unified subsidy concentrating on those with greatest need and suggests a nationwide rent setting scheme based on capital values by property to ensure consistency and encourage the private rented sector. It also argues that local authorities should be enabled to borrow more freely to build and provide tax incentives for private landlords.

12 July: Announcement of a reform to allow flat owners to own the freehold of their properties under a new commonhold system.

24 July: Report by the Joseph Rowntree Foundation argues that abolition of mortgage interest tax relief could bring lower interest rates, finance new tax cuts and boost spending on housing, claiming that the tax relief led to house price booms and the over-heating of the economy in the 1980s.

29 July: Building societies face record mortgage debt with more than 5 per cent of their total loans tied up in debts which are more than six months in arrears or which have already been repossessed.

9 Aug: *Fit for Nothing? Young People, Benefits and Youth Training*, Children's Society, reports on the difficulties facing the young homeless.

13 Aug: Series of schemes to provide hostels across country to stem the flow of young homeless to London is announced.

Lords Select Committee on the European Communities, *Young People in the European Community*, HMSO, suggests that there should be a minister for youth and that there should be more EC action to tackle young homelessness.

15 Aug: A record 36,610 homes were repossessed in the first half of 1991.

23 Aug: Department of the Environment predicts that the number of households in England will grow by about 3 million by 2010.

2 Sept: *Urgent Need for Homes*, Shelter, argues that 500,000 new housing association and council dwellings are needed by 1996 to fill the gap between projected need and provision.

11 Sept: Audit Commission, *Healthy Housing: The Role of Environmental Health Services*, HMSO, argues that more than half the houses converted into hostels and bedsits in England and Wales fall short of basic health and safety standards. It recommends the better use of enforcement powers by local authorities who should also monitor the situation more closely.

24 Sept: *A Welcome Home*, Labour Party, envisages a national housing bank to encourage more building for rent.

25 Sept: *Death Trap Housing*, National Consumer Council, says 2 million tenants live in dangerous housing – which includes 80 per cent of the estimated 334,000 multi-occupancy houses in England and Wales.

15 Oct: Tougher criminal sanctions against squatting announced.

2 Dec: *Building for the Future*, Shelter, calls for mortgage tax relief to be reallocated to help the homeless.

16 Dec: Government gives mortgage lenders 48 hours to come up with schemes to stem the tide of home repossessions. In return the government offers to introduce legislation to pass mortgage interest paid to those on income support straight to lenders.

18 Dec: Mortgage lenders put together a range of schemes to convert owners in difficulties into tenants and thus cut the rate of repossessions.

19 Dec: Government suspends stamp duty for houses under £250,000 until the end of August in an attempt to kickstart the housing market. It also announces it will introduce a bill to pay mortgage interest for those on income support directly to lenders.

Education

ALAN SMITHERS

Nineteen ninety-one was the year the new Secretary of State, Kenneth Clarke, set his stamp on education. It began with an announcement to the North of England conference in Leeds that the national curriculum was to be made more flexible and it ended with heavy hints (borne out) that there would be proposals for an important change in teacher-training at the next in Southport. In between hardly any part of the system was unaffected. Schools, further education, higher education, local authorities and the inspectorate all had to digest substantial reforms. The chairman and/or the chief executive of the School Examinations and Assessment Council, National Curriculum Council, Universities Funding Council and the National Council for Vocational Qualifications all either retired or were replaced. The two most senior officials at the DES concerned with teacher-training were moved sideways, and although a shortlist was drawn up for Senior Chief Inspector of Schools on the departure of Eric Bolton (who in each of the last three years had written a critical report suggesting, among other things, that one third of all lessons were unsatisfactory, two out of three schools had unsuitable accommodation, and there were shortages of equipment and basic textbooks) the post was not filled. The machinery restoring limited collective bargaining in negotiating teachers' salaries introduced in the School Teachers' Pay and Conditions Bill only the previous November was overturned. All was change.

John Major, the new Prime Minister, himself took a close interest in education. In February he gave a speech to Young Conservatives putting education at the top of the political agenda and emphasizing that he wanted better standards in schools and teachers to be 'fairly' rewarded. In May he personally launched a package of three white papers shaking up education for those over 16. In July he presented the Citizen's Charter where 'listing schools' achievements' was featured among such proposals as privatizing British Rail, improving health care and ending the Post Office's monopoly on letters. Schools' league tables, regular inspection of schools and parents' rights and choices were spelled out in more detail in the Parents' Charter published in September. Also in July in a speech to the Centre for Policy Studies at the Café Royal in London he signalled a return to rigorous O-level type examinations, reductions in the coursework component, pencil and paper tests in the three Rs for seven and 11 year olds and less reliance on mixed ability teaching. Such was the involvement of the Prime Minister in education at the time that the

Times Educational Supplement on 26 July 1991 rather unkindly commented that while 'the Education Secretary has decided that education is too important to be left to the educationists . . . the Prime Minister has decided that it is too important to be left to the Education Secretary'.

In all this activity the government saw itself as responding to the public mood. This was encapsulated in a speech made by the Prince of Wales in Stratford-upon-Avon to celebrate the anniversary of Shakespeare's birth. He attacked the nation's educational standards with specific criticism across the spectrum from inadequate provision of nursery education, too much emphasis on method at the expense of content, low participation in education post 16 and neglect of our literary heritage – including Shakespeare. In developing this theme the Prince was lending his voice to the criticisms made by Sir Claus Moser in his presidential address to the British Association in August 1990, which had received so much attention. In May the commission promised by Sir Claus was set up with a £1 million grant from the Paul Hamlyn Foundation. In the short run, however, it was preempted by a commission established by Channel Four whose report *Every Child in Britain* was the subject of two programmes in October and went out to all MPs, local authorities and schools. Education was also strongly represented in the other media with *The Independent* devoting several pages a day for a week in June to its own school's charter.

The Labour Party and the Liberal Democrats too sensed public disquiet and issued a number of policy documents of their own. In April the Labour Party published proposals for overhauling education 16–19, in September a Parent's Partnership document and *Governing Schools Locally* (a plan to allow schools to manage themselves locally while restoring a strategic role to the local authorities), and in October a fast track for gifted pupils to be able to move up a year and be taught alongside older pupils. But since the general thrust of these ideas including a national curriculum, testing, vocational qualifications, local management of schools and school-based teacher-training was broadly similar to that of the government, at times it had difficulty in establishing itself as a separate and alternative voice. Indeed, such was the convergence of education policy and ideas on some occasions that there were mutual recriminations about stealing each other's clothes. However, in the details there were substantial differences between the parties particularly with regard to the organization and funding of education.

Organization of Education

The government has pushed ahead with some difficulty in its plans to create diversity among secondary schools so as to offer, in its view, parental choice – underpinned by the Parents' Charter. Instead of the 20 City Technology Colleges promised by the end of 1989 there are now 13, with two more due. The first CTC, Kingshurst in Solihull, received a somewhat unfavourable report from Her Majesty's Inspectors in October saying there were 'significant areas of weakness in the teaching of designing and making'. With regard to technology, the government changed tack in December and annoucned plans to establish a network of 70-100 specialist schools that will receive grants of up to £500,000 (for which they will have had to bid), from a £25 million fund, to buy equipment and offer high quality technical and vocational courses particularly to pupils over 14.

The grant maintained scheme, in spite of the advantageous financial arrangements condemned as 'bribery' by the Labour Party, is also making slow progress. Of 24,000 state schools, 103 have opted-out of local authority control (two thirds from Conservative authorities), with 56 due to do so before next April and 112 votes in favour awaiting the Secretary of State's decision. The regulations governing grant maintained schools have been changed so that they can alter their character so as to become selective, but only a small minority were thought likely to apply. The low interest in opting out led to some slimming down of the Education Assets Board which was expected to take on the schools after overseeing the transfer of polytechnics and colleges from local authority control. Neither has the government's support for independent schools through the assisted places scheme gone entirely smoothly. In December it was reported that only 27,008 of the 33,268 places available in 1990 had been taken up, but nevertheless the National Audit Office had found an overspend of £3 million due to soaring fees. (It is in this area of school organization that Labour Party policy perhaps differs most sharply from the government's: it would return opted out schools to their former control, hand over CTCs to local authorities, and end the assisted places scheme.)

Important changes to education post 16 were announced in the May white papers and began their passage through parliament in the Further and Higher Education Bill in November. Its main proposals were: to transfer 450 further education colleges and 113 sixth form colleges in England and Wales out of local authority control; to establish new Further Education Funding Councils for England and Wales (separately) starting in autumn 1993; to allow polytechnics and colleges to call themselves universities and award their own degrees, with the Council for National Academic Awards, which previously supervised their degrees, to be abolished; and to set up Higher Education Funding Councils for England and Wales to replace the existing Universities Funding Council and the Polytechnics and Colleges Funding Council, which will be dissolved. It was mischievously suggested that while the government appeared to be trying to loosen the comprehensive system in the secondary sector it was trying to create one at the tertiary level. But the ending of the 'binary divide' seems likely – in view of the changes in research funding – paradoxically to lead to a more differentiated system with at its head some ten to 15 universities akin to America's 'ivy league'.

Curriculum

During 1991 the government continued to tidy up the unwieldy national curriculum. In January, Kenneth Clarke finally abandoned plans to make all pupils study the ten specified subjects up to the age of 16. After 14 only maths, science and English were to be compulsory and examined, technology and a modern language were to be compulsory but not necessarily examined, history and/or geography would have to be studied though not necessarily examined, art and music were to be made optional though pupils would be expected to continue with some form of PE. All subjects would however be tested at 14.

In March the regulations for history and geography were issued to operate for five, seven and 11 year olds from the autumn and for 14 year olds from autumn 1994. Both have three attainment targets. History will have a rolling 20-year deadline with more recent events being treated as current affairs. In October the National Curriculum Council (now under the chairmanship of David Pascall, a BP executive, in place of Duncan Graham) published its recommendations for a simplified national curriculum in maths and science. It put forward proposals that the number of attainment targets in maths be reduced from 14 to five and in science from 17 to four. The lists of skills and knowledge in maths are to be cut (mostly by amalgamation) from 296 to 147 and in science from 409 to 173. In November regulations were introduced to enable pupils to drop history or geography at 15. Reports of the working groups in art and music became available, but they appeared as recommendations only after substantial revisions by the National Curriculum Council in the new year. These changes are rumoured to be only the start of a sustained attempt to simplify a curriculum which in the view of the government has become in implementation too complex, demanding and prescriptive.

Testing and Examinations

The national testing of seven year olds got under way with the results duly reported in December. The NUT had threatened a boycott at its Easter conference but this was reversed on a ballot among those of its members who would be directly involved. In May the NAHT agreed that headteachers should pass on the results to local authorities providing that individual schools were not identified.

There was general agreement, however, that the standard assessment tasks took far too much time and in December, SEAC (now under the chairmanship of Lord Griffiths not Philip Halsey) described how they would be streamlined. Pencil and paper tests will replace many of the practical activities and many of the tests will be for the whole class instead of small groups. Tests in English, maths and science will be at four levels instead of three, with teachers deciding at which level the children should be tested.

In October SEAC announced the arrangements for testing 14 year olds in maths and science to be held in all schools in England and Wales on two consecutive days in June. Each subject is expected to have three written tests, each up to an hour, and the tests are to come in different versions to cater for different ability groups. Next year will be a pilot run, but schools will be required to administer the tests in 1993 when similar tests in English and technology will be added.

GCSE also came under scrutiny. In April the Secretary of State instructed SEAC (under Philip Halsey) to tighten up regulations on bad spelling for next year's papers. In November SEAC (under Lord Griffiths) responded to the Prime

Minister's call for less coursework in GCSE examinations and recommended that it usually be allowed to make up no more than 20–30 per cent of the marks. The system of grading from A–G will also disappear from 1994 to be replaced by a 10 point scale with level ten being in effect a super A-grade.

The May white papers envisaged changes in the qualifications at 18 years with an Advanced Diploma to be awarded to students taking A and AS exams and to those gaining vocational qualifications of the same standard. However, A levels are to be unchanged and the Diploma would be awarded on top of two A-level passes. A new system of general national vocational qualifications suitable for studying in school is to be implemented by the National Council for Vocational Qualifications. The Advanced Diploma, not very different on the surface from Labour's proposed Advanced Certificate of Education and Training published in April, but twin track rather than unified, was put out for consultation. In October, the NCVQ provided examples of what the general national vocational qualifications might look like in five areas – business, manufacturing, art and design, leisure and tourism, and health and care.

Participation and Performance

Standards came to the fore in 1991. Martin Turner's claim in July 1990 that reading standards were falling was borne out by HMI and a study by the National Foundation for Educational Research reported in January, and received cautious support from the Education, Science and Arts Select Committee in May. Results of the national testing of seven year olds showed that 28 per cent could not read independently and a similar proportion struggled with basic maths.

In April the government was sufficiently concerned to ask the Council for the Accreditation of Teacher Education to report by the end of the year on changes that should be introduced in the teaching of reading. But before this became available a three-man team under Professor Robin Alexander was asked, in December, to report in only two months on primary teaching methods and class organization, and specifically to look at whole class teaching, subjects rather than topic work and streaming by ability. On the particular problem of reading, both the government and Labour Party independently became attracted to the Reading Recovery Scheme that has operated successfully in New Zealand and both began 1992 announcing schemes to adopt it.

In contrast to doubts about achievement among the younger children, performance at GCSE, A level and in degree examinations continued to rise. In GCSE the proportion getting grades A–C went up from 48.3 per cent to 49.0 per cent, and grade A from 11.1 per cent to 11.6 per cent. Although there was a fall of 4.2 per cent in pupil numbers the percentage of GCSEs passed fell by only 0.9 per cent but there was a fall of 5.9 per cent in maths. At A level the pass rate continued to rise, reaching 77.8 per cent, whereas in 1980 it was only 70 per cent (where it had been for three decades). The swing away from maths, physics and chemistry continued, however. At degree level the proportion of firsts rose sharply – from 6.0

per cent in 1979 to 6.4 per cent in 1984–85 to 8.3 per cent in 1989–90. These enhanced performances were not however greeted as a success but as evidence that exams were becoming softer and examiners were being more lenient.

The improved pass rates at GCSE led to more young people continuing in education, the proportion rising from 49 per cent in 1986 to 53 per cent in 1990. More passes at A level contributed to unprecedented demand for places in universities (up by 8.7 per cent) and polytechnics and colleges (up by 16 per cent). The government has adopted this increased demand for higher education as policy and the May white papers envisaged the participation index rising from 14 per cent in 1987 to 32 per cent by the end of the century. The problems of overcrowding led to student protests and to threatened rent strikes. Ironically, this massive expansion is occurring at a time of increased graduate unemployment. The Association of Graduate Careers Advisory Services reported that unemployment rose from 4.7 per cent at the end of 1989 to 6.4 per cent in 1990, and it predicted that one in ten of 1991 university graduates would still be seeking a job at Christmas.

The silver lining to the cloud of the recession is that it became easier to recruit and retain teachers. Unfilled vacancies (though this is not a good measure of teacher supply, being a composite of resignations, posts established and applications, and subject to an annual cycle) were down from 6,494 in January 1990 to 5,600 in January 1991. In the autumn there was a considerable increase in recruits to teacher-training. Overall, 28,792 trainees began courses, a rise of 4,998 on 1990, and 20 per cent above target. Even physics was back to the level it achieved four years ago. The government claimed that the influx would enable staffing needs to be met over the next four years but to help cope with an expected extra 500,000 pupils it approved in August an Open University scheme starting in January 1994 to train 1,000 teachers at a time using distance- learning packages.

Teachers were given a 7.5 per cent pay rise in April rising in December to 9.5 per cent for classroom teachers and 12.75 per cent for heads and deputies. This still left them a long way short of where they had been relative to average non manual earnings in 1980. The government scrapped the negotiating procedures set out in the November 1990 bill and instituted a Pay Review Body under Sir Graham Day, chairman of Rover and largely made up of industrialists. In his submission to the new body, Mr Clarke invited it to consider offering bonuses (of up to 10 per cent) to those who perform well in classroom since, as he explained later, 'the one thing nobody gets paid extra for at the moment . . . is being very good at teaching children'. In anticipation of performance-related pay the NAHT commissioned a report on measuring the effectiveness of teachers from Hay Management Consultants, which recommended assessing classroom performance on a 5 point scale from exceptional to barely effective.

Throughout the year the government's concerns about teacher-training found their way into the press and this was a prelude to announcing a major shakeup of the training of secondary teachers at the beginning of 1992. Primary teacher training is also to be reformed but this awaits the outcome of the Alexander enquiry.

Finance

Some of the major clashes over education in 1991 concerned expenditure. The government continues to maintain that spending per pupil has risen by over 40 per cent between 1979–80 and 1988–89 and that capital expenditure has increased by 16 per cent, but to those in the service it does not feel like it. This is particularly the case in higher education where the expansion is being funded in part by a reduction in unit costs. Sir Edward Parkes, then chairman of CVCP, warned that continuing financial constraints were affecting quality (which sits oddly with the ever-increasing number of first class honours degrees awarded). The government is also seeking to reduce expenditure on student financial support (which accounts for nearly £1 billion per year). In September the National Association of Citizens' Advice Bureaux suggested that an increasing number of poorer students will have to abandon courses because the government has withdrawn housing and other benefits. The loan scheme, a partial replacement for maintenance grants, had been taken up by 63,682 students borrowing on average £378. But costs were heavy, each loan costing £219 to administer.

In the autumn spending round, education won an 8.6 per cent increase to be concentrated on school buildings, whose budget is to rise by 15 per cent. Both main opposition parties maintained that this will mean that education is still grossly underfunded. The Liberal Democrats have proposed a penny in the pound to be added to income tax to go to education. The Labour Party has suggested that it will allow education expenditure to rise from 4.6 per cent of GDP to 5.5 per cent, raising an extra £2.6 billion.

Quality and Accountability

In November, the government presented an Education (Schools) Bill to give effect to the Parents' Charter. It proposed: the publication of league tables giving examination and national curriculum testing results, truancy rates and school leaver destinations for all schools including independents; that schools must arrange inspection every four years; that governors ask for at least two tenders before deciding on an inspection team; a short jargon-free summary of inspection reports; a plan detailing how school governors will tackle problems highlighted by inspectors; and a teacher's written report on each child's progress each year.

The publication of league tables and the privatization of the inspectorate have aroused considerable controversy. The idea of a value-added approach rather than just raw outcomes has been widely canvassed but rejected by government on the grounds that the reporting should be as simple as possible and outcomes *are* important. Pruning the inspectorate from 480 to 175 and making it responsible for the quality control of up to 5,000 new private inspectors has also attracted a lot of criticism.

Prospect

Nineteen ninety-two will be an election year. All three parties agree that education is near the top of the political agenda but the convergence of policies makes it difficult for any one party to demonstrate the distinctiveness and attractiveness of its approach. Whichever party is elected is not likely to make much difference to the general shape of the national curriculum, testing, an advanced diploma at 18 including the technical and vocational, the expansion of higher education or school-based teacher-training.

The Labour Party would put more trust in planning than market forces and seek to reverse the diversification of secondary education and the downgrading of the LEAs. Both the Labour Party and the Liberal Democrats have promised more money for education, even if it means higher taxes. Watch this space.

Chronology

4 Jan: Announcement of a revision of the national curriculum for pupils over 14 allowing wider subject choice and the pursuit of work-related courses.
   Kenneth Clarke announces that history will only be a compulsory part of the national curriculum to age 14 and that history or geography will be alternatives at 14–16.

7 Jan: Simplified tests for seven year olds in English, mathematics and science announced.

9 Jan: HMI report says that nearly 20 per cent of seven year olds are unable to read fluently and that one in 20 of ten year olds can hardly read at all. It comments that one in five primary schools in England and Wales is failing to teach children to read satisfactorily. A National Foundation for Educational Research report also confirms that reading standards are declining. It cites the main obstacles to higher standards as staff turnover, class sizes and cutbacks in support services for slow learners and bilingual children.
   Labour announces plans to introduce a public inquiry system to deal with the school closures necessary to reduce Britain's 1.8 million surplus of school places.

11 Jan: Examining boards directed to penalize bad spelling in GCSE exams.

23 Jan: Announcement that Professor Graeme Davies is to become the new chief executive of the UFC in place of Sir Peter Swinnerton-Dyer.

29 Jan: Polytechnics and Colleges Funding Council announces funding for a further 45,000 full-time and sandwich and 20,000 part-time places in 1991–92, representing increases of 18 per cent and 15 per cent respectively.

6 Feb: Department of Employment shows that the proportion of ethnic minority young people staying in full time education is more than double that of the white population. Whilst only 11–12 per cent of whites aged 16–24 are in full time education the figure for West Indians is 15 per cent, for Bangladeshis 28 per cent and for Indians 31 per cent.

13 Feb: HMI annual report finds poor standards in one third of schools but improvements in primary science, exam results and in the numbers staying on after 16.

14 Feb: Interim report of the national curriculum music working group chaired by Sir John Manduell warns of shortages of teachers, instruments and resources.

18 Feb: HMI praise improvements in school mathematics since the introduction of the national curriculum.

19 Feb: National curriculum physical education working group produces its interim report.

20 Feb: Government to withhold £35 million from the universities, polytechnics and colleges in an attempt to force academics to agree to flexible working and differentiated pay deals.

21 Feb: Kenneth Clarke rejects proposals to raise money for higher education from students through tuition fees and taxes.

27 Feb: Plans to give every school leaver a personal 'record of achievement' are announced.

1 Mar: Alan Howarth, higher education minister, discloses that the cost of student loans is double government estimates.

10 Mar: David Harrison is appointed chairman of the Committee of Vice-Chancellors and Principals, to take up the post in August.

16 Mar: Four year teacher training courses to be abolished.

21 Mar: FE colleges to be taken out of local authority control and given freedom to compete with sixth form colleges.

1 Apr: Many schools are dirty and unhygienic as a result of contracting out of cleaning services according to a report in *Privatization News*.

2 Apr: Announcement of a new system of university funding to take effect from 1992 to encourage universities to take on students on a cheaper fees-only basis in order to increase student numbers.

3 Apr: NAS/UWT survey finds serious structural defects in 44 per cent of 500 schools surveyed.

8 Apr: St George's, Bassett, Southampton, becomes the first school to use smart cards to replace a written register.
Science Key Stages 1 and 3: A Report by HM Inspectorate on the First Year 1989–90, HMSO, points to the lack of qualified science teachers.

10 Apr: Threat of boycott of standard assessment tests at seven in England and Wales, to follow the boycott by parents and staff that severely interrupted its introduction in Scotland, recedes.

11 Apr: Inquiry into the teaching of reading ordered.

15 Apr: Proposal that schools will have to publish truancy figures in future.

17 Apr: NUT reject a no-strike deal.

22 Apr: Prince of Wales criticizes educational standards and the treatment of Britain's literary heritage and argues that recent policy changes have left teachers suffering from 'innovation fatigue', in a speech at Stratford upon Avon.
English Key Stage: A Report by HMI on the First Year 1989–90, HMSO, argues that too many children are receiving unsatisfactory reading lessons in their early years.
Schools ordered to open their own bank accounts by April 1992.
Sir Christopher Ball's report, *Learning Pays*, argues everyone should continue in formal full or part-time education until they are 18 and all should expect to achieve at least level three of the National Vocational Qualification system, equivalent to two A-levels.

24 Apr: Martin Turner, *Reading, Learning and the National Curriculum*, Centre for Policy Studies, condemns 'real books' method of teaching reading and the new standard assessment targets.

25 Apr: Government announces that opted-out schools are free to change their character.

In 1990 for the first time more than half the 16 year olds in England and Wales (53 per cent) opted to stay in schools and colleges and the proportion in education and training combined rose to 78 per cent.

29 Apr: Sir Douglas Hague, *Beyond Universities: A New Republic of the Intellect,* IEA, suggests a system of student vouchers.

Labour envisages returning to the Higginson recommendations of five A-levels instead of three and the introduction of an Advanced Certificate for Education and Training to cover the whole range of academic and vocational training undertaken by the 16–19 age group.

2 May: British Association for the Advancement of Science announces its national commission on education.

3 May: DES admits that average pupil/teacher ratios rose in 1990 for the first time since 1965.

8 May: National curriculum maths and science tests to be cut to a third of the originally envisaged size and those for 14 year olds to be postponed until 1993 to allow for further trials.

A review of the organization and role of HMI announced.

9 May: HMI calls for improvements in the teaching of humanities, saying one in four lessons is unsatisfactory and many courses are unstructured.

16 May: Education, Science and Arts Select Committee, *Standards of Teaching in Primary Schools,* HMSO, dismisses claims that standards are falling because of faulty teaching methods.

19 May: Alan Smithers, *The Vocational Route into Higher Education,* School of Education, University of Manchester, concludes there is no hope of persuading young people that vocational courses have the same status as A-levels unless vocational qualifications give them the same power in the labour market.

20 May: *Education and Training for the 21st Century,* 2 vols, HMSO, announces plans for education post 16 including general national vocational qualifications, an Advanced Diploma at 18, schools and colleges to publish their examination results, training credits for all 16 and 17 year old leavers, sixth form and further education colleges to be hived off from local authority control.

Higher Education: A New Framework, HMSO, outlines plans to increase competition for students between universities and polytechnics, allow polytechnics to change to universities and wind up the Council for National Academic Awards. Three new funding bodies for England, Scotland and Wales are to be set up.

Access and Opportunity – A Strategy for Education and Training, HMSO, the education white paper for Scotland, outlines plans for a Scottish higher education funding council, and to allow polytechnics and higher education colleges to become universities, the introduction of Scottish vocational qualifications and the removal of further education colleges from local authority control.

23 May: NUT says that standard assessment tests at seven have a detrimental effect on classroom behaviour.

24 May: Ruling in *R v Bromley London Borough Council* that it is unlawful for councils to discriminate in schools admissions policy in favour of children resident in the borough.

29 May: Anthony Lester and David Pannick, *Independent Schools: The Legal Case*, ISIS, argues that Labour and Liberal Democrat plans to remove charitable status from independent schools probably breaches the European Convention on Human Rights.

30 May: David Hart, general secretary of NAHT, urges the creation of a Royal College of Teaching, to cover the entire profession and fight for its status.

31 May: NAHT wants standard assessment tests at seven replaced by classroom assessment.

3 June: Schools have too few computers to meet the demands of the national curriculum according to a DES survey.

19 June: Audit Commission report suggests an end to the current system of free school transport.

20 June: Institute of Manpower Studies survey shows that the proportion of 16 year olds staying at school rose from 55 per cent to 60 per cent in 1990 and that there were improvements in GCSE and A-level grades. Most of the increase was in the humanities and arts.

24 June: Alec Ross and Sally Tomlinson, *Teachers and Parents*, IPPR, suggests a new grade to keep good teachers in the classroom and also advocates the introduction of a new group of 'associate teachers', part-timers to back up teachers.
Assessment: Recording and Reporting: A Report by HM Inspectorate on the first year 1989–90, HMSO, is published.

26 June: Applications for university places rose 6 per cent this year and for the first time more women than men applied.

2 July: Government admits that student loans cost twice as much to administer as forecast. HMI report on the language in the national curriculum project to raise awareness of English language teaching is withheld from publication.

3 July: John Major promises, in a speech to the Centre for Policy Studies, to make GCSEs tougher and encourage more schools to opt out.

8 July: *National Curriculum and Special Needs*, HMI, argues that poor facilities threaten standards of education in special schools, and draws attention to the deficiencies of teachers in conducting science lessons, the ways in which the children were assessed and the methods of recording results in special schools.

10 July: Duncan Graham resigns as chairman of the National Curriculum Council, to be replaced by David Pascall.

11 July: Report by Warwick University says primary teachers are so busy filling in forms and conducting other administrative duties relating to the national curriculum that they have less time teaching children to read.

15 July: Government to provide an additional £20 million over the next three years to improve literacy teaching in inner city schools.

16 July: *Language for Learning*, Assessment of Performance Unit, surveys the development of English language skills in children.

17 July: *Geography in the Early Years*, HMI, praises the teaching of the geography of the locality of the school but criticizes the lack of a wider dimension.

18 July: Philip Halsey resigns as chairman of the School Examinations Assessment Council. Sir Brian (later Lord) Griffiths is appointed to succeed him.

19 July: Government confirms it is contemplating turning HMI into an executive agency.

23 July: Increases in the examination element and a reduction in the coursework element in GCSEs is ordered by Kenneth Clarke.

24 July: Education Select Committee criticizes the current confusion over financial responsibility for education between local and central government.

29 July: SEAC bows to government pressure to penalize bad spelling in GCSEs from 1992.

6 Aug: *Every Child a Special Child: Labour's Consultation on Policy for Special Education Needs*, Labour Party, suggests bringing special education more fully into mainstream schooling.
Announcement that part-time Open University courses are to be used to train more teachers.

13 Aug: *Repair and Maintenance of School Buildings*, National Audit Office, argues that about £3 billion needs to be spent on school repairs and suggests that poor buildings might lower educational standards and increase the difficulty of implementing the national curriculum.

19 Aug: *Music for ages 5 to 14*, HMSO, calls for a balanced programme of music education. *Art for ages 5 to 14*, HMSO is also published.

21 Aug: National curriculum physical education working group recommends that all pupils should be taught swimming up to the age of 11, prompting the government to set up a survey of swimming in schools.

29 Aug: Alan Smithers and Pamela Robinson, *Staffing Secondary Schools in the Nineties*, Secondary Heads Association/Headmasters' Conference/Girls' Schools Association/Engineering Council, suggests that the requirements of the national curriculum will either mean the shedding of staff or bankruptcy for many schools under LMS.

3 Sept: *Diversification of the First Modern Language in a Sample of Secondary Schools*, HMI, says too many French lessons are poor and conducted almost entirely in English. Every school should have a teacher specializing in sex education according to a report on unplanned pregnancies by the Royal College of Obstetricians and Gynaecologists. It also calls for better training of teachers in sex education and for medical students to have practical training in communication on sex matters.

4 Sept: John Burchill, *Inspecting Schools: Breaking the Monopoly*, Centre for Policy Studies, suggests that schools should be allowed to choose their inspectors.

9 Sept: Paddy Ashdown, the leader of the Liberal Democrats, promises £1.9 billion extra spending on education, a year of preschool education, two days training per week for 16–19 year old workers and more government funding for adult education.
New diplomas to put vocational qualifications on the same footing as A levels and GCSEs are announced.

10 Sept: *Parents' Partnership*, Labour Party, outlines plans for a more positive role for parents in education and the restoration of spending on education as a proportion of GDP from the current level of 4.6 per cent to the 5.5 per cent level of 1979.

16 Sept: *Empowering the Parents*, IEA, argues for the break-up of the state education system and for schools to have the freedom to change their character.

17 Sept: Teachers are no longer to be required to serve a probationary year after qualifying.

18 Sept: Labour would scrap the assisted places scheme Jack Straw tells the Headmasters' Conference.

19 Sept: CVCP plans to move universities to a course unit and semester organization and allow students to change degree courses and colleges more easily.
Government confirms that children aged 14 will take six one-hour written tests in maths and science.

23 Sept: Tests for seven year olds are to be greatly simplified next year.

Governing Schools Locally, Labour Party, supports LMS but argues for the retention of strategic powers by local authorities and reform of the current funding formula and confused legal situation.

27 Sept: Changes to GCSE, reducing the coursework element, are announced.

Parents' Charter involving slimmed down HMI, private companies carrying out school inspections, league tables of examination results, truancy rates and success rates of school leavers and regular reports on children's progress announced.

30 Sept: *Right from the Start*, AMMA, calls for a vast increase in nursery provision.

1 Oct: *Consultation Reports: Science and Mathematics*, National Curriculum Council, proposes a greatly simplified science and mathematics national curriculum.

Oct-Dec: Wave of occupations and disturbances at various universities and polytechnics across the country about rents, overcrowding or assorted other grievances.

21 Oct: Sigmund Prais and Elaine Beadle, *Prevocational Schooling in Europe Today*, NIESR, argues that the national curriculum does little to improve the situation in technical education for older children and that one third of children should be able to opt, as in much of the rest of Europe, for more vocational forms of schooling after 14.

23 Oct: Channel Four Commission report, *Every Child in Britain*, recommends that all young children should be taught to read, write and do arithmetic at primary school even if that means repeating a year. After 14 there should be technical and vocational pathways interlocking with the academic.

24 Oct: Government trails plans for relating head teachers pay to exam results, truancy rates and job destinations.

The standard of training of primary teachers in science, history, arts and the humanities is condemned by HMI.

3 Nov: Kenneth Clarke suggests pay bonuses of up to 10 per cent for good teachers.

4 Nov: Further and Higher Education Bill published. It will transfer FEs and sixth form colleges out of local authority control, establish new further education funding councils for England and Wales, require the publication of exam results and leavers' destinations, set up higher education funding councils to replace the UFC and PCFC, allow polytechnics and higher education colleges to call themselves universities and award their own degrees, abolish CNAA and require the new funding bodies to check standards.

6 Nov: Major schools building and repairs programme heralded in the autumn statement.

Audit Commission, *Two Bs or Not? Schools and Colleges A Level Performance*, HMSO, argues that comprehensives are as good as independent schools at preparing students for A levels.

7 Nov: Education (Schools) Bill to allow schools to introduce lay inspection and reduce the role of HMI is published.

14 Nov: Liberal Democrats propose the abolition of GCSEs and A levels in favour of continuous assessment.

15 Nov: *Education Observed: The Implementation of the Curriculum Requirements of ERA*, HMI, criticizes poor assessment of pupils' performances.

26 Nov: Pupils will be able to drop history or geography at 15 under new draft regulations.

The State of Schools in England and Wales, National Confederation of Parent-Teachers Associations, shows that parents contributed £55 million towards equipment in state schools in 1990, not including responses to direct mailshots.

3 Dec: Inquiry into progressive teaching methods in primary schools under Professor Robin Alexander announced.

4 Dec: *Children in Squalor*, Labour Party, claims local authorities need £1.6 billion to fund urgent repairs on state schools.

5 Dec: Alan Smithers and Pamela Robinson, *Beyond Compulsory Schooling*, Council for Industry and Higher Eduation, shows that the education system stresses academic attainment and suggests that it should reward a wider range of talents at different levels by a system of qualifications reflecting what society wants of education and training.

19 Dec: DES publishes results of first national testing of seven year olds showing 28 per cent of seven year olds cannot recognize three letters of the alphabet and that nearly 30 per cent cannot count to 100.

Population and Society

ANNE H. GAUTHIER

Since the 1970s, the populations of all industrialized countries have undergone major changes: a decline in fertility and marriage rates, and an increase in cohabitation, divorce, and female labour force participation. In this short essay, I discuss some of the most recent changes affecting Britain's population. These changes are analysed from both a time-series perspective and a cross-national one, the emphasis being given to a comparison between Britain and the other industrialized countries. Five main areas are covered: population growth and age structure, ethnic composition, fertility, mortality, and family composition. The essay concludes with a discussion of the political issues raised by these different demographic changes.

A Slowing Population Growth

If the fear of overpopulation is still present at the worldwide level, at the national level a completely different situation is faced by the industrialized countries. While the population growth rate in the United Kingdom reached 0.74 per cent in 1960–65, it was down to 0.28 per cent in 1985–90.[1] In the long run, and under certain assumptions, the population is expected to gradually stabilize at around 61 million according to recent projections carried out by the Office of Population, Censuses and Surveys. Such a medium scenario is represented in figure 1 and is compared to two alternative scenarios; one showing an eventual decline of the population, the other a continuing increase, the population reaching nearly 65 million in 2029.

These figures are the results of some theoretical exercises, and are therefore only illustrative of some possible futures. It is nevertheless worth noting that in some countries, such as the former Federal Republic of Germany and Denmark, the number of deaths have been exceeding the number of births in recent years; making the total population growth rate entirely dependent on the net migration flow.

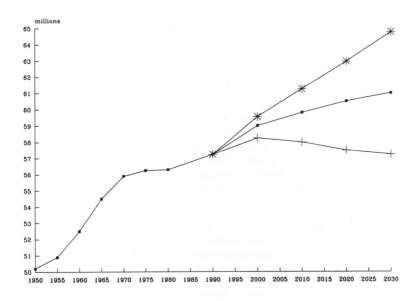

millions

Source: OPCS, National Population Projections, 1989–Based. Series PP2, no.17, HMSO, 1991.

Chart 1. Population size and projections for the UK 1950–2030

Population ageing

In parallel with this slowing population growth, all industrialized countries are experiencing a considerable ageing of their populations. While there were 10.7 per cent of persons aged 65 and over in the UK in 1950, this percentage is expected to double by the year 2026.[2] In terms of dependency ratio, this means that while there was one elderly to five working-age persons in 1950, the projected ratio is of one to three. This changing age structure of the population raises several political issues which are discussed in the last section. In order to illustrate this transformation of the age structure of the population, in figure 2 the population is represented by age group as it was in 1989, and the continuous line shows the projected population for the year 2026. While in 1989, the age structure of the population still looked like a pyramid, although with a narrow base, by 2026 we see a gradual rectangularization of the figure, the top becoming much broader as the baby-boom cohort reaches retirement age. As we mentioned above, this population ageing is not unique to Britain. In fact, it is projected to affect to a larger extent countries such as Luxembourg and the Netherlands as a result of their continuing very low fertility levels.

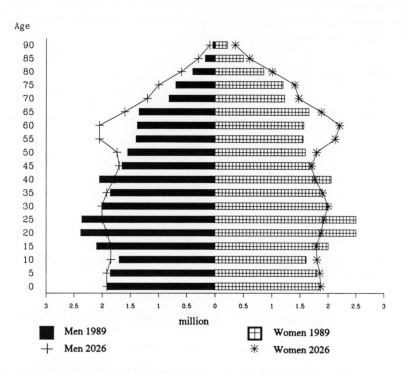

Age

Figures for 2026 based on principal projection
Source: OPCS, National Population Projections, 1989–Based. Series PP2, no.17, HMSO, 1991.

Chart 2. Population by age and sex for 1989 and projection for 2026.

Changing Ethnic Composition

In 1981, there were 6.2 per cent of foreign-born residents in Great Britain. This compares with 6.8 per cent in France and up to 26.3 per cent in Luxembourg.[3] Over time this percentage has doubled in Britain, up from 3.2 per cent in 1951. It is however more in terms of countries of origin that a major change is observed. While in 1951, 80 per cent of the foreign residents were born in the more developed countries, this has declined to 46 per cent in 1981. Conversely, the proportion of residents born in the NCW (New Commonwealth) has increased during this period from 14 per cent to 45 per cent.[4] Looking at the population by ethnicity rather than by country of birth reveals similar changes. While the non-white population represented 0.4 per cent of the total British population in 1951, by 1984-86, this had reached 4.5 per cent, among which around 40 per cent were born in Britain.[5] Indians, West Indians and Pakistanis represent the largest groups among these non-white residents. These figures illustrate well the changes in the ethnic composition of the population which have occurred during the last decades. Future changes are also to be expected as a result of growing pressures from international organizations to admit more refugees. The EC frontier-free market will moreover open the door to additional migration movements, an issue which is likely to raise important political challenges.[6]

'Fewer Babies, Longer Lives'[7]

The projected figures presented in sections 1 and 2 are based on a set of assumptions concerning fertility, mortality and migration. With regard to fertility, the current level of 1.85 children per woman in the United Kingdom in 1990 is well below replacement, and shows no sign of forthcoming increases.[8] In terms of inter-country ranking, this current fertility level places Britain near the top of the distribution as can be seen in chart 3. Only in Ireland and in Sweden is fertility still above two children per woman, although it has been declining very rapidly in the former in recent years.

These low levels of fertility contrast sharply with the very high levels observed during the baby-boom. In fact, during the period of rapid decline, or baby-bust, the total fertility rate in Britain was reduced by more than one child per woman from its peak in 1964.[9]

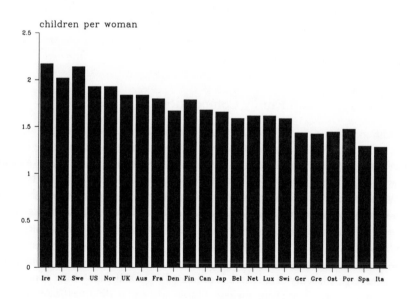

Sources: Council of Europe, Recent Developments in Europe 1991; United Nations, Demographic Yearbook 1989; C. Jones, 'Birth statistics 1990', Population Trends. 65: 9-15, 1991.

Chart 3. Total fertility rate per woman by country, 1989-90

This strong decline is the result of two factors: a decreasing average family size (intensity effect), and an increase in the average age at childbearing (timing effect). With regard to the first of these factors, two trends have been observed: a gradual disappearing of large families, and an increasing proportion of childless women. Among the 1950 birth cohort in England-Wales, it is expected that 31 per cent of women will have three or more children, while 15 per cent are expected to remain childless.[10] This compares with, respectively, 40 per cent and 11 per cent for the cohort born 10 years earlier.[11] The second factor which characterizes the change in fertility behaviour is the increase in the average age at childbearing. While in 1970, 66 per cent of first-time-mothers were less than 25 years old, in 1985 this was only the case for 51 per cent of mothers.[12] Again, this trend is not unique to Britain, and is common to all industrialized countries.

If couples have fewer children than before, they also live longer (without implying here a causal link). While the average life expectancy at birth was 68 years for males and 75 years for females in 1965–70, in 1988 it had reached, respectively, 72 and 78 years.[13] These figures place the United Kingdom in an average position when compared with the other EC countries,[14] leaving room for further improvements. This issue was in fact recently tackled by the government through its health policy which aims at first, reducing the number of deaths related to circulatory and respiratory diseases (which accounted for over 70 per cent of all deaths in 1990),[15] and second, reducing the regional and social class mortality differentials.[16] Efforts are also made with regard to AIDS which, as of March 1990, amounts to 55 reported cases per million inhabitants in the UK. This is well below the 99 cases average for the EC[17] – although international comparisons are difficult to make because of differences in detection rates.

New Household and Family Composition

In addition to these demographic changes, the family has also undergone several transformations. While a detailed analysis of these changes is not possible in this short essay, it is worth underlining three of them. First, since the 1970s we have observed a decline in marriage rates, along with an increase in cohabitation. Indeed, for an increasing proportion of people, cohabitation is now the norm, with more than half of the newly-weds in 1987 having cohabited some time before getting married.[18] For most, however, cohabitation is still a prelude to marriage rather than a definite alternative to it, as is the case in Scandinavia.

Second, this decline in the popularity of marriage has also been accompanied by the increasing instability of unions. It is estimated that for 100 marriages concluded in Britain in 1987, 37, or about one out of three, will end in divorce if rates remain at their current levels.[19] As a consequence of this trend, there has been a major increase in the number of single-parent families, doubling over the period 1971–89.[20] They are estimated to represent 15.5 per cent of all families in Great Britain in 1987–89.

Finally, a correlate of these previous trends has been the substantial increase in the percentage of children born out of wedlock. From less than 10 per cent of children until 1978, it reached 28 per cent in 1990. Such a percentage is comparable with the French figure, but is well below the 52 per cent observed in Sweden, and well above the 10 per cent observed in the former Federal Republic of Germany, and 13 per cent in Ireland.[21]

Political Issues

The demographic changes outlined previously carry obvious political implications. Three of them are examined here. First, there is the whole issue of zero or declining population growth and of population ageing. While some authors have pointed out the economic and social disadvantages of such a demographic situation, others have drawn a less pessimistic picture, suggesting ways of adjusting the economy and the institutions to the demographic trends.[22] Without entering this debate, we need nevertheless to acknowledge that the increase in the number of elderly, and especially in the ratio of elderly to each working-age person, will place additional strains on the welfare state, especially on the financing of public pension schemes and of health care. Estimates show that in order to maintain pension benefits at their current level (as a ratio of earnings), employer plus employee contribution rates would need to be increased by about 35 per cent from their present level by the year 2030 as a result of the demographic changes.[23] Of course, there will be fewer children, and one may argue that the extra expenditure implied by the ageing population could be financed by simply transferring money from the 'youth' portfolio to the 'elderly' one. However, when one considers that the public cost of each elderly person is about twice that of a child,[24] this transfer of money is clearly insufficient.

The changing family also represents challenges for society. The increasing labour force participation of women obviously calls for measures to facilitate the dual role of working parents: longer and better remunerated parental leave, more child-care facilities, and a more flexible schedule of work. On all these measures, Britain is lagging behind the other EC countries. For example, while in 1988 less than 40 per cent of children in Britain from three to school-age were enrolled in publicly funded day-care institutions, it was the case of over 95 per cent in France and Belgium, and over 50 per cent in Denmark, Greece, Ireland, Luxembourg, the Netherlands, Spain and the former Federal Republic of Germany.[25] The situation regarding those less than three years old is even more lamentable.

Finally, the increase in single-parent families and in isolated elderly people raises the whole problem of poverty and income security. In this respect, Britain compares unfavourably with the other EC countries; the incidence of poverty among children and elderly people being higher in the UK than in the Community as a whole.[26]

Conclusion

Over the past decades, the population of Britain has undergone major changes. People live longer, have fewer children, and are more likely to live in broken or reconstituted families following separation or divorce. All these changes have important implications at the political level. The increasing cost of the public pension scheme and of health care will require government to adapt institutions to the ageing population. In addition, the increase in single-parent families, and in the percentage of working mothers, is already calling for more support from the state. All these issues are already the subject of discussion at the EC level and in most of the member states. In contrast, the demographic factor seems to have attracted little attention in Britain until now. It is however not evident that the touchstones f the last decade, market forces or a policy of laissez-faire, would in this case be appropriate for dealing with the problems it presents.

Notes

1 OPCS, *National Population Projections, 1989-Based.* Series PP2, no.17, HMSO, 1991.

2 OPCS, *National Population Projections, op.cit.*

3 Eurostat, *Censuses of Population in the Community Countries 1981–1982*, Statistical Office of the European Community, Luxembourg 1988.

4 OPCS, *Demographic Review 1984*, 1987.

5 C. Shaw, 'Latest estimates of ethnic minority population', *Population Trends*, 51: 5-8, 1988.

6 *The Economist*, 1 June 1991, pp.47-48.

7 J. Ermish, *Fewer Babies, Longer Lives: Policy Implications of Current Demographic Trends*, Joseph Rowntree Foundation, 1990.

8 See C. Jones, 'Birth statistics 1990', *Population Trends*. 65; 1991, 9–15. An average of 2.1 children per woman are needed in order to replace the current generation. Recent increases in the total fertility rates have been observed in some European countries; the most striking case being that of Sweden, for which see J. M. Hoem, 'Social policy and recent fertility change in Sweden', *Population and Development Review*, 16, 4: 735–745, 1990. This reversal is partly the result of a catching-up by older women of births postponed earlier. Such a trend has not yet occurred in the United Kingdom where the total fertility rate has been relatively stable since 1981. Only a slight increase from 1.81 children per woman to 1.85 was observed between 1989 and 1990.

9 Eurostat, *Demographic Statistics 1989*, Statistical Office of the European Community, Luxembourg 1989.

10 F. Prioux, 'La Fécondité par rang de naissance dans les générations: évolution comparée en Angleterre-Galles, en France et aux Pays-Bas, depuis la génération 1930', *Population*, 4–5, 1988, pp.855–876.

11 Werner, 'Trends in first, second, third and later births', *Population Trends*, 45, 1986, pp26–33.

12 OPCS, *Period and Cohort Birth Order Statistics*, Series FM1, no.14, 1987. Calculated on the basis of the age- specific fertility rates at parity one.

13 OPCS, *Population Trends*, 65, 1991.

14 Eurostat, 1989.

15 OPCS, *Population Trends*, 65, 1991.

16 *The Financial Times*, 5 June 1991.

17 CSO (Central Statistical Office), *Social Trends*, 21, 1991.

18 J. Haskey and K. Kiernan, 'Cohabitation in Great Britain – characteristics and estimated numbers of cohabiting partners', *Population Trends*. 58, 1989, p25.

19 J. Haskey, 'Current prospects for the proportion of marriages ending in divorce', *Population Trends*, 55, 1989, pp34–7.

20 J. Haskey, 'Estimated numbers and demographic characteristics of one-parent families in Great Britain', *Population Trends*, 65, 1991, pp35–47.

21 C. Jones, 'Birth statistics 1990'.

22 Some classic references on the consequences of zero or negative population growth include J. J. Spengler, *Facing Zero Population Growth: Reactions and Interpretations, past and present*, Duke University Press, USA, 1978; and A. Sauvy, *Zero Growth*, Praeger, New York, USA, 1976. For a more recent view on this topic see P. Thane, 'Old-age: burden or benefit?' in H. Joshi (ed) *The Changing Population of Britain*, Basil Blackwell and Centre for Economic Policy Research, 1989.

23 J. Ermisch, *The Political Economy of Demographic Change*, Heinemann and Policy Studies Institute, 1983, p.207

24 P. Thane, *op.cit.*, p.63.

25 P. Moss, *Childcare in the European Communities 1985–1990*, Commission of the European Community, 1990.

26 CEC (Commission of the European Community), *Final Report on the Second European Poverty Programme 1985–1989*, Brussels, 1991.

Chronology

I. Policy statement, discussion, legislation

24 Feb: Tories' dispute over the future of child benefit.

11 Mar: Row over 'virgin births' and AID treatment to women who do not have sexual relationships with men begins.

20 Mar: The new government budget includes an increase in child benefit from October of £1 for the first child (to £9.25) and of 25p for the other children (to £7.50). Child benefits will be indexed in line with inflation from April 1992.

21 Mar: Fertility clinics are only to treat single women if they take the future welfare of any resulting children into account.

11 Oct: Decision of the High Court justifying the government in excluding employees who work fewer then 16 hours a week from protection against unfair dismissal and from the right to redundancy pay.

14 Oct: Implementation of the Children Act.

25 Oct: European court rules that employers cannot differentiate workers' pension benefits on the basis of sex.

29 Oct: Launch of the government's initiative *Opportunity 2000* which aims at increasing women's workforce participation.

1 Nov: Publication of the Asylum Bill to enable applications for asylum in the UK to be dealt with more quickly and efficiently and to tighten entry regulations (this was condemned by the UN on 14 Dec.).

3 Nov: Government announcement that maternity pay will be increased.

10 Dec: Government decides not to join the other 11 member states of the EC in signing the social chapter at the Maastricht summit.

Homosexuality

15 Feb: The Criminal Justice Bill is amended so that consenting homosexual activity should not be affected by its proposals to penalize more heavily violent and sexual offenders.

5 Mar: Insurance companies are to continue to discriminate against homosexuals because of HIV according to the Institute of Actuaries' *AIDS Bulletin.*

27 Mar: House of Keys in the Isle of Man votes by fifteen to eight in favour of a select committee which says homosexual acts in private should remain criminal offence. This prompts gay rights campaigners to call on the Home Office to intervene.

10 Apr: House of Keys throws out attempts to legalize homosexual acts between consenting adults. This was followed on 2 May by the commitment for trial in Douglas of thirteen men accused of buggery.

28 May: Legislative Council, the upper house of the House of Keys, votes by five to four against an amendment to the Sexual Offence Act which would have legalized adult homosexual acts in private.

1 Dec: Scottish Office advises authorities not to prosecute consenting males between 16 and 21 for homosexuality.

II. Statistical Reports

19 Mar: Maternal mortality rate fell by 18 per cent from 9.3 per 100,000 births in 1982–4 to 7.6 in 1985-7.

20 Mar: OPCS figures show a sharp increase in female deaths due to lung cancer and the related increase in female smoking.

17 Apr: OPCS figures in *Marriage and Divorce Statistics*, HMSO, show a sharp drop in the remarriage rate.

29 July: Family Policy Studies Centre reports that Britain's total period fertility rate has fallen to 1.8 children per woman and that of the EC to 1.6.

17 Sept: OPCS figures in *Population Trends* show that the number of one-parent families doubled in the last twenty years and that more than one child in five born in England-Wales in 1990 was born outside wedlock.

5 Dec: *Family Spending – A Report on the 1990 Family Expenditure Survey*, HMSO, finds that the average household size in 1990 was 2.48, the lowest ever recorded. The average weekly household expenditure was £247 and the average weekly income was £306.

III. Other studies

11 Jan: Study by Alcohol Research Group shows widespread disregard for licensing laws relating to underage drinking.

18 Jan: Research by Mintel International shows that 25 per cent of the population still own 75 per cent of the wealth.

4 Feb: Publication of Annette Lawson's study of contemporary adultery, *Adultery: An Analysis of Love and Betrayal*, Oxford University Press.

11 Feb: A study by the Policy Studies Institute, *One False Move . . . A Study of Children's Independent Mobility* Mayey Hillman, John Adams, and John Whitelegg shows that children's mobility has dramatically declined over the last twenty years because of traffic risks and fears of child abuse.

12 Mar: *Walls Pocket Money Monitor* shows that children are more affluent than ever with the average pocket money now at £1.69 per week.

20 Mar: *The Childhood Environment and Adult Disease*, Ciba Foundation argues that adult diseases may have their roots in early childhood, or even before birth.

2 Apr: NOP survey in *Radio Times* finds that Britons on average spend more than 50 per cent of their leisure time watching television and one in eight spends 90 per cent of leisure time watching it.

15 Apr: A Family Policy Studies Centre report, *Benefiting Europe's Children*, shows that UK lags behind Europe over child benefit.

6 Aug: A report in the *Health Education Journal* questions the extent to which gay men have modified their sexual behaviour in the light of the risk of AIDS.
Research in south west England by Exeter University's Institute of Population Studies shows that young people are not heeding calls for safe sex and analyses their sexual activities.

13 Aug: According to a Health Education Authority survey, one in three 16 year olds have lost their virginity.

16 Sept: Family Policy Studies Centre reports that current high divorce rates will lead to increases in the number of neglected and financially insecure elderly in the future, with consequent effects on health and social services.

14 Oct: The Equal Opportunity Commission report *Women and Training* shows sex bias in training.

1 Dec: Study by Family Policy Studies Centre finds that remarriage of divorced parents can take a heavier social, psychological and educational toll of children than if divorced parents stay single.

Sport

PETER BILSBOROUGH

The most prominent players in sport in 1991 were John Major, who made a reasonable contribution to progress, and a collection of composite groups and governing bodies, some of whom took useful steps forward and others who did little to help their causes. John Major's government adopted a relatively positive approach to sport. It had inherited from its predecessor a number of controversial policies and schemes which had restricted sports development. Although it left some of these intact including a range of fiscal and structural arrangements which continued to impede sports provision by some local authorities, it also attempted, albeit halfheartedly at first, to develop and improve others and in particular those concerned with programmes and resources for physical education and sport in schools. It also introduced a couple of new initiatives of its own to facilitate growth. It doubled central government's financial contribution to sport and encouraged the revival of school-aged sport. These were beneficial developments but those involved in sport were disappointed that the efforts which the Prime Minister had made to identify himself with sport were not paralleled by the production of a more cohesive set of policies, effective strategies or even greater funding. In the sports community some groups made good progress, particularly over the thorny issues of bad sportsmanship, doping and hooliganism. In contrast, some other policy-makers and influentials were involved in damaging public power plays, disagreed about strategies and procedures and sometimes failed to show that they could operate effectively.

The Status Quo

A number of the policies of Margaret Thatcher's government continued to restrict the provision of facilities and opportunities for sport and recreation in 1991. John Major made no attempts to protect sport from the damaging effect of his predecessor's fiscal policies designed to limit public spending and reduce the power and autonomy of local authorities. New financial and management arrangements continued to weaken the development of community sport and recreation.

The amount of central government grant received by a local authority is determined by the Standard Spending Assessment (SSA) set by government. Many local authorities feel that SSAs do not take adequate account of their needs and so they have had to set higher levels of community charge than might have been the case. The formula used to determine SSAs does not take account of the provision of sport and recreation, which is a non-statutory responsibility, and local authorities with well-developed collections of sport and recreation facilities have been particularly disadvantaged within the SSA calculations. Consequently, sport was an obvious and easy target for cuts by local authorities and particularly those with high community charges threatened by capping. As a result, the provision of community sport and recreation continued to be eroded in 1991 as some local authorities increased prices, reduced opening hours and let standards of maintenance slip. Another alarming trend was a weakening in the perceived importance of non-statutory sport and recreation by some local authorities.[1] This incipient drift away from providing for sport was compounded by the incremental implementation of compulsory competitive tendering to the management of sport and leisure services. It was introduced in 1989 as a value for money exercise to improve the quality of services but in 1991 it started to encourage the perception in some council chambers that sport was a peripheral activity which could be provided at arm's length by contract.

It was not all gloom and doom however. Despite many financial difficulties some local authorities did expand sports facilities and services. In 1990–1, 53 sports halls were completed and a further 45 were under construction. Fifty-five artificial turf pitches were also laid out and an additional 18 were under construction. Moreover, the local authorities in Birmingham and Sheffield were involved in some grand schemes to revitalize local economies and boost civic confidence and pride. Birmingham City Council opened a £160 million international convention centre incorporating an indoor sports arena with a capacity for 12,000 spectators. Sheffield City Council hosted the World Student Games which attracted 300,000 spectators and 5,500 competitors and officials from 111 countries.[2] The Games were well-received despite a tortured gestation and a loss of £10.5 million. Moreover, the city has been left with a range of world class sports facilities for both community and international events and the Ponds Forge International Pool has already become one of the country's most visited attractions.

Amendments

The third Thatcher government introduced the Education Reform Act in 1988 to raise standards and increase accountability. It proposed the development and implementation of a national curriculum and physical education was included as one of the ten compulsory foundation subjects. Subsequently, a national curriculum working party for physical education was established to formulate advice on programmes and attainment targets. Its interim report, published in February, recommended that pupils should learn the skills of competitive individual and team games; be able to swim 25 metres by the age of 11; be exposed to the six disciplines of athletics, swimming, gymnastics, dance, games and outdoor activities; and be taught how to appreciate and evaluate movement.[3] It was widely supported by the physical education and sports communities but at the same time they expressed concern over the availability of resources to deliver the curriculum properly.

Initially, it appeared that John Major's government would not support or finance this new curriculum. Kenneth Clarke, the education secretary, was surprisingly critical of the interim report. He suggested that there was not enough emphasis on practical activity and requested the working party 'realistically' to relate its final recommendations 'to the general level of school funding which can reasonably be expected to be available' and he hinted that resources would not be available to deliver the recommendations on swimming provision.[4]

The working party reiterated the importance of swimming in its final report published in August. Its resolve had been stiffened by the cross-party support for school swimming from a House of Commons education, science and arts committee enquiry into physical education and school sport; by an attempt by Anne Winterton, the Conservative MP for Congleton, to introduce a Private Member's bill making school swimming lessons compulsory; and by the Second Sea Lord, Admiral Sir Brian Brown, who had expressed concern about the lack of swimming ability amongst potential recruits to the Senior Service. Subsequently, the government discarded its previous stance and largely accepted the report including the recommendations for swimming. It also initiated a survey to assess the feasibility and cost of the recommended swimming provision and calculate when it should be introduced in schools.[5]

The explosion in indoor sports provision in the late sixties and seventies, and the consequent growth and development of many erstwhile 'minority' sports, led to playing fields and the pitch sports receiving little attention except from those most closely involved in management and participation. By the mid 1980s however, concern was increasingly being expressed by the sports community about the poor quality of provision and the loss of pitches. By 1990 this concern had reached a crescendo and the sports community had been joined by local authorities, politicians and the public.

At the start of 1991 the Liberal Democrats published evidence that school and community playing fields were being sold off by local councils as a way of raising money for maintenance and repairs to school buildings. Of the 63 councils who replied to its survey, 63 per cent said they were planning to sell land and 39 gave figures showing that more than 1,800 acres were up for sale.[6] Councils involved in land deals blamed Mrs Thatcher's governments for the losses. They argued that her fiscal policies had forced them to sell pitches in order to maintain statutory services and avoid rate and community charge capping. There is little doubt that the 1980 Planning and Land Act, the 1981 Department of Education and Science (DES) Instrument 909 and the 1988 Planning Policy guidance note did nothing to discourage local authorities. The 1980 act enabled local authorities to sell playing fields without making compensatory provision in the same area. The DES instrument ruled that schools did not need as much playing space as had been assumed and it gave the green light to local authorities to sell off school land for profit in the knowledge that school rolls were set to fall in the eighties. Finally, the guidance note stated that there should always be a 'presumption' in allowing planned development unless there were overriding reasons to the contrary.[7]

During 1991 John Major's government took several positive steps to prevent further losses and improve provision. Firstly, it gave the Sports Council £500,000 to establish a register of existing playing pitches to support the retention of areas of formal open space and in particular school playing fields. Secondly, it published a policy planning guidance note which emphasized that local authorities should ensure that existing stocks of playing fields and open spaces available for sport and recreation were not depleted without taking account of the long-term needs of the community for recreation and amenity open space. It also made quite clear to local authorities that playing fields should normally be protected and that local plans should include a statement on the extent of the community's requirements for sports pitches and policies on the protection of playing fields. Both initiatives were well received but some pessimists suggested that a register would be too complicated and time-consuming to create and maintain.

New Initiatives

John Major has identified himself, more than any other post-war prime minister, with sport. His particular passion is cricket. He spent his first day at the Oval in 1952 and has been a regular visitor ever since. He is also president of Surrey's youth appeal. Through his interest, sport has become a higher priority for the government and in 1991 it made moves on two fronts to facilitate development. Firstly, it made a relatively large amount of money available to a range of providers and consumers and secondly it attempted to revive school-aged sport.

The government almost doubled its contribution to sport in 1991. It gave an extra £40 million which was made available through the establishment of the Foundation for Sport and the Arts. The idea was put forward by Littlewoods, the pools firm, to buy off any idea by the government to establish a national lottery. The Foundation is underwritten by Littlewoods, Vernons and Zetters, the three big pools companies. They agreed to contribute £40 million per year and the government £20 million by reducing tax on pools' betting duty from 40 per cent to 37.5 per cent. Sport will receive £40 million a year and the arts £20 million. Tim Rice, the lyricist and cricket-lover, is the Foundation's chairman and its secretary is Grattan Endicott, a former Littlewood's executive. The Foundation awards grants to local and national clubs and organizations to build, improve and maintain facilities, purchase equipment and maintain and extend activities.[8]

The Foundation received a muted welcome although it had made the biggest ever cash injection to sport in Britain. Some of the sports community were disappointed that sports related expenditure was being used to pay for the arts. Some sports administrators also cast doubt on the ability of the Foundation to plan and act strategically. They argued that it lacked the appropriate infrastructure to deal with grant applications; queried its criteria for awarding grants and highlighted the restrictions imposed upon it by Customs and Excise which prevented money being given to a selection of Olympic sports. Perhaps most significantly, the sports community resented the way in which the pools companies had bought off the government and robbed sport of about £240 million a year. They had expected the government to establish a national lottery from which they estimated that sport would receive £300 million a year. As a result some groups continued to lobby hard for a lottery arguing that it could raise £1 billion a year for sport, art and environmental projects, create 56,000 new jobs and prevent European lotteries seizing the British market.[9] By the end of the year a considerable head of steam had been built up including support from government and Opposition MPs and most of the sports community believed that a lottery was inevitable. However, no political party had formally pledged its support and it was hinted that the pools companies could, with additional government support, increase the Foundation's funding and further scotch the lottery lobby.

During the year the government paid particular attention to promoting opportunities for school children to participate in sport. Initially, the sports minister, Robert Atkins, was moved from the Department of the Environment to the DES to strengthen the link between sport and education. This was followed by the establishment of a £700,000 pilot national coaching scheme for school children, entitled Championship Coaching, administered by the National Coaching Foundation. It aimed to provide 3,600 boys and girls between 11 and 14 years of age from 20 English local education authorities with opportunities to participate in 11 individual and team sports. It also aimed to identify gifted youngsters and coach them to higher levels of performance and excellence. There was a largely favourable reaction to the scheme but its critics argued that it was too small. They noted that it involved only 0.2 per cent of children aged 11–14 in schools and 18 per cent of English local education authorities.[10]

The increasingly positive attitude towards sport in the highest echelons of government has been welcomed but at the same time it was thought by some that John Major had not lived up to expectations. The Sports Council was particularly critical of the government's financial support. It was alarmed that the gap between what the government spent on sport and took from sport continued to widen. It was also angry, and at the same time puzzled, that its own grant had been cut in real terms for the fourth successive year. It found it hard to believe that the government's resourcing of sport had been made on the basis of a full appraisal of need. Similarly, local authority groups condemned the Prime Minister for failing to abjure existing New Right public sector fiscal policies and arrangements which were impeding community sports provision.

The government was also criticized by the Labour Party for its rather reactive and unco-ordinated policies and initiatives. It played on the government's failure to deliver its long-promised review of the structure of British sport initiated by Colin Moynihan in 1987. Labour attempted to gain the high ground with the publication of a *Charter for Sport* – the first comprehensive party policy statement since its own white paper on sport in 1975.[11] The sports community welcomed its contents but it continued to wait for the fine words from either party to be matched with deeds and resources.

Developments and Disputes

During the year some groups within the sports community made good headway in dealing with the persistent problems of bad sportsmanship, doping and hooliganism but at the same time the contributions and achievements of others were rather laboured and impeditive. Considerable progress was made to arrest the perceived erosion of the values of sportsmanship and fair play. The Central Council of Physical Recreation (CCPR) set the pace with strong support from its president, the Duke of Edinburgh. In 1990 the Council had launched a code of conduct calling for a renewal of ethical standards and acceptable behaviour throughout the practice of sport. It followed this up in 1991 with various practical measures to further its cause. Various national and international bodies declared their support for the code and began to copy and implement it in 1991. The International Cricket Committee introduced a code of conduct exhorting respect for the letter and spirit of the rules and the Football Association's (FA) plans for a premier league included a code of conduct for players and managers. Fair play was also made a deciding factor in the rugby union world cup finals if points and tries could not produce a winner. The Sports Council complemented the CCPR's ethical cause by continuing to give a strong lead on combating cheating through the expansion of measures aimed at preventing the use of performance-enhancing substances. In 1990–91 it increased its out-of-competition testing by 30 per cent and involved four more sports in this form of scrutiny. The total number of samples taken rose by 14 per cent and the number of positive tests fell from 48 to 41. The governing bodies have so far taken action in 35 of the 41 cases.[12] The use of illegal substances is steadily being eliminated.

The football authorities began to look towards a brighter future in 1991. Attendances at English League matches were up for the fifth successive season, England's fourth place in the 1990 world cup was followed by a run of 12 matches without defeat and Manchester United's win in the European Cup Winner's Cup marked a successful return by English clubs to European competition. Even more significantly, the number of arrests and ejections at Football League (FL) matches fell dramatically in 1990–91 indicating that the measures taken by the football authorities, the clubs and the police to control hooliganism were beginning to pay dividends. Arrests fell by 31 per cent from 5,945 in 1989–90 to 4,111 in 1990–91, while ejections dropped by 27 per cent from 6,973 to 5,070.[13]

On a more pessimistic note, progress was hindered by a lengthy power struggle between the FA and FL. Both governing bodies realized that despite government money from the Football Trust they had to increase their income to help clubs pay for ground improvements in the wake of Lord Justice Taylor's enquiry into the 1989 Hillsborough disaster. They both recognized that they could do more to increase sponsorship but they had their own ideas about how to raise and distribute the money. In April, several leading clubs prompted the FA to approve the establishment of a premier division of 18 clubs independent of the FL which they argued could generate £112 million a year. They wanted half of it to be retained by the new elite and the rest distributed between the remaining 72 FL clubs. The FL fought to protect the integrity of the existing structure but its case was rejected in the High Court. A new commercially independent FA premier league will start in 1992–93 and compensation of £3 million a year for five years will be paid to the clubs left behind.[14] In the short term the squabble had an adverse effect on pending commercial deals while in the long term it is feared that some lower division clubs will become part-time or go out of business and jobs will be lost.

In November the country's leading composite bodies came together to establish the British Sports Forum as a focus for the whole of sport and a lobbying body to government. However, there was a feeling that it was too little too late and that a credible corporate body should have been established 20 years earlier to provide an effective corporate advocacy for sport. Moreover, the Forum was only established after considerable rancour and the CCPR remained a reluctant member. Similarly, attempts to achieve a single voice by the three groups competing to control and present London's bid to stage the 2000 Olympic Games took so long that when a unified group did emerge, it had left itself with insufficient time to prepare a detailed and credible bid and it lost out to Manchester.[15]

In racing, a protracted dispute between the racing community and the big off-course bookmakers continued to damage the sport's attempts to climb out of recession. The former held the latter responsible for racing's financial ills. It complained that the bookmakers were not putting enough money back into the sport and asked for a more realistic percentage of their turnover. In 1989 the bookmakers gave the sport 0.9 per cent of their turnover. In most other countries bookmakers donate 3–4 per cent. The bookmakers argued that the sport could do more to help itself. They were particularly critical of the Jockey Club's management and refused to offer more money until it made attempts to improve racing. At the end of the year the gulf between them was as wide as ever. The Jockey Club and the Horseracing Advisory Council demanded a £50 million levy payment for 1992–3 while the Bookmakers' Committee offered £35.5 million.[16] The Home Secretary was handed the task of setting a figure and at the same time there were calls to disrupt racing in order to obtain more money from the bookmakers.

Notes

1 J Richardson, 'A visit from the Minister', *Leisure Manager* 9:4, 1991.

2 *Relay*, 4 Winter 1991.

3 DES and the Welsh Office, *Physical Education for Ages 5–16: Proposals of the Secretary of State for Education and Science and the Secretary of State for Wales*, National Curriculum Council August 1991.

4 Letter from the Secretary of State for Education and Science to the chairman of the national curriculum working group on physical education, 19 February 1991.

5 *House of Commons Debates*, Vol 199 Cols 993–4, 27 November 1991.
6 *Times Educational Supplement*, 1 March 1991.
7 The Sports Council, *The Playing Pitch Strategy*, The Sports Council 1991; *The Times* 27 December 1990.
8 The Foundation for Sport and the Arts, *Policy Guidelines and Criteria Approved by the Trustees*, unpublished paper from the Foundation for Sport and the Arts, 30 August 1991.
9 The Lottery Promotion Company Limited, *The National Lottery – A Legacy for Britain*, The Lottery Promotion Company Limited, September 1991.
10 *House of Commons Debates*, Vol 191 Cols 220–1, 16 May 1991.
11 *Charter for Sport*, Labour Party, September 1991.
12 *1990-1 Annual Report*, The Sports Council, 1991.
13 *The Times*, 25 July 1991.
14 *A Blueprint for the Future of Football*, The Football Association 1991; *The Times*, 1 August 1991.
15 *The Sports Industry*, March 1991; *The Times* 25 April 1991.
16 House of Commons Home Affairs Committee, *Levy on Horserace Betting Vol.1*, HMSO 1991.

Winners of Major Events 1991
Association Football
    Football League: Arsenal
    FA Cup: Tottenham Hotspur
    Littlewoods Cup: Sheffield Wednesday
    Scottish Football League: Rangers
    Scottish FA Cup: Motherwell
Athletics
    GRE British League: Haringey
    London Marathon (Men): Yakov Tolstikow (USSR)
    (Women): Rosa Mota (Portugal)
Badminton
    All-England Championships
    (Men's singles): Ardy Wiranata (Indonesia)
    (Women's singles): Susi Susanti (Indonesia)
Basketball
    National Champions: Kingston
Cricket
    Britannic Assurance County Championship: Essex
    NatWest Bank Trophy: Hampshire
    Benson and Hedges Cup: Worcestershire
    Refuge Assurance Cup: Worcestershire
Cycling
    Tour of Britain (Milk Race): Chris Walker (Great Britain)
Equestrian
    Badminton Three Day Event: Rodney Powell (Great Britain) The Irishman
Golf
    British Open Championship: Ian Baker-Finch (Australia)

Dunhill British Masters Championship: Severiano Ballesteros (Spain)
Volvo PGA Championship: Severiano Ballesteros (Spain)
Hockey
Poundstretcher National League: Havant
Hockey Association Cup: Hounslow
English Women's Champions: Sutton Coldfield
Horse Racing
1000 Guineas: Shadayid (Willie Carson)
2000 Guineas: Mystiko (Michael Roberts)
Oaks: Jet Ski Lady (Christy Roche)
St Leger: Tovlon (Pat Eddery)
Derby: Generous (Alan Munro)
Grand National: Seagram (Nigel Hawke)
Motor Racing
British Grand Prix: Nigel Mansell (Great Britain) Williams
Rowing
The University Boat Race: Oxford
Rugby League
Silk Cup Challenge Cup: Wigan
Stones Bitter League Champions: Wigan
Rugby Union
Courage English League: Bath
McEwan's Scottish League: Boroughmuir
Pilkington English Cup: Harlequins
Schweppes Welsh Cup: Llanelli
Heineken Welsh League: Neath
International Championship: England
Tennis
All-England Championships
(Men's singles): Michael Stich (Germany)
(Women's singles): Steffi Graf (Germany)

Notable Sporting Achievements 1991

21 Jan: Simon Hodgkinson, England's full-back, kicks a record seven penalties in the Five-Nations game against Wales in Cardiff.

27 Jan: Nick Gillingham breaks the world 200m short course breast stroke record in a time of 2min. 08.15s.

2 Mar: A British relay team of Linford Christie, Darren Braithwaite, Ade Mafe and John Regis break the world indoor 4 x 200m record in a time of 1min. 22.11s.

10 Mar: Stephen Hendry becomes the first snooker player to win five world ranking events in one term.

16 Mar: England achieve the Grand Slam in the Five-Nations Rugby Championship.

1 April: Scotland win the men's world curling championships in Winnipeg, Manitoba.

6 May: John Parrott, the English snooker player, wins the world title.

11 May: England win the European Nations cup in women's hockey.

15 May: Manchester United beat Barcelona 2-1 to win the European Cup Winners' Cup.

18 May: Tottenham Hotspur beat Nottingham Forrest to win the FA cup for a record eighth time.

1 June: Steve Marsh, the Kent wicketkeeper, equals the world record of eight catches in an innings in a county championship game at Lord's.

10 June: Graham Gooch, the England cricket captain, becomes the sixth Englishman to carry his bat in a Test match, and only the second against the West Indies.

20 July: Rory Underwood, the Leicester wing, becomes England's most capped player when he is awarded his 44th cap against Fiji.

27 Aug: Graham Gooch becomes the thirteenth cricketer, and only the fifth from England, to total 7,000 runs in Tests.

30 Aug: Liz McColgan wins the 10,000m and Britain's first gold medal at the world athletics championships in Tokyo.

1 Sept: At the world athletics championships in Tokyo the British men's 4 x 400m relay team of Roger Black, Derek Redmond, John Regis and Kris Akabusi beat off a strong American challenge to win the gold medal.

20 Sept: Roger Black wins the season-long IAAF/Mobil grand prix 400m title.

21 Sept: Chris Eubank wins the World Boxing Organisation's super-middleweight title.

29 Sept: Penny Way wins the women's world board sailing championship in California.

21 Oct: Nick Gillingham breaks his own world 200m short course breast stroke record in a time of 2min. 07.93s.

4 Nov: Liz McColgan records 2hr. 27min. 22s to win the New York City marathon.

Chronology

17 Jan: An England A cricket tour of Pakistan is aborted because of the outbreak of war in the Gulf.

The Sports Council and BBC Radio Sport launch a new competition to encourage fair play amongst both amateur and professional sports players.

21 Jan: Richard Griffiths, the Wales B centre, becomes the first rugby union player banned for using anabolic steroids.

24 Jan: The Rugby Football League tightens up its drug processing procedures.

31 Jan: Lord Justice Taylor, whose report on the Hillsborough disaster set the agenda for the future of British football, said that he was 'most disappointed' that more clubs were not prepared to share grounds.

8 Feb: London challenges Manchester for the UK nomination for the 2000 Olympic Games after the capital's two rival groups unite their bids eight hours before the British Olympic Association's extended deadline.

26 Feb: Simon Tuffs of Bradford Northern becomes the first rugby league player to be banned (for two years) for drug abuse.

7 Mar: Sheffield City Council, host to the World Student Games, agrees to provide an extra £5 million 'safety net', despite an earlier pledge that it would put no more funds into the financially troubled event.

19 Mar: In the Budget the Chancellor of the Exchequer, Norman Lamont, announces that he intends to establish a foundation funded by a reduction in pools betting duty and money from the pools companies. The estimated 60 million will be used to support sport and the arts.

29 Mar: A Sheffield inquest jury returns a verdict of accidental death on the 95 football fans who died in the Hillsborough disaster in 1989.

8 Apr: The Football Association agrees in principle to form a premier league within its own administration starting in August 1992. The Football League immediately declares its intentions to resist the move.

Almost two years after the Hillsborough disaster, safety experts criticize key elements of a plan by Sheffield Wednesday to reopen the Leppings Lane terraces where 95 Liverpool supporters died.

16 Apr: The three main guardians of British sports facilities – the Central Council of Physical Recreation, the Sports Council and the National Playing Fields Association – launch a joint campaign to counter the sale of playing fields. They ask central government to amend planning law and policy and local authorities to continue investing in the provision and maintenance of pitches.

19 Apr: UEFA, the European governing body of football, lifts its ban on Liverpool competing in Europe.

24 Apr: The British Olympic Association votes for Manchester to be Britain's bid to host the 2000 Olympic Games.

25 Apr: The Prime Minister makes an early declaration of support for Manchester's Olympic Games bid.

1 May: At the annual general meeting of the Marylebone Cricket Club a proposal that the club's rules be changed to allow women to become eligible for membership is defeated.

3 May: The Court of Appeal rejects claims of relatives and friends of people who died in the Hillsborough disaster for compensation for psychological damage suffered while watching the tragedy unfold on television or from nearby seats in the ground.

8 May: The Horserace Betting Levy Board announces cutbacks in spending twice as high as anticipated.

14 May: The Test and County Cricket Board rejects plans to radically alter the Sunday league but votes to introduce coloured clothing and white balls in 1992.

20 May: The Home Affairs Select Committee on the state of horseracing recommends the replacement of the Jockey Club by a new authority representative of all interests in racing, an increased levy on off-course bookmakers, extra money to be paid by bookmakers and not passed on to punters as 'deductions', racing to be permitted on Sundays, betting shops to stay closed on Sundays but allowed to open until 9pm on other days, better levels of prize money and the Levy Board to include a member who is seen to speak for the interests of the punter.

23 May: Manchester United is floated on the stock exchange.

5 June: A bill to make swimming and water safety lessons compulsory in schools is introduced in the Commons by Ann Winterton, Conservative MP for Congleton, with all-party support.

18 June: The Secretary of State for Scotland, Ian Lang, informs the Scottish Football Association that the government will offer only 'marginal support' to the £40 million project to redevelop Hampden Park.

19 June: An Education Select Committee report expresses concern at the decline of team sports in schools and recommends that teachers should be given finanical incentives to take part in extra-curricular sporting activities.

The Football Association unveils its *Blueprint for the Future of Football*. The key recommendation is the creation of a premier league with a football league of three divisions. Other ideas include: no premier league fixtures to be played on weekends preceding World Cup or European Cup qualifiers; more ground sharing; more television coverage; an increased voice for supporters in the counsels of the game; new coaching schemes for schoolboys; the establishment of a Commonwealth cup.

2 July: Plans for a £35 million redevelopment of Murrayfield are unveiled by the Scottish Rugby Union.

9 July: The government rejects calls for Sunday horse racing and more money from bookmakers to the sport.

10 July: Yorkshire decides that from next season it will drop the rule that only those born in the county can play for it.

14 July: The World Student Games opens in Sheffield. It is the largest and most expensive sports event ever held in Britain, costing about £170 million.

A Welsh XV looses 8–71 to New South Wales. It is the biggest as well as the most humiliating defeat ever recorded by a Welsh national side.

The record transfer fee between British football clubs is broken by the £2.9 million move of Dean Saunders, the Welsh international forward, from Derby County to Liverpool.

19 July: Craig McDermott, the Australian fast bowler, becomes Yorkshire's first overseas player.

20 July: The government announces stiffer penalties for those found guilty of supplying body-building drugs.

31 July: The High Court rules that the Football Association can set up and run a league of its own.

1 Aug: The High Court dismisses the Football League's case against the Football Association's establishment of a premier league

29 Aug: Grattan Endicott, the Secretary of the Foundation for Sport and the Arts, rejects the criticism of pro-lottery campaigners by commenting that the foundation is quite capable of handling and distributing money efficiently and effectively.

6 Sept: Sheffield City Council reveals that the World Student Games lost £10.4 million, the biggest deficit for any event in the history of British sport.

10 Sept: Following the disclosure of a cash crisis within the Amateur Boxing Association and the Sports Council's warning that it could withdraw grant aid of £130,000 a year, the Secretary of the British Boxing Board of Control, John Morris, calls for an 'umbrella organiaztion' to oversee boxing at both professional and amateur levels.

20 Sept: The British Boxing Board of Control grants Frank Bruno a licence to box after a successful operation for a torn retina.

21 Sept: After being knocked-out by Chris Eubank for the World Boxing Organiaztion's super-middleweight title, Michael Watson undergoes an emergency brain operation to remove a clot. This is followed by political criticism of the sport.

After the rugby world cup quarter final game in Paris between England and France, Daniel Dubroca, the French national coach, verbally abuses David Bishop, the match referee.

23 Sept: According to independent research commissioned by the Arts Council and Sports Council, there is significant interest in a national lottery amongst all sections of the population. This interest increases when it is realised that sport, arts and the environment will benefit from the proceeds.

30 Sept: A new governing body for British athletics is established. The British Athletic Federation replaces the British Amateur Athletic Board.

4 Oct: Birmingham City Council's futuristic £51 million national indoor arena is officially opened. It will stage five world championships in the next four years.

17 Oct: Neil Kinnock launches the Labour Party's *Charter for Sport* and promises 'a better deal for those millions of people who participate in sport'.

31 Oct: Following a month of negotiations between the Horserace Betting Levy Board and the Bookmakers' Committee, the task of setting the figure for next year's levy is handed to the Home Secretary, Kenneth Baker.

2 Nov: The rugby world cup final between England and Australia at Twickenham provides the first £1 million gate in the history of the game.

5 Nov: Britain's leading composite sports organisations come together to set up the British Sports Forum to provide a focus for the whole of sport and act as a lobbying body to government.

9 Dec: Sir John Quinton, chairman of Barclay's Bank, is appointed chairman of the Premier League.

Oxford United puts all its 28 professional footballers up for sale to help repay its £2 million debt to the Maxwell family, whose media empire is collapsing.

The British International Sports Committee advises Sheffield City Council that it would be 'inappropriate' for it to bid for the 1998 Commonwealth Games.

11 Dec: The government-appointed members of the Horserace Betting Levy Board recommend to the Home Secretary that bookmakers should pay £42.6 million in levy payments to racing in 1992–3 without increasing punters' deductions.

12 Dec: Jockey Club stewards approve plans for a new power-sharing structure – a British Horseracing Board.

16 Dec: The government gives £2 million to the Manchester bid for the 2000 Olympic Games to conduct a detailed feasibility study before deciding whether to back the attempts to stage the Games.

The government publishes its *Review of Sport* which contains proposals to create two new bodies from the exisiting Sports Council – an English Sports Council and a UK Sports Commission.

Race Relations and Immigration

ZIG LAYTON-HENRY

The year has been dominated by electoral considerations as the government neared the end of the Parliament. Every political crisis, whether over candidate selection, by-election campaigns or the rise in asylum seekers has been analysed in terms of its impact on the electoral fortunes of the government and the Opposition.

By September the major parties had selected almost all of their prospective parliamentary candidates. The three major parties had selected 19 Afro-Caribbean and Asian candidates compared with 29 in 1987 and 18 in 1983.[1] Of these seven were Conservatives, two of whom, Nirj Joseph Deva (Brentford and Isleworth) and John Taylor (Cheltenham) have been selected for Conservative held seats. Although both these seats can be considered marginal, these candidates have a good chance of being elected and thus being the first Afro-Caribbean and Asian Conservative MPs since post-war immigration began.[2] The controversy surrounding John Taylor's selection in Cheltenham was resolved on 10 February when his selection as the prospective parliamentary candidate was endorsed at a special meeting of the Constituency Association by 406 votes to 164. Mr Galbraith, the association member who was alleged to have said, 'I don't think we want a bloody nigger to represent us'[3] was expelled from the Constituency Association. His prosecution under the Race Relations Act was discontinued after his unexpected death on 28 October. The seven Afro-Caribbean and Asian candidates selected by the Conservatives for the 1992 general election represented a marginally higher figure than was the case for the last general election which was six. However none previously had been selected for a winnable Conservative seat.

The Labour Party has selected nine Afro-Caribbean and Asian candidates to fight the next election which is a significant reduction on the 14 selected in 1987. Those selected included the four non-white candidates elected in 1987, namely Diane Abbott (Hackney North and Stoke Newington), Paul Boateng (Brent South), Bernie Grant (Tottenham) and Keith Vaz (Leicester East). To these must be added Dr Ashok Kumar (Langbaurgh) who was elected at the by-election held on 7 November. The tensions of the approaching general election surfaced in this by-election campaign with Labour accusations that the Tories and Liberal Democrats had attempted to make 'race' an issue in the campaign. This was strenuously denied by the other parties who accused Labour of wishing to excuse a relatively poor performance. The Prime Minister had already pledged that the Tories would not play the immigration card in an election.

The fall in the number of Afro-Caribbean and Asian candidates selected by constituency Labour parties is partly explained by the dropping of some non-white candidates by the National Executive Committee in a number of by-elections in this Parliament. These included those at Kensington and Chelsea, South Staffordshire and Vauxhall. In each case a woman candidate was nominated instead. There have also been a number of controversies over parliamentary selections in Labour constituencies with large numbers of ethnic minority voters and party members. The selections at Birmingham Small Heath, Nottingham East, Ealing Southall and Birmingham Perry Barr, have all been investigated by the NEC after accusations that votes have been manipulated and the constitution violated. This shows the intense competition for inner-city nominations which tend to be safe Labour party seats. It is very likely that an Asian candidate will be confirmed in Southall and that this will raise the likely number of Labour Afro-Caribbean and Asian MPs to six after the general election.

The Liberal Democrats have selected three ethnic minority candidates for the general election, Zerbanoo Gifford in Hertsmere, Verona Marfo in Hackney North and Pash Nandhra in Ealing Southall, but none of these can be considered winnable prospects.

On 7 July the *Independent on Sunday* published the preliminary results of an NOP survey on 'race' issues for the Runnymede Trust. The sample of 1,817 people consisted of 572 Afro-Caribbean people, 479 South Asians (meaning people from the Indian sub-continent) and 766 whites. The survey was conducted through face to face interviews in areas of high ethnic minority settlement. It found that the proportions of Afro-Caribbeans and South Asians in inner-city areas who were Labour party supporters was 58 per cent and 55 per cent respectively; that support for the Conservatives was very low at 8 per cent and 12 per cent and that support for the Liberal Democrats was only 3 per cent among both groups. A large proportion, some 28 per cent, were undecided or refused to reveal their party affiliation. Labour support is increased and Conservative and Liberal Democrat support depressed by the inner-city nature of the samples, but the poll suggests that there is little evidence to support the much vaunted trend of Asians towards the Conservative party.[4]

The survey found that substantially higher proportions of Afro-Caribbeans than Asians felt discriminated against by employers, the police and the courts. 67 per cent of Afro-Caribbeans and 42 per cent of Asians thought ethnic minorities were treated worse by employers as did 38 per cent of whites. 75 per cent of Afro-Caribbeans believed that ethnic minorities were treated worse by the police compared with 44 per cent of Asians and 48 per cent of whites. 57 per cent of Afro-Caribbeans believe that ethnic minorities are treated worse by the courts compared with 19 per cent of Asians and 24 per cent of whites. Not surprisingly

26 per cent of Afro-Caribbeans agreed with the view that Britain is a very racist society compared with 6 per cent of Asians and 10 per cent of whites.[5]

Asylum Seekers and Refugees

The number of asylum applications continued to cause the government considerable concern. The numbers claiming asylum have risen from 1,563 in 1979 to 5,200 in 1988. In 1990 some 30,000 asylum applications were made and the Home Secretary informed the House in July that applications this year were running at 1,000 a week so that over 50,000 applications might be made in 1991.[6] The newspaper *The Daily Star* ran a campaign in May and June to halt the influx of foreigners who came to Britain to live off the state. It 'exposed' cases of illegal immigrants and asylum seekers and criminals involved in illegal immigration rackets. It claimed that thousands of Kurdish Turks are smuggled into Britain in lorries and that they request political asylum as soon as they arrive.[7]

On 2 July the Home Secretary announced a series of measures to cope with the increase in asylum applications. He laid before the House an order doubling the fines under the Carriers Liability Act (1987) from £1,000 per undocumented passenger to £2,000. He also announced the government would introduce an Asylum Bill to reform the treatment of asylum seekers and procedures for determining their claims. This would speed up the determination process and prevent abuses of the social security system by bogus applicants.[8] The Home Secretary also announced controversial changes in the publicly funded arrangements for advice and representation in immigration cases. The existing practice was that advice and assistance but not representation was available to those whose means qualified them under the legal aid green form scheme. In future the Home Secretary and Lord Chancellor proposed that advice and assistance and, where necessary, representation before the immigrant appellate authorities would be provided by the United Kingdom Immigrant Advisory Service (UKIAS). He argued that this would be more economical and more efficient. The Home Office grant to UKIAS would be increased to take account of the extra workload. The Home Secretary also announced that the proposed bill would provide for the accelerated handling of clearly unfounded cases. An adjudicator would be able to dismiss an appeal without an oral hearing upon deciding there is manifestly no substance to the claim. Mr Baker said, 'I believe that the rapid rejection of a large number of unfounded claims and the early departure of those applicants from this country will play a major part in deterring further abuse of the process and allow us to tackle the dramatic growth in the number of applications.'[9] He argued there was the need for a balance between obligations to genuine refugees, and obligations to the British people to control immigration.

The opposition criticized the proposals for reducing the rights of asylum seekers and making it more difficult for those in genuine fear of persecution. Mr Bernie Grant accused the government of using the numbers game on immigration and asylum matters to create a racist backlash. But Sir John Wheeler argued that without these measures a serious social problem would develop. Mr Baker utterly rejected the claim that the policy was racist.[10]

The proposals received a critical reception from the quality press[11] and interested organisations such as the Bar Council,[12] the Joint Council for the Welfare of Immigrants and UKIAS. However the tabloid press were enthusiastic in their support, *The Sun* arguing that the 'Tide of Migrants must be Turned' and that 'Britain is becoming the human dustbin of the world'.[13]

The arguments were rehearsed once again on 13 November when the Asylum Bill received its second reading. The Home Secretary argued that the numbers of people seeking asylum were posing problems throughout the world, that half a million had come to Europe this year and that the United Nations High Commissioner for Refugees estimated that there were 17 million refugees in the world. 'It would be gross irresponsibility of the government to ignore them and pretend that numbers do not matter.' Mr Baker argued that bogus applications were clogging up the system and that the central purpose of the bill and the rules were to speed up the determination process and to ensure that genuine cases are promptly identified and that rejected applicants leave the country.[14]

The Opposition spokesman, Mr Hattersley, reaffirmed the Labour Party's determination to prevent bogus asylum seekers from entering the country but criticized the bill for the arbitrary criteria against which asylum applications were to be measured and the inadequacy of the appeal system for those initially rejected. He felt that these problems would result in genuine asylum seekers being excluded. In particular Mr Hattersley attacked the proposals to transfer the representation of asylum seekers to UKIAS, to reduce the housing rights of asylum seekers, to fingerprint them and also the doubling of fines under the Carrier's Liability Act (1987). He argued that the government was introducing the Bill for the basest possible motives.[15]

The debate was heated and occasionally acrimonious with some participants ascribing the worst motives to their opponents. Bernie Grant argued that the bill was racist and suspected that the issues and the bill would feature strongly in the run up to the next general election.[16] Gerald Howarth, supporting the bill, called for the abolition of the Commission for Racial Equality as it had had the temerity to question the legality of the legislation as it indirectly discriminated against black people.[17] The government had a comfortable majority of 78 in both divisions after the debate and the bill was read a second time and committed to a Standing Committee.

The United Nations High Commission for Refugees condemned the British Asylum Bill arguing that the rules in the bill were in conflict with internationally accepted principles. The proposals to reject refugees who arrive in a group broke the UN rule that each case must be assessed individually on its merits. Also the proposal to allow immediate deportation to their own country, of people alleged to be bogus, violated the principle that each applicant should have the right to a proper appeal.

In November the Home Secretary was found guilty of contempt of court in another case concerning political asylum. In May a Zairean teacher, who claimed to have been tortured in Zaire, was expelled despite a Home Office undertaking to a judge that he could remain until his appeal had been heard. The High Court in July had accepted that a minister of the Crown could not be guilty of contempt of court but the Court of Appeal reversed this decision. Lord Donaldson, Master of the Rolls, upheld the courts' rights to protect individual rights against the state. The contention that the courts were the Crown courts and therefore that ministers of the Crown could not be in contempt was rejected. Given the constitutional importance of the case, the government has decided to appeal to the House of Lords.[18]

The Home Office was also condemned by Amnesty International for the internment of Iraqis and Palestinians at the start of the Gulf war. About 90 Iraqis and Palestinians were detained and Mr Baker justified these on the grounds that the detainees had links to terrorist groups. All the detainees were accepted as innocent by March, none were charged with terrorism and none were deported. No other Western country interned any Iraqis or Palestinians during the Gulf war. The Home Secretary's actions contributed to anti-Muslim tension in Britain which was inflamed by the tabloid press. There were numerous arson attacks on mosques in the aftermath of the outbreak of the war.

The Criminal Justice System

There has long been concern about the treatment of Afro-Caribbean people by the criminal justice system. The British Crime Survey published in September 1990 found that Afro-Caribbeans and Asians are particularly dissatisfied with the way in which their cases are handled by the police and with how they are treated when stopped in the street. Only 28 per cent of Afro-Caribbeans and 21 per cent of Asians who made 999 calls said they were satisfied compared with 53 per cent of whites. In the cases of those who visited police stations only 31 per cent of Afro-Caribbeans and 28 per cent of Asians were satisfied compared with 53 per cent of whites. There were much higher rates of satisfaction with encounters in public places with 69 per cent of whites being satisfied, 62 per cent of Afro-Caribbeans and 52 per cent of Asians. The police were found to be most likely to stop and question young men, particularly young Caribbean men. Only 12 per cent of Afro-Caribbean men described the police as very polite in pedestrian stops compared with 50 per cent of whites and Asians.[20]

The relations between the black community and the police were highlighted on 25 November when the Court of Appeal cleared Winston Silcott of the murder of PC Keith Blakelock. Shortly after, the two other men also sentenced to life imprisonment for the murder, Mark Braithwaite and Engin Raghip, were also cleared. All three had been convicted on the basis of alleged confessions to police, when denied access to solicitors. The police inquiry into the 1985 Broadwater Farm riot and PC Blakelock's murder was heavily dependent on arresting suspects and obtaining confessions. This was the case in most of the 63 prosecutions for riot and affray made after the riot. The mass arrests made after the riot deepened the gulf between young black people on the estate and the police and seriously undermined their opportunities of obtaining impartial witnesses and reliable evidence. Forensic evidence proved that the two most senior officers in the case lied on oath and conspired together to present Winston Silcott's alleged confession as a contemporaneous account and to have fabricated the note itself in pursuance of that conspiracy.[21]

Sir Peter Imbert, the Commissioner of the Metropolitan Police, said that he regretted that anyone had been wrongfully convicted of the murder of PC Blakelock but he declined to apologize to the three men who had spent six years in prison for the murder. He said that the inquiry into the murder of PC Blakelock would now be relaunched.[22] On Friday 13 December it was announced that Detective Chief Superintendent Graham Melvin, who led the inquiry, would be charged with perjury and with conspiracy to pervert the course of justice. Mr Melvin's assistant, Detective Inspector Maxwell Dingle, would also be charged with conspiracy to pervert the course of justice. Mr Melvin said he would vigorously contest the charges. He would be assisted by the Police Superintendent's Association.[23]

The Battle against Racial Discrimination

This has been another difficult year for the Commission for Racial Equality (CRE). It started with a success in that PC Surinder Singh was awarded substantial agreed damages of £20,000 by the Nottinghamshire Police Authority for racial discrimination. However, the legal costs of bringing the case were in excess of £150,000 and the CRE does not have the resources to pursue enough individual cases to make a substantial impression on the high levels of racial discrimination that are known to exist in all walks of life. For example, in January, it was reported that the Equal Opportunities Task Force's work at the King's Fund Centre from 1986–1990 had found huge levels of racial discrimination in the National Health Service and little being done to reduce it.

The high levels of cost, and the time and effort it takes to prove cases, and the generally low levels of compensation are a considerable deterrent from pursuing cases of racial discrimination. In 1989 only 1,307 people applied for assistance to the CRE to pursue complaints of racial discrimination. In 1990 this had risen to 1,381. In some cases it is hard to predict the outcome of judicial decisions, which may be an additional deterrent to bringing cases. For example, in July an industrial tribunal in Sheffield, found that an employer who refused to employ Muslims was not guilty of racial discrimination because religious discrimination was not covered by the 1976 Race Relations Act. One would have thought it would have been covered by the provisions outlawing indirect racial discrimination.

There was a similar decision by the High Court in October concerning the parents of a child who wished to move their daughter from a school with a significant proportion of Asian children to an all-white school. The Commission argued it was unlawful under the 1976 Race Relations Act for a Local Education Authority in carrying out its functions with regard to parental preference to do any act which constitutes racial discrimination. The Secretary of State for Education argued that the parents' right to choose a school of their choice under the 1980 Education Act overrode the racial discrimination provisions of the Race Relations Act. The High Court ruled in October that the Secretary of State was right and that Cleveland County Council's duty under the 1980 Education Act, to comply with the parents' wishes, overrode the provisions of the 1976 Race Relations Act. If many parents exercise their right to choose in a racially discriminatory way this will increase racial segregation in schools.

The CRE has to rely on the publicity for its successful cases making a wider impact. It also has to rely on the government giving a lead by supporting equal opportunities policies in public and by introducing monitoring procedures for appointments and promotions in the public sector, which the government has only slowly introduced. The CRE has also been pressing for amendments to the Criminal Justice Bill which would incorporate a statutory duty to be placed on criminal justice agencies to carry out and monitor their functions with proper regard to the need to avoid racial discrimination and for their activities, where appropriate, to be brought within the scope of the Race Relations Act. This seems wholly appropriate given the widespread concern with the racially discriminatory outcomes of the criminal justice system. However, the government did not incorporate these prescriptive amendments in the Act, but did impose a duty on the Secretary of State to publish such information as he considers expedient for the purpose of facilitating the performance of such persons of their duty to avoid discrimination against any persons on the grounds of race, sex or any other improper grounds.[24] Many people in the criminal justice system would have welcomed the more positive duty that the CRE amendments would have entailed.

Notes

1 The figure for 1987 includes seven selected by the Social Democratic Party. The figure for 1991 includes one Labour candidate in Southall who still has to be confirmed by the NEC.
2 There were three MPs from the Indian sub-continent elected to Parliament before World War Two. Dadabhai Naoroji was elected in 1892 for Finsbury Central as a Liberal; Sir Mancherjee Bhownagree was elected twice as a Conservative for Bethnal Green North East in 1895 and 1900 and Shapurji Saklatvala was elected twice for Battersea North, for Labour in 1922 and 1923 and as a Communist in 1924.
3 *The Sunday Times*, 10 February 1991.
4 *Runnymede Trust Bulletin*, No.247, July/August 1991.
5 Ibid.
6 House of Commons Debates, vol.194, cols 166, 2 July 1991.
7 *Runnymede Trust Bulletin* No.247, July/August 1991, p.19.
8 House of Commons Debates, vol.194, cols.166-7, 2 July 1991.
9 Ibid.
10 Ibid., col 171-172.
11 For example *The Independent* leader 4 November 1991.

12 *The Independent*, 14 November 1991.
13 *The Sun*, 31 August 1991.
14 House of Commons Debates, vol.198 cols. 1082-1085, 13 November 1991.
15 Ibid. cols. 1104-1107.
16 Ibid. cols. 1136.
17 Ibid. cols. 1163.
18 *The Independent*, 30 November 1991.
19 *The Independent*, 3 December 1991.
20 W G Skogan, *The Police and Public in England and Wales: A British Crime Survey Report*, Home Office Research Unit, 1990.
21 *The Observer*, 1 December 1991.
22 *The Independent*, 29 November 1991.
23 *The Independent*, 14 December 1991.
24 *Criminal Justice Act 1991.*, HMSO, 1991.

Chronology

2 Jan: Lord Chancellor's Department urges judges to streamline immigration appeals.

13 Jan: *Race and Criminal Justice*, NACRO, says that people from ethnic minorities are relatively harshly treated by the criminal justice system.

16 Jan: Police detain 28 Iraqis after the start of the Gulf war.

17 Jan: Further 35 Iraqis detained by the security forces.

18 Jan: Seven Palestinians are detained under Home Office deportation orders.

21 Jan: *The Work of the Equal Opportunities Task Force 1986-1990*, King's Fund Centre, finds glaring racial discrimination in the NHS and little effort to eliminate it.

25-26 Jan: Immediate release of a detained Palestinian and Iraqi ordered.

28 Jan: PC Surinder Singh wins £20,000 damages after an industrial relations tribunal finds he was refused transfer to the CID on racial grounds. Other Asian officers also receive damages awards against Nottinghamshire Constabulary.

30 Jan: Joint Council for the Welfare of Immigrants claims that deportation hearings on detained Iraqis and Palestinians will be a travesty with each hearing lasting less than 30 minutes.

1 Feb: Court of Appeal decides it has no power to intervene in the case of detained Palestinians and Iraqis.

5 Feb: *Barriers to Benefit: Black Claimants and Social Security*, NACAB, argues that people from ethnic minorities are badly served by the social security system, which does not cater well for poor speakers of English.

Refugee Council launches a charter to improve educational and job prospects for refugees.

6 Feb: Department of Employment shows that the proportion of ethnic minority young people staying in full time education is more than double that of the white population. Whilst only 11–12 per cent of whites aged 16–24 are in full time education the figures for West Indians is 15 per cent, for Bangladeshis 28 per cent and for Indians 31 per cent.

10 Feb: John Taylor confirmed as Conservative parliamentary candidate for Cheltenham by 406 to 164 votes in the constituency association.

20 Feb: Home Office Advisory Committee says attempts to intern Iraqis and Palestinians as a result of the Gulf conflict were only justified in 11 cases.

8 Mar: Remaining Arabs detained for security reasons during the Gulf war are released.

18 Mar: Judicial review in the High Court condemns London Borough of Tower Hamlets' failure to improve its housing policies towards Bangladeshis.

25 Mar: BR to review promotion tests after existing tests are shown to discriminate against those for whom English is their second language.

4 Apr: UN Human Rights Commission criticizes UK's record on immigration.

8 Apr: BBC television's *Panorama* reports on the setting up of Jewish vigilante groups on an American model to guard against anti-semitic attacks.

12 Apr: Church leaders accuse the Home Office of imprisoning refugees fleeing torture in Zaire and then making it impossible for them to get bail.

2 May: Controversy over a new selection procedure which prevents most of the current year's black law graduates from sitting Law Society examinations begins.

14 May: Survey for Victim Support argues that only a tiny proportion of racial harrassment and attacks are reported to the police, and those do not always receive serious treatment.

19 May: Vandals desecrate Muslim graves in a Bradford cemetery.

18 May: Bar Council approves a radical equal opportunities policy to ensure that at least 5 per cent of members and pupils of chambers should come from ethnic minorities and that at least 5 per cent of work sent to chambers should be given to ethnic minority lawyers.

6 June: Christopher McCrudden, David Smith and Colin Brown, *Racial Justice at Work: Enforcement of the Race Relations Act in Employment*, PSI, blames the Commission for Racial Equality for the failings of the 1976 Race Relations Act.

14 June: Bill Morris becomes the first black person elected to head a major trade union, the TGWU.

28 June: John Major calls for an urgent clamp-down on illegal immigration into the EC at the EC summit in Luxembourg.

2 July: Stringent curbs on the rights of political asylum seekers to prevent them leaving third world countries and qualifying for legal aid by Britain are announced.

25 July: Industrial tribunal finds the voluntary body, the UK Immigrants Advisory Service, guilty of arbitrary racial discrimination in its appointment of a new deputy director.

26 July: Industrial tribunal in Sheffield finds an employer who refused to employ Muslims is not guilty of racial discrimination because religious discrimination was not covered by the 1976 Race Relations Act.

31 July: UK Immigrants Advisory Service blocks the Home Secretary's plans to turn it into a government-funded monopoly agency dealing with refugees and immigrants.

5 Aug: Adoption agencies call for tighter immigration controls on babies.

15 Aug: NACAB refuses to act as the single source of legal advice for asylum seekers.

1 Oct: Immigration lawyers demonstrate outside the High Court in London against proposed changes in asylum procedures.

31 Oct: Ministers threaten to withdraw funding from UKIAS.

1 Nov: Asylum Bill to increase the burden of proof on refugees trying to claim asylum in Britain is published.

12 Nov: CRE calls for the establishment of a new criminal offence of racially-motivated violence and for racially mixed juries to try such cases.

21 Nov: Whitecraigs lawn tennis and sports club in Glasgow makes an out of court settlement after admitting discrimination against a woman applying to join because she was Jewish.

29 Nov: Court of Appeal finds the Home Secretary guilty of contempt of court over the case of a Zairean refugee deported in May.

2 Dec: Home Secretary ordered by a High Court judge to reconsider his decision to deport Karamjit Singh Chahal, a leading campaigner for Sikh independence.

10 Dec: Report for Haringey council in London alleges that there is a high degree of discrimination against the Irish community.

16 Dec: Home Office inquiry into the detention of Arabs during the Gulf war is leaked. It concluded that the security service should be neither criticized nor disciplined.

Women

VALERIE WILLIAMSON

The last two contributions on women in this annual review focused on employment issues and these have remained very much to the fore in 1991 with the espousement by 70 major employers of Opportunity 2000.[1] Despite more than a decade and a half of equal opportunities legislation there is a cumulation of evidence to show that opportunities in practice remain far from equal and a growing realization that removing barriers will not alone ensure progress. Opportunity 2000 symbolizes a commitment to positive discrimination in terms of recruitment, training and promotion and more especially, realistic retention policies which recognize family responsibilities by ensuring access to adequate child care. Demographic pressures and the consequent need of the economy for their effective contribution to the labour market, suggest that women may be able to achieve some important gains in this area. It is important however that women's interests are not seen exclusively in terms of successful labour market integration as if this was the only 'women's' issue. This could mean that a woman's dimension is omitted in the consideration of other important areas of social policy such as the radical restructuring of the NHS, which arguably has just as great an impact on women's lives.

Why NHS Reforms are of Particular Interest to Women
The past year has witnessed the beginning of a phased implementaion of the National Health Service and Community Care Act based on recommendations from the 1989 white papers, *Working for Patients* and *Caring for People*,[2] and the further implementation of the 1990 GP contracts based on the primary care working paper *Promoting Better Health*.[3] Together these developments represent fundamental changes not just to the organization but also to the culture of the NHS.

Health care is important to all of us, but it is argued that women legitimately have a special interest in the impact of the current reforms for a number of reasons. Women make greater proportionate use of health services overall, both on their own behalf and because women also seek advice and help for their families as mothers, wives and in other caring situations.[4] In addition women have health needs, principally in connection with their reproductive function, which men do not have, 'although anyone can catch a cold or break their leg, only women have babies or get cancer of the cervix and some health problems like osteoporosis and cystitis mainly affect women'.⁵ Certain health services therefore cater exclusively for women.

Yet a powerful critique of the way the NHS has served women in the past has been compiled by feminist writers . 'While the state and men undoubtedly benefit greatly from women's unpaid caring within welfare services', writes Peggy Foster 'it is far less clear that women benefit unequivocally from the caring services the state provides for them.'⁶ This critique has three main components. It is argued that:

a) The care provided reinforces inappropriate sexist ideology about the natural roles and functions of women.

b) Male dominated health care enforces social control over women particularly in instances of reproductive behaviour.

c) Certain women's health problems like premenstrual tension are marginalized and dismissed by the NHS. The critique emphasizes that the lack of sensitivity to women's needs as users in the NHS is closely related to the lack of equal opportunity for women workers within the service resulting in male domination of positions of power and responsibility in spite of their numerical superiority in the workforce (currently 79 per cent of workers in the NHS are female). It is in the context of such a critique that this review sets out to explore the likelihood of recent NHS reforms improving the position of women as users of NHS services.

Dimensions of Change – the Main Thrust of NHS Reforms

The reforms to date have not been primarily about the range of services to be provided but about the way in which provision should be made. There has been a conscious attempt to 'break the mould', to introduce competitiveness and consumer awareness in the place of presumed bureaucratic rigidities.

All three white papers have emphasized the key significance of improving information and enhancing consumer choice. In general practice, information to patients has been improved through compulsory practice leaflets and it is now easier to change doctors. Within the hospital and community services, information systems are also being enhanced, complaints procedures streamlined and quality assurance policies designed to allow for consumer feedback on service provision. Patients have had the right of access to their manual health records from November 1991.⁷

Efficiency is another keynote of the reforms. The main finding of the prime ministerial review which predated the white papers was that the NHS suffered from inefficiencies in organization rather than a shortfall in funding.⁸ To improve efficiency the government has introduced the principles of an internal market whereby the functions of purchasing and providing health care within the NHS are split, Health Authorities (HAs) and General Practice (GP) fund holders retaining responsibility for the former and the latter being devolved to directly managed units (DMUs) and increasingly to NHS trusts. Providers will then compete for purchasers' custom, thus promoting a more cost conscious service. Cash limiting is being extended into general practice through the budget holding scheme and the disciplines of such limits, if not its ultimate sanctions, through indicative drug budgets. *Working for People*, however, emphasizes that efficiency is not just about cost, but also about quality of care and there is a pervasive emphasis on effectiveness in all the white papers and subsequent government circulars, which is most directly translated into the provisions for clinical audit. A commitment to get involved in audit is now a requirement of the new GP contract and specifications concerning audit activity are expected in service agreements between HAs and provider units.[9]

Finally, the recent publication of *Health of the Nation* has emphasized the point most clearly stated in *Promoting Better Health* that health is about more than the relief of sickness.[10] It must be vitally concerned with promoting 'wellness'. Greater emphasis on health promotion is already evident in the new GP contracts which have introduced enhanced payments for health promotion clinics and for achieving targets in immunization and cytology.

Prospects for Women as Users of the NHS

Firstly, in assessing the likely impact of these reforms on women's health there is an immediate problem of gender biased statistics which inhibits any realistic assessment of the current situation. According to MacFarlane, there is a dearth of statistics on exclusively female problems like the menopause and on the socio-economic dimensions of women's health problems as social class is still inappropriately based on that of their husband's, while employment-related criteria fail to acknowledge women's differential attachment to the labour market.[11] One of the key problems in implementing the NHS reforms in general is the dearth of relevant statistics of all kinds. Departments of Public Health are being strengthened but there is little evidence that these gender specific statistical deficiencies are being addressed.

Secondly, while the emphasis on consumerism would appear to accord with feminist demands for a more participatory style of health care, under the new system choice can easily be limited to an initial choice of GP. Thereafter unless the practice is budget holding, secondary care is constrained by HA contracts with minimal scope for extra contractual referrals, leaving little scope for women to influence the nature and venue of care received. Given that 90 per cent of health care episodes take place in a primary setting,[12] additional information on GP services and the ability to change doctor more easily are important advantages for women. They are better able, if they so wish, to seek out women doctors and to choose a practice that provides special well woman clinics. In the longer term, access to medical records may also promote a more participatory doctor–patient relationship, depending on how positively the medical profession views this opportunity.

As regards secondary care, American experience suggests further caution concerning the introduction of market principles. Ostensible consumer sovereignty can thinly disguise provider manipulation.[13] Competitive DMUs or trusts may endeavour to promote profitable lines of activities such as hysterectomies, which would not necessarily be in the best interests of women. It will be important that District Health Authority (DHA) purchasers are sensitive to the real health care priorities of women and place contracts accordingly. This will require techniques of need assessment which will progressively overcome the inadequacies of existing gender based data and establish dialogue with local women's interests. Service needs vary according to demography and it is not only the needs of articulate white middle class women which should be accommodated, but also of those who are already comparatively less well served such as older women, women from ethnic minorities and disabled women. The emphasis on needs assessment opens opportunities, but the rhetoric of consumerism, unless accompanied by facilities for advocacy, could easily compound existing disadvantages for some women.

Thirdly, although efficiency in terms of better value for money would obviously be in the best general interests of all health care users, in the cash limited NHS there are potential weaknesses. It can easily degenerate into a cost cutting exercise, a major component of which is the 'rationalization' of services. If women's services do not have a high salience in the minds of planners and managers they can suffer disproportionately in such activities. A prime candidate in this field has been family planning. In 1988 it was reported that 25 per cent of HAs had made or promised cuts over the last five years.[14] Under the impetus of the new GP contracts further cuts have been introduced although research has documented that women value access to women doctors and to the impersonal ambience that HA clinics offer.[15] Whereas some services are being lost in the name of rationalization, others which affect women disproportionately are subject to cuts since they are regarded as inappropriate or unnecessary. Long-stay care of elderly people, it is being argued in terms of the *Caring for People* white paper, is better provided in smaller more community orientated settings, but the closure of geriatric wards is reducing choice for elderly residents, most of whom are women. The majority then have little option but private nursing homes. Another area where increasing privatization is occuring is fertility services. Guys Hospital, London has offered treatment outside block contract but so far only two DHAs out of 28 have confirmed they will still pay for patients referred before 1 April 1991.[16] It is not necessarily inappropriate to agree that certain services will not be provided on the NHS, provided that these decisions are taken after democratic consultations, but if the majority in powerful positions in the NHS are men there is a legitimate concern that gender bias will influence the distinction between necessities and optional extras.

Fourthly, women like men have in the past been victims of unproven/ineffective methods of health care and should welcome the encouragement of audit, but there is cause for concern over the narrowness of the definition as medical audit, rather than more broadly as the clinical audit of health care teams which would be more in line with the holistic approach advocated by feminists. It is also important to think in terms of the audit's acceptability to the patient as an additional dimension of effectiveness to clinical competence. The College of Health has argued in terms of 'consumer audit' and is doing pioneering work in this area.[17] Examples of neglect of the user perspective are the decisions made to close small maternity units on the grounds that deliveries are safer in large district general hospitals, despite the many other social and psychological factors that lead women to campaign vigorously for their retention. A user involvement in audit would seem particularly relevant in the case of long term care for chronic conditions where women are heavily involved as both unpaid carers and sufferers.

Lastly, user involvement is even more relevant in the area of health promotion. Women are recognized to have an important role here, not just concerning their own health, but as influential in the lifestyle of the whole family; 'many women have a special influential role in family health such as making decisions about the family's diet and educating children by their example'.[18] The guide also claims that 'particular emphasis has been placed on women's health'. It may be that recognition of their key role will ensure that women's views are taken into account by policymakers and that the current emphasis on positive health will lead to just that reappraisal of priorities in a holistic context that feminists have campaigned for. On the other hand there is a long and persistent history of scapegoating women and blaming them for the poor health of their families, demonstrated, for example, in the campaigns to 'educate' mothers before the first world war.[19] It is noticeable that neither poverty or social class are explicitly acknowledged as important factors in *Health of the Nation*. As Hilary Graham notes, unless social factors are acknowledged health promotion initiatives are likely to exaggerate health inequalities, 'for it is those whose health is already at risk via the cumulative effect of social and economic disadvantage who are most likely to pursue unhealthy patterns of behaviour'.[20] A clear illustration of the importance of social context is the disappointing figures last year for uptake of the national breast screening campaign (initially 60 per cent and falling). In Sweden an 89 per cent attendance rate has been achieved and death rates have fallen 30 per cent in eight years.[21] Although the new GP contracts with financial incentives for health promotion clinics including well woman clinics would appear to be supportive of women's health, feminist critiques of GP clinics argue that they overly medicalize problems. A wider professional input could perhaps be encouraged by Family Health Service Authorities (FHSAs) through their enhanced powers of allocating finance for ancillary workers.

The Potential Contribution of Equal Opportunities Policies to Improving Women's Health Care

Discussion so far would seem to suggest that whether the NHS reforms benefit women will depend to a considerable extent on the sensitivity of purchasers and providers to women's needs as they make decisions about priorities and service delivery. Feminists have long argued that an effective equal opportunities policy is the key to the transformation of the NHS. It is simplistic to equate good women's health care with care organized by women, but gender is a factor. As indicated in

Susan McRae's 1989 contribution to this annual review, demographic change and
the needs of the economy have combined in recent years to ensure a greater
appreciation of women's labour market contribution.[22] The NHS, as a very labour
intensive organization, heavily reliant on the recruitment of young women, is more
vulnerable to potential labour shortages than most employers. The situation is
aggravated by the phasing in of the new nurse training programme under Project
2000, which by making student nurses supernumerary will intensify staffing
problems on the wards.

Although the NHS has a poor record as an equal opportunity employer, greater
effort is being made in the 1990s to utilize women's talents more fully.[23]
Encouraged by the National Health Service management executive, 1991 has
witnessed a number of useful initiatives such as the £1.5 million allocated to finance
career break initiatives for doctors, and this will help women fulfil their potential.[24]
Health minister Virginia Bottomley has also introduced a 'come back to caring'
initiative involving a support package for returning nurses[25] but a report also
published this year clearly demonstrates how far the service still has to go before
there is real gender equality.[26] While accepting that 93 per cent of DHAs had an
equal opportunities policy, the report found implementation woefully inadequate,
with 84 per cent having no named manager with overall responsibility for equal
opportunity and 75 per cent no effective monitoring machinery. Part-time work has
been the traditional method whereby women endeavour to retain labour market
participation alongside child care and family responsibilities, but it can fatally
impair career prospects within the NHS. The report reveals that part-time training
was rarer than part-time posts and sometimes as in the case of medicine, such posts
were used to channel women into less prestigious specialities. There is also a
marked shortage of part-time posts for middle and senior managers and currently
only 17 per cent of unit general managers and 4 per cent of district/regional general
managers are female.

An alternative to part-time working is a greater recognition of employees' family
responsibilities through provision of flexible working arrangements and leave
entitlements, alongside comprehensive day care. Provision of the latter is still very
limited, a mere 3,500 places for a total staff of over 1 million, 79 per cent of whom
are women. An intitiative in January introduced a package of paid leave for family
sickness which DHAs may adopt,[27] but it is not a compulsory part of Whitley terms.
The problem in 1991 is that DHAs have progressively less control of the pay and
conditions of NHS workers. Responsibilities for equal opportunities are moving to
DMUs and increasingly to trusts. A report commissioned by the Department of
Health from the Office of Public Management warned in June that unless equal
opportunities policies are fully integrated with other management imperatives,
there is a danger that the pressures of contracting could make it a low priority,[28]
while in August, the Equal Opportunities Commission (EOC) argued that equal
opportunities policies (EO) must be incorporated in contractual obligations and that
granting trust status should depend on adequate EO policies and monitoring.

structures. There is however little evidence to date of such requirements being enforced. If trusts feel that equal opportunity policies will improve their competitive position, they will be enthusiastically adopted, but where the commercial advantage is not so obvious, the prospects are less encouraging. 'Social justice may be more important than the needs of the labour market but it is less pressing, therefore it is perhaps more easily shelved'.[29] There is a danger that equal opportunity measures may selectively benefit a minority of women who have managed to acquire scarce skills, while the increasingly competitive environment may actually impair the prospects for less skilled women, especially those from ethnic minorities.

Conclusion

It is not surprising that the NHS reforms do not appear to offer clear prospects of improved health care for women since there is no evidence of a specifically feminist perspective in their genesis. There are in fact many potentially worrying developments for women, especially disadvantaged women, in the new cost effective, market orientated health service. Women's health services are however acquiring a higher political saliency at home and abroad. Health minister Virginia Bottomley has committed the government to a three-pronged review of women's employment prospects in the NHS, their access to services and membership of health authority boards.[30] The contribution women make to the health care of the population as a whole is recognized by the World Health Organization (WHO) as crucial to the Health for All strategy.[31] In Vienna this summer, the Women's Health Network argued for the establishment of a European network on health for women to promote women's involvement in determining health needs and humanizing health services,[32] a potentially useful initiative in the context of 1992.[33] Such a grassroots approach to needs assessment combined with effective equal opportunity policies within the service, may yet achieve an NHS that more truly meets women's needs. As most feminists argue, the NHS is the only realistic hope for better women's health care in the UK. Despite scare stories of wholesale privatization, it remains a national service, universally available. In adapting to meet the needs of women, a more holistic and empowering approach would also better meet the needs of men.

Notes

1 See chronology, 28 October 1991.

2 *Working for Patients*, Cmnd 555, HMSO, 1989; *Caring for People*, Cmnd 849, HMSO, 1989.

3 *Promoting Better Health – the government's programme for improving primary health care*, Cmnd 249, HMSO, 1987.

4 H. Graham, *Women, Health and the Family*, Wheatsheaf, Brighton, 1984.

5 Department of Health, *Your Health: a guide to services for women*, HMSO, 1991.

6 P. Foster, 'Well woman clinics: a serious challenge to mainstream care?' in M Maclean and D. Groves (ed), *Women's Issues in Social Policy*, Routledge, 1991.

7 As from November 1991, patients have had the right of access to any manually held health records made after that date on terms similar to existing provision with regard to computerized health records and to the Access to Personal Files Act 1987 relating to social work and housing records.

8 Prime Minister Margaret Thatcher set up an internal fundamental review of the NHS following the financial crisis within the service in the winter of 1987–88. Its conclusions formed the basis of the white paper *Working for Patients*.

9 The government forced a new contract on GPs despite vociferous opposition from the British Medical Association, which came into operation on 1 April 1990.

10 *Health of the Nation*, Cmnd 1523, HMSO, 1991.

11 A. Macfarlane, 'Official statistics and women's health and illness' in H. Roberts (ed), *Women's Health Counts*, Routledge, 1990.

12 J. Fry, *Present state and future needs in general practice*, Royal College of General Practitioners, 1983.

13 A. Newbigging, *Suffering the Cuts. A survey of cuts in health services for women in London*, London Health Emergency, 1989.

14 Ibid.

15 Family Planning Review Group, *Review of Family Planning and Abortion Services*, South East Thames Regional Health Authority, 1991.

16 D. Glasman, 'Women's health services threatened by reforms', *Health Services Journal*, 2, May 1991, p.6.

17 M. Rigge, *Gynaecology in-patient services*, unpublished report to Brighton Health Authority, 1990.

18 Department of Health, *Your Health, op.cit.*

19 J. Lewis, 'The social history of social policy: infant welfare in Edwardian England', *Journal of Social Policy*, 9:4, 1980.

20 H. Graham, 'Behaving Well', in H Roberts (ed), *Women's Health Counts, op.cit.*.

21 'UK cancer screening a failure', *The Guardian*, 2 February 1990.

22 S. McRae, 'Women' in P Catterall (ed), *Contemporary Britain: An Annual Review*, Blackwell, Oxford, 1990 and 1991.

23 The chronology refers to a number of such instances.

24 'Northern RHA helps women doctors back to work', *NHSME News*, May 1991, p.11, National Health Service Management Executive.

25 'Returning nurses a vital asset', *NHSME News*, May 1991, p.10.

26 *Equality Management: women's employment in the NHS*, Equal Opportunities Commission, Manchester, 1991.

27 *Equality Managment, op.cit.*

28 *Women in the NHS*, EL(91)90, Office of Public Management, 1991.

29 Editorial in *Health Service Management*, August 1991.

30 Glasman, 'Women's health services threatened', *op.cit.*

31 *Global Strategy for Health for All by the Year 2000*, Health for All series no.3, World Health Organization, Geneva, 1982.

32 M. Tidyman, 'Women, health and urban politics', International Healthy Cities conference, Vienna, May 13–15 1991 and *Women's Health Network newsletter*, August/September 1991.

33 The creation of an internal market throughout EC countries from 1992 will facilitate internal migration of workers and their families and increase pressure for harmonization of health and welfare provision.

Chronology

7 Jan: *Drugs and Therapeutics Bulletin* argues that women up to 45 who do not smoke or have risks of heart disease can safely take the combined contraceptive pill.

9 Jan: ICI announces measures to promote equal opportunities for women employees, including maternity pay, promotion of job sharing and company pension cover during career breaks.

13 Jan: Institute of Manpower Studies report argues that the difficulties of childcare are a major reason why women are under-represented in management.

14 Jan: Nineteen women on HMS Brilliant become the first women in the Royal Navy to sail to war.

15 Jan: Bristol Appeals Tribunal rejects claims by Manufacturing, Science and Finance Union for pay comparability of speech therapists (a mainly female profession) with clinical psychologists.

18 Jan: NHS review of inequalities in pay between male and female ancilliary staff begins.

22 Jan: *Women Doctors and Their Careers*, Department of Health, points to 'gross underrepresentation' of women doctors at the top of their profession.

25 Jan: Report by Professor Robert Mansel in *The Lancet* argues that thousands of women with breast cancer are not receiving adequate treatment.

11 Mar: Philip Virgo, *Training for Jobs: Not Jobs for Trainers*, Bow Group, calls for measures to make it easier for mothers to return to employment by making child care expenses tax deductible.

25 Mar: Equal Opportunities Commission report says women have made little progress towards equal pay in the last decade.
Labour outlines plans for a women's ministry with representation in the cabinet, a network of equal opportunities ministries in the various departments and a new sex equality bill.

4 Apr: London Ambulance Service told to update and implement its equal opportunities policy after a female employee wins an out of court settlement of a sex discrimination claim.

8 Apr: Research by PSI demonstrates that twice as many women are returning to work after having a baby as a year ago.

9 Apr: Labour Party survey published on the underrepresentation of women in the upper echelons of the arts and the media and announces that a future Labour government would require equal opportunities policies from arts and media companies and the introduction of child care and flexible hours.

18 Apr: Alcohol Concern says there has been a fifteenfold increase in women's deaths owing to drink since 1960s.
Six women win a case for compensation against British Gas's decision to force them to retire from their jobs at 60, as the Lords found that the company broke EC law.

25 Apr: Lord Chancellor tells peers that single women, including virgins, cannot be denied AID.

29 Apr: Professor Richard Lynn, in a report for the Social Affairs Unit, argues women do not fill a proportionate number of senior posts because they are not as competitive as men.

16 May: Report by Sally Hughes for the Law Society finds that judicial appointments, made on the basis of informal networking amongst barristers, tend to underrepresent women on the bench.

25 May: Susan McRae, *Women into Engineering and Science – Employers' Policies and Practices*, PSI, argues that there is still discrimination against women in major scientific and engineering companies despite exemplary equal opportunities policies, partly because of an inflexible approach to career breaks, child care and maternity leave and partly because of the traditional attitudes of staff.

10 June: Catherine Marsh, *Hours of Work for Men and Women in Britain*, Equal Opportunities Commission, finds British men work the longest hours in Europe, with 42 per cent working over 46 hours per week. A lack of accessible and affordable child care facilities are seen as contributing to the long hours worked by men and women and the resulting strains on family life.

22 June: Government orders a review of work practices in the NHS by managers to tackle sex discrimination and enable mothers to resume their careers after having children.

26 June: Government commits itself to equal retirement ages for men and women after the next general election.

3 July: EC guidelines on sexual harassment at work and childcare facilities published.

1 Aug: *Equality Management: Women's Employment in the NHS*, Equal Opportunities Commission criticizes the NHS for wasting women employees by not giving them greater opportunity to combine work with parenthood.

27 Aug: *Pay at the top of the University Ladder*, Association of University Teachers, shows women professors on average receive £2,000 per annum less than their male colleagues.

3 Sept: First Division Association threatens legal action against the government over the apparent sex bias of the profit-related pay scheme introduced four years ago.

11 Sept: PSI report says that the government's decision to put responsibility for state training schemes on employers and the replacement of the TOPS scheme with the Employment Training programme for the long-term unemployed have been disadvantageous to women in the labour market.

24 Sept: *Women and Men in Britain 1991*, Equal Opportunities Commission, shows that despite a larger proportion of women in the workforce than any EC country other than Denmark the earnings gap between men and women in the UK is up to 10 per cent wider than elsewhere in the EC. On average women earn 77 per cent of male salaries and maternity rights are more restricted than elsewhere in the EC, with up to 50 per cent of working women not qualifying for them.

16 Oct: Elspeth Howe and Susan McRae, *Women on the Board*, PSI, condemns the old boy network whereby directors are chosen and calls for representation of a wider range of expertise on company boards.

17 Oct: Catherine Hakim 'Grateful slaves and self-made women: fact and fantasy in women's work orientations', *European Sociological Review*, argues that a major reason for continuing pay differentials between the sexes is that most women are not committed to full-time work and do not see a career as an important goal.

28 Oct: Opportunity 2000 launched by the Prime Minister, a commitment to achieving equality for women in the workplace signed by 50 companies and public bodies.

6 Nov: UK agrees to EC rules that give women greater financial protection for 14 weeks when on statutory maternity leave and stipulate that a woman cannot be dismissed for being pregnant.

13 Dec: Government rules out new legislation on women's employment rights.

Environmental Issues

ANDREW BLOWERS

By 1991 public, political and media concern about impending environmental catastrophe had subsided from the high peak reached in 1989. This was partly, no doubt, an inevitable reaction since 'as the years pass by and nature doesn't end, people may stop listening when environmentalists issue warnings'.[1] More fundamentally, environmental concern tends to flourish during periods of optimism and fades when recession bites and security is threatened. 'We are learning again, as in the late 1970s, that popular manifestations of concerns for the natural world are kindly spirits which cast their light upon periods of plenty and are scared off when the spectres of war or recession return'.[2] A further reason for fading interest, in Britain at least, was the general political consensus achieved as policies converged and effectively neutralized the environment as a political issue.

Nevertheless, while 1991 was a relatively quiet year for domestic environmental issues, elsewhere there was much disturbing evidence of destruction. Environmental damage was both a potent weapon and an inevitable consequence of the Gulf war yet the full impacts were obscured by 'a blanket of secrecy and a staggering lack of relevant independent scientific measurements'.[3] The firing of around 600 well heads cast a black pall over Kuwait, reducing ground temperatures by 10–15°C, releasing black rain over a region covering Afghanistan, Pakistan and Turkey and creating levels of sulphur dioxide 50 times higher than those in London. The oil slick seeping into the Gulf posed a longer term threat to the delicate ecology of the shallow basin while the oil lakes on land could result in future damage to agriculture. While the Gulf war created a regional environmental problem, further disturbing evidence of an 8 per cent depletion of the ozone layer in northern mid-latitudes brought environmental issues nearer home. The consequence, revealed in an unpublished UN Report at the end of the year, will be a rise of a quarter in the total of skin cancers to a global total of 300,000.

The threat to environmental security and health, though presently distant in place and time, was nonetheless a spur to action by government and business at national, European and international level. It was a year when the focus of attention shifted to the problems of implementing the environmental policies and programmes created during previous years. There were some new concerns such as indoor pollution and some new initiatives, notably the proposal for an Environmental Agency. In the business world there was much effort to promote environmental consciousness and to emphasize industry's role in securing sustainable growth. In essence 1991 was a year of consolidation and of preparation for the challenges of 1992 when the environment would be an issue in a national election, in the creation of the single market in Europe and, above all, the focus of the United Nations Conference on Environment and Development (UNCED), the so-called Earth Summit, the biggest international gathering of its kind ever to be held.

The Greening of Government

At least in principle, the British government regarded protecting the environment as 'comparable in its long term importance with the management of the economy and the defence of the realm'.[4] As promised it published a report in September on progress towards implementing the 350 commitments in the white paper *This Common Inheritance*. The government would 'deliver those commitments and ... stands accountable for the progress it has made'. The progress report indicated that 200 promises had been fulfilled and rolled forward 400 commitments including 100 on which work needed to be completed and 50 on which work had to be started. Secretary of State Michael Heseltine was candid about failures in some areas. 'This report does not seek in any way to disguise these; it is designed to make critical scrutiny possible'.[5] Critics were quick to seize advantage of the invitation claiming that many of the policy commitments were merely promises to participate in discussions or to implement directives, while others were vague and unspecific. Several major issues had to be resolved such as implementation of the ozone agreements or achieving reductions in greenhouse gases. But the promise of a comprehensive annual statement demonstrated the government's willingness that progress on these and other environmental issues should be monitored.

The white paper had promised that the government would itself 'integrate environmental concerns more effectively into all policy areas'.[6] Two coordinating committees of ministers were set up to ensure implementation of environmental policies, though they only met four times during the year, suggesting to critics that 'environmental policy is so unambitious that it very rarely needs to be discussed collectively by ministers.'[7] Each department has a 'green minister' responsible for overseeing its environmental impact. The Department of the Environment issued a guide for government departments explaining how they should take into account the environmental impacts of policies and programmes. There was some evidence that the problem of long run increases in the value of environmental assets was recognized. 'Rising values may result from the increasing scarcity of environmental resources or from increases in income, which means that people are better able to enjoy the environment'. This was somewhat undermined by the general adherence to the Treasury discount rate of 6 per cent though it was conceded that it undervalues long term assets and might discriminate 'unreasonably against policies which are designed to prevent long term environmental hazards'.[8]

Much less progress was made in the effort to get individual government departments to report on their stewardship of the environment. One analysis claimed that only one department had mentioned all its white paper commitments in its annual report. Two departments had failed to mention any of their commitments and all others bar one missed at least 20 per cent of their commitments.[9] Despite the inertia in some areas of government it could at least be claimed that during 1991 the government had achieved the first steps in establishing the machinery for integrated policy making.

An Environmental Agency

If general progress towards integration of government policy-making was predictably slow, in the specific area of integration of pollution control the introduction of new machinery was surprisingly fast. The white paper had argued that further amalgamations of pollution control agencies would create 'administrative upheaval at just the time when the new organizations are getting into their stride'. Yet, in his first major speech on the environment in July, the Prime Minister announced the setting up of an Environment Agency. 'It is right that the integrity and indivisibility of the environment *should* now be reflected in a unified agency', he said.[10] The intention was to bring together the recently unified pollution inspectorate (Her Majesty's Inspectorate of Pollution, HMIP) plus the Drinking Water Inspectorate, the related functions of the newly created National Rivers Authority (NRA) and the local authority waste regulation function, itself undergoing reorganization.

The creation of a unified agency was partly, no doubt, intended to remove any political advantage that Labour might gain in the coming general election campaign from its commitment to an Environmental Protection Commission. But, the timing created maximum upheaval in organizations experiencing transition. In particular there was vigorous opposition to the prospect of the NRA being dismembered and the bulk of its functions going under the Ministry of Agriculture. This would vitiate the concept of integrated river basin management covering pollution control, water supply, flood defence, fisheries conservation and recreation extolled in the white paper. Environmental interests were dismayed at the potential capture of the NRA by agricultural interests notoriously unfriendly to conservationist pressures. There was opposition, too, from local government where county councils were still grappling with the privatization of their waste disposal functions and the implications of their new role as waste regulation authorities. The new agency would remove the regulatory function from central control and accountability, further strengthening the centralization of policy making through the creation of quangos.

By the time the consultation paper on the proposed agency emerged in October four options were being canvassed. One would include only the pollution functions of the NRA while another would exclude the NRA altogether. Under a third (evolutionary) approach, the various bodies would keep their identities but be coordinated under an independent board. The fourth option envisaged full integration of the NRA, HMIP and waste regulation. The timescale had been slowed down to beyond the election but with all parties committed to change there was opportunity for more measured debate on the future shape of pollution control in the context of local government reorganization and the EC's environmental policies.

Promises and Performance

According to the government, the new agency promised a future approach to pollution control that would be 'focused, strong and independent'.[11] In terms of present performance the UK's record in 1991 showed evidence of both problems and progress. On the credit side the NRA indicated that 78 per cent of bathing beaches met minimum EC standards, up from 65 per cent in 1987. The proportion of glass recycled had doubled since 1984 to 21 per cent, but the Netherlands, Belgium, Germany and Italy had all achieved over 50 per cent and the UK was trailing behind all but two EC countries. As part of the UK's effort to achieve the target of recycling half of domestic waste (itself half of the total waste arising) by 2000, a range of schemes was introduced among nearly 100 local authorities aimed at increasing waste segregation through kerbside collection schemes. The government was proposing recycling credits, a form of incentive or rebates to local authorities who reduced the volume of waste streams and thereby the costs of disposal by removing wastes for recycling. This was part of a broader effort to minimize waste and reduce pollution through the use of market mechanisms such as tradeable pollution permits and pollution load charging.

The use of aggregates for road building, which takes about a third of the total, provides a good example of the potential for recycling. Only around half the total of aggregates used in road repairs is recycled aggregates and there is virtually no recycled material used in road construction. The total demand for primary aggregates is forecast to double over 20 years, requiring the excavation of 8.25 billion tonnes of sand, gravel and crushed rock. This is the equivalent 'to digging a hole three metres deep in an area the size of Berkshire'.[12] The increasing opposition from local communities to the destruction of landscapes, already evident in the south east, in time would constrain supply, push up prices and encourage greater use of substitutes and recycling.

Various examples of poor performance in environmental management were exposed during the year, including inadequate hazardous site maintenance, non-compliance with safety regulations in the transportation of chemicals and ignorance on the part of companies of the disposal methods being used for their wastes.[13] A survey by HMIP identified over 1,000 landfills requiring controls to prevent methane migration, a gas estimated to contribute about 5 per cent of greenhouse gas emissions as well as problems of odour and health hazards. But there was also more vigorous enforcement exemplified by the successful prosecution of South West Water for supplying water contaminated by aluminium sulphate accidentally dumped in a treatment works to 20,000 people in Camelford in 1988.

Another problem that received attention during the year was indoor pollution. A report covering 'sick building syndrome'; radon gas, tobacco smoke, damp and mould and volatile organic compounds in buildings was compiled revealing a dearth of information and significant health risks. Although the quality of air at home and work had been neglected 'people's awareness of the places in which they live and work is increasing'[14] and there was a need for a wide range of measures in this forgotten area of government responsibility.

Two policies with profound future implications were announced during the year. As had been widely predicted Sellafield was chosen in July as the preferred site for the deep geological repository for the co-disposal of intermediate and low level radioactive wastes. Geological investigations had provided sufficient justification for the choice which would save around £1 billion in transport costs in comparison to the alternative site at Dounreay. The decision would be challenged at a future public enquiry by critics who would argue the decision was premature, based on inadequate investigations and insufficient consideration of alternative management strategies. The other policy shift was indicated by Transport Secretary Malcolm Rifkind who indicated a bigger role for a privatized railway system and the need for road planning to take fuller account of environmental costs. This was a significant departure from the demand-led road planning advocated by his predecessor.

Business Burnishes its Image

The world business community endorsed a Charter for Sustainable Development at the second World Industry Conference on Environment and Management (WICEM II) in Rotterdam in April. Over 200 companies from multinational corporations as well as small and medium sized companies (with the notable exception of the Japanese) signed a declaration supporting such widely agreed goals as the precautionary approach, the transfer of technology and improved energy efficiency, though not a carbon tax. But, it was clear the business community did not endorse the need for a major shift in the overall direction of the world economy advocated by Gro Harlme Brundtland in her keynote address to the conference. The final declaration affirmed the belief in business as usual, arguing that sustainable development could be achieved through 'real economic growth', creating the capacity to solve environmental problems within the 'framework of the market economy' adapted 'to reflect environmental concerns more appropriately'.[15]

There were, though, signs of intensifying effort on the part of business to incorporate environmental criteria into production processes. There was increasing attention to product Life Cycle Analysis (LCA), a cradle-to-grave examination of raw material use, energy consumption, pollution releases and waste generation of products. Environmental auditing, the systematic self-assessment of a company's environmental performance, was becoming routinely practised, to some extent, spurred on by a prospective EC Directive. A further incentive to companies to minimize environmental impacts was the likelihood of stringent tests being applied to certain products before they could qualify for an eco label. In future the environmentally friendly claims made by companies would need to be fully justified.

Environmental requirements were having a differential impact on industries. The vehicle industry looking to its future and besieged by proposals for pollution taxes and the need for recycling, was turning some attention to research on electric propulsion and the development of plants for dismantling used cars. The iron foundry industry, a declining industry plagued by its poor record on pollution, would have to undergo further contraction before the surviving plants could meet the costs of control. For this and other industries the combined effects of recession and environmental controls could put many firms out of business, a possibility that would probably not be lost on government and the enforcement agencies when interpreting the rules.

The Environment and Europe

Throughout 1991 the EC was busy promoting drafts of new and revised Environmental Directives. The UK's practice of co-disposal of liquid and hazardous wastes with domestic refuse was frowned on by its partners. A compromise was struck allowing co-disposal of wastes provided they were compatible though the definition of what would be acceptable remained to be clarified. There were potential problems of leachate and methane migration causing pollution, risks of toxic releases and other hazards at a number of sites. Under EC criteria and the more stringent operating practices being introduced under the Environmental Protection Act only about half of the 300 co-disposal sites would be able to continue. Another proposed EC regulation seeking to make member states self-sufficient in waste disposal capacity was welcomed in principle by the UK though it did not favour tight controls on movements of non-hazardous wastes within member states. On the matter of a unified system of pollution control, the subject of another prospective EC Directive, the UK was already well ahead of most of its partners.

During the year the Directive on nitrates in drinking water was agreed, imposing tight restrictions on the application of inorganic fertilizers and livestock manure in designated 'vulnerable zones'. Further evidence of a European approach to environmental issues was the agreement on vehicle emission limits imposed on new cars. But the proposals for an energy tax would prove the acid test of cooperation. A discussion document proposing a uniform tax on all sources and a graduated tax on carbon content of fuels indicated that electricity costs could rise by about a sixth by the end of the century but the cost of coal might be two thirds higher. The tax was the means of achieving the agreed stabilization of CO_2 levels at 1990 levels by 2000. It would have a differential impact on member states based on sources of energy supply and it was bound to provoke opposition from member states, including Britain, who were jealous of their sovereignty in fiscal matters.

At one level the UK was determined to shake off the sobriquet of 'dirty man of Europe' and 'to put itself in a position where it can claim credit for laying the foundations of a more powerful Community environmental policy'.[16] The government was proposing that the Treaty of Rome should incorporate as one of its key objectives that of 'promoting throughout the Community sustainable growth which respects the environment'. There was a gap between rhetoric and practice. The UK was arguing that environmental issues should be integrated into all areas of EC policy making. At another level there appeared to be little enthusiasm among ministers for the possibility of environmental assessments of policies, plans and programmes which was being canvassed as a future EC Directive. The idea was to ensure that the environmental impact of decisions in broad policy areas such as transport, energy, agriculture, minerals, tourism and waste disposal should not escape the net.

The environment played a subsidiary role in the negotiations leading up to the EC summit at Maastricht at the end of the year. On the environment, at least, the UK was not occupying an isolated position. A conflict of interests between northern and southern EC countries was emerging. The pressure for tighter environmental controls and taxes, led by Germany, the Netherlands and Denmark, could distort the unified market and place heavy burdens on the poorer countries striving to develop their economies. The principle of qualified majority voting on environmental matters was accordingly watered down to the extent that they were described as a 'fraud' by the EC's Environment Commissioner Carlo Ripa di Meana.

The Road to Rio

North-south conflict on a global level beset the preparations for the UNCED conference to be held in Rio de Janeiro in June 1992. In his July speech, John Major underlined the importance of the Earth Summit in meeting 'global challenges which require global responses'. Yet, a week later, the G7 summit which he hosted in London failed to apply any pressure on the US to reduce its CO_2 emissions. Instead the US preferred to conceal its increases in CO_2 behind an overall reduction in greenhouse gases achieved through the phasing out of CFCs. Global environmental issues were relegated to a derisory ten minutes discussion at the summit. As one comment put it, 'The G7 have the power and the responsibility to save the earth. This summit shows they don't mind continuing to wreck it for the sake of " business as usual " '.[17]

Preparatory conferences for UNCED were held during the year in Geneva and there were national conferences to encourage the participation of NGOs, including one in London in October. These conferences were intended to establish the so-called Agenda 21 covering a broad span of issues intended to set long-term policy priorities. The negotiations over the proposed conventions on climate change, tropical forests and biological diversity to be signed ran into deadlock. The north was insisting on the protection of tropical forests while the south aimed to wrest compensating agreements on debt reduction and technology transfer. The high expectations for Rio were rapidly diminishing as the real motivations and interests of the rich and the poor became exposed.

Even where agreements had already been reached, as in the Montreal Protocols on ozone, there were doubts over implementation. With full compliance there would be a 10 per cent increase in chlorine levels in the atmosphere by 1997 and it would be some time before levels reduced thereafter. The chances of full compliance were slim and were not helped by the fact that only two of 69 countries had so far ratified the agreement for an accelerated phase-out and less than $10 million of $240 million had been paid into the ozone fund to assist developing countries with the necessary technology.

On a brighter note 1991 saw a little remarked international agreement to ban mining in Antarctica for at least 50 years. This was a further development of the Antarctic Treaty signed by 39 nations in 1988. Together the ozone and Antarctic agreements illustrated the impetus for international action to protect the global commons, hesitant at first but eventually conclusive. There were conflicts of interest, compromises to be reached and problems of securing and monitoring compliance. As 1992 approached the capacity of the international community to save itself from environmental catastrophe was about to be given its sternest test.

Notes

1 Lionel Barber, 'The Un-greening of America', *Financial Times*, 13/14 April 1991.

2 Charles Clover, 'It isn't going to last', *The Daily Telegraph*, 22 April 1991.

3 Frank Barnaby, 'The environmental impact of the Gulf war', *The Ecologist*, Vol.21,No.4, July/Aug 1991, p.166.

4 *This Common Inheritance: the First Year Report*, Cmnd 1655, HMSO, 1991, p.5.

5 *Ibid.*

6 *This Common Inheritance*, Cmnd 1200, HMSO, 1990.

7 *Environmental Data Services (ENDS)*, Report No.200, September 1991, pp.16–17.

8 *Policy Appraisal and the Environment*, Department of the Environment, 1991.

9 The Green Alliance, *Greening Government: the failure of the departmental annual reports to reflect integrated policy making*, 1991.

10 *This Common Inheritance*, p.232; Prime Minister's speech on the global environment, July 8 1991.

11 Department of the Environment, *Improving Environmental Quality*, consultation paper, October 1991, para 58.

12 *ENDS* Report, May 1991 p.15.

13 Report 1987–90 from Hazardous Wastes Inspectorate, Scotland; report on random checks on chemical vehicles in north- west in *ENDS*, July, p.10; report on survey of firms on 'duty of care' in *ENDS*, February, 1991 p.8.

14 House of Commons Environment Committee, *Indoor Pollution*, Session 1990–91, Sixth Report, HMSO, 1991.

15 WICEM II Official Report, in *Environment Strategy Europe*, Campden Publishing Ltd, 1991.

16 *ENDS*, Report No.194, March, 1991 p.3.

17 *The Guardian*, 18 July 1991.

Chronology

1 Jan: BNFL introduce a new compensation scheme for workers who develop illnesses which may be linked to radiation exposure.

3 Jan: *The Use of Herbicides in Non-Agricultural Situations in England and Wales*, Foundation for Water Research, shows 10 per cent of drinking water supplies are contaminated by herbicides over the legal limit.

5–6 Jan: At least 17 people die in gales.

8 Jan: South West Water is fined £10,000 for supplying water heavily polluted with aluminium sulphate to Camelford in Cornwall in July 1988.

28 Jan: *Environmental Indicators: A Preliminary Set*, OECD, indicates Britain's poor performance on environmental issues.

1 Feb: *The Potential Effects of Climate Change in the UK*, HMSO, predicts Britain could be 1.4°C warmer by 2030.

5 Feb: Report by the Water Research Centre (chaired by Steve Warren), argues forests contribute to the acidification of fresh water supply.

6 Feb: Britain to lead an international study on capturing carbon dioxide and disposing of it underground.

12 Feb: Oil spills into the Bristol Channel from a British Steel plant.

15 Feb: World's first plant to make the substitute for CFCs, HFC 134a, is opened in Runcorn, Cheshire.

27 Feb: New controls on water pollution announced.

5 Mar: National Rivers Authority introduces charges to cover the costs of regulating and monitoring water pollution.

27 Mar: Water will have to be pumped from the wet to the dry regions of England and Wales to avoid severe shortages in the next 20 years, the National Rivers Authority says, in warning of drought in South East England again this summer.

3 Apr: Report by HMIP warns that potentially explosive gases from landfill sites may be threatening homes at over 1,000 sites.

10 Apr: Domestic water bills would treble in the first year that water meters were installed according to the Institution of Water and Environmental Management.

18 Apr: Energy Select Committee report criticizes the Department of Transport's apparent lack of concern at CO_2 emissions from motor vehicles.

22 Apr: David Pearce, *Growth, Employment and Environmental Policy* Employment Institute, argues environmental policies can aid employment and are unlikely adversely to affect growth much, if at all.

30 Apr: Government to survey the likely impact of water metering on the elderly and infirm.

1 May: David Slater becomes director of HMIP.

7 May: Health warnings about ozone levels will be issued by the government only when it has reached 200 parts per billion, as opposed to 75 parts per billion as recommended by WHO.

10 May: Badger Bill, making it an offence to destroy or obstruct a sett, is given an unopposed third reading in the Commons.

17 May: Badgers (Further Protection) Bill, to give courts the power to order the destruction of dogs used in the offence of badger baiting, passes all stages in the Commons.

29 May: *Coming Clean on the Air we Breathe*, Liberal Democrats, suggests a 30 per cent reduction in CO_2 emissions by 2005 and a total ban on CFCs by 1994, the creation of a system of tradeable licences that set a ceiling on permitted emissions by companies, rewarding those that are most efficient in reducing pollution, the phasing out of Vehicle Excise Duty and scrapping of the remaining tax breaks for company cars, the introduction of road pricing, peak hour bans on cars in congested districts and stringent criteria for assessing the needs for new motorways.

6 June: Centre for Social and Economic Research on the Global Environment established by the ESRC at University College, London and the University of East Anglia.

14 June: New power to protect rivers, ground waters and coastal waters from agricultural fertilizers agreed by EC environment ministers.

24 June: Dr John Bowman, chief executive of the National Rivers Authority, resigns.

4 July: New curbs on noisy car alarms announced.

10 July: UN survey shows nearly half of Britain's conifers and more than a quarter of broadleaved trees are suffering moderate to severe leaf loss as a result of acid rain.

11 July: Sir Frederick Holliday quits as chairman of the Joint Nature Conservancy Commission because of his concern that the commission's powers are being undermined.

18 July: *Stratospheric Ozone 1991*, HMSO, says that the ozone layer is being depleted at twice the rate previously feared.

21 July: Drinking Water Inspectorate to inquire into how partially-treated Thames water was pumped to two million people in north and west London.

23 July: Nirex confirms it has chosen Sellafield, Cumbria as its site for a deep underground nuclear waste repository.

29 July: Cathy Read, *Pollution and Child Health*, Greenpeace, draws attention to the links between child health problems and air pollution from traffic.

19 Aug: Plans for local authorities to oversee noise levels at airports and airfields, with the exception of large international airports, are outlined.

20 Aug: National Audit Office report says HMIP remains understaffed.

24 Aug: Severe contamination of the water supply on Anglesey affects 30,000 people.

4 Sept: Royal Commission on Environmental Pollution reports that tougher controls on pollution from diesel buses and lorries are necessary.

23 Sept: A centralized agency to handle all forms of environmental pollution is to be set up in Scotland in the next three years.

7 Nov: Public Accounts Committee criticizes existing measures to prevent oil and chemical pollution at sea as 'virtually ineffective' and also condemns the inadequacy of levels of insurance cover.

8 Nov: Competition and Services (Utilities) Bill to improve services and handling of customer complaints in the water, gas and telecommunications industries introduced.

26 Nov: World Wide Fund for Nature recommends a strict speed limit of 50 mph to cut exhaust emission, reductions in toxic discharges into seas and rivers, a halt to dumping industrial waste in the sea and a cut in carbon dioxide levels to 20 per cent of 1990 levels by 2005.

12 Dec: *SSSIs: A Health Check*, Wildlife Link, argues the designation of SSSIs is failing to safeguard the wildlife of such sites.

Town and Country Planning

GORDON E. CHERRY

The British town planning movement has always been closely associated with housing matters. Planning first appeared in legislation as an appendage to a Housing Act (1909), and the first Town and Country Planning Act, independent of any reference to housing, did not enter the statute book until 1932. The early relationship between planning and housing was essentially both environmental and social, because it was concerned with the layout of dwellings in ways which broke away from the by-law regulations of the late 19th century. After 1919, planning and housing became almost inseparable in the work of local councils, both in the creation of local authority housing estates and in the control of private sector building operations. During the last ten years the situation has changed dramatically. The concerns of housing matters are now fought out on the battle ground of such questions as tenurial arrangements and housing finance, rather than on location and design. The second report of the Duke of Edinburgh's inquiry into British housing, published in June, centred on the resources necessary to tackle the problems of homelessness and bad housing conditions, and the required modifications to the housing finance system.

The problem, as ever, is the plight of the poorly housed, and how improved provision for them might be made. Between 1981 and 1991 the national housing stock increased by 9 per cent, during which time the rented sector decreased by 21 per cent. Between 1980 and 1990 housing association provision fell from 19,000 to 12,000 units a year. In 1980 the total new social housing provision was about 94,000, falling to 25,500 in 1990. With a cessation in local authority direct provision and only a modest upturn in housing association activity, the future is stark for the ill-housed. The spotlight falls on the provision of social housing and the ways in which it might be 'affordable' (that is, available at less than the full cost of its provision) and 'allocated' (that is, available to people on the basis of some agreed definition of need).

Housing is the subject of a chapter elsewhere in this volume, but the link with planning needs to be explained because of the recent attempts to tackle rural homelessness, in part through the planning system. DOE Circular 7/91 (10 May), *Planning and Affordable Housing*, deals with the policy of encouraging some building of low cost housing on land within or adjacent to existing small settlements, where housing would not normally be permitted, but where there is pressing local need. The rural problem is particularly acute, of course, because cheaper accommodation in rural areas is affected by pressure brought upon many local housing markets by wealthy newcomers. The circular states that development plans can incorporate policies specifically for low cost housing.

Rural Planning

A whole raft of issues during the year, dealing with building in the countryside and the protection of landscape, accompanied the question of affordable housing. The green belt remains the principal weapon in ensuring restraint on the release of building land in the urban fringe, and is still resolutely supported. It seemed somehow symbolic that Consortium Developments Ltd, the company set up by the UK's ten largest housebuilders to promote and build new settlements, announced their retirement from the fray in 1991, having failed to win support for their projects at Tillingham Hall and Foxley Wood in recent years. The so called 'new villages' of the Ridley era are now out of favour as the present Secretary of State seems predisposed to reject them. But pressure on green belt land around Chester and Newcastle has forced both these authorities to seek redesignation of their green belt boundaries, and various proposals for new communities up and down the country will not go off the planning agenda.

The fact is, however, that the countryside is changing and planning policies have been slow to adapt. The object of rural policies for over four decades has been twofold; to produce more cheap food and to protect the countryside from development. Success certainly attended these policies, but there are now new issues to consider: overproduction in agriculture and consequential environmental damage; and a social transformation stemming from a newcomer population. Planning still tends to see the countryside in terms of agriculture and landscape protection, but the countryside of the 21st century seems likely to be more lived-in than ever before, with communities dependent on an economy dictated not by agriculture but by manufacturing and particularly service industries.

Meanwhile, the DOE announced in June new planning controls over agricultural and forestry buildings, as forecast in the 1990 environment white paper. The discretionary controls over the siting, designing and external appearance of such buildings at present operating in the National Parks, were extended to other parts of England and Wales. Full development control was also extended to all farm holdings of less than five hectares (not ten hectares, as many consultees had advocated).

Questions of landscape protection and enhancement remained very much in the public eye. In a policy statement from the Countryside Commission on heritage coasts, their aim is that by the end of the decade there should be a litter and pollution-free coastal environment, high water quality on all bathing beaches and a continuous public footpath along each littoral. National Parks always attract attention when development is proposed: the Duchy of Cornwall was criticized when it granted the Ministry of Defence a 21-year licence for military training with live firing over 20,000 acres in the heart of the Dartmoor National Park, but opponents of the Ministry of Defence's proposed radar installation on the former St David's airfield in the Pembrokeshire Coast National Park were pleased when the government announced that the proposal had been dropped. There was general support for the government's statement in September that it is 'minded' to create independent National Park authorities for the eight National Parks currently run as county council committees. The government's 'green' credentials were further boosted by an announcement by the agriculture minister of the substantial expansion of the programme of environmentally sensitive areas (ESAs) for farming, with a doubling of the English number from ten to 22, a trebling of them in extent and quadrupling in the finance allocated to them. Political enthusiasm was shared by the environmentalists.

In July the DOE announced proposals to protect key hedgerows involving a 'Hedgerow Notification Scheme' which would require those who wish to remove hedgerows to notify their local planning authority, who may proceed to registered protection, and a separately administered scheme for hedgerow management grants. Trees in the landscape have featured strongly in environmental policy. There is a general aim of planting new forests close to selected population centres, in conformity with the national programme of the Countryside and Forestry Commissions launched in 1989. The lead forests are The Great North Forest (south Tyne and Wear/north east Durham), Forest of Mercia (south Staffordshire) and Thames Chase (east London), and in February nine, second-tier English community forests were announced: Cleveland, west Manchester, south Yorkshire, Merseyside, Nottingham, Bedford, south Hertfordshire, Swindon and Bristol. In December the delineation of the most ambitious project of all was announced: the new national forest will cover 194 square miles, straddling the edges of Staffordshire, Leicestershire and Derbyshire, taking in the sites of the ancient Needwood and Charnwood Forests.

Urban Planning

The end of an era was pronounced with the news that Milton Keynes Development Corporation is to be wound up on 31 March 1991. The task of completing Milton Keynes will be given to the Commission for New Towns which will establish a new promotions agency. But the new town era actually ended many years ago, with the transfer of public sector attention to the rejuvenation of the older cities. The latest initiative in this direction came in May when the Secretary of State for the Environment, Michael Heseltine launched a £75 million scheme for local authorities to compete for funds to regenerate urban areas. Fifteen authorities were urged to submit bids for a share in the global amount available. Meanwhile, better progress is being made in dealing with the problem of derelict land. A DOE report published in January revealed that the amount of derelict land in England fell by 11 per cent between 1982 and 1988 – the first time the Department's periodic surveys have recorded a fall. The Derelict Land Grant is being broadened in scope and flexibility, and funding increased by 23 per cent to £88 million annually.

The winding up of a development corporation compared with financial inducements for environmental recovery might suggest the demise of any notion of long term strategic planning. This was certainly suggested by the events of the 1980s, but 'strategy' is on the political agenda again. SERPLAN's *A New Strategy for the South East* published in October 1990, as advice to the Secretary of State in his regional planning guidance, continued to attract attention. Professor Peter Hall, addressing a government-organized conference on regional planning in the south east in March, highlighted three major issues for the region. These were: the polarization of London, the need to reverse the east-west imbalance, and 'rolling up the growth carpet' which has so far massively assisted the outer metropolitan fringe. These matters were addressed in Michael Heseltine's proposals for strings of mini new towns on either side of the Thames, in the so-called east Thames corridor strategy. The Secretary of State for Transport's announcement to the Conservative Party conference at Brighton in October that the Channel Tunnel rail link to London will be routed to the east of the capital, confirmed Stratford as a nodal point in the scheme of things. Planning consultants have already been appointed to carry out a study of the development capacity of the east Thames corridor.

London has dominated strategic speculation in another sense. A certain revisionism was encouraged during the year concerning local authority functions and boundaries. While the government made it clear that it had no plans to change the general local government structure of London, the Labour Party on the other hand favours a Greater London Authority, a kind of revived, streamlined GLC. In this regard, however, it is pertinent to note that in September Michael Heseltine gave the London Residuary Body final permission to proceed with the redevelopment of County Hall.

Meanwhile Prince Charles has a strategic view of things in global terms. Speaking at a European Community conference on the urban environment in Madrid in April he said that all cities need to be *sustainable* in the long term. 'That is the preeminent challenge city authorities and town planners face today. It will inevitably require a far more rigorous approach to integrated, long term planning, creating patterns of urban life that positively promote energy-saving, waste minimization, *public* transport and economic self reliance.'[1] It really does seem that the intellectual sterility of planning of the 1980s has passed.

The Planning System

The planning machine in local and central government continues to discharge its time-honoured functions. Indications are that the vast majority of district councils in England and Wales are well advanced in their work towards complete local plan coverage of their areas. In development control matters the number of appeals has been significantly reduced – a fall in the intake of new cases by 13 per cent between

April 1990 and March 1991. In the 12 months to February 1991, 32.3 per cent of appeals to the Secretary of State were allowed. The local government ombudsman's report in March continued to reveal a high proportion of complaints on planning matters – 2,601 (35 per cent of the total received, compared with 39 per cent on housing matters). Some of these related to enforcement, and it was sad to record that on 20 June Harry Collinson, principal planning officer of Derwentside District Council was shot and fatally wounded while carrying out an enforcement action in County Durham.

The year was dominated by two issues: the passing of the Planning and Compensation Act 1991, and news of a new local government commission. Within three months of the coming into effect of the 1990 Acts, which consolidated much previous legislation relating to planning, conservation areas and listed buildings, the Planning and Compensation Bill was introduced into the House of Lords. Passage through Parliament culminated in the Royal Assent on 25 July. Parts I and II respectively amend the law on town and country planning in England and Wales and in Scotland; Parts III and IV amend the land compensation code and the procedural rules governing compulsory purchase.

There is much by way of detail and technicality that would be profitless to pursue in this volume. Suffice to say, *inter alia*, that the Act largely implements the main recommendations of the report by Robert Carnwath QC (*Enforcing Planning Control*, HMSO, 1989). In development control matters, developers are allowed to enter into a 'planning obligation' either via an agreement with the local planning authority or by making a unilateral undertaking; the terminology will replace 'planning gain'. The Act also makes it clear that demolition (in certain circumstances) is now included within the definition of development. With regard to plan making, counties will be able to approve their own structure plans after a public hearing. But one of the most important sections (s26) of the Act reads: 'Where, in making any determination under the planning Acts, regard is to be had to the development plan, the determination shall be made in accordance with the plan unless material considerations dictate otherwise.' This could prove to be an epoch-making change, altering the previous presumption in favour of development; it certainly emphasizes and puts increased pressure on the process of local plan-making. It will be interesting to see whether this part of the planning system is up to it.

Finally, local government reform is in the air again. A DOE consultation paper issued in April suggested that the present two-tier system of county and district councils will become a single tier of all-purpose councils in some areas; London and the metropolitan counties (which already have single-tier authorities) will not be affected. A new, independent local government commission was foreshadowed to implement the changes. The Local Government Bill was published on 5 November. The commission, which will have a duty to recommend the most suitable local government structure for each area it examines, is expected to be in operation by June 1992. Twenty years on from the last upheaval in British local government, boundaries and function are once again under critical review.

Note
1 *The Planner*, Vol 77, no.16, 10 May 1991, p.5.

Chronology
2 Jan: David Higgens, *The Problem of Preserving Character*, University of Exeter, argues that the Lake District would be much improved by development.

31 Jan: Countryside Commission calls for an end to the cultivation of cliff-edge land and the creation of public footpaths along heritage coasts.

28 Feb: Peter Palumbo wins approval from the Law Lords for the redevelopment of the Mappin and Webb site in the City of London to a design by Sir James Stirling.

13 Mar: Michael Heseltine intervenes to revoke planning permission for a new housing development on an SSSI at Canford Heath, Poole, Dorset.
Proposals that planning authorities will have to consult the Nature Conservancy Council about applications to develop land adjoining SSSIs are published.

21 Mar: Review panel of the Countryside Commission argues that National Parks require more powers to cope with tourism and growing development pressure. It urges a new National Parks Act and makes 170 recommendations, including experimental car-free zones, restrictions on tourism development, a general National Parks authority independent of the local authorities, no further conifers and the establishment of farm woodlands in place of arable land, some low-cost housing for local need, the revival of the Hill Livestock Compensatory Allowance, the establishment of a National Park in the New Forest and the consideration of other possible sites as well.

9 Apr: Alexander Thomson Society founded to protect the buildings of Scotland's greatest architect.

16 Apr: *Encouraging the Use of Vacant Public Sector Land*, HMSO, envisages the use of tough sanctions, such as the imposition of business rates, to encourage landowners to use vacant land.

7 May: John Adams, *Determined to Dig: The Role of Aggregates Demand Forecasting in National Mineral Planning Guidance*, CPRE, critically assesses such forecasting.

15 May: *Out of Hours*, Comedia, argues that Britain's town centres are cultural and social deserts at night dominated by a pub culture and the groups of drinking male youths they generate and desolate and threatening public transport facilities.

16 May: Local authorities to be given powers to stop speculative demolition by developers of buildings that are not already protected by planning control, through an amendment to the Planning and Compensation Bill.

21 May: Labour policy document, *London – A World Class Capital*, promises to restore a strategic authority for Greater London with powers over transport, traffic control, environmental improvement and fire and police services.

14 June: *London in Prospect*, Institute for Metropolitan Studies, argues that there is no evidence for the economic decline of London.

24 May: Civic Trust warns that changes in retailing patterns and the coming of 1992 is facing many seaside towns, shopping centres, industrial areas and pit villages with steady economic decline.

23 May: £75 million inner urban fund launched.

31 May: New Catholic cathedral (designed by Quinlan Terry) dedicated in Brentwood, Essex.

3 June: Newcastle City Council publishes plans for houses and industry on green belt land around Tyneside.

5 June: Government to set up independent appeals body to vet all new applications by Scottish National Heritage for sites to be designated SSSIs.

11 June: Controls on new farm buildings in England and Wales are to be tightened but full planning controls will only apply on farms of less than 12.4 acres.

13 June: £16 million regional aid package for Cumbria announced.

20 June: Albert Dryden shoots dead Derwentside District Council's planning officer when he arrived to serve a demolition order against a bungalow Mr Dryden had built without permission.

Royal Society for Nature Conservation report calls for government payments to farmers to maintain traditional meadow and pasture.

25 June: Countryside Stewardship scheme, to help encourage farmers to conserve or recreate traditional landscapes and improve public access is launched.

1 July: *Ten Years of Docklands: How the cake was cut*, by the Labour-controlled Association of London Authorities, criticizes the lack of housing provision, community and training schemes for local people by the London Docklands Development Corporation.

2 July: Up to 100,000 farmers and farmworkers (one-sixth of the current total) will lose their jobs by the end of the century according to the Rural Development Commission as a result of changes to EC subsidies to curb over-production. This, the report argues, requires government intervention to curb the dereliction, depopulation and depression that will result.

Plans for two motorway service stations on the M40 are turned down on environmental grounds.

9 July: *A London Development Agency: Optimizing the Capital's Assets*, CBI, outlines plans for a government appointed strategic authority for the capital to plan and direct development.

10 July: Environment Select Committee criticizes the Health and Safety Executive for neglecting indoor air pollution and sick building syndrome, which costs an estimated £650 million a year in lost staff time.

25 July: Some sort of planning control to protect hedgerows suggested by the government.

31 July: Announcement that Bradford, the Dearne Valley, Lewisham, Liverpool, Manchester, Middlesborough, Newcastle-upon-Tyne, Nottingham, Tower Hamlets, Wirral and Wolverhampton have won government funding for urban regeneration under the city challenge scheme.

6 Aug: Jocelyn Stevens is appointed to succeed Lord Montagu as chairman of English Heritage.

23 Aug: Plans for a new town on Canvey Island are turned down by Michael Heseltine.

4 Sept: *Changing London for Good*, Liberal Democrats, proposes a London strategic authority, toll roads and improvements to public transport in the capital.

9 Sept: Country Landowners' Association urges members to honour their legal obligation to keep footpaths clear.

29 Sept: Mass trespass organized by the Ramblers' Association to mark its 'Forbidden Britain Day' and to protest against the illegal blocking of rights of way and the denial of access to the countryside by landowners.

17 Sept: *Population Trends*, HMSO, shows continuing trend of population movement away from the conurbations in 1981–91.

20 Sept: National Parks to be granted freedom from local authority control.

26 Sept: Duke of Devonshire and Sheffield City Council sign access agreements to their land with the Peak National Park Authority.

1 Oct: *Caring for the Countryside*, Countryside Commission, proposes that 15 per cent of land used for cereal production in England should be taken out of production and used for conservation and recreation and that there should be greater access to unused land unless this interferes with wildlife or other legitimate uses.

15 Oct: New government guidelines ask local authorities to consult the police to vet all major planning applications to ensure sufficient regard is given to crime prevention.

17 Oct: EC starts legal action against the government for failing to carry out environmental impact assessments on seven projects, including the M3 extension, the link between the M11 and the Blackwall tunnel and the East London River Crossing.

17 Dec: Britain to defy an EC block on the East London River Crossing, the M11 link to the Blackwall tunnel and the M3 extension.

Religion

GRACE DAVIE

The Waiting Game

The Ordination of Women

Forward planning in religious affairs is determined at least in part by the wider political context. In this respect, church leaders as much as everyone else are influenced by the uncertainty surrounding the result of the 1992 general election. For the Church of England this uncertainty is compounded by a further factor: in 1992 the General Synod will vote on the Priests (Ordination of Women) Measure, a crucial decision for the church, but one whose outcome is as difficult to predict as that of the forthcoming general election. Nor can anyone say with confidence what will happen whichever way the vote goes. Threats and counter-threats continue to multiply as the time for decision gets nearer.

In the meantime, most diocesan synods have voted in favour of the measure; only the dioceses of Blackburn, Chichester, London, Portsmouth, Truro, Europe and the Armed Forces have rejected it. Voting in the deaneries has been closer. It is important to bear in mind, however, that the system of voting in both dioceses and deaneries is not the same as that in the General Synod. In the former decisions are arrived at by simple majorities in the House of Clergy and the House of Laity, the synod recording a 'no' vote if the motion is lost or tied in either house.[1] In the latter a two-thirds majority is required in all three houses, voting separately. Nor does voting in the deaneries and dioceses provide a reliable indicator of what is going to happen in the General Synod next year; it was not designed with this in mind. What is does provide is some indication of opinion at a local level, opinion which varies considerably from area to area. These variations reflect differing ecclesiastical traditions which – seen positively – signify the richness of the Anglican tradition. Richness or confusion: which is it? We shall come back to this question. `

Whatever happens the vote in the Synod will either bring to an end, or prolong indefinitely,[2] a long and difficult period of uncertainty within the Established Church, not least for those women whose priesting depends on this decision.

Terry Waite's return

A very different kind of waiting did come, quite suddenly, to an end in November and provided the whole country with a welcome distraction for a day or two. Terry Waite, the Archbishop of Canterbury's special envoy, was released from captivity in Beirut on Monday 18 November after 1,763 days as a hostage. Much of this time had been spent in solitary confinement, chained to the wall for all but a few minutes each day. It was hardly surprising, therefore, that his homecoming in appalling English weather was greeted with such enthusiasm. Indeed it provoked extraordinary reactions – not least the promotion of Bunyan's *Pilgrim's Progress* to the front pages of the tabloids, alongside headlines such as 'MY GOD. You can tell he was made in Britain'. The population was, it seems, glued to their television screens to see the plane carrying Terry Waite from Cyprus touch down on British soil at RAF Lyneham. Their relief was expressed (as live coverage came to an end) in a corporate decision to put the kettle on; the surge in power was reported to be comparable to that experienced for royal weddings or the cup final!

By the beginning of December all British and American hostages had been released from the Middle East, bringing to an end an episode that influenced international politics on and off for six and a half years. The pace had quickened through the year until the final releases came so rapidly that they were almost predictable.[3] In this respect Terry Waite was but one of a group caught up in the dangerous detail of Middle East politics. He became a hostage himself as he attempted to extricate others from that predicament. For the British, however, he was a particularly high-profile captive, his case tending at times to overshadow that of others. And for the churches, he was bound to be special; for they saw him, at least in part, as a religious envoy. Candles had been kept burning since his disappearance in January 1987 and prayers for the Waite family became a regular part of worship in churches up and down the land.

The Church of England had a particular interest in the matter; Terry Waite was, after all, on the pay roll of the Archbishop of Canterbury. Exactly what he was doing in this capacity became, however, a source of considerable speculation, for there could be no doubt that a certain amount of communication with Colonel Oliver North had taken place in the period preceding Terry Waite's disappearance. The full story may never emerge, but a fuller account was offered just before Christmas once the former hostage had had a chance to adjust to his new-found freedom and to spend time with his family. This interview (given exclusively to the BBC) included an explicit expression of thanks for the lifeline provided by the BBC's World Service.

Terry Waite's release – and that of the other hostages – was but the visible tip of an unpredictable iceberg. This may be an inappropriate image for the part of the world in question, but it points to a reality that we cannot ignore. For the intricacies of Middle Eastern politics provide the backdrop for a whole series of interrelated events in the religious life of Britain in 1991.

The Middle East Factor

The Gulf War

Iraq's invasion of Kuwait on 2 August 1990 had incalculable effects on the precarious alliances that are the substance of Middle Eastern politics. Commentators at the time rightly spoke of the emergence of a new global order as the world came and continues to come to terms not only with the dramatic events in the Middle East, but with the aftermath of the 1989 revolutions in eastern Europe and with events in the USSR. Indeed the two are related, not least by the religious factor, for Islam (often in its more militant forms) straddles the border between the Middle East and the southern parts of the Soviet empire. Religious aspirations, interacting with national identity, continue to threaten the stability of that whole area.

The Gulf war was not a religious war for the West was, officially at least, defending the rights of one Muslim nation against an aggressive neighbour of the same religion. Within the dangerous and tense situation that developed, however, some confusion of terms was almost inevitable. Oil became identified with Arab and both were associated with Islam; the potential for stereotyping was alarming and the Muslim minority in this country took some of the consequences. Conversely, many Muslims – and not only Iraqis – regarded Saddam Hussein as a religious rather than a secular leader, responding to his call to support the *jihad*, or sacred mission in the defence of Islam.

How did the British churches respond to this situation? For many, the cue came from Dr Runcie's 'Thought for the Day' on the morning that hostilities started.[4] He confessed that the conventional 'Good morning' that normally precedes this two to three minute slot seemed inappropriate; no more so, however, than the use of the same adjective in the phrase 'Good Friday'. From this starting point, Dr Runcie acknowledged the sinfulness of war – the Gulf war being no exception – but at the same time, affirmed the churches and those who represent them in their duty to provide pastoral care for all those caught up in the hostilities. The churches undertook this pastoral charge in a wide variety of ways.

The wider debate about what does or does not constitute a just war gathered momentum as the political events took their course. It failed – not surprisingly – to produce any clear-cut answers. The attempt to discover whether the Augustinian criteria for a just war were met in this case produced a confusing array of responses. Was it really the 'last resort'? Did it have 'legitimate authority' and 'right intentions', and were the means 'proportionate' to the ends? Did the scale of modern warfare render the whole debate obsolete anyway? And if so, what kind of thinking should be put in its place? Nobody seemed quite to know. Increasing attention was, moreover, paid to the devastating ecological consequences of the war: the effect of war on the environment must, surely, become part of this debate.

The aftermath of the Gulf war brought no easy answers either. While everyone was grateful that the British, indeed Western casualties were low, the suffering of the Iraqi people could not be ignored and the plight of the Kurds, dramatically shown on television, prompted urgent calls for humanitarian action. It seemed that very little had been resolved by the military action apart from the removal of the Iraqis from a devastated Kuwait. In achieving this, almost as many problems were created as were solved.

Salman Rushdie

Terry Waite's homecoming has already been discussed. It was, however, brought about at least in part by the shifting balance of power between Iraq, Iran, Syria and the Lebanon. Iran's anti-western stance receded as Iraq took centre stage as the enemy. At the same time, Syria's one-time dependence on the USSR for support and finance was no longer viable as the Soviet economy came closer and closer to collapse. Both Iran and Syria began to look to the West for favours. As this stance became increasingly marked, the hostages ceased to be valuable bargaining counters in the international game; instead they became an embarrassment. They might as well go home. Home they came to great rejoicing.

But not all problems concerning Iran and Britain have been resolved. Salman Rushdie remains in hiding almost three years after the imposition of the original *fatwa* by the Ayatollah Khomeini, and the Iranians do not seem inclined or able to shift their position in this respect. Moreover, Rushdie's plight became linked to that of Terry Waite. For plans to mark Rushdie's thousandth day in hiding coincided with a crucial stage in the negotiations to release Waite, illustrating once again the very delicate balances that determine the fate of individuals. Within these balances, the religious factor – alongside a multiplicity of other pressures – is an essential ingredient. Negotiators ignore it at their peril.

Indeed the significance of the religious factor in this debate may go some way to explain Salman Rushdie's second about turn regarding his religious position, not to mention his dismay at Dr Carey's more recent remarks about toleration (on 22 November) which included a plea for a greater understanding of the Muslim position. Be that as it may, we are still no nearer, at the end of 1991, to finding a solution to the incompatibilities that lie at the heart of the Rushdie controversy. Is it, or is it not possible to reconcile satisfactorily the competing freedoms of expression and religion? Mixed with Middle Eastern politics, these incompatibilities all too easily become dangerous confrontations.

Autumnal Confusion

It seemed that one thing led to another in the middle of September. In reality, a number of quite separate issues were raised during this month, but became confused with one another because they occurred at the same time. It is important to disentangle the threads.

Early in the month, the Archdeacon of York (the Venerable George Austin) used a sermon in the Minster to call for a formal split between the Church of England's traditional and liberal wings. He argued that deep divisions of opinion should be recognised rather than papered over, allowing parishes to opt whichever way they chose. All sorts of issues were raised in this connection (issues of ministry, ethics, doctrine and liturgy) about which Anglicans are, it is quite true, at best confused and at worst in conflict.

So far, so good; Anglican disagreements – however well disguised as comprehensiveness – aren't easily contained within one institution, even one as historically flexible as the Church of England. But splitting into conservative and liberal camps will not solve the problem either, for the issues in question do not and cannot produce neat packages of liberals on one side and conservatives on the other. Those who are conservative in matters of liturgy, for example, do not always hold conservative views on ethical or moral issues; why should they? Nor can the debate about the ordination of women be used as a touchstone; indeed it has brought together unlikely combinations of people who find themselves on the same 'side' for a wide variety of reasons, with their arguments deriving from quite different principles. Most significant of all, however, there appear to be increasing numbers of churchpeople who find themselves in a category which might be labelled morally conservative but socially liberal (or moderately so anyway); a group, that is, who resist change on a wide variety of moral issues (both personal and collective) but who have at least some misgivings about the inequalities of contemporary society and want to do something about these. Where are they supposed to go in the proposed schema?

Within this confusion, the issue of homosexuality should be treated quite separately, for it invites a very different set of responses. One of these – that is to maintain a firmness of principle alongside considerable pastoral flexibility – is neither 'liberal' or 'conservative'. On the contrary, it represents a practical attempt to come to terms with a sensitive and controversial issue to which there are no easy answers. The bishops returned to this question at the end of the year, urging celibacy for the homosexual priest but not necessarily for the equivalent lay person.

The second September issue centred on the riots in Newcastle, which followed the deaths of two joyriders in a stolen car as they were chased by police. All the old *Faith in the City* chestnuts re-emerged, not least the nature/nurture controversy. Were the rioters – coming very largely from some of the most deprived estates of the north east – wholly responsible for their actions, or should society take some responsibility for their inability to participate constructively in the normal processes of living? Similarly the right or otherwise of the churches to participate in political debate had a further (inevitable) airing. Should not the churches confine themselves to teaching potential joyriders/rioters the difference between right and wrong and keep out of policy making altogether? But this is not altogether practical advice, for the churches have very little contact with the social groups in question, a paradox neatly caught by an *Evening Standard* cartoon in which would-be rioters puzzle over a headline indicating the churches' involvement on their behalf. 'What is a church?' they ask. Part of the answer lay, perhaps, in the televised funerals of the young joyriders themselves, funerals conducted by the parish priests of the area. Who else?

Coincidentally, the European Values Systems Study Group (EVSSG) chose this moment to release the outline figures for the religious aspects of their updated study on European values. The data was collected in 1990. The figures were not surprising; they showed a slight decline in the formal indices of religiosity in most of western Europe over a ten year period, though religious belief maintains itself at over 70 per cent. (The principal exceptions to the decline were the two Irelands where neither religious practice nor religious belief shows any sign of diminishing.) More interesting were the EVSSG comments about the changing role of religion in contemporary society. The churches should not, according to most people, concern themselves with private morality; that is a matter of individual choice. On the other hand, the churches should speak out on important questions of public policy, notably on the environment. It is interesting that some Conservative politicians tend to argue the reverse.

One very noticeable feature of the political aspects of the September debate was, however, a marked difference in style. Dr Carey, still feeling his way in public controversy, undoubtedly holds strong views, not least in matters educational where (once more in September) he resolutely opposed the opting-out policy so strongly promoted by the present government.[5] It was this speech on education that included some asides on the Tyneside riots which added to the confusion between topics that pervaded this month. But both the new Archbishop and Mr Major refused to be drawn into another slanging match between the churches and the Conservative government. Instead Mr Major expressed his respect for Dr Carey, underlining rather than denying the importance of the churches' participation in public debate.

Indeed the attacks on Dr Carey have, at times, come from a rather different quarter; from those within the church with decidedly short memories. A sort of 'come back Runcie brigade' who knew where they were in the reassuring world of old-boy networks and London clubs. Snide remarks by anonymous 'senior churchmen' about the new Archbishop's inexperience are not helpful; nor were previous criticisms directed, in their turn, at Dr Runcie's apparent equivocation. Both Archbishops deserve better.

The domestic year ended with two very different issues competing for attention. On the one hand those uneasy about interfaith worship organized an open letter to the *Church Times*, expressing respect for those of other faiths, but questioning the integrity of joint acts of worship. (The interfaith issue has particular resonance as the Decade of Evangelism gets under way). On the other, the rather different question of Sunday shopping – prompted as much by the recession as by changing social attitudes – gathered momentum in the run up to Christmas. Both issues, however, raise a similar principle. How should the Christian churches react when they command neither a monopoly of beliefs, nor of the social customs associated with such beliefs? Such loss of monopoly demands, as it has always demanded, a constant redefining of boundaries; a far from straightforward process.

Europe and Ecumenism

As the Maastricht summit approached, European questions asserted themselves strongly on the public agenda. The churches varied in their reactions.

Earlier in the year (July), the Church of England made a valiant attempt to address the question of a European future at 'Malvern 1991', a conference convened exactly 50 years after the original Malvern conference of the war years. 'Malvern 1941' had proved a significant, indeed prophetic, moment in the church's life, when William Temple drew together his ideas about the nature of post-war society and used the conference as a launch-pad for this philosophy.[6] 'Malvern 1991' was not comparable, and considerable conference energy was dissipated rather negatively, in patient but time-consuming attempts to accommodate the agendas of those with a wide variety of special concerns (the environment, peace, women, gay and lesbian rights, minorities, to name but a few). Nonetheless the organizers must be applauded for bringing the question of Europe to the attention of the churches and for initiating an important debate in this area.

Considerably more substantial, however, have been the discussions in the Roman Catholic church, emerging from the Synod of Bishops on Europe in Rome called for late November and from the Council of European Bishops' Conferences. (The latter has, in addition, an important non-Catholic counterpart in the Council of European Churches, their most recent ecumenical gathering taking place in Santiago de Compostela.) But even the names of the Roman Catholic organizations indicate how far behind the rest of us are on matters European; the other churches have no comparable organizational apparatus through which to engage the issues with the seriousness that the topic demands. Roman Catholics do not necessarily agree about these issues (the secular nature of western Europe, the need to build bridges between East and West and so on), nor about the policies that the church should adopt in a very rapidly changing situation. But they do point the way when it comes to serious and sustained debate about the context in which all European churches are, and will increasingly be, obliged to work; all the British churches should follow the course of these deliberations with the greatest possible attention.

Ecumenism and the European question are closely linked, for the historic divisions within the Christian church very often took territorial form, as nationhood asserted itself as the dominant mode of European politics. Nations or nation states adopted the religion of their ruler, either Catholic or Protestant, giving geographical shape to theological disagreements. But is it not possible for the diverse and varied skills, developed by the different churches through much of European history, to be offered back to the wider church in the better and more ecumenical climate that is emerging alongside a greater sense of European identity? If this is the case, the

Roman Catholics have, organizationally at least, a great deal to offer to the rest of us.

Given this potential, it is all the more discouraging that the Vatican's long-awaited response to the final report of ARCIC I has not been more positive. The response confirms that there has been 'notable progress' in the dialogue between the two communions, but does not accept that this amounts to 'substantial agreement'. There is, clearly, a good deal further to go.

Notes

1 In the Diocesan synods, the vote in the House of Bishops does not influence the final outcome. Under Article 8, voting in the House of Bishops cannot invalidate the voting in the other houses. The vote was lost or tied in 13 Houses of Bishops.

2 Even those opposed to the current legislation concerning the ordination of women admit that the issue itself cannot be so easily dismissed. It is bound to reassert itself sooner or later.

3 At the time of writing, two Germans are still being held hostage in the Lebanon.

4 The Archbishop of Canterbury's invitation to participate in Radio 4's 'Today' programme on this particular morning was, perhaps, the British equivalent – suitably understated – of Billy Graham's much more high profile presence in the White House.

5 Interestingly, Dr Carey was equally firm with respect to those Christians who 'opt out' of mainstream education into exclusively Christian schools. Such schools are, he maintained, 'socially divisive, educationally damaging and spiritually unsatisfying'.

6 See the Malvern Declaration of 1941 and Archbishop Temple's *Christianity and the Social Order*, Penguin 1942.

Chronology

4 Jan: Muslims are to set up an Islamic body roughly analogous to the Board of Deputies of British Jews.

20 Jan: National conference of Muslims in Bradford sets up a Supreme Council of British Mosques, condemns allied action in the Gulf and calls for the immediate withdrawal of non-Muslim troops in the region.

30 Jan: General Synod passes a motion calling for the setting up of a committee to consider replacing freehold tenure for incumbents with renewable contracts.
Report by the General Synod committee chaired by Rev Judith Rose stops short of recommending the ordination of women but calls for more opportunities to be created for ordained female deacons.

1 Feb: Dr George Carey succeeds Dr Robert Runcie as Archbishop of Canterbury.

19 Feb: Dr David Hope is appointed to succeed Graham Leonard as Bishop of London.

4 Mar: Peter Brierley, *Christian England*, MARC Europe, shows a decline in church attendance in 1979–89 of 14 per cent amongst Catholics, 9 per cent amongst Anglicans, 11 per cent amongst Methodists and 18 per cent in the United Reformed Church. There was a 114 per cent increase in House Church attendance and 8 per cent at Pentecostal churches.

31 Mar: A *Sunday Express* survey shows 34 per cent of people do not know the meaning of Easter Sunday and 39 per cent do not understand the significance of Good Friday, although 85 per cent claim to be Christian.

16 Apr: *Do not be afraid*, National Board of Catholic Women, argues women feel they are discriminated against in the church and want to be properly represented in its decision-making processes.

Archbishop of Canterbury floats the idea of alternative episcopal oversight for clergy opposed to the ordination of women.

19 Apr: George Carey enthroned as Archbishop of Canterbury.

2 May: Papal encyclical, *Centesimus Annus*, issued to mark the centenary of *Rerum Novarum*, offers a critique of free market economic systems.

9 May: Salman Rushdie, in a letter to *The Independent*, responds to the reaction against accepting his conversion to Islam at the central London mosque.

29 May: Rt Rev Jim Thompson, Bishop of Stepney, is translated to Bath and Wells.

31 May: New Catholic cathedral of St Mary and St Helen in Brentwood, Essex (designed by Quinlan Terry) is dedicated.

11 June: *Buried Treasure*, a report for the Methodist conference, argues that giving in the collection is insufficient.

9 July: Rt Rev Roy Williamson to succeed Rt Rev Ronald Bowlby as Bishop of Southwark.

16 July: *Good News in Our Time*, makes recommendations on the Church of England's approach to evangelism.

17–20 July: Malvern 1991 conference.

1 Sept: Jonathan Sacks becomes Chief Rabbi of Britain and the Commonwealth.

5 Sept: Calls for the Catholic Church to reconsider its opposition to divorce are made at a national convention of Catholic priests in Cardiff.

6 Sept: Chief Rabbi expresses concern about the decline of the Anglo-Jewish community.

8 Sept: Ven. George Austin, Archdeacon of York, suggests formalizing the division between traditionalists and theological liberals in the Church of England.

18 Sept: Muslims call for new laws outlawing incitment to religious hatred and discrimination on religious grounds.

19 Sept: In a speech which sparks some controversy the Archbishop of Canterbury associates the Newcastle riots with social deprivation.

24 Sept: Nigel McCulloch is appointed as the new Bishop of Wakefield.

15 Oct: Rt Rev Alwyn Rice Jones, Bishop of St Asaph, is chosen as the new Archbishop of Wales.

23 Oct: *Seeds of Hope*, Board of Social Responsibility of the Church of England, argues that the Church should take steps to rid itself of racism and encourage greater participation of and greater candidacy for ordination from young black people.

Report by English Heritage says England's 61 Anglican and Catholic cathedrals need £185 million over the next decade to cover repair costs.

25 Oct: Bishop of Oxford loses his case to require the Church Commissioners to pursue ethical investment policies even at the risk of financial loss.

5 Nov: *All God's Children? Children's Evangelism in Crisis*, Board of Education and Mission of the Church of England, warns of competition from a 'world of false values and gospels'.

12 Nov: Archbishop of Canterbury and Cardinal Hume criticize the Asylum Bill.

Government to set up Inner Cities Religious Council, to be chaired by Robert Key MP. It aims at improving church/state relations but will also include representatives of other faiths.

18 Nov: Terry Waite released, returning to Britain the following day.

22 Nov: Dr Carey gives the Morrell address on toleration at the University of York.

28 Nov-14 Dec: Extraordinary Synod of Catholic bishops from eastern and western Europe is held in Rome, to examine the religious situation in the new Europe and the problems of secularization.

4 Dec: House of Bishops, *Issues in Human Sexuality*, Church House, says homosexual relations are not acceptable for clergy but should be tolerated amongst the laity.

6 Dec: Open letter in Church Times opposes interfaith worship.

Disappointing Vatican response to ARCIC I.

The Literary Arts

DAVID MORGAN

The Novel

It was an unremarkable year for fiction. Really interesting novels were few. It is assumed that this is quite a strong period for the novel; it is still the predominant literary form. However, perspectives can change quickly. Such a year serves usefully as a reminder that the writing of fiction is a precarious business.

Perhaps the most praised work this year was Angela Carter's *Wise Children*. Her novel of theatrical twins and Shakespearean climaxes was a brilliant tour de force. It succeeded in harnessing a fertile fictive imagination to a sustained narrative whilst incorporating a great deal of humour. Carter has always written well but at times the verve of the localized making has rendered the larger structure more vulnerable. Her inventiveness and her referential idiom are characteristic of the current literary era. They also reveal a telling uncertainty about the whole process of novelistic creation. It is as though there is a need for outside assistance with the matter of fiction. This leads to a use of allusion in the widest sense. Often such a method results in a non-cohesive final product. *Wise Children* rose triumphantly above this hurdle and seems sure to amuse for some time to come.

Martin Amis is one of the most formidable of contemporary novelists. His novel of this year, *Time's Arrow*, provoked more discussion than any other. It is a strikingly fluent fiction with numerous characteristic touches of killing detail. The essential design – that of a life told backwards – was a strong idea and when it was applied to the life of a doctor in a Nazi concentration camp was always likely to promote interest and even a degree of outrage. The idea unfortunately remained an idea. Amis's work still suffers from a lack of communicable emotion. He has an undeniably brilliant style propelled by a linguistic intelligence which can dazzle almost continually. This does leave a reader very little space for feeling the emotional matter of the novel. *Time's Arrow* was a most striking work but a difficult book to love.

After a gap of some years Susan Hill published a new novel, *Air and Angels*. Hill's work, like that of Amis, has the mark of fiction that will endure. She has the great virtue of realizing a distinct subject for each novel; they are definably about something. Her latest offering – the portrait of a man's obsessive love for a much younger woman – seems less sure than some of her previous fictions but it is to be hoped that this marks a return to novel-writing for a most adept creator.

J G Ballard's *Empire of the Sun* was much praised when it appeared in 1984. Ballard published a sequel to this work in 1991, *The Kindness of Women*. It took up the autobiographical chronicle of the earlier book but seemed much more a work of purgative need. It dwelt largely on the delineation of physical relationships; it portrayed the dangers inherent in an over-familiarity with the zeitgeist. The profoundly anti-erotic results of Ballard's prose illustrate one end to which the novel has come: the assumption of sexual inclusiveness in fiction can inspire a particular weariness in the writing.

Another notable novelist whose book this year was a lesser success was Julian Barnes. *Talking it Over* employed three narrators but failed to establish adequate personalities for them. Barnes's is, however, a genial, fluent talent and it is often furthered by an enjoyable sense of experimentation.

An identifiable type of the contemporary literary artist might be dubbed the novelist of composure. These writers often present very polished narratives of social relationships. Yet they do work near to many fine lines. Anita Brookner's *A Closed Eye* was undistinguished. Penelope Lively's *City of the Mind* was a rather soft-centred and schematic work paralleling character and city. Her novel also suffered from that tell-tale sign of surface topicality: incessant reference. More successfully restrained were Jane Gardam's *The Queen of the Tambourine* – an interesting excursion into the modern epistolary novel which won the Whitbread novel award – and William Trevor's *Two Lives*. Both writers benefit from a very controlled prose style, always welcome in this era of extremes.

The British novel tends either to be a piece of small scale observation or one which talks of worlds and years. The meeting point between these two territories of fiction comes in the guise of the first person narrative, so frequent in current writing. Thus a writer may filter an ambitious, sweeping subject through one coordinating consciousness. Angela Carter, above, offered many years and one life (even with twin protagonists). This love of the first person speaks of the continually unsettling effect of Modernism. We are still listening to the post-Eliot voices of lost individuals. This, by way of contrast, explains an essential aspect of the appeal of writers such as Anita Brookner, who, even in her weaker work, seems comfortable with authorial omniscience. It is a rare treat for a reader to be guided in this fashion.

A sign of a distaste for the current sense of disintegration came when the novelist Nicholas Mosley resigned from judging this year's Booker Prize. In itself this does not appear to be a very memorable event but the terms of the debate were significant. Mosley apparently resigned because, as he saw it, no novels of character and idea were shortlisted; rather they were overlooked in favour of narratives of fragment and sprawl. This is not quite the familiar debate of modern versus traditional. His resignation did seem to describe a moment in which it was possible not to feel at home with modern fiction, however, to resent the automatic sense of the quirky. The Booker Prize itself went to Ben Okri's *The Famished Road*. This was a magical narrative of an African spirit child.

Other established writers who published this year were Margaret Drabble (*The Gates of Ivory*) and Michael Frayn (*A Landing on the Sun*). Beryl Bainbridge's *The Birthday Boys* took a characteristically tangential look at a famous subject – on this occasion the discovery of the South Pole. Pat Barker's latest work *Regeneration* was a rarity in being an impressive war novel, based upon the figure of Siegfried Sassoon. David Lodge was typically humorous in *Paradise News*. James Kelman was as bleak as ever in the stories of *The Burn*. Alan Judd's *The Devil's Own Work* was an accomplished ghost story. The first novel which drew most praise was Gordon Burn's *Alma Cogan*.

Veteran novelist William Cooper published the dangerously entitled *Immortality at any Price*. His classic *Scenes From Provincial Life* (published in 1950) still seems an important work; it managed a particular tone of detached observation which still seems very appropriate today. Will the reader in 2020 regard Carter, Amis or another with a similar appreciation of the novelist's foresight?

The Bestseller

Having spoken already of the overriding sense of continuity which predominated in 1991 it might be appropriate to consider the area of book production which is marked by a yet more specific and absolute consistency – the realm of the bestseller. Here it is that the same names always feature. (A useful digest of the sales figures may be found in an article in *The Guardian*, 9 January 1992, by Alex Hamilton.) The nation thrills with Jack Higgins and Dick Francis and romances with Catherine Cookson and Danielle Steele. The preoccupations with dieting and astrology endure. The new and bizarre phenomenon of converting an author's name into a registered trademark takes this inescapable sense of continuum to one logical extreme. Thus the 'new' Virginia Andrews may appear after the author's death, written by another hand. When a more overtly literary novel sells on a scale even approaching this the result is striking. A S Byatt's *Possession* and Ian McEwan's *The Innocent* sold well in 1991. That is success.

Current critical theory would refute any such distinction between popular and literary fiction – and *theoretically* such a refutation would seem inevitable. In practice, the perceived difference persists. It is a feature of the current literary situation which it would be disingenuous to deny. Institutional response to this fact was furthered this year by, amongst other examples, Frederick Forsyth's *The Day of the Jackal* appearing on the London Board A-Level English syllabus. This gesture seemed less an attempt at imparting a spurious respectability to the work in question than a submission before the inexorable force of the readily assimilable artefact.

As a whole, sales figures for books were down. Even the bestseller suffered numerically. The literary community must await with some trepidation the consequences of attempts to introduce a free-pricing policy which would end the

Net Book Agreement. It seems likely that such a move would result in a greater standardization of the books on offer. More and more books were discounted in 1991. In context, and perhaps also in content, this would appear to have been a recession year.

World Fiction

English abroad often challenges the productions of British writers. Nineteen ninety-one was a quiet literary year elsewhere too, however. Australian Peter Carey brought his characteristic metaphorical lucidity to bear in *The Tax Inspector*. Canadian Margaret Atwood is another notably impressive manager of modern meaning and she offered the stories of *Wilderness Tips* in 1991. The Nobel prize was awarded to the South African novelist Nadine Gordimer. Gordimer's work is written in an impressive plain style. As always with such awards there seems the presence of political as well as aesthetic consideration behind the choice. Her volume of stories *Jump* showed the vulnerability of her writing but as with other Nobel laureates the literary phenomenon she constitutes appeals for recognition.

Literature in translation is most popular when it originates from Latin America or eastern Europe. The former region this year offered Gabriel Garcia Marquez's *The General in his Labyrinth*, a historically magical novel based upon the life of Simon Bolivar. The next generation includes accomplished writers like Isabel Allende, author this year of *The Stories of Eva Luna*. Mario Vargas Llosa reapproached literature from politics with *In Praise of the Stepmother*. Eastern Europe is in turmoil; the sort of turmoil which makes such a regional generalization specifically inappropriate. Czech novelist Milan Kundera had his latest novel *Immortality* translated here. Critical response was mixed but this was a distinguished piece of fiction, much more comfortable in its fragmentary state than many. One strength of such writing is a total lack of self-consciousness about its strategies for avoiding closure. The excellent Ivan Klima shares much of Kundera's powerful awareness of fictional and historical irony. His novel this year was *Judge on Trial*.

An interesting voice in the making is that of the Israeli writer David Grossman. His *The Smile of the Lamb* was a less certain work than the previous *See Under: Love* of 1990 but this is a talent whose development seems certain. His better known compatriot Amos Oz provided *To Know a Woman*. The Jewish-American novelist Isaac Bashevis Singer died this year. A Nobel laureate, Singer is esteemed but perhaps not as widely read here as he deserves to be. Whilst the volume of 1991, *Scum*, was not his most convincing Singer is a powerful chronicler of detail. His finest work has the absolute sureness of touch, the skill of selection and the understanding of importance on all scales which merits a wider readership.

The Swiss novelist and dramatist Max Frisch also died in 1991. His blackly allegorical plays are still performed here – *Andorra, Biedermann und die Brandstifter* (The Fire Raisers) – but the novels are less known. Perhaps the relative obscurity of fine fictions such as *Stiller* is a sign of current taste which enjoys a tale of political ferment – particularly one located elsewhere – to the slower forces of creeping insecurity at work in Frisch's Swiss writing.

America

American fiction can be very exciting. This year some of its most publicized products undermined this by their very scale. Harold Brodkey took a great many years to write the lengthy *The Runaway Soul*. Norman Mailer's new book *Harlot's Ghost* was equally capacious. At the opposite extreme a posthumous volume of terse pieces, *No Heroes Please*, came from Raymond Carver. This was a reminder of the loss of a formidable talent. Much publicity surrounded Bret Easton Ellis's *American Psycho*. This chronicle of modern distress included scenes of notorious violence which instigated outrage and ensured large sales. The literary merit of the novel itself appears uncertain but there does seem a healthy vigour about the spectacle of substantial offence. It is at least heartening to know that the contemporary reader is not immune to all forms of provocation.

The American novelist has always seemed more at home with the technological complexities of the current moment. One of the most interesting writers across the Atlantic, Don DeLillo published *Mao II*. This was an ambitious and angst-ridden attempt to probe the connections between fiction and terrorism. It did not entirely cohere as a novel but this work certainly gave the impression of asking necessary questions. It also recorded some of the most perplexing of modern phenomena not least a mass wedding in a football stadium. Another interesting American novelist is William Wharton. This year's *Last Lovers* paired two striking protagonists and illustrated the writer's not inconsiderable ability to focus upon a modern individual. This is a skill possessed also by Anne Tyler whose brilliantly quirky portrayals entertain with truth, on this occasion in *Saint Maybe*.

Poetry

Two books dominated the year in poetry. Seamus Heaney's *Seeing Things* was one of his finest works and drew considerable acclaim. Heaney is the poet of the current period. This volume included some of the most persuasive of his work, amongst others in the central sequence of twelve-lined sonnets 'Squarings'. As its title suggests the anthology is much concerned with the centrality of vision, the potential for epiphany and for spiritual recognition in the daily occurrence. As such its thesis was powerfully old-fashioned. In addition to the quality of its contents *Seeing Things* was marked out in part by the praise it received. The material showed the poet's confidence, his ability to merge the personal and the aesthetic. This was the effort of earlier volumes but they did not always succeed in escaping the contemporary manner of fragmentary narrative. Now the final accomplishment of formal control silenced any such objection. The other book was Michael Longley's *Gorse Fires* which won the Whitbread poetry award and was the writer's first for some years. Longley writes with a strong sense of the specific and this volume shared with Heaney some of the thrust of celebration. Roy Fuller was another writer who could impress with the faithful clarity of detail and the good-humoured domesticity of his writing. Fuller died in 1991 and his lucid poetic voice will be missed.

There were, of course, other books of poems this year. One might note the continuing struggle with heritage and place in R S Thomas's *Counterpoint* and the deftly witty writing of D J Enright in *Under the Circumstances*; but it was not an easy year for poets to assert themselves. To say as much might sound as if excessive store is set by public response. The nature of current poetry, however, is such that it specifically requires a degree of tolerance and faith to succeed. It is as though one needs to believe that the poems will satisfy – almost before reading them – in order that they may escape the impression of arbitrariness. Few current poets – Heaney is exceptional here – seem able to speak with an imposing voice. More usual is a tone which appeals to a reader, asking for a benign fidelity of attention. It is difficult to imagine that Heaney's progress has not been helped by the breadth of favourable reaction his work commands. If one could trust more poets more consistently perhaps the field would widen further.

Drama

In this the poet has much in common with the would-be dramatist. It is never a good year for new writing in the theatre. This must stem in large part from the lack of performance spaces open to untried plays and the allied overbearing difficulty of economic constraints. It is hard to avoid the impression that there is an increasing desperation about the whole theatrical situation as far as new work is concerned. The most notable exponents at work this year included Harold Pinter. *Party Time* was his first new play for some time and was a reminder of former glories when his acute ear for unstable dialogue was at its best. Christopher Hampton's *White Chameleon* had an autobiographical foundation but met with less favourable response.

David Hare's *Murmuring Judges* continued his anatomization of the institutional aspects of contemporary Britain. Hare is one of the most notable recorders of current values. Yet, as with other politically concerned writers at present, the difficulties of avoiding stereotype are often revealed to be considerable.

More consistently favourable attention was paid to Alan Bennett's *The Madness of George III*. Bennett's is one of the strongest theatrical voices of the current era. It resides largely in his talent for empathy, for animating a distant individual. Another striking phenomenon at work here is that there is often a sense that the audience enjoys the play as a re-enactment of another aspect of the same composite character, one which stars in all his dramas. Whether this unifying appeal is autobiographical in foundation or not it appeals to the relish for similarity rather than difference.

Something new and interesting usually comes from Bennett, often from Hare; and there is always a new Ayckbourn. This year a pair of plays, *The Revenger's Comedies*, continued his progress into more startling and ambitious areas, supported by an absolute craftsmanship. Another interesting premiere was that of a new play by Arthur Miller. *The Ride Down Mount Morgan* took bigamy as its subject. A new Miller play will always be notable but this did not seem one of his most impressive pieces. His decision to give the play its first performance in London was due to his dissatisfaction with the opportunities for serious theatre in America. This restrictive situation only adds to the theatre's problems here as few, if any, strong dramas cross the Atlantic.

The strongest push of theatrical concern at present is that towards an interest in spectacle in the broadest sense. This can manifest itself in an emphasis upon staging, upon the use of space, movement, music: the totality of the dramatic experience. This naturally promotes an interest in non-western theatrical traditions. It is reflected by such phenomena as the London International Festival of Theatre, a most vigorous happening. Such a preoccupation is rejuvenating but it also threatens to make the vulnerability of text-based drama all the greater. Given the testing situation for new plays in Britain – one which is exacerbated by the temptations for the dramatist of other media (Stephen Poliakoff's latest film, *Close My Eyes*, appeared this year) – the literary community must look to its laurels and nurture the new writing which does raise its voice.

Biography

Biography thrives. This year Michael Holroyd completed his three-volume (not including a fourth for references) work on Shaw which seemed itself a monument to monumentality. Much praised also was John Richardson's book on *Picasso*; this was the first of four projected volumes. Can production on this scale be continued? Is the time right for the spare, incisive memoir?

Literary figures always feature strongly in the lists of notable biographical works. This year saw memorable incarnations of, amongst others, *Samuel Butler* (by Peter Raby), *Hopkins* (by Robert Bernard Martin), *G H Lewes* (by Rosemary Ashton), *Goethe* (Volume 1 by Nicholas Boyle) and *Patrick White* (by David Marr). Kenneth Pople's book on Stanley Spencer was a work which reflects the current revaluation which the artist has attracted in good measure. Literary biographies often seem to appear for no apparent reason; artists are less frequent subjects and thus tend to aspire to current fashion. It was a relatively thin year for works in the political sphere, save the inevitable instant John Majors. The most striking work was Alan Bullock's *Hitler and Stalin: Parallel Lives*.

There may seem to be a dwindling field of subjects for biographical treatment but two essential truths remain. Firstly, a biography can never entirely contain its subject. Unlike novels, biographies can always be rewritten – by someone else, indeed. The most prescient of writers was newly described by Michael Shelden. This latest Orwell was a rather more mild mannered figure than the testy character of Bernard Crick's earlier portrait. Some figures seem tailor-made for biography; another (and impressive) book on D H Lawrence appeared this year (Volume 1 by John Worthen). A related phenomenon is the simultaneous appearance of two or more versions of the same life. Unlikely duos this year included two Bulgakovs and two H M Stanleys. At present there appears to be a biography of Trollope for each year.

Secondly, the appeal of biography is in part that of providing what the novel often does not: a solid character, a clear narrative line. If one's taste is gratified by such things then the considerable comfort of knowing the ending seals the argument. The reader of most biography need not fear digression, or a change of narrator. He may relax into the safety of chronology. (Peter Ackroyd's *Dickens* was a rare exception to this in 1990.) The title of this year's *The Death and Life of Sylvia Plath* by Ronald Hayman did announce another exceptional gambit rather boldly. Plath like Lawrence seems destined always to be ripe for biography.

In the world of autobiography Laurie Lee's *A Moment of War* continued his celebrated sequence and fulfilled many expectations. Kingsley Amis provided some notable gossip in his *Memoirs* and contributed to a partial portrait of our literary times. John Osborne's second volume of autobiography was more substantial. *Almost a Gentleman* showed that he provoked still. The same gestural stance was evident. More compassionate was Philip Roth's *Patrimony*. This book on the death of the novelist's father had a raw materiality which evoked the dignity and the pain of everyday detail.

Literary Studies and Salman Rushdie

Criticism has reached a state of compromise in which it often seems excessively comfortable. Now knighted, Frank Kermode is one of the most celebrated and impressive of current practitioners. Kermode's writing reflects the established position enjoyed by theoretically based work. Once a source of much objection, theory now resides quite happily in the circles of accepted doctrine and practice. Kermode published an excellent volume of essays this year, *The Uses of Error*. Similarly Terry Eagleton, another formidably intelligent critic, writes with a great sense of sweep and surety in his new volume, *Ideology*. As holder of an Oxford professorship he is a deservedly established figure. An equally impressive portrait of the old/new way of seeing was Frederic Jameson's *Postmodernism*. In either case there is little to unsettle in these volumes.

Another interesting version of merger is illustrated by two small American books which appeared this year; Nicholson Baker's *U and I* and Simon Schama's *Dead Certainties*. In both cases fictional freedoms were applied to other modes of writing, in the former to criticism and biography and in the latter to history and family memoir. These were quiet challenges to established practices but perhaps this is the way of the moment: development by attrition; the arrival of the insidiously new.

The essay is far from being a current form. John Gross's *Oxford Book of Essays* ably illustrated the paucity of modern expansive reflection. Yet Salman Rushdie's case remains *the* current literary issue. He has now been in hiding for over 1,000 days and his volume of essays, *Imaginary Homelands* was inevitably interesting.

It included some of his most eloquent defences of *The Satanic Verses* (such as 'In Good Faith' discussed here last year) and showed above all the deep-rooted political sensibility behind all his fantastic fictions. From early essays (such as the striking invective of 'Outside the Whale') to the present, Rushdie has voiced his perception of the inevitable political complicity of the artist. In large part this may be the crime for which he is now being punished.

Graham Greene and Angus Wilson

Graham Greene died in April 1991. Angus Wilson died in May 1991. Two major novelists, who both present powerful, complicated relationships with their times, they are also rather contrasting cases.

Greene's books have always been popular. His finest work is powered by a strong narrative drive and an unerring understanding of novelistic space; in essence a true appreciation of what the market will bear. His work is made attractive by its consistent delight and dread in settings and the most manageable versions of philosophy he offered to his readers. He could tell a very good tale whilst suggesting that there was actually more to it than that. A world figure, his best work – *Brighton Rock, The Power and the Glory, The Heart of the Matter* – was always economic and traditional. Yet he regarded himself as an outsider in a sense, despite great success. His outspoken political views created for him an offset position which could be used to be artistically central.

Angus Wilson's later years seem to have been overshadowed by his sense of being undervalued. He was always an accomplished writer, of early stories and social comedies: *The Wrong Set, Anglo-Saxon Attitudes* and of later darker works, *The Old Men at the Zoo*. It is to be hoped that the very formidable imaginative talent at play in these fictions will be revalued now that his oeuvre can be begun to be seen as a whole. Wilson's fiction moved with the times but was in a sense left behind, Greene was a steadfastly traditional writer whom the times chose to take with them. Both were very fine novelists. Neither has an obvious successor at present. As we achieve a certain distance from their writing it is certain that their strength will become all the clearer. Greene and Wilson wrote ambitious works in which the ambitions were realized. This is what is rare in 1991.

Chronology
8 Jan: Sorley McLean, the Gaelic poet, wins the Queen's 1990 Gold Medal for poetry.
22 Jan: Nicholas Mosley wins the Whitbread Book of the Year award for his novel *Hopeful Monsters*.
13 Feb: Report by the British Market Research Bureau argues that books are promoted in too upmarket a manner, aimed almost exclusively at middle-class readers.
14 Mar: Death of Margery Sharp.
16 Mar: Ray Monk's *Ludwig Wittgenstein: The Duty of Genius*, Cape, wins the John Llewellyn Rhys Prize.
3 Apr: Graham Greene dies.

17 Apr: Death of the playwright and scriptwriter Michael Pertwee.

29 May: Claire Tomalin wins the 1990 NCR Book Award for non-fiction for *The Invisible Woman*.

31 May: Death of the novelist Sir Angus Wilson.

15 July: Death of the poet Terence Hards.

27 Sept: Death of the poet Roy Fuller.

22 Oct: Ben Okri wins the Booker Prize for his *The Famished Road*.

27 Oct: Deaths of the poet George Barker and the novelist Catherine Heath.

5 Nov: Death of the Welsh dramatist Gwenlyn Parry.

15 Nov: Death of the novelist Elizabeth Ayrton.

18 Nov: Michael Frayn wins the *Sunday Express* Book of the Year award for his novel, *A Landing on the Sun*.

26 Nov: William Boyd wins the McVitie prize as Scottish writer of the year for his *Brazzaville Beach*.

The Political Economy of the Arts

ROBERT HEWISON

The political and economic uncertainties caused by the Gulf war contributed to the mood varying between depression and grim endurance felt in most sectors of the arts economy during 1991. Following a long standing tradition, the Imperial War Museum commissioned the painter and photographer John Keane to act as official war artist in the Gulf, although the results of his controversial work were not exhibited until March 1992. An early casualty of the conflict was a major exhibition at the Victoria and Albert Museum, 'The Art of Death', which the museum's trustees decided in January to postpone on the grounds that the subject was 'inappropriate at present'. A more long term and significant casualty was Britain's largest theatrical and sporting ticket agency, Keith Prowse, which collapsed in September, owing more than £9 million.

The receivers for Keith Prowse attributed the collapse to 'the downturn in the travel, tourism and hospitality industry as a result of the Gulf war', but the general economic recession that had begun to make itself felt in the autumn of 1990 was undoubtedly the underlying factor affecting cultural activity. In September the chairman of English Heritage, Lord Montagu of Beaulieu warned that the recession was as big a threat to historic houses as the redevelopment boom of the 1980s. Lord Montagu was obliged to stay on an extra six months as chairman of English Heritage, as a result of the difficulty of finding a successor. He was succeeded in April 1992 by Jocelyn Stevens, former rector of the Royal College of Art. In October English Heritage announced details of just over £2 million in grants to 35 cathedrals to help with repairs, the first in a new programme giving government assistance to cathedrals for the first time. It was a measure of the general economic climate that in June St Paul's introduced a compulsory charge to visitors.

In general, major art exhibitions – notably the Constable exhibition at the Tate Gallery – did not attract the anticipated crowds. Audiences in the West End fell by 14 per cent between mid-February and mid-March, recovering slowly to an expected equivalent of the 1989 level, down on 1990's record 5.3 million. In August the Edinburgh Festival found itself with a loss of £250,000 as a result of poor attendances. Britain's art trade suffered from a 70 per cent fall in the number of works sold. The drop in inflation and reduction in interest rates eased pressure on overdrafts and deficits, but theatres and concert promoters were not helped by the rise in VAT to 17.5 per cent at the beginning of April.

The Subsidized Arts

The unexpectedly generous increase in the grant-in-aid to the Arts Council for 1991–92 announced in the autumn of 1990, which permitted an average increase of 8 per cent in the core grants of most of the Arts Council's clients, enabled most recipients to hold the line against inflationary and recessionary pressures. The specially devised 'enhancement' grants, totalling £7.5 million, began to be distributed to 45 specially selected clients, many of whom had considerable deficits. The largest tranche, of £1.35 million, went to the Royal Shakespeare Company, which in March was able to resume performances at its London base in the Barbican. The company's previously perilous position was further improved by an extension of Royal Insurance's sponsorship for another three years and a £1.35 million increase over three years in subsidy from the City of London, which also committed an additional £400,000 to the resident orchestra at the Barbican, the London Symphony Orchestra. On 1 March Adrian Noble formally took up his post as artistic director of the RSC. His own productions during the year were well-received, but his choice of freelance directors to replace the former system of RSC associate directors was less sure.

One company notable for its absence from the 'enhancement' list was Welsh National Opera, which threatened that it would have to close with the loss of 250 jobs if more money were not found for its work. At the end of January the Arts Council awarded WNO an additional £300,000, while in a separate move the Welsh Office contributed a further £840,000 to clear the company's deficit. This direct intervention by government was commented on as an abrogation of the 'arms-length' principle. WNO's general director, Brian McMaster later left the company to succeed Frank Dunlop as director of the Edinburgh Festival, Dunlop having decided that the 1991 Festival was to be his last, following a dispute with Edinburgh District Council. McMaster was succeeded at WNO by the American agent and impresario Matthew Epstein. Scottish Opera, facing a deficit of £675,000 saw the enforced departure of Richard Mantle, who was replaced as managing director by Richard Jarman.

Musical chairs were something of a theme throughout the year. In April the triumvirate running the English National Opera, music director Mark Elder, productions director David Pountney and general director Peter Jonas all announced that they would be leaving the company, though in all three cases this was for reasons of career, rather than the difficulties facing ENO, which was forced to cancel a second planned production and cut its performance budgets in the light of a cumulative deficit of £1.3 million. The BBC television executive Dennis Marks was appointed to replace Peter Jonas as general director in 1993, when Jonas moves to the Bayerische Staatsoper in Munich. Sian Edwards, the first woman to conduct at Covent Garden, was appointed music director of the ENO from 1993.

The Royal Opera House, Covent Garden, had another difficult year. In September the government formally gave its permission for the long-delayed redevelopment scheme, due to start in 1996, but significantly stressed its unwillingness to contribute to the anticipated £200 million cost. In April, as a result of the sale of property and the loss of some 50 jobs, the general administrator Jeremy Isaacs was able to announce that the long term deficit had been reduced to £1.7 million, but that ticket prices would have to rise by 11 per cent, with the top seat costing £113. In June Covent Garden's opera director Paul Findlay announced that he would not be renewing his contract in 1993 – Nicholas Payne of Opera North was appointed to succeed him – and in August Lord Sainsbury, a critic of the Arts Council's policy towards the Opera House, stepped down as chairman in favour of Angus Stirling, who continued to serve also as secretary-general to the National Trust.

At the end of October the Opera House's finances were once more placed in jeopardy when performances were suspended for two weeks on the grounds that the orchestra, which had rejected an offered pay increase of 5.5 per cent, was not prepared to work normally. The dispute itself was settled relatively inexpensively, but the lockout meant the loss of some £600,000 in revenue. Emblematically, the delayed production of Meyerbeer's *Les Huguenots* was ill received, with booing in parts of the house. In an attempt to exploit the fashion for 'arena opera' launched by the pop promoter Harvey Goldsmith with productions of *Carmen, Tosca* and *Aida* (plus a concert in Hyde Park by Luciano Pavarotti), Covent Garden's expanded production of *Turandot* was given ten performances at Wembley Arena at the end of the year.

In January, the Liverpool Playhouse, with debts of £800,000, went into administrative receivership, but was able to stay open as a result of a partnership with the commercial producer Bill Kenwright, and fresh funds from local authorities and the Liverpool pools firm, Littlewoods. Nonetheless there were 14 redundancies and a shift towards 'safer' programming. In March Michael Rudman was forced to resign as director of the Chichester Festival Theatre as a result of the previous year's deficit and dissatisfaction with his programme plans. In September, Mark Brickman, director of the Sheffield Crucible Theatre (run in tandem with the neighbouring Lyceum, reopened at the beginning of the year for the World Student Games) resigned on the grounds that he was being required to introduce more 'popular' programming. At the Royal Court in London Max Stafford-Clark, artistic director since 1979, fought a long battle to have his contract renewed. In November agreement was reached with the board of the English Stage Company that he should continue, but working in tandem with Stephen Daldry, artistic director of the Gate Theatre, who would eventually succeed him.

In January Extemporary Dance Theatre announced its closure after the loss of its Arts Council funding. Two small unconventional companies, Gay Sweatshop – whose patron the actor Ian McKellen was knighted in the New Year Honours list – and Second Stride narrowly avoided extinction when the Arts Council was persuaded not to cut off their funding altogether. The black theatre company Temba lost its status as a regular revenue client, but another black company, Talawa was able to announce that it was to become a building-based company, having reached an agreement with the London Institute to refurbish the Jeanetta Cochrane Theatre.

In April the Oxford Playhouse reopened under a new funding arrangement between Oxford University, the Arts Council and local authorities, while Oxford's Old Fire Station theatre opened with the help of funds from the highly successful producer of musicals, Cameron Mackintosh. In April the Arts Council announced the creation of a 'new collaborations' fund of £200,000 to encourage experimental and interdisciplinary projects. Second Stride, having been refused funding by the dance panel, was able to obtain support from this new source.

Local Authority Funding

While most existing Arts Council clients were able to survive – though at the cost of reduced budgets and less adventurous activity – the smaller fry of local theatre companies, youth theatres, theatre-in-education and children's theatre suffered slow attrition as a result of central government pressure on discretionary local authority spending. The Audit Commission published two separate critical reports on local authority arts and museums policies. In a speech to the annual meeting of the Museums Association in July the arts minister Tim Renton called for the release of local museums from bureaucratic controls, but the Association, many of whose members worked in local authority museums, angrily rejected the minister's suggestion that local galleries and museums were adequately funded. In October a report by the Policy Studies Institute on amateur arts activities suggested that these too were suffering as a result of cutbacks by local authorities.

The PSI report calculated that local authorities were spending a rough total of £300 million on the arts (including £3.5 million on amateur activities). The pattern of expenditure was extremely uneven. With an annual budget of £27 million, Birmingham took the lead from Glasgow in terms of cultural investment, with the opening of a new concert hall, commissions for sculptures and the refurbishment of Birmingham Repertory Theatre. On the other hand Derbyshire County Council cut its £450,000 arts budget completely, closed 11 libraries and was expelled from membership of the Museums Association after it had sent 19 works of art from Buxton Museum for sale at auction to contribute to general funds. (At the end of the year it was learned that the government had drafted a bill that would allow all national museums to sell off works.) In Bristol Paul Unwin and his associate director Timothy West, who had fought a long campaign to keep the Bristol Old Vic going in the face of local authority cuts, resigned in March when it became clear that funding would continue to be insufficient.

London was especially hard hit by the effect of local authority spending cuts on the London Borough Grants Committee. This committee, involving all 33 London boroughs, was established in 1985 to look after cross-borough funding of local voluntary agencies following the abolition of the Greater London Council. A hundred arts organizations and more than 600 voluntary bodies received a proportion of their funding from the LBGC, but political differences between the

boroughs meant that it was unable to set a budget until 8 May, after the financial
year had begun. The compromise figure of £28.625 million was a cut of 17 per cent
in real terms, and was intended to fall disproportionately on arts organizations,
including the Hampstead Theatre, Greenwich Theatre, Bush Theatre, the Almeida,
the King's Head Theatre Club, the Chisenhale Dance Studio, the Institute of
Contemporary Arts, the Whitechapel Art Gallery, the London Film Festival, Dance
Umbrella and the London International Festival of Theatre. While not all of these
lost their funding immediately, the Almeida Theatre, which under new
management had abandoned its festival of new music and acquired a reputation for
fashionable productions of the classics, faced imminent closure as a result of the
loss of £54,000, 20 per cent of its grant. A contribution of £100,000 from the
composer Andrew Lloyd Webber to its funding appeal helped keep the theatre
open.

In spite of a successful appeal the Young Vic continued to be menaced by
closure. Funding for arts organizations in London was further limited by the Arts
Council's decision to award only a 2.5 per cent increase to Greater London Arts,
the regional arts association replaced by the London Arts Board during the year.
The Museum of London introduced admission charges, and laid off large numbers
of archaeologists following the withdrawal of funds from English Heritage and the
downturn in the construction industry, where developers had paid for the
investigation of development sites.

A Search for New Sources of Funding

With recession and government policy indicating that box office revenue and
conventional subsidy would see, at best, zero growth, the search for alternative
sources of funding the arts became more urgent. In November, the Association for
Business Sponsorship of the Arts announced that to the end of the financial year
1990–91 business sponsorship of the arts had risen to an estimated £57 million
(sports sponsorship stood at about £200 million). This showed an increasing
dependency on a source of funds that could well decline as businesses trimmed
their budgets to cope with the recession.

The effects of the recession was given as one reason for the lack of progress in
fund raising by the Arts Foundation, a new organization launched in May under
the chairmanship of the chairman of the Arts Council, Lord Palumbo. The
foundation was created after a bequest in 1989 of £1.1 million to the Arts Council
from the estate of a Swiss banker who had been a refugee in Britain during the war.
The Council however decided that a separate organization should be established
in order to encourage private patronage of the arts. A target of £20 million was set,
and the former director of the Design Museum, Stephen Bayley, was appointed
part-time director. The foundation announced its commitment to encouraging
innovation, but during 1991 the policies of the Arts Foundation remained unclear.

Ironically, a more secure form of fresh funding proved to be gambling. While
the Arts Council joined with the Sports Council to promote the idea of a national

lottery, UK Lotteries Ltd were the first in the field in February with an 'instant' lottery ticket scheme in London, the south east and north west, which raised £3.6 million in its first six months of operation for a wide range of charitable organizations, including some 20 arts organizations.

As the budget approached, speculation mounted that a national lottery would be in place by 1993, when European Community lotteries would be free to operate in Britain. The minister for the arts lent support, but hopes were dashed when the Chancellor announced that in return for a 2.5 per cent cut in betting levy, the private companies promoting football pools would form a foundation for sport and the arts which would distribute £20 million a year to arts applicants and £40 million to sports. Though a welcome addition, this sum was considerably less than the £600 million a year that advocates of a national lottery argued their scheme could produce.

While the future for private patronage seemed as uncertain as ever, a number of schemes involving private patrons reached their spectacular fruition. The Victoria and Albert Museum opened its new Chinese gallery, with the help of £1.25 million from T T Tsui; the Royal Academy opened its new Sackler Gallery; the Heinz family contributed £2 million to the National Portrait Gallery, and the National Gallery opened its new wing, designed by the American architect Robert Venturi, and paid for with £35.5 million from the Sainsbury family. While the exterior was considered almost too discreet, the interior was praised as a fine, temple-like setting for the gallery's early and Renaissance holdings. Earlier in the year the National Gallery's insistence on a policy of free entry helped it to secure the long term loan of Hanz Bergruuen's collection of impressionist paintings.

In Edinburgh, where the Fruitmarket Gallery closed and a campaign was mounted for the creation of a National Gallery of Scotland on a single site, the Museum of Scotland announced the result of an architectural competition to build a new wing. The successful design, by Alan Forsyth and Gordon Benson, did not meet the approval of the Prince of Wales, who resigned from the museum's committee of patrons when the result was announced. Later in the year the Prince himself ran into criticism when he launched his modified and reduced plans for a model development outside Dorchester, master-planned by Leon Krier.

The director of the National Museums of Scotland, Dr Robert Anderson, was appointed to succeed Sir David Wilson as director of the British Museum. The new British Library building in St Pancras meanwhile continued to experience difficulties. The retiring chief executive, Kenneth Cooper, predicted that the new library would be 'second rate' because of government financial restrictions, while the move of books to the new building was delayed when the new sliding shelving was found not to work properly. In October the government abandoned its plans to spend £1 million on commissions for works of art to embellish the new building, saying the money, which was already allocated, should be transferred to a contingency fund instead.

The National Arts Strategy

In September the Arts Council began to release the first of 45 discussion documents on almost all aspects of arts and media policy, commissioned from administrators, practitioners, journalists and academics. This was in response to a request in March 1990 from the then minister for the arts, Richard Luce, that a new national strategy for the arts and media be devised to govern arts policy for the decade. Organized by the Arts Council (with similar exercises conducted by the Scottish and Welsh Arts Councils) the scheme also involved the British Film Institute, the Crafts Council and the Regional Arts Boards, all of whom contributed to discussion documents and organized seminars and debates as part of a consultation process which ended in December. A further consultation was scheduled to take place in spring 1992, when a draft based on the discussions of 1991 would be published, prior to the completion of a final document during the summer. The exercise, though subject to delays, did set off a national debate about arts policy, prompting several meetings and conferences outwith the officially organized discussions.

The parallel (some would say preemptive) structural changes to arts administration decided in advance of the emergence of a national arts strategy continued. On 1 October the ten new Regional Arts Boards, replacing the previous 12 English Regional Arts Associations, officially came into being. In May a further 24 Arts Council clients were told that they would be devolved to their respective RABs in 1992, but the process both of restructuring and devolution proved to be a longer process than anticipated. The minister for the arts was concerned that the end result should be a saving in administrative costs – savings that were not at first forthcoming – and set the Arts Council a target of £1 million for savings in administration throughout the system by 1993–94.

In March the Council launched Arts 2000, a 'national celebration of the arts', dedicating the succeeding years up to the millennium to the promotion of a particular art form, and inviting cities, groups of towns or regions to nominate themselves for particular association with each of the years and art forms in question. The programme began in 1992 when the City of Birmingham, whose symphony orchestra under Simon Rattle had already launched its own 'towards the millennium' decade by decade survey of 20th century culture, became City of Music.

Arts 2000 should not be confused with Lord Palumbo's millennium project for the refurbishment of Britain's stock of cultural buildings, which he proposed in 1990, but which still had not received any formal government support by the end of 1991. Lord Palumbo – whose interests were reflected at the Arts Council by the creation of an architecture unit – continued to produce new ideas for future celebrations, calling for artistic events to mark the opening of the Channel Tunnel in 1993, a world fair in the year 2000 and a third festival of Britain in 2001.

The Autumn Settlement

The minister for the arts repeated his warnings against excessive administration costs in November, when he announced an unexpected increase of nearly 14 per cent in the Arts Council's grant in aid for 1992–93, following the Chancellor of the Exchequer's announcement of the government's spending plans for 1992. This increase of £27 million was the largest in the Council's history, bringing it to £221.2 million for the following year. The Arts Council was quickly able to announce grants above the rate of inflation for most of its revenue clients, with substantial increases going to touring and the new Regional Art Boards, where increases averaged more than 15 per cent, with particular attention being paid to the eastern, southern and south east Arts Boards. The Young Vic and the London International Festival of Theatre received significant increases, but the Royal Opera House (including the Royal Ballet and Birmingham Royal Ballet) although receiving just over £1 million, found its increase was only 6.5 per cent. The 45 'enhancement' clients were not especially favoured, having had substantial increases in 1991. A significant exception in the round of increases was the Royal Philharmonic Orchestra, which protested at receiving a 13 per cent cut in its grant.

Museums, galleries and the heritage industry did less well out of the proposed total central government cultural spending package of £609.498 million. Funding for national museum running costs rose by 5.5 per cent, and there were some selective grants for refurbishment and special projects, but purchase grants for national museums and galleries remained frozen at their level for 1984–85. During the year both the Museums and Galleries Commission and the reviewing committee on the export of works of art expressed alarm at the inability of British museums and galleries to compete with foreign buyers for important items such as Canova's *Three Graces* or the Badminton cabinet, because museum purchase grants were so low. The minister asked the reviewing committee to submit a report on the operation of the Waverley system governing the export of works of art, which in the committee's opinion was in danger of breaking down.

When asked why the government had decided to increase its funding for the arts, especially the performing arts, the minister pointed to the economic difficulties felt as a result of the recession. More cynical members of the press pointed to the imminence of a general election. In December the government announced that it would be holding a European arts festival in 1992, to coincide with Britain's presidency of the European Community from July to December. The festival was to have a budget of £6 million and be organized by John Drummond, the outgoing controller of BBC Radio Three.

In September the Labour Party published a comprehensive policy document, *Arts and Media: Our Cultural Future*, which proposed a strengthened Ministry of Arts with responsibility for all the cultural industries and an enhanced role for local authorities in arts policy making. The most radical proposal in the document was that local authority arts funding should become a statutory requirement, qualifying for central government rate support grant, but specifying no minimum expenditure.

The document was significantly light on figures, and fell short of promising a place in the Cabinet for an arts minister, or guaranteeing that control of broadcasting would be taken over from the Home Office.

The Japan Festival

While the bicentennial of the death of Mozart provided the occasion for many discussions and performances, the Japanese festival, launched on 4 June and scheduled to run into 1992, quickly justified its claim to be the largest of its kind ever staged in Britain. Costing some £20 million, with over 350 events in more than 200 venues throughout the United Kingdom, the festival embraced both high and popular Japanese traditional culture, from Hokusai at the British Museum and Grand Kabuki at the National Theatre to sumo wrestling at the Albert Hall, but also sought to represent contemporary cultural developments, most notably the synthesis of spiritual values, high technology and sheer economic energy reflected in the _Visions of Japan_ exhibition at the Victoria and Albert Museum. Promoted by a group of British businessmen with interests in stimulating Anglo-Japanese trade and Japanese inward investment in the UK, the festival attracted the sponsorship of many Japanese firms operating in Britain. Whatever the aesthetic and educational impact of the Japan Festival, the political message required little decoding: Britain was to experience the cultural salesmanship and economic penetration that it had once so confidently exported.

Chronology
8 Jan: Liverpool Playhouse placed in the hands of administrators.

Welsh National Opera meeting with Lord Palumbo, Chairman of the Arts Council, fails to resolve it funding crisis.

Cinema audiences in 1990 were at a ten year high of 91 million according to Rank Screen Advertising.

23 Jan: Frank Dunlop resigns as director of the Edinburgh Festival following disagreements with the city council.

24 Jan: _Local Authorities: Entertainment and the Arts_, Audit Commission, argues that councils should monitor their arts subsidies more closely since too much of their subsidies goes to venues offering an unfocused mixture of arts and popular entertainments.

29 Jan: Announcement of the Sainsburys awards for arts education, worth £250,000.

31 Jan: Welsh Office and Arts Council save Welsh National Opera with a £1.5 million cash injection.

7 Feb: National Gallery unveils its rehung and refurbished west wing.

14 Feb: _The Road to Wigan Pier? Managing Local Authority Museums and Art Galleries_, HMSO, criticizes conservation and poor quality marketing and displays in the local services.

4 Mar: Tara Arts, Britain's leading Asian theatre company is to close its London base after Wandsworth council axed its £55,000 grant.

15 Mar: Report by British Invisibles shows that arts and culture won £6 billion overseas earnings in 1990, 50 per cent up on 1984-5.

19 Mar: A new trust to benefit arts and sport is to be set up by reductions in pools betting duty and through the contributions of the pools promoters.

26 Mar: Kenneth Cooper, chief executive of the British Library, attacks government underfunding.

13 Apr: Work begins on converting a derelict gasworks in St Ives, Cornwall into the Tate Gallery's second regional branch.

15 Apr: National Art Collection Fund launches scheme to enable regional collections to buy twentieth century art.

17 Apr: *Local Authorities and Museums,* Museums and Galleries Commission, says local authority museums are usually underfunded and low priority.

10 May: UK Film Commission to be set up to entice more film-makers to Britain. It will be headed by Sydney Samuelson.

16 May: Robert Anderson appointed to succeed Sir David Wilson as director of the British Museum.

17 May: Government spurns appeals to assist fundraising to prevent the Badminton cabinet, one of the finest pieces of eighteenth century furniture in Britain, being exported.
Brian McMaster appointed to succeed Frank Dunlop as director of the Edinburgh Festival.

29 May: New arts funding and promotion body, the Arts Foundation, is launched with Stephen Bayley as director.

12 June: Public Accounts Committee criticizes the wastage of money and inadequate storage and other facilities in a report on the progress of the new British Library.

26 June: Museums Association calls for a long-term investment and planning strategy towards museums and art galleries.

8 July: National Gallery announces that Nicholas Baring will replace Lord Rothschild as its chairman in 1992.

9 July: The new Sainsbury wing of the National Gallery opened.

23 July: Tim Renton, the Minister for the Arts, says more local authority museums should consider charging in a speech to the Museums Association.

24 July: The Other Place, the Royal Shakespeare Company's new £1.8 million theatre in Stratford-upon-Avon, opens.

13 Aug: Prince Charles resigns as president of the patrons of the National Museum of Scotland over the procedure adopted in selecting the design for the new museum.

11 Sept: Labour pledges an end to admission charges at national museums, as part of its manifesto for the arts.

18 Sept: Foundation for Sport and the Arts announces its first grants, worth £6 million in total.

24 Sept: Dennis Marks is to be the new general director of the English National Opera.

27 Sept: Reviewing committee on the export of art launches a stinging attack on the government's record on curbing art exports in its annual report.

24 Oct: *Amateur Arts in the UK,* PSI, finds that whilst arts and crafts groups have increased considerably over the last 25 years subsidies to them are currently being cut. The report calls for greater spending on the amateur arts.

7 Nov: Arts Council grant to rise by nearly 14 per cent.

3 Dec: Reviewing committee on the export of works of art suggests a register of the most important items (which could not be exported) be compiled.

9 Dec: Government announces a European arts festival to be held from 1 July to 31 December 1992.

Science

MICHAEL KENWARD

The political event of 1991, the collapse of Communism and the Soviet Union, left its mark in scientific circles. During the year, Britain's leading scientific body, the Royal Society, forged new links with individual republics. Lithuania started the trend in February 1990. In 1991 the academies of science in Georgia, Estonia and Ukraine also signed joint memoranda of understanding with the Royal Society. One positive outcome of these agreements will be an influx of scientists to Britain from the republics. This will do little to solve the plight of science in what remains of the Soviet Union, at one time a leading scientific nation. Scientists in the remains of the USSR faced two key pressures. The state could no longer afford to pay their salaries, nor could it justify, or find the money for, a massive defence research programme. And this is one area where, even if it were a roaring success, the growth of a market economy would have little impact.

The British government, that most ardent of privatizers, has found it difficult to sell all of its scientists into the private sector. Those researchers whose employer did make the transition to privatization – British Telecom and the Central Electricity Generating Board, to pick the most obvious – saw their numbers, and budgets, decline as the once state-owned organizations took a more cost conscious view of R&D and abandoned their roles as supporters of research for its own sake.

Soviet scientists faced far grimmer fortunes. Never well paid, they encountered two parallel pressures. Economic chaos hit them as hard as anyone else in the old union. The declining fortunes of the military establishment, a large employer of scientific manpower in the USSR, produced fears that redundant weapons scientists would find themselves unemployed and unemployable and would rush to countries that wanted to develop nuclear weapons. Social upheavals exerted other pressures on Soviet science. The new-found freedom of people to think for themselves, and to do so openly without fear of repression, had an unexpected side effects, according to Sergei Kapitza. A leading light in Soviet science and a member of the Soviet Academy of Sciences, Kapitza complained of a growing anti-science trend among the general public, with what he regarded as an unhealthy rise in interest in religious cults and 'fringe sciences' such as parapsychology. To a certain extent, the move against science was partly in response to such disasters as the Chernobyl reactor accident. Whatever the causes, the result was that scientists in the Soviet

Union suddenly found themselves in the same position as many scientists in the West – facing a public with little faith or interest in science.

It is easy to see the state of Soviet science as a recent phenomenon. In reality, science has suffered many of the depredations that led eventually to the collapse of the political system. In a review of the state of Soviet science Kapitza paints a tale of more than 20 years of neglect.[1] He highlights his own area of science, particle accelerators, and describes long-delayed projects: he could have used an even more powerful example, and one that gave science its largest splash in the British media during 1991.

Hot Fusion

In November, the fusion research project at Culham near Oxford finally achieved something that scientists in this area had been working towards for over 40 years. In the Joint European Torus (JET) machine a mixture of atoms of deuterium and tritium underwent nuclear fusion. Fusion is the physical process that powers the sun and the stars. Previously the only man-made fusion reactions of any note have been in thermonuclear weapons, hydrogen bombs. The attraction of fusion lies in its ubiquitous fuel. Deuterium and tritium are isotopes of hydrogen – chemically the same but with slightly heavier atoms. Deuterium is an ingredient of ordinary water. Tritium is radioactive and scarce in nature, but it can be made by promoting the right sort of nuclear reactions in lithium, a light metal that is relatively abundant.

The scientific challenge has been to create in the laboratory the physical conditions under which atoms of deuterium (D) and tritium (T) will merge, fusing to form a heavier atom, of helium, releasing energy in the process. One condition needed for fusion to happen is a temperature over 100 million degrees. This makes it impossible to hold fusion fuel in any physical container. At these temperatures, atoms disintegrate: their electrons and nuclei are separated, producing a state of matter known as a plasma. For 40 years scientists have been trying to construct a system of magnets to hold a plasma, making use of its magnetic properties. A major breakthrough in magnetic confinement, the science of devising stable magnetic bottles that do not leak plasma, came in the 1960s when the Soviet scientist Lev Artsimovich devised the tokamak configuration of magnetic fields. Even then there were doubts about the quality of Soviet science: the fusion world reserved its judgement on the claimed breakthrough until a team of researchers from Britain took a planeload of sophisticated equipment – in effect a gigantic thermometer built around a laser – to the USSR to make more refined temperature measurements. Artsimovich was right. Over the next two decades, research teams around the world built tokamaks, culminating in JET in Europe and the Tokamak Fusion Test Reactor at Princeton in the USA. JET produced its first plasma in 1983. Since then the project has moved inexorably towards the conditions needed for DT fusion. As well as a high temperature, the plasma has to be dense enough and long-lived enough for fusion reactions to take place before the whole system falls apart. Since 1983, fusion research has concentrated on experiments with plasmas of hydrogen and deuterium. There was never any rush to try it with DT. The very success of DT fusion would pose problems that the research team did not want to deal with early on.

DT fusion on any scale produces copious streams of neutrons, and when these hit the metal surrounding the plasma the result is to make the material radioactive. The associated radiation hazards will limit the time that researchers can spend working inside JET, thus reducing the opportunities to change the experiment and to try out new ideas. In the event, JET operated just two brief shots with a mixture of DT inside the machine. Even this was enough to keep scientists out of the machine itself for some months, while the radiation settled to a more acceptable level. During those months, the machine reverted to experiments with deuterium. While the JET's results made headline news, the media did not deliver the uncritical reports that characterized earlier episodes. There were a number of reasons for this healthy scepticism. To begin with, the 1950s had brought tales of inexhaustible and cheap energy, only to see them dashed as the neutrons turned out not to be the product of thermonuclear reactions.

Fusion may not have some of the undesirable attributes of nuclear fission – its output of radioactive waste is less of a problem for example – but it is still a high-tech approach to energy technology. And despite last year's scientific confirmation that fusion will work, a practical power station remains some way off. The research community accepts that it will be perhaps half a century before fusion can contribute to the world's energy scene. The case for thermonuclear fusion was not greatly helped by the cold fusion saga of 1989, when a pair of chemists claimed to have achieved, in an experiment little larger than a jam jar, something that had consumed billions of dollars in building machines you could drive around in.[2]

Carbon Chemistry

While fusion may have grabbed the biggest headlines in the popular media, inside scientific circles some genuine chemistry provided the most consistent talking point of 1991. In 1985 a group of chemists had put forward the idea that carbon atoms could come together in a new form. Diamond and graphite are familiar forms of carbon. They differ in that their atoms are joined to one another in different ways. With four 'hooks' that it can hang on to a neighbouring atom, each carbon atom can connect with its neighbours in a number of ways and can form sheets of atoms (graphite), or stacked crystals (diamond). The new form of carbon comes about when hexagons and pentagons of carbon atoms join up in an ordered way to form a closed empty sphere.

The 1985 suggestion was that the new type of carbon would consist of a 'cage' of 60 atoms. Because of the resemblance to the geodesic domes made famous by Buckminster Fuller, the new molecule was dubbed Buckminsterfullerene, buckyballs for short. Until 1990, buckyballs were little more than a chemical

442   *Contemporary Britain*

curiosity. Chemists had made the molecules, but only in minute quantities, far too little for any serious science.

Then a German group, made up of physicists rather than chemists, which had spent years working on what happens to carbon in space, came up with a way of making buckyballs in relatively large amounts. They vaporized carbon and tried various ways of turning it back into a solid. When this happened in helium, the result was a soot containing a few per cent C60. It was then relatively easy, although tedious, to extract fullerene. It subsequently turned out that C60 was but the first member of a whole new family, now known as the fullerenes. C70 came after C60, followed by a stream of other molecules whose shape departed from the pure sphere of C60 depending on how many carbon atoms they held – C70 is shaped somewhat like a rugby ball.

The leading American journal *Science* dubbed C60 its 'molecule of the year' for 1991 and estimated that the material cost something like $2,000 a gramme to produce. Throughout the year, research journals carried a stream of papers on the fullerenes and their physical and chemical properties. Interesting enough in their own right, fullerenes throw new light on the chemistry of carbon, the element that is the basis of all living organisms. Thoughts naturally turned to possible industrial applications of the fullerenes. It is far too soon to know if there will be a growth in fullerene technology, but in the USA at least corporate laboratories were quick to join their academic colleagues and to set up research programmes on C60.

Critical Reactions

A new area of scientific interest such as the fullerenes inevitably leads to demands for funds, as the research community flocks to the new frontier. The continuing plight of British science is such that it cannot respond adequately to such demands. The fullerenes were no exception, with only one team seriously active in the area, albeit it a team led by Harry Kroto, one of the scientists involved in the early work on C60 in 1985.

One of the year's more significant analytical reports on science on the United Kingdom came from the Advisory Council on Science and Technology. ACOST is perhaps the most high-powered advisory body on science, working as it does out of the Cabinet Office. Yet its critique of the state of British science was as strident in its way as those from more outspoken groups. That the council offered its interpretation in a public document was itself something of a victory for those who did not like the way that the government was running things. In 1987, ACOST delivered its thoughts to the world at large. Then Margaret Thatcher, who had always taken a close personal interest in the committee's deliberations, decided that the council should be free to offer confidential advice. Pressured by the House of Lords Select Committee on Science and Technology, Mrs Thatcher conceded that ACOST could deliver a 'state of the nation' review of science and technology when a new chairman took over.

Last year's report was Sir Robin Nicholson's review and plan of action for the next three years. The topics that ACOST highlights are interesting enough in their own right, but read behind the nimble linguistic footwork and you can detect well-aimed poisoned arrows. And the arrows fly in several directions. As ACOST says, how a country allocates its R&D budget is at least as important as the size of that budget. Historical considerations, says the council, may have exerted too strong an influence. And this is where reading between the lines becomes important. This is doubtless hidden support for the view held by many scientists that grandiose international projects gobble up far too much money. One big international project whose ability to soak up money arouses considerable discussion within the scientific community is the European Organization for Nuclear Research, CERN, the particle physics factory in Switzerland. CERN looks increasingly like the plaything of the old guard of megalomaniac scientists. With Japan holding out against pressure to help fund the plans of the USA to build its next big particle-smashing toy, the Superconducting Supercollider, perhaps physicists will start to use their brains to find out what is going on in the world.

Because it names no names, ACOST can doubtless claim that it had other historical accidents in mind when it called for 'thorough reviews of the extent to which the current distribution of funding has been determined by history and what changes might be desirable to reflect current national needs'. It might, for example, have been thinking back from a point made elsewhere in the report. Britain has an organization called the Medical Research Council. It might be more honest to change the name to Biology Research Council, such is its cursory attention to what happens in Britain's hospitals. Considering both the absence until early last year of anything approaching a coherent R&D strategy on the part of the NHS itself and the growing dependence of medical research on money raised by the medical charities, it is only common sense for ACOST to suggest that researchers should investigate treatments that reduce health costs. There could, however, be problems if the charities were to throw money at academics in search of cheaper medicine. Universities have, in recent years, done well in attracting money for research from industry, the government and charities. This has not brought the financial rewards that it might. In another unspoken sideswipe at government, ACOST says that universities have been less successful in recovering the full cost of research that they have carried out for third parties. The council doesn't say so, but some of the government's own departments are notoriously mean when it comes to paying for overheads. And unlike industry they don't have the excuse that they already pay for the universities through taxes.

My favourite passage of the report is its comments on the need to create the right climate for science and technology. I am as mystified as ACOST as to how the public has come to see science and technology as a part of the problem 'rather than as the key to a solution'. Yet again, this seemingly innocent query is built on a sideswipe at another typically British problem. Young people increasingly want jobs 'with high ethical values and a clear view of their long term purpose', says

ACOST. There are those who will be puzzled by the report's implicit pat on the back for Japanese companies, which express their missions 'in terms of profound ethical and social values which provide an orientation and sense of purpose to all involved, while most British companies express their goals merely in terms of profit'. And that piles the blame on to another part of society. So in one slim report ACOST has quietly put the boot into academics, the government and industry, among others.

Military Connections

No review of science and technology in 1991 can avoid at least a passing reference to the Gulf war. This demonstration of the obvious supremacy of Western military technology may do something to slow down the pace of change in military research. It cannot, however, halt the inevitable move away from military R&D as the Soviet threat diminishes. If nothing else, the West will have to rethink the allocation of its vast military R&D budgets.

Another significant report of 1991 came from the Parliamentary Office of Science and Technology. A child of the Parliamentary and Scientific Committee, POST has been quietly building a reputation for itself as a valuable source of impartial advice for Parliament. During the year, POST produced its own report on military R&D; it also commissioned a supporting study by the Science Policy Support Group.

Since the 1960s something like a quarter of the country's R&D spending has gone on defence. In 1988–89, the Ministry of Defence (MoD) employed 22,000 people as scientific and technical staff and accounted for around 45 per cent of the £4,500 million that the government invested in R&D. In the West, only the USA and France can match this devotion to military R&D. The first thing that becomes clear from the two reports, particularly that of the SPSG, is public uncertainty as to where the MoD's money goes or how effectively it is spent. To a certain extent, obscuring the facts on spending confuses the enemy. Less easy to justify is the fact that 'data on industry's own ("private venture") funding for defence are not available'. But this is one of those perennials and is no more than an extension of industry's general reluctance to tell the world about its R&D spending. Equally frustrating is 'the substantial discrepancy between the figures given by the MoD for R&D performed in industry and industry's own estimates'.

When accused of not playing fair by science, governments are quick to cite statistics to prove just how well Britain compares with other countries. If the claimed level of spending on military R&D crumbles into dust the closer you look at it, 'it would then be much harder for the government to maintain that British spending on R&D overall is well up to the standards of its main competitors', as the SPSG's report puts it. There has certainly been long-standing suspicion about the way in which the MoD categorizes R&D. If a significant portion of the claimed spending on development actually goes into 'repetitive flight testing and safety tests', then the country's R&D budget shrinks before your eyes.

The SPSG says that 'there is evidence that much that is counted as development work is not true development'. The report says that this could account for as much as half of the defence R&D budget. In other words, more than £1,000 million of Britain's £4,500 million public spending on R&D just might evaporate into thin air. Much as this provides a fine debating point, it isn't going to change patterns greatly. It does though underline the importance of looking closely at the pattern of defence R&D. Does research for military objectives lead the way and spin off ideas into civil technology? A number of changing factors suggest that even if this used to be the pattern it is no longer the case. As POST's own report points out, the military market is less important than it was. Ten years ago the world's semiconductor companies earned 8 per cent of their revenue from the military market: today that figure is 4 per cent.

Perhaps more significant is the different timetable that applies in the civil sector. Military projects tend to be long and drawn out; it can take many years to develop new equipment for the defence sector. If anything that delay in reaching the marketplace has grown as the hardware has become more sophisticated. This is in complete contrast to civilian technology where competitive advantage comes from being the first into the market. There is, however, a more fundamental obstacle in the way of transferring technology between the military and civil sides of industry. Other governments make positive attempts to squeeze everything they can out of their military R&D and to use it to improve the quality of technology throughout industry. In Britain it is almost as if the government wants to keep the two apart. 'The present and recent governments', says POST's report, 'do not see the MoD as having a role in supporting the general national technology base or in fostering technological work that is unrelated to defence requirements.' Once again, everyone's *bête noire*, the Treasury and its rules, come under suspicion. Financial accountability requires that each government department eschew any spending for activities that are outside its remit. This makes it difficult for the MoD to support work that may benefit the Department of Trade and Industry, for example. Of course, the MoD is not ignorant of industry's needs. It has tried various schemes to flush out science and technology that might find civil application, but these programmes have not been hugely successful.

It is important to look closely at this transfer of technology between the civil and military sectors. It could become even more important in the future as the defence game changes, for one possible outcome of the decline in weapons sales could actually be an increase in the need for R&D. As POST puts it: 'One option would be to maintain strong R&D teams and to fund technology demonstrator programmes. This would, in principle, allow the UK to move rapidly into procuring state-of-the-art weaponry (should circumstances so require) without incurring the expense of deploying field quantities of armaments, providing the original demonstrator phase has included the necessary production engineering preparation'. This policy begs all sorts of questions. How 'rapidly' could industry leap into action, for example? But it is certainly a strategy that Britain should consider as it contemplates its response to the changing military position on the planet.

A policy of preparedness has significant implications for the way in which we fund R&D. The government wants industry to do more of the R&D that goes into weapons systems. But industry cannot afford to do this if there will be no production run at the end of the development process. One option would be for the government to pay industry to do the R&D that would underpin new military systems. But industry in Britain has no track record of earning a living from doing R&D on contract. These are, then, interesting times for the research side of the defence business as well as for industry. Until recently, the number of unasked questions far exceeded the number that had yet to be answered. At least the debate is now getting under way.

Notes

1 *Scientific American*, June 1991, p.96.
2 Michael Kenward, 'Science', in P. Catterall (ed.), *Contemporary Britain: An Annual Review 1991*, Blackwell, 1991.

Chronology

1 Jan: Professor Arnold Wolfendale is appointed Astronomer Royal.

9 Jan: Royal Society launches an inquiry into the state of scientific research.

11 Jan: Education, Science and Arts Select Committee, *Science Policy and the European Dimension*, HMSO, criticizes Britain's opaque, difficult-to-monitor system of funding science research, calls for a 50 per cent increase in the civil science budget, better facilities to match Europe, and for a study of the extent and causes of the brain drain. It argues that research and development spending should be raised from 0.6 per cent to the 0.9 per cent of GDP of France and Germany, but rejects the idea of a cabinet-level Minister of Science.

14 Jan: The space-experiments element in the Juno programme to put a British cosmonaut in space with a Soviet mission is abandoned.

15 Jan: Researchers at Edinburgh University announce that they have succeeded in cramming all the technology for a video camera onto a single silicon chip.

18 Jan: Government introduces a bill to privatize its patent licensing organization, the British Technology Group.

22 Jan: Report by the Centre for Exploitation of Science and Technology argues that Britain is losing out to foreign competitors in the growing market for equipment and services to combat pollution.

23 Jan: More than 250 scientists launch a campaign against what they say are secret plans to stop nuclear physics research in Britain.

6 Feb: Science and Engineering Research Council cuts research funding by £28 million from its 1991–92 budget.

18 Feb: Researchers at St Mary's Hospital Medical School claim in an article in *Nature* to have found a link between Alzheimer's disease and a genetic mutation.
British Scientists Abroad, in an open letter to John Major, warn that the country risks 'severe economic and social damage' unless more money is devoted to science.

11 Mar: *Science Watch* argues that British science has declined in quality in the 1980s and is now behind Germany in terms of the number of citations gained.

14 Mar: Nuclear Structure Facility at Daresbury, Cheshire is to close because of lack of funds.

15 Mar: Researchers in Britain, the US and Japan claim to have isolated the gene which causes bowel cancer.

21 Mar: Survey in *British Medical Journal* associates childhood leukaemia with preconceptual exposure of fathers to wood dust, radiation and benzene. However another survey by Scottish Health Service and Royal Hospital for Sick Children, Edinburgh, finds no link with fathers' occupations.

25 Mar: Lords Select Committee on Science and Technology, *Science Budget 1991–92*, HMSO, criticizes cuts in science budgets and calls for a cabinet committee on science and technology, to be chaired by the Prime Minister.

30 Mar: Report in *The Lancet* says injections of magnesium have been used successfully to treat chronic fatigue syndrome.

8 Apr: Successful treatment of breast cancer by using implants of irradiated wires is reported in *European Journal of Cancer*.

25 Apr: Professor Raymond Levy announces in *The Lancet* that significant progress has been made in treating Alzheimer's disease using the drug tacrine.

29 Apr: Advisory Council on Science and Technology report calls for changes in science and technology courses to improve scientists' communication skills.

2 May: Details of the transcervical resection developed at the Royal Free Hospital, London as an alternative to hysterectomy are published in *The Lancet*.

8 May: Dr Peter Goodfellow of the Imperial Cancer Research Fund and Dr Robin Lovell-Badge of the National Institute for Medical Research announce in *Nature* their success in locating and identifying the gene which determines gender.

8 May: *Evaluation of the Alvey Programme for Advanced Information Technology*, HMSO, criticizes the failure to invest sufficient to take the R&D success of the programme through to production. Other criticisms were company obstructivenes and poor planning and management.

18–26 May: Helen Sharman becomes the first Briton in space on a Soviet space mission.

5 June: Report by the Science and Engineering Research Council's Industrial Strategy Panel says funds for equipment are inadequate and postgraduate research funds are 'unacceptably low'.

11 June: *Pushing Back the Frontiers*, Labour Party, suggests setting up a new non-cabinet post of Minister for Science, Technology, Research and Statistics with a budget of more than £1 billion, tax credits to persuade companies to invest more in R&D, and a minister of technology in the DTI responsible for industrial R&D. It also suggests a Defence Diversification Agency to redeploy to the civilian economy defence related skills and assets, improved relations between higher education and industry, an increased science and technology content in the schools curriculum and in higher education, and the movement of the Meteorological Office from the Ministry of Defence to a Ministry of Science. Labour would also establish a Humanities Research Council and an independent Office of Technology Assessment to advise Parliament on the consequences of new technologies.

Science and Innovation: The Cultural Revolution, Conservative Research Department, defends the government's record on science.

18 June: Centre for the Exploitation of Science and Technology report contrasts British and German technology and industrial strategy and recommends the expansion of regional technology policy and the introduction of a legal requirement to train staff.

30 June: Announcement of the successful development of insulin which is inhaled rather than injected by the Radcliffe Infirmary, Oxford.

11 July: Announcement in *The Lancet* of a new test enabling doctors better to predict breast cancer, developed by researchers at University College Hospital and the Middlesex Hospital in London.

17 July: Committee chaired by Brian Fender recommends that the Science and Engineering Research Council spends £6 million per annum on nuclear structure physics, £3.7 million more than the SERC had budgeted for.

24 July: Astronomers at Jodrell Bank claim to have discovered the first planet orbiting around a star other than the Sun.

7 Aug: *Mathematics: Strategy for the Future*, SERC, calls on the government to double the money spent on methematics research and to improve its teaching in schools.

12 Sept: *Nature* attacks the government's narrow and short-sighted approach to science, calling for a cabinet-level minister of science to promote research and its application to industry, the doubling of research grants, less specialized school education, four year degree courses and better pay for academics.

27 Sept: Licences for scientists over 70 to experiment on animals are to come under annual review after a case earlier in the year when an 89-year old researcher was found guilty of causing unnecessary suffering to rabbits.

7 Oct: British Antarctic Survey has to cut research because of a cash crisis.

9 Nov: JET fusion research reactor in Culham, Oxfordshire produces fusion energy for a few minutes.

25 Nov: *Science and Technology Issues*, Advisory Council on Science and Technology, complains university scientists are under-resourced and that British companies spend too little on research and warns that Britain has a 'two-tier workforce with a highly educated élite and a poorly trained population'.

16 Dec: Science budget for 1992–3 set at £1,002 million, a 2.5 per cent rise in real terms.

Scotland

JAMES G. KELLAS

The Constitutional Question

Although the Scottish Constitutional Convention did not meet in plenary session in 1991, having 'reported to the Scottish people' on 30 November 1990, the constitutional issue in Scotland was still alive in 1991. Indeed, in November it re-emerged in dramatic form when the Conservatives lost the Kincardine and Deeside by-election on 7 November to the Liberal Democrats and were reduced to only nine seats in Scotland out of 72, making them the third party in terms of seats, after Labour and the Liberal Democrats.

This released an avalanche of political rhetoric on both sides of the border. The Liberal Democrat victor, Nicol Stephen, in his speech on election immediately called for a Scottish Parliament, claiming that the Tories had lost their mandate to govern Scotland. This theme was echoed by the party leader, Paddy Ashdown, and was taken up in editorials in London-based newspapers such as the *Sunday Times* and *The Observer* on 10 November, with the former running a large headline 'Home Rule for England'. The editor, Andrew Neil (a Scot) also called for a reduction in the number of Scottish MPs, since Scotland was 'over-represented' in Parliament in terms of population share. Later in the week, the Scottish question also appeared in editorials in the *Daily Telegraph* and the *Financial Times*, which again sought some constitutional change. The problem of Conservative representation was now acute in the House of Commons at Scottish Question Time, for there were only four Scottish Tory backbenchers to ask questions, with 63 MPs on the Opposition benches. This meant that English Tories had to be continually enlisted to ask Scottish questions. The Speaker tried to give both sides some measure of equality but this deeply offended some Scottish MPs, who resented having to give way to MPs with no constituency interest in Scotland. The Speaker, and some Tories, reminded the Opposition Scots that Parliament was a 'United Kingdom Parliament', but the fact was that the procedures of that Parliament were linked into the balance of the parties in Scotland. If there were too few Scottish MPs on one side of the House then Scottish business was in difficulties. Already, since 1987, the Select Committee on Scottish Affairs had lapsed for lack of Conservative participation, and now the other parts of Scottish business looked increasingly precarious. If the number of Conservative MPs in Scotland was to be further reduced at the next general election, and the Conservatives formed the government, there might not be enough Scottish Conservative MPs to run the Scottish Office. This would provoke an even more extreme version of the 'Doomsday Scenario' than that after the 1987 election.

It was this seemingly desperate situation for the Conservatives in Scotland which made some of them seek to alter the current links between Scotland and England. One way forward might be devolution or even independence for Scotland, and another to reduce the number of Scottish MPs. This, according to some English Tory MPs, should be done straightaway, despite the report of the Select Committee on Home Affairs in December 1986[1] that no change in the number should be made at present, and the acceptance of this by the Conservative government in February 1988 in its reply to the Committee's report.[2]

If devolution were to be granted, the Conservatives and Liberal Democrats maintained that a further reduction in the number of Scottish MPs would be in order. Of course, independence would get rid of the problem altogether. The *Sunday Times* backed each of these propositions in turn, and the theme of Scottish 'over- representation' was taken up by several English Conservative backbenchers during Scottish Question Time on 13 November, Prime Minister's Question Time on 14 November and the Scottish Secretary's statement on Scottish Office spending on 4 December. However, the Scottish Office ministers did not favour a reduction in the number of Scottish MPs in the present circumstances, perhaps because this might actually deplete the Scottish Conservative ranks as well as those of the other parties. On 8 December, Ian Lang, the Scottish Secretary, called for a debate on Scotland's future in the United Kingdom to be held in the Scottish Grand Committee. This was a clear sign that the Conservative Party was now more sensitive to the constitutional issue, although the official policy was that it would not support a half-way devolution option.

The choice was between total independence and the status quo (defined as 'the Union'). This was despite survey evidence showing around half of Conservative voters supporting a Scottish Parliament, and some prominent Conservative devolutionists with roots in local government such as Struan Stevenson (former leader of Kyle and Carrick District Council and parliamentary candidate for Edinburgh South), Councillor John Young (leader of the Conservatives in Glasgow District Council), and Councillor Brian Meek (former Convener of Lothian Regional Council and Vice President of the Scottish Conservative and Unionist Association). In the Borders, a group of Tories led by the Prospective Parliamentary Candidate, Lloyd Beat, produced a pamphlet in April advocating 'all-round devolution' coupled with a single-tier local government structure and the enforced opt-out from public control of education and health.[3] Other Conservative devolutionists who spoke up towards the end of the year included Sir Russell Fairgrieve (former Scottish Office minister and former chairman of the Scottish Conservative Party), and there were also those who, while not clearly devolutionists, wished the subject discussed, such as Councillor Christine Richards (leader of the Conservatives on Edinburgh District Council) and some members of the Scottish Tory Reform Group.

The result of the by-election revived the whole issue of devolution and independence at a time when the Constitutional Convention was relatively inactive, and the SNP was making only a slight impact on the political scene. It was the reaction to the Liberal Democrat by-election victory which raised the temperature, and put Scotland once more onto the political agenda in London, and not any activity by the Constitutional Convention or the SNP. This pointed to the interaction between the Scottish and British political systems and the vital importance of votes and seats in Scotland to English MPs and opinion-leaders. If Scottish and English voters diverge too starkly and the government is left badly under-represented in Scotland, then it becomes sensitive to the demands for constitutional change.

In Scotland itself, the constitutional debate was also taking place in the executive of the Scottish Constitutional Convention, and in the political parties. Several questions relating to devolution remained unresolved, including the electoral system, the position of the Scottish Office, and the number of Scottish MPs at Westminster. After the Kincardine and Deeside by-election had reopened the debate generally, a split was revealed in the Convention between the Liberal Democrats and Labour. The former were prepared to reduce the number of Scottish MPs to around 60 under devolution, while Labour wanted to retain the present 72. Moreover, the Liberal Democrats wanted to see 'the eventual abolition' of the Scottish Office, while this was not on Labour's programme. Lastly, the electoral system for the devolved Parliament remained unsettled. Labour was still undecided as between the 'additional member system' of PR as in Germany and the alternative vote system. The Liberal Democrats did not accept the alternative vote system as PR, and continued to press for the single transferable vote system. However, they would probably settle for the additional member system to maintain a consensus. Meanwhile, in November, the Convention embarked on a publicity campaign in the press, with an appeal for financial support.

The electorate in Scotland remained fairly steady in its support for a Scottish Parliament, according to the surveys in 1991. A typical survey, in *The Scotsman* of 17 September, gave the following results: independence separate from both England and Wales and the EC, 11 per cent; independence separate from England and Wales but in the EC, 26 per cent; devolution within the UK, 41 per cent; no change, 19 per cent; no opinion, 3 per cent. However, some doubts remained. In May, the devolution figure was as low as 33 per cent, and the no change option was 28 per cent. Independence (two options) was the same at 37 per cent. Should a Scottish Parliament lead to higher taxes then only 43 per cent said they would support setting one up, with the same number against, and 15 per cent having no opinion.[4]

Contemporary Britain

Parties and Elections

In a quiet year for elections in Scotland (there was only one parliamentary by-election, and there were no local general elections), the Kincardine and Deeside by-election on 7 November provided not only a 'shock' result but also a reopening of the constitutional debate and welcome copy for the Scottish media. The by-election was caused by the death of Alick Buchanan-Smith, a former minister, devolutionist and critic of the governmment on several issues. The Conservative candidate, Marcus Humphrey, continued the former MP's independent line by opposing the proposed trust status of the Foresterhill hospital group in Aberdeen and the merger of the Gordon Highlanders regiment, but this strategy could not prevent the loss of the seat. The swing from Conservative to Liberal Democrat (11.4 per cent) was not as great as at some recent by-elections in England such as Ribble Valley in March (24.7 per cent), but the fact that the Tories were now the third party in Scotland in terms of seats provoked (as we have seen) a vigorous constitutional debate. There was evidence of tactical voting, as the Labour vote dropped by 8.2 per cent, presumably as a result of transfers to the Liberal Democrats, who rose by 12.7 per cent. The SNP nearly doubled its share of the vote to 11.1 per cent, which showed that it had partly resisted tactical voting, even if it had come only third.

Table 1. Kincardine and Deeside by-election, 7 November 1991

Candidate	Votes[1]	Percentage of vote	Change in vote share
Nicol Stephen (Liberal Democrats)[2]	20,779	49.0	+12.7
Marcus Humphrey (Conservative)	12,955	30.6	−10.1
Allan Macartney (SNP)	4,705	11.1	+4.6
Malcolm Savidge (Labour)	3,271	7.7	−8.2
Stephen Campbell (Scottish Green)	683	1.6	+1.0

[1] Turnout 67 per cent
[2] Liberal Democrat majority 7,824

Meanwhile, opinion polls in 1991 showed support for the parties within the following ranges: Labour: 41–51 per cent; Conservative: 18–30 per cent; SNP: 17–25 per cent; Liberal Democrats: 6–14 per cent; Greens: under 1–3 per cent. These fluctuations were related to specific events such as the Gulf war (in late January, Conservative support rose to 30 per cent, but by December it had fallen to 18 per cent), the Budget, the Kincardine and Deeside by-election, and the Scottish party conferences. These conferences gave the parties welcome publicity in the media in Scotland, although they also revealed their splits. The Labour Party Scottish conference in Aberdeen (8–10 March) endorsed 'proportional representation' for a Scottish Parliament, but no particular scheme was adopted then or later in 1991. The conference endorsed the proposal that at least 50 per cent of the seats in a Scottish Parliament be allocated to women, but again how this was to be achieved was not made clear. In fact, Labour in Scotland was divided on both these issues, and another division was over the poll tax non-payment campaign. Local government leaders now attacked this, despite the fact that some had participated in it at first. A motion to show solidarity with non-payers was rejected on the advice of the executive.

The Conservative conference at Perth (8-11 May) met shortly after the government had announced the coming end of the poll tax. It was at the Scottish conference in 1986 that the seething discontent over rates revaluation had first been displayed which led directly to the introduction of the poll tax, at first in Scotland, and then in England and Wales. The demise of the tax was hardly likely to arouse enthusiasm, and the proposed council tax was met with some scepticism. Yet most Scottish Tories had come to realise that there were no votes to be won by persisting with the poll tax. Other divisions were seen on the government's policy on fishing, the failure to transfer government oil safety jobs to Aberdeen, and devolution. The last subject was largely kept within the confines of a fringe meeting of the Scottish Tory Reform Group, and Scottish Secretary Ian Lang told the conference that even Bill Walker MP's mild 'Scottish Senate' proposal could not be entertained.

The SNP conference in Inverness (18–21 September) opened with a declaration that the target date for independence was 1 January 1993, when the single European market comes into full operation. While this was seen by many delegates as unrealistic, even more were worried that the Party's new symbol seemed to resemble the Nazi swastika. This was partly offset by the satisfaction engendered by securing the film actor Sean Connery's voice for the party political broadcast on 16 September. Connery was later to make other public statements in favour of the SNP and Scottish independence. Another charismatic figure, Jim Sillars MP, beat incumbent Alastair Morgan by 279 votes to 184 for the post of deputy leader (Senior Vice-Convener), although the latter was supported by the Convener, Alex Salmond. The post has the task of running the general election campaign, and Sillars wished to give it a high profile. Other splits in the party had been revealed earlier in the year. The party abandoned its poll tax non-payment campaign at a special national conference at Govan on 23 March by 244 votes to 132, amidst complaints. The leader of the non- payment campaign, Kenny Macaskill, accepted the decision but promised to continue his non-payment and was now effectively marginalized in the party. Another split continued over the policy of 'independence in Europe'. Those supporting independence outside Europe had formed the Scottish Sovereignty Movement, along with members of the Scottish Green Party. This attracted disaffected nationalists such as the former Vice-Convener Jim Fairlie, who had left the party in 1990, to a fringe meeting in Inverness.

The Scottish Liberal Democrat conference in Pitlochry (5–7 April) was divided on various issues. A three-option referendum (independence; devolution; status quo) after the general election was rejected 'amidst confused scenes'[5] and the conference narrowly decided to continue the party's commitment to phase out nuclear power. Some delegates claimed that the party was more committed to market principles than the Conservatives, and urged members to buy shares in the electricity companies. Paddy Ashdown echoed English Conservative sentiments in seeking to reduce the number of Scottish MPs to around 57 if devolution were introduced. But the Scottish party's commitments to 'Eurofederalism' and a 'Europe of the regions', to proportional representation, and to a local income tax, along with its opposition to national primary school testing and a two-year Higher Grade examination, marked it off from the other parties in Scotland on one or more of these policies.

The Government of Scotland

At the beginning of the year, the Scottish Office announced that it was changing the names of its constituent departments, on the advice of an advertising agency. All departments would henceforth start with the words 'Scottish Office' (as in 'The Scottish Office Education Department', previously the Scottish Education Department). A completely new name was given to the Scottish Development Department – The Scottish Office Environment Department – but the other departments retained their core titles. What difference these changes would make was not clear, but more substantial innovations were under way with the start of Scottish Enterprise and Highlands and Islands Enterprise on 1 April, and their associated local enterprise companies (13 in the case of Scottish Enterprise). The privatization (flotation of shares) in June of the former electricity boards, the South of Scotland Electricity Board and the North of Scotland Hydro-Electric Board, as Scottish Power plc and Scottish Hydro-Electric plc respectively, considerably reduced the Scottish Office's responsibilities in energy, though Scottish Nuclear Ltd was still governmment-owned. After some hesitation, the Scottish Office supported the setting up of a promotional office in Brussels, Scotland Europa, to be run by Scottish Enterprise, but without the participation of local authorities.

A fundamental reform of further and higher education was announced on 20 May, and a bill, the Further and Higher Education (Scotland) Bill, was introduced on 26 November. This aimed to set up a Scottish Higher Education Funding Council, to take the place of the Universities Funding Council in Scotland. From 1993, Scottish universities and higher education colleges would get their finance from the Scottish Office through the mediation of the new Scottish council. Four Scottish 'central institutions' were given permission to become universities: Robert Gordon's Institute of Technology in Aberdeen, Napier Polytechnic in Edinburgh, Paisley College of Technology, and Glasgow Polytechnic. Glasgow College and Napier College had already in 1991 been allowed to change their names from 'college' to 'polytechnic', the latter up till then an English title. Local authority further education colleges would under the bill look to the Scottish Office for their finance, and would be run by college councils appointed by the Scottish Secretary instead of the local authorities. In the school sector, school boards remained controversial, with around a quarter of schools failing to elect them in 1991. Moreover, the progress towards 'opting out' of schools from local government control was zero in 1991, since not one school had opted out. Parental resistance was also seen to the government's policy of testing primary school pupils. This was left to the will of the parents in 1991, and between a half and two-thirds did not put their children forward for the tests. They were no doubt influenced in their decision by the militant anti-testing campaign waged by the teachers' unions and the education authorities. None of the latter were controlled by the Conservatives. The government promised to make such tests more strictly compulsory in 1992. All this amounted to a kind of 'revolution' in Scottish education, at least in administration if not in content. The latter remained enmeshed in talk of changing the 'Highers' at some future date (a committee under the chairmanship of Professor John Howie was considering the matter), and of improving the 'modules' in the Scottish Certificate of Vocational Education.

In the health service, three hospitals (Foresterhill Group, Aberdeen; South Ayrshire Group; Royal Scottish National Hospital, Larbert) were given permission by the Secretary of State on 3 December to establish trusts in 1992 (Aberdeen, South Ayrshire) and in 1993 (Larbert). These decisions were highly controversial, and Labour promised to undo them if elected. The number of Health Councils was reduced from 44 to 18 in April.

Local government continued to suffer from the effects of the community charge (poll tax). Three million warrants for recovery of non-payment had been issued betweeen the start of the tax in 1989 and the end of 1991, and 64 per cent was unpaid at the end of October 1991, compared to 59 per cent at the same time in 1990. In October, 22 per cent remained unpaid for the financial year 1990–91, compared with 12.9 per cent for the financial year 1989–90.[6] On 7 May, Lothian Regional Council was chargecapped by the Secretary of State for Scotland, Ian Lang. Other financial troubles came with the collapse of the Bank of Credit and Commerce International in July. Several local authorities had invested heavily in the Bank, none more so than the Western Isles, which stood to lose over £23 million. After an enquiry by Professor Alan Alexander of Strathclyde University, the Convener, Rev. Donald Macaulay resigned on 2 September. A 'day of humiliation' was observed in the Isles on 12 December, and the council dismissed its Chief Executive and Director of Finance on 16 December.

In Orkney Islands Council, there was much trouble and publicity over the 'taking into care' of nine children from four families on 27 February when the social work department and police uncovered an alleged network of child abuse involving parents and the local minister on the island of South Ronaldsway. When no court proceedings were instituted, a judicial inquiry was held under Lord Clyde, starting on 26 August. This was still sitting at the end of 1991, and was set to go on well into 1992, with the Scottish Office, after pressure, meeting part of the considerable bill for lawyers' expenses.

During 1991, there was much talk of a radical reform of local government. Paradoxically, in view of the events in the Western Isles and Orkney (both all-purpose authorities), there was near unanimity in the parties that a single-tier system should be introduced. The 'home rule' parties wanted this to accompany the settting up of a Scottish Parliament, but the Conservatives proposed it not along with devolution but with a radical transfer of functions such as education to central government.

Society and Economy

At the start of 1991, it was reported that for the first time in over twenty years there had been positive net migration (+6,000) to Scotland during 1989. However, the overall population had dropped by 30,000 to 5.09 million, and there was an even greater drop of 60,000 in the total registered electorate. This was perhaps related to electors trying to avoid liability for the poll tax.

The state of the Scottish economy is partly responsible for migration. A revival in North Sea oil output and prices until November attracted labour to north-east Scotland, but for central Scotland the Scottish Development Agency painted a bleak picture of the prospects for the steel industry on 24 January. This was borne out when workers were laid off at the Ravenscraig hot strip steel mill on 15 February, with formal closure of the mill on 5 April. The rest of the plant was guaranteed by British Steel until 1993, 'subject to market conditions'. (British Steel announced on 8 January 1992 that Ravenscraig would close entirely in September 1992.) The decision to close the Ravenscraig hot strip mill was severely criticized by the House of Commons Select Committee on Trade and Industry on 14 March. The closure within the next five years of another steel mill, the Dalzell plate mill, was announced on 2 July. This promised effectively to kill off the steel industry in Scotland.

More industrial bad news came when the US Navy decided in February to close its Holy Loch base, and a leak revealed that the government intended to close the Rosyth naval base. After a furious backlash, the government reprieved the Rosyth base on 16 July, but 900 jobs were lost, and 1,000 others were transferred to other bases. In the same month it was announced that Scotland's infantry regiments were to be cut by one-third, with famous regiments such as the Gordon Highlanders to be merged. At the end of the year, there was better news when Kvaerner Govan, the shipbuilders, announced on 18 December orders worth £200 million, which would guarantee the workforce employment for four years.

In the media, a new popular Sunday newspaper, *The Sunday Scot*, was launched on 10 March by Scottish businessman David Murray, but it closed on 11 July with the loss of £3 million. The bi-monthly political magazine, *Radical Scotland*, closed in June with its 51st issue. According to the editorial, the Scottish political situation had developed so much in the years of the magazine's existence that its *raison d'etre*, self-government, 'has been accepted in all but the darkest corners of Scotland'.[7] In March, Radio Clyde took over Radio Forth, and in October the independent television franchises were re-awarded to STV and Grampian. The former had no competitor, and won the franchise for a nominal annual fee of £2,000. In December, *The Daily Record* and *The Sunday Mail*, two of Scotland's most popular papers, were put up for sale as part of Mirror Group Newspapers. A bid for these was promised by the Scottish employees. On a happier note, Gaelic broadcasting on TV was boosted by the grant of an additional £1.5 million in January to the £8 million already announced by the government. This would make a further 200 hours of Gaelic TV programmes from 1992, a total of 300 hours a year, compared with 100 hours in 1991. This money would also provide work for several hundred media people in the Gaelic-speaking community, which amounts to a mere 1.5 per cent of the Scottish population.

In the arts, changes in management and financial troubles marked the year. The director of the Edinburgh Festival, Frank Dunlop, was replaced and left his post in August with an attack on Edinburgh District Council for its lack of financial support. His successor had been named in May as Brian McMaster of Welsh National Opera. Scottish Opera and the Royal Scottish Orchestra were no better off, and each finished 1991 with a debt of £800,000. This led to the Opera's new managing director, Richard Jarman, cancelling the 1992 production of *Tristan and Isolde*. In part the financial shortfall had resulted from the poor funding from the Arts Council of Great Britain, which regarded Scottish Opera as a 'visitor' in England, and would not fund its English performances at the level of those of Welsh National Opera, which was regarded as a 'resident'.[8] The Royal Scottish Orchestra (renamed in 1991, replacing the old name Scottish National Orchestra and the short-lived name Royal Scottish National Orchestra) also had a new chief executive, Christopher Bishop, whose poor relations with the players became notorious during 1991. In the visual arts, Edinburgh's Fruitmarket Gallery closed in January, and Glasgow's Third Eye Centre in June. Perhaps theatre was the most happy of the arts in 1991, with the reopening in August of Edinburgh's Empire Theatre as a home for operatic and other performances.

The churches were badly split over the Gulf war, with the Moderator of the General Assembly of the Church of Scotland, the Rt Rev. Professor Robert Davidson, and the Roman Catholic Archbishop of Glasgow, the Most Rev .Thomas Winning, expressing reservations about the use of military force. When the minister of Glasgow Cathedral, Rev. Dr William Morris, announced that the official service of remembrance would be held on 4 May in the Cathedral with the Archbishop of York, Dr John Habgood, delivering the sermon, the Bishop of Edinburgh (Scottish Episcopal Church), the Rt Rev. Richard Holloway, issued a condemnation on the grounds that the views of the Scottish Church leaders were being flouted, and their position usurped by English clerics.[9] In the event, the service was attended by the church leaders in Scotland, as well as by the Queen and the Prime Minister.

Notes

1 Select Committee on Home Affairs, HC [1986-87] 97–I.
2 Government reply to the report of the Select Committee on Home Affairs, Cmnd.308.
3 *The Scotsman*, 8 April 1991.
4 *The Scotsman*, 9 May 1991.
5 *The Scotsman*, 8 April 1991.
6 *The Scotsman*, 23 October 1991.
7 *Radical Scotland*, no. 51 (June/July 1991), p.3.
8 Letter in *The Glasgow Herald* from Anthony Everitt, Secretary-General, Arts Council of Great Britain, 13 December 1991.
9 *The Scotsman*, 8 April 1991.

Chronology

6 Feb: US nuclear submarine base at Holy Loch in the Clyde to close from January 1992.
15 Feb: Ravenscraig hot steel mill workers laid off.
1 Apr: Scottish Enterprise and Highlands and Islands Enterprise replace Scottish Development Agency and Highlands and Islands Development Board respectively, and take on functions of the Training Agency in Scotland.
5 Apr: Closure of Ravenscraig hot strip steel mill.
7 May: Lothian Regional Council charge-capped.
18 Jun: Flotation of shares in Scottish Power (ex-South of Scotland Electricity Board) and Scottish Hydro-Electric (ex-North of Scotland Hydro-Electric Board).
4 Jul: British steel announces closure of Dalzell steel plate mill within five years.
16 Jul: Rosyth naval base reprieved after lobbying by Scottish MPs, but 900 jobs to go and 1,000 to be transferred to other bases.
7 Nov: Liberal Democrats gain Kincardine and Deeside from Conservatives in by-election.
26 Nov: Further and Higher Education (Scotland) Bill debate opens.
3 Dec: Secretary of State for Scotland Ian Lang announces that three hospital groups are to be allowed to establish trusts.
18 Dec: Kvaerner Govan shipyard announces £200 million orders.

Wales

DENIS BALSOM

Any clichéd scene of Wales would have three essential components – coalminers, rugby players and a choir. For generations this stereotype has persisted and, although never applicable to all of Wales, has become part of an internal self image as much as an external identity. In 1991 coal is no longer mined in the Rhondda and indeed, the future of the remaining tiny coal industry in Wales appears bleak and unlikely to survive any move towards privatization. Nineteen ninety-one also saw the publication of a report lamenting the demise of the traditional Welsh choir. Once a symbol of community spirit and vitality, a source of keen competition between towns and villages, the choirs are now in decline, with shrinking membership, an ever higher average age and minimal recruitment of younger singers. Even worse, Wales were humiliated in the rugby World Cup. Having finished in a creditable third place in the 1987 inaugural competition, in 1991 Wales failed to progress beyond the opening round. This national disgrace was then further compounded by the success of England in reaching the World Cup final. Does anything remain that is truly Welsh?

Unique to Wales of course, is the language. Nineteen ninety-one proved to be a relatively uneventful year for this issue, which for so long has been central to Welsh politics. In April the decennial census enumerated the Welsh speaking population, but the results are not expected to be published until 1993. This assessment of the Welsh speaking population is a crucial indicator of the viability of the culture and thus the figures are keenly awaited by all those active in linguistic politics – for and against. It is highly likely that the results of the 1991 census will not be supportive of language activists in Wales and may thus encourage the adoption of an even more defensive attitude. The long running arson campaign, attributed to the shadowy group, *Meibion Glyndwr*, against second homes and in-migration to Wales, was fairly dormant by the standards of recent years. But neither however did the police make any significant headway in resolving the case, after their embarrassing harassment of a leading Welsh television star concerning the arson attacks in 1990. A rather unpleasant copycat incident in Anglesey, involving letter bombs, was solved and prosecutions are imminent.

Direct action in support of the language has always been the hallmark of *Cymdeithas yr Iaith Gymraeg* (The Welsh Language Society), though strictly eschewing any acts of personal violence. *Cymdeithas yr Iaith Gymraeg* has spearheaded the campaign for reforms in provision for the Welsh language since the mid 1960s, during the course of which many of its members have served custodial sentences. The current campaign is to secure a Property Act for Wales which would give some special status to local purchasers in the Welsh speaking heartland areas and thus help combat the pressures of in-migration and financial exclusion from the market experienced in many rural areas of Wales. In promotion of this cause two members of *Cymdeithas*, chairman Alun Llwyd and Branwen Nicholas, attacked government offices in north Wales in January, were brought to trial in September and sentenced to imprisonment. The government has always refused to negotiate with *Cymdeithas* whilst it remained committed to breaking the law, but recent indications suggest the government may be relenting, in return for a 'truce' being called by the activists. Such official recognition of the issue, and of those advancing its case, suggests that some government action may soon be forthcoming.

Government action has not been forthcoming, however, on the principal linguistic issue of the recent past, and focus of many earlier direct action campaigns – the demand for a new Welsh Language Act. The official Welsh Language Board, appointed by the Secretary of State for Wales in July 1988, produced a draft Welsh Language Bill after an extensive consultation exercise. All political parties are committed to some measure of reform to the official status of the Welsh language in Wales and it was therefore a major disappointment that the Queen's speech, at the opening of Parliament in November, contained no pledge to bring forward this legislation in the current session. This and other linguistic issues, in education for example, will form a distinct Welsh sub-agenda in the forthcoming general election campaign.

Welsh Politics

As the phoney war between the main political parties continued, in heightened anticipation of the general election, two by-elections took place in Wales during the year – at Neath and at Monmouth. These two events illustrate well the continuance of a distinct Welsh politics. In April, at Neath, following the death of the worthy, but undistinguished, Labour backbencher Donald Coleman, Peter Hain was elected for Labour with a substantial, if reduced, majority. Given the electoral history of Neath this was an unremarkable outcome and was always likely to be so. However, runners-up to Labour were Plaid Cymru, the Welsh nationalist party, repeating their good performance at the previous by-election at Pontypridd in 1989. Neath is an intensely Welsh community, but defined by its industrial history and culture rather than its language, though a residual 10 per cent or so of the population still speaks Welsh. Such areas have for generations exhibited an almost tribal loyalty to Labour, and in doing so have contained support for Plaid Cymru to the linguistic fastness of north and west Wales. Labour's representatives from industrial Wales have been mostly Welsh working class politicians, often with a trade union background, who were later replaced by a post-war generation of, by now, middle class professionals, but children of a similar proletarian background. The hierarchy of personnel in the Labour Party, and the governments of 1945, 1964, 1966 and 1974, affirm the importance of this Labour cadre. In drafting Peter Hain, a South African born, well known anti-apartheid campaigner and prominent former Young Liberal, the Neath Labour Party was doubtless endorsing its commitment to many commonly held principles, but it also appeared that the local party was being used as a borough in the leader's pocket to ensure the election of one of his coterie of metropolitan political friends. Loyalty to Labour prevailed, and will continue to do so for some time, but the substantial showing by Plaid Cymru is a reminder that there are distinct elements to politics in Wales that should not be taken for granted.

The second by-election of the year was a much more national affair with the entire upper echelons of all parties descending to spend most of May contesting the by-election in Monmouth which followed the death of Sir John Stradling-Thomas. Sir John had enjoyed a safe majority since 1966 and had pursued a successful political career reaching middle-rank ministerial office before withdrawing to the backbenches and assuming the mantle of a 'Silent Knight'. He had been deselected from his constituency for the next election prior to his untimely death. In the bifocal world of Welsh politics, Neath should have been an entirely local affair, but succumbed to the radical chic. Monmouth belongs to the wholly British, Westminster dimension of Welsh politics yet revealed a latent Welshness in its support for Labour. Monmouth is a prosperous, Border constituency analogous to many in the south and west of Britain. At a by-election in the fourth year of a Conservative government, following the heady victory of the Liberal Democrats in Ribble Valley, this should have been a repeat of Ryedale or Crosby, a mid-term third party triumph to be enjoyed until the resumption of normal politics at the next general election. In defiance of this rather well-worn scenario, Labour's Huw Edwards was victorious in a campaign that appeared to preview many of the issues and arguments which will dominate the coming general election. In these unlikely surroundings it appeared that a residual Welshness gave Labour a victory it could never have anticipated in, say, neighbouring and not dissimilar Hereford.

The new Conservative leadership's abandonment of the poll tax resurrected the issue of local government reform in Britain. In Wales this issue goes further in that devolution and the spectre of a Welsh assembly are never very far from the surface in any such discussions. Secretary of State for Wales, David Hunt, issued a consultative paper on local government reform and called for responses, but did not initiate a full-scale inquiry such as is to occur in England. Whilst the collective organizations of Welsh counties and Welsh districts disagree as to the appropriate model for the future, there is consensus advocating a return to single-tier unitary authorities with an all-Wales strategic authority of some kind. All the opposition parties also envisage some all-Wales institution being created and even the Minister of State, Sir Wyn Roberts, perhaps inadvertently, hinted that a Welsh assembly of some sort might be imminent from the government. Although the final government proposals are still awaited, there was a sense of disappointment when, in the shadow of the Maastricht conference, Mr Hunt claimed that Welsh representation on a European regional body would make a Welsh assembly redundant.

Other Events

As elsewhere in Britain, Wales suffered from the effects of recession in 1991. The levels of unemployment remain stubbornly higher than the national average and the increases have been felt particularly keenly in many areas that were previously the growth points of the 1980s. The impact of recession and unemployment is less concentrated than that previously experienced. Where specific industries, such as steel and coal, were especially hard hit in earlier recessions, in 1991 the impact appeared remarkably widespread and uniform. The economic downturn has also eased the pressure in rural areas of inward migration, but the publication of the first preliminary results of the 1991 census shows that the expanding areas of Wales are the coastal and rural districts of north, west and mid Wales whilst the traditional industrial areas of south Wales continue to lose population. Overall the population of Wales has grown to 2,780,000 since 1981, an increase of only 0.2 per cent, but this ranges from a growth of 12.9 per cent in Colwyn to a decline of 8.8 per cent in Port Talbot.

The sporting year was dominated by the further travails of the national rugby team. In the home championship Wales failed to record a single victory. The summer tour to Australia saw embarrassingly large defeats inflicted upon Wales by Queensland, New South Wales and the Australian national side. Changes in management were introduced prior to the World Cup in the autumn, but to little avail. Wales succumbed to Western Samoa and Australia, to be dismissed early from the competition. For many years Welsh soccer has lived in the shadow of Welsh rugby, within Wales, and of England and Scotland within football itself. Although failing to qualify for the last World Cup, or for the 1992 European Nations championships, Wales did manage several giant-killing results, beating world champions West Germany in June and Brazil in September. In golf, Ian Woosnam won the US Masters tournament at Augusta in April.

For Wales, as elsewhere, 1992 will be dominated by the general election, whenever it is called. Neil Kinnock could become the first Welsh Prime Minister since Lloyd George. Whilst any future Labour government will contain many Welsh ministers, the centre of gravity within the Labour Party has generally moved to Scotland. Many senior government posts would be held by Scots and Labour's constitutional proposals guarantee an immediate Scottish Parliament, but are less specific concerning Wales. Whatever the national outcome of the election, Wales will predominantly support the Labour Party. Against a sitting Conservative government Labour will monopolize the traditional anti-establishment ethos of radical Wales. This legacy, however, would pass to Plaid Cymru should a Labour administration be elected and Plaid have previously shown their capacity to act as a catalyst to Welsh politics. An inconclusive election result at Westminster would give added status to all the minor parties for the duration of the impasse and out of this may yet emerge genuine constitutional change which will enhance the status of Wales.

Chronology

4 Jan: Welsh Language Society launch their campaign of direct action against the Welsh Office to secure a Property Act. Alun Llwyd and Branwen Nicholas are arrested for causing damage to the Property Services Agency offices at Rhos-on-Sea.

7 Jan: Dafydd Elis Thomas, the leader of Plaid Cmyru, announces that he will retire at the next general election.

14 Jan: Assembly of Welsh Councils reveals its plans for local government reorganization. They include reducing local authorities from 45 to 18 with an elected Welsh assembly.

31 Jan: Welsh Office and Arts Council save Welsh National Opera with a £1.5 million cash injection.

11 Feb: Draft bill by the Welsh Language Board is published which would make Welsh valid for all official purposes, allow employers to make ability to speak Welsh a condition of employment and set up a Language Board for Wales with powers to make grants or loans to promote the language.

14 Feb: Seasonally adjusted unemployment figures go over 100,000 for Wales.

22 Feb: Hoover at Merthyr Tydfil announce 450 redundancies.

6 Mar: Plans for a £1 billion international airport in Wales near Newport are announced.

16 Mar: Euromet's chemical waste storage plant in Rhymney, South Wales, has its licence revoked.

21 Mar: Welsh Secretary David Hunt calls on local government chiefs to devise a system of single-tier authorities as part of local government reform.

4 Apr: Peter Hain elected as MP for Neath following the death of Donald Coleman.

17 Apr: Cardiff Bay Barrage Bill is defeated in the House of Commons.

1 May: Pembrokeshire Health Authority became the first in Wales to apply for NHS trust status.

16 May: Monmouth, previously a safe seat for the Conservatives, goes to Huw Edwards of Labour in the by-election following the death of Sir John Stradling-Thomas.

6 Aug: Two firebombs outside a Conservative party office and an army recruiting centre are defused in Bangor, north Wales.

Einir Jones won the crown at the Bro Delyn National Eisteddfod in Mold.

7 Aug: Angharad Thomas won the prose medal at the National Eisteddfod two days after being arrested on the Eisteddfod field for daubing as part of the campaign for a Welsh Language Act.

8 Aug: Robin Llwyd ab Owain won the chair at the National Eisteddfod.

9 Aug: Royal National Eisteddfod ends in Mold, Clwyd, with a call from the poet R S Thomas for support for *Meibion Glyndwr*.

2 Sept: A dispute between two shopkeepers led to youths rioting in the Wilson Road area of Ely, Cardiff. Disturbances continued for four consecutive nights.

5 Sept: *Cymdeithas yr Iaith Gymraeg* members Alun Llywd and Branwen Nicholas are jailed for six months each for breaking into and damaging the PSA offices at Rhos-on-Sea in January.

8 Sept: Firebombs in Bala and Anglesey.

20 Sept: In a *Western Mail* interview, John Major opposed devolution and stated that consultation on a new Welsh Language Act would continue.

1 Oct: Neil Kinnock tells the Labour Party conference that a Labour government would introduce devolution, 'first to Scotland and then progressively with consent to Wales and the regions of England'.

10 Oct: Welsh Secretary David Hunt calls for an EC regional assembly in Brussels rather than a Welsh assembly.

12 Oct: Wales go out of the rugby World Cup, beaten 38–3 by Australia.

15 Oct: Rt Rev. Alwyn Rice Jones, Bishop of St Asaph, is elected as the new Archbishop of Wales.

16 Oct: HTV retain their Wales and west of England independent television franchise.

25 Oct: Protests at the 'second division' devolution on offer for Wales (as opposed to Scotland) from Labour at the Plaid Cymru conference.

6 Dec: Four firebombs are discovered at a postal sorting office in Bangor.

Northern Ireland

PAUL ARTHUR

Nineteen ninety-one began with a whimper and ended with a bang – in fact a series of bangs. In that respect it was not dissimilar to most other years over the past two decades . . . except, of course, for the whimper. It was a whimper of hope, a still small voice urging us towards finding the means to make political progress. We cannot put it more strongly than a whimper because optimism is a scarce commodity in this hostile environment. In any case we had enough bangs in the form of explosions and politically motivated murders to remind us not to raise our expectations above the level of the gutter. While others marvelled at the Gulf war, the disintegration of the USSR and Yugoslavia, the opening of the political process in South Africa, and the implications of Maastricht, we concentrated on the dreary steeples of Fermanagh and Tyrone. Our unemployment figures remained depressingly high; we took little consolation from the fact that the recession did not bite as deeply here as in the other regions of the United Kingdom; and our paramilitaries maintained their impressive level of productivity. The problem continued to diminish the quality of democracy in the UK. There was no peace dividend in Northern Ireland.

The Economy

By the end of the year there were 102,000 (or 14.2 per cent of the work force) claiming unemployment benefit, the thirteenth consecutive increase and up by 6,000 on twelve months ago. The economy minister Richard Needham blamed this increase in the seasonally adjusted figures on bomb and incendiary attacks on industrial and commercial premises, particularly in the latter end of the year: 'I am the first to recognize that areas such as north and west Belfast have a very serious unemployment problem and spend much of my time trying to create employment there. The actions of Sinn Fein's colleagues in the IRA work against the people I am trying to help'. Mr Needham's remarks have some validity. In the previous six years it has been estimated that between £400 and £500 million had been invested in the commercial development of Belfast city centre. It was beginning to resemble any British High Street and had attracted many of the prestige companies to open up there. 'Normality' appeared to be around the corner. It was to demonstrate that

Northern Ireland was indeed a place apart that the IRA revived their firebomb attacks on retail outlets at the beginning and end of the year.

The devices ranged from a simple but deadly cassette, easy to plant and difficult to detect, to the massive car bomb – 'cut price terrorism' in the argot of the authorities. And if a ring of steel was thrown round Belfast the paramilitaries simply moved their campaign to large suburban shopping centres. Over 200 incendiary devices were planted in Northern Ireland during 1991 – six times more than the number for 1990, and more than the total for all of the previous nine years. The drain on the exchequer was massive: projected figures for compensation payments suggest that they are expected to rise to record levels and in real terms may be the highest since the mid 1980s. Preliminary estimates put the cost of property damage at over £33 million, an increase of 50 per cent on the previous year, and personal injury claims at around £23 million. (Admittedly this is a fraction of the costs in the 1970s but it remains a worrying statistic.) In addition arson attacks are meant to induce demoralization and divert the security forces from their normal pattern. Thus some of the devices were hoaxes: on 23 August, for example, 42 devices were planted – each had to be treated as a real device and many hours would pass before all of them were cleared.

But it would be a mistake to blame unemployment solely on the bombing campaign. Northern Ireland's peripherality has always been an obstacle to economic development. One of the reasons why recessionary effects have been less in Northern Ireland than the other regions is because the Northern Ireland economy entered the recession at a lower base, a fact acknowledged in the Northern Ireland Economic Council's autumn report: 'The relative immunity of the local economy from the full effects of the UK recession is more likely a reflection of its underlying weaknesses rather than its strength'. The report recognized as well that because local industry is relatively well supported by public funds Northern Ireland did not experience the same impact of high interest rates and exchange rate problems as other regions; and it benefited from employment provided by the public service – proportionally twice the size of that in the rest of the UK.

The advent of the single European market offers opportunities to overcome some aspects of peripherality. Largely for political reasons Northern Ireland accounts for only 4 per cent of imports into the Irish Republic and remains largely dependent on Britain; whereas the Republic's trade has taken on a distinctly continental flavour since joining the EC – Europe accounts for over 50 per cent of its exports. Both governments recognize the advantages to be gained from increased cross border trade, and one source estimates that the present level of north-south trade could increase by as much as 75 per cent and generate more than 60,000 new jobs if the right steps are taken. Hence in 1991 the first computerized database of over 10,000 Irish companies was established.

The political implications of the single European market might worry some traditional unionists, a worry underlined by his presidential address to the Fianna Fail party conference in March when Mr Haughey cited Europe as a way to 'find a solution to the centuries-old deeply embedded problem that still persists in Northern Ireland'. His comment that, as enthusiastic Europeans, 'we are the new unionists' will add to their sense of woe; as will the decision to treat the island of Ireland as a single entity under the European Economic Area Treaty. The treaty will establish a 19 nation free trade zone of EC and EFTA countries by 1993. The *Financial Times* on 23 October commented that the treaty is an 'historic advance (paper not real) for Irish unity. Since Efta objected to giving cohesion money to the UK a sneaky sub-clause in the treaty says Northern Ireland will become beneficiaries through the entitlements of the island of Ireland'.

Campaigns of Violence

In 1991 the Troubles claimed 75 civilians and 19 members of the security forces, an increase of 12 on 1990 and the same figure as that for 1988. The small number of security deaths (fewer than in any year since the IRA campaign began in 1971) demonstrates that the IRA spent much of the year concentrating on economic targets and in a retaliatory campaign of assassination against loyalists. That latter fact is indicative of increasing activity by loyalist paramilitaries. They are credited with 40 murders, their highest level since the late 1970s. Most were innocent Catholics although three were members of Sinn Fein and one the member of an extremist republican faction, the Irish People's Liberation Organization (IPLO).

Ironically it was the success of the Stevens Inquiry (established to examine charges of collusion between loyalist paramilitaries and the security forces) which helps to explain the upsurge in loyalist violence. Stevens removed three key loyalist commanders and replaced them with younger, more ruthless men who preferred the anonymity of collective leadership to the charismatic cult of the personality, as well as removing a key informer from inside the UDA. This hampered easy penetration of loyalist groups by the security forces. The UDA reorganized itself and began a policy of political co-operation with the UVF. To some degree loyalist violence was a reaction to an assassination campaign waged by the IPLO. It had been founded in 1986 and followed a policy of targeting specific loyalist leaders. The IPLO's reputation was such that in August the RUC stated that the IPLO was involved in drug smuggling, and in December Sinn Fein ordered them to disband describing them as a 'criminal gang'.

Another aspect of paramilitarism were frequent charges of racketeering, so that accountants became another weapon in the battle against terrorism. Anti-racketeering officers attached to the Northern Ireland Office (NIO) claimed in December that they had diverted more than £1 million from republican and loyalist groups who had been using false accounting in 28 drinking clubs in Belfast. Under the Registration of Clubs (Northern Ireland) Order which came into effect in 1987 eight republican and four loyalist clubs were forced to close in the last year and 11 others have had stringent accounting practices imposed upon them. Other clubs have closed down voluntarily when they found that they could not satisfy the new arrangements.

The IRA remains the most dedicated paramilitary group, with a seemingly inexhaustible supply of weapons. By launching a mortar attack on the Gulf war cabinet in February and planting a series of incendiary devices in London in December they demonstrated their resourcefulness. But in some respects 1991 was not a good year for republican paramilitaries. It has been calculated that over 600 IRA personnel are in prison, probably the largest number since the ending of internment in the mid 1970s. They are having to rely on less experienced operatives: the two bombers who blew themselves up in November were unknown to the authorities. We have seen that a more determined loyalist campaign was making life more uncomfortable for the IRA and their fellow travellers.

And finally the British and Irish authorities were cooperating more closely on extradition procedures. At a meeting of the Anglo-Irish Conference on November 20 the Irish government agreed to introduce amendments to the Extradition (European Convention on the Suppression of Terrorism) Act 1987 'as soon as possible'. This followed a decision in the Irish courts that an IRA man was guilty of the extraditable offence of kidnapping but since, in effect, he had served his sentence already he was to be released. The Irish agreed to seal off loopholes identified by the previous week's Supreme Court decision and to address the concerns expressed by the British government. In return the British authorities undertook to formalize the arrangement of 'speciality' under which extradited persons could not be charged with new offences as had happened earlier in the year when a London magistrate introduced new charges after the extraditable offence had been thrown out.

The republican campaign had a major problem with public relations. Some IRA activity was deemed to be counterproductive by the electorally conscious Sinn Fein. After the IRA killed a civilian in a London mainland station in February Sinn Fein's northern chairman, Mitchell McLaughlin, described it as 'catastrophic'. In fact throughout 1991 Sinn Fein distanced itself from IRA actions. At a press conference in January the Sinn Fein general secretary made it clear that the party would not in future respond to individual IRA actions: '. . . Sinn Fein is not the IRA. The IRA is capable of speaking for itself'. And at their annual conference a few days later Gerry Adams called for the development of a peace initiative and for negotiations without precondition; and in November he told a university debating society, 'I think we'll have to give and take. I think we'll have to come to an arrangement which won't necessarily fulfil the republican objectives. But I am quite convinced that process will start'.

The rhetoric of peace sat uneasily beside IRA actions. Shortly after the IRA killed two soldiers and injured many others including a five year old girl at Musgrave Park hospital in Belfast in November, Adams issued a statement warning of the consequences of allowing a major Belfast hospital to opt for trust status. This was too much for one Belfast morning newspaper, is influential in nationalist circles. An *Irish News* editorial on 4 November commented that by any standards this 'was an extraordinary statement. Mr Adams is the head of the political wing of the IRA which has now decided that hospitals are legitimate targets'. Although Sinn Fein had had two surprising by-election victories in 1991 it was conscious that as an all-Ireland party it lacked a 'sound republican base' in the Republic. In the Irish local government elections in July its vote fell from 3.3 per cent in 1985 to 2.1 per cent. There was no doubt that the campaign of violence was a major reason.

Another unwelcome development during the year was the attention that human rights groups were now paying to paramilitary violence. In the past they had concentrated solely on the misdemeanours of the authorities. But in a report from the US based Helsinki Watch in October there was the warning that 'human rights violations are persistent and ongoing, that they affect Protestants and Catholics alike, and that they are committed by both security forces and paramilitary in violation of international human rights . . .'. Some paramilitary actions were described as 'barbaric' and 'particularly gruesome'. In addition Amnesty ('the respected human rights group' according to Sinn Fein) announced that in future it would 'confront the atrocities' committed by 'political opposition groups' including the IRA. Helsinki Watch had specifically mentioned punishment shootings or kneecappings. During the year there had been about 200 such punishments and the IRA had come under pressure from such groups as Families Against Intimidation and Terror (FAIT) to desist from these practices so that by December *Republican News* announced that it was IRA policy to 'sharply reduce physical punishments' and to 'implement in their place a wide range of non-physical responses'. It may be that this decision was influenced by Helsinki Watch.

The Brooke Initiative

One of Gerry Adams' major concerns was the worry that the Brooke talks among the four major constitutional parties in Northern Ireland – the Alliance Party, the Democratic Unionist Party, the Social Democratic and Labour Party, and the Ulster Unionist Party – might succeed and leave Sinn Fein the loser. There were not too many optimists, hence the year opened with a whimper. But on 26 March the Secretary of State was able to tell the Commons that after 14 months of painstaking negotiations he had got the agreement of the parties to address the totality of relationships within these islands by examining the three strands which encompassed the problem: relationships within Northern Ireland, between Northern Ireland and the Republic, and between the Republic of Ireland and the UK as a whole. Discussion was to take place in a ten week gap between meetings of the Anglo-Irish Conference and the four parties were to nominate ten members each for the negotiations. All recognised the historic import of the talks and the Rev. Ian Paisley praised Mr Brooke for conducting his dealings 'in honesty, uprightness and with great openness'.

It had not been easy to get to even that stage. One of the major stumbling blocks had been when Strand Two talks would begin, that is when the Irish government would be brought into play. The unionist parties had been insistent that 'substantial progress' had to be made on the first strand dealing with matters inside Northern Ireland, whereas the Dublin government had understood from their talks with Mr Brooke that they would be brought in within a matter of days. Eventually Dublin offered a compromise whereby it accepted that Mr Brooke would decide when they were brought into the process. It was agreed that the talks would begin on 30 April with a series of bilateral meetings between the Secretary of State and the party leaders to finalize 'housekeeping arrangements' such as the location of the talks, and the length and frequency of inter-party meetings. The Secretary of State expected that these bilateral meetings would be 'fairly brisk'. In the event they turned out to be anything but brisk so that the first plenary session did not take place until 12.52 pm on 17 June and the talks whimpered to a collapse on the evening of 2 July.

Essentially the talks did not move beyond the procedural level and little of substance (beyond well rehearsed party positions) emerged. The first major problem concerned the venue for Strand Two talks. The SDLP and Dublin wanted them somewhere on the island of Ireland but the unionists suggested London or abroad because they refused to sit down with an Irish government on the island unless it rescinded or amended Articles Two and Three of the Irish Constitution which claimed jurisdiction over Northern Ireland. Then a problem arose as to the chairman of the second strand. Dublin assumed that their Foreign Minister, Gerry Collins, would be in charge but were prepared to rotate it between Collins and Mr Brooke. The unionists wanted Mr Brooke solely in charge and Mr Paisley denounced the idea of an independent chairman as 'an absolute farce'. In time they accepted an independent chairman but believed that the first choice of Lord Carrington was at the very least mischievous because unionism despises the Foreign Office and all its machinations. After scouring the world and considering about 30 names Sir Ninian Stephen, former Governor General of Australia, emerged as the chairman. But that threw up another procedural problem. What were to be the standing orders and under what terms of reference was the chairman employed?

Hence the long delay in getting to the first plenary session during which much bad blood was spilt. The two unionist leaders even went over the head of Mr Brooke and held a meeting with John Major on 15 May to attempt to break the deadlock. There was not even agreement as to the outcome of that meeting and Rev. Paisley told the press that 'Our faith in him [Mr Brooke] has been rudely shattered'. Against this background it was not altogether surprising that the Secretary of State brought the proceedings to a close on 2 July although he told the Commons on the following day that 'foundations had been laid for progress in the future which neither cynics nor men of violence will be able to undermine'. He said that he would 'listen for rustling in the undergrowth' and that he hoped to pick up the process in the autumn. By the end of the year he was still trying to get the show on the road again with no evident success.

If that cursory account suggests that the whole business was no more than the equivalent of two bald men fighting over a comb it would do an injustice to the deep-seated animosities which paralysed the protagonists. All had made concessions to get to the negotiating table. The Taoiseach, Charles Haughey, who had described Northern Ireland as a 'failed political entity' was tacitly admitting that a devolved system could emerge from Strand One and was conceding privately that Articles Two and Three would be discussed during the talks. The SDLP and the Irish government had allowed for a gap in intergovernmental conference meetings even though they suspected that unionists would indulge in procrastination. Indeed the Unionist MP for Strangford, John Taylor, claimed on 26 April that the Agreement had been suspended and that it could never be 'de-suspended' and continued as if nothing had happened. In an effort to prevent an outbreak of mutual recrimination and allowing that the Orange marching season was upon them, Mr Brooke brought the proceedings to a halt to enable an intergovernmental conference to proceed as planned on 16 July.

The unionist parties were conscious of a degree of paranoia inside their community. The UDA believed that the party leaders were totally unprepared for the talks and one small loyalist faction produced a poster of the two party leaders with the message WANTED FOR TREASON. The Belfast morning newspaper *Ulster News Letter* cautioned on 31 May that the NIO has manipulated sections of the media by portraying 'the talks as being synonymous with peace. It may be nearer the mark to say they are synonymous with movement towards a united Ireland and fragmentation of the United Kingdom'. They knew too that if they failed that the Anglo-Irish Agreement would stay in place. All were conscious that their negotiating skills were rusty, a fact which became apparent in the early days of the talks and which was confirmed in an opinion poll conducted for the Rowntree Reform Trust in July. The poll confirmed that the electorate wanted the talks to continue, and when it came to apportioning blame for their breakdown the unionists were seen as the chief culprits.

When the talks did break down an *Irish Times* editorial suggested that the 'Brooke talks had reached a hiatus, not a conclusion'. By the end of the year it was difficult enough to sustain that view. At his party's annual conference in October the UUP leader, Mr Molyneaux, quoted from Mr Brooke's Commons statement on 3 July: ' "I hope it might be possible for fresh talks to take place." We stand on common ground with the Secretary of State, who never used the word "resume". He, too, is prepared to put the past behind'. In other words the unionists assume that fresh talks will take place under different ground rules. In addition a British general election is approaching and there are some suspicions inside the SDLP that the Conservatives are prepared to do a deal with the unionists in the event of a hung parliament. They point to an interview Mr Brooke gave to *The Irish Times* on 27 September, and to speeches made at the Conservative Party conference by Mr Brooke and Douglas Hurd. In all of this they believe that overtures are being made to the unionists which raises questions about Mr Brooke as an honest broker. If the ground rules are changed it is unlikely that the SDLP will re-enter talks.

The year ends therefore with two intriguing questions. Is there a 'peace party' inside the republican movement and can it be sustained to allow for a cessation of violence? Can that be reconciled with a statement made by the deputy leader of the DUP, Peter Robinson MP, at the end of October when he said that the Union 'no longer exists in any worthwhile recognizable form' and that unionists should prepare to consider 'alternative forms'?

Chronology

4 Jan: IRA revives firebomb attacks against retail outlets in Belfast.

5 Jan: Catholic man shot dead in Lurgan, County Armagh by the UVF.

21 Jan: A retired RUC man is murdered.

24 Jan: IRA shooting and bombing of an army rifle range in Staffordshire.

27 Jan: Catholic man shot dead by loyalist gunmen.

4 Feb: 'Human bomb' attack on the UDR base at Mayherafell, County Londonderry. No one was seriously injured.

6 Feb: RUC accuses the main loyalist paramilitary groups of becoming the principal agents of drug trafficking in the province.

7 Feb: IRA launches mortar attack on Downing Street, narrowly missing the Cabinet Room in which the cabinet had just convened.

The Lords reject legal challenges to the ban on direct-speech interviews with terrorist groups.

18 Feb: Two bomb attacks by IRA on London rail termini with one fatality.

25 Feb: IRA bomb blast on the main line between London and St Albans.

1 Mar: Soldier killed and three others injured by a land mine in South Armagh.

3 Mar: Four Catholics shot dead in a public house in Lurgan, County Armagh.

4 Mar: Catholic taxi driver murdered by loyalists in Belfast.

UDR soldier killed in an IRA rocket attack.

Kenneth Baker rejects a Labour offer of talks on a replacement for the Prevention of Terrorism Act.

5 Mar: IRA bomb explodes inside Shorts complex, the fifth such incident in two years.

15 Mar: Twenty man team set up to hunt the real Birmingham bombers after the release of the Birmingham Six.

19 Mar: Decision to close two army outposts in Northern Ireland and draft in 500 extra troops announced.

20 Mar: Northern Ireland power industry to be privatized and broken up.

22 Mar: IRA attack a woman civilian in Londonderry, whose husband they killed four years previously.

25 Mar: Unionist leaders announce their acceptance of Peter Brooke's terms for talks on Northern Ireland.

28 Mar: Archbishop Cahal Daly questions the use of the UDR in nationalist areas.

UVF gunmen kill three Catholics, two of them teenage girls, in a mobile shop in Craigavon, County Armagh.

5 Apr: Firebomb attacks in central Manchester.

8 Apr: Off-duty RUC officer is killed by a car bomb in Ballycastle, County Antrim.

9 Apr: A relative of the DUP MP, Rev. William McCrea, is shot dead in Coagh, County Tyrone.

10 Apr: Father Peter McVerry makes allegations in the Irish press that homeless boys are being procured in Dublin and taken to act as male prostitutes for British army officers in Northern Ireland.

IRA man killed by police whilst trying to mount a mortar attack on Downpatrick.

13 Apr: A Protestant man is shot dead by the IRA. On 17 Apr the Gardai acknowledge that leaks of information passed to them by the RUC may have been responsible for his death.

17 Apr: Loyalists announce a ceasefire to coincide with the Brooke talks on the future of Northern Ireland.

A challenge to the Irish Republic's ban on broadcast interviews with members of proscribed organizations, including Sinn Fein, fails before the European Commission on Human Rights.

22 Apr: Fair Employment Commission survey shows that Catholics constitute 35 per cent of the workforce in the public and private sectors in the province, but are under-represented as a community in the senior levels of some sectors and in the security forces.

30 Apr: Brooke talks begin in Stormont.

6 May: Unionists hold talks with Fine Gael in Dublin on the political future of Northern Ireland.

13 May: A prominent Orange Order leader is killed by a booby trap bomb in Armagh city.

15 May: Successful Unionist meeting with John Major keeps the Brooke initiative going.

21 May: IRA guns down a Protestant businessman at his Belfast office.

25 May: Soldier killed and another seriously injured in a bomb attack on a barracks in West Belfast.

30 May: Unionists reject nomination of Lord Carrington to chair the Brooke talks.

2 June: Senior official of the Northern Ireland Industrial Development Board is injured by a car bomb.

3 June: Three man IRA unit is wiped out in an SAS ambush in County Tyrone.

6 June: IRA kill an alleged police informer in Londonderry.

17 June: IRA kill a part-time member of the UDR.

All-party talks begin in Belfast. Agreement on Sir Ninian Steven as chairman of the second phase of the talks is reached.

20 June: Unionists warn that they will pull out of the Brooke talks if scheduled Anglo-Irish talks go ahead on 16 July.

28 June: Announcement that the Maze prison is to close.

29 June: Former Ulster Defence Association commander Cecil McKnight is shot dead by the IRA at his Londonderry home.

30 June: INLA kills a member denounced as a RUC informer.

1 July: High Court rules that a Catholic family in a Protestant area of Belfast who left their home because of attacks upon them made themselves intentionally homeless.

3 July: Brooke talks wound up.

4 July: Loyalist paramilitary call off a ten week ceasefire.

18 July: Member of RNVR shot dead by Irish People's Liberation Organization in his shop in centre of Belfast.

19 July: Catholic taxi driver shot dead by loyalists in west Belfast.

21 July: Alleged informer abducted in Irish Republic and shot dead by IRA. Widespread local protests about the killing.

23 July: UDR and the Royal Irish Rangers to merge.

25 July: The cases of the UDR four, soldiers gaoled in 1986 for the murder of a Catholic, are referred to the Court of Appeal.

5 Aug: IRA kills a Protestant in County Tyrone.

9 Aug: IRA kills a man in Londonderry, alleging he was a member of the UVF.

10 Aug: Catholic shopkeeper killed by loyalists in Falls Road, Belfast.

12 Aug: Loyalist gunmen kill a republican in County Tyrone.

15 Aug: A Belfast Catholic is accidentally killed by an IRA bomb.
A Protestant former member of UDR is killed by IRA in County Tyrone.

16 Aug: Sinn Fein member shot dead by loyalists in County Londonderry.
IPLO member is shot dead by loyalists in west Belfast.

17 Aug: Soldier killed by a landmine in South Armagh.

18-27 Aug: Two men take sanctuary in Newry Catholic cathedral from the IRA.

20 Aug: Three members of a family take refuge from 'intimidation' by the security forces in a church in Cookstown, County Tyrone.

28 Aug: Massive IRA bomb all but demolishes the RUC station in Markethill, County Armagh.

29 Aug: Amnesty International report condemns RUC interrogation procedures.

3 Sept: Catholic man shot dead by loyalists in west Belfast.

8 Sept: Peter Brooke announces he will try to revive the talks.

10 Sept: Man shot dead by IRA in south Belfast.

16 Sept: Leaks suggest that the government has set up a committee to review the use of lethal force by the security forces.
A Sinn Fein councillor in Londonderry is killed by loyalists.

17 Sept: RUC officer killed by an IRA mortar attack in Swatragh, County Londonderry.

28 Sept: Catholic shopkeeper killed by UDA in Belfast.

29 Sept: Catholic student shot dead by RUC. The following day an investigation into the circumstances of the killing is launched.

2 Oct: Channel 4's *Despatches* alleges that some RUC officers have been involved with loyalist terrorist activity.

10 Oct: IPLO kill a man in the Shankill Road area of Belfast. Loyalist gunman kill a Catholic taxi driver.

14 Oct: One man killed and another critically injured by loyalist terrorists in Belfast.

20 Oct: Charles Haughey urges an early restart to the Brooke talks.

25 Oct: Catholic killed at gunpoint in County Tyrone.

6 Nov: UDR soldier killed in County Londonderry.

13 Nov: Four Protestants killed in separate IRA attacks in Belfast.

14 Nov: RUC to be increased by 440 and 100 more troops to be sent to the province.

15 Nov: Two people killed in IRA bomb attack at a concert by the band of the Blues and Royals in St Albans, Hertfordshire.

20 Nov: Irish government pledges to review its extradition laws after the Dublin Supreme Court freed Anthony Sloan, an IRA suspect, having ruled that certain crimes were political and not open to extradition.

24 Nov: Loyalist prisoner killed and eight others injured (one of whom later dies) in an explosion at Crumlin Road gaol in Belfast.

25 Nov: UDR soldier killed in south Armagh by IRA.

27 Nov: Five hundred extra troops sent to Northern Ireland.

2 Dec: IRA begins its Christmas campaign with firebombs in London's west end.

7-9 Dec: Firebombs in Manchester's shops.

13 Dec: Craigavon police station wrecked by a 2,000 pound bomb.

14-15 Dec: Firebombs in London stores.

21-22 Dec: Five killed by gunmen in weekend of violence in Ulster.

23 Dec: Firebombs in London followed by an IRA announcement of a Christmas ceasefire.

Index